CLINICAL HANDBOOK OF
Marital Therapy

THE GUILFORD FAMILY THERAPY SERIES
Alan S. Gurman, Editor

CLINICAL HANDBOOK OF
Marital Therapy

Edited by
NEIL S. JACOBSON
University of Washington

ALAN S. GURMAN
University of Wisconsin Medical School

THE GUILFORD PRESS
New York   London

PRINTED IN THE UNITED STATES OF AMERICA
Third printing, September 1987

Library of Congress Cataloging in Publication Data

Main entry under title:

Clinical handbook of marital therapy.

    (The Guilford family therapy series)
    Includes bibliographies and indexes.
    1. Marital psychotherapy—Handbooks, manuals, etc.
I. Jacobson, Neil S., 1949–   .   II. Gurman, Alan S.
III. Series.   [DNLM: 1. Marital Therapy.   WM 55 C641]
RC488.5.C585   1986   616.89′156   85–31539
ISBN 0-89862-067-8

Contributors

CAROL M. ANDERSON, PhD   Western Psychiatric Institute and Clinic, University of Pittsburgh, Pittsburgh, Pennsylvania

ROBERT C. AYLMER, EdD   Lifecycle Center, Newton, Massachusetts

DONALD H. BAUCOM, PhD   Department of Psychology, University of North Carolina, Chapel Hill, North Carolina

ELLEN M. BERMAN, MD   Department of Psychiatry, University of Pennsylvania, Philadelphia, Pennsylvania, and Marriage Council of Philadelphia, Philadelphia, Pennsylvania

GREGORY BROCK, PhD   Department of Psychology, University of Wisconsin–Stout, Stout, Wisconsin

LAURA S. BROWN, PhD   Private practice, Seattle, Washington

JOHN F. CAHALANE, ACSW   Western Psychiatric Institute and Clinic, University of Pittsburgh, Pittsburgh, Pennsylvania

LARRY L. CONSTANTINE, MSW   Private practice, Acton, Massachusetts

JEANETTE COUFAL, PhD   Department of Psychology, University of Wisconsin–Stout, Stout, Wisconsin

JAMES C. COYNE, PhD   Department of Family Medicine, University of Michigan Medical School, Ann Arbor, Michigan

CHRISTOPHER DARE, MD   Department of Children and Adolescents, the Maudsley Hospital, Denmark Hill, London, England

WILLIAM J. DOHERTY, PhD   Department of Family Medicine, University of Oklahoma Health Sciences Center, Oklahoma City, Oklahoma

CELIA JAES FALICOV, PhD   San Diego Family Institute, and Department of Psychiatry, University of California, San Diego, La Jolla, California

LARRY B. FELDMAN, PhD   Department of Psychiatry, Loyola University Medical School, Maywood, Illinois

v

FRANK J. FLOYD, PhD   Department of Psychology, Illinois Institute of Technology, Chicago, Illinois

SHARON W. FOSTER, PhD   Department of Pediatrics, University of Wisconsin Medical School, and University of Wisconsin Hospital and Clinics, Madison, Wisconsin

MARTIN GOLDBERG, MD   Department of Psychiatry, University of Pennsylvania, Philadelphia, Pennsylvania, and Marriage Council of Philadelphia, Philadelphia, Pennsylvania

LESLIE S. GREENBERG, PhD   Department of Counseling Psychology, University of British Columbia, Vancouver, British Columbia, Canada

BERNARD GUERNEY, JR., PhD   Department of Human Development, The Pennsylvania State University, University Park, Pennsylvania

ALAN S. GURMAN, PhD   Department of Psychiatry, University of Wisconsin Medical School, Madison, Wisconsin

R. JULIAN HAFNER, MD   Department of Psychiatry, Flinders Medical Centre, Bedford Park, Australia

JULIA R. HEIMAN, PhD   Psychiatry and Behavioral Sciences, Harborview Community Mental Health Center, University of Washington School of Medicine, Seattle, Washington

JEFFREY A. HOFFMAN, PhD   Department of Psychology, University of North Carolina, Chapel Hill, North Carolina

AMY HOLTZWORTH-MUNROE, MS   Department of Psychology, University of Washington, Seattle, Washington

NEIL S. JACOBSON, PhD   Department of Psychology, University of Washington, Seattle, Washington

SUSAN M. JOHNSON, PhD   Department of Counseling Psychology, University of British Columbia, Vancouver, British Columbia

MELVIN R. LANSKY, MD   Department of Psychiatry, UCLA Medical School, Los Angeles, California, and Brentwood Veterans Administration Medical Center, Brentwood, California

HAL C. LEWIS, PhD   Department of Psychology, University of Denver, Denver Center for Marital and Family Studies, Denver, Colorado

E. JAMES LIEBERMAN, MD   The Family Institute, Washington, D.C.

SUSAN B. LIEBERMAN, MSW   The Family Institute, Washington, D.C.

GAYLA MARGOLIN, PhD   Department of Psychology, University of Southern California, Los Angeles, California

HOWARD J. MARKMAN, PhD   Department of Psychology, University of Denver, Denver Center for Marital and Family Studies, Denver, Colorado

ANN L. MILNE, ACSW   Private practice, Madison, Wisconsin

TIMOTHY J. O'FARRELL, PhD   Department of Psychiatry, Harvard Medical School, Boston, Massachusetts, and Veterans Administration Medical Center, Brockton, Massachusetts

K. DANIEL O'LEARY, PhD   Department of Psychology, State University of New York at Stony Brook, Stony Brook, New York

DOUGLAS J. REISS, PhD   Western Psychological Institute and Clinic, University of Pittsburgh, Pittsburgh, Pennsylvania

DAVID G. RICE, PhD   Department of Psychiatry, University of Wisconsin Medical School, Madison, Wisconsin

JOY K. RICE, PhD   Departments of Educational Policy Studies and Women's Studies, University of Wisconsin–Madison, Madison, Wisconsin

ALAN ROSENBAUM, PhD   Department of Psychology, Syracuse University, Syracuse, New York

CLIFFORD J. SAGER, MD   Jewish Board of Family Services, New York, New York, and Department of Psychiatry, New York Hospital–Cornell Medical Center, New York, New York

SCOTT M. STANLEY, MA   Department of Psychology, University of Denver, Denver Center for Marital and Family Studies, Denver, Colorado

THOMAS C. TODD, PhD   Marriage and Family Therapy Training Program, Bristol Hospital, Bristol, Connecticut

DON ZIMMER, MEd   Private practice, Seattle, Washington

Preface

In 1978, the two of us were involved in a spirited debate that was published in the journal *Family Process*. In that debate, we disagreed on the relative merits of a behavioral approach to marital therapy. If asked, we are certain that our colleagues would have assumed that we were not speaking to one another. No one (including ourselves at that time) would have predicted that we would ever collaborate on a book.

How did we move from ideological adversaries to co-editors in seven short years? One of us would like to believe that the other was a closet behaviorist all along, and simply saw the light. The alleged "closet behaviorist" attributes the rapprochement to the other's personal analysis. While there is probably no resolution to this debate, the reconciliation can not be denied. This book is the result.

In actuality, as we became friends and exchanged ideas over the past seven years, we learned that there were several common elements to our practices, despite rather fundamental differences in case conceptualization. More importantly, as we continued to study, teach, and utilize marital therapy techniques, we became increasingly sensitive to the common denominators and bottom lines imposed by acutely distressed couples seeking therapy. Although differences in technique certainly exist between therapists, it is possible to bring any group of experienced marital therapists together and find much common ground. Most of this common ground arises from work in the trenches. However disguised it might be by jargon which is theory-specific, there is a collective pool of clinical wisdom from which experienced marital therapists draw.

Unfortunately, it is hard to find this clinical wisdom in the literature. Despite a growing body of articles and books on the research and practice of marital therapy, there are few detailed guides to clinical practice, and even fewer that are comprehensive in their scope. This book is an attempt to rectify this deficiency in the current literature. It is the first comprehensive guide to the clinical practice of marital therapy.

As we explain in Chapter 1, the book includes five parts: "Major Models of Marital Therapy"; "Emerging Models of Marital Intervention"; "Interventions with Various Populations and Relationally Defined Problems"; "Marital Therapy and Selected Psychiatric Disorders"; and "Special Issues." Without exception, the contributors are noted authorities on their topic areas of focus, and they were all given an outline to guide them in their writing. Although the outlines varied somewhat from section to section, they were all geared toward a focus on clinical issues. In particular, authors were asked to discuss characteristics and attributes of good marital therapists, strategies used to overcome common clinical roadblocks, and examples of "bad therapy."

We are delighted by the outcome. We hope that others are as well.

NEIL S. JACOBSON
ALAN S. GURMAN

Contents

PART IV: MARITAL THERAPY AND SELECTED PSYCHIATRIC DISORDERS

Marital Therapy: From Technique to Theory, Back Again, and Beyond

1

ALAN S. GURMAN
NEIL S. JACOBSON

Only two decades ago, one observer of the marital therapy scene referred to the field as "a technique in search of a theory" (Manus, 1966), for while psychotherapists were increasingly treating couples with marital problems, there was little conceptual clarity or coherence to their work. Manus's assessment of the state of the field was provocative and largely accurate. At that time, psychotherapy with couples was indeed a hodgepodge of unsystematically employed techniques grounded tenuously, if at all, in partial theories at best. The only coherent theory of human behavior that had been applied frequently to the clinical study and treatment of marital problems was the psychoanalytic perspective (e.g., Mittelman, 1944; Oberndorf, 1938), and the only identifiable long-term, in-depth clinical project involving this area of study (Dicks, 1964, 1967) that has had any enduring impact on contemporary thinking in the field was grounded in object relations theory. Indeed, Manus's (1966) assessment 20 years ago of the state of the relationship between theory and practice in marital therapy may have been an understatement, for while psychoanalytic theory and object-relations theory were obviously already at relatively advanced stages, there were few clearly developed implications for clinical technique that had been derived from these schools of thought (Gurman, 1978, 1981) and then, as now, "psychodynamic" conjoint marital therapy regularly called upon technical operations that were in no way derived from psychodynamic principles for understanding human behavior or conducting the psychotherapeutic experience.

Though marital therapy of the 1960s lacked a coherent conceptual grounding, it did not lack a history. Indeeed, it had multiple, independent

Alan S. Gurman. Department of Psychiatry, University of Wisconsin Medical School, Madison, Wisconsin.
Neil S. Jacobson. Department of Psychology, University of Washington, Seattle, Washington.

histories. Several historians have mapped the beginnings and the evolution of the field in great detail (e.g., Broderick & Schrader, 1981; Gurman, 1978; Haley, 1984; Nichols & Everett, 1986; Olson, 1970), and have even traced the progression of emerging ideas and clinical practices in the field as revealed in the professional literature (Gurman, 1973). Like the history of any significant movement, the history of marital therapy is defined by the historian, so there is no single tale to be told (cf. Haley, 1984; Nichols & Everett, 1986). Marital and family therapists are now quite clear on the virtues of the "double description" (Bateson, 1979) of relationships, through which a more complex, and richer, appreciation of a marital or family system may be generated. Such a polyocular perspective of "the" history of marital therapy is likewise commended to the reader, who may consult the writings of the authors referred to earlier to distill his or her own meaningful history.

Perhaps the most controversial issue in constructing the history of marital therapy, and one which relates centrally to the rationale for why the present volume was needed, involves the relationship between "marital therapy" and "family therapy" (Gurman & Kniskern, 1979; Haley, 1984). The simple act of punctuating the relationship between the two by separating them with the word "and," as in the preceding sentence, itself grammatically isolates the core issue at hand: are "marital therapy" and "family therapy", in fact, separable? Haley (1984) has provocatively argued the case against such a distinction, based largely on the grounds that "The dyad does not seem to be a conceptual unit on which theory can be built" (p. 3), and that "a focus on a dyad forces the observer to ignore the structure in which the dyad functions" (p. 8), that is, the broader systems of interlocking triangles in which the dyad is inevitably embedded, including that of the clinical triangle of couple-plus-therapist.

We both agree with and disagree with the position reflected by Haley (1984). We agree (Gurman & Kniskern, 1979) that "marital therapy" is best conceived as a particular variant or subtype of family therapy. We do not agree that a conceptual and technical focus on the marital dyad precludes clinically useful theory-building. All models of "marital" (or "family" or "individual") therapy necessarily address the nature and meaning of the relationship between the therapist and his or her patients because that relationship, and the relationship between the therapist and each individual patient participant, is the vehicle and the medium through which more specific therapist actions, that is, "techniques," set the occasion for the possibility of desired change. The fact that marital therapy is typically conducted in a triangular interpersonal arrangement (Gurman, 1985) does not, however, preclude the study of the marital dyad qua dyad. Indeed, as we believe this volume attests, there have been very considerable conceptual and empirical advances in the development of clinically useful theories of the marital dyad since the time when Manus (1966) proclaimed his depressing assessment of the field. There now exist several coherent theories of marital interaction and dysfunction (see Part I, "Major Models of Marital Therapy," and Part II, "Emerging Models of Intervention"), and within each of these theories, systematically derived therapeutic techniques have been developed and refined. Moreover, the application of these models to the treatment of both explicitly relational problems (see Part III, "Interventions with Various Populations and Relationally Defined Problems") and to problems of adults traditionally defined in individual diagnostic terms (see Part IV, "Marital Therapy and Selected Psychiatric Disorders"), has been made increasingly clear in the last decade or less. In addition, several very important and clearly articulated models and methods of marital intervention in domains typically seen as falling outside the purview of "marital therapy" (e.g., prevention and enrichment programs) have been developed both conceptually and technically.

In fact, therein lies the essential rationale for the need in the field of family therapy for a volume which comprehensively addresses the application of clinical strategies for working with couples. We agree with Haley (1984) that exclusive or predominant training in psychotherapy with couples does not adequately prepare neophyte therapists to work effectively with larger social units (the nuclear family, the extended family, etc.). We would also argue that exclusive training for clinical work with such larger social systems does not adequately prepare therapists for effective work with couples (Gurman, 1985). Beyond the issue of the training of neophyte therapists, we would note that most psychotherapists who refer to themselves as "family therapists," in fact, devote an enormous amount of their clinical time to work with couples, perhaps even a majority of their time. In addition, there is a large constituency of clinicians in all the mental health professions who practice as "generalists" and spend large portions of their face-to-face clinical hours with couples.

Still, most textbooks on the theories and practices of family therapy pay only very limited attention to clinical work with couples (e.g., Gurman & Kniskern, 1981; Hoffman, 1981; Nichols, 1984; Wolman & Stricker, 1983). Thus, for both confirmed family therapists and neophyte family therapists, as well as for the general practitioner of psychotherapy, there seemed to be a need in the literature for a broad coverage of clinical interventions for working with couples. Thus, this volume was conceived with the aim of bringing together detailed specifications of treatment models, strategies and techniques, and demonstrating how these approaches are grounded in theory. In keeping with this decidedly clinical emphasis, the two concluding chapters (see Part V, "Special Issues") on the assessment of outcome and ethical issues in marital therapy also reflect this clinical focus.

MAJOR MODELS OF MARITAL THERAPY

Part I of this *Clinical Handbook* presents detailed considerations of what currently appear to be the dominant and most influential models of marital therapy, that is, psychodynamic, behavioral, structural/strategic, and Bowenian. As in the chapters in Parts II and III, on the treatment of explicitly relational problems, and on the marital treatment of psychiatric disorders, the aim in Part I was to articulate the direct linkages between theoretical models of marital relationships and strategies of intervention. Each author was asked to address the following issues:

1. The theoretical model of marital distress/dysfunction;
2. The theory of therapeutic change:
    a. rationale for how the treatment approach follows from the model of distress;
    b. overall strategy for bringing about relationship change (e.g., diagnostic/assessment procedures, typical goals, typical structure of therapy sessions, hypothesized active ingredients of the approach);
3. Specific techniques (including discussion of obstacles to successful treatment and how they are dealt with, and limitations and contraindications of the approach);
4. The role of the therapist (including discussion of typical technical errors); and
5. Common significant clinical issues (e.g., working with "difficult" couples, managing resistance and noncompliance, handling acute marital distress, the role and use of individual sessions and/or other therapeutic adjuncts, termination).

While each author of the chapters in Part I is firmly committed to a specific theoretical model, there emerges in this section as a whole, a most fascinating pattern. Each of these major models is shown clearly to be sufficiently conceptually coherent and flexible to be able to incorporate effectively both specific treatment techniques and therapist stances that are typically associated with alternative models. Thus, for example, Dare (Chapter 2) provides a rationale for the use of both directive and paradoxical techniques in the context of couples therapy firmly rooted in psychoanalytic thinking; within a social learning/cognitive ("behavioral") framework, Jacobson and Holtzworth-Munroe (Chapter 3) emphasize the importance of the therapist's capacity to provide "emotional nurturance" to couples, and to remain attuned to the need for attention to "individual" issues; Todd (Chapter 4) offers solid conceptual justification for the inclusion of communication and problem-solving skill training in structural/strategic therapy; and Aylmer (Chapter 5) makes clear that couples therapy from a Bowenian perspective can comfortably incorporate both direct and indirect therapist interventions, and can be responsive to both the short-term crisis management needs of couples, and to longer-term desires for change in multigenerational family systems. The repeated theme in Section I of technical flexibility paired with conceptual integrity is consistent with recent explicit efforts in the field to integrate apparently incompatible theories and methods of treatment (e.g., Feldman, 1985; Gurman, 1978, 1981; Pinsof, 1983; Stanton, 1981), and, in our view, signals the commendable recent thrust in the field to identify common mechanisms and methods of facilitating therapeutic change.

EMERGING MODELS OF MARITAL INTERVENTION

A clear example of such attempts to integrate divergent views of intimate relating, and to integrate clinical concern with both the intrapsychic/affective and interpersonal/interactional dimensions of marital relationships, is provided by Greenberg and Johnson (Chapter 11). While their chapter illustrates well such newly emerging interests in the field toward integration, it also signals what appears to be a genuine re-emergence of interest in experiential theories and methods of relationship change. Likewise, the Liebermans' contribution on group couples therapy (Chapter 10) rekindles our awareness of the potency of such methods of working with couples.

In addition to those two chapters, which reconnect us to certain views and approaches that have unfortunately fallen into a state of relative neglect in the field, Part II also presents detailed discussions of four more recently developed domains of marital intervention which are typically seen as outside the boundaries of "marital therapy," yet which, from the perspective of public health policy, reflect the need for the development of clear models of professional involvement. Importantly, recent developments in all four of these domains (enrichment: Guerney, Brock, & Coufal, Chapter 6; prevention: Markman, Floyd, Stanley, & Lewis, Chapter 7; divorce mediation: Milne, Chapter 8; family medicine: Doherty, Chapter 9) place a very strong emphasis on empowering clients via education and skill training. And all four of these intervention models simultaneously address both the resolution of current concerns and the lowering of the probability of being at risk for future difficulties. It will be interesting to observe the extent to which the educational–preventive emphases of marital intervention models such as these come to influence the practices of marital "therapy" in the years ahead.

INTERVENTION WITH VARIOUS POPULATIONS
AND RELATIONALLY DEFINED PROBLEMS

In our view, the scope of marital therapy may be heuristically conceived as comprising two major domains. The first domain is that which addresses the application of various treatment methods to problems which are probably consensually seen as interactive and interpersonal and constitute, more or less, the "standard fare" of marital therapy. The second domain, treated in Part IV of this volume, addresses the application of clinical methods to the treatment of problems that are traditionally viewed in the mental health professions as disorders of individuals.

Part III includes nine chapters that may be roughly grouped into three clusters. The first three chapters by Rice and Rice (Chapter 12, "Separation and Divorce Therapy"), Berman and Goldberg (Chapter 13, "Therapy with Unmarried Couples"), and Sager (Chapter 14, "Therapy with Remarried Couples") constitute what may be called the "coupling–uncoupling–recoupling" cluster. As a group, these chapters address clinical problems involving predictable and nodal events and processes in the formation, dissolution and modification of the emotional and structural bonds of marriage.

What is especially salient in each of these chapters is the explicit recognition of the fact that while couples stressed during any of these periods of developmental transition share common dilemmas and issues, there are multiple configurations of relationship difficulty within each general category, and consequently, there is the need for tailoring treatment interventions to different types of couples' needs. For example, clinical work with couples in the coupling-uncoupling-recoupling context probably requires as much sustained attention to the dynamics of individuals as any commonly occurring marital problems, and requires especially carefully balanced attention and sensitivity to both individual dynamics and structural dynamics.

The second cluster of chapters in Part III, including those by Feldman (Chapter 15, "Sex-Role Issues in Marital Therapy"), Falicov (Chapter 19, "Cross-Cultural Marriages"), and Brown and Zimmer (Chapter 20, "Therapy Issues of Lesbian and Gay Male Couples"), may be called, "the role of values in couples therapy." While the values of therapists and patients operate in significant ways in any psychotherapy encounter (Jacobson, 1983), some problems brought to therapists have especially great value salience in two ways. First, increasing numbers of couples seek help in resolving conflicts which explicitly involve deeply held personal values in areas such as gender role expectations and cultural differences based on ethnicity, religion, etc. Second, while any presenting problem has the potential to elicit untoward antitherapeutic reactions from the therapist, especially in the form of coalitions between the therapist and one partner against the other partner, some, such as those involving issues of sex role identity and cultural identification, have greater potential to do so than others. And some intimacy issues carry additional potential for complicating, and even precluding the establishment of, a working alliance with both members of a couple, when they are attached to powerfully socialized values. Perhaps nowhere is this more likely than when "straight" therapists work with gay male or lesbian couples.

The final triad of chapters in Part III, by Heiman (Chapter 16, "Treating Sexually Distressed Marital Relationships"), Constantine (Chapter 18, "Jealousy and Extramarital Sexual Relations"), and Rosenbaum and O'Leary (Chapter 17, "The Treatment of Marital Violence"), may be called, "problems of passion." These areas of marital difficulties are linked by the intensity of affect inherent in presenting problems in these areas, and may also be linked concurrently or sequentially in distressed marriages. Though not unique in this regard among marital problems, this triad of difficulties reminds us, often dramatically, that "relationship problems" often exist on a foundation of individual psychological conflict, and that explicit therapist attention to such individual conflict that predates the marriage is often called for, in addition to the attention that needs to be directed to current interactional forces that maintain marital disharmony. As Constantine (Chapter 18) emphasizes in his discussion of the problems of jealousy and extramarital relations, "Regardless of the therapist's commitment to a 'systemic formulation,' individual dispositional factors need to be taken into account."

MARITAL THERAPY AND SELECTED PSYCHIATRIC DISORDERS

Constantine's view that a genuinely systemic approach to treatment necessitates attention to multiple levels of psychological experience is fundamental to the chapters in Part IV of this *Handbook*, including those by Hafner (Chapter 21, "Marital Therapy for Agoraphobia"), Coyne (Chapter 22, "Strategic Marital Therapy for Depression"), O'Farrell (Chapter 23, "Marital Therapy in the Treatment of Alcoholism"), Anderson, Reiss, and Cahalane (Chapter 24, "Marital Therapy with Schizophrenic Patients"), Lansky (Chapter 25, "Marital Therapy for Narcissistic Disorders"), and Foster (Chapter 26, "Marital Treatment of Eating Disorders"). Each of these problems has been traditionally viewed as largely, if not exclusively, residing within individuals, both in terms of their origins and their maintenance. Logically, then, psychotherapy for such problems has, in the main, emphasized the treatment of such troubled individuals apart from the current interpersonal context in which their problems are manifest. Contemporary clinical systemic theory, by contrast, seems often to bypass attending to such problems as disorders in their own right, or even to deny the existence of such "disorders." Since our own view is that these problems involve genuine disorders which exist apart from, as well as in significant connection with, relationship dynamics, we requested that, in addition to the issues to be considered in the chapters in Part I ("Major Models of Marital Therapy") which were identified earlier, authors of chapters in Part IV also address the following questions:

1. What is the usual definition of this problem?
2. How do relationship issues contribute to this (individual) problem?
3. How does the (individual) problem contribute to marital discord?
4. What nondyadic factors, if any, play an important role in either the etiology or maintenance of this disorder?
5. Are there limitations of a purely "marital therapy" approach to treating this problem?
6. Are other interventions (e.g., medications) used in treating this problem within a maritally focused therapy?

Perhaps the most controversial issue in the realm of systemically sensitive treatment of psychiatric disorders is whether "individual" problems are functional for relationships, that is, serve functions in the marital system or in other, larger systems in which the marriage is embedded. Perhaps a more pragmatically important variation of this question, and a conceptually more challenging one to consider, is not whether individual symptoms serve interpersonal functions, but when do they do so? Posing the issue in this way allows for the possibility (indeed, in our view, the likelihood) that (a) some individual symptoms are routinely, or at least often, interpersonally functional; (b) some individual symptoms are never, or at least rarely, interpersonally functional; and (c) some individual symptoms are more variably interpersonally functional. Whatever the eventual status of evidence on this matter may be, it is quite clear that, at least for the marital and family treatment of some individual psychiatric disorders, such as schizophrenia, intervention not based on the assumption of the functions of symptoms is currently the preferred method of treatment (Gurman, Kniskern & Pinsof, 1986).

ETHICAL AND EMPIRICAL ISSUES IN MARITAL THERAPY

The field of marital therapy has clearly progressed in the last two decades from one in which clinical techniques hungered for solid conceptual foundations (Manus, 1966) and, as this volume attests, now articulates numerous coherent theories of marital distress and treatment, and technical innovations with direct theoretical linkages. Thus, it might be said that marital therapy has gone from technique to theory, and back again. In addition, marital therapy has also gone beyond technical and theoretical innovation and clarification, and now has accumulated a substantial body of empirical research (Gurman, Kniskern & Pinsof, 1986) which both documents the efficacy, in general of (conjoint) couples therapy, and provides an empirical basis for at least some important and recurrent decisions that must be made in clinical practice, as Baucom and Hoffman (Chapter 27, "The Effectiveness of Marital Therapy") show in Part V of this volume.

Marital therapists have also moved beyond attending to considerations of technique and theory with increasing public confrontation of the enormously significant and complex ethical issues involved in the practice of marital therapy (see Margolin, Chapter 28, "Ethical Issues in Marital Therapy"), and Kaslow and Gurman (1985) have recently written in detail about ethical considerations in marital/family therapy research. These ethical issues touch on virtually every aspect of clinical practice by requiring the field's attention to such fundamental matters as the competence of therapists; the therapist's responsibility to both the individual partners in a relationship and to"the relationship"; confidentiality and privilege; informed consent; and therapist values. Undoubtedly, such ethical issues should, and in all probability will, receive increasing scrutiny in the years ahead. Indeed, one of the major ethical challenges in the field, that of our collective professional accountability for the efficacy of marital therapy (Foster & Gurman, 1985), forms a direct link between the issues considered in the final two chapters of this *Handbook*, and therefore is ultimately relevant to all the theoretical and technical matters considered elsewhere in this volume.

REFERENCES

Bateson, G. (1979). *Mind and nature: A necessary unity*. New York: Dutton.

Broderick, C. B., & Schrader, S. (1981). The history of professional marriage and family therapy. In A. S. Gurman & D. P. Kniskern (Eds.), *Handbook of family therapy*. New York: Brunner/Mazel.

Dicks, H. V. (1964). Concepts of marital diagnosis and therapy as developed at the Tavistock Family Psychiatric Clinic, London, England. In E. M. Nash, L. Jessner, & D. W. Afse (Eds.), *Marriage counseling in medical practice*. Chapel Hill: University of North Carolina Press.

Dicks, D. V. (1967). *Marital tensions*. New York: Basic Books.

Feldman, L. B. (1985). Integrative multilevel family therapy. *Journal of Marital and Family Therapy*, *11*, 357–372.

Foster, S. W., & Gurman, A. S. (1985). Social change and couples therapy. In C. Nadelson & M. Polonsky (Eds.), *Marriage and divorce: Contemporary perspectives*. New York: Guilford.

Gurman, A. S. (1973). Marital therapy: Emerging trends in research and practice. *Family Process*, *12*, 45–74.

Gurman, A. S. (1978). Contemporary marital therapies: A critique and comparative analysis of psychodynamic, behavioral and systems theory approaches. In T. Paolino & B. McCrady (Eds.), *Marriage and marital therapy*. New York: Brunner/Mazel.

Gurman, A. S. (1981). Integrative marital therapy: Toward the development of an interpersonal approach. In S. Budman (Ed.), *Forms of brief therapy*. New York: Guilford.

Gurman, A. S. (Ed.) (1985). *Casbook of marital therapy*. New York: Guilford.

Gurman, A. S. & Kniskern, D. P. (1979). Marital therapy and/or family therapy: What's in a name? *American Association for Marriage and Family Therapy Association Newsletter*, *10*(3), 1, 5–8.

Gurman, A. S. & Kniskern, D. P. (Eds.) (1981). *Handbook of family therapy*. New York: Brunner/Mazel.

Gurman, A. S., Kniskern, D. P., & Pinsof, W. M. (1986). Research on the process and outcome of marital and family therapy. In S. Garfield & A. Bergin (Eds.), *Handbook of psychotherapy and behavior change* (3rd ed.). New York: Wiley.

Haley, J. (1984). Marriage or family therapy? *American Journal of Family Therapy*, *12*, 3–14.

Hoffman, L. (1981). *Foundations of family therapy*. New York: Basic Books.

Jacobson, N. S. (1983). Beyond empiricism: The politics of marital therapy. *American Journal of Family Therapy*, *11*, 11–24.

Kaslow, N. J., & Gurman, A. S. (1985). Ethical considerations in family therapy research. *Counseling and Values*, in press.

Manus, G. I. (1966). Marriage counseling: A technique in search of a theory. *Journal of Marriage and the Family*, *28*, 449–453.

Mittlemann, B. (1944). Complementary neurotic reactions in intimate relationships. *Psychoanalytic Quarterly*, *13*, 479–491.

Nichols, M. P. (1984). *Family therapy: Concepts and methods*. New York: Gardner Press.

Nichols, W. C., & Everett, C. (1986). *Family therapy: An integrative approach*. New York: Guilford.

Oberndorf, C. P. (1938). Psychoanalysis of married couples. *Psychoanalytic Review*, *25*, 453–475.

Olson, D. H. (1970). Marital and family therapy: Integrative review. *Journal of Marriage and the Family*, *32*, 501–538.

Pinsof, W. M. (1983). Integrative problem-centered therapy: Toward the synthesis of family and individual psychotherapies. *Journal of Marital and Family Therapy*, *9*, 19–36.

Stanton, M. D. (1981). Marital therapy from a structural/strategic viewpoint. In P. Sholevar (Ed.), *Handbook of marriage and marital therapy*. New York: Spectrum.

Wolman, B. B., & Stricker, G. (1983). *Handbook of family and marital therapy*. New York: Plenum.

I

MAJOR MODELS
OF MARITAL THERAPY

2

Psychoanalytic Marital Therapy

CHRISTOPHER DARE

PSYCHOANALYSIS AND MARRIAGE

The ideas expressed in this chapter do not derive from a specialist practice of marital therapy. I am a psychoanalyst and child psychiatrist, and in my professional work my interests focus on the effort to identify a range of psychoanalytic psychotherapies appropriate to a mixed practice of child and adolescent psychiatry and private consulting psychoanalytic psychotherapy. That is, my practice is in two distinct halves. First, I work with children and adolescents in a National Health Service facility (in a university setting of a postgraduate teaching and research hospital). The second setting for my clinical work is a private practice in which the main referral is of adults who span an age range from young adulthood to midlife and who, for the most part, request psychoanalysis or psychotherapy.

From the outset of my clinical practice I have been involved with the development of a rigorous conceptualization of the psychoanalytic therapeutic process (Sandler, Dare, & Holder, 1972). At the same time, I have been strongly influenced by my attempts to apply psychoanalytic conceptualizations of therapy and personality to the spectrum of problems and motivations for which help is requested in the National Health Service facility.

Psychoanalysis provides a wide-ranging scope for the description of the individual personality (Dare, 1981) and is a rich framework for the conceptualization of individual development (Dare, 1985) and the therapeutic process (Sandler *et al.*, 1972).

Christopher Dare. Department of Children and Adolescents, The Maudsley Hospital, Denmark Hill, London, England.

Nevertheless, after some years of training in psychoanalytically based child psychiatry, I became convinced that psychoanalytic psychotherapy addressed to a child or young person as an individual had only limited applications within child psychiatry, being effective in perhaps 10% of referrals. The inapplicability to the broad range of cases does not stem from an inability to form a psychoanalytic understanding of the cases, which is always essential and illuminating, but largely reflects the relatively high level of motivation and necessarily long time span that the therapy requires if it is to have a chance of being successful. These emerging considerations led me into the field of crisis treatments and conjoint therapies. The latter revealed a limitation of psychoanalytic theory in the conceptualization of interpersonal relationships. As Rycroft (1956, p. 62) has said, ". . . the knowledge and theories that we have about inter-relationships between individuals . . . have never been satisfactorily incorporated into metapsychological theory." I believe that the problem of incorporating a more thoroughgoing interpersonal framework within psychoanalysis calls for the development of a further supplement to the "metapsychological points of view" (Freud, 1915) and that this additional framework can be supplied by general systems theory (von Bertalanffy, 1950), as utilized by family and marital therapists.

It must be emphasized that this view of the current limitations of psychoanalysis in providing a full theory of interpersonal and family functioning is not intended as a destructive criticism but as a pointed reminder of the need for developments in the theory and practice of psychoanalysis to take seriously the special features of interpersonal processes as distinct from intrapsychic psychology. I am drawing attention to a difference between frameworks for understanding, on the one hand, the internal workings of a person's mental life, and on the other hand, the structure of their personal relationships. I believe that some psychoanalytic writings (e.g., Blanck & Blanck, 1968) fail to make this distinction. This is relevant not simply for the purposes of understanding what goes on between people, but, even more, for the deployment of effective therapy. A failure to take careful account of this distinction results in what I regard as crass attempts to apply psychoanalytic treatment methods designed for the individual to families and couples. The context and *dramatis personae* of a therapeutic endeavor should shape the qualities of that endeavor. The contrast between psychoanalytic therapy for adults and that for young children shows that "orthodox" psychoanalytic practice is capable of encompassing this distinction. In the development of a psychodynamic understanding of the couple, I have been most influenced by other therapists who have made the transition from individual to conjoint work but have not abandoned an appreciation of their psychoanalytic roots (e.g., Dicks, 1967; Framo, 1982; Skynner, 1976; Whitaker, see Neill & Kniskern, 1982), and by work from the Institute of Marital Studies in London (Bannister & Pincus, 1965; Pincus & Dare, 1978).

According to general systems theory (e.g., Katz & Kahn, 1966; von Bertalanffy, 1950), the rules that govern the individual separate functioning of the different elements of a system are not predictive of the rules governing the overall interactional organization of the system made up of the totality of the elements. Psychoanalytic understanding of the individual and systems understanding of the marriage and family relationship can be integrated by making a careful distinction between the interior mental workings of the individual as a description of the *elements* of the system and the currently impinging interpersonal context as the superordinate *system.*

The inadequacy of the explanations of the mechanisms and dynamics of interpersonal functioning, as a preconscious awareness, may be a reason why the most influential and prestigious psychoanalytic journals (e.g., *Journal of the American Psychoanalytic Association, International Journal of Psycho-Analysis, Quarterly Journal of Psychoanalysis*) are noticeably lacking in even passing references to marriage as an important feature of people's psychological life. A search through the titles and indexes of volumes of these three journals in the last 10 years reveals no articles on marriage, although there are copious references to other family dyads; no extensive accounts of psychological features or causations of marital relations; and only passing references to the fact that many of the people represented in the case histories, so extensively reported, are married. The main psychological insights offered by current psychoanalysis, in the journals surveyed, is in linking partner selection ("object choice") to earlier patterns of relations, especially mother–child, father–child, and oedipal configurations.

There is a contrast between the "official" presentation of psychoanalysis in the printed literature and discussions with practicing psychoanalysts about their patients. Such discussions make it very clear that, at least in the British Psycho-Analytical Society, there is a strong acceptance of the intensity and mutually determined rigidity of the marital relationships of the patients in treatment. In informal clinical descriptions marriages, like neurotic symptoms, are seen as multiply determined compromise formations. Conflicts are seen to exist between currently ego-syntonic object-related needs and relationship tendencies organized around importations into the current life of the patient of elements of past relationship experiences. Unconscious and preconscious motivations for marital choice are usually seen as distorted by, if not wholly determined by, the transformations of instinct-driven fantasies.

The links between marital object choice and earlier object-related experiences are very important for my understanding of the current structure of marital relationships and contribute to part of my practice in marital therapy. These links are considered in greater detail later in this chapter.

SYSTEMS THEORY AND PSYCHOANALYTIC MARITAL THERAPY

Having said how important it is to integrate the psychoanalytic understanding of individual psychological development, personality structure, and object choice, I must also emphasize that there is actually only a relatively small body of literature on the application of systems thinking to the marital system. For example, in Paolino and McCrady's (1978) comprehensive volume on marriage and marital therapy, Steinglass (1978) offers an extremely useful summary of some principles of the application of the systems approach to marriage, but he draws on very little work actually addressed to the marital dyad as opposed to the general literature of the family as a system (within the general systems theory definition). Olson's (1975) and Gurman's (1978) classifications of contemporary marital therapies place systems therapy alongside psychoanalytic and behavioral approaches as one of the three major groups, yet identify relatively few published discussions that focus on the marriage using systems theory thinking.

From the point of view of this chapter, systems theory, as it is usually mobilized in the theory of family therapy, has implications both for the psychoanalytic model of marriage and for psychoanalytic marital therapy.

Marriage as a Transactional, Interpersonal Structure

A systems orientation emphasizes the need to see the couple as a reference point in its own right and not simply as an arrangement of two separate and not necessarily impinging psychopathologies. What goes on in the marriage, whether or not both partners are overtly implicated, must be considered as though it were an expression of aspects of each partner. Each individual is assumed and expected to have an investment in the attitudes, activities, expectations, and symptomatic qualities of the partner, regardless of what their conscious wishes and beliefs would suggest to the contrary. Each individual is also assumed and expected to engage in behaviors, to take up conscious and unconscious attitudes, and to modulate affects and the expression of sexual drives in ways that diminish the direction and amplitude of change in their partner and in themselves. That is to say, homeostatic negative feedback mechanisms are constantly brought into play. The couple will be likely, therefore, to have long-term features, demonstrating the stabilizing aspects of these mechanisms. Systems observers, from Haley (1963) onward, have noted the balance of complementarity and symmetry in a given marriage, and at one time it looked as if it would indeed prove possible to establish a "taxonomy" of marriage (Goodrich, 1968). Although such descriptions of the patterns of relationships from moment to moment are useful, they rarely seem relevant to an understanding of the sustained, persistent qualities of a marital relationship.

Hierarchy and Control

Minuchin (1974) has clearly demonstrated and articulated the importance of the hierarchy of power and control in the systemic understanding of the structure of a marriage that is in the parenting phase. Stanton (1981), in an illuminating chapter on the applications of techniques that is akin to Minuchin's approach, makes it clear that in working with couples without children, concepts of hierarchy and control are not given a central role. In my experience, couples from cultures in which the husband is customarily given rights to control his wife rarely come forward for marital therapy. I have worked with couples in which one partner comes from a Hindu or Muslim culture. In those cultures, the traditional pattern of marriage is one of highly differentiated marital roles, with a balance of power and control residing in the husband. This cultural tradition is incorporated in the gender identity of the members of the culture, although it is opposed by values acquired in adulthood, and is often in conflict with the expectations of the spouse of North European culture. Psychoanalytic marital therapy seeks to explore conflicts deriving from the cultural differences rather than to establish the hierarchy.

Boundaries

Boundary issues, which are also so characteristic of the theoretical, structural concerns of systemic therapists (e.g., Minuchin, 1974), and whose properties are so actively sought and addressed in structural family therapy, are as much a feature of marital therapy as of whole-family therapy, whether or not children are present in the family. In marital therapy, however, the crucial boundaries that must be the concern of the therapist are those between the couple and the outside world, and the couple and their families of origin, as much as those between the couple and the children of the marriage.

The central point here is that understanding features of the marriage from a systems point of view addresses issues of importance to the psychoanalytic marital therapist that are not readily describable in psychoanalytic language, and need not be so. The psychoanalytic therapist needs to be aware of these issues, can use the customary systems language to describe them, and can seek to understand the implications for the constraints and qualities of these features for the internal psychological functioning of the marital partners. At the same time, the therapist needs to be concerned with the ways in which such systemic processes will be adapted to personality structures derived from long-standing expectations and attitudes deriving from object-related experiences.

THE DISTINCTION BETWEEN PSYCHOTHERAPY AND PSYCHOANALYSIS

Marital therapy can be a legitimate form of psychoanalytic psychotherapy, and to describe it I wish to draw a general distinction between *psychotherapy* and *psychoanalysis*. I propose that psychotherapy can be regarded as an activity spanning a broad spectrum that can merge with "pure" psychoanalysis as a clinical activity. As Paolino (1978) has emphasized, psychoanalysis is a word denoting a body of theory as well as a clinical practice. In my practice, however, I make a distinction between psychotherapy and psychoanalysis by both the initial and continuing motivation that brings the patient into treatment. In general, the more an individual presents with specific symptoms from which relief is urgently requested, as the first and persisting motivation for therapy, the more that therapy will tend to be on the psychotherapy end of the spectrum. The more the individual presents with a conscious or latent wish to understand himself or herself, the more the process will resemble "pure" psychoanalysis. This distinction is never absolute. However urgent their need for symptomatic relief, few people are completely uninterested in the development and workings of their own mind. Similarly, no one who ostensibly seeks enlightenment about himself or herself (a "training analysis") does not also harbor some wish to change important and even fundamental aspects of the self. I am not aware of any general acceptance of this distinction, but it is important in my practice. I think that the request for enlightenment is a legitimate one for the patient–client (the analysand) to make and an honorable one for a practitioner to attend to, and I believe it to be highly beneficial in the development of a psychotherapist's skills. But the request for insight, as an end in itself, is not the same as a request for symptomatic or characterological change. A central precept in the psychoanalytic theory of treatment is that therapeutic change in adults (but not in young children) is in some way mediated by insight. It is also clear that, on the one hand, much else goes on with significance for change within psychoanalysis, as Haley (1963) has written about so eloquently, and that, on the other hand, as Sandler *et al.* (1972) have emphasized, there are limitations to the role of insight in psychoanalysis. It is my experience that it is rare for a psychotherapy that benefits the patient (in my practice, "the patient" is a shorthand phrase to include an individual, a couple, a family, or even a stranger group) not to include or result in some changes in the subject's self-understanding. I think this is true for all psychological therapies, even those in which there is no conscious intention on the part of the therapist to make interpretations or communicate insight. For example, the experience of obtaining relief from a phobic state by an exposure program of graded desensitization or by implosion communicates a certain view as to the nature of the person undergoing the treatment and results in a change in the subject's self-understanding. My observations have been that such behavioral treatments may also result in some changes that, as a psychoanalyst, I would describe as "structural."

The importance of distinguishing motivations for insight and motivations for symptomatic relief lies in the implications for activity on the part of the psychoanalyst. In a psychotherapy, the psychoanalyst will use the psycho-dynamic formulation about the nature of the problem to devise a therapeutic strategy. The implementation of the strategy would not preclude the proffering of interpretations with the aim of developing "insight." At the same time, and perhaps principally, the therapist will give support, advice, or strategic directives based on the psychodynamic hypothesis whereby the individuals and their interpersonal relationship patterns are to be understood, and whose nature and timing will be determined by the analyst's perceptions of the current state of the transference. A strong positive transference, for example, may provide an opportunity to suggest to the patient the making of some significant life changes, in the expectation that the transference will allow the patient to feel safe about undertaking the activity. The changes advised will have been determined by the therapist's notion that the changes are likely to be within the patient's current capacity but will extend the range of activities and sublimations of the patient. In like manner, a strongly ambivalent transference can be taken advantage of to make a statement that may have the form of an interpretation but that is strategically devised to have a paradoxical intent. For example, the "interpretation" may contain a prediction that the patient cannot do what is said to be intensely sought for, with a psychodynamic explanation as to why that is the case.

In a psychoanalysis, by contrast, the therapist is not nearly so constrained by the pressure to achieve change into devising motivating interventions. The process is a collaborative exploration of the meaning and development of the patient's inner life and external relationship experiences. In an analysis, the therapist is always attempting to help the patient enlarge his or her awareness of the potential for achievements, relationships, and recreation, but the vehicle is the increasingly accurate perception of what is inside the self of the person.

As a rule, patients seen as couples are rarely motivated by a simple wish to enlarge their personal self-awareness though such couples are encountered occasionally. Mostly, couples seek urgent relief from the symptomatic state of one partner, or they suffer from overt marital distress. For this reason, communication of insight-promoting interpretations are given, not simply for the understanding they contain, but for strategic, change-provoking reasons (Gurman, 1981). The therapy is psychoanalytic in that the understanding of the individuals is psychoanalytically informed, and many of the interventions are couched in terms that make them resemble interpretations. That is, the interventions contain information that overtly refers to processes both within and between the individuals, and that is assumed by the therapist to reflect an accurate understanding of these individual and dyadic processes.

INDICATIONS FOR PSYCHOANALYTIC MARITAL THERAPY

Life-Cycle Considerations

If the interventive style of a particular piece of psychoanalytic psychotherapy is determined by the major motivation for therapy, then considerations of who is to be engaged in the therapeutic sessions is determined by the life-cycle location of the person or persons presenting with difficulties or requests for help.

Martin (1977) suggested an approach to the problem of determining whether an individual or a conjoint therapy was indicated. She identified the optimum training case, sought around the world by psychoanalytic training institutes, as a young adult, separated from and living relatively independently of the family of origin, whose presenting problems could be understood to have prevented the development of ties into a family of creation. By the contrary argument, the more a potential patient is closely involved in, and by implication "neurotically" snarled into, a family of origin or a family of creation, the less psychoanalysis is predicted to take a straightforward course (and hence to be a "suitable training case"). By the paradigm that Martin suggests, family therapy is indicated for problems presenting in people, notably children and adolescents, who are living with and closely absorbed in their families of origin. Individual therapy is indicated for young adults who have psychologically separated from their families of origin sufficiently to live independently, but who have not yet settled into long-term cohabiting love relationships.

By this analysis, marital therapy is sensibly contemplated in all cases when the presenting problem is located within someone who is in a partnership that has not yet produced children. For a married or cohabiting couple who have children, the indication for marital therapy must be determined by the extent to which the children are or are not actively and persistently drawn into the marital interactions. Clearly, no therapist is likely to believe that any child can be exempted from some psychological participation in his or her parents' marital arrangement, and so the judgment has to do with the degree of involvement. My rule of thumb has to do with symptomatology. If a child is symptomatic, then the therapist should assume that a whole family investigation is essential, however much the parents proclaim a marital problem. Marital therapy should not be prescribed on account of the therapist's observations of marital disharmony when the presenting problem is ascribed to a child of the family. Marital therapy may well be indicated when a couple who have children complain vigorously of their relationship problems.

Marital Therapy with Childless Couples

The most likely indication for marital therapy is for those couples (married or not) who have not yet had children. This is, indeed, the most common occasion for marital therapy in my practice. These couples present in two ways. The first mode of presentation is that the partners come jointly, asking for help because of marital tensions and rows. The question whether to break up or stay together and have children is apparent immediately or rapidly. In family life-cycle terms, the couple is trying to decide whether to enter the next phase, that is, to become a three-person, parenting structure.

The alternative is to separate and start again in order to reach, eventually, the parenting phase with another partner.

The second mode of presentation of childless couples is that they come via one partner asking for individual therapy (either, by my definition, for psychotherapy or psychoanalysis). The initially presenting partner may have a variety of symptoms ranging from persisting depressions or anxieties to a lack of success and satisfaction in work. The partner leading the request for help may be in professional training that carries with it a tradition of receiving personal therapy, that is, in a helping profession that uses counseling or psychotherapeutic skills. However the referral is organized, whether it be an overt request for symptomatic relief or a training experience in which insight is sought openly, I try, first, to see the partners together. Even with diverse requests, located in the individual, it is often quite explicit that the issue between the couple is whether to have children. For example, when one partner to a marriage requests an analysis for training purposes (as part of an institutional requirement or out of personal interest), there is often a discussion about whether their joint financial resources should be used on having a baby or for one of them to have an analysis. This comes out, usually in a straightforward way, when the therapist asks direct questions about their plans to have children. To my mind, there is an ethical issue in not seeing the couple when one partner requests an analysis unless it is fairly obvious that the decision not to have children has been very fully worked out by the couple. There is also an ehtical dilemma for me in taking into analysis an individual who is married or in a long-term partnership, knowing, as I do, that a psychoanalysis is a potentially powerful intrusion into married life. For this reason, most of the married people I have in analysis have had a previous marital therapy.

In summary, there are three indications for psychoanalytic marital therapy in a couple who have not yet had offspring: (a) when both members of a partnership are asking for an understanding of the nature of their relationship and of the problems that trouble them within it; (b) when one member of the marriage is seeking "insight" therapy, but there is not good evidence that the implications for his or her marriage have been seriously worked through; and (c) when one member of a partnership has symptoms for which psychoanalytic psychotherapy is indicated; that is, there are symptoms for which there is neither an urgent clamor for relief nor an obviously efficacious but as yet unprescribed safe medication, or a behavioral technique that is likely to be effective.

Marital Therapy with Couples with Children

The main indications for psychoanalytic psychotherapy in a couple with children is for serious marital problems, especially with people who come from a milieu in which a reflective evaluation of personal relationships and self-understanding are expected and appreciated. The therapist has to be sure that there are no significant involvements of children in the marital problem, as demonstrated by their symptomatic states. In my practice, either one or both members of such couples are also members of a profession or a culture in which individual psychoanalytic psychotherapy is the customary resort for all personal and relationship problems, and for whom therapy without accompanying offers of insight development from the therapist would be alien and unacceptable.

THE COURSE OF PSYCHOANALYTIC MARITAL THERAPY

The Setting and Subject Matter of Therapy

THE STRUCTURAL PROBLEM OF MARITAL THERAPY

In marital therapy, a consistent difficulty that is an inevitable concomitant of a three-person group has to do with the danger of alliance formations and taking sides. So strong is the problem of asymmetry—a couple consists of a man and a woman, and the therapist has to be either male or female— that it may be an indication for co-therapy. The relatively nondirective nature of psychoanalytic marital therapy is itself compatible with a co-therapy mode, provided the two therapists have a basic alignment in their theoretical orientation and in their technique (Rice, Fey, & Kepecs, 1972). I find co-therapy congenial in marital therapy (for reasons of the difficult countertransference issues raised in a subsequent section), but I also think that there are many problems inherent in working out the co-therapy relationship, and so, in practice, I rarely engage in co-therapy except with my wife as therapeutic partner.

In the absence of co-therapy as a solution to the inherent structural problem of marital therapy, the therapist must exercise constant surveillance of all the practices of the therapy in order to counteract the attendant risks. The hour arranged for the therapeutic meetings should be arranged with strict regard for equalizing the importance of the activities of both partners. I always try to negotiate with both members of the marriage, asking them to use two telephone extensions, if possible, in scheduling our initial session. In the therapy room, the chairs should be located so that there is no apparent favoring of one partner, and social graces should be deployed symmetrically in, for example, deferring politely on the threshold. For patients seen in private practice, I find it important to leave the bill in a neutral spot in the room so that the couple can decide who picks it up, rather than hand it to one or the other of them. It is crucial to be symmetrical in body orientation, tone of voice, balance of affective responsiveness, and so on. At every session, and many times in each session, the therapist has to review the interaction pattern between therapist and couple to identify any imbalance, both as a

source of information about the current state of the couple and to avoid a
bias in the therapeutic relationship (see Gurman [1981] for further discussion
of establishing early therapeutic alliances in marital therapy).

As to the frequency of therapy sessions, once a week or once a fortnight
is the most customary. Each session lasts the analytic hour (i.e., 50 minutes).
A longer time is necessary for some couples in crisis, but a shorter time is
too brief to establish a theme and see it through to a sense of having done
a clear piece of work.

THE EARLY STAGE OF MARITAL THERAPY

The couple is usually left to begin the session, commonly starting with a
summary of a conspicuous disagreement in the time since the previous
contact or, if one or the other is symptomatic and the therapy is still focused
thereby, a description of symptoms occurring in the interval. From the
beginning of the therapy, the couple can be "trained" to talk to each other,
for the most part, rather than to the therapist, both by being told so to do
and by the therapist's looking toward the silent, listening member of the
couple when one spouse is talking. By this means, the therapist can observe
the couple's interaction and is less often put on the spot by attempts on the
part of one or the other spouse to gain alliance with the therapist. As the
couple get under way in the session, the therapist may have to redress the
balance of utterances pouring from one spouse by urging the speaking
member of the couple to get a response from the silent spouse. The need
to obtain symmetry is a consistent feature and an example of the constant
need for a directive element in marital therapy. The therapist has to avoid
being treated as a witness to grievance, or worse, as a judge in the marital
disagreements. The attempt by a spouse to gain the therapist as an ally has
to be countered by openly disavowing any intention of taking sides and by
confronting the couple with each attempt to get the therapist in alliance
against a spouse.

LATER STAGES OF MARITAL THERAPY

Later in therapy, an exploration of childhood experiences of one or the
other spouse in being a confidant, a helpless observer, or a scapegoat of a
parent in interparental marital disputes may be undertaken and made the
subject of reconstructive interpretations. However, the therapist must give
attention to ensuring a balance between the exploration of the origins of
attitudes and roles within the marriage out of the spouses' individual childhood
experiences and attending to the here-and-now interactions. Reconstruction
of childhood origins of the marriage is important a little way into the therapy
in order to take the heat out of a persisting quarrelsome episode and invite
some sympathy on the part of each spouse for the other. A formal genogram
is useful for this purpose. Part of the insight that will usually be evolved in
the therapy is some understanding of the parts of their childhood that

structure the marriage, both insofar as there are aspects of childhood that they seem compelled to repeat in the marriage and parts that they attempt to "cure" by rigorous avoidance.

In the course of any discussion about current conflicts, or in the examination of past influences on the present, the therapist can be identifying processes between the couple. The way into process is by noting, first, the affective tone of both partners in an interchange, seeing how it moves in the course of discussion, and identifying repetitive sequences. The couple's tendencies to get into patterns (e.g., of attack and defensiveness, defeatism and contempt, injury and succour) are observed. Once seen, the therapist has the option of pointing out the sequence; of amplifying the pattern by encouraging more open expression of the affects; of urging one member of the couple to help the partner to break the pattern by noticing what is happening; of exploring what reminiscence of family of origin is represented in the sequences; or of encouraging exploration of the personal psychodynamics of the pattern. These options show that directive and interpretative possibilities reside in most of the material, and the therapist, at each point in the session and in the overall span of the therapy, must make decisions about where the balance should lie, in urging more interaction, encouraging mutual reflectiveness, forcibly opposing compulsively repeated sequencess, or interpreting individual conflicts and patterns of attitudes.

The Balance of Directive and Intepretative Interventions

As has been made clear here and elsewhere (Gurman, 1978, 1981), however much the therapist uses a psychoanalytic understanding of the individuals of the marriage and their interaction, psychoanalytic marital therapy cannot be as exclusively interpretive as a psychoanalysis seems to be. The repetitive sequences between the spouses are likely to be so forceful and compelling that interpretation alone will neither interrupt them in full flight nor eliminate them. Within the session, the therapist may have to block them by open prohibition while encouraging the couple to undertake their own control, within the session, of unproductive patterns of nagging and intimidation, on the one hand, or collusive, anxiety-reducing "assistance," on the other. For particularly rigid and intensely conflictual aspects of married life, pushing the couple to discuss solutions to out-of-session areas of conflict or symptomatic activities may be necessary, and it is essential to return to these areas in subsequent sessions to see if the couple have kept to their agreements. Failure to keep to agreed-on solutions is a rich source of material for enlightening the couple as to their unwitting commitment to painful patterns that, at a conscious level, they would like to avoid and is therefore a way into and a signal for further exploration of the unconscious origins of marital disharmony.

There are no fixed rules about whether a pattern can best be handled by the therapist by questioning and exploration; by reconstructive interventions about interactions or personal dynamics; by prescriptive or prohibitive directives, injunctions, or interpretations; or by straightforward task setting. That is, there is no "ideal" interpretation as the preferred mode of intervention that is "pure" and, therefore, right. The task of the therapist is to help the couple alter patterns in their marriage that they dislike and that prevent them achieving current satisfactions, and of taking advantage of individual life-cycle possibilities. Interpretation may give the couple the freedom they seek to be more fully together or to separate (if that seems right), but so may either a straightforward or paradoxical task (see Gurman [1982] for a discussion of the use of paradoxical interventions in psychdynamic marital therapy). A task or paradoxical prescription can be given because it may be a more forceful communication of the psychodynamics of the couple than an explicit interpretation (Skynner, 1981). To tell a couple to teach a wakeful child to have "happy" dreams, which, of course, contain scenes of graceful swooping movements in the warm sun and sea, may be as good a way to get them in a mood for mutual sensual pleasure as explicit sexual therapy or an interpretation of the origins of their sexual inhibitions. The dynamic meaning of each of these interventions is the same. The form is chosen according to the couple's cultural and intellectual style, the inventiveness and preference of the therapist, but, above all, what seems to be liberating for the couple at the moment.

The Issues of Transference and Countertransference

TRANSFERENCE

In psychoanalytic psychotherapy of the individual, the dyadic nature of the meeting and the relative neediness of the patient or client enhances the development of transferences of a parent–child sort. For this reason, in the psychoanalytic literature the evolution of technique has emphasized working with archaic infantile transferences, seemingly revealing aspects of the earlier phases of psychological life. The setting of couples therapy is, by its three-person nature and by the presence of the couple with their actual or potential sexual life, much more likely to give rise to oedipal transferences, with all the issues of alliances, coalitions, rivalries and jealousies, boundary formations, and triangulation that that stage implies. But it must be noted that although the couple as individuals may, in their neediness, have potential child transferences to the therapist (and this certainly occurs), the major inherent transference is to the therapist as an intruding child or adolescent, as a rival sib, or as a parent who will resent the oedipal child's closeness to the other parent. These transferences need to be observed (and produce complex countertransferences), but their interpretation is rarely therapeutically indicated. They are best managed by ensuring that the spouses interact with each other and are pushed into having as symmetrical a relationship as possible with the therapist.

Nevertheless, the concept of transference, although strictly concerned with the relationship of patient to therapist, is relevant to phenomena occurring between the spouses. Indeed, Gurman (1981) has noted that the husband–wife transferences are the central transferences in marital therapy requiring the therapist's active attention and intervention. The relationship between a couple always contains elements of child to parent (especially to mother) features derived from the infancy and childhood of the partners in their families of origin. In this sense, a great deal of "transference" interpretation goes on in psychoanalytic marital therapy as the therapist unfolds the infantile origins of qualities of married life.

COUNTERTRANSFERENCE

Most of the manuevers to gain a symmetrical relationship described thus far deal with the complex countertransferences that evolve in marital therapy. Inevitably the therapist, especially if trained in individual therapy, will be put in the position of the helping adult to the needy client or patient. This position is comfortable and gratifying. To be drawn into the position of intruding child or parent, or of disruptive adolescent, is bewildering and can lead to poor technique. Commonly, when the therapist is viewed positively, he or she will find that there is a sort of "grandparent" transference, whereby the couple attempt to use the therapist (perhaps appropriately) to gain freedom from superego prohibitions and ideals.

This complex web of countertransferences is compounded by what is the most specific and uncomfortable aspect of marital therapy for the therapist, namely, the recurring theme of the threat of divorce (Gurman, 1983, 1985). Few marital therapies, whether initiated for overt marital disharmony or on account of the symptoms of one spouse, will avoid coming up against the possibility of separation. Indeed, most couples seem to need to get to the point of realizing that divorce is possible for them to make significant movement in their relationship. This produces very painful and disequilibrating countertransferences in therapists, who so often have, from their backgrounds, persisting parentified child self-expectations. To oversee a couple who are likely to part is, for many therapists, a disabling reenactment of vivid childhood fears. It is one reason why personal psychotherapy, in which countertransferences from current therapeutic work are examined, is such a valued concomitant of training in marital therapy. Similarly, regular supervision, including review of video or audio tapes of sessions, is also valuable.

CONCLUSION

As described in this chapter, psychoanalytic marital therapy is not a pure form. The main stress lies in the conceptual framework whereby individual psychodynamics are postulated as structuring the marital relationship by unconscious family-of-origin motivations of transference-like qualities. These processes can by interpreted, and thus elements and variations of psychoanalytic psychotherapeutic techniques are employed. The major part of the therapy, like all marital therapies, is dominated by the need to gain a symmetrical relationship with the couple. This is all the more important the more the therapist tends to passivity. Because all activities on the part of the therapist have meaning, interpretations can be expressed explicitly as verbal statements communicating the therapist's understanding of the couple to the couple; or the meaning can be communicated analogically by tasks, injunctions, or enactments by the therapist (expressing rage, pain, hopefulness, restlessness, bewilderment, or whatever). The actual pattern of therapeutic activities will be altered by the phase of a session or therapy. Preexisting cultural and intellectual tendencies in the couple, the pressure of symptoms and intercurrent life events, will also affect the therapist's style; while the ever-present possibility of separation, divorce, or other major life changes will also have important technical implications.

REFERENCES

Bannister, K., & Pincus, L. (1965). *Shared phantasy in marital problems: Therapy in four-person relationship*. London: Tavistock Institute of Human Relations.

Blanck, R., & Blanck, G. (1968). *Marriage and personal development*. New York: Columbia University Press.

Dare, C. (1981). Psychoanalytic theories of the personality. In F. Fransella (Ed.), *Personality: Theory, measurement and research* (pp. 24–36). London: Methuen.

Dare, C. (1985). Psychoanalytic theories of development. In M. Rutter & L. Hersov (Eds.), *Child and adolescent psychiatry: Modern approaches* (pp. 204–215). Oxford, England: Blackwell Scientific Publications.

Dicks, H. V. (1967). *Marital tensions*. London: Routledge and Kegan Paul.

Framo, J. L. (1982). *Explorations in marital and family therapy*. New York: Springer.

Freud, S. (1915). *The unconscious*. Standard edition, *14*, 161–215.

Goodrich, W. (1968). Towards a taxonomy of marriage. In J. Marmor (Ed.), *Modern psychoanalysis*. New York: Basic Books.

Gurman, A. S. (1978). Contemporary marital therapies: A critique and comparative analysis of psychoanalytic, behavioral and system theory approaches. In T. J. Paolino & B. S. McCrady (Eds.), *Marriage and marital therapy* (pp. 455–566). New York: Brunner/Mazel.

Gurman, A. S. (1981). Integrative marital therapy: Toward the development of an interpersonal approach. In S. Budman (Ed.), *Forms of brief therapy*. New York: Guilford Press.

Gurman, A. S. (1982). Using paradox in psychodynamic marital therapy. *American Journal of Family Therapy, 10*(1), 72–74.

Gurman, A. S. (1983). The therapist's personal experience in working with divorcing couples. *American Journal of Family Therapy, 11*, 75–79.

Gurman, A. S. (1985). The therapist's role in couples' decision to divorce. *Family Therapy Networker*, in press.

Haley, J. (1963). *Strategies of psychotherapy*. New York: Grune & Stratton.

Katz, D., & Kahn, R. L. (1966). Common characteristics of open systems. In *The social psychology of organizations* (pp. 14–29). New York: Wiley.

Martin, F. (1977). Some implications from the theory and practice of family therapy for individual therapy (and vice versa). *British Journal of Medical Psychology, 50*, 53–64.

Minuchin, S. (1974). *Families and family therapy*. Cambridge, MA: Harvard University Press.

Neill, J. R., & Kniskern, D. P. (Eds.). (1982). *From psyche to system: The evolving therapy of Carl Whitaker*. New York: Guilford Press.

Olson, D. H. (1975). Marital and family therapy: A critical overview. In A. S. Gurman & D. G. Rice (Eds.), *Couples in conflict* (pp. 7–62). New York: Jason Aronson.

Paolino, T. J. (1978). Introduction: Some basic concepts of psychoanalytic psychotherapy. In T. J. Paolino & B. S. McCrady (Eds.), *Marriage and marital therapy*. New York: Brunner/Mazel.

Paolino, T. J., & McCrady, B. S. (1978). *Marriage and marital therapy*. New York: Brunner/Mazel.

Pincus, L., & Dare, C. (1978). *Secrets in the family*. London: Faber and Faber.

Rice, D. G., Fey, W. F., & Kepecs, J. G. (1972). Therapist experience and "style" as factors in co-therapy. *Family Process, 12*, 1–12.

Rycroft, C. (1956). The nature and function of the analyst's communication to the patient. In *Imagination and reality* (pp. 61–68). London: Hogarth Press.

Sandler, J. J., Dare, C., & Holder, A. (1972). *The patient and the analyst*. London: George Allen and Unwin.

Skynner, A. C. R. (1976). *One flesh: Separate persons*. London: Constable.

Skynner, A. C. R. (1981). An open systems, group-analytic approach to family therapy. In A. S. Gurman & D. P. Kniskern (Eds.), *Handbook of family therapy*. New York: Brunner/Mazel.

Stanton, M. D. (1981). Marital therapy from a structural/strategic viewpoint. In G. P. Sholevar (Ed.), *The handbook of marriage and marital therapy* (pp. 303–334). New York: Spectrum.

Steinglass, P. (1978). The conceptualization of marriage from a systems theory perspective. In T. J. Paolino & B. S. McCrady (Eds.), *Marriage and marital therapy*. New York: Brunner/Mazel.

von Bertalanffy, L. (1950). The theory of open systems in physics and biology. *Science, 3*, 23–29.

3

Marital Therapy: A Social Learning–Cognitive Perspective

NEIL S. JACOBSON
AMY HOLTZWORTH-MUNROE

The approach to marital therapy described in this chapter has evolved from early versions of what has come to be known as behavioral marital therapy (BMT). Whereas behavioral marital therapy has generally been defined as the application of social learning and behavior exchange principles to the treatment of marital problems (Jacobson & Margolin, 1979), our version of BMT has evolved to the point where a new label seems appropriate. Over the last 10 years there has been a distinct trend toward broadening the conceptual and technical domains of BMT to include an analysis of cognitive and affective variables; this has been true not only in our own work (Holtzworth-Munroe & Jacobson, 1985; Jacobson, 1983a, 1984; Jacobson, McDonald, Follette, & Berley, 1985; Wood & Jacobson, 1985) but also in the work of others (Baucom, 1981; Fincham & O'Leary, 1983; Margolin, Christensen, & Weiss, 1975; Margolin, 1983; Schindler & Vollmer, 1984; Revenstorf, 1984; Doherty, 1981; Weiss, 1980, 1984). With the development of a sophisticated clinical literature on marital therapy from a behavioral perspective, it has gradually become clear that treating couples is more complicated than early behavioral formulations would have had us believe (Jacobson, 1983a, 1983b; Jacobson & Margolin, 1979; Liberman, Wheeler, deVisser, Kuehnel, & Kuehnel, 1981; Margolin, 1983; Stuart, 1980). Moreover, research findings have tended to point us away from parsimony, as it has become apparent that nonmediational models account for relatively little variance in marital satisfaction (Jacobson & Moore, 1981). Perhaps what is most important, one inescapable conclusion from the wealth of controlled-outcome research

Neil S. Jacobson and Amy Holtzworth-Munroe. Department of Psychology, University of Washington, Seattle, Washington.

in BMT is that standard behavioral techniques are not always effective
(Jacobson, Follette, Revenstorf, Baucom, Hahlweg, & Margolin, 1984).
With this broadening and expanding of the model, the term *behavioral*
seems to have been eclipsed. Yet the commitment to empirical investigation,
which has until now distinguished behavioral from nonbehavioral models,
remains unaltered.

SOCIAL LEARNING—COGNITIVE (SLC) MODEL
OF MARITAL DISTRESS

Social learning theories have been characterized by a dual emphasis on the
social environment and cognitive–perceptual processes as determinants of
behavior (Bandura, 1977). The SLC perspective on marital distress certainly
falls within that tradition. First and perhaps foremost is a continued belief
in the preeminence of the social environment as a determinant of marital
satisfaction. Both marital stability and subjective marital satisfaction are seen
as determined by the relative frequency of positive and negative behavior
exchanges between spouses (Jacobson & Moore, 1981; Stuart, 1969; Weiss,
Hops, & Patterson, 1973). This model of marital satisfaction has been
described as both functional and hedonistic. Functionality is implied by the
emphasis on the relationship between behaviors emitted by spouses in a
marital relationship and the environmental antecedents and consequences.
The model is hedonistic because it begins with a straightforward proposition
that benefits received determine whether or not couples will stay in relationships. Indeed, there is abundant evidence that nondistressed couples
exchange higher frequencies of rewards, and lower frequencies of punishers,
than do their distressed counterparts (Birchler, Weiss, & Vincent, 1975;
Gottman, 1979; Jacobson, Follette, & McDonald, 1982; Margolin, 1981;
Margolin & Wampold, 1981; Markman, 1979; Vincent, Weiss, & Birchler,
1975; Vincent, Freidman, Nugent, & Messerley, 1979).

In addition to differing in the amount and degree of exchanged reinforcement and punishment, distressed and nondistressed couples can be
distinguished by the pattern of reinforcing and punishing exchanges. Distressed
couples are highly *reciprocal* in their exchanges of negative behaviors (Gottman,
1979; Margolin & Wampold, 1981; Schapp, 1984); when one spouse delivers
a punisher to the other, the latter is very likely to reciprocate, which begins
a chain of escalating coercive interaction (Hahlweg *et al.*, 1984). Moreover,
distressed couples are highly *reactive* to immediate relationship events, whether
they are rewarding or punishing (Jacobson *et al.*, 1982). This means that
punishers have an immediate impact that is more punishing, and rewards
have an immediate impact that is more rewarding, for distressed than for
nondistressed couples. Thus, punishing behavior has a particularly deleterious
impact on distressed spouses and is highly likely to lead to escalation. In
contrast, happily married couples are relatively unlikely to reciprocate punishing

behavior (Gottman, 1979). Moreover, couples who are happy seem to be less reactive to immediate events in a relationship (Jacobson *et al.*, 1982). Thus, these couples exhibit both a resilience and a relative independence from immediate contingencies that are absent in couples who are not getting along.

The expansion of the model has been primarily in two directions: away from a nonmediational and toward a mediational theory; and from a purely functional model that is basically content free to one that attempts to specify some of the topographical parameters in marital satisfaction–distress. More specifically, movement toward a mediational model is reflected primarily in an emphasis on the cognitive and perceptual processes associated with marital distress (Baucom, 1981; Doherty, 1981; Fincham & O'Leary, 1983; Holtzworth-Munroe & Jacobson, 1985; Jacobson, McDonald, Follette, & Berley, 1985) and a more recent emphasis on the role of affect in controlling both functional and dysfunctional marital processes (Gottman, 1982; Levenson & Gottman, 1983). Cognitive research has focused on the role of causal attributions in producing, maintaining, and exacerbating marital distress. The research cited above indicates that distressed couples tend to attribute their partners' negative behavior to factors that maximize its negative impact and at the same time undermine the impact of positive behavior through causal attributions that deny the partner credit for it. This is simply one example of an area of research that suggests it is not only the things that spouses do and say that cause them problems but also how those events are construed and perceived. Attention to the role of affect is even newer to the literature, but recent research by Gottman and his associates appears to offer some promising new directions. For example, Gottman (personal communication, 1984) recently offered an escape conditioning model to explain why conflict-avoidant tendencies exist in distressed couples. This model is based on evidence that husbands manifest strong sympathetic nervous system arousal during conflict exercises and that the duration of intense sympathetic arousal is greater for men than it is for women. Gottman believes that there may be sex differences in the aversiveness of negative affect.

Finally, the undernourished skeleton of traditional behavioral models has been nourished in recent years by attempts to characterize the topography of marital satisfaction and distress. Much of this work has involved the specific kinds of deficiencies that exist in distressed relationships. As one example, specific deficits in communication skills seem to characterize distressed couples (Gottman, 1979). These deficiencies are especially evident in strategies that distressed couples use for dealing with conflict, a fact that serves as the rationale for teaching couples conflict-resolution skills in marital therapy (Gottman, 1979; Jacobson & Margolin, 1979; Margolin & Wampold, 1981; Schaap, 1984). Moreover, topographical analyses based on spouse reports of behavior in the home show that communication problems are better predictors of daily marital satisfaction than complaints in other areas (Jacobson & Moore, 1981). In addition to research elucidating the role of communication deficiencies in marital conflict, theoretical speculation exists in a number of areas. Weiss (1980), for example, has identified skill deficits in pinpointing, providing supportive and understanding communication, and negotiation of behavior change; he has suggested that these skill deficits, as well as those in the area of problem solving, best differentiate distressed from nondistressed couples. Jacobson (1983b) has identified traditional sex-role structures as conducive to marital distress and has provided recent evidence that such patterns predict a negative response to marital therapy (Jacobson, Follette, & Pagel, 1984).

In short, conceptual research and theorizing in the SLC area is occurring in a number of different laboratories all over the world (cf. Hahlweg & Jacobson, 1984). It appears that the relationship between theory and practice is reciprocal rather than unidirectional. Many examples of theoretical developments have produced clinical innovations, as the paragraphs below indicate. However, clinical observations have also been a plentiful source of research findings (Jacobson, 1984).

A THEORY OF THERAPEUTIC CHANGE

Our version of marital therapy is one of many that have been developed in various clinical research laboratories around the world under the "behavioral" rubric. After the pioneering work of Richard B. Stuart and the collaborative effort between Gerald R. Patterson and Robert L. Weiss at the University of Oregon, marital treatment programs from this perspective have been studied by K. Daniel O'Leary and associates at Stony Brook, Gayla Margolin and Andy Christensen in Los Angeles, John Gottman at the University of Illinois, Donald H. Baucom at the University of North Carolina, Kurt Hahlweg and Dirk Revenstorf at the Max Planck Institute in Munich, Paul Emmelkamp in Holland, Howard Markman in Denver, and elsewhere. For the remainder of this chapter, we focus on our own version of marital therapy from an SLC perspective. Despite some differences between the various approaches cited above, some overriding technical and conceptual similarities make the choice of which model to focus on somewhat arbitrary. Since ours is the one with which we are the most familiar, it receives primary attention.

The SLC marital therapist derives treatment strategies from a number of sources. He or she is familiar with the conceptual framework discussed in the previous section. During assessment phases, attention tends to focus on behaviors and problems identified in research studies as those that discriminate between happy and unhappy couples. In other words, although these areas do not automatically receive attention in marital therapy, they always receive close scrutiny during a marital assessment.

Based on the research findings that distressed couples actually exchange fewer rewarding and a greater number of punishing behaviors than nondistressed couples, one initial goal of marital therapy is to increase the ratio of positive to negative behavior exchanges. This is accomplished mainly through focusing on increasing positive instead of decreasing negative behavior. There is evidence that positive and negtative events are relatively independent (Wills, Weiss, & Patterson, 1974) and that negative behaviors tend to diminish automatically during successful marital therapy, even if they are not the main focus of therapeutic interventions (Margolin & Weiss, 1978). The assumption is that if a supportive environment can be created for the acceleration of positive behaviors, not only will behavior changes occur but cognitive and affective changes will result. Thus, in attempting to produce increases in the exchange of positive behavior, primary attention is focused on creating a context for the occurrence of such changes that will also produce cognitive and affective changes that reinforce the behavior changes.

In short, the SLC approach is based in part on the assumption that behavior change is not only important in its own right but offers a lever for producing cognitive and affective changes. While a therapist working within this framework might be more inclined than others to insist on behavior change before being willing to designate a case as successful, this same therapist would not claim success, despite fundamental behavior changes, unless couples report that they are happier with the relationship. Thus, the emphasis on behavior change is a means to an end as much as it is an end in itself.

A second premise of the SLC approach is that skills are required in order to maintain a satisfactory intimate relationship over a long period. No matter how attracted two people might be to one another initially, and no matter how "legitimate" the basis for attraction, love and attraction are not enough to sustain a relationship across the myriad of obstacles and hurdles that life throws in one's path. Couples need a variety of skills, including the ability to deal constructively with conflict, provide support and understanding to one another, and perform a variety of instrumental and affectional tasks. The SLC perspective attempts during the assessment phase to identify the areas of deficiency and target those for change during marital therapy.

The area of skill deficiency most commonly emphasized is that of conflict resolution. When couples enter therapy manifesting dysfunctional strategies for resolving conflict, the therapist usually has no way of knowing whether these performance deficits bear a causal relationship to other marital problems. Thus the categorization of these deficiencies as skill deficits is as much for heuristic purposes as it is because the label is believed to be literally true. The advantages of such a categorization are, first, that the reattribution of marital problems as manifestations of skill deficiencies is generally more benign than the attributions made by the spouses themselves in attempting to account for their difficulties; and second, it allows the therapist to focus on training in problem-solving and conflict-resolution skills during marital therapy. Problem-solving training is a very effective therapeutic technique when used as part of a marital therapy regimen, whatever the rationale for its use (Jacobson, 1984; Jacobson & Follette, 1985). Among other things, when couples can sit down and deal with conflict constructively with one another they are much better able to function as their own therapists when conflict arises in the future. In short, besides the immediate therapeutic impact of conflict resolution training strategies, they also serve a preventative function.

The other major category of intervention that follows from the SLC conceptual framework involves an attempt to overcome *reinforcement erosion*, which refers to the tendency for spouses in a long-term relationship gradually to lose their ability to gratify one another. The causes of reinforcement erosion are numerous, but at times habituation is a sufficient explanation. The SLC marital therapy helps override the effects of reinforcement erosion by teaching couples to track relationship quality on a day-to-day basis and devote the time and attention to it required to maintain high levels of marital satisfaction.

Stages of Therapy

To some extent, it is antithetical to the SLC perspective to discuss "stages" because one of the central features of the model is its emphasis on a functional analysis, which implies an idiographic approach to assessment and treatment. Conceivably, the stages of therapy could differ dramatically from one couple to another. In practice, however, marital therapy does tend to follow a well-defined structure that reflects in part the clinical research context in which much of the technology was developed and the common denominators that unite many kinds of marital problems despite divergence in content.

STAGE 1: ASSESSMENT

The SLC marital therapy distinguishes assessment from therapy. Unless couples enter therapy in a state of acute crisis, two to three sessions are devoted exclusively to assessment and evaluation. During the assessment phase, couples are told that no commitment has been made by either side to work together in therapy. Rather, the purpose of the evaluation is to determine whether marital therapy is the optimal plan, and if not, for the therapist to recommend alternative courses of action (e.g., individual therapy for one or both spouses). Couples are further told not to expect improvement in their relationship during the evaluation, since the focus is on collecting information rather than on interventions aimed at relationship enhancement.

The specific tactics and strategies used to conduct an SLC marital assessment include a variety of self-report questionnaires, both conjoint and individual spouse interviews, daily data collection by spouses at home, and a systematic evaluation of communication patterns. These techniques are well described elsewhere (Jacobson, Elwood, & Dallas, 1981; Jacobson & Margolin, 1979; Margolin & Jacobson, 1981; Weiss & Margolin, 1977).

The important point is that many techniques can be used to achieve the same goals, which are to understand what the determinants are of a particular couple's current dissatisfaction. Assessment is comprehensive and at the same time focused on those areas of relationship functioning that receive particular emphasis within an SLC framework: communication and problem-solving skills; both potentially and actually exchanged reinforcing and punishing behaviors; patterns of escalation and coercion; areas of instrumental skill deficiency; cognitive schema, beliefs, and attributional processes; and repetitive interactional themes.

The process of assessment has several noteworthy features besides the information-gathering function. First, the information-gathering procedures often have a therapeutic effect, despite the therapist's insistence to the contrary. Since the focus is on relationship strengths as well as problem areas, and since every effort is made to understand the basis for a given couple's attachment to each other, the questions asked by the therapist often facilitate spouses' attention to more positive aspects of the relationship. Given that couples often enter therapy selectively tracking negative aspects of the relationship, this refocusing of attention can often bring relief and some positive affect. Moreover, the experience of being in therapy and talking to a neutral, objective third party about relationship problems can in and of itself mitigate feelings of hopelessness and enhance positive expectancies about the relationship.

Second, the outcome of this assessment process could be a decision not to proceed with marital therapy. The recognition of "no therapy" as a viable option is very important for a marital therapist because unless such options are actively explored, the danger exists that couples will be inadvertently maneuvered into marital therapy even when it is not in the best interests of one or both of them (Jacobson, 1983a). For example, at the time that Jack and Connie entered marital therapy, Connie had already spent 6 months disengaging from the relationship in various ways including more independent activities with other people, the acceptance of a job that required more traveling, and some emotional withdrawal from Jack. Given Jack's long history of physical abuse, the disengagement process seemed to the therapist to be healthy and in need of support. A treatment program oriented toward enhanced intimacy would have required a greater degree of reinvestment in the relationship than was warranted at present, given all of the assessment information. Thus it was very important that the option of continued dis-engagement be thoroughly considered and explored during the assessment phase.

ROUNDTABLE DISCUSSION

After the therapist has completed the evaluation, she or he presents the couple with a formulation of the problems, an assessment of their strengths as a couple, and a proposed treatment plan. If marital therapy is indicated, both therapist and spouses agree on a time-limited course of treatment with specific goals. Only once this treatment regimen has been agreed upon can it be said that therapy has begun.

INSTIGATION OF INCREASES IN POSITIVE BEHAVIOR

Very often therapy begins with an emphasis on the generation of positive changes in the natural environment. These interventions are designed to have short-term but immediate effects on the relationship, to provide couples with a shot in the arm. Typically, the interventions feature directives from the therapist regarding assignments to be implemented at home. Following implementation, the couple return for the subsequent session and the home-work assignment is debriefed. The content of this next session is determined by the outcome of the previous homework assignment. If the assignment went well, the couple are ready to move on to the next step. If it went poorly, some troubleshooting might be necessary in order to remediate whatever difficulties the couple had with the assignment.

The primary purpose of these instigative interventions is to produce short-term increases in positive behavior exchanges. Relationship skills designed to extend these benefits over time are deemphasized. If the therapist were to stop treatment following a successful round of such instigative interventions, the probability of relapse would be great (Jacobson, 1984; Jacobson & Follette, 1985). However, it is not completely correct to say that these interventions are devoid of skill-training components. As we elaborate in the following section, couples learn to pay daily attention to the quality of the relationship, identify problem areas when they exist, and intervene in efficacious ways to enhance daily marital satisfaction. These skills are often novel to couples who enter therapy without understanding that relationships require care and attention in order to succeed.

SKILL ACQUISITION

The bulk of therapy session time in the typical case is devoted to the acquisition of new behaviors generally conceptualized as skills. Most often, the primary focus in this phase is on communication skills, especially problem-solving skills. Less often, but not infrequently, other skills receive primary attention, such as parenting or sexual enrichment skills. During the skill-acquisition phase of therapy, the therapist is quite directive, the sessions highly structured, and the techniques largely psychoeducational.

GENERALIZATION AND MAINTENANCE

Since the ultimate goals of therapy involve changes in the relationship that persist independently of the therapist, it is important that his or her influence begins to subside once the skills have been acquired. The skills are designed to allow the couple to function independently of the therapist; but in order for couples to acquire the necessary independence, strategies for generalization and maintenance must be inserted into the treatment program. The influence of the therapist must fade, couples must assume increasing responsibility for managing their own affairs, and the therapy session itself must gradually cease to be the focus of all important relationship issues. This last phase of therapy attempts to foster couples' independence through a variety of technical and clinical procedures.

The attempt to train spouses to become their own therapists has been only partially successful. Recent evidence indicates that while the skills taught to couples within the SLC framework do extend the benefits of therapy over time, even with this focus the effects gradually fade for many couples. Thus we are currently in the process of experimenting with some clinical innovations designed to enhance long-term outcomes. Included among our current efforts are the use of booster sessions beginning 6 months following formal termination. The underlying principle behind our current efforts is that the former expectation regarding the permanence of our treatment effects was naive. Why should a short-term treatment program result in permanent changes in a relationship subjected to numerous influences other than therapy? In an attempt to cope with this debunking of our omnipotence myths, the concept of marital therapy is being gradually altered. Instead of the idea that therapy is intensive, discrete, and has a specific termination date, long-term relationship enhancement may be more likely with a model that deemphasizes formal termination. In this model a relationship is formed between a couple and a therapist, but it is considered ongoing even beyond the end of weekly sessions. It is expected that couples will return for periodic visits, much like the regular visit to a dentist.

OVERVIEW

In clinical research settings, where a relatively standardized treatment package is used, therapy consists of 20 sessions, 60 to 90 minutes each, once per week. During the generalization and maintenance phase, sessions occur less frequently. The sessions themselves tend to be highly structured, beginning with an agenda negotiated between the therapist and the couple. After the agenda is set for a given session, homework from the previous session is discussed and debriefed. Most sessions include a main body of "new business," which to some extent follows from the previous week's homework. Sessions usually end with some sort of recapitulation of the events of the session, and conclude with the presentation of a new homework assignment.

SPECIFIC TECHNIQUES

The therapist working within an SLC framework has a wide assortment of techniques from which to select. The assessment process and roundtable session establish the specific goals to which both therapist and couple have committed themselves to work in therapy. From that point on, techniques can be chosen that are most appropriate to meeting those goals. The techniques to be discussed in the present section are commonly used, and they will be discussed in the order in which they usually appear. Nevertheless, it is important to keep in mind that treatment plans are tailored to the needs of individual couples, and we organize according to techniques primarily for convenience and ease of presentation.

Behavior Exchange Techniques

Therapy often begins with a few sessions devoted to instigating increases in the rate of positive behavior exchange. After months or years of focusing selectively on the negative events in the relationship, an early emphasis in therapy on pinpointing and increasing positive behavior can help overcome this perceptual bias. In addition, behavior exchange (BE) techniques can be effective in countering spouses' feelings of helplessness at the beginning of therapy, which usually manifest themselves in the expressed conviction that there is nothing they can do to improve the quality of the relationship. One version of this conviction is the claim that the other's behavior is solely responsible for how the relationship is going. Another is that feelings of satisfaction and dissatisfaction are ineffable and are unrelated to the occurrence or nonoccurrence of specific behaviors. The BE techniques help couples pinpoint the behaviors associated with their own and their partners' subjective satisfaction and dissatisfaction with the relationship. They also learn to use their own behavior to enhance the quality of the relationship on a day-to-day basis. When the interventions have the desired effect, not only do they result in short-term increases in marital satisfaction but also a sense of control over the course of the relationship on a day-to-day basis. The concept that maintaining marital satisfaction requires daily vigilance and attention is introduced, as is the notion that even small changes in behavior can have a major impact on marital satisfaction. Although it is not uncommon for couples to complain about the artificiality of some exercises, the therapist can usually reassure them by insisting that such premeditated attention is necessary when the goal is to modify long-standing, habitual behavior patterns.

At the beginning of therapy, couples are often so entrenched in their habitual patterns of blaming one another for the marital problems that the collaborative set necessary for the successful resolution of long-standing issues is virtually impossible to establish. Initially, BE does not focus on major areas of conflict, and as a result is less demanding and therefore more likely to pay off during the early stages of therapy. Tasks and assignments are graded in such a way that partners can experience success without having to change high-cost behaviors. Subsequent to their experience of enhanced satisfaction, they are often more collaborative and therefore willing to take on some of the demanding tasks that comprise the latter stages of therapy.

Behavior exchange relies heavily on homework assignments as a vehicle for enhancing relationship quality. In fact, the therapy sessions revolve around the previous week's homework assignment: The beginning of a session is spent debriefing the previous assignment; the middle of the session is often spent troubleshooting those aspects of the assignment that did not work well; and the latter part of the session is spent presenting a new assignment that emerges in part from the just-completed discussion of the prior assignment. One of the underlying messages of BE is that marital therapy is not simply attending a session for an hour a week; indeed, from the beginning couples learn that the work at home is much more central to the success of the therapy enterprise than what transpires during the therapy session. This may be one of the central differences between the SLC perspective and other theoretical frameworks. Other techniques, such as communication–problem-solving training, utilize the session itself as a vehicle for change; with BE, the vehicle for change is the home environment.

The BE techniques typically begin with the request that both spouses focus on themselves. This means that each spouse is asked, in a number of different ways, how she or he is contributing to the problems in the relationship, and what power she or he has to improve its quality by making behavior changes. The commitment to focusing on oneself is sought during the roundtable discussion and before therapy actually begins. By encouraging both spouses to avoid blaming their partners for the paucity of gratification currently existing in the relationship, and by insisting on solutions that involve each spouse targeting his or her own behavior for change, the therapist interrupts a long-standing and unproductive pattern involving both passivity, with each spouse feeling powerless and waiting for the partner to "change first," and excessive preoccupation with one's own victimization. The self-focus activates spouses and restructures their efforts to improve the relationship. Once couples have committed themselves to focusing on their own behavior, time is spent teaching them to "pinpoint" behaviors in their repertoires that have a salutary impact on daily marital satisfaction. Behavior-change directives are then delivered by the therapist, in which each spouse is asked to increase the frequency of some of these pinpointed behaviors and to observe the impact of these increases on the partner's daily marital satisfaction, which is being continuously recorded. Each spouse engages in this task independently but simultaneously, and so the behavior-change directives are at once parallel and unilateral. Of special interest here are two dimensions of this assignment that deviate from typical behavior exchange directives: First, both spouses are initially asked to come up with their own hypotheses about what will be reinforcing for their partner, as opposed to the usual method of asking each spouse what she or he wants from the other; second, instead of directing spouses to change particular behaviors, the therapist delivers rather general instructions to increase the frequency of "some" behaviors from a pool of potential reinforcers. The rationale for both of these modifications is that they maximize the amount of choice for each spouse regarding what behaviors to accelerate. Based on social-psychological reactance theory, choice should decrease the likelihood of resistance to the directive on the part of the giver. More important, choice renders it more likely that any behavior change that does occur will be viewed by the recipient as internally motivated, voluntary, reflective of a positive attitude, and likely to continue (Holtzworth-Munroe & Jacobson, 1985). Thus, BE is structured, not merely to encourage behavior change, but also to maximize the likelihood that occurring behavior changes will be supported by corresponding cognitive and perceptual shifts.

There are a number of variants on the basic BE themes. Stuart (1980) asks spouses to hold "caring days," where each spouse is to act as if she or he cared for the other and accordingly engage in behaviors designed to be pleasing. Weiss, Hops, and Patterson (1973) instruct spouses to hold "love days," where on certain days, without announcement to the partner, spouses double or triple their rates of positive behaviors. Liberman, Wheeler, deVisser, Kuehnel, and Kuehnel (1981) teach pinpointing by encouraging their couples to "catch your spouse doing something nice" as an early homework assignment, and foster accelerations in positive behavior using the "perfect marriage fantasy," where partners generate ideas for possible ways of improving the relationship.

To illustrate our use of BE procedures, we shall use an example where hypothesized reinforcers and punishers are derived from the Spouse Observation Checklist (SOC). The SOC is a daily checklist of marital behaviors completed by each partner once a day. It was originally developed by Patterson, Weiss, and their associates (Patterson, 1976) and has been revised by Weiss and Perry (1979). Our version (Jacobson, Follette, & McDonald, 1982; Jacobson & Moore, 1981; Jacobson, Waldron, & Moore, 1980) consists of 409 items divided into 12 categories of marital behavior (e.g., Companionship, Sex, Household Responsibilities). The task is to report retrospectively over the past 24 hours whether or not a particular behavior has occurred and then to rate its impact (positive, negative, or neutral) if it occurred. Thus, if each spouse completes the SOC nightly for a week, you have a daily record of the positive, negative, and neutral events that occur. Furthermore, when each spouse is asked to rate the overall marital satisfaction for that day on a 9-point Likert Scale, daily frequencies of particular types of events can be correlated with subjective satisfaction to generate hypotheses regarding the potent reinforcers and punishers in the relationship. Couples can be taught to generate hypotheses using the SOC. Later, they are asked to test those hypotheses by increasing their delivery of some hypothesized reinforcers and then observing their impact on the partner's marital satisfaction ratings. Again, as we mentioned above, each spouse chooses from a list of reinforcers the behaviors to deliver; and each spouse generates her or his hypotheses regarding what behaviors would increase the partner's satisfaction rating, without input from the partner. Later, when the couple return for their next session, input from the recipient is added regarding behaviors that she or he would like to see increased.

The following is a portion of an early therapy session where BE techniques were utilized. The therapist is reviewing a homework assignment from the preceding week, which had involved each spouse's attempting to generate, from the partner's SOC, a list of behaviors that appeared to be associated with high marital satisfaction ratings. Later that same week, they were to increase the frequency of four or five of these hypothesized reinforcers.

THERAPIST: O.K., so we've agreed to spend most of the session reviewing which behaviors each of you thought increased your partner's satisfaction with the marriage and whether your ideas were correct. I'd like to know which items from the SOC you put on your list of behaviors that might please your spouse. Would you like to start, Bob?

BOB: Sure, I made a pretty long list.

THERAPIST: Good. That means there are lots of ways you might be able to please Ann.

BOB: Yeah, and I noticed that a lot of them were under the Communication section of her form. Like, "Spouse talked to me about his day" and "We discussed a problem." Those were all marked with a plus sign when they occurred. Except the items about arguing.

THERAPIST: So, you think that area of your relationship, communication, might be important to her?

BOB: Seems to be. I mean, I didn't even remember talking about some things until I looked at her list. That stuff isn't stuff I normally think about.

ANN: That's true. I really noticed that I was marking lots of communication items and Bob wasn't. That sort of upset me that he didn't even notice.

THERAPIST: That's important information and very common . . . what pleases one person may not be exactly the same as what pleases another person. I should have warned you about that last week, before you examined each other's SOCs, but I'm glad you brought it up now. Often with couples some of the things they enjoy overlap and some are different. And that's normal. . . . After all, your task is to please your spouse, so what's important is knowing what will do that, since it may not be the same as what pleases you.

ANN: I guess so. I mean, I know it's really nice for me when Bob brings me flowers, but he wouldn't be thrilled if I brought him flowers. Right, Bob?

BOB: Yeah.

THERAPIST: O.K., that's a good example. And the point is that even though getting flowers may not thrill Bob, it's important that he knows it thrills you, Ann, so that he can please you. Now, let's get back to Bob's finding out that communication is important to Ann.

BOB: Well, I also kept track of her—what is it?—daily marital satisfaction rating, DSR.

THERAPIST: Yes, DSR.

BOB: Yeah, and it was higher on days when we talked a lot. Like the first couple of days her DSR was a four and then, on Sunday, we had a long talk about my problems at work and her DSR for that day was a six.

ANN: That was a good talk. Bob never seems to want to do that any more. It's not like when we first—

THERAPIST: O.K., I'm going to ask you to stop, Ann, and try to focus on the positives right now, because it sounds like there are some of those. Also, I want to remind you to focus on yourselves and your own behavior during this discussion. You did have a good talk this week.

ANN: Yeah, you're right.

THERAPIST: O.K., so it looked like those items were ways to please Ann. Did you test your theory?

BOB: Yeah, the last couple of days I've been better about talking.
THERAPIST: Can you give me some examples?
BOB: Well, every day when I got home I asked her how her day was.
THERAPIST: Great. Anything else?
BOB: Yesterday she was upset about a phone call with her mother, and I asked if she wanted to tell me about it. That was about all.
THERAPIST: That seems like a good start. Did those things seem to increase Ann's satisfaction?
BOB: Well, her DSR had been a five or six recently.
THERAPIST: You mean since you started asking her how her day was and asked about the phone call?
ANN: Yeah, it's really true. Plus I told him that I liked it.
THERAPIST: Great, it's really nice when you let someone know you appreciate their efforts. Sometimes couples who are mad let each other know but forget to tell each other when they are feeling good about something the other person did. How did that make you feel, Bob?
BOB: Good. You know what, after a fight with her mom, I often try not to get involved, and we have an argument later 'cause she's still upset about the fight. But that didn't happen this time.
THERAPIST: So it seems like by asking her to talk you were able to prevent an argument.
BOB: Yeah, I guess so.

The session continued with a focus on Ann and the behaviors she tried to increase.

This brief excerpt illustrates many facets of BE, along with many of the clinical issues that generalize to other domains of marital therapy. First, the therapist keeps each spouse focusing on herself or himself. Second, the emphasis is on increasing positive behavior and tracking positive aspects of the homework assignment; although couples often tend to dwell on the one day when things did not go well or the one argument they might have had, the therapist wants to maintain their focus on the positive aspects of the relationship in order to build on those and modify their biased, negative tracking. Third, the therapist encourages the spouses to be specific so that each person understands exactly what behaviors were attempted and so that successful experiences can be replicated. Fourth, the therapist normalizes differences between spouses in their preferences, thus suggesting that people do not have to be identical in order to be compatible. Fifth, the therapist not only underscores and specifies the successful experiences but also attempts, whenever possible, to state the general principle underlying the specific experiences. In this case, the therapist pointed out that a new method for dealing with the wife's stormy relationship with her mother may have emerged.

These examples are in no way meant to be a comprehensive list of BE techniques. The BE techniques can be used not only to generate positive exchanges at the beginning of therapy but can also be extended to cover major areas of discord. In short, BE involves any instigative intervention where the goal is to generate behavior change between spouses at home. It is to be distinguished from the more process-oriented communication–

problem-solving training to be discussed in the next section. For some couples, BE will be a sufficient treatment. Most couples require tactics in addition to BE, however, because BE does not directly address the quality of marital interaction. Thus it provides little basis for weaning couples from the therapy environment. What it does provide is relief from the feelings of hopelessness that often pervade the decision to seek marital therapy, practice in pinpointing currently existing resources, and the important lesson that relationship quality can be directly affected by changes in relatively low-cost behaviors. Most frequently, it is designed to pave the way for the more intensive process-oriented work to be discussed below.

Communication–Problem-Solving Training

Perhaps the one therapeutic technique found universally in marital therapies, regardless of theoretical orientation, is communication training. Research supports the widespread utilization of such techniques. Distressed couples exhibit a variety of dysfunctional communication patterns (Gottman, 1979). Moreover, there is some evidence that these faulty communication patterns not only precede but actually predict subsequent marital distress (Markman, 1979). Finally, recent studies show spouse-reported communication to be the content category most highly correlated with daily marital satisfaction (Jacobson & Moore, 1981). Thus, even if none of this research proves that communication deficiencies are causally related to subsequent marital distress, they show that both observers and spouses report pervasive deficiency in communication dissatisfaction with communication, or both, in amounts that are directly proportional to the overall functioning of the marriage.

The distinguishing characteristic between communication training from an SLC perspective and that of other theoretical schools is its use of direct teaching strategies to promote positive communication. With the exception of Guerney's work (see Chapter 6, this volume), no school of marital therapy other than the SLC relies on behavior rehearsal as a primary component of the training (cf. Jacobson & Margolin, 1979). The SLC method of communication training is complicated and multifaceted; it involves didactic instructions, practice by the couple, and feedback from the therapist based on the practice sessions. There is good reason to believe that such tactics are necessary to promote the acquisition of new communication skills: Jacobson and Anderson (1980) found that only the complete package produced increments in communication growth relative to no training; neither instructions alone, instructions and rehearsal without feedback, nor instructions and feedback without rehearsal produced any notable changes in interactional performance.

This section pays special attention to problem-solving training, which is communication training oriented toward enhancing the ability of marital partners to talk to one another about conflict issues in the relationship.

Problem-solving training (PS) has played a central role in our model throughout its history. However, before discussing PS, some attention will be devoted to other forms of communication training, particularly the teaching of receptive and expressive skills. These latter areas have been increasingly emphasized in our own work and have long been a major component of both behavioral and other kinds of marital therapy (Guerney, 1977; O'Leary & Turkewitz, 1978; Weiss *et al.*, 1973).

TEACHING RECEPTIVE AND EXPRESSIVE COMMUNICATION SKILLS

Historically, behavioral marital therapists taught listening and expressing as preludes to working on problem solving and behavior change. They once played a subordinate role in our work. In recent years, however, we have begun to focus more explicitly on these skills as important targets for therapeutic change in their own right. There are two main reasons for this renewed emphasis. First, our clinical experience told us that the exclusive focus on the more instrumental communication skills taught during PS was clearly helping our couples to become better companions, but it was less clear that it was producing greater emotional closeness and intimacy (Jacobson, 1983b; Margolin, 1983). Teaching couples to share feelings with one another in a supportive, understanding way seems to complement nicely the more rational, cognitive emphasis of PS. Second, we have begun to view communication training as a powerful method for promoting egalitarianism. Since we believe that relationships with unequal power are almost guaranteed to promote continued distress to one if not both partners, the movement toward egalitarianism is believed to be inherent in all our work with couples. Therefore, anything that promotes it is clinically useful to an SLC perspective.

The techniques themselves are highly derivative and not in any way unique to our model. In fact, in large part they are the same skills emphasized by Guerney and his associates (this volume) in their relationship enhancement approach. We have also been influenced by Gottman and his associates (Gottman, Markman, Notarius, & Gonso, 1976). Often, we begin by teaching listening skills that include paraphrasing, reflecting, and validating. Most of the couples who come to us for therapy do not listen to one another carefully, fail to indicate to the other that the latter has been heard, or both. We emphasize the value of these skills as ways to promote clarity of communication, but also their utility in communicating care and concern. Most people in marital relationships find it gratifying to be understood by their spouse. The therapist discusses and models nonverbal methods as well as the more obvious verbal ways to communicate attention and interest. Nonverbal emphases include the use of eye contact, expressiveness in the face, body language, and nodding the head as methods to indicate to the speaking partner that she or he is being tracked. Verbal attention is taught using Guerney's (1977) tactic of creating discrete roles of "speaker" and "listener" and having spouses alternate those roles during training. Listeners are not to interrupt speakers; listeners are to listen carefully while the speaker is talking and then rephrase or restate what the speaker has said. After paraphrasing, the listener asks the speaker whether the paraphrase was accurate. If so, the speaker can either elaborate or give up the floor so that the listener has an opportunity to become the speaker; if not, the speech is repeated, followed by the paraphrase, with this cycle continuing until the speaker is satisfied that he or she has been understood.

Expressive skills are usually taught after listening skills. Speakers are taught to use "I statements," which qualify and emphasize the subjective reality of their perspective (e.g., "As I see it, Mexico is a better choice than Tacoma for a vacation; at least, I think that I would have a better time in Mexico"). The self-reference technique helps the speaker avoid presenting the perspective as if it were objective reality. Otherwise, the listener may dispute the truthfulness of the message rather than simply listen and attempt to understand the speaker's perspective. The use of these expressive techniques promotes the idea that one's experience of the world is subjective, and often what are perceived as "facts" in relationships are perceptions that can understandably diverge from the perceptions of another human being, whose subjective experience of the world is bound to be unique. Speakers are also encouraged to identify their feelings and communicate them to the listener as part of the "I statement." By including affective expressions whenever appropriate, the speaker accomplishes many tasks at once, all of which promote closeness and intimacy.

To illustrate the functions of including affective expressions as part of an "I statement," consider Jack and Clara, a couple in therapy. One of their repeated arguments involved Jack's menacing, intimidating manner of speech. Whenever he grew frustrated or disagreed with Clara, he began to raise his voice and point his finger at Clara. At the beginning of therapy, Clara would complain about Jack's behavior by saying, "You shouldn't act that way; I'm not going to tolerate violent behavior." In response to such statements, Jack would raise his voice, point his finger at her, and insist, "I am not acting violent; I am just disagreeing with you to make sure that you understand my point." Her "I statement" after some communication training was, "When you raise your voice and point your finger at me, I get scared, probably because even though you may not intend violence, it appears menacing and intimidating to me." In that one remark, Clara is now disclosing something about herself that is probably going to make her position more understandable to Jack, that promotes intimacy through self-disclosure, and that is almost inherently more likely to induce sympathy than a remark that emphasizes the behavior of the other person. Here, Clara is revealing something fairly intimate about herself, emphasizing that her perception of his behavior is subjective and may actually be an inaccurate reaction given his intentions. Intimate self-disclosures involving affective expression are much less likely to lead to continued escalation than statements devoid of such expression and that fail to acknowledge the subjective reality.

Expressive skills training may also include learning to make constructive requests for behavior change. Couples can be taught to request change without the typical overgeneralizations, character assassinations, and irrelevancies that so frequently contaminate the behavior change requests made by people in dissatisfying marriages. Instead, the request is specific, oriented toward increasing positive rather than decreasing negative behavior, and takes the form of, "If you would do X [specifically defined], in situation Y, I would feel Z [sharing feelings and positive consequences]." Of course, even these very concise, polite requests will not always be accepted by a partner; thus, teaching couples palatable ways of saying no are also important to this exercise.

In training couples to use these communication skills, modeling is often used. Spouses sometimes find it easier to try out these new strategies with a therapist than with the partner. The therapist needs to be active, directive, and persistent in stopping destructive communication while aiding in the acquisition of these new communication skills. Once skills are practiced effectively in the therapy session, couples are given homework assignments to practice them at home. It is not suprising that home practice often uncovers difficulties that either failed to emerge or had ostensibly been resolved during the therapy sessions. We would almost never ask couples to practice a skill that has not been successfully mastered in the therapy session.

In structuring therapy sessions to facilitate the acquisition of these skills, it is often easier to begin with nonconflict issues. We often begin with having couples talk about the time when they return home at the end of a day. Neutral topics allow couples to focus on the process itself, rather than become distracted by the content of an emotionally loaded issue. It should also be pointed out, however, that neutral or make-believe topics without emotional fallout may not provide practice that will generalize to the major conflict areas. Moreover, too much time spent on trivial topics can promote disengagement from the therapy process, particularly for high-conflict couples who need some immediate relief.

Before concluding this section, we want to mention our newest application of communication training. As we said above, communication training can be a powerful tool for restructuring relationships along egalitarian lines. Our hypothesis is that patterns of dominance and power often manifest themselves in the habitual roles that each spouse assumes during everyday conversation. Often, when a therapist intervenes in this conversation process and encourages each spouse to assume different roles, these new behaviors have powerful ramifications for current patterns of dominance, and in fact often are completely inconsistent with those patterns. This creates the possibility that the patterns will change, depending on how skillful the therapist is in promoting equal power in other areas of the treatment program.

We have recently experimented with interventions that used the discussion of the couple's day as a vehicle for both observing and altering patterns of dominance. When spouses reunite at the end of the day to exchange information and communicate about what has happened to each of them in the time they have been apart, two patterns of dominance tend to emerge.

In one pattern, the dominant partner is the one who does most of the talking. The "dominance through talking" (DT) pattern shows a speaker preoccupied with himself or herself who consumes most of the interaction time absorbed in details of his or her day, with little apparent interest in eliciting information from the partner's day. When the listening partner does bring up an event from his or her day, the speaker either does not pay attention or quickly returns to his or her own day. The listener reinforces this self-preoccupation by seldom offering information about his or her day, and by encouraging the speaker to elaborate. The expressions of support, the undivided attention, and the requests for elaboration all serve to provide for the speaker a green light to debrief thoroughly all events that have transpired in his or her day. It is as if everything that happened to the speaker is important and worth recounting in detail, while both spouses seem to agree that the events in the listener's day were trivial. Husbands are more commonly speakers in this pattern.

The second dominance pattern that manifests itself in discussions regarding events of the day if the "dominant listener" (DL) pattern. Here, the listener dominates the conversation by a lack of interest in what the other is saying, and by concomitant witholding of any information. The listener is disengaged; she or he leans away from the speaker, does not look directly at the speaker, and appears bored and uninterested in the conversation. The speaker talks about a variety of topics, but there is the sense that the speaker could be talking to himself or herself. In this pattern, wives are usually the speakers.

During training in receptive and expressive communication skills, the therapist's directives shift the interaction away from these habitual patterns of dominance. For example, the therapist might say, "Now I would like you [the dominant listener] to paraphrase everything she says with your eyes maintaining contact with hers, while sitting up in your chair and leaning slightly forward." Usually, both partners are at least somewhat uncomfortable with such directives, and the key to success with this task is for the therapist to be both persistent and willing to explore each spouse's inhibitions to engaging in the task. Cognitive and affective explorations often reveal cognitions such as, "Nothing that happens to me is important" or "My job is to elevate the self-esteem of everyone else in the family; that is all I am good for," and affect involving fear of change, of ambiguity, of becoming vulnerable. The point is that the task provides a vehicle for exploring and later modifying rigid, stultifying patterns of interaction that seem to have implications beyond those initially intended in communication-training exercises.

PROBLEM-SOLVING TRAINING

Conflict-resolution skills are typically taught after couples have mastered basic listening and expressive skills. The focus is on facilitating spouses' ability and willingness to discuss conflict areas constructively and reach viable solutions to them. The hope is that they will use these skills after therapy is over to deal with future conflicts that arise.

Conflict-resolution skills taught in the SLC framework represent a structured, highly specialized kind of interaction. There are specific concepts for
couples to learn, rules for them to follow, and a format in which problems
are to be discussed. As an introduction to the format, the rules, and the
concepts, they read a manual written for couples and taken from the Jacobson
and Margolin (1979) book. The manual provides a detailed discussion of
the problem-solving process.

Then the skills are taught during therapy sessions, with the therapist
playing the role of teacher and coach. Often, the therapist will begin by
modeling the skill, explaining the principle involved, and providing the
couple with feedback as they practice the skill. When the skill is performed
incorrectly, or when spouses lapse into their destructive, maladaptive patterns,
the therapist interrupts them and provides them with further feedback. Once
spouses can perform a particular skill adequately in the therapist's office,
they are given homework assignments to practice the skill at home.

The problem-solving process is divided into two distinct phases: the
definition phase and the resolution phase. Couples are taught first to define
the problem, during which time they avoid suggesting possible solutions,
and then to focus *exclusively* on solutions and avoid further elaborations on
what the problem is. This distinction is maintained because couples often
falter in their conflict-resolution discussion through a contamination of these
processes: If solutions are suggested prematurely, that is, before the problem
has been properly defined, often the wrong problem is being discussed;
conversely, by continuing to redefine the problem during the discussion of
solutions, couples effectively avoid the more difficult task of deciding what
they are going to *do* to solve the problem.

Problem definitions are characterized by the following rules:

1. *Problem identification should be preceded by expressions of appreciation.*
These expressions place problems in perspective. Most people find it easier
to accept criticism when it is placed within the context of overall appreciation
for one's positive attributes and qualities. Thus, for example, "You forgot
to empty the garbage" is more likely to elicit a defensive, noncollaborative
response than "I really appreciate the help you've been giving me around
the house lately, even though I do get angry when you forget to take out
the garbage."

2. *Problems should be identified specifically, in behavioral terms, and
without derogatory adjectives or personality-trait labels.* Instead of "You are
disgusting and inconsiderate," the PS format would favor, "You often fail
to call me to tell me what time you'll be home."

3. *When defining problems, include direct expressions of feeling.* When
one or both spouses pinpoint problem behaviors to the other, they are
encouraged to make explicit the affect associated with the behavior. For
example, instead of saying, "It is not nice to flirt with other women at
parties," partners are encouraged to include expressions such as, "When
you flirt with other women at parties, I feel hurt and angry." Feeling

expressions tend to be disarming; the recipient of a complaint that includes a feeling expression is less likely to countercomplain or deny responsibility and more likely to accommodate to the feeling.

Validation, Collaboration, and Acceptance of Responsibility

Conflict-resolution discussions are most likely to break down shortly after the problem is first defined. The habitual response to a complaint is to defend oneself through denials, cross-complaints, excuses, or justifications. The problem-solving format precludes such responses and substitutes one of many possible collaborative responses; empathy, admissions, apologies, and recognition of the other's feelings are possible alternatives. It is equally important that spouses who have identified problem behaviors in the partner are willing to acknowledge whatever role they play in either creating, maintaining, or exacerbating the problem.

When defining problems, the rules in the training program are designed to circumvent all of the habitual maneuvers that lead to a breakdown in the discussion. The definition phase is where problem-solving discussions usually die in distressed relationships. Most of the rules are designed to promote engagement and collaboration in the couple by generating changes in the way complaints are expressed and received. Complaints are expressed in such a way as to maximize the likelihood that the recipient will receive the complaint in an engaged and collaborative manner; in addition, spouses are encouraged to receive complaints not as challenges or threats but as relationship problems that are in the interests of both of them to solve.

Here is an example of a couple, Ed and Sue, defining one of their remaining problems at home during the latter stages of therapy.

SUE: Ed, I have been delighted by the way you've been reading to the children in the evenings. They love it. On the weekends, it still makes me angry that you don't spend more time with them.

ED: So you're saying that you do appreciate that I spend some of my evening time with Tom and Kathy, but since I don't spend time with them on weekends, you feel angry. Is that right?

SUE: Yeah.

ED: You're right that I don't spend much weekend time with the kids, and I can understand why that would be upsetting to you.

SUE (*after paraphrasing*): I realize that some of the responsibility is mine, since I often get on your case about getting chores done on weekends, which takes away from time that you could be spending with the children.

ED (*after paraphrasing*): Let's figure out what we can do about this.

After the problem has been defined, the couple moves into the solution phase of the discussion, where they move sequentially through three tasks: brainstorming, identifying the components of a contract, and forming a written contract.

BRAINSTORMING

During brainstorming, a list of solutions is generated, from which a contract will eventually be formed. The instructions to the couple are to generate a list of possible solutions by verbalizing all ideas that enter their consciousness, without censoring anything. Evaluative comments are not allowed during the brainstorming exercise. The purpose of this exercise is to allow partners the opportunity to generate ideas without having to evaluate them. They are told not to worry about the quality of the idea at this point in the discussion, and in fact the therapist reinforces this lack of concern with quality by suggesting some absurd, and probably humorous, solutions. This exercise is designed to counteract the couple's tendencies to censor themselves and evaluate all ideas negatively before seriously considering them.

Here is the list of solutions generated by Sue and Ed regarding the problem identified above:

1. Sue could scan the newspaper and come up with a list of children's activities available for an upcoming weekend and then ask if Ed would like to take the kids to any.
2. Ed could agree to spend every Saturday afternoon with the kids.
3. Sue and Ed could give the kids up for adoption.
4. Ed and Sue could take the kids to the park together on Saturday afternoons.
5. Ed could take 30 minutes on Friday night to think of home activities (such as puzzles or drawing) and then play with the kids sometime over the weekend, in the activity he chooses.
6. Sue could accept Ed's limitations as a father and withdraw the complaint.
7. Sue could help Ed with some of the weekend chores so that he would have more time for the kids.
8. Ed could give up his Saturday morning baseball games to make sure he has more time to spend with the kids.

IDENTIFYING THE COMPONENTS OF A CONTRACT

From the list of proposed solutions generated during brainstorming, the partners eliminate those that are patently absurd. Then each of the remaining proposals are discussed from each of two perspectives: (a) Were this proposal to be adopted, would it either solve or contribute to a solution to the problem; and (b) were this solution to be adopted, what would be the benefits and costs to each of the spouses. After each perspective is considered, a decision is made regarding the disposition of the proposal under discussion. Three dispositions are possible. Either the proposal is to be included as a component of a contract, eliminated because the costs outweigh the benefits, or tabled for reconsideration after other proposals on the list are considered. Eventually, this process generates a set of components to be combined systematically into a change agreement or contract.

FORMING A WRITTEN CONTRACT

This final step in the problem-solving process involves synthesizing the component proposals into an integrated, specific change agreement. The final agreement should specify the behaviors to be changed, the situations in which the changes will occur, and the cues that the couple plans to adopt to maximize the likelihood that the agreement will be carried out. All change agreements are implemented on a trial basis and renegotiated if either partner turns out to be dissatisfied with them. Each spouse signs the agreement and agrees to reassess it at a specific time on a specific day.

The first draft of the agreement by Ed and Sue was as follows:

> Sue will scan the newspaper for children's activities for an upcoming weekend.
> Ed will watch the TV weather on Friday evening to see if the weekend might be good for going to the park. He will also come up with some activities at home in case the weather forecast is bad.
> On Friday evening, Ed will ask Sue to help him with one weekend task, which should not require more than an hour of her time. At this time, Friday evening following the news, Ed will plan activities for the following afternoon.
> Ed will follow through with the ideas by spending Saturday afternoon with the kids between 1:00 and 4:00 p.m. If Ed has to work on Saturday, the plans automatically are implemented on Sunday instead. Planning for them is still done on Friday evenings.

All three phases of the problem-solution discussion are goal oriented and designed to promote a specific, systematic agreement that will eliminate the problem. In order to arrive at such an agreement, partners must maintain a collaborative set and avoid some of the alienating interactions that typically stand in their way when conflict-laden issues are discussed. In addition to the guidelines for resolving conflicts that we have focused on in this section, some general communication guidelines pervade the problem-solving discussion, whether it is definition or solution that is currently being addressed. The two most important are the use of paraphrasing and the avoidance of sidetracking. Paraphrasing skills serve the same function here as they do in any other area of communication. However, they seem particularly useful as a pacing device in conflict-resolution discussions. Sidetracking is very common among distressed couples, and if couples can be successfully induced to discuss only one problem at a time, their chances of being able to resolve a given problem are greatly increased.

Other Techniques

Although behavior exchange, communication training, and problem-solving training are commonly used within the SLC framework, they are by no means ubiquitous. For example, quite often parent training or other behavior management techniques are used to help partners with conflicts over child rearing. Sex therapy is also often used to supplement and in some cases preempt these other techniques. A further discussion of technique is included below in the section on still unresolved clinical issues. This upcoming section includes recent clinical innovations.

THE ROLE OF THE THERAPIST

The successful SLC marital therapist must maintain a perpetual focus on two different levels: First, she or he is delivering a technology designed to help couples enhance relationship satisfaction; second, the therapist, through clinical skills and personal attributes, is creating a context for the technology that will facilitate the learning and implementation of those skills by clients. Throughout the development of this approach, there have been efforts to technologize the practice of marital therapy, to reduce the proportion of outcome variance attributable to nonspecific therapist characteristics. By building into the structure of treatment regimens rules that guide the therapist's behavior through rough clinical terrain, we attempt to reduce the incidence of bad clinical judgment or clinical errors. But try as we might, therapist variables continue to mediate outcome, and even within the SLC framework numerous choices and clinical decisions are made without the benefit of rules or guidelines.

The present section is devoted to five classes of therapist behavior that we believe are particularly important in mediating a positive response to marital therapy. These classes were derived from an analysis of cases treated in our clinical research setting at the University of Washington.

Structuring Skills

Successful marital therapy from an SLC perspective requires highly structured therapy sessions with an active, directive therapist. This requirement is based on two considerations: First, time must be used efficiently if the therapeutic tasks are to be accomplished within a relatively brief, time-limited format; second, directiveness from the therapist is often required to prompt successful collaborative interaction between partners. Rules are often used to foster structure and collaboration during therapy sessions. But not all therapists are equally adept at enforcing rules. When spouses take control of the treatment sessions, agendas do not get accomplished, and destructive interaction patterns are perpetuated. When behaviors occur that deviate from the planned agenda for that session, the therapist must squelch them when appropriate. The skillful SLC marital therapist will stop couples in such a way that they not only redirect their behavior at the time they are being stopped but also regulate it more successfully in the future. The best way to foster such learning is to make sure that clients understand why they are being stopped when the therapist does, in fact, interrupt them. By therapists' asking the question, "Why am I stopping you?" partners develop an awareness of the rules and participate in the process of critiquing their own rule violations. In this way, they gradually learn to regulate their own behavior. Frequent prompts from the therapist are also helpful, including an explicit setting of an agenda at the beginning of each session. These agendas should not be imposed on the couple; rather, they should be negotiated and mutually agreed on. Once they are set, however, it is up to the therapist to make sure that they are implemented as planned.

Structuring skills also pertain to the ability to direct the flow of the therapy process across sessions. Couples enter therapy with presenting problems, and the treatment plan is oriented toward solving these problems. It is up to the therapist to make sure that the problems are receiving proper attention and that therapy is focusing on the issues that are consistent with expectations. Of course, treatment goals often change during the course of therapy, and new problems emerge. When these changes occur, however, treatment plans should be renegotiated, and structuring skills should be brought to bear on these emergent problems.

One tactic that facilitates this across-session structuring is the frequent practice of "taking inventory." This refers to assessing outcome formally with respect to each treatment goal at the beginning of the therapy session. In our work, every three or four sessions we suggest an agenda item such as the following:

> One thing I'd like to do today is check our progress in each of the areas we decided to work on during the roundtable. We decided to work on sex, parenting, financial management, and trust. Could we take a few minutes and assess where things stand in each of those areas? I am interested in your perceptions of what things have changed for the better, what changes still need to be made, and so on.

It is important to recognize that clients cannot be relied on to initiate work in the areas that are most salient. Frequently, when the therapist asks, "What would you like to work on today?" clients answer impulsively, and the session ends up focusing on whatever the couple have argued about most recently rather than those fundamentally important, recurring issues that brought them into therapy. Therefore, it is up to the therapist to safeguard discussion of the major issues in the couple's relationship.

Instigative Skills

Of course, controlling the flow of therapy sessions is a means to an end rather than an end in itself. Enhancing relationship quality in the natural environment is ultimately the standard one must use to evaluate the success of marital therapy. Structuring skills, in and of themselves, by no means guarantee that change will be instigated in the natural environment. Instigative skills can be divided into three subcategories: inducing a collaborative set, fostering compliance with homework assignments, and promoting generalization and maintenance of treatment effects.

INDUCING A COLLABORATIVE SET

This may be the most important clinical skill for therapists working within an SLC framework. Distressed couples are seldom willing to collaborate when they first enter therapy. Yet successful marital therapy depends on their willingness to work together. The marital therapist must establish and then foster maintenance of a collaborative set by, first, providing spouses with a convincing conceptualization of their marital problems that defines them in terms of the relationship and implies mutual responsibility. Then, after presenting this alternative theory about what is "wrong" with the relationship, the therapist offers a treatment plan requiring a bilateral commitment from both partners to work together, focus on what they can do as individuals to improve the relationship rather than wait for the partner to change "first," and agree to the value of principles such as "compromise" and "behavior change." Although it would be grossly unrealistic to expect couples to drop their adversarial posture based on the therapist's mere presentation of an alternative model, it is possible to induce a commitment to collaborative behavior, despite reservations that spouses might have about the therapist's model. Once this commitment is obtained, actual collaboration is much more likely, since violations of the commitment can be labeled as such. Usually the commitment is obtained following a discussion such as the following:

> I know that neither of you sees the problems in your marriage the same way I do at present; I am not concerned about that. What I do need from you, however, is a commitment to proceeding in therapy on the assumption that my model is correct. From my model, the correct treatment plan involves collaboration, compromise, and change. Each of you does what you can to improve the quality of the relationship, without waiting for the other to change first. If you both commit yourselves to this, I am confident that eventually you will come around to adopting my model. Let me tell you more specifically what I mean by collaborative behavior, and then I need to check with each of you to see if you feel comfortable making this commitment. . . .

Finally, assuming that the therapist is able to present the alternative model effectively and induce a commitment to collaboration, the third and final prerequisite to effective inducement of a collaborative set is that positive changes must occur fairly rapidly in therapy. The credibility of the therapist's model hinges to a large extent on its value to both spouses, which translates into some tangible signs of relationship improvement early in therapy. BE interventions are often used to facilitate such rapid, relatively low-cost changes.

INSTIGATING COMPLIANCE WITH HOMEWORK ASSIGNMENTS

Homework plays a critical role in marital therapy from an SLC perspective. Most of the important interventions are mediated through between-session assignments. Therapists vary in their abilities to produce compliance, and the microskills involve the choosing of appropriate assignments, providing clear rationales for and explanations of them, gaining commitments from spouses to completing them, and dealing effectively with noncompliance when it occurs despite the therapist's best efforts.

Noncompliance occurs at a fairly high rate. Nevertheless, most of the time it is either preventable or modifiable given skillful clinical interventions. Rather than view noncompliance as evidence of unconscious resistance to the goals of marital therapy, SLC therapists assume that, most of the time, more parsimonious explanations are available. In some instances, the aversive consequences of changing one's behavior are immediate, whereas the benefits to be derived, such as an improved relationship, are delayed. These consequences include not only the expenditure of time and effort but, and more important, the willingness to take risks and enhance one's own vulnerability. At other times, assignments are not completed because couples forget about them, misunderstand them, or underestimate their importance. The likelihood of incomplete homework is greatly reduced if all these factors are taken into account when the assignment is presented.

Stimulus-control strategies describe attempts to prevent noncompliance rather than deal with it after the fact. Most of these strategies are designed to enhance the salience of the homework for clients. Therapists often communicate in subtle ways that the task is not important, by presenting the assignment tentatively or apologetically. Salience is maximized by verbally explicating the rationale for the assignment; eliciting explicit commitments for compliance from both spouses; anticipating and repudiating potential excuses for noncompliance; anticipating and even exaggerating the aversiveness of the task; providing clients with verbatim, written descriptions of the assignment to take home with them; and calling clients during the week to check on adherence. Therapists who diligently enact all these strategies rarely see noncompliance.

Response-control strategies include all methods designed to deal with noncompliance after it has occurred. These strategies tend to be antithetical to the message that noncompliance is O.K. Therapists who support and sympathize with explanations offered by couples for noncompliance are likely to see it repeated. Therapists who go on with business as usual despite noncompliance with homework are implying that homework is peripheral to marital therapy. Therefore, we typically announce that the agenda for the therapy session that was to occur on that day must be postponed until the following week—or until the homework has been completed. This response is practically required of a therapist working within an SLC framework because the agenda often emerges from an analysis of the homework. Instead of the planned agenda, the focus shifts to a direct discussion of the compliance problem and how it can be solved; this is the only issue discussed at that session. Alternatively, unless the homework cannot be practically or ethically completed during the therapy hour (e.g., sensate focus exercises), the therapist might instruct the spouses to complete the assignment right there in the therapist's office during the therapy hour. Once the therapist suspends the treatment program and shifts to the compliance issue, couples understand that the assignment is the "ticket" to the session. Rarely does this tactic need to be employed more than once during the course of a marital case.

PROMOTING GENERALIZATION AND MAINTENANCE

One of the central dilemmas of the SLC approach is that in spite of a highly structured treatment regimen with a directive therapist, couples are supposed to develop autonomy and learn to function as their own therapists. As couples are acquiring new repertoires during the early and middle stages of therapy, the therapist must be maximally active and directive. Once these skills are acquired, however, the therapist's influence must gradually fade. Generalization and maintenance of positive changes can be fostered through technology and through clinical skill. Techniques include increasing the length of the interval between therapy sessions; holding follow-up booster sessions subsequent to the end of active treatment; substituting couples' home therapy sessions (which we call "state of the relationship" sessions) for weekly contact with the therapist; and tailoring the standard techniques to fit the idiosyncratic characteristics of particular couples. The clinical skills are more subtle and difficult to describe, but generally involve restraint. Instead of jumping in and giving couples more input than they need to solve particular problems, generalization and maintenance are more likely to be fostered by allowing them to grapple on their own, assuming, that is, that they have the requisite skills. Often, the most therapeutic intervention available is to inform a couple that they have the ability to solve a problem themselves.

Teaching Skills

The SLC marital therapist is a teacher. Therapists who simply prompt interactional changes in the therapy sessions can generate impressive short-term changes, but when therapy is over the couple will be bereft of the skills that the program is attempting to impart. When therapy is having the intended effect, couples should leave therapy with principles applicable to new problems that come up. Being a good marital therapy teacher means frequently shifting from specific examples to general principles, and then back to specifics. For example, when spouses are presented with feedback, the feedback should be connected with a principle: "Hank, I'd like you to try it again with the inclusion of an expression of appreciation. Remember that the appreciation reminds her that your complaint is confined to a particular behavior, that in other ways you think she's just fine the way she is." Whenever possible, not only should the therapist state the principle but also the rationale for the principle.

Another aspect of good teaching in marital therapy involves the willingness to repeat oneself frequently. Therapists who are shy when it comes to repetition forget that most clients are not mental health professionals and do not process information about psychological issues as quickly as do the therapists. In our work, therapy sessions are punctuated by frequent restatements of rules, guidelines, and rationales.

Another tactic that facilitates the acquisition of principles is actively involving clients in the learning process. Instead of preaching or lecturing, the effective SLC teacher has couples do most of the work. For example, at the conclusion of a therapy session, the therapist may ask the clients to summarize the events that occurred during the session and state the important principles manifested along with their rationales.

Ultimately, the SLC therapist is most concerned with fostering a stance toward therapy that is active and engaged rather than passive and quiescent. When the therapist is either working harder or seems more invested in therapy than the clients, something is wrong. A good teacher ensures that the clients will perform the bulk of the therapeutic work.

Inducing Positive Expectancies

If spouses are not optimistic about the ultimate outcome of marital therapy, they are unlikely to behave collaboratively during the therapy sessions, and they are less likely to comply adequately with homework assignments. In order to instill positive outcome expectancies, therapists must strike a balance between optimism and sobering realism: On the one hand, the therapist must be encouraging; on the other hand, the therapist must make it clear that marital therapy is a difficult undertaking and that maximum success requires hard work and the ability to withstand valleys that unfortunately rear their ugly heads in the wake of peaks. If clients expect miracles, they may become passive and simply await the "cure." If therapy does not progress as smoothly as they expect, they may become demoralized.

Spouses must be prepared for the crises and downward spirals that often occur along the jagged path toward relationship enhancement. By providing couples with advance warnings regarding these probable "relapses," spouses are less likely to discard their positive outcome expentancies when regressive periods actually occur. The warnings must be especially prominent during the early phases of therapy when the honeymoon is in effect, or any time when therapy success is predominant. The transition from BE to PS is a time when relapse is particularly common, since couples move from focusing on increasing low-cost pleasant events to discussing conflict-laden issues; thus this transition period constitutes an ideal time for reminding couples that a relapse is to be expected.

The paradox in the expectancy induction art is that, quite often, client expectancies are best maintained by the therapist's providing sobering reminders, urging caution, and predicting relapses. At the other extreme, the therapist must remain upbeat, enthusiastic, and resilient when therapy is not going well. Not only must the therapist sell the couple on the model of therapy, but his or her excitement and enthusiasm about the potential of the treatment program *for them* is an essential prerequisite to their buying into the paradigm. This optimism and enthusiasm for the approach lends an upbeat quality to the therapy sessions; without it, the therapy sessions lose their vitality and become "depressing" to all participants.

Finally, along with enthusiasm and optimism, the ability to inject levity and humor into the sessions is highly facilitative. Therapy is hard work, and spouses are prone to approach the tasks with earnestness and sobriety. There is, however, often a lighter, more ironic side to marital problems, and the therapist who can induce some laughter can help mitigate the frequent negative emotional response to these important relationship issues being discussed.

Providing Emotional Nurturance

With a treatment regimen that is as highly structured as BMT, there is always the danger that the therapist will "overregulate." The dangers of "underregulating" notwithstanding, effective BMT requires that the therapist provide sufficient latitude and flexibility that the clients do not experience emotional frustration. The credibility of the therapist and the treatment program can be safeguarded only to the extent that clients are allowed effective expression. This expression includes not only a positive emotional response to the treatment procedures but also an opportunity to communicate to the therapist the depth and variety of reactions that each spouse has to therapy and to the partner during the course of therapy.

One major aspect of this emotional nurturance involves the frequent taking of each spouse's "affective temperature." Periodically, during the course of therapy, the therapist should make contact with the clients to ascertain their degree of emotional involvement in therapy and their reactions to the changes that are occurring in therapy. First, during our roundtable or interpretive session, when the therapist presents to the couple his or her perspective on the problems in the relationship, these formulations must be carefully "cleared" with each spouse. In other words, the therapist must actively check out her or his perceptions with each spouse and be prepared to respond to their disagreements, reservations, and misgivings regarding what the therapist is saying. Second, throughout the sessions, the therapist must be attentive to the clients' nonverbal responses to the events of therapy. When the apparent affective response does not seem commensurate with the events, the therapist must do some probing. For example, one spouse remained relatively bland and unexcited despite the occurrence of an agreement that seemed to solve the client's major concern about the marriage. The alert therapist commented on the discrepancy between the importance of the event and the absence of an emotional response, to which the client admitted to incredulity regarding the effectiveness of the agreement. If the therapist had not been attentive to the client's emotional state, the agreement would have remained unaltered, and the client would have been dissatisfied, unbeknownest to the therapist. Third, the therapist must engage in "search and destroy" missions, by frequently inquiring how each spouse is reacting to therapy. This way concerns, reservations, and equivocal reactions can be ferreted out and subjected to cognitive interventions.

In addition to tracking clients' emotional responses during the course of therapy, the therapist must avoid repudiating or disqualifying strong emotional reactions on the part of spouses that are not conducive to collaboration. Here the therapist must demonstrate that she or he understands the spouse's feelings and at the same time not allow those feelings to serve as an excuse for noncollaborative behavior. One of the many common examples of this dual role occurs when clients express anger and frustration and then attempt to justify noncollaborative behavior on that basis. If the therapist cuts off prematurely, or in other ways disallows the venting of these feelings, the client is likely to feel even more frustrated and may disengage from therapy. Feelings can be allowed adequate expression and then acknowledged by the therapist without detracting from the continued emphasis on collaboration.

CURRENT STATUS, UNSOLVED PROBLEMS, AND NEW DEVELOPMENTS

After only 15 years of research and clinical development, much progress has been made in the treatment of marital problems from the SLC perspective. As Baucom and Hoffman (Chapter 27) illustrate, numerous controlled experiments have been conducted evaluating the efficacy of behavioral marital therapy. There is more evidence supporting its efficacy than exists for all other models of marital therapy combined. Cumulatively, this literature tells us that, across the populations of couples treated in clinical research projects, the SLC approach has a statistically significant impact that cannot be reduced to nonspecific or placebo factors (Jacobson, 1978, 1979). No other major model of marital therapy, with the exception of Guerney's (this volume) relationship enhancement procedures, documents its effectiveness in this way, by appealing to a series of controlled studies replicated independently of the laboratories in which the techniques were developed.

Estimates of how often the SLC approach leads to relationship improvement vary considerably depending on the source. Recently, Jacobson, Follette, and Revenstorf (1984) developed some relatively objective criteria for evaluating whether or not a case had improved, and the extent to which the improvement was clinically significant. These criteria were then applied to a reanalysis of previously completed outcome studies (Jacobson, Follette, Revenstorf, Baucom, Hahlweg, & Margolin, 1984). The results diverged from study to study, but overall about half the couples seemed to be benefiting from current applications of marital therapy from the SLC perspective. In our own recently completed study, 72% of the couples showed improvement, with 58% ending up within the happily married range on measures of global satisfaction. By the 6-month follow-up, two-thirds of the couples receiving our complete, standardized treatment package were happily married; this percentage was reduced to 50% by the time of the 12-month follow-up. Although none of these couples had split up by this time, it is evident that a substantial proportion of them were not benefiting substantially from our clinical research treatment package.

In attempting to understand these relatively low success rates, several issues seem relevant. First, these are very stringent criteria for success and failure, by far the most stringent that have been applied in the marital therapy literature until now. Yet they seem appropriately conservative; it is questionable whether couples who are "less miserable" when they leave therapy but still not "happy" should be considered successes. Moreover, while divorces would never automatically be considered failures in our clinical practices, neither can they be assumed to be successes, particularly in a research context where an experimenter cannot have it both ways. Since most couples enter therapy hoping for an improved relationship as an outcome, it seems most suitable for research purposes to count divorces as failures. Second, since all the couples treated in this study were in a research project, and given a standardized treatment package administered by an inexperienced graduate student therapist, it might be argued that these results constitute an underestimate of the success that occurs when the SLC perspective is applied in clinical practice. Third, research has been surprisingly unproductive at coming up with variables that predict a positive response to therapy (see Chapter 27). In a recent study of our own, only one variable predicted a positive outcome at the 6-month follow-up. When couples entered therapy exhibiting a traditional sex-role constellation with respect to their preferences for interpersonal versus autonomous activities (Jacobson, Follette, & Pagel, 1984), the prognosis was poor. This is not much predictive power in an area where individual differences between clients are expected to account for the preponderance of variance in outcome. Thus, although we have intuitive guesses as to what constitutes a couple that is likely or unlikely to benefit from marital therapy, most of our intuitions are either unsubstantiated or, worse, refuted by empirical research.

Where does all this leave us in our efforts to develop treatments that are more effective and applicable to a broader array of couples? A number of future directions suggest themselves as possible areas of emphasis. We have chosen to explore a number of avenues simultaneously, each one reflecting an area of clinical deficiency based on either clinical experience, experimental evidence, or preferably both. In the remainder of this chapter, we explore five areas that are believed to constitute gaps in our current treatment technology and recent clinical innovations designed to fill in the lacunae.

Strategies for Dealing with Escalation of Negative Affect

As Gottman (1979) and others (e.g., Margolin & Wampold, 1981) have shown, couples seeking marital therapy are characterized by rapid, reciprocal, and often explosive escalation of negative affect. Hahlweg and his associates (1984) demonstrated that this tendency toward rapid escalation stays with clinical couples even after an apparently successful regimen of marital therapy. These findings gibe with our clinical experience. It is relatively easy to teach communication skills that can be enacted in an anticipated, structured format. Often couples acquire these skills without much generalization to the situations outside the formal structured exercises where arguments usually occur.

For many years, our attention was focused on clinical strategies that could be used to stop these arguments. We attempted to induce couples to generalize their communication–problem-solving skills to these naturalistic occurrences. Many couples simply failed at this endeavor, despite being excellent communicators and problem solvers in other situations. The next step involved attempts to teach cognitive coping skills that could be employed during the argument to promote deescalation (Epstein, 1982; Schindler & Vollmer, 1984). For example, after learning to recognize the early signs of an angry altercation, spouses might be trained to emit self-statements to calm themselves down and redirect the conversation. Based on our clinical experience, these techniques were usually unsuccessful. Couples had little trouble producing such self-statements outside the emotional context, but it often seemed that when embroiled in the heat of battle, neither was sufficiently willing or able to disengage from the process long enough to engage the coping skills. When asked about their lack of utilization after the fact, at times spouses would say that they forgot about the coping skills, and at other times they remembered but chose not to employ them. It often seemed that other reinforcers prevailed, despite the spouses' ability after the fact to recognize that these quarrels had a destructive impact on the relationship.

Finally, after devoting years to developing a technology for deescalation of negative affect, we began to experiment with alternatives. One exciting development has been a technique called *troubleshooting*, although a more appropriate label might be *exploration and troubleshooting*. In many ways, troubleshooting (TS) is the antithesis of our past efforts: Whereas all techniques until now attempted to interrupt and diffuse the coercive interaction, in TS there is no explicit effort to modify the escalation process. Instead, the primary goals are to (*a*) explore cognition and affect that accompany the escalation process; and (*b*) examine possible behavioral options that exist in such explosive situations, given the emergent cognitions and emotions.

The exploration approach bears striking similarity to the work of Greenberg and Johnson (this volume), as well as that of Wile (1981); both Wile's ego analytic framework and the Greenberg and Johnson "emotion-focused" framework seek to develop rather than squelch expression during emotional interchanges. The first step is to induce the couple to "get into" the dispute during a session. If they have had an unresolved argument during the week, this can usually be accomplished simply by asking them to continue the discussion. Alternatively, the therapist might simply capitalize on a recurring dispute that occurs during a session, so that induction is unnecessary. The process seems to be most productive when the exploration occurs around issues that are both common and prototypical for a particular couple. The second step is for the therapist to interrupt the escalation process by engaging in sequential dialogues with each spouse. These dialogues are aimed at an elaboration of the thoughts and feelings that transpire as the issue at hand is being discussed. The therapist attempts to elicit from each spouse the meaning that this issue has for her or him, and the unexpressed affect associated with it. While the therapist elicits this information from one spouse, the other is asked simply to sit quietly and listen. Once both spouses have had the opportunity to elaborate thoroughly on their cognitive and affective states, the third step involves a retrospective analysis of the escalation process around this issue, with the aim of identifying behavioral options that each spouse has in this situation, given the thoughts and feelings that were just pinpointed.

Although our conclusions must remain tentative until controlled studies have been conducted, the TS process seems to be a very productive way to use the material generated by escalation. Based on about 2 years of clinical experience with the technique, it seems to be associated with reduced rates of destructive escalation much more often than the prior techniques aimed at interrupting or stopping the process. Our guess is that each step plays an important role: The first step ensures that any learning that occurs will be in a situation that is maximally relevant to the situations that present problems for the couple in the natural environment; the second step offers each spouse the opportunity to elaborate on his or her "position" (Wile, 1981) without interruption, something spouses rarely have the opportunity to do when the therapist is not around; the third step fosters the understanding that behavioral options exist despite these powerful thoughts and feelings. As each spouse alternates in the role of speaker and listener, the therapist is able to capitalize on the unique advantages of each. The speaker has the experience of being "understood" and "listened to," which in turn decreases the desparation and intensity of expression around the issue. The listener receives a great deal of information that renders the speaker's position more understandable and sympathetic.

Troubleshooting will be investigated much more systematically in the next few years. The results thus far have been impressive and certainly warrant greater attention.

The Incorporation of a Focus on Individual Issues into Marital Therapy

We have spoken elsewhere of the unfortunate tradition within behavioral marital therapy to focus exclusively on dyadic issues. This tradition is unfortunate because an exclusively relationship-oriented therapy ignores the needs of individuals within that relationship, needs that can and often do conflict with the dyadic goals set during marital therapy. The most common example of such a conflict is one spouse who has disengaged from a relationship that has been destructive to her or him and has developed greater self-esteem, not to mention life satisfaction, as a result of the disengagement process. To the extent that marital therapy fosters greater involvement and intimacy, participation may not be in the interests of this hypothetical spouse, especially when the likelihood that the partner will accommodate to these individual changes is low.

This example is just one of the complications that can result when a marital therapy regimen is too inflexible to take into account the psychological issues for each spouse, even those that may conflict with the typical goals of marital therapy. We believe that the clinical flexibility of the SLC perspective is enhanced to the extent that these individual issues can be incorporated into the treatment plan. To take one example, whenever one spouse has some sort of behavior problem that is either incapacitating or consumes a great deal of relationship attention, it is doubtful whether an exclusively dyadic or marital therapy focus will eradicate the individual problem; in fact, inattention to the individual problem may impede progress on the relationship front as well. We do not believe that problems such as depression, agoraphobia, and alcoholism are routinely solved by marital therapy alone. Nevertheless, as the chapters in Section IV of this volume indicate, the marriage should be taken into account in treating a great variety of individual problems because, at the least, the relationship has been disrupted by them.

Clinical innovations designed to remediate this problem include a thorough assessment of individual issues during routine pretreatment marital therapy assessments; the willingness on the part of marital therapists to deal with individual problems either as presented or as they emerge during a relationship-focused treatment program; and the inclusion of treatment plans that incorporate both individual and dyadic treatment goals in one program. These innovations would be nothing new to psychodynamically oriented marital therapists (cf. Gurman, 1978), but they have not been emphasized in the SLC perspective.

Two ramifications must be emphasized. First, we are now much more likely to include individual sessions with one spouse during the course of a marital therapy regimen. Second, if the presenting problems include both marital and individual issues, we are much more inclined than we used to be to treat both sets of issues as part of an integrated package. Five years ago, the standard strategy would have been to bifurcate the treatment effort by referring one spouse for individual therapy and concurrently treating the marital problems ourselves. By uniting the treatment efforts around one therapist and one integrated therapy regimen, the chances that the two sets of issues will work at cross purposes are greatly reduced. Such a strategy requires that marital therapists possess a variety of skills and that they be capable of working with nondyadic, individually based problems.

The Use of Molar Contracts and Problem-Solving around Thematic Issues

One of the "hottest" innovations pervading our clinical research right now is the use of relationship themes as a therapeutic vehicle. This idea came directly from the work of Greenberg and Johnson (this volume); although these relationship themes were always part of our case conceptualization, their identification and direct use as an intervention vechicle have been attempted only recently. As Greenberg and Johnson point out, across the multitude of content areas that serve as the stimuli for marital conflict, it is usually possible to identify one or two recurring themes that unite these diverse content areas. In fact, there are probably a few major themes that categorize all marital disputes. One of them, described by Jacobson and Margolin (1979), involves one spouse constantly seeking more intimacy while the partner is seeking more autonomy. When couples report after 10 weeks of therapy that the major issues are not getting addressed, they are often alluding to these themes, although they rarely articulate them in the ways that we are describing here. In many cases, we have found it useful to identify such themes as they are percieved by the therapist during the pretreatment assessment, encourage the couple to identify their occurrence during periods of conflict, and even to problem-solve them during the latter stages of marital therapy. The recognition of these patterns as they occur helps to disengage people from highly destructive arguments. Even if they are identified after the fact, they help the couple process the discussion and help reinstitute positive interaction. Often, the problem is not the argument itself but the couple's lack of resiliency. Instead of staying angry and withdrawn from one another for weeks, an identification of the recurrent pattern can facilitate closure.

Beyond this identification, it has been a pleasant surprise to discover that some couples can change these patterns through problem solving and the formation of change agreements. The surprise results from the fact that both the discussion and the product (i.e., the change agreement) seem to fly in the face of sacred rules such as the importance of specificity. To the extent that issues can be discussed thematically, such interventions are to be encouraged, since they are not only cost effective but also promote generalization. This emphasis on themes has been particularly helpful with highly intellectualized clients who view the micro approach as not doing justice to the complexity of their problems.

Integrating Sex Therapy and Marital Therapy

A widely accepted but false piece of clinical lore is the belief that sexual problems do not require direct attention if they "result from" nonsexual marital problems; the notion is that sexual problems will take care of themselves provided that the nonsexual roots receive adequate attention. Melman and

Jacobson (1983) discovered that this was untrue by looking at the effects of behavioral marital therapy on couples' sexual complaints. It was discovered that improvement in the sexual area was extremely rare, even when all other areas of the relationship showed improvement. The lesson from this study was that sexual problems require direct attention in order for therapy to result in their alleviation. They do not disappear automatically, even when therapy is successful in other domains.

The next question becomes, What type of direct attention is needed? When the problem is a discrete dysfunction such as premature ejaculation or primary orgasmic dysfunction, the standard techniques developed by Masters and Johnson (1970) with recent modifications (Heiman, Chapter 16; Heiman, LoPiccolo, & LoPiccolo, 1981) seem to be highly successful. The great majority of our couples present with sexual problems that are much more diffuse, however, and more refractory to treatment than the diagnosed sexual dysfunctions. Complaints involve generalized dissatisfaction in quantity and/or quality, low sexual desire, and discrepancies in spouses' ideal frequency. Although much attention has been devoted to the treatment of low sexual desire, there is very little evidence as to the efficacy of any techniques currently described in the literature. In fact, what research has been done suggests that the changes that do occur as a result of such treatments are of dubious clinical significance (e.g., Heiman & LoPiccolo, 1983).

Another deterrent to progress in this area is the tendency for sex and marital therapies to be discussed in two separate literatures, as if they were distinct and unrelated problems. In fact, some marital therapists even refer couples to a sex therapist instead of handling the sexual issues themselves, and, even more commonly, sex therapy specialists send their clients elsewhere for marital therapy. These practices reflect an age of specialization that has run amok. We feel strongly that progress in the area of integrating sex and marital therapies cannot begin in earnest until the field desists from this artificial and misleading distinction.

We have been experimenting with a variety of techniques for enhancing the quality of couples' sex lives. First, by including a routine program called "sexual enrichment" in all our work, we normalize the desire for sexual enhancement and negate some of the discomfort that still inhibits many couples from admitting to sexual difficulties. Second, we extend many of our other techniques to the sexual area, thus dealing with sexual issues as we would any other marital problems. Much can be done to improve a couple's sex life by dealing with communication about sex. For example, clarification of and communication about the initiation and refusal of sexual activity can sometimes have dramatic consequences. Furthermore, explicit change agreements for creating a more erotic environment around the house can enhance both the quality and quantity of sex lives. Finally, many of the exercises described by Barbach (1983) have proven to be quite useful. In particular, communication exercises where couples share fantasies regarding ideal sexual experiences can be valuable sources of information, and if handled properly within a supportive, therapeutic environment, can produce positive shifts in couples' sexual practices.

This remains an area of much experimentation. We seem to be much better at producing companions than we are at eroticizing relationships. Other prominent sex therapists are exploring numerous alternatives, including the systemic approach described by Heiman in this volume. Obviously, this is an area in need of much clinical innovations as well as research.

Termination: An Obsolete Concept?

It seems appropriate to end a chapter on marital therapy with a reexamination of the concept *termination*. The SLC perspective is fundamentally suspicious of quick fixes. It is based on a premise that instigating change through therapist directives is at best a short-term solution to long-standing relationship problems. For marital therapy to result in long-term changes, couples must learn to function as their own therapists.

Our research has not disproven this premise; if anything, it has suggested that the skill orientation underlying the SLC perspective is necessary but not sufficient. Without it, many couples relapse rather routinely and quickly; with it, more couples maintain their treatment gains. For some couples, however, the ultimate determining factors will be the life events that they are exposed to subsequent to termination. It strikes us as naive to believe that any form of marital therapy, however potent its initial impact, will routinely have a permanent and lasting effect regardless of the numerous life stresses and events that occur subsequent to termination. These subsequent events gradually predominate relative to a marital therapy regimen, so that the longer the follow-up, the less variance in satisfaction remains to be accounted for by our treatments. This prediction is testable, although it has never been tested because so few long-term follow-ups have been conducted. The important point is, to the extent that we hope to have a permanent impact on most couples, the model of intensive treatment followed by termination is unlikely to accomplish the task.

Instead, we have been moving toward a model in which the marital therapist operates more like an accountant or a dentist than a physician. Accountants and dentists form relationships with their clients, solve their most pressing problems, and then meet with them periodically to provide checkups, crisis intervention, and further consultation. In the same way, marital therapists often meet with a couple for 2 to 4 months. Rather than expect this therapy regimen to have permanent and sweeping effects, it might be more prudent, and certainly more consistent with the evidence, to stop for a while and encourage people to come back when the time is right. This type of relationship deals more effectively with a clinical reality known to every practicing marital therapist: Couples often stop therapy independently of the therapist's agenda. If they are encouraged to come back when ready, and if the therapist avoids the temptation to broaden excessively the treatment goals in an effort to solve every problem at once, couples are more likely to use therapy as a resource rather than view a return to therapy as a sign that the original regimen failed.

This redefinition of the marital therapist's role places booster sessions in an important position. We are currently exploring the efficacy of booster sessions from three perspectives: First, we expect them to reduce termination anxiety; second, we expect them to result in greater adherence to treatment prescriptions between the last intensive treatment session and the booster; third, we expect the booster sessions themselves to prolong the effects of therapy.

Ideally, the final product will involve briefer intensive therapy because the initial treatment goals will be more modest. The total amount of therapist time is expected to be about the same as it is now because couples will utilize booster sessions, which, at the least, will include annual marital "checkups." This model calls into question the meaningfulness of the termination concept as applied to marital therapy.

The attempts to respond more effectively to distressed couples' escalation tendencies, better incorporate individual and sexual issues, adopt a more molar focus, and prolong the effects of marital therapy are at the forefront of our current work. Other exciting developments, including the integration of various marital therapy models (Feldman, 1982; Gurman, 1981; Segraves, 1982), loom on the horizon. In this chapter, we have attempted to describe the current technology of the SLC approach and also provide a sense of the dynamic interchange between research and clinical practice that uniquely characterizes this model. The developmental process of this mode leads to one safe prediction: When this volume is revised, this chapter will read quite differently from the way it reads now.

REFERENCES

Bandura, A. (1977). Self-efficacy: Toward a unifying theory of behavioral change. *Psychological Review*, 84, 191–215.

Barbach, L. (1983). *For each other.* New York: New American Library.

Baucom, D. H. (1981, November). *Cognitive behavioral strategies in the treatment of marital discord.* Paper presented at the annual meeting of the Association for the Advancement of Behavior Therapy, Toronto.

Birchler, G. R., Weiss, R. L., & Vincent, J. P. (1975). A multimethod analysis of social reinforcement exchange between maritally distressed and nondistressed spouse and stranger dyads. *Journal of Personality and Social Psychology*, 31, 349–360.

Doherty, W. J. (1981). Cognitive processes in intimate conflict: I. Extending attribution therory. *American Journal of Family Therapy*, 9, 5–13.

Epstein, N. (1982). Cognitive therapy with couples. *American Journal of Family Therapy*, 10, 5–16.

Feldman, L. B. (1982). Dysfunctional marital conflict: An integrative interpersonal–intrapsychic model. *Journal of Marital and Family Therapy*, 8, 417–428.

Fincham, F., & O'Leary, D. K. (1983). Casual inferences for spouse behavior in maritally distressed and nondistressed couples. *Journal of Social and Clinical Psychology, 1,* 42–57.

Gottman, J. M. (1979). *Marital interaction: Experimental investigations.* New York: Academic Press.

Gottman, J. M. (1982). Temporal form: Toward a new language for describing relationships. *Journal of Marriage and the Family, 44,* 943–962.

Gottman, J., Markman, H., Notarius, C., & Gonso, J. (1976). *A couple's guide to communication.* Champaign, IL: Research Press.

Guerney, B. (1977). *Relationship enhancement.* San Francisco: Jossey-Bass.

Gurman, A. S. (1978). Contemporary marital therapies: A critique and comparative analysis of psychodynamic, systems, and behavioral approaches. In T. J. Paolino, Jr., & B. S. McCrady (Eds.), *Marriage and marital therapy: Psychoanalytic, behavioral, and systems theory perspectives.* New York: Brunner/Mazel.

Gurman, A. S. (1981). Integrative marital therapy: Toward the development of an interpersonal approach. In S. Budman (Ed.), *Forms of brief psychotherapy.* New York: Guilford Press.

Hahlweg, K., & Jacobson, N. S. (Eds.) (1984). *Marital interaction: Analysis and modification.* New York: Guilford Press.

Hahlweg, K, Revenstorf, D., & Schindler, L. (1984). Effects of behavioral marital therapy on couples' communication and problem-solving skills. *Journal of Consulting and Clinical Psychology, 52,* 553–566.

Heiman, J. R., & LoPiccolo, L. (1983). Clinical outcomes of sex therapy: Effects of daily versus weekly treatment. *Archives of General Psychiatry, 40,* 443–449.

Heiman, J. R., LoPiccolo, L., & LoPiccolo, J. (1981). The treatment of sexual dysfunction. In A. S. Gurman & D. P. Kniskern (Eds.), *Handbook of family therapy.* New York: Brunner/Mazel.

Holtzworth-Munroe, A., & Jacobson, N. S. (1985). Causal attributions of married couples: When do they search for causes? What do they conclude when they do? *Journal of Personality and Social Psychology, 48,* 1398–1412.

Jacobson, N. S. (1978). Specific and nonspecific factors the effectiveness of a behavioral approach to the treatment of marital discord. *Journal of Consulting and Clinical Psychology, 46,* 442–452.

Jacobson, N. S. (1979). Increasing positive behavior in severely distressed adult relationships. *Behavior Therapy, 10,* 311–326.

Jacobson, N. S. (1983a). Beyond empiricism: The politics of marital therapy. *American Journal of Family Therapy, 11,* 11–24.

Jacobson, N. S. (1983b). Expanding the range and applicability of marital therapy. *Behavior Therapist, 6,* 189–191.

Jacobson, N. S. (1984). A component analysis of behavioral marital therapy: The relative effectiveness of behavior exchange and problem solving training. *Journal of Consulting and Clinical Psychology, 52,* 295–305.

Jacobson, N. S., & Anderson, E. A. (1980). The effects of behavior rehearsal and feedback on the acquisition of problem solving skills in distressed and nondistressed couples. *Behavior Research and Therapy, 18,* 25–36.

Jacobson, N. S., Elwood, R., & Dallas, M. (1981). Assessment of marital dysfunction. In D. H. Barlow (Ed.), *Behavioral assessment of adult disorders* (pp. 439–479). New York: Guilford Press.

Jacobson, N. S., & Follette, W. C. (1985). Clinical significance of improvement resulting from two behavioral marital therapy components. *Behavior Therapy 16,* 249–262

Jacobson, N. S., Follette, W. C., & McDonald, D. W. (1982). Reactivity to positive and negative behavior in distressed and nondistressed married couples. *Journal of Consulting and Clinical Psychology, 50,* 706–714.

Jacobson, N. S., Follette, W. C., & Pagel, M. (1984). *Predicting who will benefit from behavioral marital therapy.* Unpublished manuscript.

Jacobson, N. S., Follette, W. C., & Revenstorf, D. (1984). Psychotherapy outcome research: Methods for reporting variability and evaluating clinical significance. *Behavior Therapy, 15,* 336–352.

Jacobson, N. S., Follette, W. C., Revenstorf, D., Baucom, D. H., Hahlweg, K., & Margolin, G. (1984). Variability in outcome and clinical significance of behavioral marital therapy: A reanalysis of outcome data. *Journal of Consulting and Clinical Psychology, 52,* 497–504.

Jacobson, N. S., & Margolin, G. (1979). *Marital therapy: Strategies based on social learning and behavior exchange principles.* New York: Brunner/Mazel.

Jacobson, N. S., McDonald, D. W., Follette, W. C., & Berley, R. A. (1985). Attributional processes in distressed and nondistressed married couples. *Cognitive Therapy and Research, 9,* 35–50.

Jacobson, N. S., & Moore, D. (1981). Behavior exchange theory of marriage: Reconnaisance and reconsideration. In J. P. Vincent (Ed.), *Advances in family intervention, assessment, and theory* (Vol. 2). Greenwich, CN: JAI Press.

Jacobson, N. S., & Moore, D. (1981). Spouses as observers of the events in their relationship. *Journal of Consulting and Clinical Psychology, 49,* 269–277.

Jacobson, N. S., Waldron, H., & Moore, D. (1980). Toward a behavioral profile of marital distress. *Journal of Consulting and Clinical Psychology, 48,* 696–703.

Levenson, R. W., & Gottman, J. M. (1983). Marital interaction: Psychiological linkage and affective exchange. *Journal of Personality and Social Psychology, 45,* 587–597.

Liberman, R. P., Wheeler, E. G., deVisser, L. A. J. M., Kuehnel, J., & Kuehnel, T. (1981). *Handbook of marital therapy: A positive approach to helping troubled relationships.* New York: Plenum Press.

Margolin, G. (1981). Behavior exchange in happy and unhappy marriages: A family cycle perspective. *Behavior Therapy, 12,* 329–343.

Margolin, G. (1983). Behavior marital therapy: Is there a place for passion, play, and other non-negotiable dimensions? *Behavior Therapist, 6,* 65–68.

Margolin, G., Christensen, A., & Weiss, R. L. (1975). Contracts, cogntition, and change: A behavioral approach to marriage therapy. *Counseling Psychologist, 5,* 15–25.

Margolin, G., & Jacobson, N. S. (1981). Assessment of marital dysfunction. In M. Hersen & A. S. Bellack (Eds.), *Behavioral assessment: A practical handbook* (2nd Ed.) (pp. 389–426). London: Pergamon Press.

Margolin, G., & Wampold, B. E. (1981). Sequential analysis of conflict and accord in distressed and nondistressed marital partners. *Journal of Consulting and Clinical Psychology, 49,* 554–567.

Margolin, G., & Weiss, R. L. (1978). A comparative evaluation of therapeutic components associated with behavioral marital treatment. *Journal of Consulting and Clincial Psychology, 46,* 1476–1486.

Markman, H. J. (1979). Application of a behavioral model of marriage in predicting relationship satisfaction of couples planning marriage. *Journal of Consulting and Clinical Psychology, 47,* 743–749.

Masters, W. H., & Johnson, V. E. (1970). *Human sexual inadequacy.* Boston: Little-Brown.

Melman, K. N., & Jacobson, N. S. (1983). The integration of behavioral marital therapy and sex therapy. In M. L. Aronson & L. R. Wolberg (Eds.), *Group and family therapy.* New York: Brunner/Mazel.

O'Leary, K. D., & Turkewitz, H. (1978). The treatment of marital disorders from a behavioral perspective. In T. J. Paolino & B. S. McCrady (Eds.), *Marriage and marital therapy: Psychoanalytic, behavioral, and systems theory Perspectives.* New York: Brunner/Mazel.

Patterson, G. R. (1976). Some procedures for assessing changes in marital interaction patterns. *Oregon Research Institute Bulletin, 16.*

Revenstorf, D. (1984). The role of attribution of marital distress in therapy. In K. Hahlweg & N. S. Jacobson (Eds.), *Marital interaction: Analysis and modification* (pp. 325–336). New York: Guilford Press.

Schaap, C. (1984). A comparison of the interaction of distressed and nondistressed married couples in a laboratory situation: A literature survey, methodological issues and an empirical investigation. In K. Hahlweg & N. S. Jacobson (Eds.), *Marital interaction: Analysis and Modification* (pp. 133–157). New York: Guilford Press.

Schindler, L., & Vollmer, M. (1984). Cognitive perspectives in behavioral marital therapy: Some proposals for bridging theory, research, and practice. In K. Hahlweg & N. S. Jacobson (Eds.), *Marital interaction: Analysis and modification* (pp. 309–324). New York: Guilford Press.

Seagraves, R. T. (1982). *Marital therapy: A combined psychodynamic-behavioral approach.* New York: Plenum Press.

Stuart, R. B. (1980). *Helping couples change: A social learning approach to marital therapy.* New York: Guilford Press.

Stuart, R. B. (1969). Operant-interpersonal treatment for marital discord. *Journal of Consulting and Clinical Psychology, 33,* 675–682.

Vincent, J. P., Freidman, L. L., Nugent, J., & Messerly, L. (1979). Demand characteristics in observations of marital interaction. *Journal of Consulting and Clinical Psychology, 46,* 557–566.

Vincent, J. P., Weiss, R. L., & Birchler, G. R. (1975). A behavioral analysis of problem-solving in distressed and nondistressed married and stranger dyads. *Behavior Therapy, 6,* 475–487.

Weiss, R. L. (1984). Cognitive and strategic interventions in behavioral marital therapy. In K. Hahlweg & N. S. Jacobson (Eds.), *Marital interaction: Analysis and modification* (pp. 337–355). New York: Guilford Press.

Weiss, R. L. (1980). Strategic behavioral marital therapy: Toward a model for assessment and intervention. In J. P. Vincent (Ed.), *Advances in family intervention, assessment and theory* (Vol. 1, pp. 229–271). Greenwich, CN: JAI Press.

Weiss, R. L., Hops, H., & Patterson, G. R. (1973). A framework for conceptualizing marital conflict, technology for altering it, some data for evaluating it. In L. A. Hamerlynck, L. C. Handy, & E. J. Mash (Eds.), *Behavior change: Methodology, concepts, and practice* (pp. 309–342). Champaign, IL: Research Press.

Weiss, R. L., & Margolin, G. (1977). Assessment of marital conflict and accord. In A. R. Ciminero, K. D. Calhoun, & H. E. Adams (Eds.), *Handbook of behavioral assessment.* New York: Wiley.

Weiss, R. L., & Perry, B. A. (1979). *Assessment and treatment of marital dysfunction.* Eugene, OR: Oregon Marital Studies Program. Write to Robert L. Weiss, Department of Psychology, University of Oregon, Eugene, Oregon 97403.

Wile, D. B. (1981). *Couples therapy: A nontraditional approach.* New York: Wiley.

Wills, T. A., Weiss, R. L., & Patterson, G. R. (1974). A behavioral analysis of the determinants of marital satisfaction. *Journal of Consulting and Clinical Psychology, 42,* 802–811.

Wood, L. F., & Jacobson, N. S. (in press). Clinical applications of behavioral marital therapy. In D. H. Barlow (Ed.), *Behavioral treatment of adult disorders.* New York: Guilford Press.

4

Structural–Strategic Marital Therapy

THOMAS C. TODD

This chapter presents an integrated structural–strategic model of marital therapy. Since the possibility and desirability of such an integration is a topic currently under considerable debate (Fraser, 1984b), it seems appropriate to preface the body of the chapter with a brief discussion of the two models and the basis for integration that forms the backbone of this chapter.

As Stanton (1981a, 1981b) has noted, structural and strategic therapies share many common features.[1] Similarities and differences in the models are mentioned only briefly in this section, since they constitute the bulk of the chapter. In the material presented in the remainder of this chapter, assumptions and techniques that are common to both structural and strategic therapies are presented without comment. When the two models differ, these differences are commented on.

Structural and strategic therapies share many assumptions that differentiate these two forms of therapy from many others presented elsewhere in this book. Both emphasize the importance of current context, as opposed to history. The family life cycle is viewed as an important developmental framework within which the couple (and family) evolves. Symptoms are viewed in this developmental context and are seen as maintained by the system, while also maintaining it.

---

1. According to this author (Todd, 1983), much of the confusion related to the integration of structural and strategic therapies has been, at least in part, a result of confusing different models of strategic therapy. Throughout this chapter, the model of strategic therapy that is primarily considered is the distinctly paradoxical therapy characteristic of Haley (1963, 1976, 1984), Rabkin (1977), and Madanes (1981, 1984). As MacKinnon, Parry, and Black (1984) have described in detail, these models differ considerably from the Milan model or that of the Mental Research Institute.

Thomas C. Todd. Marriage and Family Therapy Training Program, Bristol Hospital, Bristol, Connecticut.

In both models, therapy is an active, directive, and goal-oriented process. Diagnosis is not separate from intervention, and the view of the system necessarily includes the therapist. Both models tend to be brief, problem focused, and pragmatic.

Important differences between the two models have contributed to the difficulty in integrating them. Structural therapy places greater emphasis on the importance of having the therapist "join" with the couple or family, as well as encouraging the therapist to employ personal influence to achieve therapeutic goals. In strategic therapy, the goals of therapy are typically less obvious, with progress toward these goals achieved by indirection or even provocation, rather than by straightforward therapeutic influence. Structural therapy emphasizes a larger time span and tends to view interaction as relatively stable or static in its patterning. By contrast, in strategic therapy much briefer sequences of behavior are emphasized, especially those sequences that involve symptomatic behavior.

Several models for integrating structural and strategic therapies have been proposed (Coyne, 1984; Fraser, 1984a; Liddle, 1984; Stanton 1981a, 1981b). The present model is similar to the structural–strategic model of the family therapy of drug abuse developed by Stanton and Todd (Stanton, Todd, & associates, 1982), and to the marital therapy model of Stanton (1981a). In its crudest form the latter has been characterized by Liddle as "structural first, strategic second" (Liddle, 1984, p. 73). This is an accurate shorthand summary of Stanton's general rules: (a) Initially deal with a couple through a primarily structural approach, (b) switch to a predominantly strategic approach when "structural" techniques either are not succeeding or are unlikely to succeed (Stanton 1981a).

For ease of explication, the terms *structural* and *strategic* are used as if these forms of therapy were used in their pure form. In this integrated model, however, they are seen as two extremes in a continuum; in actual clinical practice, it is rare for either to be used in its pure form.

THE MODEL OF MARITAL DISTRESS

Structural and strategic therapies share a common view of marriage as a relatively stable interactional system. Viewed as a system, the behavior of the marital dyad (or any other stable dyadic system) is seen as governed by the state of each of the partners, the feedback between them, and the impact of the "environment," which includes children, the respective families of origin, friends, work systems, and so on. The dyad is considered to be a goal-oriented system that attempts to satisfy the competing needs of the individual partners, the couple as an entity, and those of the environment.

Within limits, the couple is seen as doing the best it can to satisfy these competing demands. The system is also evolving and is not a closed system. New stages in the family life cycle (Carter & McGoldrick, 1980; Liddle,

1983) and the individual developmental cycles of the marital partners (Sheehy, 1976; Levinson, 1978) demand changes in the behavior of the marital dyad. One of the primary sources of marital distress is the failure of the system to adapt to these new requirements. Such marital distress can take two major forms: a stable unsatisfactory situation or a marital crisis.

A STABLE UNSATISFACTORY SITUATION

The most common form of marital distress is when the partners find themselves trapped in a stable but unsatisfactory situation. The distress may manifest itself in any number of ways. Often these include seemingly individual symptoms, such as depression or alcoholism. Other symptoms may be much more clearly interactional in nature, such as family violence, constant bickering, or sexual difficulties. There may be no clear-cut symptoms; rather, complaints of a vague nature, such as "There is no feeling left" or "Is this all there is to marriage?"

In the structural–strategic view, such symptoms are most often a response to life-cycle demands. As the context of the marriage changes, it becomes increasingly obvious that the marital relationship must itself change, yet for a variety of reasons change is too threatening. Classic examples of stressful transitions include the "empty nest" syndrome and the midlife crisis.

It is a mistake to regard the behavior of the couple as completely static, even though the spouses seem to be obviously stuck. When observed more closely, the behavior of the couple is seen to consist of a series of stages that make up a repetitive sequence (DeFrank-Lynch, Rigazio-DiGilio, & Todd, 1985; Haley, 1976). Within this sequence or cycle, symptomatic behavior plays a key regulatory role, signaling a shift back to the usual range of behavior. Unfortunately, such shifts can keep the couple trapped within a relatively narrow range of behavior.

Consider, for example, the response of a relatively traditional couple to the prospect of the "empty nest." As children grow and become more independent, it becomes increasingly obvious that the marital relationship will assume more importance to both partners and that the nonworking wife may need to find other sources of gratification to replace her diminishing role as mother. These changes require major readjustment for any couple, changes that are usually accomplished by a combination of trial-and-error experimentation, explicit negotiation, and marital distress.

In a clinically "disturbed" couple, this process breaks down and is replaced by an increasing reliance on "symptoms" (in the broadest sense) to define what is permissible. When the wife approaches her husband and makes it obvious that she needs more from him, he may withdraw into work. Further pursuit may be met with anger from him and criticism of her as too demanding. When she begins to move outside the home and test her wings, one or both partners may become anxious, or messages may be received from the extended family that such behavior is not acceptable. While such initial "corrective feedback" is encountered in any family or couple, in clinical couples it seems too risky to continue in the face of such opposition. With each repetition of the cycle, the role of the symptoms becomes more deeply entrenched.

The second major form of marital distress that typically confronts the therapist is that of a couple in obvious marital crisis. Something has happened, either in the environment or between the partners, that has created a "new ballgame." This may have occurred in the form of a sudden "trigger event," such as the death of a family member or an unexpected job transfer. Alternatively, the situation may have developed gradually, but the response to that situation may have exceeded the threshold of "permissible" behavior in a radical way. One of the most frequent examples of the latter is the extramarital affair. The marital relationship may have been deteriorating noticeably over a period of years, accompanied by individual distress and marital disharmony. When one of the partners has an affair, the relationship may be radically transformed, possibly in ways that may have an irreversible effect (which is not to imply that such changes are necessarily or inherently undesirable or maladaptive).

In both forms of marital distress, the therapist is typically faced with seemingly impossible, contradictory demands. In the stable unsatisfactory relationship, the implicit demand is, "Help us change, but without our having to disrupt anything" or "Help us maintain the status quo, while meeting these new demands." In the case of marital crisis, the couple seem to be asking, "Help us return to the old ways (even though that is impossible)."

In both situations, the problem is often implicit in the couple's definition of the situation, as well as their definition of what behavior is permissible. They are often blocked by their definition of the situation from trying new behavior and utilizing skills and strengths that they are capable of using successfully in other contexts. As we see in later sections of this chapter, the job of the structural–strategic marital therapist is to redefine the situation in more useful ways and help the couple gain access to existing skills and strengths.

Specific Concepts

The model of marital distress presented thus far is generally consistent with the assumptions made by most interactionally oriented marital therapists who work within the overall framework of general systems theory (GST) (von Bertalanffy, 1968).[2] However, certain key concepts that are characteristic of the structural–strategic view of marital distress set this model apart from other interactional models.

2. An extraordinary range of marital and family therapists describe their therapy as based on GST, including such diverse practitioners as Bockus (1975, 1980), Bowen (1978), Bross (1983), Jackson and Lederer (1968), Satir (1967), and Sluzki (1978).

A prominent example is the concept of power. Both Haley (1963) and Madanes (1981) have written eloquently on the role of power in the marital relationship, especially the importance of symptoms in regulating the balance of power. This is consistent with the above description of the regulatory function of symptomatic behavior, in which the symptomatic spouse unwittingly employs symptoms to achieve changes that presumably could not be effected through more direct means.

Other systems concepts are incorporated in the work of Minuchin and other structurally oriented therapists (Aponte & van Deusen, 1981; Minuchin, 1974; Minuchin & Fishman, 1981). The boundaries of a subsystem such as the marital dyad are "the rules defining who participates, and how" (Minuchin, 1974, p. 53). The couple may have little or no integrity as a separate subsystem (too "diffuse" a boundary) or may be too "rigid" about preventing outside contact and outside influences.

Closely related are the concepts of enmeshment and disengagement (Minuchin, 1974), which refer to typical interactional styles within the couple and in their interactions with others. At the enmeshed end of the continuum, there is little sense of separateness or autonomy. Spouses seem to talk and think for each other and have few individual positions on issues. Along with this, they are typically highly reactive to changes in the partner. Hoffman (1975) describes enmeshment as the "too richly cross-joined system," suggesting how hyperreactive the system can become to small changes in one member. At the opposite extreme of disengagement, there is little sense of connectedness and support. Autonomy is easily achieved, but at the expense of loyalty or commitment to the marital unit. Thus, even extreme fluctuations in the behavior of one partner produce little or no response in the other.

As Minuchin has cautioned (1974), it is important to recognize that neither enmeshment nor disengagement is regarded as either "healthy" or "pathological." It is more useful to view these characteristics as predisposing the system to difficulties in responding to particular environmental demands, while playing a more adaptive role in other situations. Enmeshed systems, for example, react poorly to situations requiring individual autonomy and often go into crisis around transitions such as leaving home. Such systems are, however, quite sensitive to changes and correct many situations before they get too extreme.

Disengaged systems, on the other hand, offer little mutual support at times of increased external stress. The lack of a sense of collective responsibility and loyalty means that there is little tendency to compensate for each other (e.g., if one spouse is tired or sick) and that accountability is loose for the actions of other family members, such as children. Disengaged systems, however, readily allow individual autonomy and can add or subtract members quite flexibly. They have thus provided considerable stability in poverty-level families, in situations where external factors may make a particular caretaker unreliable.

While the primary focus of this chapter is on the marital relationship, it is important to remember that this relationship always exists in a wider context. Almost invariably, the characteristics of the marital dyad are consistent with those of the context within which it is embedded. It is rare, for example, to find an enmeshed couple for whom intrusions from the extended family are not an issue, or in which children are not allowed to become inappropriately involved in parental and marital issues.

Alliances and coalitions are extremely important in the structural–strategic framework. Although these terms are often confused in popular usage, they are technically different. Hoffman (1981, p. 108) notes that alliances are affiliations between two people based on common interests and not involving a third party. In coalitions, by contrast, two people join together against or to the exclusion of a third. Haley (1976) has placed particular emphasis on alliances and coalitions, stressing the inherently triadic nature of relationships. In his view, the marital dyad is an unrealistic abstraction, which seldom exists in pure form. As we see in later sections, this presents particular problems for the marital therapist, who is hard-pressed to avoid becoming part of a triangle.

AN OVERVIEW OF STRUCTURAL–STRATEGIC MARITAL THERAPY

Therapeutic Rationale

The role of the therapist in bringing about change is logically related to the model of the marital system and marital distress. If therapy is successful, the therapist will help the marital system to find a new adaptation that will be more satisfactory for all concerned. This new set of behaviors will allow the couple to respond more successfully and more flexibly to the demands of the "environment" while meeting their own needs as individuals and as a couple. A key indicator of this success is the reduction in individual symptoms and marital distress.

The therapeutic model emphasizes health and adaptation. This means preserving the healthy aspects of the couple's current functioning to the maximum extent possible, as well as finding ways of activating existing strengths of the couple in new contexts where these strengths were previously underutilized. The therapist needs to maintain the view that the system is doing its best to meet conflicting demands but that there are factors that prevent the couple from finding a more satisfactory solution on their own. The therapist will need to be active and directive in helping the couple move away from old patterns. Despite this active role, the emphasis should always be on establishing a healthy, self-sufficient system and allowing the system to choose its own solution as much as possible.

Consistent with this emphasis on promoting a healthy, self-sufficient system, the therapist should intervene as economically as possible while still achieving major therapeutic goals. Ideally, this means identifying and activating skills already possessed by the couple. Failing this, the therapist may need to instruct the couple in necessary skills, such as communication or problem solving.[3] If the therapist senses ambivalence and reluctance about the prospect of change, yet feels that such changes are within the therapist's grasp, the personal influence of the therapist may be used to motivate the couple. Finally, when there is clear evidence that direct efforts to produce change are counterproductive, more strategic techniques may be necessary.

The two forms of marital distress described in the model of marital distress dictate somewhat different therapeutic responses, although the goals remain the same. In the stable unsatisfactory situation, the initial goal of the therapist must be to destabilize the situation in order to make a new solution possible. In the situation of marital crisis, this is not necessary. Whether the crisis already exists or is generated in part by the therapist, the therapist will need to moderate the crisis to keep it within manageable limits so as to prevent the couple from returning to old patterns out of fear. At the same time, some level of crisis must be maintained in order to propel the couple to search actively for new alternatives so that the possibilities for growth[4] inherent in any crisis situation are not lost.

The Therapeutic Model

In this section the basic framework of the therapeutic model is outlined, along with a typical case example, leaving the elaboration and specific technical aspects for later sections. By providing this overview of the therapeutic model, it is hoped that specific techniques can be understood more easily, rather than viewed in isolation.

Structural–strategic therapy emphasizes carefully planned action on the part of the therapist toward specific goals. This begins with the process of joining with the couple. Joining is a deliberate process in which the therapist initially accepts the couple's organization and style and blends with them (Minuchin, 1974, p. 123). This includes accommodating to typical communication patterns, tracking familiar content, and adopting the couple's affective style and nonverbal behavior. Joining is not therapy, however, and

---

3. Such skill training is rarely acknowledged in "pure" examples of structural and strategic therapy (cf. Haley, 1976). Viewed within the context of encouraging the self-sufficiency of the system, however, skill training is a logical addition to the skills a structural–strategic therapist should possess and employ. The therapist must be careful, however, to use skill training as a means of empowering the couple, rather than as a subtle putdown of one or both spouses.

4. Both Minuchin (1974) and Haley (1976) define growth similarly in viewing the goal of therapy as enhancing the variety of options and flexibility of response of the family members.

the structural–strategic therapist moves quickly to establish the therapist's role as that of change agent. On the other hand, a failure to join effectively may prevent the therapist from establishing the necessary influence to become a change agent.

Structural–strategic therapy is distinctly goal oriented in nature. This is not to imply that goal setting is easy, especially with couples in conflict. The therapist will begin the process of goal setting early in therapy, knowing full well that considerable shaping and redefinition will be necessary in the early stages of therapy. Later, as goals are fully or partially achieved and as new issues emerge, a new therapeutic contract may be explicitly negotiated. Haley (1976) has emphasized strongly that renegotiation must take place before new issues are tackled.

At the beginning of therapy, each spouse is asked to state his or her own goals and hopes for therapy. As Haley and others have noted (Haley, 1976; Fisch, Weakland, & Segal, 1982), these patterns of problem definition have one thing in common, namely, that unless they are modified, they will not be useful in helping the couple to solve their problems. Often the definition of the problem is a major part of the problem. A major task of the therapist therefore becomes restating these definitions into the form of a solvable problem.

When the initial goal statements of the two spouses are compared, they can fall into three patterns that are problematic for the therapist:

1. A combination that is typical of couples in open conflict is for the spouses to have incompatible goals and views of the situation, particularly for each to blame the other for the situation and see the other as the only one who needs to change.
2. When one spouse is overtly symptomatic, both spouses often agree that the symptomatic spouse is "it" and is the only person who needs to change.
3. Finally, both spouses may agree on a vague description of the situation, such as "We don't communicate," "We just lead parallel lives," or, "The feeling is gone between us."

In each of these possible combinations, the therapist hopes to bring the couple to a point where they both agree on specific goals—goals that involve change on the part of both partners and that are interactional in nature (as opposed to describing individual symptoms or traits).

Assessment

The process of assessment in structural–strategic therapy is multipronged and begins immediately; thus it is inextricably linked to the change process. While this form of marital therapy is relatively ahistorical, it does proceed from the assumption that the spouses are unsuccessfully trying to adapt to new demands placed by life-cycle transitions and individual issues such as retirement and illness. Similarly, the therapist looks for critical events in the recent past, such as significant losses or changes that have led the couple to seek therapy at this particular time.

A second major prong of the assessment process is observing the pattern of interaction that is characteristic of the couple. This includes relatively stable and static patterns, such as a chronic lack of conflict resolution, constant interruptions and bickering. Of potentially greater therapeutic significance is the discovery of repetitive sequences of behavior that maintain dysfunctional behavior (Haley, 1976). The therapist will be alert to the role of symptoms and analogues of the symptom[5] in regulating such sequences, since these transitional points in the sequence will be key points for therapeutic intervention.

Finally, the process of assessment must include testing the couple's response to the therapist and observing the role of the therapist in the therapeutic system of couple plus therapist. This includes noting the efforts of the spouses to induct the therapist into their system and sensing the role that each wants the therapist to play. It also includes probing the willingness of the spouses to shift behavior and take direction from the therapist, as well as testing how cooperative and responsive they are to the efforts of the therapist to find and develop strengths in the couple.

Contracting

As the processes of joining, goal definition, and assessment proceed, the therapist will usually attempt to establish clear therapeutic goals and strategies for achieving these goals. How much these goals and strategies will be shared with the couple depends on how "strategic" the therapist must be.

In the integrated structural–strategic model proposed in this chapter, it is considered ideal for the therapist to negotiate an explicit treatment contract with the couple. If it is clear that the therapist can establish an interpersonal connection and therapeutic alliance with each spouse, and if the therapist has been sucessful in developing tentative hypotheses and therapeutic strategies, it is appropriate for the therapist to share these with the couple and have the spouses function as full partners in the treatment plan.

"Full disclosure" is not always necessary or desirable. For example, interpreting the function of a symptom may engender unnecessary resistance; instead, it may be more effective to block the symptom or find an alternative rationale for a therapeutic directive that is more palatable and less confronting.[6] (For example, an overinvolved parent may be given a "vacation" or described

---

5. For example, it is unusual for an alcoholic spouse to drink during a session, but it is not unusual for one of the spouses to bring the drinking into the session at crucial moments. This may take the form of threats to drink, references to drinking, or nonverbal reminders of behavior when drunk.

6. See Haley (1976, pp. 201–217) for an extensive discussion of the clinical and ethical issues involved in disclosing or withholding information.

as overloaded rather than accused of being intrusive.) In fullblown strategic cases, most of the strategy will be kept hidden and even denied if the couple confront the therapist. Always, however, the therapist should be able to specify therapeutic goals that match those of the couple and should be able to demonstrate the connection between these goals and the strategies adopted.

Once the therapist has established an overall treatment plan, whether "structural" or "strategic," the structure of the therapy, including the structure of each session, becomes much more predictable. The typical stages of subsequent sessions are (a) reviewing homework and significant events since the preceding session; (b) gathering new data and generating new ideas related to overall strategy and goals; (c) having the couple interact directly in the session, with coaching from the therapist;[7] and (d) assigning new homework tasks to be performed before next session.

This session structure is common to the full spectrum of structural and strategic approaches, but with important variations. When working predominantly structurally, the therapist will usually hope that the homework assignment will be performed successfully in a straightforward way. Similarly, the therapist will emphasize straightforward changes in the couple's pattern of interaction during the session.

When working more strategically, the therapist needs to be much more neutral in the evaluation of the outcome of previous directives and homework. Whether the task succeeds or fails, the therapist should avoid praise or criticism that might reveal the therapeutic agenda. If anything, the therapist should be skeptical of positive changes and positively validate failure to do the task. During the session, behavior in relation to the therapist is at least as significant as the behavior of the spouses toward each other. The therapist will not push for positive changes in their interaction but will observe and probe their interactive behavior in a neutral fashion.

Termination

The process of termination in structural–strategic therapy is consistent with the health orientation of this model. Many characteristics of this form of therapy combine to make termination straightforward and a relatively easy process. Presumably, the therapist has consistently emphasized the importance of having the couple do tasks with each other, especially outside the sessions, and has made it clear that this is the real work of therapy. This makes it easy to give the credit for change to the couple (Stanton, 1981d). A major part of the termination process is the review of what the couple learned and

---

7. At times, mere coaching and exhortation from the therapist may be insufficient to produce the desired shift in behavior. As mentioned, it may be necessary to instruct the couple in specific skills. Modeling by the therapist and role playing may also be helpful. In all such "teaching" interventions it is crucial for the therapist to consider how this role may establish an undesirable coalition with one spouse or place the therapist in an unproductive "one-up" position.

what they did, especially with a view toward using these same skills to meet new situations.

If the therapy has been predominantly strategic in flavor, it is even more imperative for the therapist to refuse credit for positive changes. (The couple will rarely give such credit anyway!) Instead, the therapist will express puzzlement or grudging admiration at changes that have occurred. Since these changes have not occurred at the therapist's direction, or have even seemed to be contrary to the therapist's directives and warnings, this attitude of the therapist will seem genuine. The therapist's final action, when working strategically, will usually be to caution against a relapse or "side effects," perhaps scheduling a follow-up call or a session in the future to see whether these pessimistic predicitons are justified. In most cases in which the therapist has thrown down the strategic gauntlet, the spouses welcome such an opportunity to prove the therapist wrong.

The time parameters of structural–strategic therapy also aid in the termination process. From the beginning, the therapist should make it clear that the therapy is expected to be relatively short-term (e.g., 10 to 15 sessions) and focused on specific problems and goals. When these are achieved, the therapist will get out as quickly as possible, rather than look for new problems or accepting a vague contract. As mentioned, this does not mean that the therapist is opposed to renegotiating a new contract in response to issues raised by the couple; what is to be avoided is drifting into long-term therapy or "fishing" for new problems.

As therapy begins to be successful in achieving the agreed-upon goals, the sessions are usually spaced at wider time intervals, such as moving to alternate weeks and progressing to once a month. This allows the spouses to do more of the work themselves and helps ensure that they can maintain the changes without the therapist. When termination occurs, it is with the understanding that further problems are a normal part of life. While the therapist hopes that the spouses can meet these new challenges without further therapy, they can certainly return for a few "booster" sessions. The expectation is clearly conveyed that any additional therapy is likely to be extremely brief, since the spouses have successfully dealt with problems.

Case Example

The following case example illustrates many of the general points of the therapy model:

> Mr. and Mrs W. sought therapy after 35 years of marriage. Mrs. W., the caller, said, "I'm beginning to think that we have never loved each other all this time." It became obvious that several major life transitions had propelled them to this crisis point. Mr. W. had been forced to retire at age 62 because of a corporate takeover in the large firm in which he had been a top executive. They had sold their large house in the Boston suburbs and moved to a much smaller house in western Massachusetts that had previously

been their weekend getaway. Mrs. W. had been conducting an antique business there on weekends, but these changes allowed the couple to realize their dream of going into the antique business together. Unfortunately, their dream now seemed to be a nightmare. They were together constantly and fought nonstop, leading both to believe that they hated each other.

It was apparent that their expectations and interpretations were aggravating the problem. Several highly stressful life transitions had combined to produce severe marital distress. It was also obvious that Mr. and Mrs. W. were amplifying this distress by assuming that they should be happy and by interpreting their fighting as evidence that they did not love each other. (They thought that perhaps they had been too busy working to notice that they really hated each other.) Evidence collected in the first session did not support this assumption, since the two of them were able to recall many happy moments together, enjoyed vacations, were supportive to each other, and so on. The therapist succeeded in dramatically reducing their stress level by normalizing their distress, explaining to them how stressful life transitions can be, even those that have been happily anticipated.

In the second session, an unexpected area of strength was discovered, somewhat by chance, which was to form the basis for the remaining therapy. The spouses described how they managed money with a system that had proven very successful for them. They had three separate bank accounts for purchasing antiques—hers, his, and joint. This system had prevented any second-guessing of each other about purchases, yet seemed to provide an acceptable level of togetherness.

We applied this paradigm to the issue of antique shows, one of the consistent sources of fights. Rather than have both of them work all the shows together and squabble about whose selection, whose arrangement, and the like, would prevail, they agreed to divide the show calender into "his" and "hers." The off-duty partner could come to the other shows only in the status of helper. In addition, both agreed that the person not in charge should not spend much time at such shows. The next session was scheduled in a month to determine the effectiveness of this intervention.

The couple reported with pleasure that the agreement had totally eliminated the stress produced by the shows. They had further refined the agreement to eliminate other sources of friction, and they had even been able to offer advice to each other, within the safety provided by this structure, without producing fights. We went on to examine other conflictual areas, including the allocation of space in their tiny house to allow some "private time" and the division of tasks around the business to make their roles more distinct. Again, they were enormously relieved to learn that other couples found such issues stressful, and they were easily able to negotiate new ground rules. The final session, over a month later, proved to be merely a "checkup" to confirm the sense that theirs was a sound relationship that was now back on track. We reviewed what they had learned and how they could apply it to other situations that might occur.

This is an unusually clear example of the role of stressful transitions and how a "healthy" couple feel trapped in a cul de sac that requires professional help to escape. The health orientation of this therapeutic model was clearly helpful in preventing this from becoming a long-term case, feeding into their fears of deep relationship problems. Instead, their view of the problem was changed to one that identified them as a normal couple reacting predictably to stressful transitions. The therapist's role was to help them discover strengths that they were already using in other contexts, to devise tasks and agreements that made use of these strengths, to see that these changes had the predicted positive effect, and to leave the system as soon as possible.

Assumptions

Although many of the assumptions of this model are implicit in the material presented thus far, it may be helpful at this point to identify the basic assumptions explicitly:

1. The primary job of the therapist is to find ways to get the couple to attempt new forms of behavior toward each other.
2. While insight may follow such new behavior, insight is not necessary to produce behavioral change. Relabeling may be useful to set the stage for behavioral change, but not because of its "truth value."
3. The most valuable part of therapy is behavioral change outside the therapy session, but it is rarely possible for the couple to achieve this without the help of the therapist. Behavioral changes in the session can be useful in preparing for similar changes outside the session.
4. The therapist needs to be active and directive, helping to devise conditions within and between sessions that will allow the couple to interact in a new way. While some instruction on the part of the therapist may be necessary, the primary emphasis is on creating the context for the activation of existing skills and motivating them to use these skills.
5. Symptoms are presumed to serve an adaptive function in the system, but at the expense of preventing the system from adapting more successfully to changing circumstances.
6. With the therapist's help, the couple can find a new solution that is "better"—one that allows the couple to meet the competing needs of the situation more satisfactorily, without the need for symptomatic behavior.
7. Once such a solution has been found, it tends to be self-maintaining and in fact often generates further positive changes.

Overcoming "Obstacles" to Therapy

Since structural–strategic therapy emphasizes doing rather than merely talking, it is relatively easy to recognize noncompliance with treatment recommendations. When faced with such lack of compliance, the therapist has three major choices of response. They are listed below in the ideal order in which they should be applied, although in actual practice there will often be some degree of overlap in their application.

INTENSIFY JOINING EFFORTS AND ACCOMMODATE TO CLINICAL FEEDBACK

Anderson and Stewart (1983) have noted that Minuchin and other structural therapists place particular emphasis on *joining* as an antidote for resistance. While joining is not the only remedy, failures in joining should always be examined first. Indications of difficulty may be obvious, such as threats to quit therapy, challenges to the treatment plan, or intensified emphasis on individual symptoms; or they may be more subtle, such as halfhearted compliance with assignments. Several forms of inadequate joining may be responsible for the difficulties, such as moving too fast or being too aggressive in attempting to shift from an individual problem to an interactional one. The difficulty may be more general, such as a lack of warmth and a mechanical quality to the therapist's actions, or some other form of affective mismatch. Finally, the joining problems may be on an individual level, where the therapist is unsympathetic or even antagonistic to one of the spouses.

In the structural view, the reasons for the therapist's failure to join adequately are not important. What is important is that the therapist must take responsibility for accommodating to the feedback from the couple, viewing "resistance" as a property of the therapeutic system rather than residing within the spouses. Joining is considered to be a deliberate effort to match the therapist's behavior to that of the couple or individual. As such, it can be consciously altered when obstacles are encountered. It may be sufficient to alter the therapist's nonverbal behavior. If, however, the therapeutic situation has deteriorated seriously or is in danger of dissolving, more extreme measures are called for. The therapist can apologize for pushing so hard and can devote time and effort to "understanding" the couple's situation better. Similarly, when the therapeutic relationship with one spouse is in jeopardy, an individual session with that spouse is very often an effective remedy for previously inadequate joining.[8]

In addition to improved joining, the therapist should consider other techniques at his or her disposal to reduce the degree of threat perceived by the couple or one spouse. These can include normalizing their difficulties with a theoretical explanation or comparing their situation with that of other couples. Self-disclosure on the part of the therapist or the co-therapy team can have a similar effect.

REFINE STRUCTURAL TASKS

When both spouses seem to have adequate rapport with the therapist and yet task compliance is uneven or nonexistent, the tasks themselves may be

8. Here it is important to remember the distinction between alliances and coalitions. The purpose of the individual session is to develop a therapeutic alliance by developing greater empathy for that spouse. Bids for a coalition against the other spouse are to be avoided, including the revelation of secrets or one-sided presentations of events.

at fault, or task-specific motivation may need to be increased. The therapist may need to "sell" the task better, or relabel it to make it more clearly relevant to the spouses' goals.[9] Second, the task may be simplified and made less demanding, or the contract may be made more specific through agreement on where, when, and how the task will be performed. Finally, if these measures fail, it may be obvious that the task is off-target, making recontracting for a different task necessary.

Consider the following case example:

The author was asked to provide a one-session consultation with a couple who had originally sought family therapy and were now having difficulty making the transition to couple sessions. Bob and Alice were both in their early 30s and both in their second marriage. They had been seen for 10 family therapy sessions to deal with problems concerning Alice's teenage daughter from her first marriage. Although both spouses agreed that the primary problems were between them, couple sessions had been unproductive, with Alice making vague complaints about Bob and with both spouses more comfortable talking about children, ex-spouses, and other absent parties.

Discussion with the therapist revealed two dominant themes from previous sessions—Bob's drinking and his lack of involvement with Alice's two younger daughters. In the consultation session, discussion of Bob's drinking was inconclusive, with Alice giving mixed messages about whether it was a problem or whether she simply felt excluded and ignored. Discussion shifted to his lack of involvement in the family. With considerable prodding, Alice identified that she wished that Bob would spend some pleasant time with the girls instead of coming home in an irritable mood. Further negotiation got Bob to agree what nights and times he could play with the girls, and what they would do together.

In this case, there was no need to wait for the next session for the task to fail. Alice sat quietly through this negotiation process with her arms folded in an extremely closed and unyielding posture. Concerned about this, I asked her whether the task we had just negotiated would be constructive or if it was just a side issue. She quickly labeled it as a side issue, and we began the contracting process all over again. She stated clearly (with therapeutic help) that she wanted more support from Bob. Now it was Bob's turn to resist an assignment. He felt that Alice's need for support had begun a year previously, subsequent to the death of her father. Bob stated that he was not the kind of man who could fill that need for Alice, and that she had known that when they had gotten married. Alice was helped to scale down her requests to make it obvious that they were within Bob's capabilities. Bob still adamantly refused. I then joined with him, identifying him as a "man of action" like myself, one who found it difficult to hear about a problem without offering a solution. Alice agreed that she valued his active problem solving but made it clear that she needed his affection first. He said that if he became emotional, "Then there would be two of us in the soup instead of one." I noted that unless he showed some emotion, she

<hr/>

9. See Haley (1976, pp. 54–57) for guidelines for increasing the motivation of family members to follow directives.

*would never listen to his suggestions, which she agreed were excellent. We
concluded with my noting that both of them would find this new pattern
difficult and that both would need considerable help from the therapist to
learn to put it into practice.*

SHIFT TO STRATEGIC TECHNIQUES

Stanton (1981a) has established general principles for deciding whether and
when to use a structural or a strategic approach with couples. In general,
Stanton advocates beginning with a predominantly structural approach,
switching to a strategic approach only when (*a*) the structural approach is
not working; or (*b*) it seems obvious that the structural orientation is doomed
to failure (e.g., with a couple with an extensive history of unsuccessful
treatment).

These two general principles seem to cover the major transitions between
structural and strategic therapies when one or the other is used almost
exclusively. In practice, it seems difficult to categorize most cases so neatly,
and even the most extreme cases are seldom "pure." It seems more useful
to consider therapeutic strategies (and cases) as falling on a continuum from
almost purely structural to almost purely strategic. Not only can cases occupy
any point along this continuum, but it is also typical for a case to move
along this continuum from session to session and even within a session.

Another way of labeling this continuum, and one that makes it easier
to understand these shifts, has been proposed by White (1983). He labels
as "radical" structural and other techniques that are straightforward requests
for change. At the opposite extreme are "conservative" interventions that
support the status quo. In the context of psychotherapy, these are usually
considered strategic or paradoxical, since advocating the status quo seems
contrary to the stated purpose of therapy. Viewed within this framework, it
is not surprising that pure cases are rare and that shifts along the continuum
are usually necessary. All "radical" interventions engender some resistance.
Increased joining (which is actually an implicitly conservative intervention)
may be sufficient to dispel this resistance, but often a more pronounced
shift is necessary. The therapist can then employ one of the strategic techniques
listed below, such as positioning or restraining, on a temporary basis, shifting
back when the resistance is diminished. With more resistant couples, a
different "mix" may be necessary, in which the therapist is consistently
conservative but may stop short of paradoxical directives. Figure 4-1 illustrates
some of the possibilities along this continuum.

A Brief Catalogue of Paradoxical Techniques

The author has identified six key ingredients of a strategic or paradoxical
approach. Space permits only a brief presentation here; for further details
and examples, the reader is referred to publications specifically addressed
to paradoxical techniques (Todd, 1981, 1984; Todd & LaForte, in press).

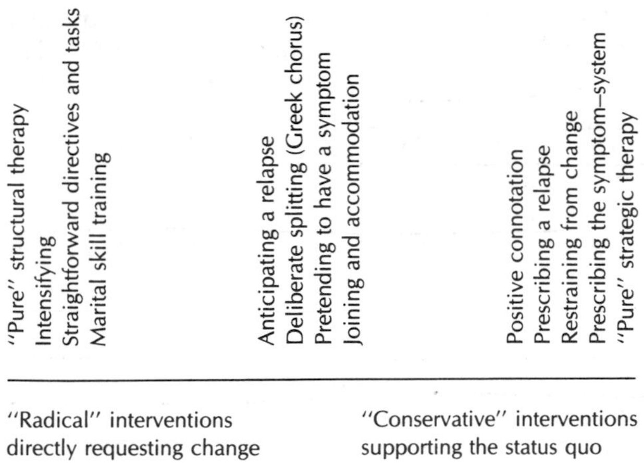

FIGURE 4-1. The structural–strategic therapy continuum with illustrative examples. Note that all scaling is *extremely* approximate.

RELABELING

It should be clear by now that relabeling plays a major role in structural–strategic therapy. The most important strategic variant of this technique has been described as "positive connotation" (Selvini-Palazzoli, Cecchin, Prata, & Boscolo, 1978, pp. 55–66) and "positive interpretation" (Stanton, 1981c). This is often applied to symptomatic or other behavior typically considered undesirable. Instead, the behavior is described as having a positive effect or at least as being based on positive intentions, which Stanton and Todd (1979) characterize as "ascribing noble intentions." In its ideal form, the positive motivation attributed to the patient or the villain should be secretly aversive to him or her. For example, a husband's swearing and verbal abuse might be relabeled as a protective effort to make his wife look good by contrast, for which she should be grateful. The closer such relabeling resembles the "truth" of the situation, the more power it will have, although such relabeling is presumed to be effective through blocking the behavior it refers to, rather than through the production of insight.

POSITIONING

A closely related technique is positioning, in which the therapist takes a stance that seems the opposite of the assumptions that the therapist is expected to make. The use of this technique is crucial whenever the therapist senses that assumptions are being attributed to the therapist that would drastically curtail therapeutic flexibility and that would be used to advantage by one spouse. A typical example is the spouse who says with apparent innocence, "Doctor, we are supposed to be totally honest here, aren't we?" shortly before unloading on the unsuspecting partner. A strong case can be made that, in some contexts, each of the "sacred cows" of marital therapy can be unsuitable or harmful, including honesty, open communication, dropping past grievances, and even seeing the couple conjointly instead of separately.[10]

Positioning is also important in setting the tone of therapy, particularly when the therapist senses that he or she is working too hard or is pumping optimism into the marital sessions. Here the work of Fisch and his colleagues at the Mental Research Institute is particularly instructive in illustrating how the therapist can take a pessimistic and "one-down" position rather than be "set up" to prove himself or herself (Fisch *et al.*, 1982).

RESTRAINING

It is rarely a mistake to advise a couple to "go slow," especially when they appear to be making progress or when they seem too tolerant of an intolerable situation. The most typical mistake is to point out negative consequences of change that actually are more terrifying than the current situation. ("If you spent more time together, you might get depressed, and your husband would probably have a heart attack.") It is better to imply that they are not ready to tolerate apparently positive consequences and to point out "negative" consequences that the spouses would argue are positive (Papp, 1984). For example, "If you stopped being depressed, you might find new life in your sexual relationship, and I'm not sure that either of you are ready for that."

DELIBERATE SPLITTING

While these strategic techniques can be effective when used appropriately, many therapists find it difficult to be consistently pessimistic, to argue against change and to espouse symptomatic behavior. There is also the danger that the therapeutic relationship will become unnecessarily antagonistic. Fortunately, it is possible to have one's cake and eat it too, by having the therapeutic team appear to be split and argue both sides of the dilemma (Papp, 1980). One faction can argue that change is dangerous, that the symptoms are positive, and so forth, while the other side is more optimistic and advocates change. This splitting can be accomplished even when working solo, by attributing the pessimistic stance to an absent supervisor or psychiatrist, to the accepted wisdom of the field, or simply by having the solo therapist "be of two minds" (Bergman, 1982). As the couple begins to change, "public opinion" can gradually shift to validate their changes.

PRESCRIBING

"Prescribing the symptom" typically has been considered the hallmark of paradoxical therapy, even though it is rarely useful in simplistic form. Instead, as the Milan associates have shown so elegantly (Selvini-Palazzoli *et al.*, 1978), it is much more effective when the behavior of the whole

---

10. It is true that these sacred cows have developed over the history of marital therapy for good reasons, and the inexperienced therapist kills them at his or her own peril. The principles themselves are not being questioned, only their rigid and unquestioned application.

system is prescribed and amplified. The whole interactional pattern is pre-scribed, under the therapist's control, possibly at assigned times or in a particularly ritualized manner. For example, a jealous husband might be assigned to conduct a detailed investigation of his wife each time she came home, while she was instructed to act deliberately evasive and encourage his doubts. In more extreme cases, particularly when a strategic team is used, written prescriptions can be powerful applications of this technique (Todd, 1981; Todd & LaForte, in press).

PRETENDING

The work of Madanes (1981, 1984) on pretending has created a multitude of new opportunities in strategic therapy. With compliant couples, rituals of pretending can be assigned that will break an old pattern or introduce humor and absurdity. Asking a spouse to pretend to have the symptom avoids arguments with the therapist about conscious control and can be equally effective whether or not the patient complies. For example, an alcoholic can be instructed to act drunk at random times during the week, with the spouse instructed to attempt to differentiate between real and simulated episodes. Regardless of the degree of compliance, such an assignment typically disrupts the usual patterns of both spouses.

Limitations and Contraindications

There are few absolute contraindications to the structural–strategic approach. Even in integrative models such as that of Pinsof (1983), the structural–strategic approach is an optimal initial one, with a shift to other approaches seen as necessary only if structural–strategic therapy is ineffective. The structural–strategic approach offers the advantage of connecting immediately with the couple in terms of their stated complaints and concerns and working quickly to get results. This makes the model useful for a wide range of couples, including those who are unsophisticated about therapy and expect prompt recommendations and results. There are, however, a few typical situations in which the use of this model may not succeed and in which the therapist should apply the model with caution. While each of these situations presents problems for many, if not most, forms of marital therapy, there are factors that make them particularly problematic for structural–strategic therapy.

First, under some circumstances it may be inadvisable to see the couple in sessions together. This is particularly true when the spouses are separated or divorced, and there is little or no contact outside the sessions. Not only may the therapy sessions become the equivalent of a date, more of a social occasion than a therapy session, but also there is little opportunity for work to occur with the couple between sessions. Since structural–strategic therapy places a heavy emphasis on having the couple work at changes in their behavior, particularly between sessions, this is a significant problem. A partial remedy for this situation is to work out the details of a structured separation, including regular "dates" and homework assignments (Granvold, 1983).

In other situations, seeing the couple conjointly may create a misleading impression of priorities, particularly regarding the goals that must be addressed first in therapy. The most obvious example of an error in this regard is the therapist who continues to do marital therapy with a couple in which an alcoholic spouse is continuing to drink. In this situation, or with other forms of substance abuse, a few conjoint sessions may be used to underscore the need for treatment. After this groundwork has been done, the priority must shift to abstinence as the primary issue (Berenson, 1976). Treatment resources in addition to marital therapy are usually necessary, such as inpatient detoxification and rehabilitation and self-help groups such as Alcoholics Anonymous. A similar concern has been voiced in the area of spouse abuse, where many practitioners believe that seeing spouses conjointly while active abuse is continuing may give the appearance of condoning the abuse.

A second problem for the model is created by spouses who have incompatible expectations for therapy, which make it impossible to identify common goals and establish a mutually satisfactory contract. Such incompatibility and hidden agendas create difficulties for any form of marital therapy. They create a particular danger for a highly directive form of therapy such as structural–strategic therapy, especially if the therapist imposes assignments and structures interaction without paying attention to the feedback from both spouses. When one spouse has little or no investment in continuing the marriage and has no real intention of changing, this spouse may still keep up appearances by seeming compliant in therapy. This will eventually come to light because of failure to do the homework or cooperate fully during the sessions. It is often quicker, however, to see each spouse individually for one diagnostic session early in therapy to ascertain the level of motivation for conjoint therapy and provide an easy opportunity for information about outside relationships to be revealed.[11]

The third problematic situation for using structural–strategic therapy is dealing with a couple in which one or both spouses refuse to drop the past and are unable to focus on the present and future. This can be a problem for any form of therapy that emphasizes work in the "here and now" and that focuses on achieving positive changes. A spouse who refuses to drop past grievances will typically be uncooperative with tasks and will tend to minimize any positive changes. Initially, a move to more strategic methods may be attempted to break this impasse, such as prescribing intensified suffering (Todd, 1984). In such techniques, the therapist prescribes the usual behavior of the couple in extreme form, in this instance by prescribing a

---

11. The therapist must establish the ground rules for such individual sessions carefully. Such sessions are not confidential from the other spouse, and the therapist should reserve the right to reveal information obtained or press the spouse to do so.

ritual form of suffering. If such strategic techniques fail, however, it is often necessary to work individually with each spouse to motivate each to make changes that are not contingent on the changes of the other, or to decide to leave the relationship. This individual work can be done in a manner that is consistent with a structural–strategic framework by agreeing to see the spouses individually in a time-limited contract, reconvening the couple after a specified interval to assess progress and ascertain the possibility of resuming conjoint sessions.

THE ROLE OF THE THERAPIST

Structural–strategic therapy has often been accused, at least informally, of ignoring the therapist and overemphasizing technique. This criticism has some merit, but no one who has watched sessions conducted by experienced structural therapists would maintain that the therapist is unimportant. The distinctive aspect of structural–strategic therapy is its assumption that the behavior of the therapist is subject to deliberate control, including the planned use of self and the cultivation of a personal therapeutic style. This form of therapy is highly teachable and applicable to a wide range of therapists as long as the therapist is willing to take an active role and try new behavior. Several major skills must be developed to conduct this form of marital therapy with maximum success.

Since structural–strategic therapy is so goal oriented, it is critical for the therapist to be able to identify clear goals and keep the therapy consistently goal related. To do this, the therapist must be able to collect systematic data concerning symptomatic behavior and other target behavior and to use these data to develop hypotheses relating these observations to interactional patterns involving the couple. As therapy continues, progress toward therapeutic goals must be monitored continuously. The therapist must also be able to evaluate the interaction of the couple, the feedback to the therapist from each spouse, and the reactions of the therapist, and to utilize this information to revise previous hypotheses and develop new strategies.

To be successful at structural–strategic therapy, the therapist must be active and directive. The therapist cannot afford to be a passive observer or mere commentator while the family continues its familiar, unproductive patterns. Instead, the therapist should begin to intervene to change these patterns as soon as she or he has begun to develop tentative therapeutic hypotheses. In particular, this means giving the couple explicit directions to behave differently toward each other during the session. Naturally, since the spouses have had difficulty shifting their behavior toward each other in the past, the therapist must be prepared to give additional coaching to one or both partners to maintain this new behavior.

This directive role requires many component skills. The therapist must be able to revise hypotheses and strategies on the spot, in response to feedback from the couple. Directions must be precise and action oriented and should not invite further discussion with the therapist. Since directives often are not readily accepted, the therapist must deliver them in a manner that will make it most likely that they will be followed—sometimes crisply authoritative and at other times tentative and exploratory. Knowing and adopting the couple's world view and language will also be extremely helpful in this process. Finally the therapist should use the results of in-session tasks to develop homework assignments for the couple between sessions.

Becoming active and directive creates the danger that the therapist will become too central and remain too involved in the interaction during the session. For the therapist to become an effective observer, there must be times when the therapist will orchestrate a particular scene or task between the spouses and then sit back and observe. At the same time, however, the therapist must be constantly ready to intervene quickly and forcefully to redirect the interaction or to block unproductive patterns. Few therapists are equally adept at both intense involvement and detached observation, yet it is this combination that is so critical to the success of structural–strategic therapy. Minuchin is particularly skilled at this. In the film *Anorexia Is a Greek Word* (Minuchin, 1980), for example, he interacts directly and intensely to provoke the wife, implying that she has been wrong and is responsible for her daughter's being in the hospital. When he succeeds in getting her to respond angrily, he disengages and diverts the fight to the husband, where it really belongs.

Finally, the therapist needs the intangible quality of courage of conviction. In this therapeutic model, the task and responsibility of the therapist are to help the couple move beyond their familiar patterns of behavior to a new pattern. This process is bound to be stressful and anxiety provoking for them, and for the therapist as well. The therapist must be courageous enough to move beyond this inevitable distress and to resist the couple's efforts to persuade the therapist to allow them to return to the status quo. At the same time, however, the therapist must remain open to the possibility that the therapeutic hypotheses may be inaccurate.

Somewhat different skills are required in this process, depending on whether the therapist is working predominantly in a structural or a strategic mode. When working structurally, the therapist needs to direct the interaction and intensify the affect to move the couple beyond its usual threshold, using the techniques outlined in the earlier section. When positive changes are achieved with the structural approach, the therapist can support and validate them.

When working strategically, it is particularly difficult for the therapist to stick with the chosen strategy when there is no initial success. Not only is it necessary for the therapist to persist, but it is also frequently necessary to exaggerate and escalate even further in the chosen direction. Positive results also present a potential trap for the strategic therapist. When working strategically, it is a mistake to react positively. Instead, it is necessary to maintain a consistent posture of restraint and skepticism. In extreme cases, the therapist may need to complete the entire course of therapy without giving or receiving direct positive validation. This requires a very different therapeutic relationship from that to which most therapists are accustomed.

Therapist Error

As Bross (1983) has pointed out, there is a definite distinction between the errors made by beginners and those of more experienced therapists. For the most part, the errors mentioned in this section are typical of relatively inexperienced therapists, although few therapists are completely immune to them. Many forms of behavior that would be mistakes when performed by inexperienced therapists are not necessarily errors when utilized by an experienced therapist. For example, students of the author have noted that, despite all of the author's emphasis on having the spouses talk to each other, in many situations he continues to have the spouses talk to him. This behavior would probably be regarded as an error if the session was to be conducted by a student, since the student would have much more difficulty seeing the underlying patterns while remaining so central. As we see below, certain forms of error are reduced by the appropriate application of the structural–strategic approach, while other errors are probably aggravated or made more likely. Furthermore, there are several differences between structural and strategic therapy concerning the concept of therapeutic error.

Contracting errors are important sources of initial difficulty in both structural and strategic therapies. Both therapeutic models require a clear acceptance of the presenting problem as the criterion of therapeutic success. In structural therapy, the usual mistake is to attempt to move too quickly to redefine the problem in interactional terms, especially if both spouses agree that the problem is an individual one, such as the wife's depression. Of course, it is equally serious simply to accept a definition of the problem that leaves one spouse completely uninvolved.

Strategic therapy is often selected for severe presenting problems. The severity of the presenting problem may make it seem obvious that it should be the target of therapy, yet it is a major mistake to accept this too readily. First, the couple should be required to demonstrate to the therapist that the symptom is truly intolerable. Second, by slowing down the agreement on the problem, the therapist can obtain crucial data on the interactional significance of the symptomatic behavior.

In the structural approach, consistent therapist centrality is a common and serious error. When most of the interaction is between the therapist and one spouse or the other, there are several unfortunate consequences. First, it is difficult for the therapist to see the couple's pattern of interaction or modify it directly. Second, when the therapist must react to every statement of each spouse, the probability of taking sides increases dramatically. Similarly, the therapist will find himself or herself answering questions and evaluating issues that belong more properly between the spouses. Finally, if the therapist remains such an integral part of the pattern, there is much less carryover when the spouses interact outside the session. All these problems can be easily avoided by having the couple interact directly with each other under the therapist's direction.

A second major error in structural therapy results from a loss of the systemic perspective, which can produce a tendency to take sides and blame one spouse more than the other. A frequent contributing factor is for the therapist to become immersed in the particular content, rather than pay primary attention to the interactional patterns. The primary difficulty is recognizing that taking sides and thinking linearly are occurring. Once this error has been detected, whether by the therapist or by a colleague or supervisor, the remedy is a straightforward combination of two ingredients. First, the therapist can make a deliberate effort to ascertain the contribution of the "victim" or "innocent party" to maintaining a circular pattern of interaction. Second, the therapist can overcome side taking by conscious efforts to join with the spouse who has been allied against, even if this requires an individual session to develop more rapport.

The final major error to which the structural approach is prone is the use of "more of the same," described in popular language as "using a bigger hammer." This error is particularly frequent with beginning therapists who have received an introduction to the structural approach and think that the change process is simple. They seem to think that the structural approach implies that there is a "right" way for a couple or family to be, and that all the therapist needs to do is to push them forcefully toward that goal. When they encounter resistance, they simply push harder and escalate their demand (the "bigger hammer"), instead of backing off and resorting to more strategic techniques.

Strategic therapy has its own characteristic forms of error, which are probably a product of the kind of therapists (like the author) drawn to this approach and the kind of cases that seem to require it. One of the most common mistakes is becoming unnecessarily fancy and complicated, or even worse, using the strategic approach when little or no resistance is encountered and a more straightforward approach would suffice (Papp, 1980). Often these errors are relatively harmless and result only in considerable amounts of unnecessary work on the part of the therapist. In more extreme cases, misapplication of the more dramatic strategic techniques can produce unnecessary resistance.

A related form of error, which seems common to strategic practitioners at all skill levels, is the development of interventions that are unnecessarily complex. It is all too easy to become intrigued with novel interventions, or to compete with other team members to see who can develop the most sophisticated intervention, losing sight of the goals of the intervention and the immediate priorities for intervention. It is not uncommon, for example, for the brainstorming of a strategic team in the first or second session to produce enough possible interventions to suffice for the next six sessions, even though only one or two interventions are appropriate for that session. Often the appropriate intervention, especially in an early session, seems disappointingly simple.

Both structural and strategic therapies place heavy emphasis on between-session tasks. The advantages of such tasks have been outlined above, but they also have their disadvantages. If the final intervention and homework begin to assume too much importance for the therapist, there are several unfortunate consequences. The therapist tends to tune out during the session, focusing attention on the intervention and losing connection with the couple. Often the therapist will overlook evidence during the session that would indicate that the task will fail. (In structural therapy, this is a result of ignoring the important principle that some analogue of the task should be tried in the session before assigning it as homework.) Final interventions that are insufficiently connected to the session itself are unlikely to be very successful, and in the meantime the therapist will probably have missed multiple opportunities to promote change during the session.

ADVANCED STRATEGIES FOR DIFFICULT COUPLES

The structural–strategic approach seems uniquely appropriate for working with certain "difficult" couples and problematic situations. Examples of these applications, including any necessary modifications of the approach, are listed briefly in this section, although they by no means exhaust the possibilities.

THE DISENGAGED MARRIAGE

With good reason, most therapists dread working with couples whose relationship has lost all feeling and energy. The usual trap for the therapist is to attempt to pump energy and optimism into the sessions, only to find that the primary result is the exhaustion and depletion of the therapist and eventually anger and frustration at the couple. Several structural–strategic techniques are useful in avoiding this trap. The therapist can ensure that the couple does most of the work by having them talk to each other rather than the therapist. Assigning tasks makes it clear whether or not the couple intends to work in therapy, although the therapist must avoid the temptation to keep developing new tasks when previous tasks fail for lack of effort. Finally, the therapist should always be ready to resort to positioning. If the therapist has already offered a clear direction for change and clear guidance concerning how that change would take place, and if the couple remains demoralized and pessimistic, then it is definitely time for the therapist to adopt an even more skeptical and pessimistic stance than the couple, even suggesting that therapy is futile under the present conditions. Whether this has a paradoxical effect or not, it allows the therapist to escape from a thankless and unproductive role as the sole provider of energy and hope.

POLARIZED COUPLES

Few clinical situations are more frustrating than working with couples who are extremely polarized. Often it seems that such couples cannot agree on anything, including the content, goals, or ground rules of therapy. Several strategic approaches suggest themselves. (For further discussion of these and other techniques, see Todd, 1984.)

Working solo, the therapist may need to adopt an extreme "one-down" position, expressing a desire to help the couple but not knowing where to begin in the face of their seemingly complete lack of agreement. If this is insufficient to provoke any movement and agreement on goals, it may be necessary to be more provocative, for example by labeling their failure to agree as protection of each other. Finally, the couple can be challenged that they could not tolerate the consequences of making progress in therapy.

Co-therapy from a strategic perspective offers unique advantages with polarized couples. One of the most effective techniques is for the two therapists to take extremly polarized positions on issues similar to those that divide the couple. Mild forms of this technique may prompt the spouses to soften their positions in reaction to seeing them presented in exaggerated form, or to seeing the therapists model flexibility. With the most stubbornly stuck couples, it may be necessary to frustrate them by deliberately immobilizing the therapy because of apparent disagreements between the therapists.

RESISTANCE

Todd (1984) describes a variety of strategic techniques for dealing with "resistance" from a couple. All these techniques attempt to utilize the resistance by accepting and modifying it, instead of opposing it directly. In addition to examples given in other sections of this chapter, this principle can be extended to deal with basic issues, such as who should be involved in therapy or what the aim of therapy is. In a case described more extensively in that article, when the husband, George, pressed to discontinue marital sessions because of his anxiety attacks, this was relabeled as a "generous sacrifice" on his part to protect his wife, Martha. Whenever both marital partners collude to make the problem an individual one—depression, bulimia, alcoholism, and so forth—it is usually prudent to accept this problem initially and enlist the spouse as a "helper" in the early stages of therapy. When changes begin to occur, even if they are ostensibly only changes in the "patient," interpersonal material will usually emerge that the therapist can use.

LOW-SES COUPLES

Structural family therapy was originally developed to deal with low-SES (socioeconomic status) families and has been shown to be effective with them (Minuchin *et al.*, 1967). Similarly, the structural approach is particularly applicable for couples from such a background. While all stereotypes are dangerous, it does seem to be generally true that these couples tend to be more skeptical about therapy and to be more interested in specific (and fast) results. Several characteristics of structural marital therapy match these expectations—the focus on specific goals, the emphasis on beginning the change process in the first session, and the use of concrete homework tasks. These factors are particularly helpful in the initial engagement process. Once some specific achievements have been accomplished and trust in the therapist has been established, it may be possible to contract for less immediate goals.

VALUE ISSUES

Issues of values are particularly troublesome when working with couples, triggering reactions from the therapist concerning such issues as how intimate a marriage should be, the comparative merits of marriage and divorce, and whether affairs should be condoned. The structural approach provides a clear "out" for the therapist, since it emphasizes that the couple needs to do the major work of therapy directly with each other. Therapy can be clearly framed as a situation in which the couple must decide how they will live their lives. The therapist will help, but the therapist will do so by intervening on the process level, rather than pass judgment on particular content issues. At times this may take the form of reaching for areas of agreement or disagreement ("Do you really agree with that? Tell your husband why not"). At other times, the couple may need coaching to break out of unproductive patterns ("Could you put that in the form of a statement to your wife, rather than a question?").

COUPLES IN CRISIS

Couples in crisis are particularly apt to be ripe for immediate change, and an active form of therapy such as the structural approach can capitalize on this readiness. The emphasis on health and building on strengths make it more likely that changes can be achieved without creating an unnecessary dependency on long-term therapy. There is, however, one significant danger when working with any directive form of therapy in a crisis situation: It is important not to miss the opportunity for creating a significant change, which is a danger if the therapist makes the couple too comfortable too quickly. The therapist must analyze carefully why this crisis is occurring now. Such an analysis should help the therapist decide what structural changes are necessary to prevent the crisis from recurring. These changes become the immediate goals for intervention, which can often be accomplished with surprising ease when the couple is in crisis.

The Role of Alliances

Both structural and strategic therapies assume that alliances with the therapist can be consciously controlled. The therapist has available a wide variety of techniques that can be used to create or enhance an alliance with one spouse or the couple. These include deliberate selection and modification of content, body language, use of metaphor and imagery, speech style, and the "ground rules" of therapy. (See discussions of "joining" in Minuchin, 1974, pp. 123–129; and Minuchin & Fishman, 1981, pp. 28–49.)

In marital therapy, with its inherent potential for developing triangles (Haley, 1976, pp. 151–168), particularly careful attention must be paid to alliances. Often it is necessary for the therapist to make deliberate efforts to create an alliance that will counteract a natural alliance with one spouse, or to recruit a "reluctant customer." In the latter case, the spouse who is more skeptical or less "therapy-wise" is at an inherent disadvantage in the therapy situation. Usually it is possible to make a considerable effort to ally with this spouse without risk of alienating the more enthusiastic spouse.

The Role of Therapeutic Values

No form of therapy is truly value free, and this is particularly true of a directive, goal-oriented therapy such as structural–strategic therapy. Two issues are particularly problematic. First, the therapist may feel a strong pull to side with one spouse (e.g., in cases of spouse abuse). Unless a more neutral position, based on a systemic understanding of the situation, can be found, it is unlikely that either spouse will be helped. Second, certain situations may place the therapist at odds with the couple, for instance when they choose to remain together despite a seemingly dreary or perverse relationship or in spite of severe consequences to the children.

In all such cases, it is important for both sides of the ambivalence to be stated openly. In mild situations, it may be sufficient to include a co-therapist who has a natural alliance with the other spouse. In more severe cases, or when the situation of the couple is abhorrent to both therapists, it is often necessary to resort to the "deliberate splitting" technique. In this technique, both sides of the argument are stated in extreme, polarized fashion. The two positions can be argued by the two therapists, or between the therapist and the team behind the mirror, or between the therapist and a supervisor or consultant (real or imagined).

Consider the following case example:

> *A beginning marital therapist was seeing an unmarried couple with a long history of violence, frequent separations, and hospitalizations of the female*

partner. Both partners were divorced from former spouses in which the patterns of interaction were similar to this relationship. The therapist was naturally horrified to learn that the couple planned to get married in the near future. Unfortunately, the therapist felt constrained from expressing her reservations for a variety of reasons; the couple seemed adamant about their plans, in spite of the opposition of families, friends, and other "helpers" in the system. The therapist was afraid that voicing her reservations might destroy her tenuous therapeutic relationship with the couple, causing them to leave therapy, although her unexpressed fears were interfering with the therapy. She requested a consultation with the strategic team in the hopes of resolving this dilemma. The response of the consultant and team was predictable but effective: The team took a strong position opposing the marriage and blaming the therapist for failing to prevent this disastrous step. In this and future sessions, the therapist was able to remain allied with the couple, invoking the advice of the team whenever setbacks occurred ("Now I'm beginning to see what the team was warning me about"). The team was also able to predict specific problems and identify ways in which the couple (and the therapist) could prove the consulting team wrong in their dire predictions.

In less extreme cases, working within a structural framework, the impact of the therapist's values can be minimized by constantly attempting to have the couple talk to each other, rather than talk to the therapist. The therapist should avoid making any value-laden pronouncements, such as "That's good" or "He has a good point there." Instead, any approval should be reserved for the process level, such as congratulating the couple for moving beyond their usual conflict to reach agreement on an issue.

Concurrent Individual and Marital Therapy

Having one or both spouses involved in individual therapy concurrent with their marital therapy can present difficult problems for the marital therapist. When other therapists are involved, it is almost inevitable that the agendas will compete and loyalty issues will develop. In one extreme example, the author received a referral for marital therapy from the wife's individual therapist, who felt she was "too allied" with the wife to conduct the marital therapy. On further investigation, it was learned that the individual therapy predated this marriage by 3 years and that the husband had been asked to agree never to come between the wife and her therapist as part of the wedding vows! (Unsurprisingly, neither the author nor the husband was able to break this bond.)

Concurrent individual therapy can be successful (if difficult) when the therapy is performed by the marital therapist. If co-therapists are conducting the marital therapy, each can see one spouse. In either situation, several conditions are important to maximize the chances of success and minimize the inherent problems:

1. The individual sessions are not confidential. The spouse may be encouraged to reveal important material, with the therapist reserving the right to reveal it if the patient refuses.

2. The scheduling of individual sessions in relation to couple sessions will be established according to the judgment of the therapist(s). It is particularly important to avoid long stretches of individual therapy without conjoint sessions to measure progress.

3. In most cases, it is ideal for the individual sessions to be balanced, with both spouses participating equally. This is especially important if a solo therapist is attempting to do both marital and individual sessions, in order to avoid a strong alliance with the spouse who receives the most individual attention.

4. The therapist must be careful to enforce the contract that only individual issues will be discussed in the individual sessions. Issues involving the spouse are best reserved for the conjoint sessions. These issues can be admissible if the therapist can keep the patient focussed on why that situation is a problem for her or him, rather than on the absent spouse, and what the patient intends to do about it.

With severe individual symptoms it may be impossible for the therapist to avoid individual sessions, and some of these ideal conditions may be impossible to achieve. This is most likely to be true when the problems are extreme and when both spouses agree that therapy is only for the symptomatic spouse. In such circumstances "true" marital therapy, in which both partners are "legitimate" patients, may be impossible, and it may be necessary to include the spouse as a "helper" or "objective observer."

The author almost invariably recommends individual sessions (always as few as possible) in two situations:

1. When working solo with a couple and finding onself allied and identified with one spouse. A few individual sessions will usually help the therapist develop more sympathy with the other partner.
2. When it is impossible to break through a pattern of intense blaming, extreme reactivity, or unproductive conflict. Individual sessions can often help each spouse to examine his or her own contribution to the problem, if the therapist vigilantly enforces the rule blocking complaints about the absent partner.

The final use of individual therapy as an adjunct to marital therapy is to consider it as "graduate training," somewhat akin to the position of Whitaker (Napier & Whitaker, 1978, p. 73). When the couple's goals have been achieved and new patterns have stabilized, it often happens that one spouse will be much more interested in continuing therapy than the other spouse. A shift to individual therapy can be made with the least risk of repercussions with the couple or sabotage from the spouse when the therapist is the former marital therapist, since the successful marital therapy usually develops a sense of trust on the part of the spouse. It is still preferable for the therapist to "touch base" with the less-involved spouse and have occasional conjoint sessions to review progress.

Concurrent Group and Marital Therapy

The most useful form of group therapy as an adjunct to marital therapy is a couples group, rather than a group of unrelated individuals. A couples group can be most useful with couples such as the following: (a) relatively healthy couples, or couples who have benefited sufficiently from therapy to avoid recurrent crises and unproductive conflict, who can benefit from seeing others interact and who can contribute to the group; (b) couples who present themselves as healthy but who are actually highly defensive, such as couples with psychosomatic complaints, who may be more willing to listen to input from peers; (c) couples whose problems are typical of couples in their developmental stage, who will receive normalizing feedback.

Occasionally, structured groups are helpful for specific purposes, such as assertiveness training. The marital therapist who has a systemic frame of reference will quickly recognize the importance of monitoring and validating the effects of such groups, in conjoint sessions with the spouse. Assertiveness practiced with strangers often will collapse when addressed to the spouse; if successful, it may create severe stress in the marital relationship. Both dangers can be avoided when the spouse supports participation in the group and participates in the homework.

Evidence of Effectiveness

Controlled-outcome studies of the effectiveness of structural–strategic marital therapy are rare. This form of marital therapy is unfortunately in the same position as most other forms of marital therapy—with the exception of behavioral marital therapy and marital enrichment—of having to rely on the strength of theoretical articles and case studies. This is not meant to imply that the comparative efficacy of behavioral marital therapy has been demonstrated or that the effectiveness of these forms of therapy have been shown with more distressed couples (see Gurman & Kniskern, 1981).

Indirect support can be tentatively obtained by extrapolating from the results of family therapy outcome research. As has been noted elsewhere (Gurman & Kniskern, 1981; Todd & Stanton, 1983), structural family therapy has produced some of the few controlled outcome studies, especially for psychosomatic symptoms of children (Minuchin, Rosman, & Baker, 1978; Rosman, Minuchin, Liebman, & Baker, 1976) and for drug addiction (Stanton *et al.*, 1980; Stanton *et al.*, 1982).

As the author has noted elsewhere (Todd & LaForte, in press), research on strategic therapy presents unique problems. It has been mentioned earlier in this chapter that the therapist who is working strategically needs to be neutral about outcome, or even to appear to promote an outcome diametrically opposed to that sought by the therapist (and presumably by the couple). It therefore becomes difficult to conduct research that seems to imply that a particular outcome is "good." Even worse, the implication that the therapist values the outcome could work to undermine therapy.

Needed Future Developments in Structural–Strategic Marital Therapy

1. The need for adequate research in structural–strategic marital therapy has already been noted. What makes this even more imperative is that the current climate in marital and family therapy often produces extravagant claims of success, especially among the newer forms of brief marital and family therapy. Often these claims are substantiated only by a few case studies or a dramatic videotape.

2. Although structural and strategic therapists have contributed significantly to the family therapy literature, there is relatively little written specifically about marital therapy from this perspective. In view of the number of practitioners working significantly or even predominantly with couples, this is most unfortunate.

3. It has become a commonplace assumption that conventional diagnosis is of little or no value when working with relationship problems. What is needed is a more relevant form of "diagnosis" based on marital and family interaction. Promising steps have been taken in the analysis of videotaped "family tasks" originally developed for research (Minuchin et al., 1967; Minuchin et al., 1978; Stanton et al., 1980). As these methods become more clinically useable and less time-consuming, they will be more valuable to practicing clinicians.

4. Closely related to this last point is the need to ask more refined questions of the model; for example, what information is needed to select a particular intervention for a particular couple (e.g., reframing) or a particular model (e.g., strategic)? While informal guidelines are developing, including this chapter, more systematic efforts would be valuable.

5. Structural family therapy has been characterized by its emphasis on putting the therapist in the picture when mapping family interaction and structural goals. This emphasis on the therapist's position is even more crucial in marital therapy than in family therapy. Unfortunately, the therapist's role is more subtle and, therefore, more difficult to characterize; systematic efforts to do so would be extremely valuable.

6. It is the author's definite impression that structural–strategic therapy is alive and well! It is obvious from a cursory examination of recent publications in the marital and family therapy journals that this area is developing rapidly on every front, including its epistemological and theoretical base and clinical methodology. Creative applications of structural–strategic methods abound, and even controversial issues are discussed publicly. We hope that this

chapter will encourage this development further, but this model seems to be undergoing healthy growth and development even without this stimulus.

REFERENCES

Anderson, C. M., & Stewart, S. (1983). *Mastering resistance: A practical guide to family therapy*. New York: Guilford Press.

Aponte, H. J., & van Deusen, J. M. (1981). Structural family therapy. In A. S. Gurman & D. P. Kniskern (Eds.), *Handbook of family therapy*. New York: Brunner/Mazel.

Bergman, J. (1982, March). *Strategic therapy with resistant families: Working without a team*. Workshop presented at American Orthopsychiatric Association annual meeting, San Francisco.

Berenson, D. (1976). Alcohol and the family system. In P. J. Guerin (Ed.), *Family therapy: Theory and practice*. New York: Gardner Press.

Bockus, F. (1975). A systems approach to marital process. *Journal of Marriage and Family Counseling*, 3, 251–258.

Bockus, F. (1980). *Couple therapy*. New York: Jason Aronson.

Bowen, M. (1978). *Family theory in clinical practice*. New York: Jason Aronson.

Bross, A. (Ed.) (1983). *Family therapy: Principles of strategic practice*. New York: Guilford Press.

Carter, E. A., & McGoldrick, M. (1980). *The family life cycle: A framework for family therapy*. New York: Gardner Press.

Coyne, J. C. (1984). Introducing structural interventions into strategic therapy: A caution. *Journal of Strategic and Systemic Therapies*, 3, 23–27.

DeFrank-Lynch, B., Rigazio-DiGilio, S., & Todd, T. C. (1985). *Mapping the cycle of interaction: A structural descriptive recording of system behavioral sequencing*. Manuscript submitted for publication.

Fisch, R., Weakland, J., & Segal, L. (1982). *Tactics of change*. San Francisco: Jossey-Bass.

Fraser, J. S. (1984a). Process level integration: Corrective vision for a binocular view. *Journal of Strategic and Systemic Therapies*, 3, 43–57.

Fraser, J. S. (Ed.) (1984b). Special issue on integration/disintegration. *Journal of Strategic and Systemic Therapies*, Fall, 3.

Granvold, D. K. (1983). Structured separation for marital treatment and decision-making. *Journal of Marital and Family Therapy*, 9, 403–412.

Gurman, A. S., & Kniskern, D. P. (1981). Family therapy outcome research: Knowns and unknowns. In A. S. Gurman & D. P. Kniskern (Eds.), *Handbook of family therapy*. New York: Brunner/Mazel.

Haley, J. (1963). *Strategies of psychotherapy*. New York: Grune & Stratton.

Haley, J. (1976). *Problem-solving therapy: New strategies for effective family therapy*. San Francisco: Jossey-Bass.

Haley, J. (1984). *Ordeal therapy: Unusual ways to change behavior*. San Francisco: Jossey-Bass.

Hoffman, L. (1975). "Enmeshment" and the too richly cross-joined system. *Family Process*, 14, 457–468.

Hoffman, L. (1981). *Foundations of family therapy: A conceptual framework for systems change*. New York: Basic Books.

Jackson, D., & Lederer, W. J. (1968). *The mirages of marriage*. New York: Norton.

Levinson, D. (1978). *The seasons of a man's life*. New York: Knopf.

Liddle, H. (Ed.) (1983). *Clinical implications of the family life cycle*. Rockville, MD: Aspen Systems Corporation.

Liddle, H. (1984). Toward a dialectical–contextual–coevoluationary translation of structural–strategic family therapy. *Journal of Strategic and Systemic Therapies*, 4, 66–79.

MacKinnon, L., Parry, A., & Black, R. (1984). Strategies of family therapy: The relationship to styles of family functioning. *Journal of Strategic and Systemic Therapies*, 3, 6–22.

Madanes, C. (1981). *Strategic family therapy*. San Francisco: Jossey-Bass.

Madanes, C. (1984). *Behind the one-way mirror: Advances in the practice of strategic therapy*. San Francisco: Jossey-Bass.

Minuchin, S. (1974). *Families and family therapy*. Cambridge, MA: Harvard University Press.

Minuchin, S. (1980). *Anorexia Is a Greek Word*. Videotape distributed by Boston Family Institute.

Minuchin, S., & Fishman, H. C. (1981). *Family therapy techniques*. Cambridge, MA: Harvard University Press.

Minuchin, S., Montalvo, B., Guerney, B., Rosman, B., & Schumer, F. (1967). *Families of the slums*. New York: Basic Books.

Minuchin, S., Rosman, B., & Baker, L. (1978). *Psychosomatic families*. Cambridge, MA: Harvard University Press.

Napier, A. Y., & Whitaker, C. A. (1978). *The family crucible*. New York: Harper & Row.

Papp, P. (1980). The Greek chorus and other techniques of family therapy. *Family Process, 19*, 45–57.

Papp, P. (1984). *The process of change*. New York: Guilford Press.

Pinsof, W. (1983). Integrative problem-centered therapy: Toward a synthesis of family and individual psychotherapies. *Journal of Marital and Family Therapy, 9*, 19–35.

Rabkin, R. (1977). *Strategic psychotherapy: Brief and symptomatic treatment*. New York: Basic Books.

Rosman, B. L., Minuchin, S., Liebman, R., & Baker. L. (1976). Input and outcome of family therapy in anorexia nervosa. In J. L. Claghorn (Ed.), *Successful psychotherapy*. New York: Brunner/Mazel.

Satir, V. (1967). *Conjoint family therapy*. Palo Alto, CA: Science and Behavior Books.

Selvini-Palazzoli, M., Cecchin, G., Prata, G., & Boscolo, L. (1978). *Paradox and counterparadox: A new model in the therapy of the family in schizophrenic transaction*. New York: Jason Aronson.

Sheehy, G. (1976). *Passges: Predictable crises of adult life*. New York: Dutton.

Sluzki, C. E. (1978). Marital therapy from a systems perspective. In T. J. Paolino & B. S. McCrady (Eds.), *Marriage and marital therapy*. New York: Brunner/Mazel.

Stanton, M. D. (1981a). Marital therapy from a structural/strategic viewpoint. In G. P. Sholevar (Ed.), *Marriage Is a family affair: A textbook of marital and family therapy*. Jamaica, NY: S. P. Medical and Scientific Books.

Stanton, M. D. (1981b). An integrated structural/strategic approach to family therapy. *Journal of Marital and Family Therapy, 7*, 427–439.

Stanton, M. D. (1981c). Strategic approaches to family therapy. In A. S. Gurman & D. P. Kniskern (Eds.), *Handbook of family therapy*. New York: Brunner/Mazel.

Stanton, M. D. (1981d). Who should get credit for change which occurs in therapy? In A. S. Gurman (Ed.), *Questions and answers in the practice of family therapy*. New York: Brunner/Mazel.

Stanton, M. D., & Todd, T. C. (1979). Structural family therapy with drug addicts. In E. Kaufman & P. Kaufmann (Eds.), *The family therapy of drug and alcohol abuse*. New York: Gardner Press.

Stanton, M. D., & Todd, T. C. (1982, April). *Integrating structural and strategic therapy*. Workshop conducted at the Philadelphia Child Guidance Clinic.

Stanton, M. D., Todd, T. C., & Associates. (1982). *The family therapy of drug abuse and addiction*. New York: Guilford Press.

Stanton, M. D., Todd, T. C., Steier, F., VanDeusen, J. M., Marder, L., Rosoff, R. J., Seaman, S. F., & Skibinski, E. (1980, December). *Family characteristics and family therapy of heroin addicts: Final report, 1974–1978*. Grant No. R01 DA 0119. Report prepared for National Institute of Drug Abuse.

Todd, T. C. (1981). Paradoxical prescriptions: Applications of consistent paradox using a strategic team. *Journal of Strategic and Systemic Therapies, 1*, 28–44.

Todd, T. C. (1983, October). *Structural and strategic therapy: The case for integration*. Washington, DC: National Council on Family Relations.

Todd, T. C. (1984). Strategic approaches to marital stuckness. *Journal of Marital and Family Therapy, 10*, 373–379.

Todd, T. C., & LaForte, J. (in press). *Paradoxical prescriptions: The use of written prescriptions in strategic therapy*. New York: Guilford Press.

Todd, T. C., & Stanton, M. D. (1983). Research on marital and family therapy: Answers, issues, and recommendations for the future. In B. B. Wolman & G. Stricker (Eds.), *Handbook of family and marital therapy*. New York: Plenum Press.

von Bertalanffy, L. (1968). *General system theory: Foundations, development, applications*. New York: Braziller.

White, M. (1983). Anorexia nervosa: A transgenerational system perspective. *Family Process, 22*, 255–273.

Bowen Family Systems Marital Therapy

ROBERT C. AYLMER

The history of the development of Bowen's thinking about family process is well documented, and the interested reader is referred to his collected papers (Bowen, 1978). For the purpose of this chapter, however, it is worthwhile to note some of the major developments in Bowen's systems theory, particularly as they pertain to marital therapy. In the 1950s, Bowen was one of the pioneers in the family study of schizophrenia (Bowen, 1960) that is largely responsible for the birth of family therapy in general (Guerin, 1976). In the tradition of the then current psychodynamic notions of maternal deprivation and the schizophrenogenic mother, Bowen began by investigating mother–child symbiosis. He and his staff hospitalized mothers along with their schizophrenic offspring on a research ward at the National Institute for Mental Health (Bowen, 1976). Bowen quickly noted how "the mother-child relationship was a dependent fragment of the larger family unit" (Bowen, 1976, p. 57), however, and modified his research design to incorporate fathers and well siblings, who then also lived on the research ward.

Out of this effort came several key elements in Bowen's theory, especially the notion of *fusion*, or the inability of some individuals to distinguish "between the subjective feeling process and the more objective intellectual process" (Bowen, 1976, p. 59). For Bowen, this capacity for the differentiation of thoughts from feelings is the key parameter of emotional maturity. Differentiated individuals keep a separation between emotional and intellectual functioning whereby ". . . intellectual functioning can retain relative autonomy in periods of stress" (Bowen, 1976, p. 65). Such individuals are thought to be "more flexible, more adaptable and more independent of the emotionalism

Robert C. Aylmer. Lifecycle Center, Newton, Massachusetts.

about them . . . [they] cope better with life stresses, their life courses are more orderly and successful and they are remarkably free of human problems" (Bowen, 1976, pp. 65–66).

Studying such individual psychological variables in the context of hospitalized whole families led Bowen naturally to extensions of the theory to family systems. Thus, families whose members are characterized by a high degree of fusion, or emotional immaturity, can be thought of as emotionally immature systems. Bowen (1976) coined the term *undifferentiated family ego mass* to describe such systems.

By observing whole families on the research ward, Bowen was also able to chart some of the process and structures that made up the "undifferentiated family ego mass," and began developing the concept of *triangles* in 1955 (Bowen, 1976). The function of triangles in a family system is to reallocate stress so that overloaded dyadic relationships are protected and the family system's equilibrium is maintained (see Figure 5-11).

In the triangle's simplest form, individuals in a stressed relationship will bring in (or "triangle") a third party through whom the emotional process can be rerouted. Such patterns are frequently seen in the nuclear family dynamics surrounding symptomatic children; for example, the mother of the symptomatic child is overinvolved with the child, with the father distant from the child, to compensate for a marital problem. Multigenerational extended-family triangles are readily apparent in the clinical observation of spouse selection and marriage, for example, marriage soon after the death of a parent (Aylmer, 1977).

Clearly, the relative ability of individuals and family systems to tolerate stress and maintain problem-solving functions (differentiation), and to handle relationship issues without triangling, are major determinants of how, who, and when individuals marry and how well spouses then deal with the problems of living in a committed intimate peer relationship. Bowen maintains, for example, that individuals generally marry someone at approximately the same level of differentiation, but then shift into "pseudo-self," reciprocal postures in which one spouse functions at an apparent higher level of independence or power than the other (Bowen, 1978).

THE BOWEN MODEL OF MARITAL CONFLICT

In the Bowen model, marital conflict, like individual problems in adults or children, is thought to emerge out of interactive influences in the *self system*, the *extended-family system* (families of origin), and the *couple–nuclear family system*.

The Self System

Self issues can be divided into the areas of *developmental issues, personality factors*, and *family-of-origin programming. Developmental issues,* and for marital conflict in particular, *adult* development issues, play a central role in the conceptualization of individual and relationship problems. Such terms as "Catch-30," "mid-life crisis," and "male menopause" are well documented and described by a number of life-span researchers as well as popular writers (Kegan, 1983; Levinson, 1978; Sheehy, 1977). Clearly, sudden changes in the identity, physical capacity, career, and social position of spouses throughout the life cycle place severe stresses on their relationship and require ongoing modification of rules, roles, and expectations throughout the course of any marriage (Stanton, 1981).

Personality factors are probably most extensively studied in the psychodynamic model of marital therapy (Dicks, 1967; Sonne & Swirsky, 1981), which describes relationship patterns in terms of "interlocking neuroses," as in the well-known obsessive–hysteric marriage (Ackerman, 1958). Bowen family systems therapists, in contrast, prefer to describe individuals in terms of interactive relationship patterns, such as the *emotionally oriented pursuer* or the *object-oriented distancer*.[1]

> An emotional pursuer is a people-oriented communicator of feeling who tends to take the lion's share of responsibility for maintaining relationships, has an internal and interpersonal rhythm that runs on two speeds, full speed ahead and dead stop. The emotional pursuer tends to be a night person as opposed to a morning person and to value free access across boundaries into others and their own personal space. The emotional pursuers of the world enthusiastically undertake new tasks and adventures, taking more than reasonable risks with unbridled optimism. Errors made are errors of commission. Apology and making things explicit come easy, while endings and good-byes come hard.
>
> The emotional distancer on the other hand is an object-productivity-oriented person with little proclivity for communicating personal thoughts and feelings and a rhythm that is steady and predictable. He tends to be a morning person who would prefer that you not ask into his personal space and will gladly return the favor by rarely if ever asking into yours. Temperamentally he approaches new tasks and adventures cautiously and with a "healthy" seasoning of pessimism. Errors committed are usually errors of omission. Apologies come especially hard, while leaving things implicit is easy, and endings and separations appear to cause much less proximate upset and emotional pain. (Guerin, 1982, p. 19)

The closest Bowen family systems therapists come to a noninteractional theory of personality is in Fogarty's existential writings on self in the family system (Fogarty, 1971). He describes zones or areas of investment in the individual that are *People, Objects, Depth,* and *Time.* Yet, on closer examination, the *People, Objects,* and *Time* dimensions all reflect interactive tendencies (e.g., movement toward objects) in the context of a relationship (e.g., movement away from people); only in the *Depth* dimension is Fogarty describing what could be considered intrapsychic events.

Fogarty deals with the depth dimension most eloquently in his landmark papers "On Emptiness and Closeness" (Fogarty, 1976a, 1976b). Here he

---

1. This may in part stem from Bowen's prohibition of psychiatric jargon in the 1950s among his research team at the NIMH (Bowen, 1976).

describes the difficulties that emerge in relationships as stemming from individual's unwillingness or inability to come to terms with the core experience of *emptiness*, which Fogarty sees as an unavoidable aspect of human existence. Rather than deal with emptiness, people attempt to fill themselves with success, material rewards, and ultimately in relationships. Since emptiness is basically unfillable, when these unrealistic expectations are unmet, the personal distress that emerges is often projected onto the relationship, as if one's personal satisfaction is the other's responsibility and one's unhappiness is the other's fault.

Thus, Fogarty places considerable emphasis on personal responsibility, expectations, projection, and experiential–existential self-awareness in his assessment and treatment of couples. This process is most clearly evident in his "expectations–alienation" progression wherein unrealistic expectations for the spouse and for marriage proceed through stages of *disappointment, hurt, sadness, anger,* and finally *alienation* and *isolation* (Guerin, 1982).

Family-of-origin programming is the major determinant of the content (and some of the intensity) of these dysfunctional expectations; it also determines many of the attitudes, orientations, and self-concepts that affect individuals' behavior in a marriage. This programming is thought to take place through the multigenerational mechanism of the family projection process (Bowen, 1978).

In the family projection process, family members are imbued with the characteristics ("serious," "irritable," "overresponsible," "unreliable") and emotional obligations ("take care of mother," "make up for wastrel uncle," "replace dead sibling") of predecessors with whom relationship issues in the family are unresolved because of incomplete mourning (Paul & Paul, 1975), family loyalties (Boszormenyi-Nagy & Spark, 1973), divorce (Aylmer, 1977), or cut-offs (Carter & Orfanidis, 1976). Thus, individuals come out of their family of origin into the world and marriage "programmed" to reenact roles and characteristics belonging to people, relationships, and events long buried.

In addition to inheriting aspects of this complex multigenerational saga, individuals grow up in the immediacy of a nuclear family in which emotionally charged reciprocal interaction patterns with each parent or *primary parental triangles* set up special potentials and limitations for other relationships.

For example, a man growing up in a typical parental triangle of harsh, critical distance father and overinvolved, smothering mother (who has given up on reaching her husband) may come to adult intimate relationships with an *emotional allergy* to closeness that he will experience as invasion and loss of independence, and a compensatory distant critical stance that was modeled by his father (Figure 5-1).

Correspondingly, a woman growing up in another typical primary parental triangle with an aloof, idealized father and a punitive, critical mother who competed with daughter for father's limited affection might come to adulthood with an *emotional addiction* to distant men, whom she pursues but never succeeds in catching, and an inability to relate to women (Figure 5-2).

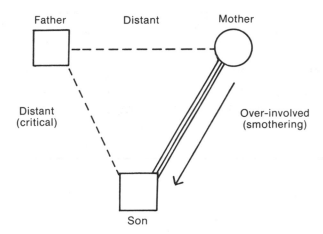

FIGURE 5-1. Nuclear family triangle: closeness sensitive.

Finally, men and women grow up in a system of brothers and sisters (or lack thereof), and the experience of this *sibling position* is another powerful determinant of adult relationship behavior. Toman (1969) has demonstrated, for example, that marriages that are *complementary* (e.g., a younger brother of a sister marrying an older sister of a brother) have a much higher probability of enduring and producing children than noncomplementary marriages.

These pieces of "unfinished business" with parents, siblings, and extended kin are statistically normal, if less than optimal. The more intense these unresolved issues are, however, and the more they are dealt with via distance

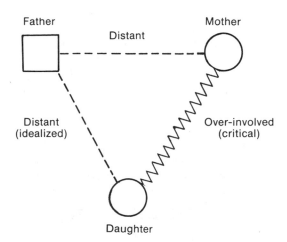

FIGURE 5-2. Nuclear family triangle: distance sensitive.

and cut off from the family system in which they developed, the more they overload the marital relationship and predispose it to distress (Figure 5-3).

The Extended-Family System

The preceding section described how some ways of growing up in a family can predispose individuals under stress to re-create predictable relationship patterns and react to these patterns in predictable ways. However, a model of marital conflict also needs to specify how such patterns are triggered and what sustains the obviously dysfunctional and painful interactions that characterize such patterns in marital conflict (Guerin & Fay, 1982).

A psychodynamic view of marital conflict holds that under the press of reality in day-to-day cohabitation, spouses' idealized views of each other erode and disillusionment sets in, with a corresponding unrealistic, projective negativity toward the other spouse (Sonne & Swirsky, 1981).

A structural–strategic view would be that changes in the family life cycle (e.g., having children) render established marital interactional patterns or rules obsolete, and the spouses will have conflict until they establish new, more appropriate rules (Stanton, 1981).

The Bowen family systems view is that the ongoing anxiety level, ways of handling anxiety, and the severity of recent stressors or nodal events (which intensify anxiety and anxiety processes) in the extended-family systems surrounding the marriage are the major determinants of the timing, intensity, and persistence of marital conflict. For example, in family systems with a high degree of *fusion*, as discussed above, anxiety levels are chronically high because the stresses and strains of normal life are not dealt with effectively. Moreover, in such systems, dysfunctional structures emerge to deal with the inordinately high levels of chronic anxiety. Among these reciprocal structures are *triangles* (described above), *reactive distance*, and *cut-offs*, whereby portions of unpleasant emotional process (e.g., disappointment) or toxic issues (e.g., unresolved grief) are avoided by ceasing to deal with important members of the family system who represent the toxic issues. Correspondingly, *reactive closeness* and *enmeshment*, wherein certain individuals are prevented from normal separation and autonomous functioning, often compensate for emotional needs in other relationships that are being

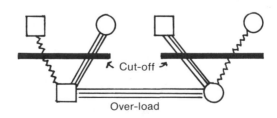

FIGURE 5-3. Family-of-origin cut-off and marital overload.

dealt with via reactive distance. The reciprocity of these structures is apparent in observations that triangles in families are often composed of one cut-off and two enmeshed individuals (see Figures 5-1 and 5-2).

In addition to such clinical observations, research on stress and illness indicates that ongoing interactions with the family of origin play a significant role in the onset of physical symptoms. For example, how well individuals are currently getting along with their parents is a major predictor of stress-related illness, and postpartum depression is more common among women who are physically and emotionally distant from their extended families or for whom there has been a recent death in the family of origin (Freeman, 1983).

The role of family members' death in postpartum depression illustrates the second major extended-family factor in marital conflict, namely, *nodal events* or stressors. Nodal events can be *recent* (conflict over care of aging grandmother) or *remote* (dispute over grandfather's will 10 years ago); *instantaneous* (heart attack in father) or *long-standing* (Alzheimer's disease in mother); *positive* (birth of a child) or *negative* (death of a sibling); *serious* (threat of nuclear war) or *mild* (child starts nursery school). Nodal events may also occur at the level of an *individual* (job loss); a *relationship* (sister's divorce); a *social group* (women's liberation); or *society as a whole* (the energy crisis).

Nodal events, therefore, are either family phenomena *per se* (marriage, divorce, birth, death, etc.) occurring within the systems or nonfamily phenomena (employment, social changes, etc.) that intrude on family members from outside. In either case, nodal events can influence marital distress by raising the anxiety level in the extended-family system(s), thereby intensifying the operation of dysfunctional family patterns (triangles, cut-offs, enmeshments), which increase stress on individual family members (including the spouses) and simultaneously decrease their range of relationship options and appropriate connectedness in the kin network.

Moreover, at a content level, the nature of specific nodal events may trigger vulnerable and toxic marital issues that are not being addressed (e.g., sister's divorce may threaten the stability of other marriages in the system).

In summary, the higher the frequency and severity of nodal events in the extended-family system, and the lower the emotional maturity (differentiation and connectedness) of that system, the higher the level of anxiety and the greater the likelihood of individual or relationship symptoms, including marital conflict.

Couple/Nuclear Family System

Finally, sources of marital conflict arise out of the couple relationship itself and other nuclear family issues. Some of these factors, including incompatibility of sibling position, unrealistic expectations, and reciprocal reactive triangles (pursuit–distance, over- and underfunctioning), are difficult to isolate from the interconnected contexts of the self and extended family. Such factors overload the marital relationship and predispose it to dysfunction under stress (see Figure 5-3).

Of course, even if these complicated legacies and limitations were not present, the many compromises, negotiations, adaptations, and new learnings that must occur in order for two unrelated people to live together and perhaps have children are formidable. McGoldrick (1980) states:

> Marriage requires that a couple renegotiate together a myriad of personal issues they have previously defined for themselves or that were defined by their parents, including everyday decisions like when and how to eat, sleep, talk, have sex, fight, and relieve tension. They must decide about vacations, and how to use space, time, and money. Then there are the familial decisions about which traditions and rituals to retain from each family of origin and which ones the partners will develop for themselves. These and thousands of similar decisions can no longer be determined solely on an individual basis. They must be worked out compatibly so the two can fit together. The couple will also find themselves having to renegotiate their relationships with their parents, siblings, friends, and other relatives in view of the new marriage. (pp. 93–94)

Once these hurdles are passed, as time and new stages of the family life cycle buffet the couple, various parameters of the marital relationship may undergo stress. Guerin (1982) lists the following important "relationship maintenance functions" that can break down under stress: communication, information exchange, self-disclosure, credibility, and relationship time–activity. More generally, these functions are manifestations of the couple's emotional climate, patterns of movement (pursuit–distance, over- and underfunctioning), and central triangles (Burden & Gilbert, 1982).

In general, when stress impacts a marriage (from any of the systems described above), the ongoing transactional patterns that may be adaptive, or at least benign, become more reactive and exacerbated, and dysfunction will appear in some area of the family system. In couple systems in which the primary reactive reciprocity is on the horizontal axis of *pursuit–distance*, the progression is generally from active pursuit–distance (Figure 5-4) to reactive distance by the pursuer (Figure 5-5) to reactive pursuit by the distancer (Figure 5-6) to mutual aggrieved shutdown with fixed distance, interrupted by occasional stormy battles (Figure 5-7) (Guerin, 1982). In such couples, extramarital and child triangles are common, leading to ongoing marital conflict in the former and symptomatic children in the latter (see Figures 5-8, 5-9).

Distance   Pursuit

FIGURE 5-4. Pursuit–distance reciprocity.

FIGURE 5-5. Reactive distance by pursuer.

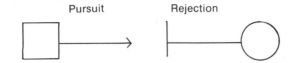

FIGURE 5-6. Reactive pursuit by distancer; rejection by pursuer.

FIGURE 5-7. Fixed distance.

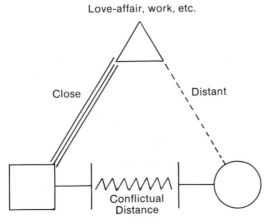

FIGURE 5-8. Marital triangle.

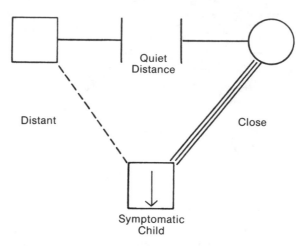

FIGURE 5-9. Child triangle.

Couples in which the primary reactive transactions have been on the vertical axis of *over- and underfunctioning* often develop symptoms in one spouse or ritualized transactions around substance abuse when stress impacts the system (see Figure 5-10).

Summary

Individuals physically leave their families of origin with *emotional allergies* and *emotional addictions* (in the form of expectations or reactivity) to certain types of individuals or relationships (see Figures 5-1 and 5-2). When these emotional patterns with parents are not renegotiated in adulthood and are

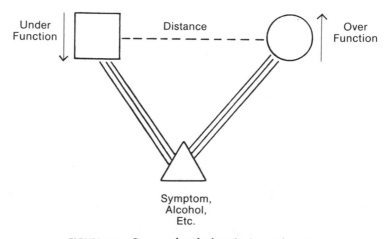

FIGURE 5-10. Over- and underfunctioning reciprocity.

simply allowed to persist behind a cut-off, the expectations and reactive potentials are displaced on to the marriage, in the fantasy that the spouse will "make it all better." This results in an overinvestment in the couple relationship, including unrealistic expectations, censoring in communication, and intensification of anxiety about the relationship (see Figure 5-3) (McGoldrick, 1980; Satir, 1967).

Under *stress* (which may arise from anywhere in the nuclear–extended-family system or social–physical environment), existing *reciprocal reactive patterns* (pursuit–distance, over- and underfunctioning, and/or triangles) are intensified; *relationship distortions* (fixed distance, cut-offs, and/or enmeshment) occur, locking in and intensifying emotional process and creating *system dysfunctions* (marital conflict, a symptomatic child, and/or a symptomatic spouse) (Figure 5-11).

THE BOWEN MODEL OF THERAPEUTIC CHANGE

Given that the Bowen family systems model of marital conflict focuses on a dysfunctional cascade of extended-family, self, and marital processes (Figure 5-12), it follows that the model of treatment would focus on *arresting* and, insofar as possible, *reversing* the downward flow (Figure 5-13).

The general rationale for marital treatment, therefore, is to *track* the emotional process between the spouses and then *shift* the emphasis from a marital level (i.e., focus on the other spouse) to a *self-level* (i.e., focus on one's own behavior and contribution to the problem). In doing so, as aspects of self-process emerge out of the reactive, projective marital process, they are examined against the multigenerational matrix of the *extended-system* level (focus on the patterns of cut-off, enmeshments, triangles, toxic issues, and nodal events that contribute to the problem). In the last phase, equal attention is paid to the historical ways in which previous generations have created family patterns as well as to current manifestations of those patterns throughout the family system. In addition, the family focus is trained on both the *nuclear* family of origin (i.e., the spouses' parents and siblings) and the *extended* kin network (i.e., grandparents, aunts, uncles, cousins).

The goals of treatment are similarly allocated across the marital, self, family, and social levels. At the *marital* level, the therapist works toward change in the emotional climate (affect and communication), reciprocal reactive movement patterns (pursuit–distance and under- or overfunctioning), and key triangles (extramarital, child) (Burden & Gilbert, 1982). At the *self* level, therapy moves toward increasing self-focus (vs. projection and blame) and clarifying and emphasizing the spouses' awareness of and comfort with their inner systems (dimensions of self, emptiness). At the *family* system level, therapy attempts to open up options for connectedness (vs. distance and cut-off), defuse enmeshed relationships, sort out and neutralize key multi-generational triangles, and detoxify taboo issues. Finally, at the *social* level,

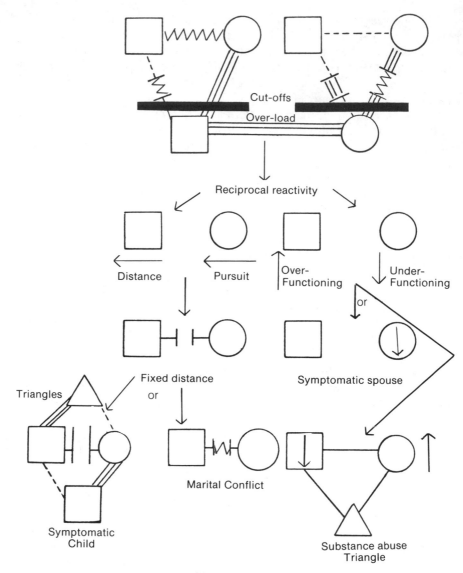

FIGURE 5-11. Multigenerational emotional process.

therapy assists spouses to improve their personal networks, examine and perhaps revise their career options, and commit to personal or political causes free of marital triangulation.

Diagnosis and Assessment

The first stage in any assessment process is to evaluate and intervene in any severe *crisis* the couple is experiencing. More detailed diagnostic procedures

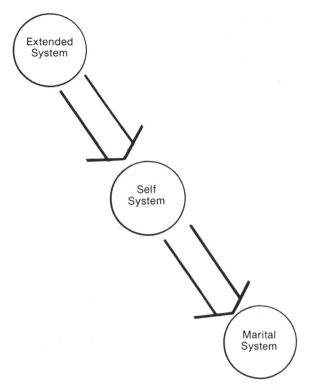

FIGURE 5-12. Downward flow of stress across systems.

may need to be deferred, while immediate issues such as physical abuse, active alcoholism, psychotic symptoms, or suicide are at least contained enough via legal, medical–pharmacological, and organizational interventions for therapy to begin. Once the couple is no longer functioning at a life or death survival level, assessment can proceed.[2]

The *genogram* (see Figure 5-14) is the primary assessment procedure used in the Bowen family systems model (Guerin & Pendagast, 1976; Pendagast & Sherman, 1977). Basically an annotated family tree, the genogram allows the clinician to collect data about the family system, its individual members, and their relationships in a rapid, efficient manner, reducing all events to a common calendar time frame, and allowing rapid access to, and retrieval of, important data. It usually contains the names, ages, and geographic location of all family members, from children to grandparents, on both sides. The genogram also should include exact dates for major events in the system, such as births, deaths, serious illnesses, or hospitalizations;

2. In some cases, of course, the assessment methods can be used in crisis intervention as well, for example, using a genogram to develop a suicide watch network for a depressed spouse, or finding a sympathetic sibling for a battered spouse to stay with temporarily. For clarity, this presentation does not deal at length with such extreme circumstances and assumes therapist control over the clinical situation.

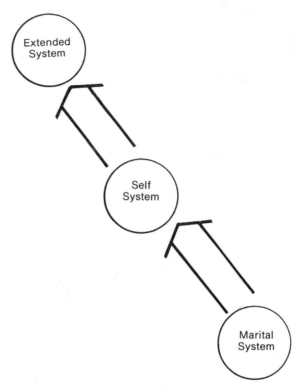

FIGURE 5-13. Upward flow of stress resolution.

marriages, separations, and divorces; retirements, job changes, and family moves. Collecting data in this way allows problems or symptoms to be seen in the context of the whole family's developmental cycle in addition to that of the individual presented as the problem.

Usually, the couple is seen together from the beginning,[3] and the first session is devoted to taking a complete genogram for both spouses. It is often useful to schedule a double appointment for the first session, to allow time for each spouse's genogram and some exploration of the presenting problem. Normally, after introductions, the therapist says something like: "As a way of beginning, I'd like to find out some background informations about you and your family, to better understand the problem. Now, when were you two married?"

Although therapists differ as to which spouse should be interviewed first (the one who made the appointment, the symptomatic one, the asymptomatic

3. Some therapists separate the couple for the evaluation phase, thinking that the spouses will be more open or connect more fully to their family experience without the observing spouse (Paul & Paul, 1975). Bowen sometimes sees spouses separately for family-of-origin work if the reactivity in the couple slows down progress too much (Bowen, personal communication, 1983).

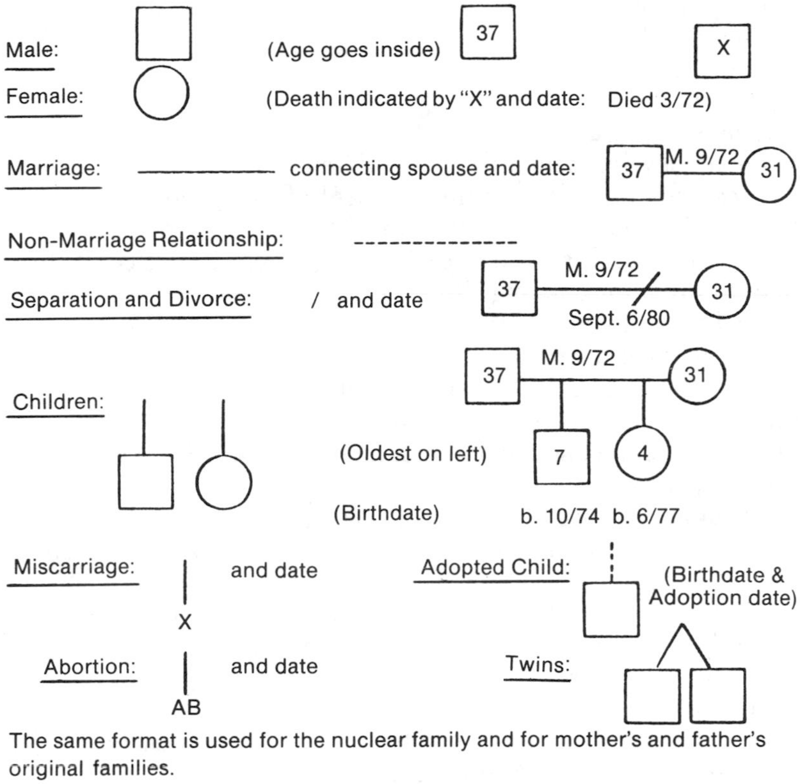

Male: ☐   (Age goes inside) [37]   [X]

Female: ○   (Death indicated by "X" and date: Died 3/72)

Marriage: ———————— connecting spouse and date: [37] M. 9/72 (31)

Non-Marriage Relationship: – – – – – – – – – –

Separation and Divorce: / and date   [37] M. 9/72 / Sept. 6/80 (31)

Children: (Oldest on left)   [37] M. 9/72 (31)

(Birthdate)   [7] (4)   b. 10/74 b. 6/77

Miscarriage: | and date   Adopted Child: ☐ (Birthdate & Adoption date)
             X

Abortion: | and date   Twins: ☐☐
          AB

The same format is used for the nuclear family and for mother's and father's original families.

FIGURE 5-14. Genogram symbols.

one, the same-sex spouse, the opposite-sex spouse, the husband, the wife, etc.), the author prefers to see who answers this first question, and begin with the genogram of that spouse. Following this, the other spouse's genogram is elicited, and assessment of the problem proceeds. In the course of the genogram[4] the therapist should try to collect the following information at the level of self, nuclear family, extended family, and the couple itself.

Self level
  Brief physical and psychological health history including present involvement
       with or need for care or consultation
  Life-cycle stage and personal nodal events
  Social functioning (job, friends, etc.)
  Level and quality of emotional reactivity
  Degree of self-focus versus projection
  Characteristic emotional position

4. For a detailed transcript of questions actually asked in taking a genogram, see Guerin and Pendagast (1976).

Pursuer–distancer
Over- or underfunctioner
Sibling position
Nuclear family
Life-cycle stage of family
Functional–developmental level of children
Physical–emotional health (involvement of caregivers)
Social adjustment (school, work, peers)
Relationship of each spouse to each child (close, distant, conflictual)
Relationships among siblings
Key nuclear family triangles
Extended family (each spouse)
Cultural, ethnic, social-class background
Family size and sibling constellation
Geographic location and communication of members (frequency, method, quality)
Functional level of each member (education, occupation, health, social)
"Personality" sketch and/or relationship position of key members (e.g., "the black sheep," "the go-between," "everybody's darling")
Relationship of each spouse to each parent, each sibling, and other key family members (close, distant, cut-off, enmeshed)
Ambient anxiety level
Vulnerability to stress
Family patterns of reaction to conflictual stress (e.g., distance, fighting, alcohol, somatic symptoms, cut-off, divorce)
Toxic issues (e.g., deaths, former marriages, affairs, symptoms, money, sex)
Major multigenerational triangles

Once these contextual parameters are clarified, the therapist can move toward examination of the presenting problem and assess process issues in the couple itself.

Couple issues
Relationship problem versus symptoms in one or both spouses
Reciprocal reactive patterns surrounding the problem or symptoms (pursuit–distance, over- or underfunctioning)
Openness of communication (safety vs. attacking and defending; ongoing exchange vs. shutdown)
Intensity of bilateral projection between spouses
Ability to disengage or engage approximately and under control
Degree of relationship deterioration (separation, involvement of legal system)
Extramarital triangles (affairs, peers, "movements," substance abuse)

In addition to collecting valuable data, beginning therapy with the genogram helps structure the therapeutic process for the working sessions to come. Spending considerable time with each spouse in getting the family picture facilitates joining and the development of therapeutic rapport. In addition, having the other spouse present for this phase helps prevent the development of real or perceived alliances or triangles in the therapy system itself, which would be much more likely if spouses were seen separately. Moreover, while the therapist is interviewing one spouse, the other must sit quietly and listen (occasionally with some gentle but firm reminder from the therapist). This sets a tone of reduced reactivity and safety in the session and may in time allow spouses to hear each other more empathically as they learn more about each other's emotional context outside the marriage.

The Structure of the Therapy Session

Bowen family systems therapy with couples occurs in two main formats: *conjoint meetings*, in which one couple meets with the therapist; and *multiple-family therapy groups*, in which three couples usually meet together with the therapist. In both formats, meetings are generally held once or twice a month.

In the multiple format, the therapist divides the session equally among the couples, spending approximately 30 or 40 minutes interviewing each couple, while the others observe. There is no interaction or communication among the couples. Bowen (1971) maintains that the modeling and indirect learning this observation component provides makes the multiple group much more effective than the standard conjoint format.

According to Bowen (1971), the format of a typical session might go as follows:

> I might open by asking the husband what kind of progress he has made since the last session and to give me his most objective report. If his report has reasonable content, I would then turn to the wife and ask for her *thoughts* while he was talking. Early in the course of therapy, my questions are designed to elicit the intellectual process by asking for thoughts, opinions, or ideas. In other situations I might ask for her response or reaction which is a little less intellectual. Only much later in therapy, and in special situations, would I ask for a reading from her subjective inner feelings. After the wife has spoken, a question would be directed to the husband, such as, "What was going on in your thoughts while she was talking?"
>
> There are occasional "clean" sessions in which the therapist does nothing more than direct questions from one to the other. There are situations in which the husband's comments might be too minimal for an adequate response from his wife. Then I would ask sufficient questions to get him to elaborate his ideas before asking the wife for her thoughts. If the wife responded with minimal comments, there would be more questions to get her to elaborate before turning to the husband again. If feelings build up and one responds emotionally and directly to the other without waiting for my questions, I increase the directness and tempo of the questions to return the process to me. I am always dozens of questions ahead of them. There is always a backlog of theoretical assumptions about the family about which I have questions. During sessions I keep notes about new areas for questions when there is a lull. When obvious feelings are stirred up during a session, the

goal is to get them *talking about* the feelings rather than expressing it. For instance, if the wife suddenly became tearful, I might ask her husband if he noticed the tears or what was going on in his thoughts when he saw the tears. An overall goal for the questions is to touch on areas known to be emotionally important for them and to get calm, low keyed responses. (pp. 194–195)

This pattern of keeping the sessions calm and routing all communication through the therapist contributes to the essential therapeutic conditions of *reduced reactivity, safety, and empathy.* Throughout the sessions, questions are directed to each spouse separately, instead of encouraging the couple to communicate directly with each other. Bowen (1971) observes that in highly emotional relationship systems, an attempt to solve problems by "talking it out" only "stirs up the emotional reactiveness and drives (the spouses) further apart" (p. 193).

The therapeutic structure of routing all communication through the therapist, who remains detached though involved, stems from several key assumptions about emotional systems and about therapy. These assumptions are, first, that therapy is a learning process that occurs best in a climate of low anxiety; second, that the important interactions are those that go on in the family *outside* the consulting room; and third, that in order to be effective, the therapist must control the session and avoid being triangled by the couple's emotional process.

Staying de-triangled from the couple occupies considerable therapist attention in this model and is considered the most powerful therapist input. Bowen (1971) states, "The emotional problem between two people will resolve automatically if they remain in contact with a third person who can remain free of the emotional field between them, *while actively relating to each*" (p. 196). The tendency of systems to avoid change by constantly triangling in new relationships is thereby blocked, and the spouses are able to develop a more responsible, differentiated way of dealing with each other.

Another way of staying de-triangled involves the use of casual comments, humor, or reversals, although Bowen points out that once triangled, or emotionally involved, a therapist's use of humor will come across as sarcastic and mean. He explains:

A reversal, which is a comment that focuses on the obvious or opposite side of an issue, or that picks up the casual or slightly humorous aspect, is a most effective way of decompressing an overserious situation. One wife, for example, becomes more emotionally uptight in describing the dominating, nagging mother. I made a casual comment about her lack of appreciation for the mother's lifelong effort to make her be a good daughter; the spouses laughed, the tension was decompressed, and I had communicated awareness that there was another side to the issue. When the therapist can remain casual about such serious situations, it is usually not long before the spouses can begin to get outside themselves to a more objective view of the situation. (Bowen, 1971, p. 197)

While pursuing such questioning, getting reactions from the spouses, and keeping the tone of sessions calm and light, the therapist will explore all the different levels of self, couple, family, and social network. He or she will, for example, track carefully a sequence of transactions that led to a fight, inquire into inner states of feeling and thinking, question parallels with other relationships in the family system, teach some relevant family systems principles, or suggest an experiment that might help resolve or illuminate a problem area.

While *phases* of therapy are not greatly emphasized in the Bowen model, work with couples can be conceptualized as falling into three distinct, though overlapping, stages. The first stage, or *assessment stage* (1 to 5 weekly sessions), consists of taking each spouse's genogram, eliciting their views of the presenting problem, and establishing a therapeutic structure. The second stage, or *problem stage* (5 to 10 biweekly sessions), involves exploring relationship dynamics via deliberate "experiments" in changing behavior sequences, with the couple shifting the problem focus from the relationship and the other to self. Most couples will have achieved symptom relief by this stage, and some will terminate therapy because they now feel better. Such couples often return later when the next crisis develops, either for another brief problem-solving consultation or for more extensive work on themselves.

Some couples will remain in therapy for the third and final *differentiation-of-self stage* (20 or more biweekly or monthly sessions) in which self issues are reworked in the context of ongoing family-of-origin relationships. In this stage, the therapist acts primarily as a "coach" reviewing and guiding the spouses' efforts to understand and change their fundamental patterns of emotional functioning by restructuring their functional positions in their extended-family system.

Such therapeutic efforts require a great deal of motivation and commitment compared to brief, symptom-focused approaches. Moreover, the amount of calendar time involved can be substantial, up to 4 years (or more) for a completed therapy with well-motivated, upper-middle-class couples (Bowen, 1971). However, it should be noted that, compared to other personal growth-oriented models, the amount of therapy time is minimal, frequently no more than 10 to 20 hours a year, with an average total therapy time for a couple generally under 50 hours.

The therapist must recognize that not all couples will pursue therapy to the level of differentiation in the family of origin. Some will take what benefit they can from the therapist's de-triangled interaction with them. Others will be helped somewhat by tasks or experiments suggested in the marital or nuclear system. As long as this natural variance in capacity for change is accepted, there are no specific indications or contraindications for the approach.

SPECIFIC TECHNIQUES

The following case illustrates how the foregoing concepts of the Bowen family systems therapy are applied in marital treatment.

Harry and Sue, a childless Jewish couple in their mid-30's and married
about 5 years, were referred for therapy by Harry's internist, because Harry's
symptoms of sleeplessness, respiratory problems, and gastrointestinal distress
were not responding to either medication or traditional group therapy.
Despite Harry's and Sue's reluctance to be seen together for "his problem,"
a series of conjoint evaluation sessions was scheduled. In the first session,
a genogram (see Figure 5-15) was taken along with a history of the presenting
problem. Harry's and Sue's reactive, over- and underfunctioning was apparent
in this review. Harry had developed anxiety symptoms since leaving the
family business when his father retired and sold the company. Harry had
taken a job with a boss very much like father, with whom he felt intimidated
and powerless. At the time of referral, Harry was so incapacitated by anxiety
and exhaustion that he would bring work home to Sue, who would do it
at night, after completing her own demanding professional and domestic
responsibilities. Although this reciprocal interaction of overfunctioning women
and underfunctioning men was clearly visible in both Harry's and Sue's
parents' marriages as well as their own (see Figure 5-16), neither could see
this as a pattern. Instead, they reiterated their focus on Harry's symptoms
and wondered if individual therapy wouldn't be better than couples work.

Therefore, a therapeutic reversal was employed, in which Sue was told
that Harry's symptoms were indeed worse than the therapist had been led
to believe, that she was not doing enough for him, and that she needed

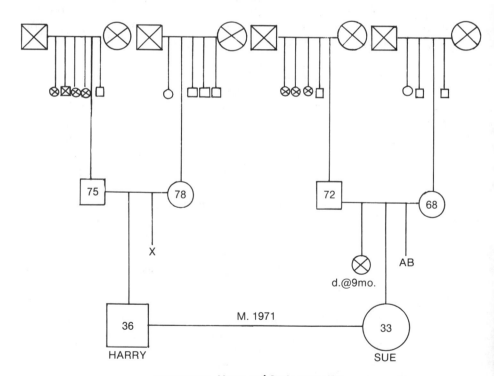

FIGURE 5-15. Harry and Sue's genogram.

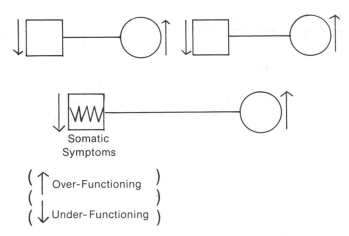

FIGURE 5-16. Reciprocal under- and overfunctioning.

guidance on how to take even better care of him (e.g., by laying out his clothes each night and making him breakfast). One week later, the couple returned with Sue in revolt, exclaiming, "He's a grown man and it's about time he started taking care of himself. I've got too much to do to baby him day and night." Harry's anxiety symptoms improved, and he began taking on more responsibility for his own affairs.

This shift in the marital process almost immediately triggered a shift in Sue's self process. Not having Harry's problems as her primary focus, she became depressed and more upset about his lack of affection (pursuit–distance reactivity) and their long-term problems with infertility (see Figure 17).

Once at least one spouse has made the shift from *marital focus to self focus,* the therapist should direct most of the attention to this spouse, clarifying and expanding the self focus and beginning to connect issues in self to issues in the family of origin. If the other spouse is motivated to do the same, some gentle family-of-origin work can be begun with this spouse as well, but it is wise not to push or hurry the process out of a naive belief in parity between the spouses. Usually, spouses do not shift from marital to self to family-of-origin issues at the same rate. Often it takes one spouse's dramatically

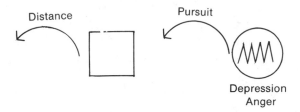

FIGURE 5-17. Reciprocal pursuit–distance.

altering behavior in the relationship for the other to have or notice a change in experience. This therapeutic shift may occur spontaneously (e.g., a pursuing wife may become depressed and withdrawn when therapy focuses on her grief for her dead mother, leading to acute loneliness in her distancing husband). It may also occur strategically (e.g., when an overfunctioning husband is coached deliberately to back off from making decisions for his wife, leading to a shift in her from helplessness to dissatisfaction about lack of intimacy in the marriage). Of course, change in one spouse's behavior may also not lead to any apparent change in the other's experience or behavior, indicating that more time or more aggressive intervention is called for.

> Getting out of her overfunctioning, pseudomaternal role with Harry allowed Sue to reconnect to her urgency about their difficulties in having a child, which itself was intensely interwoven with the couple's struggles over intimacy. As a frustrated emotional pursuer, Sue was primed to substitute connection to the longed-for child for the affection she wasn't getting from Harry (see Figure 5-18).
>
> The fertility project, as Sue's territory, ritualized and reified the pursuit–distance dynamic, since she was in charge of the clock–calendar bedroom routine, and Harry was perforce at her beck and call. Several years of these forced "command performances," as Sue referred to their lovemaking, had effectively destroyed whatever playfulness and spontaneity had existed in Harry's and Sue's sexuality, and toxified the affection between them as well.
>
> Therefore, although Sue was fairly ready to pull back from her pursuing role (once she spontaneously gave up her maternal overfunctioning role), the intimate space in the couple was so toxic that Harry did not begin to move toward Sue. His focus remained angry and projective and he seemed to enjoy his sense of power in denying her satisfaction (see Figure 5-19).
>
> Sue, meanwhile, was becoming more depressed, and was encouraged to work on the distant relationship with her father. This was explained to her as a way of helping, first, to learn about getting close to a man in a less stressful context than her current relationship with Harry; second, to become less dependent on and desperate about closeness with Harry, since

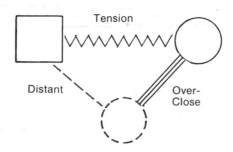

FIGURE 5-18. Incipient child triangle.

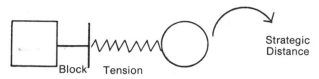

FIGURE 5-19. Coached retreat by pursuer.

he would no longer be the only man in her life; and third, to give her an alternate focus for her emotional energy so that she wouldn't slip back into pursuing Harry (see Figure 5-20).

In assisting a couple through these levels of marital, self, and family processes, the therapist must always be sensitive to issues of sequence, pacing, and relevance.

Sequence and *pacing* refer to the probability that spouses will change in different ways, at different rates, on different issues, and the corresponding need for the therapist to individualize the stance toward each spouse. The therapist must be prepared to let one spouse "stay on the sidelines," while the other works more actively toward change in self, in participation in the marriage, or in the family system. The therapist must also be alert and able to respond to subtle shifts in the "uninvolved" spouse's behavior, affect, or cognition as changes in the more active one radiate into the relationship space and begin to permit bilateral change.

Finally, the therapist must recognize that stress usually cycles and recycles throughout the family system over time before lasting change occurs. For example, in Harry and Sue's case, what began as a physical symptom in one spouse shifted to psychological distress in the other spouse and then to tension in one side of the extended family, before erupting into overt marital conflict. Failing to anticipate this process as appropriate and normative to systems therapy, and to communicate this *in advance* to the couple, runs the risk of unnecessarily raising the therapist's or the couple's anxiety level,

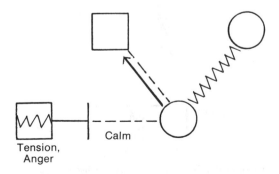

FIGURE 5-20. Connecting pursuer to extended family (change in marital system).

or of dismissing them prematurely from therapy in the belief that short-term symptom relief equals systemic change.

The therapist must also be sensitive to the issue of relevance as attempts are made to redirect the spouses' focus away from the marital fusion toward more workable issues in the self, couple, and family systems. One way to accomplish this is to predict some of these likely intersystem shifts in stress areas described above. Such predictions can be softened by using indirect communication. For example, in the early stages of work with Harry and Sue, the therapist would occasionally pose offhand comments or questions to Harry such as, "How long would it take your mother to get mad at you if you got really close to Sue, or would she go after Sue first?" and, "Do you think your father could handle your mother on his own if she finally gave you up, or would he start pressuring you to get back in line and take care of her for him?"

Another strategy to maintain relevance involves creating what Bowen has called "the tempest in a teapot" (1978, p. 510). By arranging experiments that deliberately evoke more heated experiences or transactions in cooler areas of the self, couple, or family systems, the therapist assists the spouses to see the multigenerational linkages to their perceived problems.

> One such "tempest in a teapot" was used to help Harry detoxify the intimate space between himself and Sue and allow him to move closer to her. A hypothesis was formulated that Harry needed to de-triangle more from his overinvolvement with his mother, and to find a less toxic field in which he could begin to experiment with direct expressions of affection. He was therefore given the task of warming up his relationship with his father, by shifting their greetings and partings from distant, stiff handshakes to warm, close hugs (see Figure 5-21).
>
> The effect of this project on Harry was substantial. Although closeness continued to be difficult for him, he was able to make affectionate moves

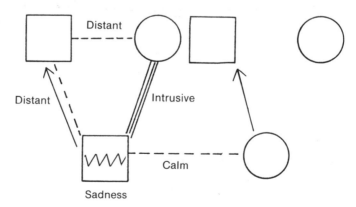

FIGURE 5-21. Primary parental de-triangulation connecting distancer to family system and change in self system: (son).

toward his father that had not been possible with his wife. In doing so, Harry began to experience (rather than reenact) his reluctance to get close and to discover what its sources were in his life. Describing "the jail cell I build around myself," Harry recalled with considerable emotion his time away from home in prep school. He would spend long evenings in his room trying to study and listening to the other boys in the dorm laughing and having a good time while he sat lonely but scared to make contact. Harry was encouraged to share this memory with his father as a beginning exploration of their mutual problem of emotional distance. As he continued this project, Harry found himself finally able to begin approaching Sue affectionately with less fear (see Figure 5-22).

This vignette illustrates how directed tasks in the family of origin can elicit significant insight and emotional experience in the *self* system (Harry's memory of loneliness in prep school), and how such information can be used to de-triangle relationships in the *family* system (sharing this memory with his father), leading to change in behavior in the *couple* system (more comfort with closeness). However, the *recycling* of stress frequently leads to temporary regression in either spouse or their extended-family systems when positive change has occurred. Therefore, following significant movements anywhere in the three-level system, the therapist needs to be alert for the emergence of new system configurations and to respond appropriately to the reemergence of stress and symptoms in different system areas. The following case segment illustrates several therapeutic strategies for dealing with such developments.

As the relationship with his father improved and he began moving closer to Sue, Harry's mother's anxiety level began rising (see Figure 5-23). This aspect of the process had been anticipated in the coaching of Harry to stay "involved but detached" with his mother by devoting his relationship time with her to asking many questions about her own family experience and extended system. However, this was not entirely successful, due to Harry's high level of anxiety about changing the relationship with his mother. The usually palliative effect of extended-family exploration with an overclose

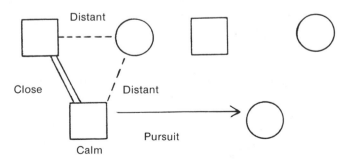

FIGURE 5-22. Change in marital system following de-triangulation.

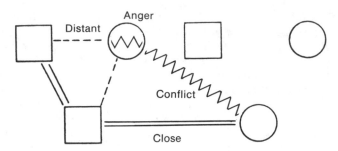

FIGURE 5-23. Change in self system: (mother): creation of new triangle.

parent was weakened somewhat by the heavy-handed and blaming way
Harry asked the questions, and by his triangling the stress with his mother
by revealing that he was only doing what his therapist had told him to do.
The therapist instructed Harry to tell his mother what a good job the
therapist thought she had done in raising Harry and that he thought the
main problem was that Harry wasn't close enough to his mother.

Soon, increased stress began to develop between Harry's mother and
Sue. The therapist's reversal in praising Harry's mother and allaying her
anxiety about therapy, had succeeded in de-triangling the therapy and
returning stress to the family system (see Figure 5-23).

The form the new stress cycle took, i.e., a triangle between Harry, his
mother, and Sue, allowed the therapy focus to shift to Sue and her family
system. Although Sue had begun to move toward her father by writing him
directly, Sue's relationship with her father continued to operate through her
mother, in part because her mother was also primarily responsible for her
ill husband's care. Moreover, Sue maintained her reciprocal enmeshed position
with her mother by participating in the cut-off from her mother's siblings
(see Figure 5-24).

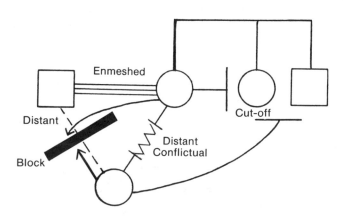

FIGURE 5-24. Primary parental triangle: stable configuration.

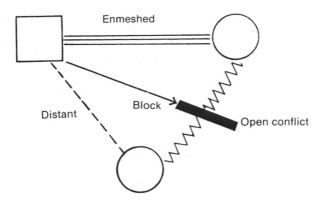

FIGURE 5-25. Primary parental triangle: conflict configuration.

The negative side of the enmeshment surfaced only during Sue's annual visits to her parents' sunbelt home some distance away. At these times, Sue and her mother would almost immediately begin squabbling over who was in control of housekeeping and cooking arrangements, only taking a break when Sue's father would flush and announce that his blood pressure was getting dangerously high, illustrating his reciprocal blocking of Sue's relationship with her mother (see Figure 5-25).

Sue would return from the visits "an emotional two-year-old" and would spend the rest of the year in polite but angry distance from both parents. She was indeed ripe for an intense in-law triangle that allowed her to stay distracted from problems with her own mother while reenacting the same issues with Harry's mother (see Figure 5-26).

Sue's work with her family system illustrates some alternate routes to de-triangulation when direct routes are blocked. In such cases, clients are often coached to use reversals, or indirect strategies, on parts of the system where they are stuck.⁵ Sue was coached in two reversals, one with Harry's mother and one with her own. One of the issues between Sue and Harry's mother was that the mother kept appearing at the couple's home with unrequested food and supplies, while Sue fumed helplessly, feeling put down and invalidated. She was instructed to thank Harry's mother lavishly for her gifts, both at the time they arrived and again each time Sue anticipated a visit from Harry's parents. At that time, she was also to request help in preparing one of Harry's favorite dishes "just like mother used to," and to specify which items his mother should include in the next grocery delivery. While this strategy did not curtail Harry's mother's intrusiveness, it calmed Sue down enough to begin looking at her own mother problem. It also de-triangled Sue out of the relationship between Harry and his mother so that Harry could continue his efforts to deal with his mother on his own.

5. While sometimes paradoxical in nature, these therapeutic reversals differ from other "paradoxical techniques" in that the client, not the therapist, is in charge of the paradoxical move, and the goal is to shift the client's experience of his or her situation, rather than to manipulate others' behavior.

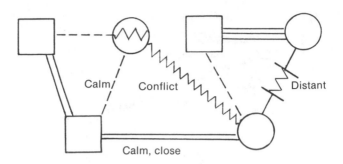

FIGURE 5-26. Mother/mother-in-law triangle.

Reversals require a modicum of calm clearheadedness if they are to be successful and not come across as sarcastic and hurtful (though even successful reversals may be labeled negatively by a change-resisting recipient). In situations in which triangles are extremely intense, *straddling moves* to lower intensity may be necessary as a precondition for a de-triangling reversal (see Figure 5-27).

> *She could perform a reversal with Harry's mother more readily than with her own mother because the intensity of the relationship was much less with her mother-in-law and she had less to lose. In order to allow her to do the same with her own mother, she first had to broaden her relationship options to the point that her mother was not her only family connection, and she could risk some temporary disturbance between them. This shift was accomplished by Sue's reconnecting with her mother's siblings, with whom both her mother and Sue had been cut off. Although they all lived quite close to Harry and Sue, Sue had to master considerable emotional reactivity and reluctance before being able to differentiate from her mother in this way.*

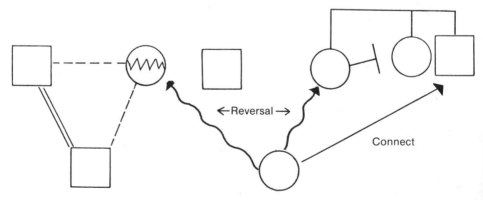

FIGURE 5-27. Primary parental de-triangulation: straddling to extended system with reversal in nuclear and in-law systems.

Reversals often take the form of going with or intensifying a noxious transaction instead of engaging in one's typical resistance. This position prevents bilateral escalation (although the other may escalate considerably to elicit the old reaction) and allows for a different emotional experience in the reverser, a different outcome in the dyadic interaction, a shift in a key triangle surrounding the dyad, or all three.

Sue's primary overt difficulty with her mother involved conflicts over authority when Sue visited her parents (see Figure 5-25). Rather than squabble, Sue was coached not to make a single move in her mother's house without asking for permission and advice (see Figure 5-27).

In making tea, for example, Sue was to ask whether to draw water from the hot or cold water tap, whether to use the small or large burner on the stove, and whether to preheat the teapot. (On other visits, she would have stubbornly asserted which alternative was right, while her mother attacked and criticized whichever way Sue was going about the task until her father's symptoms intervened.) Sue was to ask similar questions about what to wear, how to drive to familiar places, etc.

After 2 days of this, Sue's mother began laughing every time Sue asked for advice, and telling Sue to act more like a grown-up. She returned from her weekend visit reporting that for the first time she had gone through an entire visit without fighting with her mother and had actually had a good time. Mysteriously, Sue's father began answering her letters directly (rather than her mother's doing so for him), and he and Sue were able to discuss his illness and her fear of his dying. Equally mysteriously, Sue's mother reopened relationships with her siblings and went to visit them for the first time since moving away 10 years previously. Calmer about her own mother, Sue no longer reacted to Harry's mother's anger, and, as Harry took on the job of handling his mother directly, her competitive jealousy ceased to be a toxic issue in the marriage.

Family system changes represented by shifts in the primary parental triangles lead to higher levels of differentiation in the self system and thereby create the conditions for less fused, nonreactive behavior in the couple system. Having neutralized toxic issues and replaced triangles with person-to-person relationships, spouses can approach each other and their relationship with less unfinished business, fewer unrealistic expectations, and more ability to tolerate differences. Under such conditions, symptoms and relationship problems often clear up automatically or respond to straightforward teaching about the functioning of emotional systems.

Having improved their relationships with both sets of parents, Harry and Sue began functioning at a more mature emotional level, as Sue put it, "more like husband and wife than brother and sister." They no longer took vacations automatically with one set of parents or the other, and operated with more of a boundary (in contrast to reactive distance) between their marriage and both extended families. Within the marriage, struggles over intimacy and closeness lessened, and they were able to pursue plans to adopt a child. Sue's overprotectiveness toward Harry ceased, and he remained free of his anxiety symptoms. Finally, Harry undertook a series of career assessment procedures that allowed him to leave his unfulfilling job and managerial relationship for a more rewarding and less stressful position.

THE ROLE OF THE THERAPIST

The need for the therapist to stay out of triangles with the couple, to maintain a detached–involved position, to lighten the atmosphere, to teach principles of emotional functioning, and to track emotional process through self, couple, and family system levels has been described above and in considerable detail elsewhere in the literature (e.g., Bowen, 1971; Burden & Gilbert, 1982). Until recently (Burden & Gilbert, 1982; Guerin, 1982), however, unlike more symptom-focused schools of family therapy, practitioners of the Bowen model have not specified how this is done or how therapists should learn the necessary techniques.

At a more descriptive level, however, it is also possible to examine the therapist characteristics that seem most congruent with the model. Clearly, a well-honed, slightly ironic sense of humor is of major importance in maintaining the "distant but friendly" position of the Bowen model therapist. It is also important that the therapist be comfortable with authority and structure (though with an egalitarian and somewhat pessimistic view of human imperfection). Preferring logical clarity and certainty to ambiguity and amorphous detail, such a therapist would deal in cool rather than heated transactions. Viewing this set of factors from the standpoint of ethnicity (McGoldrick, Pearce, & Giordano, 1982), it is not surprising that many practitioners of the Bowen family systems model are Irish Catholic in origin.

Rather than stress technique, the Bowen model has always emphasized the development of the therapist's capacity for objectivity, freedom from personal emotional reactivity, and knowledge of family system principles by directed efforts at "differentiation of self" in the therapist's own family of origin (Carter & Orfanidis, 1976). Therefore, a significant component in Bowen family systems training involves therapists-in-training ongoing work in their families of origin.

While most marital and family therapy training pays some attention to the therapist's own family, most deal with this issue as a static, internal, countertransference phenomenon to be resolved through catharsis and insight. Thus, in many programs, trainees sculpt their family experience, engage in role play or psychodramatic recreations of their relationships and events, and in general spend time emoting and "understanding" how they carry their family experience with them in their personal and professional lives. In the Bowen model, however, trainees are required to return to the family emotional field *in vivo* in order to examine and redefine their current functional position in the family and restructure their current relationship behavior in conformance with the principles of emotional functioning described by the model. For example, rather than simply "understand" or even "experience" how one's negative attitude to mother's bossiness interferes with current personal and professional functioning, a trainee in the Bowen model would be coached in how not to react predictably and automatically to mother's bossiness, and how to assess and neutralize the nuclear and extended-family triangles underlying this transaction, by redefining his or her position in these other relationships as well.

Work in one's own family of origin is a rich context in which to learn the principles of emotional systems that a therapist needs to function competently. However, many models of training teach system principles effectively, and it is primarily in the quality of *clinical application* of theory that family-of-origin work becomes critical.

Foremost in this domain of applied theory is the capacity to think clearly in the midst of a highly charged emotional field. Practicing objectivity, desensitizing oneself to emotional triggers, and learning to "think on one's feet" in the crucible of one's own family field prepares the therapist to do likewise in the intense encounter with clinical families. Such preparation acts as insurance against the misuse of clinical work to express or enact aspects of the therapist's unresolved family issues. It also maximizes the likelihood that systems principles will be applied in a thoughtful, logical manner, preventing loss of therapeutic leverage through impulsive, random interventions.

Second, family-of-origin work teaches convincingly the universality of family process. The direct experience of the struggles to free oneself from entrenched family patterns leaves Bowen family systems therapists relatively unencumbered by the "us–them," "normal–pathological" dichotomies that often characterize practitioners of psychodynamic and problem-solving approaches.

Third, the therapist's level of optimism and clarity when suggesting family-of-origin tasks to couples is a major determinant of their receptivity to such novel and anxiety-arousing ideas. Personal experience with the range of family projects and situations allows the therapist to be both specific and confident in conveying this information to the couple. Threrapists without such experience often hesitantly suggest vague proposals, such as, "Get closer to your family," or worse, they encourage regressive emotional expression, such as, "Go home and tell them how angry you are." These misapplications of systems principles support resistance rather than change and only maintain the system's ongoing reactive patterns.

Fourth, the difficulties and anxiety levels attendant to seemingly simple changes in one's relationship patterns are absolutely impossible to appreciate without "having been there." Unless a therapist has experienced the sweaty palms, accelerated heart rate, intestinal flip-flops, and sleepless nights involved in reaching out to a distant parent, deliberately disappointing an overclose parent's expectations, having overture after overture ignored, or opening up a toxic issue that has not been explored in 30 years, he or she cannot appropriately pace, support, and empathize with individuals attempting to do the painful and difficult work of differentiation. Instead, the therapist will be glib, unsympathetic, and ultimately unsuccessful in assisting the differentiation effort.

COMMON CLINICAL ISSUES

While the Bowen model is relatively consistent in its approach to different problems or families, there are some clinical situations that have engendered specific approaches or principles. Most of these involve avoidance of various triangles in the family or therapy systems, and some of the specifics of dealing with such situations are discussed next.

Affairs

A spouse actively engaged in an extramarital affair will be encouraged to terminate the affair, at least for the duration of therapy. Doing so will allow both spouses to experience more directly their emotional positions in the marriage and avoid the confusion, ambivalence, and rage inherent in such triangles. Also, by preventing the leakage of emotionality and information, a more accurate and comprehensive picture of the marital and family system can be drawn and more energy is available for change.

Direct work with a spouse who will not end an affair is minimized, while the other spouse is coached (often in individual sessions) on how to respond. Such response might include developing and communicating an "I position" about willingness to continue the marriage if the affair persists; exploring multigenerational patterns in both spouses' families regarding affairs, divorce, and other marital dysfunction; or consulting an attorney for guidance in obtaining a legal separation. Once the uninvolved spouse is able calmly and forcefully to take such steps, the affair often is dropped, and marital therapy can begin. In some cases, this means that the breakdown of the marriage is acknowledged, and steps can be taken to disengage from the relationship appropriately (Guerin, 1982).

Alcoholism

Therapy with alcoholic couples proceeds through several discreet phases (Berenson, 1976a, 1976b; Bowen, 1973). The first phase focuses on attaining stable sobriety. In doing so, however, the therapist needs to be careful not to get caught in the same overresponsible or enabling trap that characterizes most nonalcoholic spouses. This de-triangling by the therapist may include "I positions," such as refusing to meet with an intoxicated individual or making therapy contingent on the spouses' involvement with AA or Al-Anon (Guerin, 1977).

Often, work in this initial stage is aimed primarily at helping the non-alcoholic spouse become less focused on controlling the alcoholic and more focused on self issues, such as emptiness (Fogarty, 1976a, 1976b). Berenson states:

> The goal is for the spouse to hit bottom before the alcoholic does . . . once the non-alcoholic spouse distances or detaches, the alcoholic usually becomes worse. If the spouse sticks to the plan, and does not get pulled back into the fusion of homeostasis, the alcoholic will usually take his turn to hit bottom and then stop drinking. (1976b, pp. 292–293)

Berenson goes on to cite the therapeutic paradox:

> The more a spouse takes a position for herself, the more likely the alcoholic is to stop drinking: the more the spouse takes a position in order to get the alcoholic sober, the more likely such a move is going to be a failure. (1976b, p. 293)

After sobriety is established, the couple frequently enters what Berenson calls a "walking on eggs" state in which an artificial distance compensates for the fear that expressing feelings will trigger another drinking episode. Often a 6- to 12-month hiatus from therapy is prescribed, in which the couple uses AA and Al-Anon to maintain sobriety without the added stress of relationship change. Alternatively, couples can be seen intermittently for supportive therapy aimed at restraining change and intimacy until sobriety is well established. Following this stage, a second phase of therapy can then be aimed at decreasing the emotional distance without having the drinking resume and freeing one or both spouses from continuing disruptive input from the extended-family system.

Attorneys

Once couples have engaged lawyers and begun legal processes toward divorce, marital therapy becomes quite difficult. Guerin (1982) has even labeled this process as a separate stage of marital conflict, with the goal of therapy being amicable divorce rather than reconciliation. Unfortunately, the adversarial foundation of the legal system supports and intensifies the polarized and projective aspects of marital fusion. This makes the therapeutic aim of self focus and shared responsibility for marital difficulties impossible and frequently intensifies the couple's anger and blaming to a level that precludes couples therapy.

For this reason, couples are generally discouraged from involving attorneys in the problem until a clear decision to end the marriage is reached therapeutically. Exceptions to this principle include abuse situations in which protective documents are necessary, "information only" consultations with attorneys to educate spouses about the logistics and impact of the divorce process, and the use of legal consultation as strategic communication, e.g., all else having failed, a pursuing spouse may get the distancer's attention by scheduling an appointment with an attorney, leaving an attorney's card on the kitchen table (especially if it lists a Family Law specialty) or having the attorney send the spouse a memo regarding the session.

Dead or Disengaged Marriages

When both spouses profess that the marriage is dead, that they have nothing in common, that they are not interested in each other, and in general paint a bleak picture of their relationship, the therapist should sympathetically agree, ask if they have considered divorce, and offer to help in any way possible. Couples who genuinely wish to separate but are frightened or need permission will welcome this attitude and proceed to do so, with or without therapeutic assistance. On the other hand, couples who are using a hopeless stance as an emotional poker chip will find no game available in the therapist's office and will have to revise their position in favor of more productive issues or find a therapist more willing to triangle with them. The paramount principle here, as in all therapy, is that the therapist should never be more motivated for change than the client.

It is more often the case, however, that one spouse (either the distancer or the pursuer in reactive distance) is all for divorce while the other is all for marriage. In such cases, the therapist needs to avoid taking sides, and to connect relevantly to both sides of the dispute. He or she might convey that the eventual outcome of such situations is unpredictable and that both divorce and reconciliation are frequent occurrences. The therapist should, however, avoid inappropriately raising hopes of reconciliation, by warning that while it takes two to make a marriage, it only takes one to end it, if that one is determined to do so. The therapist may use this argument to help the marriage-focused spouse begin to prepare for life alone by enhancing relationships with family and friends, exploring career and living alternatives, and generally reversing direction from pursuit to calm distancing. In marriages that are truly over, such preparation calms that spouse's desperation and panic, and allows a divorce to proceed with less bitterness and fallout on the spouses and children.

In contrast, when one spouse is using threats of divorce to control or hurt the other, the switch from desperate pursuit to calm distance will often trigger a reverse toward closeness in the divorce-focused one, so that both are re-engaged and therapy can proceed.

Fundamental Value Difference

Particularly in the aftermath of the sexual revolution and women's liberation, many couples in the 1980s are faced with crises of commitment regarding marriage and childrearing. Men and women, who at age 20 welcomed the freedom to live together without legal ties or fear of illegitimate children, at age 30 or 35 desperately listen to the "biological clock" tick away the last seconds of safe childbearing years.

Also, in this era of advances in equal opportunity for the sexes and enhanced professional roles for women, couples (married or not) are often faced with potentially bitter disputes over whose career is to come first, or who will make the necessary adaptations to cover the domestic front. This issue is particularly difficult for the current generation of young adults, who, for the most part, were raised in traditional households. They are therefore caught in an ambivalent position in which their intellects say they should share responsibility and negotiate differences, but their emotions continue to dictate traditional sex roles.

Therapy involving such highly charged issues should proceed from the assumption that a well-functioning couple can deal effectively with most life issues and that these are best resolved in a calm climate, detached from extraneous factors. Therapeutic suggestions to promote calmness might include talking to married siblings or friends about the tradeoffs, frustrations, and satisfactions of marriage and children; exploring with parents what their ambivalence was about marriage, childrearing, or career questions, and how they have resolved personal or relationship conflict; asking parents' opinion of the prospects of the partner as a spouse or parent, and eliciting their picture of the "perfect mate" for their child; researching patterns of career, marriage, and childbearing in the extended-family system; and envisioning life without the partner, perhaps by taking a separate vacation or other break from the relationship (this is particularly useful if initiated by the marriage-focused partner). Ultimately, the partners will have to declare "I positions" about the bottom-line conditions regarding marriage, children, career, or other issues that would be necessary for their continued participation in the relationship. Decision deadlines, such as, "We'll work on this question of commitment for six months, but if there's no wedding date set by then, I'm leaving," are often useful in concentrating the issues and mobilizing energy for change.

Resistant and Highly Conflictual Couples

The Bowen model does not pay much explicit attention to the question of resistance, except for the usual guidance to the therapist to avoid triangulation into an overresponsible position. The therapist's ability to use humor, reversals, and the detached–involved position are particularly important in maintaining an atmosphere of calm in the high-energy field such couples create (Burden & Gilbert, 1982). The therapist needs to be especially consistent in keeping control of the interview, and may see spouses separately for part or all of some interviews if necessary to control their reactivity. The therapist must also be prepared to take firm "I positions" about physical or verbal abuse when these disrupt the therapeutic process in or outside the consulting room. With couples whose apparent resistance reflects high anxiety and marital crisis, such calming tactics are often useful in establishing a more workable therapeutic environment.

With couples whose resistance is more integral to their basic functioning, a light, playful tone that acknowledges the subtleties of their dance and gently teases their commitment to continue it will sometimes allow such couples to experiment with more positive approaches to their problems. However, the therapist must constantly stay reminded that not all couples may wish to change, and certainly not always in the direction the therapist might wish.

Individual Therapy

A Bowen family systems therapist may, for reasons of strategy or efficiency, spend considerable portions of therapy time with spouses separately. However, such separate sessions generally follow the same guidelines for conjoint meetings described above, and individual therapy as it is conventionally understood, that is, intensive, insight oriented, and transferential, is explicitly excluded from the model (Carter & Orfanidis, 1976). In the Bowen model, such an approach makes the therapist and the therapy relationship much too central and like other dysfunctional triangles, such as affairs, drains off needed energy from family process. The dangers of this triangling in promoting fusion and maintaining the status quo are especially prevalent when a couple has separate individual and marital therapists. Most Bowen model therapists, therefore, will not treat couples who are involved with other therapists.

Another problematic potential therapy triangle involves the spouse who intitially consults a therapist individually.[6] Whether or not therapy continues with both spouses, it is useful to have a conjoint meeting as soon as possible (preferably the first contact) to avoid the spouses' triangling the therapist as the ally of one. This maneuver also facilitates the involvement of both spouses in therapy at a later date if necessary.

Termination

Because of the relative infrequency of therapy sessions, the cool therapy atmosphere, the avoidance of transference, and the focus on emotional relationships *outside* the therapy situation, termination is not a significant issue in Bowen family systems therapy. Moreover, since differentiation is seen as a lifetime self-process with one's family, rather than a time-limited process with a therapist, couples never really terminate the effort. Furthermore, it is not uncommon for individuals or couples to return for brief "refresher"

6. This is important even when the presenting problem involves so-called individual issues, as is illustrated in the case of Harry and Sue, described earlier in this chapter.

coaching as personal or family changes present new problems and/or opportunities for growth.

EXTENDED-FAMILY OBSTACLES

In addition to the foregoing special clinical problems of couples that require modification or selective emphasis of the model, additional situations in the extended-family system can complicate therapy. These include parents who are dead or severely disabled or have been physically abusive, intense bitterness in individuals about past hurts at the hands of a family member, and extremely cut-off or estranged family systems. A detailed treatment of techniques in these situations is beyond the scope of this chapter, but a few guidelines can be presented here.

Dead Parents

Resolving unfinished business with a parent who is dead or cannot reciprocate relationship efforts is problematic. Although the net result is probably never as complete as with *in vivo* efforts, considerable therapeutic impact has been observed via attempts to complete and reality-test distorted images of the parent by researching his or her identity through family members, friends, and colleagues; healing cut-offs and system dysfunction by reconnecting with key members of the parent's extended family; and by detoxifying and finishing arrested grief processes by writing letters to the parent, visiting the grave, nursing home, or mental hospital; and other means of fostering an emotional connection to the dead parent (Paul & Paul, 1975; Williamson, 1978).

Abuse, Bitterness, and Fear

Parents who have physically or sexually abused their children create barriers of fear and anger that are difficult to cross. Yet as long as the "child" is controlled by that negative image of the parent, his or her own emotional functioning and relationship potential in adulthood will be limited. Here, the focus first needs to be on recognizing and validating the anger and sadness at the mistreatment; neutralizing the reactivity to such memories of the parent; attempting to understand the behavior in the context of the parent's life; assuming some responsibility for continuing the bitterness and cut-off long after the events had ended; carrying out some ritual of forgiveness and reconciliation with the parent; and learning to interact with the parent in an adult, unfrightened manner. In making such efforts it is helpful to remember that one is ultimately responsible for one's own emotional position and conduct in relationships, and that cut-offs and angry isolation, however seemingly justified, are damaging to all parties involved.

Severely Estranged Families

In some families, physical or emotional distance is so extreme as to seem insurmountable. Families in which no members live within hundreds of miles of one another, or who have not spoken to one another in decades, are not uncommon, especially in highly mobile Anglo-Saxon sectors of American society. In dealing with such families, the therapist must model and communicate perseverance, tolerance for rejection, patience, and low expectations, all seasoned with a strong dose of humor. The therapist should remind clients that change is a slow, long-term process; that change in one-half of a relationship is still change; that conditional change ("I'll do A if you do B") is rarely successful; and that change in movement or direction between people is more important than change in content or feelings. The importance of relationship building, which allows family members to get to know one another gradually and get over initial awkwardness or suspicion before addressing important issues, cannot be overemphasized. Finally, seemingly small gains, such as meeting a distant relative for lunch, going to a ballgame with father alone, or sending mother a birthday card, if continued, should be recognized for the significant system changes they reflect.

LOOKING TO THE FUTURE

Research Findings

Despite Bowen's strong emphasis on scientific objectivity as the distinctive foundation of his model, very few studies exist that actually test the efficacy of multigenerational therapy (Gurman & Kniskern, 1978). This may in part reflect Bowen's disclaimer that his model involves "therapy" at all or the difficulty in operationalizing complex multidimensional variables such as *differentiation*. In any case, with the exception of Bowen's early studies on schizophrenia (collected in Bowen, 1978), he and his immediate colleagues at the Georgetown (University) Family Center seem to emphasize theoretical elaborations of the model (Friedman, 1978); analogic parallels to scientific fields such as animal behavior (Kleiman, 1978), biofeedback (Kerr, 1978), and virology (Winer, 1978); and occasional clinical research relating family systems phenomena to life events such as divorce (Cristofori, 1978) or bereavement (Hollister, 1978; Kuhn, 1978). The few actual therapy studies done by the Bowen group focus more on *process* factors, such as predicting changes in speech patterns of family members during therapy (Winer, 1971) or developing systems for graphing and tabulating these and other in-therapy behaviors (Moynihan & Ingraham, 1971; Schiebel, 1971), than on therapeutic effectiveness or *outcome*.

Nevertheless, some outcome studies of multigenerational family-of-origin marital therapy have been performed outside Bowen's immediate group. In one study (Burden & Gilbert, 1982), therapy outcomes and background data were tabulated for 48 couples in severe marital difficulty. Burden and Gilbert found substantial positive outcomes (either improvement in the marriage or "divorce with progress") in 56% of the couples, while 44% showed little or no change, or simply got divorced without any progress. It is noteworthy that all but one of the "no change" couples, and all but one of the "divorce without progress" couples, were either still active in therapy at the time of the study or, if therapy was completed, were below the mean length of treatment (13.4 months). In cases with a duration of more than 13 months (whether still active or not), the success rate approximated 80%. Though possibly confounded by rater bias, this finding suggests that therapy is more effective when couples remain in treatment longer. Possible rater bias is a major weakness of this study, however, since the only outcome variable was the therapist's or supervisor's rating of how well the couple did in therapy.

In another study (Williamson, Bray, & Malone, 1984), couples in multigenerational family-of-origin marital therapy were compared to a control group of couples in systems-oriented psychotherapy dealing primarily with current social and nuclear family relationships. Change was measured by several self-report instruments and therapists' ratings of outcome. These authors report no differences between the two groups in either satisfaction with or perceived effectiveness of therapy. Given the strong emphasis on differentiation and individuation in both the Bowen (1978) and Williamson (1981, 1982a, 1982b) models, however, it is interesting that the multigenerational therapy clients reported more change in *individuation* (defined as independent functioning and responsibility for one's own behavior) between spouses and from parents, while the control-group clients reported more *intimacy* (defined as trust, fondness, self-disclosure, and commitment) between spouses (Bray, Williamson, & Malone, 1984b). This study also represents one of the first applications of a research instrument developed by Williamson's group that attempts to operationalize intricate multigenerational concepts such as fusion, differentiation, and triangulation (Bray, Williamson, & Malone, 1984a).

Implications for Continuing Development of the Model

While these studies demonstrate that multigenerational concepts can be operationalized and applied to therapy outcome in ways that seem to validate the internal consistency and efficacy of the model, there are many as yet untested questions about how, and how well, the Bowen family systems model works in marital therapy and therapy in general.

For example, after reanalyzing the Burden and Gilbert (1982) data described above, McGoldrick and Rohrbaugh (1983) posed several interesting treatment questions, such as whether marital conflict or dysfunction is more likely to emerge out of changes in the behavior of the *pursuing* or *distancing* spouse, and whether it is easier (in therapy) to teach a pursuer to distance or a distancer to pursue. It would also be interesting to explore whether there are differential implications for therapeutic outcome of each type of intervention.

Finally, once these and other concepts are reliably and validly measured, as Williamson and his colleagues have begun to do, research could proceed to test and elaborate some of the cherished assumptions of the Bowen model, including the specific impact of reworking family-of-origin issues on current personal and interpersonal functioning; prediction, further specification, and implications for therapeutic strategy of individuals' readiness to become involved in family of origin work; and perhaps most central, demonstration of the specific contributions of work on the therapist's own family to professional competence.

In the area of clinical development, several efforts (Aylmer, 1984; Carter & Orfanidis, 1976; Williamson, 1982a) have been made to operationalize and extend Bowen's unique and creative ways of working in the multigenerational model. By organizing, describing, and illustrating the specifics of applying the model in different clinical contexts, Bowen's work can be made more accessible to interested clinicians who heretofore have had difficulty in making the translation directly from his ideas to their own work. Still, for the researcher, theoretician, or clinician who is intrigued by these extensions of Bowen's work, there is no substitute for the rich lode of his original contributions available in his collected papers (Bowen, 1978) or the many examples of his clinical work and teaching in the Georgetown Family Center videotape library.

REFERENCES

Ackerman, N. W. (1958). *The psychodynamics of family life*. New York: Basic Books.
Aylmer, R. C. (1977). Emotional issues in divorce. *The Family*, 4, 3–7.
Aylmer, R. C. (1984). A taxonomy of coaching: Work in progress on operationalizing the multigenerational model. Paper read at the 1984 American Orthopsychiatric Association annual meeting, Toronto, Canada.
Berenson, D. (1976a). A family approach to alcoholism. *Psychiatric Opinion*, 13, 33–38.
Berenson, D. (1976b). Alcohol and the family system. In P. J. Guerin, Jr. (Ed.), *Family therapy: Theory and practice*. New York: Gardner Press.
Boszormenyi-Nagy, I., & Spark, G. (1973). *Invisible loyalties*. New York: Harper.
Bowen, M. (1960). A family concept of schizophrenia. In D. D. Jackson (Ed.), *The etiology of schizophrenia* (pp. 346–372). New York: Basic Books.
Bowen, M. (1971). Principles and techniques of multiple family therapy. In J. O. Bradt & C. J. Moynihan (Eds.), *Systems therapy*. Washington, DC: Groome Child Guidance Center.
Bowen, M. (1973). Alcoholism and the family system. *The Family*, 1, 20–25.
Bowen, M. (1976). Theory in the practice of psychotherapy. In P. J. Guerin, Jr. (Ed.), *Family therapy: Theory and practice* (pp. 42–90). New York: Gardner Press.
Bowen, M. (1978). *Family therapy in clinical practice*. New York: Jason Aronson.
Bray, J. H., Williamson, D. S., & Malone, P. E. (1984a). Personal authority in the family system: Development of a questionnaire to measure personal authority in intergenerational family processes. *Journal of Marital and Family Therapy*.

Bray, J. H., Williamson, D. S., & Malone, P. E. (1984b). PAFS: *Personal authority in the family system, questionnaire manual*. Houston: Houston Family Institute.

Burden, S., & Gilbert, J. (1982). Stage III marital conflict. *The Family*, 10, 27–39.

Carter, E. A., & McGoldrick, M. (1980). *The family life cycle: A framework for family therapy*. New York: Gardner Press.

Carter, E. A., & Orfanidis, M. M. (1976). Family therapy with one person and the therapist's own family. In P. J. Guerin (Ed.), *Family therapy: Theory and practice* (pp. 193–219). New York: Gardner Press.

Christofori, R. H. (1978). Modification of loss in divorce: A report from clinical practice. In R. R. Sagar (Ed.), *Georgetown family symposia*, Vol. 3 (1975–1976), *A collection of selected papers* (pp. 211–220). Washington, DC: Georgetown University Press.

Dicks, H. V. (1967). *Marital tensions*. New York: Basic Books.

Fogarty, T. (1971). A four dimensional concept of self. In J. Bradt & C. Moynihan (Eds.), *Systems therapy* (pp. 82–88). Washington DC: Groome Child Guidance Center.

Fogarty, T. (1976a). On emptiness and closeness (Part 1). *The Family*, 3, 3–12.

Fogarty, T. (1976b). On emptiness and closeness (Part 2). *The Family*, 3, 39–49.

Freeman, I. (1983). Factors in post-partum depression. Paper presented at the Massachusetts Psychological Association annual meeting, Boston.

Friedman, E. H. (1978). Culture and family process. In R. R. Sagar (Ed.), *Georgetown family symposia*, Vol. 3 (1975–1976), *A collection of selected papers* (pp. 158–167). Washington, DC: Georgetown University Press.

Guerin, P. J., Jr. (1976). *Family therapy: Theory and practice*. New York: Gardner Press.

Guerin, P. J., Jr. (1977). A systems view of the alcoholic family. *The Family*, 4, 29–36.

Guerin, P. J., Jr. (1982). The stages of marital conflict. *The Family*, 10, 15–26.

Guerin, P. J., Jr., & Fay, F. (1982). The envelope of marital conflict: Social context and family factors. *The Family*, 10, 3–14.

Guerin, P. J., Jr., & Pendagast, E. (1976). Evaluation of family system and genogram. In P. J. Guerin (Ed.), *Family therapy: Theory and practice* (pp. 450–464). New York: Gardner Press.

Gurman, A. S., & Kniskern, D. P. (1978). Research on family therapy: Progress, perspective and prospect. In S. L. Garfield & A. E. Bergin (Eds.), *Handbook of psychotherapy and behavior change*. New York: Wiley.

Hollister, M. (1978). Families who experience the loss of a child. In R. R. Sagar (Ed.), *Georgetown family symposia*, Vol. 3 (1975–1976), *A collection of selected papers* (pp. 205–210). Washington, DC: Georgetown University Press.

Kegan, R. (1983). *The evolving self*. Cambridge, MA: Harvard University Press.

Kerr, M. E. (1978). Aspects of biofeedback physiology and its relationship to family systems theory. In R. R. Sagar (Ed.), *Georgetown family symposia*, Vol. 3 (1975–1976), *A collection of selected papers* (pp. 98–109). Washington, DC: Georgetown University Press.

Kleiman, D. G. (1978). Monogamy in mammals. In R. R. Sagar (Ed.), *Georgetown family symposia*, Vol. 3 (1975–1976), *A collection of selected papers* (pp. 1–51). Washington, DC: Georgetown University Press.

Kuhn, J. S. (1978). Realignment of emotional forces following loss. In R. R. Sagar (Ed.), *Georgetown family symposia*, Vol. 3 (1975–1976), *A collection of selected papers* (pp. 193–204). Washington, DC: Georgetown University Press.

Levinson, D. J. (1978). *The seasons of a man's life*. New York: Ballantine Books.

McGoldrick, M. (1980). The joining of families through marriage: The new couple. In E. A. Carter & M. McGoldrick (Eds.), *The family life cycle: A framework for family therapy* (pp. 93–119). New York: Gardner Press.

McGoldrick, M., Pearce, J. K., and Giordano, J. (Eds.). (1982). *Ethnicity and family therapy*. New York: Guilford Press.

McGoldrick, M., & Rohrbaugh, M. (1983). Analysis of 48 couples with severe marital conflict. Unpublished paper.

Moynihan, C. J., & Ingraham, B. (1971). Toward a definition of change. In J. O. Bradt & C. J. Moynihan (Eds.), *Systems therapy. Selected papers: Theory, technique, research* (pp. 218–233). Washington, DC: Groome Center.

Paul, N. L., & Paul, B. B. (1975). A *marital puzzle*. New York: Norton.

Pendagast, E., & Sherman, C. (1977). A guide to the genogram. *The Family, 5*, 3–14.

Satir, V. (1967). *Conjoint family therapy*. Palo Alto, CA: Science and Behavior Books.

Schiebel, D. (1971). Observing and charting family process. In J. O. Bradt & C. J. Moynihan (Eds.), *Systems therapy. Selected papers: Theory, technique, research* (pp. 253–267). Washington, DC: Groome Center.

Sheehey, G. (1977). *Passages*. New York: Bantam Books.

Sholevar, G. P. (Ed.). (1981). *The handbook of marriage and marital therapy*. New York: Spectrum Publications.

Sonne, J. C., & Swirsky, D. (1981). Self-object considerations in marriage and marital therapy. In G. P. Sholevar (Ed.), *The handbook of marriage and marital therapy* (pp. 77–102). New York: Spectrum Publications.

Stanton, M. D. (1981). Marital therapy from a structural/strategic viewpoint. In G. P. Sholevar (Ed.), *The handbook of marriage and marital therapy* (pp. 303–334). New York: Spectrum Publications.

Toman, W. (1969). *family constellation* (2d ed.). New York: Springer.

Williamson, D. (1978). New life at the graveyard: A method of therapy for individuation from a dead former parent. *Journal of Marriage and Family Counseling*, 93–101.

Williamson, D. S. (1981). Personal authority via termination of the intergenerational hierarchical boundary: A "new" stage in the family life cycle. *Journal of Marital and Family Therapy, 7*, 441–452.

Williamson, D. S. (1982a). Personal authority via termination of the intergenerational hierarchical boundary. Part II: The consultation process and the therapeutic method. *Journal of Marital and Family Therapy, 8*, 23–38.

Williamson, D. S. (1982b). Personal authority in family experience via termination of the intergenerational hierarchical boundary. Part III: Personal authority defined, and the power of play in the change process. *Journal of Marital and Family Therapy, 8*, 309–323.

Williamson, D. S., Bray, J. H., & Malone, P. E. (1984). Personal authority in the family system: An evaluation of intergenerational consultation. Unpublished paper.

Winer, L. R. (1971). Some efforts in defining and assessing change. In J. O. Bradt & C. J. Moynihan (Eds.), *Systems therapy. Selected papers: Theory, technique, research* (pp. 234–252). Washington, DC: Groome Center.

Winer, L. R. (1978). Cancer: Analysis of virus-host-cell systems and family system. In R. R. Sagar (Ed.), *Georgetown family symposia*, Vol. 3 (1975–1976), A *collection of selected papers* (pp. 141–157). Washington, DC: Georgetown University Press.

II

EMERGING MODELS OF MARITAL INTERVENTION

6

Integrating Marital Therapy and Enrichment: The Relationship Enhancement Approach

BERNARD GUERNEY, JR.
GREGORY BROCK
JEANETTE COUFAL

Marital therapy does not live up to its full potential unless it empowers couples with the attitudes and skills that will enable them to interact compassionately, supportively, harmoniously, and lovingly—that is, unless it enriches couples' relationships. We do not think that an integration of enrichment and therapy needs, on average, to cost more in either time or money than traditional forms of therapy. Perhaps more often than not, such an integration will save time and money. The reasons we believe it will not cost more in time or dollars—and in fact may cost less—is that we do not see enrichment as something that should be added on to traditional therapy as an "extra."

We are not advocating the grafting on of a new branch to the present therapy tree; we are advocating a new, and we think stronger, therapy tree, one in which enrichment flows from the roots up, strengthening the whole structure. It is our belief that such a holistic therapy is one that will be more beneficial not only in the long run (i.e., at follow-up years later) but also in terms of immediate outcome.

What we are advocating in pressing for such a holistic marital therapy is that marital therapy join the revolution we believe has recently commenced in the realm of psychotherapy as a whole. We see this revolution as one that has begun to create the second major historical shift in the treatment of personal and interpersonal disturbances. The first shift was from a spirit

Bernard Guerney, Jr. Department of Human Development, The Pennsylvania State University, University Park, Pennsylvania.
Gregory Brock and Jeanette Coufal. Department of Psychology, University of Wisconsin–Stout, Stout, Wisconsin.

151

(demon possession) model to a medical (illness) model. We see the current shift as being away from the medical model toward an educational (skill or competence) model (Guerney, 1977b, 1982a).

The medical paradigm for treatment—the orientation toward pathology and toward fighting invading organisms or traumas that constitute disease and create symptoms—is a model extremely well adapted to problems that involve physiological and biochemical events. It is not at all an appropriate model for relationship problems. Why not? Because no gal ever went to a singles bar looking for a streptococci to inhale. No guy ever joined a dating service to get himself into an intimate situation with a hookworm. The couple coming to a marital therapist *sought each other out.* They decided to embrace each other, to intertwine their lives. The couple did this because they *wanted* something and felt the other person could provide them with that something. They had very *positive* goals. Their situation is painful now only because those goals have come to be frustrated, perhaps even largely forgotten.

In order for enrichment to be integrated successfully with therapy, the medical model usually followed by marital therapists needs to be replaced by the educational model. The therapist who follows an educational model immediately helps the client to see what *positive* relationship goal the client wants to reach. The client is helped to see that when the positive goal is reached, it will eliminate a pain or complaint. The positive goal is sometimes merely the other side of the coin from a current pain. For example, "I'd like him to spend more time talking to me" can replace "I'd like him to stop being so obsessed with his work." Often though, even in the initial interview, the client can be helped to draw on experiences remembered from the springtime of the relationship—experiences that now may seem completely out of reach—to state deeper positive goals. For example, "I want him to feel it is great pleasure and fun to be alone with me, to feel affectionate when we are alone, and to show me his affection in lots of little ways—as he did when we were courting and first married."

The holistic therapist, oriented by the educational model, wants to give the client a strong positive motivation for therapy. Such a therapist is unwilling to settle for the lesser motivation provided by the simple prospect of removing pain or frustration. He or she wants positive goals writ large in the mind's eye of the client right from the beginning.

Instead of diagnosing the faults of the relationship, the holistic therapist helps a couple to define, as early in therapy as possible, the kind of relationship they would like to have. The therapist then teaches them the skills they need in order to reach these goals. (Almost always, in the United States today, the requisite skills are those that promote intimacy, honesty, compassion, harmony, and love.) It is usually obvious to couples that if these skills are learned and the desired relationship is attained as a result of their use, the pain and complaints that brought them to therapy also will have been eliminated on the way.

The holistic marital therapist provides the clients with the know-how, the process skills, they need to learn; although the therapist may offer input, basically the clients are in charge of designing and constructing their relationship as they want it to be. No marital therapist can make diagnoses as can a physician or laboratory technician. Unlike medical diagnoses, the diagnoses made by marital therapists are *inevitably* based on the therapist's schooling, cultural background, and personal preferences, or the personal preferences of the individuals who made up the theory or the measuring instruments the therapist chooses to use. For a therapist to try to get couples to meet the goals of his or her own favorite psychological or relationship theorist or test designer, instead of meeting their own goals as a couple, seems to us to be a miscarriage of justice as well as a good formula for frequent failure.

The holistic marital therapist does not use the curative, subtractive model of traditional medicine but strives to add knowledge, skills, and confidence in dealing with a loved one. The teaching, enrichment, holistic goal becomes the major goal of the marital therapist. The appropriate professional model here is not the physician but the teacher.

Relationship Enhancement (RE) provides one example of a method of marital therapy that follows such a holistic model. The effectiveness of RE is more striking with severely troubled couples than with less troubled clients (Ross, Baker, *et al.*, 1985), but it has been empirically found to be an effective strategy for the severely disturbed, for those clients who are less disturbed, and for those who desire enrichment only.

This effectiveness has been demonstrated for a variety of RE formats. Effectiveness of group marital RE in a once-a-week format in comparison with randomly assigned waiting control list group showed that RE produced significantly greater gains in marital communication, marital adjustment, and the quality of marital relationship (Ely, Guerney, & Stover, 1973; Collins, 1977). Group marital RE in a marathon format (4- and 8-hour sessions) demonstrated that clients in RE showed greater gains than they had during the waiting period of comparable duration (Rappaport, 1976). These gains were in communication, behaviors, general communication patterns, marital harmony, relationship quality, trust and intimacy, and client perceptions of their ability to resolve their problems.

A number of studies have been conducted comparing RE to other kinds of interventions with couples. These include behavioral (Wieman, 1973), Gestalt (Jessee & Guerney, 1981), traditional discussion treatments (Ridley, Jorgenson, Morgan, & Avery, 1982) the Couples Communication Program, and another communication–problem-solving skill-training program (Brock & Joanning, 1983). In each of these studies, RE was found to be superior to the alternate treatment either in outcome measures (e.g., marital adjustment, quality of the relationship, quality of the communication, and ability to resolve problems) or on process variables (e.g., client perceptions of the depth, worthwhileness, strength, fairness, and importance of the method to the alternate treatment). On no variables was RE found to be a less potent approach than an alternative approach. Ross and Baker *et al.* (1985) compared RE with the preferred flexible therapeutic approaches of experienced marital therapists in a community mental health center. After the therapists received 3 days of training in RE, marital cases were assigned to them by random means to receive either RE or the therapists' preferred therapy. The couples receiving RE gained more on each variable studied: marital adjustment, quality of relationship, and quality of communication. Results of the studies comparing RE to other treatments indicate that the improvements found for RE therapy cannot be attributed to artifacts (e.g., repeated testing) or to nonspecific treatment effects, such as placebo, Hawthorne, thank-you, and experimenter-demand effects.

Maintenance of gains—and in some studies, maintenance of the superiority of gains—in comparison with groups receiving alternate treatments, has been shown with mother–daughter dyads (Guerney, Vogelsong, & Coufal, 1983) and with premarital couples (Avery, Ridley, Leslie, & Milholland, 1980), as well as with marital couples (Weiman, 1973; Brock & Joanning, 1983). In our view, RE owes a large measure of its potency to the fact that it follows the holistic, educational, enrichment approach outlined earlier.

THEORETICAL FOUNDATIONS OF RE THERAPY

It has been a source sometimes of amusement and sometimes of concern to RE therapists to find themselves classified, in terms of method, by some as behavioral, by others as client centered, and by still others as experiential. In terms of theory, RE has been described by some as based in communication theory, by others as behaviorist, and by still others as based on social learning theory. We think the label "interpersonal" would be better than any of those. However, if a label need be found for RE, we think the best classification would be "integrated," because the theoretical foundations of RE derive from what are generally considered to be the three major schools of psychotherapy plus one that we think should also be considered a major school but usually is not.

The three major schools we refer to are the psychodynamic, the humanistic, and the behavioral schools; the fourth is the interpersonal. We view the theoretical foundation of RE as an integration of these theoretical positions. We have attempted to make the processes of selection and rejection from each of these theoretical frameworks fit both the world of clinical reality and the world of research evidence, and we see each of the components selected as fitting very well with one another, indeed building on one another, instead of merely being an eclectic hodgepodge. However, here space allows us only to provide a broadly sketched account of the major theoretical features that we have selected or rejected from each of these psychotherapeutic orientations.

From the psychodynamicists, the Freudians in particular, RE has drawn these major concepts: the importance of the unconscious, the power of defense mechanisms, the value of self-understanding (insight), and the positive power of catharsis. All of the RE skills in interaction, but most notably the guidelines for Expressive skill, were constructed to (a) increase a client's awareness and understanding of poorly differentiated, unrecognized, and sometimes unconscious attitudes, perceptions, desires, and feelings; (b) permit the client to express these inner realities to intimates in a way that is cathartic; and (c) does not arouse the psychological defense mechanisms of those intimates any more than is absolutely necessary while still conveying truth. In addition, a major psychodynamic concept is drawn from Adler to help explain the power RE has to hold and to change clients: Human behavior is understood best in the context of goal seeking, and the powerful drive toward mastery that characterizes individuals and groups seeking goals.

Rejected from psychodynamic theory is the view that defense mechanisms and their accompanying distortions of reality operate primarily to protect us against recognizing early fantasies and traumas. Also rejected from psycho-dynamic theory is the view that methods of choice for promoting catharsis or overcoming defenses, or increasing self-understanding, should include gathering historical information, questioning, probing, free association, dream interpretation, and interpretation of dynamics.

From within the humanistic school, we draw exclusively on Rogerian theory. In place of the rejected psychodynamic view that early traumas, observations, and fantasies of early childhood are of central importance in triggering the self-deceptions brought about by defense mechanisms, we accept Rogers's view that defenses operate mainly in order to protect one's self-concept. In RE theory, the threat of being judged to be different from one's self-image is seen as the key ingredient of defensive distortion. Rogerian therapeutic methods—empathy, acceptance, respect, and understanding— are built into one of the central skills (Empathic Responding) taught to clients in RE therapy. These Rogerian hallmarks are seen as methods of choice for reducing another's defensive distortions, for promoting self-un-derstanding and insight, and for encouraging constructive catharsis. They are the attitudes and techniques taught to clients in preference to teaching them psychodynamic attitudes and techniques.

Rejected from client-centered theory is the notion that the relationship climate created by the therapist plus the client's inherent capacities are alone sufficient to produce therapeutic–enrichment change. We believe that clients should be assisted in therapeutic progress by teaching them appropriate skills.

From learning theory in general, and from behaviorism in particular, RE takes a good deal of its central rationale and methodology. These are the rationale and methods that involve helping clients to change their ideas, their attitudes, and their patterns of behavior, and helping clients learn to help others change. We also believe that the unconscious and all of the defense mechanisms are better understood in terms of learning theory, as explicated by Dollard and Miller (1950), than they were explained by the Freudians.

Perhaps the two most central concepts as far as RE technique *per se* is concerned are modeling and reinforcement. These principles and techniques are associated primarily with Bandura and Skinner, respectively. Modeling and reinforcement are sedulously practiced by the therapist in teaching RE skills. Also, these techniques are taught to the clients for a number of reasons: to help them teach their intimates the skills that they have learned; to help them change their own behavior in ways that they wish to change it; and to help them help their spouses change behaviors that the spouse has agreed to change.

Rejected from behavioral thinking is the idea that reinforcement is central or sufficient to make relationships (or therapy) work well. Affection, caring, and a willingness to give (all without emphasizing contingencies) are viewed in RE theory as being at the heart of effective therapy, as well as at the heart of love, and therefore at the heart of good marital relationships. Contingent reinforcement should be the servant of love and caring; if ever contingent reinforcement instead becomes the master, then intimacy, trust, love—and therapy—are all likely to be subverted.

Also rejected from behaviorism is the view that catharsis is, at best, something to be ignored and, at worst, something that is quite harmful. We believe catharsis *can* be harmful but that, skillfully done, catharsis can be a vital ingredient of growth to an individual or a relationship.

We now come to what we think should be viewed as a fourth major school of psychotherapy. We believe it is the school of thought that, if one had to be chosen to the exclusion of all others, is the one marital therapists would be forced to choose. We refer to the "interpersonal" school of thought. This is a theoretical position that can effectively integrate intrapsychic, psychodynamic, and behavioral components and that is by its very nature a system-oriented theory. The theory originated, of course, with Harry Stack Sullivan (1953). But the much more highly systematic, comprehensive, and empirically based elaboration of Sullivanian theory by Timothy Leary (1957) is the version that we rely on to increase our understanding of how RE methods work to effect interpersonal and individual change. The following central propositions from Sullivan and Leary are present in RE (see Guerney, 1982b, 1984).

Significant persons in our environment condition and train us to become what we are. We, in turn, similarly train others in our intimate interpersonal environment. We seek to train others to feed us interpersonal responses that will allow us to respond comfortably to them in ways that reduce our own anxieties. Such conditioning of others is possible because stimulus–response patterns in interpersonal interactions are sufficiently predictable for people in general (Shannon & Guerney, 1973)—and probably even more so for particular individuals—to permit us unconsciously to learn what particular interpersonal responses on our part generally elicit particular responses from others. Just as others respond to us in "reflexive" ways, we also respond reflexively to the interpersonal stimuli others feed to us as they seek to "train" us. The styles of interpersonal response we prefer to use to elicit responses from others that allow us to feel comfortable in using our own preferred responses constitute our "personality." Reshaping these patterns to fit the conscious desires and goals of the individual and his or her spouse better is, in our view, central to effective marital therapy.

Thus, in RE therapy clients are taught—in effect, but not in the same language—the laws that govern "reciprocal interpersonal reflexes" (Leary, 1957). Responses that they previously made without awareness, that is, reflexively, are brought into the realm of conscious choice and action. RE therapy trains clients in the behavioral skills necessary to emit the interpersonal behaviors they need to emit to further their conscious goals. Such conscious choices replace the reflexive, anxiety-reducing reactions that otherwise would determine their interpersonal initiatives or responses. By learning, first, the most important predictable relationships among interpersonal responses, and by learning conscious control over the responses that they make, individuals and couples can successfully reshape their relationships (and personalities) to fit their aspirations better.

What we reject from Sullivanian–Learian theory is the position that the reduction of anxiety through the unconscious control of interpersonal responses is the sole explanatory concept necessary to explain personality, interpersonal relations, and "psychopathology." Rather, we add from behaviorism the notion that reinforcement can also be extremely useful in explaining these phenomena. Based on empirical research, we also reject certain specific hypotheses set forth by Leary in terms of which interpersonal responses elicit what interpersonal responses from others and in their place substitute other relationships based on empirical research (Shannon & Guerney, 1973).

METHODS AND STRATEGIES FOR CHANGING CLIENTS

Therapy–Enrichment Goals of RE

The goals of marital RE therapy are to teach clients the skills that they need to master in order to strengthen love: attitudes and feelings centering on caring, giving, understanding, trusting, sharing, being honest, and being open, compassionate, and harmonious. Research has shown that these are the same sorts of goals that clients generally set for themselves (Fisher, Giblin, & Hoopes, 1982). These goals are perhaps most succinctly reflected in the criteria used by RE therapists in discussing with clients their readiness to terminate therapy. The criteria are these: (a) Any critical presenting relationship conflict and problems have been resolved; (b) the skills of the couple are sufficient to resolve any remaining, less critical problems and serious conflicts or interpersonal problems that may arise in the future; (c) the couple have integrated their skills into daily living within and outside the relationship; (d) the couple have set aside times for regular use of skills; and (e) the skills have generalized sufficiently so that clients use the skills not only to resolve problems and conflicts but also to enrich their relationship with greater love (i.e., with greater openness, trust, understanding, compassion, and harmony).

Range of Application and Formats

Clinical experience has shown that RE therapy is useful whenever working on the marital relationship seems indicated. Skill-training methods seem to be appropriate for all levels of education and socioeconomic status, but relative to other methods seem to be especially appropriate for the less educated, lower socioeconomic client (Goldstein, 1973). RE marital therapy appears to be particularly effective also in work with more severely distressed individuals and couples (see Ross, Baker, et al., 1985; Vogelsong & Guerney, 1980; Brock & Joanning, 1983; Vogelsong, Guerney, & Guerney, 1983; Waldo & Guerney, 1983).

Marital RE therapy can be used with an individual, a dyad, or a group of individuals or dyads. (Even when used with an individual or with a group of unrelated individuals, we consider RE to be a conjoint approach in that the sessions are devoted to preparing the individuals for specific interactions with their spouse. Such interactions are rehearsed in sessions, implemented at home, and then supervised on the basis of detailed client reports.) In the RE paradigms presented later, we have chosen to illustrate the dyadic rather than the unilateral format. RE therapy can be conducted in an *intensive* format, which means using mini-marathon sessions (3 or 4 hours) or marathon sessions (more than 4 hours). The intensive format can be used only in the early stages (which we call "front loading"), or it can be used throughout the entire course of the therapy. Of course, marital RE therapy also can be conducted in an *extensive* format, in which sessions last 45 or 90 minutes, once or twice a week, for many weeks. *Time-limited* formats are frequently used with RE programs offered to those seeking prevention or enrichment. The fixed time for such a program might run, for example, for 1 weekend, for 3 days, for 2 weekends, or for 12 or 15 weeks of 2-hour sessions.

"Time designated" (Guerney, 1977a) is the format typically used for marital RE therapy. In this format an informal contract is made with clients who agree to a minimal time commitment (anywhere from 2 to 20 sessions). At the designated time, progress is evaluated in terms of the therapist's and the client's views on the advisability of termination. If it is decided that more time is needed, another time is designated for the next evaluation.

The Skills Taught to Clients

To bring about the changes we expect in individuals and couples, we believe it is necessary and sufficient to teach clients nine sets of skills. Specific operational guidelines clarifying each skill may be found elsewhere (Guerney, 1977a; Preston & Guerney, 1982). Here the skills are described only in terms of the purpose each serves.

1. *Expressive.* This skill equips the client (*a*) to understand his or her emotional–psychological–interpersonal wants and needs better; (*b*) to express such wants and needs to intimates in ways that do not incite unnecessary anxiety, defensiveness, conflict, and hostility, but instead tend to engender respect, understanding, and cooperation; and (*c*) to deal with conflicts and problems with less anxiety, promptly, assertively, positively, and in terms of one's own specific goals and needs.

2. *Empathic.* This skill equips the client (*a*) to understand the emotional–psychological–interpersonal needs of others better; and (*b*) to elicit from others more prompt, frequent, honest, relevant, open, trusting, and intimate behaviors.

3. *Discussion/Negotiation* ("*mode switching*"). This skill enables the client to preserve a positive emotional climate when working on problems and conflicts. It helps the client avoid unnecessary or damaging digressions from the central topic, and to bring discussions quickly to basic issues.

4. *Problem–Conflict Resolution.* This skill enables the client to develop, and to help his or her spouse develop, creative solutions to problems. Clients learn to develop solutions in which the needs of both husband and wife are met as much as is possible. As a result of their *mutually* fulfilling nature, such solutions are likely to prove enduring.

5. *Self-Change.* This skill enables clients to implement successfully agreements and plans that they have worked out with their spouse. It helps them by teaching them how, more quickly and consistently, to change their own attitudes, feelings, and behaviors in accord with such agreements.

6. *Helping Others Change.* This skill enables one spouse to help the other spouse to change attitudes, feelings, and behaviors in such a way as to enable the other, more successfully and consistently, to implement agreements and plans that they have worked out together.

7. *Generalization–Transfer.* This skill enables the client to train himself or herself to use relationship enhancing skills in daily life.

8. *Teaching Supervisory (Facilitative) Skill.* This skill enables the client to train others (including others not attending) to use RE skills more consistently in daily life when the skills are called for. That is, this skill trains a client to train others to treat the client in ways that are likely to enhance the client's individual self-image and psychological well-being, and to improve the relationship.

9. *Maintenance.* This skill enables the client to maintain usage of the skills over time for problem prevention, problem solution, and enrichment.

Methods

PARADIGM FOR TRAINING

In teaching RE skills, the following training paradigm is used. Although sometimes adjacent categories are intermingled, the steps are generally followed in the order shown:

1. Be sure you have motivated the client as much as possible.
2. Explain the rationale underlying the skill and how that relates to client goals.
3. Explain to the client as many of the essential guidelines for the skill, and as much of the rationale for each skill as the client's attention span permits. (The guidelines omitted initially can be worked into the teaching as practice progresses.)
4. Use demonstration audiotapes, videotapes, or live role playing with the client or with a co-therapist to demonstrate the skill. Have the client point out the significant features and then add on important features that the client did not detect.
5. Supervise the client's practice of the skill word by word within the therapeutic session.
6. When a high enough level of competence in the skill has been reached, give the client assignments that require practicing the skill in his or her natural environment.
7. Supervise these assignments very closely via audiotapes or detailed self-reports.
8. Provide transfer–generalization assignments that will help the client learn to use the skills spontaneously in the course of ordinary daily living.
9. Closely supervise the assignments designed to bring about spontaneous, everyday usage.
10. See that the skill is incorporated in a skill-maintenance regimen.

PARADIGM FOR TOPIC SELECTION

The paradigm used to guide the choice of topics for marital RE therapy is as follows: In the sequence shown, clients discuss (a) strongly felt views and feelings that do not involve the spouse (such topics are used only during the very early stages of mastering empathic skill); (b) positive views and feelings concerning the spouse; (c) suggestions for enhancement or enrichment issues—that is, suggestions for improving the relationship that the other person may also find pleasant or, at least, is not likely to find strongly objectionable; (d) mild problems; (e) moderate problems; (f) serious problems; (g) enhancement–enrichment issues again. If problems need to be solved immediately, the therapist may employ various RE techniques (e.g., doubling) to see that they are quickly resolved even before the client has learned any or all of the skills. Once resolved, the therapist returns to the sequence described.

PARADIGM FOR THE TYPICAL SESSION

After the first few hours, the therapist typically does the following things in the order shown: (a) Reviews and supervises home assignments; (b) conducts follow-up inquiries regarding solutions to previous problems that are now due for follow-up evaluation; (c) asks the couple to share good feelings generated by their spouse's attitudes, characteristics, and behaviors (an optional, but generally advisable procedure); (d) reviews the issues chosen by the clients as being the most important to the relationship and, if necessary, supervises the revision of such topics, occasionally making suggestions about an omitted issue the therapist deems important; (e) supervises the use of RE skills as the couple work to resolve the chosen issue; (f) follows each issue through to its resolution within the session, and if it is not fully resolved within the session, tells the clients whether or not they should continue to work toward a solution at home or wait until the next supervised session; (g) helps the couple prepare for the home assignment.

RE-APPROPRIATE THERAPEUTIC RESPONSES

Aside from friendly social responses at the beginning of the therapy sessions, the occasional injection of humor into the therapeutic process, all the RE-appropriate responses that a therapist should make may be classified into the categories that follow.

REINFORCING RE RESPONSE—VERBAL

Here, the therapist, by showing his or her approval, socially reinforces a client for following one of the guidelines for RE behavioral modes or for making a good effort. Examples are "Very good"; "Terrific"; "Wonderful"; "Beautiful"; "Good"; "You're trying very hard, which makes me feel very good." Reinforcement should be the single most frequent therapist response. It is used to reinforce effort, good responses, self-corrections, and every adherence to therapist prompts and suggestions. Such responses are especially frequent and important in the early stages of training but are carried on throughout therapy. In RE therapy the purpose of social approval for making RE responses is used as much to bring a general feeling of success and to provide encouragement as it is to reinforce and shape particular behaviors contingently.

REINFORCEMENT OF RE RESPONSES—NONVERBAL

These reinforcements are used in the same manner as the verbal responses outlined above. In some cases, especially early in therapy, these may take the form of patting the client on the back or on the arm as a sign of approval.

Most often, nonverbal responses take the form of head nodding and facial expressions and manual signals commonly interpreted in the culture as indicating approval. Nonverbal reinforcements are very valuable in that they can be inserted quickly, without interrupting the flow of the dialogue, to reinforce subcomponents of a client's ongoing statement. Neither verbal nor nonverbal signs of approval are ever given to the perceptions or ideas being expressed; rather, approval is directed only toward process—how well the RE guidelines have been followed in expressing those perceptions or ideas.

STRUCTURING

Structuring responses explicitly explain guidelines for RE modes and procedures, or remind participants of those guidelines.

DEMONSTRATING RE RESPONSES

Demonstrations also are used to explicate RE response guidelines and procedures. The difference between demonstration and structuring may require some explanation. Structuring is simply a statement (or restatement) of a guideline. In a demonstration, the therapist illustrates the points he or she is making through role playing or by playing an audiotape or videotape. Demonstration is a situation set up specifically to show how the modes and procedures of RE are incorporated into lifelike situations.

MODELING RE RESPONSES

Modeling, like demonstration, helps the client see what a guideline looks like in action. Modeling differs from Demonstration in that the situation is real. The therapist feeds a modeling response to the client during an ongoing dialogue. Modeling not only serves a general teaching purpose like Demonstration but also improves the therapeutic quality of the dialogue. It does so because the therapist uses it whenever anticipating that his or her own modeling response, by being a higher-quality RE response, will be significantly more effective in helping clients understand one another or resolve a conflict or problem than the clients' own response has been or is likely to be. The therapist also uses a modeling response when a client hesitates or looks to the therapist for help.

ENCOURAGING–PROMPTING RE RESPONSES

Encouraging–prompting responses are reminders or suggestions made to the client in order to encourage the client to follow RE procedures or guidelines. Unlike structuring, encouraging–prompting responses are not intended to correct an outright error or remind the client about a particular rationale or principle. Rather, encouraging–prompting responses simply serve to stimulate the client to make a particular kind of response or to refine one just made. Encouraging–prompting responses are different from modeling responses in that such responses are open-ended; they do not suggest to the participant a particular way of saying something but serve as a general reminder.

DOUBLING

Doubling is an attempt by the therapist to speak for the client when the client is unwilling or unable to speak for himself or herself, or to speak in a sufficiently skillful way. The therapist takes the role of spouse A and addresses spouse B in a far more composed and skillful way than the spouse A could do at that moment. When the therapist is doubling, the spouse for whom the therapist is doubling is instructed to assent to the therapist's statement by nodding, or to make corrections if the statement does not accurately reflect the spouse's thoughts and feelings. The therapist might double for a spouse only for a response or two, or for a whole session. The technique differs from a modeling response in this respect: Doubling is a *takeover* of the role of the client. The client is not expected to repeat the statements made by the therapist, as would be the case in modeling responses.

TROUBLESHOOTING—CLIENT REACTION

Troubleshooting in response to a client reaction occurs whenever the client is either unwilling or unable to follow standard RE procedures. If it is an instance of the client's being *unwilling* rather than unable to follow the procedures, the therapist repeatedly responds empathically to the doubts and difficulties being raised by the client in order to draw out the client's resistant feelings and thoughts fully. After this, the therapist uses Structuring (i.e., presenting underlying rationale for the method, empirical evidence, experience, etc.) to try to persuade the resistant client to return to RE procedures. The leader then solicits the client's views and returns to empathic responses to make certain that the client's doubts have been assuaged. If the client is now comfortable with going back to RE procedures, troubleshooting is over. If the client still has doubts, the process is repeated. The entire chain of responses just described that a therapist makes in trying to return the client to RE procedures are categorized "Troubleshooting—Client Reaction."

Another type of Troubleshooting—Client Reaction response occurs when the client is *unable* to follow RE procedures because the client is emotionally overwhelmed, for example, by anger or by sorrow. Here the therapist responds empathically to the client to help the client deal with those feelings. When the client regains composure, the therapist will move to Structuring responses to bring the client back into routine RE procedures.

TROUBLESHOOTING—THERAPIST REACTION

This response is very rare. We would not expect an RE therapist to use it at all with most clients. However, by their very nature, the times at which the responses occur are likely to be rather critical points in the therapeutic process. Therefore, despite the infrequency, a category has been made for this response. A Troubleshooting—Therapist Reaction response occurs mainly in two situations.

The first situation is one in which the therapist feels it is absolutely necessary for him or her to make some suggestions to the client as to how a problem might be dealt with. Now, for whatever reason, the therapist has come to believe that the clients cannot understand or see a solution on their own that the therapist believes would be an effective solution satisfying to both parties. Such a situation might be expected to occur when a solution needs to be arrived at very quickly because of the urgency of the circumstance involved. (In making such a suggestion the therapist would, of course, use Expressive skills, such as speaking subjectively.)

The second situation in which the therapist might express feelings or ideas of his or her own (again always remaining in the Expressive mode) would be when firm decisions have been made by the clients that run counter to the law or to strongly held moral principles of the therapist. An example would be a decision made by a couple that would involve neglect or abuse of their child.

ADMINISTRATIVE—RE

There are responses that implement features characteristic of RE therapy as distinct from other therapies. For example, "Ruth, you began as Expresser last session, suppose you let David begin as the Expresser today," or, "Let's review the tape of your home practice session of Empathic skills." "Administrative—Neutral" responses are not classified as RE-appropriate. These would be administrative responses that might occur in any type of therapy. For example, "I'm feeling a bit warm. Would you mind if we opened the window?"

Illustration of RE-Appropriate Responses

The following "transcript" of a couple in dyadic marital RE is partly real and partly constructed so as to illustrate a great number of RE-appropriate responses in a brief space. All RE-appropriate therapist responses are illustrated except Administrative-RE, Doubling, Troubleshooting, and Demonstrating responses. The categories are noted in brackets after each response. In addition, we have shown, again in brackets, the type of RE responses the clients' have made.

THERAPIST: Before we were interrupted, Mary, you were in the Expressive mode, and you were talking about not feeling very much in tune with the way Pete is feeling these days. How about if we pick it up there? [Administrative-RE]

MARY: O.K. Pete, I have seen you feeling excited and optimistic like this before when you have laid off drinking. I am sorry I am not as enthusiastic as you are, but I guess I'm in a sort of wait-and-see mood. [Expressive]

THERAPIST: Good. [Reinforcement—Verbal]

PETER: You think this time will be like the other times—I stay off the booze for a while and then, bingo, right back I go. [Empathic]

THERAPIST: Beautiful. [Reinforcement—Verbal] Let's get at the underlying feelings, too.

[Structuring] Add this: "You're *afraid* to trust me. Because if you get your hopes up high, it'll hurt all the more if I go back to drinking." [Modeling, for the Empathic Responder]

PETE: You're afraid to trust me. You don't want to be hurt so badly again.

THERAPIST (*nods head vigorously*): [Reinforcement—Nonverbal for Empathic Responder]

MARY: Yes, that's right. Also I don't really know what's changed. You are not drinking and that's changed; but outside of that, we seem to be the same, I mean us, the relationship. [Expressive]

PETE: Well, these things take time. . . . [Wrong Mode]

THERAPIST: You need an Empathic response, Pete. [Encouragement–Prompting]

PETE: You, ah, feel, ah—(*pause*). You feel depressed about changing what goes on between us. [Empathic] I would like to switch. [Request for Mode Switch]

MARY: Yes, go ahead. [Approval for Mode Switch]

PETE: I know things in the past have been hard on you, but you don't seem to realize that I *am* different now. . . .

THERAPIST: Be subjective. She may not agree that you've really changed. [Structuring]: "I'm convinced I'm different now." [Modeling Expressive Statement]

PETE (*to therapist*): Right, sorry. (*Then, to wife*): I really am completely confident that I've changed now. I—

THERAPIST: Good. [Reinforcement—Verbal]

PETE: —don't think we need to always be looking back. I don't want to do that.

THERAPIST: Very good, Pete. [Reinforcement—Verbal] Would you add how it makes you *feel* when she seems to you to be looking back? [Encouraging, Prompting]

PETE (*to Mary*): I feel dragged down. Sometimes . . .

THERAPIST: Very good. [Reinforcement—Verbal]

PETE: Right. I think I need to put it behind me. And I want you to put it behind you too, because I think you get bummed out when you talk about the past. [Expressive]

THERAPIST: Good. [Reinforcement—Verbal] You kept it your *perception* of her feelings. [Structuring] How about being more *specific* about your own Interpersonal Message and tell her *why* it's important to you that she not talk about the past; how it makes you feel when she talks about the past. [Structuring; Encouraging–Prompting]

PETE (*to Mary*): When you feel down, it makes everything more difficult for me. I feel like I'm carrying you and me at the same time. I get overwhelmed. [Expressive]

MARY: You don't feel strong enough to carry us both. [Empathic] I would like to switch. [Request for Mode Switch]

PETE: O.K. [Permission to Mode Switch]

MARY: I just want to scream! I feel like I've carried you for the past four years, and now when I want a little support, you say that *you're* overwhelmed!

PETE (*after a pause*): You think I'm ungrateful, that I'm not willing to give you support, even though you stuck by me when I needed you.

MARY: You're sure right about that! I want you to stand up for a while. I feel like I'm entitled to sort of recover for a while. I'm tired of being down and depressed. I need some breathing space from the burden of holding you together. You don't, and you can't, appreciate how much the past has cost me, and all of it directly on account of you. [Expressive]

THERAPIST: Mary, let's do some of that over again. There is a lot you stated there that Pete might disagree with, so you need to make it subjective. You *feel* like you've been holding him together; you don't *think* he appreciates you, or the price you've paid. [Modeling Expressive Statement] Stay subjective. [Structuring] And I think you're experiencing a lot of resentment—a sense now of injustice, of unfairness. You want him to show you more of the understanding and support that you feel you have given to him. His love and support mean a great deal to you. Would this statement be accurate? "I want you to show me that you love me and will give me support, just as I've shown my love and support to you. Feeling your love and getting your support is extremely important to me." [Modeling Expressive Statement] Do you feel ready yet to bring in the underlying positive feeling like that? [Structuring]

MARY (*tearfully*): I've shown you my love. I do love you. I think you love me. I want you to show it more. I'm not feeling any of it now. I want to feel it. And I feel entitled to that. It doesn't do me a lot of good that your act is supposedly together if showing me that kind of support is not a part of your having your act together. [Expressive]

THERAPIST: That's great, Mary! [Reinforcement—Verbal]

CLINICAL ISSUES

Dealing with Resistance

We will consider five kinds of resistance: (*a*) resistance to the therapy or the therapist; (*b*) resistance to change in the relationship out of fear that one will be placed at a disadvantage or lose an advantage in the relationship; (*c*) the use of defense mechanisms to resist recognition of one's own anxiety-provoking thoughts and feelings; or (*d*) the use of defense mechanisms to resist recognition of the thoughts and feelings of one's spouse that are anxiety provoking; and (*e*) resistance to work mainly because it's work.

We here coin the term "iatrogenic resistance" to refer to resistance to the therapy or the therapist because of the nature of the therapy. We believe RE avoids most iatrogenic resistance. Why? Because the nature of RE therapy is so obviously nonanalytic, nonjudgmental, and impartial. Other therapies may also be nonanalytic, nonjudgmental, and impartial in fact, but their diagnostic, or solution-finding orientations—which lead to probing, question asking, and sometimes suggestions, advice, and persuasion about clients' lives—often make clients think and feel otherwise. The possibilities for such misinterpretation in a skill-training therapy such as RE are virtually nil.

Resistance to RE therapists is almost nonexistent for similar reasons. Since (with rare exception) RE therapists do not concern themselves with the content of the issues the clients discuss—not even by asking a question—it is all but impossible for clients to interpret or misinterpret the therapists' behavior as judgmental or as favoring one spouse over the other.

Thus, RE is readily seen by clients as a learning process and not as a process in which they will be analyzed and possibly found wanting or wrong. Another reason for minimal resistance to therapy or the therapist is that it is amply clear to clients that they maintain control over the decisions and that there will be no subtle attempts by the therapist to steer decisions this way or that. The warmth and unconditional positive regard for the clients and the confidence the therapist shows in them are, we believe, other reasons for the general lack of this first type of resistance in a holistic, skill-training, humanistic therapy such as RE.

What about resistance to the therapy precisely because of some of its skill-training aspects? Frequently, non-RE therapists contemplating RE say that their clients would resist the idea of postponing work on serious problems for the first few hours of therapy while they learn the basic skills. We almost never encounter client resistance of that nature. If it is encountered, however, there are RE techniques—including the use of the "front-loaded" format mentioned earlier—for going to work immediately on serious problems when clients or therapists believe that they must not delay (Vogelsong & Guerney, 1982).

We now move on to consider the second type of resistance. First, we explore the question of resisting change out of fear that one will be placed at a disadvantage in relation to one's spouse. This type of resistance is quite infrequent in RE. We believe the reason for this is that every aspect of the process and of the skills are designed to assure that each person will be heard fully, be understood fully, and have his or her needs considered in depth by the spouse. The skills also are designed to assure that conflicts will be resolved in such a manner as to meet the needs of *both* members of the pair as much as possible. Thus, once clients have learned the guidelines for problem–conflict resolution and have been walked through the process by the therapist once or twice, they rarely fear being placed at a disadvantage by the therapeutic process.

One might think that such strong equalitarianism might in itself create resistance in those who hold a dominant position. That is, it is not surprising that clients who resented being dominated by the spouse experience a great sense of relief and satisfaction as a result of the equality achieved through the use of the RE skills they are learning; but what about a partner who previously had been successful in domineering? Theoretically, such a partner might resist the process to protect the "advantage." We have given considerable thought to the question of why this seldom happens. We think such resistance generally fails to arise because of the increased benefits the previously dominating partner quickly gains from the general improvement in the relationship. Such a partner is getting more of his or her own needs met as the skills are brought into play. It seems that most domineering partners are capable of seeing that by being more fair, they themselves gain more than they lose. Apparently, they generally feel the gains more than compensate for any loss of "advantage" in being domineering. Often, they did not recognize that they were perceived as unfair or domineering to begin with. It is not something they consciously desire to be, and this too allows them to give up this "advantage" with less resistance than we might have predicted. (If such resistance should occur, like other forms of resistance, it is handled by means of Troubleshooting, as described in the section on specific RE techniques.)

The third and fourth types of resistance—resistance through the use of defense mechanisms—are considered inevitable components of any therapeutic process. As we stated earlier, all RE skills are designed to reduce the arousal of such defense mechanisms. Also, the warm, empathic, nonjudgmental, and nonthreatening behavior of the therapist is seen as reducing the use of defense mechanisms. As we indicated in our discussion of theory, it is our belief that probing, indirect leads, questioning, interpretations, suggestions, advice, persuasion, and the like increase and strengthen defense mechanisms, and these techniques are therefore avoided. Also, as part of Expressive skill, clients learn introspective skills and learn to welcome—for the helpful information it provides—even negative expressions of feelings as long as such feelings are not acted out destructively. This acceptance of their own and their partner's inner realities, and the recognition that feelings need not be acted out, seems to reduce clients' defense mechanisms to comparatively low levels.

The fifth and last form of resistance is that of resisting work mainly because it's work. Clients definitely tend not to do their first one or two home assignments. This initial work resistance is so frequent in RE that we have come to consider it a natural part of the therapeutic process rather than a problem. When the therapist takes the appropriate steps, homework generally commences in earnest. These steps are careful structuring, getting commitments as to specific times and places for doing the homework, giving the clients tangible things (feedback, reports, tapes) to hand in, and mild troubleshooting exchanges.

In summary, the methods used for any and all types of resistance are Structuring, Doubling, or Troubleshooting (see section "RE-Appropriate Therapeutic Responses"). It might be reiterated here that Troubleshooting is used (infrequently) to make suggestions to clients that they discuss certain problems or issues. This is done in the course of the regular review of the Relationship Questionnaire, in which clients list discussion topics.

Application to Individual Problems

By individual problems, we refer to the problems of one spouse that seem to be neither attributable to, nor exacerbated by, the relationship between the couple. We feel that the potential of marital therapy to help resolve an individual's intrapsychic or behavioral problems generally has been underestimated, both by individually oriented therapists and by marital therapists.

The first reason underlying our belief that very often marital therapy can reduce individual intrapsychic problems is that we think that level of stress is a significant determinant of the degree to which individual problems manifest themselves. To that observation add the observation that stress level and marital adjustment are doubtless correlated fairly strongly. Thus, it seems reasonable that individual problems often can be ameliorated if the marriage relationship can be improved.

Second, we believe holistic marital therapy has great potential for helping clients with their individual problems in more specific ways. For example, in RE therapy clients are trained to be highly sensitive to the feelings and needs of the other partner and to be supportive of those needs. Indeed, participants are trained to help each other with their individual problems and, in effect, to administer client-centered therapy to one another under circumstances where only one partner has a problem (be it a situational problem, a behavioral problem, or an interpsychic problem).

Both empirical evidence (D'Augelli, Deyss, *et al.*, 1974) and much clinical experience indicate that with respect to variables that have been demonstrated to make an important difference in therapy outcome—empathy, warmth, and genuineness—the skill levels of couples trained in RE reach the level of the average professional counselor rather quickly. When a client is so trained, his or her spouse, in effect, has a trained client-centered therapist on call around the clock. Couples in RE also receive some training in skills based on behavior therapy; skills for self-change and for helping another to change. The client-centered skills help clients to help their spouses with feelings, attitudes, and decision making. Once a decision has been made about the direction of behavioral change desired (if any), clients can bring the behavior-changing behavior skills learned in RE therapy into play to help their spouse bring about those changes.

We have had many pleasant surprises about the extent to which RE marital therapy can help out with "individual" problems. Here is an example: Workers in an alcohol and drug counseling received 3 days of RE training. As a result, they decided to introduce the methods within their agency to replace the kind of nonholistic marital work they had been doing. They were able to get every single spouse to attend the RE sessions regularly. In the first 20 cases that have gone at least 2 months past therapy termination, they have not had a single instance of relapse in drug or alcohol abstinence. In a similar span of time before introduction of RE, they estimate that by this time the relapse rate in the group would have been about 50% (P. Matter & W. MacAllister, personal communication, 1983).

We hypothesize that holistic, skill-training, enrichment-oriented therapies will prove to be of even greater benefit than other marital approaches appear to be in helping "individual" problems. We refer to problems ranging from anxiety reaction through depression to helping prevent schizophrenics from relapsing and requiring rehospitalization.

The "Unmotivated" Client

A husband who does not wish to be "dragged in" or who "wants out" of the relationship, or a wife who is being court-referred for alcoholism, or a husband who is court-referred for spouse abuse, often seems to be "unmotivated." We put the word in quotes because the "unmotivated" client certainly is not unmotivated in general, and he or she may or may not be unmotivated to change in the desired direction; in fact, what he or she is unmotivated to do is to take on the particular client role that the therapist has in mind. And, in our view, therapy cannot proceed efficiently and effectively until the client *becomes* motivated; that is, wants to take on the type of client role the therapist feels he or she should.

Almost all therapists seem to feel put out about having to stimulate and arouse motivation in clients. This too probably is, in part, a hangover from the medical model. When patients come to physicians for treatment, they usually feel terrible and are greatly worried. They are, for sure, highly motivated to assume whatever position the physician desires them to assume. Those who operate within the medical model come to expect this and to feel resentful when clients are "unmotivated" to assume the position the therapist prefers.

Good teachers, on the other hand, always look on motivating the student as simply the first and foremost part of their daily job. That is how the issue is viewed by the holistic, RE therapist. Motivating *all* clients is the number-one task. What's more, *keeping* them motivated is always task number two. Both often are not easy. The trick is to find out what the clients *want* and what they do *not want* for themselves, and then to show them that the things you wish to teach them will help them to get what they want and avoid what they do not want. This is done by all the means mentioned in the section on therapist skills.

When all else fails, the RE therapist simply tries to get the client to willingly "go through the motions" as an experiment for X minutes, hours, or weeks. The therapist then strives mightily to see to it that the experiences the client has during that "X" period are positive enough to convince the client that there is everything to gain and nothing to lose by learning the skills. We believe RE is, comparatively speaking, extremely successful in holding and helping "unmotivated" clients, and we attribute that to the advantages of a skill-training, holistic approach as earlier outlined.

CONCLUDING COMMENT

We believe that with respect to complex interpersonal relationships, it can be accepted as a psychological–behavioral law that people work harder, learn better, and are far less resistant and deceptive when they are striving to achieve positive goals than when merely striving to avoid pain. The proposed adaptation of this law to marital therapy is as follows: *The acquisition of skills and positive marital experiences—as opposed to the simple elimination of pain—greatly strengthens client motivation and learning and therefore enhances the effectiveness of marital therapy.*

REFERENCES

Avery, A. W., Ridley, C. A., Leslie, L. A., & Milholland, T. (1980). Relationship Enhancement with premarital dyads: A six-month follow-up. *American Journal of Family Therapy, 8*, 23–30.

Brock, G. W., & Joanning, H. (1983). A comparison of the Relationship Enhancement program and the Minnesota Couple Communication program. *Journal of Marital and Family Therapy, 9*(4), 413–421.

Collins, J. D. (1977). Experimental evaluation of a six-month Conjugal therapy and Relationship Enhancement program. In B. G. Guerney, Jr. (Ed.), *Relationship Enhancement: Skill-training programs for therapy, problem prevention, and enrichment.* San Francisco: Jossey-Bass.

D'Augelli, A. R., Deyss, C. S., Guerney, B. G., Jr., Hershenberg, B., & Sborofsky, S. (1974). Interpersonal skill training for dating couples: An evaluation of an educational mental health service. *Journal of Counseling Psychology, 21*(5), 385–389.

Dollard, J., & Miller, N. E. (1950). *Personality and psychotherapy.* New York: McGraw-Hill.

Ely, A., Guerney, B. G., Jr., & Stover, L. (1973). Efficacy of the training phase of conjugal therapy. *Psychotherapy: Theory, Research, and Practice, 10*(3), 201–207.

Fisher, B. L., Giblin, P. R., & Hoopes, M. H. (1982). Healthy family functioning: What therapists say and what families want. *Journal of Marital and Family Therapy, 8*, 273–285.

Goldstein, A. (1973). *Structured learning therapy: Toward a psychotherapy for the poor.* New York: Academic Press.

Guerney, B. G., Jr. (1977a). *Relationship Enhancement: Skill training programs for therapy, problem prevention, and enrichment.* San Francisco: Jossey-Bass.

Guerney, B. G., Jr. (1977b) Should teachers treat illiteracy, hypocalligraphy, and dysmathematica? *Canadian Counselor, 12*(1), 9–14.

Guerney, B. G., Jr. (1982a). The delivery of mental health services: Spiritual vs. medical vs. educational models. In T. R. Vallance & R. Sabre (Eds.), *Mental health services in transition: A policy sourcebook.* New York: Human Sciences Press.

Guerney, B. G., Jr. (1982b). Relationship Enhancement. In E. K. Marshall & P. D. Kurtz (Eds.), *Interpersonal helping skills.* San Francisco: Jossey-Bass.

Guerney, B. G., Jr. (1984). Relationship Enhancement therapy and training. In D. Larson (Ed.), *Teaching psychological skills: Models for giving psychology away.* Monterey, CA: Brooks/Cole.

Guerney, B. G., Jr., Vogelsong, E., & Coufal, J. (1983). Relationship Enhancement versus a traditional treatment: Follow-up and booster effects. In D. H. Olsen & B. C. Miller (Eds.), *Family studies review yearbook.* Beverly Hills: Sage.

Jessee, R., & Guerney, B. G., Jr. (1981). A comparison of Gestalt and Relationship Enhancement treatments with married couples. *American Journal of Family Therapy, 9*, 31–41.

Leary, T. (1957). *Interpersonal diagnosis of personality.* New York: Ronald Press.

Preston, J., & Guerney, B. G., Jr. (1982). *Relationship Enhancement skill training.* University Park, PA: Individual and Family Consultation Center. Xeroxed.

Rappaport, A. F. (1976). Conjugal Relationship Enhancement program. In D. H. Olsen (Ed.), *Treating relationships* (pp. 41–66). Lake Mills, Iowa: Graphic Publishing.

Ridley, C. A., Jorgensen, S. R., Morgan, A. C., & Avery, A. W. (1982). Relationship Enhancement with premarital couples: An assessment of effects on relationship quality. *American Journal of Family Therapy, 10*, 41–48.

Ross, E. R., Baker, S. B., & Guerney, B. G., Jr. (1985). Effectiveness of Relationship Enhancement therapy versus therapist's preferred therapy. *American Journal of Marital and Family Therapy. 13*(1). 11–21.

Shannon, J., & Guerney, B. G., Jr. (1973). Interpersonal effects of interpersonal behavior. *Journal of Personality and Social Psychology, 26*, 142–150.

Sullivan, H. S. (1953). *The interpersonal theory of psychiatry.* New York: Norton.

Vogelsong, E. L., & Guerney, B. G., Jr. (1980). Working with parents of disturbed adolescents. In R. R. Abidin (Ed.), *Parent education and intervention handbook.* Springfield, IL: Charles C Thomas.

Vogelsong, E., & Guerney, B. G., Jr. (1982). Relationship Enhancement in clinical practice. *American Journal of Family Therapy, 10,* 73–77.

Vogelsong, E., Guerney, B. G., Jr., & Guerney, L. F. (1983). Relationship Enhancement therapy with inpatients and their families. In R. Luber & C. Anderson (Eds.), *Communication training approaches to family intervention with psychiatric patients.* New York: Human Sciences Press.

Waldo, M., & Guerney, B. G., Jr. (1983). Dyadic marital Relationship Enhancement therapy in the treatment of alcoholism. *Journal of Marital and Family Therapy, 9*(3), 321–323.

Wieman, R. J. (1973). *Conjugal relationship modification and reciprocal reinforcement: A comparison of treatments for marital discord.* Unpublished doctoral dissertation, Pennsylvania State University.

Prevention

HOWARD J. MARKMAN
FRANK J. FLOYD
SCOTT M. STANLEY
HAL C. LEWIS

7

The purpose of this chapter is to present a rationale and methodology for working with couples who are planning marriage in order to reduce the occurrence of relationship distress and dissolution after marriage. According to current divorce-rate data (e.g., Glick & Norton, 1976) about 4 of 10 first marriages will end in divorce. This alarming figure, in human terms, means an enormous amount of personal distress, disruption and dislocation of lives, vulnerability to physical and mental disorders, and growing strain on social institutions (Markman, Floyd, & Dickson-Markman, 1982). An even gloomier picture is provided by Mace and Mace (1980), who estimate that among marriages that do not end in divorce, 50% are not happy marriages and only 10% of all marriages reach their full potential. The traditional response to these problems, represented by the majority of the chapters in this book, is treatment for distressed couples. An alternative approach is to intervene with preventive programs before problems develop.

Preventive intervention currently receives inadequate attention from marital therapists and treatment agencies. Instead, the clergy and church- or synagogue-affiliated groups almost exclusively assume responsibility for providing preventive services to couples. These services typically are limited to educating couples about maintaining religious practices in the home and providing guidance and advice about current problems or anticipated future problems as uniquely expressed by each couple (see Markman *et al.*, 1982). In contrast, the preventive intervention that we describe represents a more

Howard J. Markman, Scott M. Stanley, and Hal C. Lewis. Department of Psychology, University of Denver, Denver Center for Marital and Family Studies, Denver, Colorado.
Frank J. Floyd. Illinois Institute of Technology.

generic approach. It focuses on issues that are relevant to all marital relationships, attempting to alter relationship behaviors and beliefs that generally are associated with the development of marital problems and distress.

Preventive interventions with couples must be clearly distinguished from both marital treatment and relationship enhancement. Unlike treatment, prevention intervenes with couples *before* any symptoms of relationship distress develop. Preventive intervention is future oriented and only indirectly addresses any current difficulties premarital couples may be experiencing. Similarly, although prevention programs intend to enhance the relationships of couples who are already experiencing relatively high levels of relationship satisfaction, this activity is directed toward the goal of preventing future problems. In a sense, all interventions that enhance couples' current relationships probably serve a preventive function, and relationship enhancement can be considered as one form of preventive intervention. However, prevention also includes interventions that may be of little value to couples currently, but are designed to help them in the future. A wide range of preventive intervention programs have been established and preliminarily investigated. These programs vary broadly in terms of theoretical orientation and focus of intervention (see Markman, Floyd, & Dickson-Markman, 1982, for a review). In the present chapter we focus on the approach to preventive intervention with *premarital* couples established at the University of Denver's Center for Marital and Family Studies.

THEORETICAL FRAMEWORK

Our rationale for working with couples before they are married is partially based on family developmental theory. The family life cycle as a framework for viewing family development and family transition across the life span has been receiving increased attention from both family researchers and family therapists (Carter & McGoldrick, 1980; Duvall, 1977; Haley, 1972; Lewis, 1984; Napier, 1980; and Nock, 1979). Delineation of the tasks and transitions that families face as they negotiate a course through life can contribute to a better understanding of healthy, growth-inducing family functioning, as well as unhealthy, growth-inhibiting family functioning. We focus on one segment of the family life cycle, the transition to marriage, as a critical period in family development and an opportune target for preventive clinical efforts. This focus reflects our belief that the transition to marriage is a precedent-setting stage entailing a number of complex developmental tasks, the successful resolution of which may lay the foundation for future family development and growth (see Lewis, 1984, for details). In contrast, incomplete or maladaptive resolution of the transition to marriage may set a pattern for future disturbance and problematic family functioning.

The manner in which this early phase of the family life cycle is handled may have far-reaching consequences for the psychological adjustment of both children and parents. If the transition to marriage is poorly resolved, then the couple may look to the birth and development of a child as a means to stabilize their relationship, to derive personal satisfactions that have not been found in the marital relationship, or to divert attention away from interpersonal issues with which the marital relationship is unprepared to cope. Such triangulation processes (Bowen, 1978) may continue in varying degrees throughout the child's lifetime, having deleterious effects on the child's development and mental health. This phenomenon has led family theorists to examine the generational transmission of psychological problems and to propose that a vast majority of mental health problems are multi-generational in nature (Bowen, 1978; McGoldrick, 1980; Paul & Paul, 1975; Terkelsen, 1980).

Placing the Transition to Marriage within a Model of the Family Life Cycle

A model of the family life cycle within which the transition to marriage can be located is presented in Figure 7-1. This model is a synthesis of concepts from many sources, including Lewis (1984), McGoldrick (1980), and Carter and McGoldrick (1980).

The general thrust of this model indicates that the family life cycle can be thought of as a developmental track. This track is hazardous in the sense that change and adjustment are periodically required by horizontal stressors. These horizontal stressors are either predictable family transition phases or unexpected external events such as an untimely death, natural disaster, or sudden economic setback. Because of such hazards, the family developmental track is bumpy, and derailment from the track is frequent. Derailment (as depicted by the slanted arrow) can occur at any point along the developmental track and will generally lead to family distress, may lead to individual pathology, and will make it much more difficult for the family to progress along the developmental track.

An important influence on a family's progression along the developmental track is the relative balance of family resources versus family liabilities, or, as represented in the model, vertical supports versus vertical stressors. The vertical stressors tend to make it more difficult for the family to negotiate successfully the developmental track, whereas the vertical supports tend to facilitate successful passages along the track. Lewis (1984) identifies four levels of vertical stressors and supports. These are (a) social system influences such as level of social support, qualities of the social environment, effects of political–economic and social issues such as sex-role shifts, employment patterns, effects of changing attitudes toward marriage, divorce, and parenting; (b) transgenerational influences such as residual parent–child issues, in-law issues, multigenerational family myths, attitudes, behavior patterns, and the like; (c) elements of the evolving nuclear family system such as level of family cohesion, level of family adaptability, communication–interaction

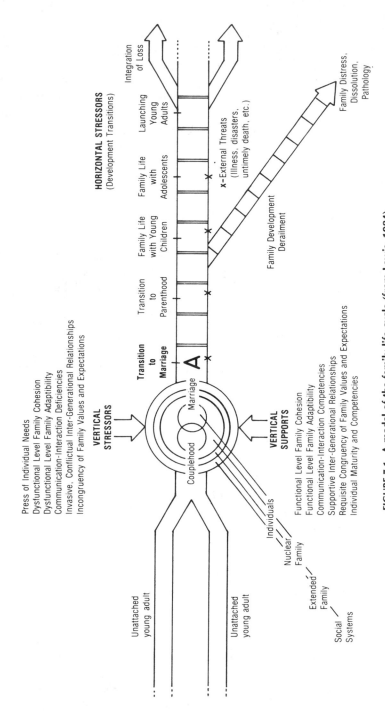

FIGURE 7-1. A model of the family life cycle (from Lewis, 1984).

patterns, behavioral expectations and compatibility of such expectations; and (d) individual personality components such as interpersonal maturity, degree of self-differentiation, and various behavioral competencies. Factors at various levels may have reciprocal influences on one another. For instance, intergenerational interferences may affect patterns of communication in the nuclear family, or societal pressures may influence the level of adaptability in the family. Individual personality factors and relational dynamics or systems components may influence each other reciprocally. If the vertical stressors heavily outbalance the vertical supports, then pressure will be exerted on the family toward derailment. If this occurs at a point when horizontal stressors are intensified, then derailment will become much more likely; that is, if a preponderance of vertical stressors converge on a point of horizontal stress, then the family system is likely to break down and become dysfunctional in some respects. Further, if the horizontal stressors are extensive enough, almost any family will appear dysfunctional, at least temporarily. Frequently, the very responses that lead to short-term relief of distress and anxiety caused by horizontal stressors (e.g., triangulation, denial, scapegoating) subsequently become vertical stressors that contribute to future problems.

Tasks of the Transition to Marriage

Figure 7-1 graphically depicts the pivotal position (point A) of the transition to marriage phase within the family life cycle. The newly formed couple is embarking on a journey along the developmental track with few guarantees of eventual outcome. Horizontal stressors are immediately encountered in the form of the developmental tasks that inhere in the transition to marriage. We can describe at least six such developmental tasks that immediately confront the couple and may set a tone for future marital and family functioning. These are

1. To develop and engage in constructive communication and conflict resolution skills
2. To develop realistic, constructive, compatible attitudes and expectations regarding relationship and marriage
3. To develop behavioral–interaction patterns that satisfy the basic emotional and psychological needs of each partner
4. To move toward one another (and sometimes away from their families of origin) as primary sources of gratification and anxiety reduction
5. To develop constructive mechanisms for regulating closeness–distance and dependency–independency (cohesion) within the relationship
6. To develop constructive mechanisms for regulating the pace and path of change (adaptability) within the relationship

As the list makes clear, the couple in the transition to marriage phase is presented with an imposing array of developmental tasks. It is virtually impossible to overestimate how complex and demanding these tasks are. Unless the sum of vertical supports on all four levels (i.e., social environmental, transgenerational, interpersonal, and intrapersonal) is greater than the sum of vertical stressors, it is unlikely that the couple will have much success accomplishing these transitional tasks. Thus, our rationale for a preventive approach presumes the stressfulness and fluidity of the transition to marriage as normative and strives to create "buffers" (social supports, interactional competencies, relationship enhancement techniques, and the like) that will help the evolving couple remain on a healthy, growth-promoting developmental track.

Viewed this way, the transition to marriage period is a time of relationship crisis, with "crisis" defined as a period of change and flux when previous responses and solutions to problems are no longer appropriate or effective (Caplan, 1964). At this time the relationship is less crystallized and less resistant to change than it either has been in the past or will be in the future after marital roles, rules, and patterns of interaction become entrenched. This transition period is, thus, an opportune time to intervene by helping couples learn attitudes and behaviors that contribute to adaptive adjustment in the short run and enhance their ability to cope with new relationship stressors in the long run. While we recognize that we cannot intervene at every level of vertical support (e.g., without a more in-depth approach, we cannot hope to alter significantly individual maturity levels or transgenerational issues), there are several types of relationship competencies and supports that we believe can be bolstered effectively. The specifics of an intensive preventive program that reflects the above theoretical position are presented in the pages that follow.

INTERVENTION MODEL

In contrast to most prevention programs for couples developed on the basis of common sense and clinical intuitions, we have based the content of our program on the above theoretical model and empirical foundations laid by cross-sectional and longitudinal research on relationships. In particular we incorporate into our program the results of research conducted within the cognitive–behavioral tradition (see Markman *et al.*, 1982, for details of our prevention model). These findings indicate that dysfunctional interaction patterns *precede* the development of relationship dissatisfaction and that early signs of impending distress are potentially recognizable in premarital interaction, *independent* of the couples' premarital relationship satisfaction and problems (Markman, 1979, 1981). Other studies show that once dysfunctional interaction patterns form, they are hard to modify (Raush, Barry, Hertel, & Swain, 1974). The fact that communication deficits may be apparent *before* marriage suggests that premarital couples might benefit from training in skills usually taught in marital therapy early in their relationship as a prevention strategy, rather than wait until severe marital conflict develops. Put succinctly, our distillation of relevant research suggests three main foci for an effective and comprehensive preventive program. These are (a) the development and guided practice of constructive communication and conflict resolution skills; (b) the clarification and modification of relationship beliefs and expections; and (c) the expansion of sexual–sensual knowledge and attitudes.

THE PREMARITAL RELATIONSHIP ENHANCEMENT PROGRAM

The Premarital Relationship Enhancement Program (PREP) is a cognitive–behaviorally oriented intervention for couples who have made a commitment to marry in the near future. The program was originally designed for couples who are marrying for the first time, although it is also applicable to remarital couples. We have recently begun to consider the special issues of previously married couple members, such as integrating children from a previous marriage into a new family system. Derived from a behavior–competency model of marital success, PREP views happily married couples as possessing competencies (i.e., communication and problem-solving skills) that less successful couples lack (Markman et al., 1982). The program helps premarital couples develop these competencies before marriage to increase the probability that they will achieve successful marriages. Further, by providing the couples with success experiences in solving low-conflict relationship problems, we hope to increase their confidence in their ability to solve more serious problems in the future. Notarius and Vanzetti (1984) demonstrate that increased relationship efficacy, defined as confidence in solving problems, is positively related to relationship satisfaction for married couples.

Over the past 7 years the program has been implemented and evaluated with several cohorts of couples. Initial versions of the procedure are presented in earlier publications (Markman & Floyd, 1980; Markman, Floyd, Stanley, & Jamieson, 1984). Evaluation data have indicated that intervention, as compared to control couples, demonstrated increased communication skills and relationship satisfaction immediately after the program. At 1- and 3-year follow-ups, the intervention couples, compared to no-treatment control couples, not only maintain these gains but also increase their relationship satisfaction and communication quality. The short-term findings have been replicated recently by Blew and Trapold (1982). Several factors have led us to modify the PREP model continually. These factors include (a) our increased experience working with premarital couples; (b) the growth in the field of cognitive–behavioral interventions with couples to encompass a wider range of relationship dimensions; and (c) the accretion of new research and treatment-outcome data. Below we present the most recent version of PREP. More detailed descriptions, as well as training materials, are available from the authors.

Areas of Intervention

COMMUNICATION AND CONFLICT-RESOLUTION SKILLS TRAINING

This area is the largest component of the PREP program because competency in marital interactional skills is the most widely documented factor associated with marital success. Studies comparing the interactions of distressed and nondistressed married couples repeatedly demonstrate that happily married couples exhibit more positive communication skills than distressed couples (Birchler, Weiss, & Vincent, 1975), that they evaluate the impact of their interactions more positively (Floyd & Markman, 1983; Gottman, Notarius, Markman, Bank, Yoppi, & Rubin, 1976), and that they engage in fewer destructive patterns of interaction (Gottman, Markman, & Notarius, 1977; Revenstorf, Hahlweg, & Schindler, 1984). More important, longitudinal studies indicate that couples' interactional styles remain stable from early in marriage to 5 years later (Raush et al., 1974) and that satisfying premarital interactions predict future marital satisfaction (Markman, 1979, 1981).

The effectiveness of communication training for couples is documented by a large body of treatment-outcome studies with distressed married couples (see Jacobson, 1978, for a review). Additionally, recent outcome data from premarital communication-based interventions show promising results. Our own data, reviewed earlier, indicate that premarital couples who complete the PREP program exhibit more positive communication skills following intervention than do control couples (Markman, Jamieson, & Floyd, 1983) and experience higher levels of relationship satisfaction 1 and 3 years after intervention (Markman, 1982). A pre–post evaluation study by Blew and Trapold (1982) compared communication training with an attention placebo condition. The results indicate that although the premarital couples in both conditions demonstrated increased relationship satisfaction as they moved closer to marriage, only couples who received the communication training showed increased satisfaction with their interactions. These findings suggest that communication training is an important, effective component of intervention for altering high-risk destructive interactions.

COGNITIVE RESTRUCTURING

The PREP program includes interventions designed to alter couples' cognitions that may interfere with their engaging in positive interactional exchanges. The development and refinement of this component draws on emerging data indicating that irrational relationship beliefs and destructive attributional sets are associated with marital distress (e.g., Eidelson & Epstein, 1981). Further, an outcome study by Margolin and Weiss (1978) suggests that intervention is more effective when couples are instructed to focus on their interactional behaviors and attribute relationship problems to faulty interactions. Our own data with premarital couples have preliminarily confirmed this finding. An investigation of the congruity between couples' and objective assessments of interaction (Floyd, 1983) indicates that couple members who are relatively more reactive (or responsive) to their partners' communication skills have more positive outcomes following intervention. As yet, however, we have only begun to examine how cognitions change as a result of intervention. Ongoing research on marital expectations, beliefs, and attributions in relation to couples intervention (e.g., Baucom, 1981) should lead to further refinements of our intervention techniques.

SENSUAL–SEXUAL ENHANCEMENT

The rationale for focusing on sexuality is simply that sexual functioning is an important component of all marital relationships, yet couples receive little anticipatory guidance in this area. Preliminary data (Rosenthal, Floyd, & Markman, 1981) suggest that we are able to increase couple members' knowledge of human sexual functioning, and decrease misconceptions, without intruding on their moral beliefs.

Screening and Assessment

The PREP program is designed as a primary preventive intervention that is appropriate for all couples who are planning marriage. Thus there is no need to screen for specific types of couples or specific relationship problem areas. Nevertheless, the intervention is most effective for couples who meet two general criteria. First, the couple members should have a strong commitment to the stability of the relationship, with clear intentions to marry in the near future. Dating couples who have not made such a commitment will be less responsive to the future orientation of the program and probably will be less likely to follow through on homework assignments. Second, PREP is not designed to treat couples who are experiencing major, current relationship problems. These couples are referred to treatment agencies for a more individualized, problem-focused intervention.

Assessment procedures are used primarily to specify the emphasis of the individualized meetings with the paraprofessional consultants who work with each couple. For example, if a couple exhibit a relatively high rate of negative verbal and nonverbal expressions prior to intervention, the consultant may emphasize the use of editing skills during the individualized communication training sessions. We conduct comprehensive, multidimensional pre- and post-intervention assessments, as well as multiple follow-up assessments, for basic research purposes and to guide modification of the intervention program (see Markman et al., 1983). In more applied settings such extensive assessment procedures would not be necessary. The most important assessment procedures are summarized below.

1. *Relationship satisfaction and areas of agreement–disagreement.* A premarital version of the Locke–Wallace Marital Adjustment Test (Locke & Wallace, 1959), called the Premarital Adjustment Test (PMAT; Markman,

1979), is used to assess the overall level of relationship satisfaction for each couple member. This instrument also provides information about relationship areas in which couple members perceive themselves as agreeing or disagreeing (e.g., finances, displays of affection). This information is supplemented by couples' responses to a problem inventory (Knox, 1971), on which couple members rate the magnitude of each of 10 commonly experienced relationships problem areas and add other problem areas not included in the list.

2. *Communication proficiency.* Both subjective and objective assessments of problem-solving interactional skills are obtained. Couple members employ the Communication Box (Markman & Floyd, 1980) to evaluate the impact of each other's statements while interacting. In settings where this apparatus is not available, paper-and-pencil measures of interaction (e.g., Snyder, 1979) may be a useful alternative method for obtaining similar information. Videotaped samples of the couples' interactions are also evaluated with the CISS objective observational measure (Notarius & Markman, 1981). We developed the Communication Skills Test (CST; Floyd and Markman, 1984) as an objective economical alternative to CISS ratings for use in applied settings. The CST enables an evaluation of the verbal and nonverbal communication proficiency displayed by couple members (based on a five-point rating scale applied to microsegments of interaction samples).

3. *Relationship beliefs and expectations.* The Marital Expectation Form (Markman, 1977) is used to evaluate expectations about children, careers, and role responsibilities.

4. *Sexual knowledge and attitudes.* Subscales of the Sex Knowledge and Attitudes Test (Leif & Reid, 1972) provide information about the couple members' sexual knowledge, attitudes toward sexual relations and auto-eroticism, and sexual misconceptions.

Program Format

The PREP program occurs in five 2-hour sessions that take place weekly over a 5-week period. Several components are present in each session: lectures, work with consultants, homework, and homework review. Typically, schedules are arranged so that three or four couples participate in the program together. In most cases two paraprofessional consultants work with each couple (see section on therapist factors for details). The couples meet as a group for the lecture portions of the sessions, but meet alone with their consultants for all other aspects of each session.

The first two sessions of the program deal primarily with communication skills training. The third session focuses on problem-solving skills and negotiation patterns. The fourth session is designed to help the participants make a detailed examination of their relationship expectations. Finally, the last session focuses on sexual education, sexual communication, and enhancement.

Much of the material covered in the lectures of the program is also covered in a book, A *Couples Guide to Communication* (Gottman, Notarius, Gonso, & Markman, 1976). Couples are given a copy of this book in the first session. At the end of each session a homework assignment is given. Many of the homework assignments involve reading material and doing exercises from this book. Feedback from participants indicates that this book is written on a practical, understandable level and is very readable and applicable to couples' lives.

Program Content by Session

SESSION 1

When the couples arrive, they are warmly greeted and introduced to the consultants who will be working with them. As soon as all the couples have arrived and are comfortable, the first lecture of the program is delivered. This lecture covers two primary areas: (a) the philosophy and goals of the program; and (b) the definition of many of the communications skills taught in the program.

The goals, explained in educational terms, include teaching communication skills, teaching problem-solving skills, helping participants gain awareness of their relationship expectations, and educating the couples about human sexuality and communication about sexual issues. A focus on the relationship rather than the individuals is stressed, and partners are encouraged to view their relationship as an interdependent system. Emphasis is placed on the fact that all couples have problems and on the notion that it is *how* these problems are dealt with that differentiates happy couples from unhappy couples. Finally, the rationale for relationship enhancement and prevention of relationship problems is discussed.

To facilitate the teaching of communication skills, a model of communication is presented. The "speaker" is defined as the one who has a message to convey, and the "listener" is designated as the one to receive that message. Good communication is defined as when the speaker's intended message equals the impact that it has on the listener (except in cases where the speaker's intent is specifically aimed at harming the listener). Within this model, a variety of speaking and listening communication skills are presented, both nonverbal (good eye contact, body posture, and voice tone) and verbal (speaking for self, expressing feelings, staying on the topic, paraphrasing and summarizing, checking out the intent of the message with the speaker, avoiding mindreading, and stopping negative interchanges). Obviously, these communication skills should be useful in premarital and marital relationships, but some couple members have also reported generalizing these skills to other settings, such as the workplace. Here is what one man had to say during a follow-up interview a year after participating in the PREP program:

> Communication is so important that it is taken for granted. You never take a course in communication, and it comes up constantly at work. I mean, the biggest excuse for failures in any kind of organization is communication breakdown, but nobody ever goes out and says, "If there are all these breakdowns, we should improve our communication."

A distinction between regular communication and problem-discussion communication is made. It is suggested that couples need to "engage their communication skills maximally" when discussing problems, but that during regular or free communication sequences a focus on using skills is not usually necessary.

A major goal of communication within our model is to understand and validate the partner's position (including thoughts, perceptions, and feelings). Toward this end, a distinction is drawn between problem discussion–clarification and problem solution–negotiation. We stress that an adequate phase of problem discussion, wherein each partner strives to understand (without trying to change) the other's view and feelings about the problem, is essential to achieving a satisfying, validating solution to significant problems. Problem solution should be attempted only after both partners fully understand the issue from both their own and their partner's perspective.

In the next phase of the first session the couples have an opportunity to exercise the skills discussed in the lecture. First, they discuss a neutral topic as poorly as they possibly can, doing the opposite of what has just been defined as good communication. This serves the dual purpose of facilitating the acquisition of the definitions of the skills and putting the couples at ease. Next, the couples observe a videotape of themselves discussing an issue (taped in an assessment session). With the consultant's help, they are able to identify both skills and deficits in this videotaped communication segment. The final exercise asks the couples to discuss a neutral issue again, but this time to employ as much skill as possible. Consultants attempt to point out what the couples are doing well and what they could try differently.

In the final part of the session the consultants go over the homework assignment with the couples. They are asked to read sections from A Couple's Guide to Communication (Chapters 1 and 2) covering the material discussed in the session and to do exercises from the book.

SESSION 2

When they return for the second session, the couples are asked about their reactions to the homework assignment. The next part of this session is spent in a lengthy videotape feedback session with consultants. This allows a much deeper analysis of their communication than was possible in the first session. With the consultants' assistance, each couple is encouraged to analyze and improve on the communication skills they observe on the videotape. Suggestions for improvement are forwarded and tried in the session. The videotape segment used in this task is of the couple discussing a problem in their relationship (again, recorded in an earlier assessment session). It is not unusual for couples to continue these discussions (begun on tape) and come to a more skillful and satisfying understanding of the issues involved. Almost all couples seem to find this sort of videotape work exciting, enriching, and powerfully educational. For example, the male in one couple going through the program found this exercise particularly enlightening. He had prided himself on his ability to communicate effectively, having routinely made comments to the effect that he used good communication skills such as those taught in the program. In watching the videotape, he was struck by a sequence wherein his partner tried to get her point across three times in a row (with building frustration and anger), while he assumed she was saying something quite different from what she intended to say. He was able to profit from this presentation and continue the discussion begun on the tape with his partner. He was able to validate her viewpoint, and they went on to reach a positive resolution of this problem.

The lecture in Session 2 is a presentation of communication skills that bear directly on the ability to discuss and resolve problems. For instance, we focus on the use of "XYZ statements," communicating what specific behavior (X), performed when (Y), resulted in what feeling (Z). Participants are shown how XYZ statements can be constructively used for expressing feedback about both positive and negative partner behaviors. Other skills covered are "editing" (politeness), "leveling" (constructive honesty), and how to monitor specific problem behaviors. In the last exercise of this session, couples work with their consultants on the skill of transforming global, nebulous negative statements into specific XYZ statements.

This skill is practiced by using global negative statements from A Couple's Guide to Communication to keep the exercise nonthreatening. The homework assignment requires couple members to read more about XYZ statements, leveling, and editing (Chapters 3 and 4). Each couple is asked to practice these skills at home.

SESSION 3

After a review and discussion of the homework assignment, couples practice expressing minor irritations in the XYZ format. Next, a brief lecture is delivered on the theme of problem-solving skills. The concepts of positive behavior change, behavioral contracting, and compromise are presented. Great emphasis is placed on the value of structure in problem solving. Specifically, it is suggested that, especially during stressful times, it is most advantageous to focus on use of the communication skills taught in the program. Structuring such processes with the use of skills increases the chances of good communication at times when anger or frustration would normally impede effective communication. To facilitate the development of good problem-solving skills, couples are taught to play a problem-solving board game (see Markman et al., 1984, for details). The steps of this board game correspond to the steps of successful problem solving the couples have learned in the program, namely, problem discussion, problem negotiation, compromise, and contracting. Couples play through the game twice, each time selecting a different problem they want to work on.

Couples usually view this game as an excellent device to aid in the consolidation of the skills taught in the program. One couple moved toward solving two of the most annoying, recurring problems in their relationship by playing this game with the facilitation of the consultants. Using the structure of the game, the female was able to discuss her concern about their sexual relationship. Through adequate problem discussion, each was able to understand the other's view of the problem, a process that was extremely validating for each partner. Subsequently, this couple were able to work out a way to solve the problem, and they left the session feeling confident that they would be able to work out future problems.

Another short lecture at the end of the third session introduces the topic and homework for the next session, which is designed to help the participants examine, in detail, their expectations for their relationships (see Sager, 1976). This preparatory lecture explains how persons have an array of relationship expectations at various levels. Some expectations are conscious and are expressed verbally to one's partner; other expectations are conscious, but have not been expressed; and some expectations are out of awareness and cannot be expressed. Couples are taught to see that all expectations affect their relationships in one form or another, regardless of whether these expectations are available to their current awareness or have been discussed yet between couple members.

The homework for this session is to complete a workbook (adapted from Sager, 1976) that encourages participants to consider various expectations they may or may not hold. The workbook is broken down into two segments: one examining expectations held about marriage and one examining expectations held about the needs and desires of the individual with respect to the relationship. The workbook lists common expectations or issues in these areas and stimulates participants to explore their expectations in these areas. The workbook encourages participants to indicate both the degree to which they are aware of various expectations, and which expectations have been directly expressed to their partner. Couple members are also asked to identify areas in which they feel they may have expectations of which they are not fully aware.

SESSION 4

Session 4 begins with a lecture on the concept of expectations and the effects they can have on a relationship. Couples again are told that all expectations have relationship effects and that such effects may be more negative when expectations are vaguely understood and poorly expressed. The fact that expectations can lead to disappointment and communication problems is discussed, with numerous examples from our experience and the couples' own experiences.

The remainder of Session 4 is spent having the couples discuss some of their expectations with the facilitation of their consultants. These discussions serve two purposes. First, the couples have an opportunity to explore the expectations they hold and how these may affect their relationships. Second, this process brings to light emotionally charged material that the couples can discuss using all of the communication skills they have learned in the program. The consultants attempt to facilitate this process with minimal input, allowing the couples to utilize and consolidate all of the communication skills covered. For example, here are excerpts from one couple's discussion of expectations they have for each other regarding chores. They start "mind-reading" (assuming that they know how their partner feels), a potential sign of trouble. They then recognize this and refocus their conversation in a way that allows them to reach a mutually satisfying decision concerning how to resolve this problem:

FEMALE: You expect me to be a maid.
MALE: No I don't.
FEMALE: Well, I was mad because you weren't doing anything and you saw I was making the bed and didn't care.
MALE: But I fully intended to do those chores later, after the football game was over.
FEMALE: But I didn't know how long I would have to wait.
MALE: Well, what we got going on in cases like this is a little mindreading. . . . I sort of had it all planned out but I didn't say anything to you. . . . I wanted you to sleep in. . . . I think it's definitely something that we need to talk about.

For homework, couples are asked to set aside a few hours for the purpose of continuing their discussion of expectations and to read Chapters 5 and 8 in the book. Reports from many couples who have set aside some special, uninterrupted time together for such discussions have been very positive. Couples often report that they experience a great degree of closeness and understanding through this type of structured interchange.

SESSION 5

After a brief discussion of the previous week's homework and interaction, a lecture aimed at sexual education, enhancement, and the prevention of sexual problems is delivered. The lecture covers the human sexual response, sex differences, sexual dysfunction, birth control, and various perspectives on sensuality. One of the key emphases in this lecture (and group discussion) is that communication skills are very important in sexual intimacy and satisfaction and that many of the same concepts and principles that apply to other communication settings apply here as well. A slide projector is used throughout this lecture to aid in the presentation of the material.

After this lecture, the couples practice a sensate-focusing communication exercise on a nonsexual body area (e.g., a hand). This exercise helps couple members to see the value of specific, direct feedback in sexual communication.

The final part of this session is allocated to reviewing the couples' overall experience in the PREP program. Couple members' subjective reactions to various aspects of the program are solicited, and personal feelings regarding the ending of the program and the consultant–participant relationship are exchanged. Ways in which material mastered during the PREP experience may serve the evolving relationship are anticipated and reinforced.

THERAPIST FACTORS

One feature of PREP that distinguishes it from most treatment programs for couples is the use of both professional and paraprofessional staff to implement the program. Duties are divided among professional and para-professional staff in order to make the program more economical for delivery to a large number of couples. A professional staff member is needed to deliver the lectures, direct discussion, and answer questions in the group meetings, and to provide supervision for the paraprofessional consultants. The paraprofessionals (consultants) are responsible for conducting sessions with an assigned couple, including guiding couples through in-session exercises and reviewing homework assignments.

Program consultants have come from a variety of backgrounds, including graduate and undergraduate students in psychology, counseling, speech communication, and nursing. Each consultant must be thoroughly familiar with the material covered in the program and, if lacking previous experience, must be trained to use effective facilitative interviewing skills for working with couples. The consultants receive intensive training, comprised of in-doctrination in the goals and philosophy of the program, education about specific communication skills and other content areas of the program, and training in the role and techniques of communication-skills consultation. We have found that consultants can be trained adequately with as little as 20 hours of didactic and role-play instruction, supplemented by reading assignments. Also, although the consultants must be closely supervised by the professional group leader, one leader can efficiently direct a group of up to six couples. The division of duties thus makes PREP a viable program for use in service agencies where costly professional staff time is scarce, or in community settings such as church groups where volunteers can serve as paraprofessional consultants.

Three broad therapist (consultant) attributes distinguish our intervention model. The most important of these factors is a competency orientation toward intervention. Our leaders and consultants are most effective when they are able to maintain a consistent focus on expanding couple members' competencies in the program's targeted skill areas. Some couples are eager to talk about either limitations in their relationship or personal problem areas, and even experienced therapists may be tempted to begin treating these problems as they are identified. Doing so is beyond the scope of the intervention program, however, and may produce deleterious effects for the couple member when identified problems are explored but cannot be resolved adequately within the limited time frame. We believe that although limitations can be identified in almost every relationship, a number of unacknowledged strengths can also be identified. Our staff is encouraged to maintain steadfastly a focus on helping the couple capitalize on these available competencies and learn new problem-solving strategies that can enhance the relationship without attempting to treat problems that may be present.

Group leaders and consultants are also trained to maintain a "process focus" throughout the program. The PREP program is designed to teach couples skills and attitudes that will help them adapt effectively to future relationship stressors. In order to accomplish this goal the intervention must focus on the process of the couples' interactions, attempting to enhance their general ability to cope with a wide range of stressors rather than merely focus on current stressors. For example, many couples experience disagreements about how to manage family members who are trying to influence them about upcoming wedding plans or about plans for financial expenditures. A solution to this problem may seem obvious to the consultant. Nevertheless, offering the couple advice about dealing with family members would not enhance the couple's own ability to resolve such disagreements and generate mutually satisfying solutions on their own. Instead, the consultant must direct his or her efforts to improving the manner in which the couple communicate about this topic, perhaps helping them begin to generate some rules for dealing with pressures from their family members. The consultant's ability to maintain this focus conveys the meta-message that it is unlikely that disagreement about any one issue will threaten the stability of the relationship. In certain stages of marital therapy, the therapist may find it necessary to advise the couple about a temporary solution to a conflict that has reached a standoff point. In our preventive program the need for immediate solutions is not present, and the consultant can take advantage of the opportunity to begin working on the *process* of the couples' interactions from the outset of intervention.

The third broad therapist characteristic involves adopting a teacher–consultant role in relation to the couple members. In view of the relatively brief time for intervention, couples are discouraged from becoming dependent on the consultant or group leader for help in discussing important relationship issues or resolving conflicts. After instructing couples about the skills presented in the program, the staff member's task is to encourage and support the independent use of the skills and the incorporation of these skills into each couple's customary style of interacting. This supportive function is accomplished in the context of a consultative relationship, where couples assume primary responsibility for experimenting with new methods of interacting and consultants help clarify and resolve any difficulties they may experience in doing so. To this end, consultants are taught to work for relationship change in the specific, limited target areas of such a psychoeducational program. Specifically, they are trained to teach couples the skills covered in the program and to facilitate each couple's ability to use these skills.

In addition to these three characteristics, the group leader's and consultant's basic relationship-building skills are crucial, just as in treatment settings. In their review of marital and family therapy outcome research, Gurman and Kniskern (1978) conclude that the therapist's ability to establish a positive, supportive relationship with clients is the single therapist factor that is most consistently associated with positive therapy outcomes. This also holds for behavioral interventions (Barton & Alexander, 1981). As discussed, structural aspects of the therapist's role in premarital prevention differ from more traditional treatment approaches; nevertheless, the couples' receptiveness to preventive intervention is probably largely determined by their acceptance of the group leaders and consultants as understanding, caring, and genuine. Unfortunately, the quality of the client–therapist relationship, as well as other therapist characteristics associated with PREP, has not yet received empirical attention. We hope that future research will help clarify and refine many of the clinical impressions presented here.

CLINICAL ISSUES

The issues covered in this section are unique to preventive and enhancement programs. There are obviously other clinical issues that we face in our prevention work with couples; however, these issues are not distinct from the issues faced by other cognitive–behaviorally oriented therapists. The reader is referred to other chapters in the book for a discussion of these issues.

Deterioration Effects

Many couples enter prevention programs feeling very good about their relationship, although they may be "at risk" for future distress. Prevention programs must be particularly concerned with the potential negative effects (deterioration effects) that might be associated with interventions. While deterioration effects are of concern to all intervention programs (Gurman & Kniskern, 1978), they are particularly problematic under conditions where the couple is feeling good about their relationship at the start of the program. For example, Gurman (1980) argued that premarital intervention that "teaches couples how to express directly their doubts and disatisfaction" (p. 93) is dangerous because it directly attacks the development of idealization that is a critical developmental prerequisite for couples to manage successfully the transition to marriage stage. We have responded to this critique in detail elsewhere (Markman, Jamieson, & Floyd, 1983), pointing to the empirical data suggesting that (a) the program does not negatively impact on idealization; (b) the couples in the program do not show negative short-term and long-term effects; (c) couples who do not receive the program do show deterioration over time that is consistent with normal developmental trends for couples during the early stages of marriage. Even though couples may experience an increase in conflict, the intervention seems to channel this experience in a positive manner. For example, Blew and Trapold (1982) suggested that raising conflict-laden issues in a couples assessment may produce negative outcomes for untreated couples. Couples who also received intervention following the assessment, however, failed to show any negative effects. Nevertheless, we continue to be vigilant to the issues raised here, and feel that it is an important ethical responsibility to monitor continually the potential for raising problems that couples have not previously experienced.

Motivation

One of the most frustrating clinical issues in our prevention work concerns the *motivation* of premarital couples to take advantage of the preventive interventions that we have to offer. Unfortunately, the couples who need the intervention most seem to be those who are least receptive to the program. Although 95% of the couples who have been solicited for PREP initially expressed interest, only 50% eventually completed the program. Examination of the "completers" versus "decliners" indicated few clear differences on measures of relationship functioning. However, interviews with these couples and subsequent research have suggested a few hypotheses. First, the major difference between the two groups may be their *commitment* to the marital relationship, with accepters having higher levels of commitment than decliners. Second, accepters may have relatively high levels of communication skills, which enable them to negotiate disagreements that seem to exist for most couples, concerning whether or not to participate in the program. Finally, since females are generally more willing to participate in the program, the differences in the male's level of commitment may be the key factor in terms of which couples take advantage of preventive intervention. Currently we are following up on these ideas by developing a measure of relationship commitment that includes an assessment of relationship priorities (Stanley & Markman, 1984).

On a more pragmatic level, in order to increase participation we have been obtaining ongoing feedback from couples concerning what were the most enjoyable and least enjoyable parts of the program. We have used this information to design changes in the program that attempt to increase the "hedonic relevance" of the program for the couple. At the same time, we have been cognizant of the need not to oversell a generally untested product (e.g., by telling couples that if they participate in the program, they will not experience marital or family problems). One of the challenges facing prevention programs is to work on techniques and strategies to communicate the potential benefits of the program to couples and to make the programs more widely available to couples. One strategy that we have used successfully is to disseminate programs to community agencies (e.g., religious institutions) that serve couples during the relevant transition periods.

Information Retention and Overload

In short-term skill-training programs such as ours, the potential problems of information overload and retention must be considered. Although this problem should be addressed by all intervention programs, most remain silent on the issue. In our program we attempt to enhance learning by using multiple methods to present information and by providing many opportunities (during the sessions and at home) to practice the new skills. Our research indicates that couples are learning the skills and will function better in the future than control couples will. Nevertheless, the question of how couples *best* learn and then make use of the information we provide should be addressed in the future.

Distressed Couples and Prevention

Finally, an important issue we have encountered is, What should be done for couples who seek out prevention programs when they appear to need therapy programs? Since we conduct rather extensive screening of our couples, we are usually able to discover the "distressed" couples who may need more than prevention. Nevertheless, our measures of "objective distress" may not be consonant with the couples' own experience of distress. This seems to be particularly the case with younger couples. Our decision has been to treat these couples like any others. If they bring up the need for treatment of relationship problems, however, then we advise them that this is not the best intervention program for them and provide referrals to more appropriate treatment agencies. This usually comes up in the midst of (or after) problem discussions that wind up in extremely negative interactions. Thus we generally take the position that couple members should be the ones to bring up their distress and that we should avoid imposing our perceptions of distress on these couples. Our outcome data indicate, perhaps not surprisingly, that our preventive intervention program is in some cases particularly helpful for couples who are relatively low on objective measures of relationship functioning. Thus, adopting the strategy of not identifying distress for couples and not referring them for therapy does not seem to be harming them.

In this chapter we have tried to explicate our firm belief in the value of early, primary prevention of martial distress. We have presented the basic rational and methodology of a program designed to prevent relationship problems before they develop. The results of empirical evaluations conducted thus far indicate that we have the potential to help couples develop competencies that enable them to cope with the transition to marriage. Nevertheless, we plan to modify our program continually, based on the empirical results emerging from our longitudinal research as well as the experiences of those who participate in our program or utilize similar methods.

REFERENCES

Barton, C., & Alexander, J. (1981). Functional family therapy. In A. S. Gurman & D. Kniskern (Eds.), *Handbook of family therapy*. New York: Brunner/Mazel.

Baucom, D. (1981, November). *Cognitive Behavioral Strategies in the Treatment of Marital Discord*. Paper presented to annual meeting of the Association for the Advancement for Behavior Therapy, Toronto, Canada.

Birchler, G. R., Weiss, R. L., & Vincent, J. P. (1975). Multimethod analysis of social reinforcement exchange between maritally distressed and nondistressed spouse and stranger dyads. *Journal of Personality and Social Psychology, 31,* 349–360.

Blew, A., & Trapold, K. (1982, November). *Fixing what isn't broken: Methodology and ethical considerations in premarital interventions*. Paper presented at the Annual Meeting of the Association for the Advancement of Behavior Therapy, Los Angeles.

Bowen, M. (1978). *Family therapy in clinical practice*. New York: Jason-Aronson.

Caplan, G. (1964). *Principles of preventive psychiatry*. New York: Basic Books.

Carter, E. A., & McGoldrick, M. (1980). *The family life cycle: A framework for family therapy*. New York: Gardner Press.

Duvall, E. (1977). *Marriage and family development*. Philadelphia: Lippincott.

Eidelson, R., & Epstein, N. (1981, November). *Cognition and marital maladjustment: Development of a measure of unrealistic relationship beliefs*. Paper presented to annual meeting of the Association for the Advancement of Behavior Therapy, Toronto, Canada.

Floyd, F. (1983, August). *Cognitive factors in behavioral intervention with couples*. Paper Presented to annual meeting of the American Psychological Association, Los Angeles.

Floyd, F., & Markman, H. J. (1983). Observational biases in spouse observation: Toward a cognitive/behavioral model of marriage. *Journal of Consulting and Clinical Psychology, 51,* 450–457.

Floyd, F., & Markman, H. (1984). An economical observational measure of couples' communication skill. *Journal of Consulting and Clinical Psychology, 52,* 97–103.

Glick, P., & Norton, A. (1976). Number, times and duration of marriages and divorces in U.S. In *Current Population Reports*, Series P-20, No. 297, Bureau of the Census.

Gottman, J. M., Markman, H. J., & Notarius, C. I. (1977). The topography of marital conflict: A sequential analysis of verbal and nonverbal behavior. *Journal of Marriage and the Family, 39,* 461–478.

Gottman, J. M., Notarius, C. I., Gonso, J., & Markman, H. J. (1976). *A couple's guide to communication*. Champaign, IL: Research Press.

Gottman, J. M., Notarius, C. I., Markman, H. J., Banks, D., Yoppi, B., & Rubin, M. E. (1976). *Journal of Personality and Social Psychology, 34,* 14–23.

Gurman, A. S. (1980). Behavioral marriage therapy in the 1980's: The challenge of integration. *American Journal of Family Therapy, 8,* 86–96.

Gurman, A. S., & Kniskern, D. P. (1978). Deterioration in marital and family therapy: Empirical, clinical, and conceptual issues. *Family Process, 17,* 3–20.

Haley, J. (1972). Critical overview of present status of family interaction research. In J. L. Framo (Ed.), *Family interaction: A dialogue between family researchers and family therapists*. New York: Springer.

Jacobson, N. S. (1978). Specific and nonspecific factors in the effectiveness of a behavioral approach to the treatment of marital discord. *Journal of Consulting and Clinical Psychology, 46,* 442–452.

Knox, D. (1971). *Marriage happiness*. Champaign, IL: Research Press.

Leif, H. J., & Reid, D. M. (1972). *Sexual knowledge and attitude test* (2d ed.). Philadelphia: University of Pennsylvania School of Medicine.

Lewis, H. (1984). *A test of a developmental model of the transition to marriage stage of the family life cycle*. Unpublished dissertation, University of Denver.

Lewis, H. C. (1984). *Ego development, self-differentiation, and family cohesion in the transition to marriage phase*. Unpublished doctoral dissertation, University of Denver.

Locke, H., & Wallace, K. (1959). Short marital adjustment and prediction tests: Their reliability and validity. *Marriage and Family Living, 21*, 251–255.

McGoldrick, M. (1980). The joining of families through marriage: The new couple. In E. A. Carter & M. McGoldrick (Eds.), *The family life cycle: A framework for family therapy*. New York: Gardner Press.

Mace, D., & Mace, V. (1980). Enriching marriages: The foundation stone of family strength. In N. Stinnett, B. Chesser, J. DeFrain, & P. Knaub (Eds.), *Family strengths: Positive models for family life*. Lincoln, NE: University of Nebraska Press.

Margolin, G., & Weiss, R. L. (1978). Comparative evaluation of therapeutic components associated with behavioral marital treatments. *Journal of Consulting and Clinical Psychology, 46*, 1476–1486.

Markman, H. J. (1977). *A behavior exchange model applied to the longitudinal study of couples planning marriage*. Unpublished doctoral dissertation, Indiana University.

Markman, H. J. (1979). The application of a behavioral model of marriage in predicting relationship satisfaction of couples planning marriage. *Journal of Consulting and Clinical Psychology, 4*, 743–749.

Markman, H. J. (1981). Prediction of marital distress: A 5-year follow-up. *Journal of Consulting and Clinical Psychology, 49*, 760–762.

Markman, H. J. (1982, July). *The short-term results of a cognitive-behavioral program designed to prevent marital distress*. Paper presented to the International Conference on Personal Relationships, Madison, WI.

Markman, H. J., & Floyd, F. (1980). Possibilities for the prevention of marital discord: A behavioral perspective. *American Journal of Family Therapy, 8*, 29–48.

Markman, H. J., Floyd, F., & Dickson-Markman, F. D. (1982). Toward a model for the prediction and primary prevention of marital and family distress and dissolution. In S. Duck (Ed.), *Personal Relationships 4: Dissolving personal relationships*. London: Academic Press.

Markman, H. J., Floyd, F., Stanley, S., & Jamieson, K. (1984). A cognitive/behavioral program for the prevention of marital and family distress: Issues in program development and delivery. In K. Hahlweg & N. Jacobson (Eds.), *Marital interaction: Analysis and modification*. New York: Guilford Press.

Markman, H. J., Jamieson, K., & Floyd, F. (1983). The assessment and modification of premarital relationships: Implications for the etiology and prevention of marital distress. In J. Vincent (Ed.), *Advances in family intervention, assessment and theory*. Greenwich, CT: JAI Press.

Napier, A. (1980). Primary prevention: A family therapist's perspective. In N. Stinnett, B. Chesser, J. DeFrain, & P. Knaub (Eds.), *Family strengths: Positive models for family life*. Lincoln, NE: University of Nebraska Press.

Nock, S. (1979). The family life cycle: Empirical or conceptual? *Journal of Marriage and Family, 41*, 15–26.

Notarius, C. I., & Markman, H. J. (1981). The Couples Interaction Scoring System. In E. Filsinger & R. Lewis (Eds.), *Assessing marriage: New behavioral approaches*. Beverly Hills: Sage.

Notarius, C., & Vanzetti, N. (1984). The marital agenda protocol. In E. Filsinger (Ed.), *Marital and family assessment*. Beverly Hills, CA: Sage.

Paul, N. L., & Paul, B. B. (1975). *A marital puzzle: Transgenerational analysis in marriage counseling*. New York: Norton.

Raush, H. L., Barry, W. A., Hertel, R. K., & Swain, M. A. (1974). *Communication, conflict and marriage*. San Francisco: Jossey-Bass.

Revenstorf, F. D., Hahlweg, K., & Schindler, L. (1984). Interaction analysis of marital conflict. In K. Hahlweg & N. Jacobson (Eds.). *Marital Interaction: Analysis and modification*. New York: Guilford Press.

Rosenthal, A., Floyd, F., & Markman, H. (1981). The short-term evaluation of a sexual enhancement program for couples planning marriage. Unpublished manuscript, University of Denver.

Sager, C. J. (1976). *Marriage contracts and couple therapy: Hidden forces in intimate relationships*. New York: Brunner/Mazel.

Snyder, D. K. (1979). *Marital satisfaction inventory*. Los Angeles: Western Psychological Services.

Stanley, S. M., & Markman, H. J. (1984, July). *Commitment as facilitator and constraint in the maintenance of close relationships*. Paper presented to the Second Annual International Conference on Personal Relationships, Madison, WI.

Terkelsen, K. G. (1980). Toward a theory of the family life cycle. In E. A. Carter & McGoldrick (Eds.), *The family life cycle: A framework for family therapy*. New York: Gardner Press.

8

Divorce Mediation: A Process of Self-Definition and Self-Determination

ANN L. MILNE

THE MULTIDIMENSIONAL NATURE OF DIVORCE SETS THE STAGE

Historically, divorce has been viewed by mental health professionals as being outside the domain of psychotherapy. The psychodynamic model, with its focus on unconscious conflicts and intrapsychic pathology (Brown, 1982), did not allow couples in conflict to be treated in a clinical setting through direct negotiations. The traditional schools of therapy (psychoanalytic, hypnotherapy, Adlerian, Jungian, Ericksonian, etc.) do not direct themselves to the psychological and emotional issues of the divorcing family; instead, they see divorce as a legal process that begins on termination of the marriage. The public has also viewed divorce as a legal entity. Couples who engage in marital therapy and who reach the decision to divorce often terminate the counseling process at the point that they initiate the legal process of divorce and view the need for psychological intervention as being complete.

In contrast to therapists who work from an insight-oriented model, therapists from the behavioral, rational, and Gestalt schools focus more on product than process. The goal of treatment with couples in conflict is on reaching agreements to lessen the stress and conflict of the relationship.

Within the past decade, we have begun to see therapists identifying themselves as divorce counselors specializing in services directed toward the mental health concerns of the divorcing family. Therapeutic interventions with divorcing couples combine an insight approach with the action-oriented focus of the behaviorists. Divorcing spouses attempt to resolve relational

Ann L. Milne. Private practice, Madison, Wisconsin.

conflicts to effect a satisfactory postdivorce adjustment. Out of this has come a body of emerging theory directed toward the emotional–psychological process of divorce (Bohannan, 1970; Brown, 1976; Federico, 1979; Kessler, 1975; Weiss, 1975; Wisemann, 1975). This divorce theory has moved us from the one-dimensional view of divorce as a legal process to a more practical view of divorce as a multidimensional process.

To view divorce as unidimensional and solely within the purview of the legal discipline is to ignore the intricacy of the divorce process and the multiplicity of tasks involved in the full resolution of divorce. Similarily, to view divorce as solely a psychological restructuring of the family is to ignore the contractual and legal issues inherent in the divorce process. As Bohannan's stations of divorce illustrate (Bohannan, 1970), a more realistic notion of divorce is that of a restructuring or recasting process in which certain defined tasks need to be accomplished that will allow for a balance between the ongoing nature of the relationship and the need to establish autonomy.

The development and institutionalization of a service that allows for the psychological dissolution of the marriage and the contractual definition of independent and shared responsibilities seem in order. The advent of divorce mediation is an attempt to accomplish this task and provide a professional service that reflects the multidimensional nature of divorce.

THE HISTORY AND INSTITUTIONALIZATION OF DIVORCE MEDIATION

The concept of mediation whereby a neutral facilitator aids two or more parties in resolving a dispute has a lengthy history. Mediation has been practiced in a variety of cultures, and its anthropological history is noteworthy. Gulliver (1979) traces the existence of mediation from primitive societies to the present.

In Africa, an institution known as the community "moot" provided a type of mediation service to assist in resolving a variety of interpersonal disputes. Mediation was a common means of resolving disputes in ancient China and is still used today to resolve issues, including divorce and child-custody disputes. Chinese immigrants to the United States in the mid-nineteenth century brought this tradition with them and established the Chinese Benevolent Association to resolve disputes in their community through mediation (Brown, 1982). The ancient Hebrews used a Jewish Religious Court, which exists today as the Jewish Conciliation Board, first established in 1920 in New York City to provide assistance in dispute resolution (Milne, 1982).

In 1974, O. J. Coogler, an attorney and marriage and family counselor, established the Family Mediation Center in Atlanta, Georgia. Spurred by his own emotionally and financially costly divorce, Coogler began to institutionalize the idea of divorce mediation through the publication of a book, *Structured Mediation in Divorce Settlements* (Coogler, 1978). The book proposed a framework for third-party mediators to assist a couple in resolving contractual issues such as finances, property division, support, and child custody, using communication and intervention techniques borrowed from labor mediation and the social sciences. The focus of the relationship between the mediator and the couple was transposed from an examination of past events and causative factors to the examination of future needs and the development of a contractual agreement. Coogler later established the Family Mediation Association as an organization of individuals interested in the development and advancement of divorce mediation as a viable means of resolving divorce related disputes.[1] Other organizations, such as the Academy of Family Mediators,[2] have emerged to promote the concept of divorce mediation and provide a network for practitioners.

The refinement of divorce mediation was furthered with the publication of *Divorce Mediation: A Rational Alternative* by Howard Irving (Irving, 1980) and *Divorce Mediation: A Practical Guide for Therapists and Counselors* by John Haynes (Haynes, 1981). Each new publication and journal article continues to add to the definition and development of this new field of practice.[3]

Most states now provide for some form of no-fault divorce. The underlying premise of no-fault divorce is that the responsibility for determining whether a divorce is warranted is made by the parties, as opposed to the court. This trend toward empowering the parties to retain their decision-making responsibilities is also found in the provisions for *pro se* divorce and joint custody. Each is premised on some degree of mutuality and cooperativeness, and lessens the decision-making authority of the court (Milne, 1982). The introduction of divorce mediation as a means of allowing divorcing individuals to develop their own financial, property, and parental agreements continues the philosophy of returning decision making to the family (Milne, 1983b).

The social sciences have turned their collective attention to mediation as a viable means of assisting family members with interpersonal disputes. From a tradition in which the individual was treated in isolation from other family members, we have seen psychotherapy grow to include couples coun-

1. The Family Mediation Association (c/o William G. Neville, President, No. 10 Cogswood Road, Asheville, North Carolina 28804). Following the death of FMA Founder, O. J. Coogler, efforts have been made to merge the Family Mediation Association with the Academy of Family Mediators.

2. Academy of Family Mediators, P. O. Box 246, Claremont, California 91711.

3. F. Bienenfeld, *Child Custody Mediation, Techniques for Counselors, Attorneys and Parents* (Palo Alto: Science and Behavior Books, 1983); R. Coulson, *Fighting Fair, Family Mediation Will Work for You* (New York: Free Press, 1983); J. Folberg & A. Milne, *Divorce Mediation: Theory and Practice* (New York: Guilford Press, in press); J. Folberg & A. Taylor, *Mediation: A Comprehensive Guide to Resolving Conflicts Without Litigation* (San Francisco: Jossey-Bass, 1984); J. Lemmon (Ed.), "Mediation Quarterly," *Journal of the Academy of Family Mediators* (San Francisco: Jossey-Bass, 1983); D. Saposnek, *Mediating Child Custody Disputes* (San Francisco: Jossey-Bass, 1983).

seling, family therapy, divorce counseling, and now divorce mediation. The emphasis on the understanding and actualization of past events in one's life has evolved to include forms of therapy that are less insight focused and instead emphasize the resolution of behavioral issues (working outside the home, financial arrangements, parenting relationships, etc.) and future contractual relationships (conciliation agreements, pre- and post-nuptual agreements, and mediated divorce stipulations). These behavioral and contractual forms of therapy address quasi-legal issues reflecting the growing awareness among individual and family therapists that relationships are not only psychogenic in nature but also psycholegal (Kressel, Lopez-Morrilas, Weinglass, & Deutsch, 1978; Kaslow, 1979–1980; Folberg & Milne, in press)

The extension of mediation into the area of divorce is a natural progression consistent with the historical roots of mediation and the attitudinal and conceptual changes that have occurred in the social sciences and the law. The emergence of divorce mediation is unique because of the interdisciplinary nature of its development and the multidimensional nature of divorce. This multimodal aspect has caused confusion and difficulty when it comes to actually defining what divorce mediation is and what it is not.

DEFINING THE PROCESS

Mediation is generally defined as a means of resolving conflict through the use of a neutral, third-party mediator whose role is described as that of a facilitator of communication, a guide toward the definition of issues, and a settlement agent who works toward the resolution of those issues by assisting the disputants in their own negotiations (Milne, 1982).

Different from the judicial–arbitration process, the parties retain control of the outcome, rather than turn the decision making over to a judge or arbitrator (Milne, 1982). Different from traditional forms of therapy, mediation does not focus on obtaining insight into the history of conflict, nor does it attempt to change personality patterns. Although these may both occur, they are fringe benefits of the mediation process. Different from the behavioral forms of therapy and divorce counseling, the goal of mediation is not to restructure relationships nor lessen anxiety and stress. Again, this may be a net result, but it is not the primary purpose of the process.

Mediation is not treatment. No diagnoses are made, and the parties do not analyze past behaviors but reach agreements that provide for the future (Milne, 1982).

Mediation is a contracting process between disputants. Divorce mediation focuses on the dissolution of the marital corporation and the allocation of the marital resources including property, finances, and children. The mediator serves as a guide to the parties as they define the issues in dispute and negotiate an agreement.

In 1973, social psychologist Morton Deutsch presented his findings on the nature of human conflict and the use of a third party in conflict resolution (Deutsch, 1973). Two years later, Jeffrey Rubin and Bert Brown added to Deutsch's conceptual framework on conflict resolution with a detailed analysis of the process of negotiation and bargaining. Their description of how mediation facilitates conflict resolution provides an operational definition of the process (Rubin & Brown, 1975). Mediation is described as a means of

> reducing irrationality in the parties by preventing personal recriminations by focusing and refocusing on actual issues; by exploring alternative solutions and making it possible for the parties to retreat or make concessions without loosing face or respect; by increasing constructive communication between the parties; by reminding the parties of the costs of conflict and the consequences of unresolved disputes and by providing a mediator model of competence, integrity and fairness. (D. Brown, 1982, p. 14)

Because divorce mediation borrows from the disciplines of law, psychology, and the fields of traditional negotiation and mediation, attempts to define it succinctly and differentiate it from other processes, such as therapy, vary in success. How divorce mediation is defined is largely dependent on what is being mediated, who is doing the mediating, and the setting in which the mediation is offered (Folberg, 1982). The mediation of financial and property issues may, for example, be referred to as a nontherapeutic, task-oriented process where budgets are presented and a settlement is reached by compromise and is based on need and ability to pay (Coogler, 1978). The mediation of custody and visitation issues may be described by others as a therapeutic process during which the parties realign their relationship from that of spouses and parents to solely that of parents. This process may include not only discussions about plans for the children but also a discussion of the marital relationship and events leading up to the divorce (Milne, 1978; Haynes, 1981; Milne, 1983b).

The background and training of the mediator has a direct effect on how mediation is defined. Mediators from a mental health background typically fall on the therapeutic end of the therapy–not therapy debate.

> While the social work mediator helps settle the economic division, he/she also helps the couple place the marriage behind them, deal with the emotional issues that caused the divorce, and look forward to the future. (Haynes, 1978, p. 7)

Mediators from a legal background tend to define mediation as more behavioral and contractual and less therapeutic. H. J. Folberg (1983) defines mediation as a nontherapeutic process

> by which disputants attempt to reach a consensual settlement of issues in dispute with the assistance and facilitation of a neutral resource person or persons . . . the

process consists of systematically isolating points of agreement and disagreement, developing options, and considering accommodations. (p. 8)

Christopher Moore, a social psychologist and respected trainer in the field, also defines mediation as an agreement-producing, contractual process

of intervention into a negotiation session of an acceptable, impartial third party with no decision making power, but who works with contending parties to find a mutually acceptable solution to their dispute. (Moore, 1982, p. 2)

The setting of mediation also affects its definition. When mediation is used within the context of a therapy setting, it tends to be defined in a more clinical fashion.

Throughout the bargaining process the professional makes a unique contribution. Therapeutic or counseling training teaches him/her to be self-aware, empathic to the clients, and understanding of past issues that may never have been resolved. By creating a therapeutic atmosphere, therefore, s/he can assist the clients to identify personal blocks and internal problems. (Haynes, 1981, p. 11)

Perhaps most confusing is the difference between divorce counseling and divorce mediation. Divorce therapy has been described as a new profession or a new speciality within the existing profession of marriage and family therapy (Brown, 1976; Hunt, 1977; Framo, 1978; and Brown, 1982).

[Divorce therapy] is concerned with helping an individual or a couple disengage from the marital relationship, to adjust to the stress of separation, and to cope with such emotions as anger, hostility, resentment, anxiety, guilt, rejection, regret, grief, and depression. . . . Divorce therapy can also help individuals better understand what went wrong in their marriage, to help bridge the transition to single life, to prepare for future, post divorce relationships, including single parenting, and to be more aware of the effect of divorce on their children and the need of children for continuing relationships with both parents. (D. Brown, 1982, p. 30)

As the literature on divorce mediation grows, we see a clearer distinction between divorce therapy and divorce mediation.

Divorce therapy may be differentiated from divorce mediation in that the former is focused more on stress relief, individual behavior change and increased self understanding, while the latter is focused more on dealing with specific problems, resolving disputes and negotiating differences inherent in the dissolution of the marital state. While successful divorce therapy may facilitate mediation and while successful mediation may be therapeutic, these two processes should be clearly separated. (D. Brown, 1982, pp. 30–31)

In spite of commentators who tend to blur the distinguishing features of mediation, therapy, and the practice of law, there is a growing consensus that divorce mediation is in an evolutionary definitional process similar to what has occurred in the fields of marital and family therapies. This definitional process will likely recognize that divorce mediation borrows from other fields and is influenced by the issues being mediated, the setting of the practice, and the discipline of the mediators; but it is clearly a separate and distinct practice from its parental figures.

We are seeing divorce mediation grow up and out of the disciplines of law and social sciences into a new and separate field reflective of its roots. An operational description of mediation techniques and models of practice will provide further definition as divorce mediation continues to evolve into a separate and unique field of practice.

MEDIATION TECHNIQUES—INTERVENTIONS FOR AGREEMENT MAKING

Several authors (Brown, 1982; Gulliver, 1979; Kessler, 1978; Moore, 1983) have described the mediation process as a linear series of stages. Kessler (1978) describes mediation as a four-stage process: (a) setting the stage; (b) defining the issues; (c) processing the issues; and (d) resolving the issues. For the sake of simplicity, this four-stage approach will be used in this chapter as a means of describing the interventions and techniques of divorce mediation.

Setting the Stage

The theater for mediation may be established long before the disputants enter the mediator's office. Frustrations with the legal system, recommendations by friends and other professionals, and media attention may have "primed the pump" and alerted the couple to the idea that mediation is an alternative means of resolving divorce-related conflicts.

The stage for mediation is officially set when the parties and the mediator first make contact. This typically occurs when one or both parties phone the mediator to inquire about the service, the availability of the mediator, and the fees. This initial contact provides an opportunity for both parties and the mediator to gather some initial data about each other, to explore individual expectations, and to formulate the beginning of the mediation relationship (i.e., "Does this person sound like someone I can work with?"). This initial testing of the waters goes both ways—the client assessing the mediator and the mediator assessing the client.

At the initial meeting between the couple and the mediator, the stage continues to be set as the mediator introduces himself or herself and asks the parties to tell something about themselves, what brought them to mediation, and what they define as the issues to be settled. Important here is the establishment of the relationship between the parties and the mediator based on a sense of trust, respect, empathy, and interest. As this is accomplished, the mediator builds credibility with the parties and begins to explain the mediation process, what it can and cannot accomplish, and how it may or may not be of help to them, based on their description of the issues in dispute.

As the parties and the mediator jointly assess the appropriateness of mediation, a "buy-in" process is initiated where the parties are assisted in determining their commitment to the process of mediation. When mediation is presented in such a voluntary fashion, the parties have the opportunity to discuss the various settlement processes available to them (i.e., interpersonal negotiations, negotiations through an advocate, therapy, litigation, and adjudication). Parties who choose mediation have already reached their first agreement—to mediate.

Typically, the mediator, in offering his or her services, will also clarify the role of the mediator with the parties. By defining the mediator's role as that of a consultant, contracted by the parties to facilitate their communication and settlement process, the mediator marks the role as that of an expert in assisting them in reaching a resolution, instead of determining a resolution for them. Most experienced mediators will emphasize that the final responsibility for settlement lies with the parties and that the job of the mediator is similar to that of a coach's calling on a particular set of plays and strategies that will assist the players on the field.

By defining the mediator–client relationship in such a manner, the mediator further sets the stage by foreshadowing (Kessler, 1978) some of the elements of mediation—the need for flexibility, a willingness to negotiate and compromise, a willingness to settle the issues, and an acknowledgment of the typical stumbling blocks to mediation. This foreshadowing process furthers the definitional task of the mediator and assists the clients in committing themselves to the process (Kessler, 1978). As the parties become aware of their responsibility for the final outcome of mediation, they must confront the issues of trust and risk taking. How vulnerable are they willing to be with the other spouse? This question is probably answered by most couples according to how much trust they are willing to invest in the mediator and their sense of the mediator's expertise and understanding of them.

We have now come full circle in setting the stage for mediation and return to the relationship between the parties and the mediator. This is not surprising, for if the relationship between the parties was unimpeded, they would likely have resolved the issues between them without the need for third-party intervention. Because this is not the case, the parties have sought an outsider to assist them with the process. Thus the initial tasks in this preliminary stage of mediation are those that relate to the relationship between the mediator and the clients, the establishment of the limits of the mediation process, and the definition of the role of the mediator.

Some mediators rely on a very structured mediation process including the use of a written agreement to mediate that sets forth the rules of the process (Coogler, 1978). These rules govern the mediation process and the relationship between the parties and the mediator. The rules define the issues to be addressed in mediation—typically limited to property division, child support, spousal maintenance, and child custody; identify the information and homework required of the parties to allow for the negotiation of these issues, such as preparing budgets, reviewing previous tax returns and obtaining appraisals; identify the context of the mediation process including whether the parties will be seen separately or together, phone calls, length of session, fees; and determine the process to be used in finalizing the agreement, whether the parties will consult with separate legal counsel, use a single advisory attorney recommended by the mediator, or process the agreement on their own, without legal counsel. Other mediators find the adherence to such a structured process and the use of rules unnecessary and instead clarify the working relationship either by distributing a brochure setting forth the expectations or summarizing the working contract in a letter to the parties (Milne, 1978, 1981; Elson, 1982).

Many of the aforementioned tasks in this stage of the mediation process are the same goals that a therapist hopes to accomplish initially: establishing trust and rapport, and defining the relationship. The difference lies with the focus of the process. Mediation focuses on the issues that need to be addressed to finalize a divorce agreement: the division of property, the economic support of children and spouses, and the arrangements for ongoing care of the children.

The resolution of these contractual issues differentiates mediation from therapy but causes it to become suspect as the practice of law as these issues have historically been the domain of the legal profession. Further, the negotiation of these issues is typically not accomplished in a vacuum. Although the resolution of hurt, anger, fear, guilt, and rejection is not the purpose of divorce mediation, these relationship issues are often germane to the mediation process. This then leads us to the next stage of mediation.

Defining the Issues

When a mediator first asks the parties to define the issues in dispute, most parties do so by answering with their solution—or with their final position: "Well, the dispute is about custody—I want custody and so does he"; or, "I think I should have the house because _____, and he thinks he should have the house because. . . ." This positional bargaining (Moore, 1983; Fisher & Ury, 1981) is typically a dead end or at best leads the parties into a contest of wills to see who can convince or wear down the other.

The mediator's task is now twofold: to move the parties from this positional posture to a discussion of basic needs and interests, and to surface any underlying conflicts that may inhibit the mediation process. This typically occurs through a questioning process, such as, "What is it that you are unhappy about?" or "What is it that you are really looking for?"

As this questioning process proceeds, the couple begin to surface a number of other issues, often of long-standing duration, related to the marital relationship or issues that are individual and specific to each spouse. As noted in previous sections, divorce is a psychogenic and emotional process. Reflective of this will be the identification of conflicts of a personal and relational nature. The task of the mediator is to assist the couple in cataloging the various kinds of conflicts. Kessler (1978) offers three categories: (a) topical issues; (b) personal issues; and (c) relational issues.

Topical issues may be described as the "point-at-ables" of divorce (i.e., division of property, finances, how the children will spend time with each parent). They are issues that are often physical and observable and make up most divorce stipulations.

Personal issues may be described as those internal conflicts and concerns that each individual brings with them to mediation. These may be historical issues rooted in family of origin, such as self-esteem, power, anger, or loss of love objects. Mediation often opens the door to these personal issues of long-standing duration. These personal issues may also appear in the form of the "new me" (e.g., "I was never able to assert myself in the marriage, and I'm not going to let him walk all over me now"). The need to turn over a new leaf and act differently is often observed in divorce mediation.

Relationship issues are the accumulated marital–divorce issues not resolved during the marriage that continue to be unresolved as the couple move from being spouses to being former marital partners. The hurts, the angers, the unfulfilled expectations, and the unmet promises of the marriage are the substance of relationship conflicts and are often at the root of disputes brought to mediation.

The task of the mediator is to validate these topical, personal, and relationship issues as legitimate conflicts but apprise the parties that mediation is a process that focuses on topical issues. Individual or couple counseling may be more appropriate for personal and relationship issues. Mediation resolves the external conflicts as it manages and acknowledges the internal conflicts. The goal is not the resolution of personal and relationship issues but how to manage these issues as they become roadblocks to the resolution of the topical issues.

As the probative questioning of the mediator surfaces the issues, the mediator will help the parties to catalogue the issues and begin a self-definitional process wherein the parties can identify the issues appropriate for mediation. This sorting process allows the parties to translate the conflicts as initially defined in positional terms into manageable issues of needs and desires. For example, "What I really want is an opportunity to be involved with the children, to feel that I have a place in their lives and a hand in their growth and development," or, "Our house feels like home to me; I need this kind of security and comfort right now to adjust to the divorce." This definitional process—defining the issues, cataloging them, and recombining them into needs and interests as opposed to positions, brings the parties to the next stage of the mediation process.

Processing the Issues

As the mediator assists the parties in focusing on the topical issues of the divorce and redefining them as interests or needs, the parties are able to move into the stage of processing the issues. Alternatives now become evident. There is a lot more room to negotiate when a parent's interest is in wanting to be involved with the upbringing of the children than there is when a parent identifies the issue as that of wanting custody of the children. This reframing process allows for a discussion of the issues in a manner conducive to settlement rather than the competitive push—pull routine that results from the taking of a position.

The mediator can now attend to the parties' communication—negotiation processes. Typical of most parties new to mediation is a communication process reflective of their behavior during the marriage. It did not prove to be workable then and probably is ineffective now as well. The task of the mediator is to demonstrate this to the couple and provide them with more effective communication tools.

The mediator may point out patterns of rhetorical conflict (expanding conflict for its own sake) that result in an impasse and contrast this to such techniques as active listening, "I statements," paraphrasing, modeling, and role reversal. By asking one party to take the other's position, the mediator reinforces an understanding of the other's needs and goals. Even a modicum of understanding and empathy begins to eat away at an adversarial, competitive relationship.

Blockages to communication typically result from the appearance of personal and relationship issues, as noted above. For some couples, mediation is a *double entendre*. It provides a means of continuing a relationship with one's spouse, while its goal is that of separating from the relationship. Some couples seem to relish the mediation process but avoid reaching any agreements.

The mediator must attend to relationship issues while processing topical issues. Reestablishing the parties' commitment to the process of mediation and identifying the issues relevant to mediation and those more appropriate to therapy are ways of managing the emotional climate. A time out from mediation and a referral to therapy may be appropriate.

Acknowledging the relationship issues and asking the parties to develop ways of dealing with these issues so that they do not inhibit the process of mediation is a management technique used in the mediation process. Often the mediator will be confronted with the relational issues of power and control. Power may lie with a party's having a verbally aggressive style or a better ability to articulate, or with a spouse who possesses more information about such things as finances or child development. Rarely are parties evenly matched in all areas. Often, though, this imbalance provides a solution to the conflict, assisting parties in combining their assets (their power) in a cooperative decision-making process that can work to their mutual gain, as opposed to the more destructive end of sole enhancement.

By reorienting the parties toward mutual goals and overlapping interests, the mediator moves the parties along the resolution continuum. Fisher and Ury (1981) analogize this reorienting process as one of having the parties move from sitting at opposite ends of the negotiation table to sitting at the same side of the table, as though they were two judges, faced with having to make a joint determination on a particular issue. Moving the parties to the same side of the table allows for the continuation of the resolution process. This occurs by the mediator's assisting the parties in developing a list of possible solutions and options that could potentially meet their identified needs and interests. This is done without evaluating any of the options on the table. This brainstorming process reinforces the mutuality of the problem and assists the parties in separating their interests from the solutions (Fisher & Ury, 1981).

It may become evident that the parties need more information to move to the resolution stage of the mediation process. Homework, sharing information, and consulting with outside experts may help with this. Once the options are generated and the parties have access to information pertinent to the issues, they will likely enter the resolution stage of mediation.

Resolving the Issues

Once alternatives have been generated, the couple can begin the matching and mutual accommodation process inherent in resolving the issues. A building-block process begins when needs and interests are matched with solutions (Moore, in press; Fisher & Ury, 1981). This building-block process is simplified when issues are dealt with in a singular fashion instead of allowing issues to be linked so that the resolution of one issue is dependent on the determination of a different issue. This is sometimes a luxury in divorce mediation, for plans for children and financial arrangements can be dependent on each other.

Often, solutions are reached by parties combining proposals, reaching tentative agreements (eliminating the need to overcommit to something a party does not yet feel comfortable with), and agreeing to agree in principle. The combining of options is similar to a sounding-out process in which if we extend Fisher and Ury's (1981) analogy of the two judges, we find the parties working to fit pieces of the options together to fashion an agreement whose fabric will cover both their shared and separate interests.

As the agreement begins to take shape, the mediator helps the parties develop a plan for finalizing the agreement and providing for its implementation. It is often helpful to add to the mediation agreement a periodic review procedure and to define a means of resolving future disputes. As divorce is a time of change, it is not unusual that agreements may need to be changed and reevaluated as the parties' situations change and the needs of children change over time.

   This final stage in the mediation process is the culmination of a set of previously accomplished tasks that fall within the linear stages of mediation. The reliance on creativity and the generation of options in this final stage allow the parties to complete a means–end shift whereby the parties shift their focus from the desired end to the means to that end (Moore, in press). This shift breaks the deadlock that often occurs between parties who become enmeshed in the personal and relationship issues and who have positioned themselves to have to defend their separate stakes.

   Critics who state that mediation is only a whitewash of the more substantive interpersonal and psychological issues may have a point. Yet many couples do not wish to engage in a psychotherapeutic process and find that mediation is a means to an end that satisfies their interests in reaching a settlement. The resolution of the contractual issues provides the emotional distance and clarity that many couples need to separate physically and emotionally.

PROFESSIONAL ISSUES

As divorce mediation continues to define itself as a field of practice, accompanied by an emergence of conceptual theory, models of practice, and supportive research, it will also begin to confront an increase in professional issues and concerns. Some of these issues are already being discussed in the literature (Silberman, 1981, 1982; Milne, 1983a,b) and through professional forums such as symposiums on standards and ethics,[4] conferences,[5] and committees.[6] Professional issues include the definition of appropriate users of the service, the definition of the role of the mediator, the relationship between the mediator and the clients, the nature of the agreement and its formal implementation, and the qualifications and training of the mediator.

4. The Association of Family and Conciliation Courts has sponsored three Symposiums on Divorce Mediation Standards and Ethics: December 1982 (San Diego), May 1983 (Toronto) and May 1984 (Denver). Delegates from over 30 professional organizations attended, to assess the need for certification and begin to develop parameters of practice for divorce meditors. Model Standards of Practice for Family and Divorce Mediators were completed at the May, 1984 symposium. The Model Standards are now available for organizations to subscribe to, endorse, or to be used as a resource document for the development of specific standards of practice. Copies are available from the Executive Director of the Association of Family and Conciliation Courts, c/o Oregon Health Sciences University, Department of Psychiatry, Gaines Hall, Room 149, 3181 S.W. Sam Jackson Park Road, Portland, Oregon, 97201.

5. The Association of Family and Conciliation Courts Conference, Fort Lauderdale, Florida, December 1981, and Williamsburg, Virginia, December 1983. American Bar Association, Alternative Means of Dispute Resolution Conference, Arlington, Virginia, June 1982 and Los Angeles, California, June 1983.

6. American Bar Association Arbitration and Mediation Committee of the Family Law Section, Leonard Loeb, Chairperson. American Orthopsychiatry Task Force on Mediation, Elizabeth Koopman and Mark Lohman Co-Chairpersons. Mediation Committee of the Association of Family and Conciliation Courts, Ann Milne, Chairperson.

Appropriate Users of the Service

The matter of appropriate users of mediation services raises two questions: For what types of clients is mediation likely to be most successful, if success is defined as resulting in an agreement? For which clients is divorce mediation an ethically appropriate practice? Limited research exists regarding the definition of appropriate and successful users of divorce mediation services.[7] Practitioner surveys indicate that service providers believe mediation is inappropriate for clients when (a) there are allegations or evidence of child abuse or neglect; (b) there have been multiple social agency or psychiatric contacts for the parents and/or children; (c) there exists considerable postdivorce conflict accompanied by frequent court appearances; and (d) one or more of the parties has evidenced serious psychological problems or has demonstrated erratic, violent, or severely antisocial modes of behavior (Pearson, 1983; Salius, 1978).

Kressel, Jaffee, Tuchman, Watson, and Deutsch (1980) examined a small sample of divorcing couples in an attempt to describe the relationship pattern between couples and apply this to mediation. Couples were found to fit into four separate categories: enmeshed, autistic, direct conflict, and disengaged.

Enmeshed couples were described as those exhibiting extremely high levels of overt conflict and ambivalence about the divorce and who engaged in prolonged conflict over minutiae and appeared to expand conflict for its own sake. Autistic couples were those with a relative absence of overt conflict accompanied by minimal communication and mutual avoidance during the decision-making stages of the divorce. Direct-conflict couples engage in overt conflict and communicate directly with each other, including about the decision to divorce. Disengaged couples display a low level of ambivalence about the divorce, appear ready to terminate the marital relationship, and display a lack of interest in each other. According to Kressel *et al.* (1980), direct conflict and disengaged couples have a greater likelihood of reaching an agreement through mediation than those couples exhibiting enmeshed and austic relationships.

---

7. The Divorce Mediation Research Project was funded by a grant from the Children's Bureau of the Administration for Children, Youth and Families. This project was directed by Dr. Jessica Pearson, Denver, Colorado, and was administered by the Association of Family and Conciliation Courts. This author served as a Field Researcher for the Project. Survey questionnaires were mailed to more than 1000 agencies and individuals providing divorce mediation services. In addition, site visits were made to Boston, Portland, San Francisco, Los Angeles, and Atlanta where divorce mediators, judges, lawyers, therapists, and clients were interviewed in an effort to gain a comprehensive view of divorce mediation in context. The project included an extensive analysis of the mediation of custody–visitation disputes at the court sites of Los Angeles, Minneapolis, and in the statewide system of Connecticut. The project has evaluated the long- and short-term effects of mediation, the components of effective mediation including an analysis of the characteristics of successful and unsuccessful disputants, and identified the factors and key policy issues involved in the organization, establishment, and delivery of divorce mediation services in the public and private sectors.

The appropriateness of clients for mediation will continue to be addressed through philosophical exchange. This issue includes the willingness of the parties to mediate, the ability of the parties to contract, and the diversity of power between the couple.

Mandating parties to mediate who have no desire to effect an agreement and instead wish to continue to battle is a waste of time and an infringement on a disputant's right to due process. Educating the parties about mediation and making it available as one alternative among a smorgasbord of dispute-resolution processes allows for a self-selection process that will eliminate individuals who do not wish to resolve conflict using the tenets of cooperation and compromise. Allowing parties to choose whether they wish to litigate or mediate respects the rights of couples in conflict.

Individuals who are unable to understand the terms of an agreement to mediate, and who are unable to represent themselves satisfactorily and ascertain their own interests and the interests of their children, are unable to contract effectively for mediation services. This would include individuals displaying severe psychological disturbance and a history of antisocial behaviors, as well as those couples chronically enmeshed in conflict and who, as a result, are unable to effect a contract to work together.

An imbalance of power between the parties is often central to the debate regarding who should and should not mediate. This objection to mediation is frequently raised by feminist groups. Diversity of power is central to most relationships. Rarely are two individuals evenly matched in skill and background. Mediation provides a reasonable means of attending to power. The adversarial system is predicated on the assertion of one individual over another through displays of power, wearing the other party down, and putting forth a better case. Such is power. The mediator, on the other hand, assists the parties in combining their strengths toward the goal of resolving an issue and educates parties to use their strengths effectively for settlement as opposed to dominance. In essence, power imbalances in relationships are a given. Mediation provides a means of addressing and managing these issues with the parties to effect an agreement-producing process.

The Role of the Mediator

The role of the mediator and the relationship between mediator and clients raises several professional and practice issues. The clients' perception of the mediator as a therapist or as a lawyer may cause them to expect that the mediator will be able to resolve certain issues normally beyond the scope of mediation. For example, a therapist mediator may be sought in the hopes of working out a reconciliation, or a lawyer mediator may be looked to for legal advice regarding the merits of a particular offer. It is incumbent on the mediator continuously to clarify the role of the mediator. This becomes more difficult when the mediator does things that are typically identified with lawyers or therapists (e.g., drafting agreements or meeting with parties individually).

Changing roles midstream, when mediation either reaches an impasse or is terminated, is also problematic. This would include the mediator who switches to the role of a custody evaluator when custody mediation is unsuccessful or the therapist who provides counseling during a break in the mediation process. Although this is usually done with the best interests of the clients in mind, these activities cause problems with confidentiality and trust and often result in a conflict of interest.

Legal critics of the mental health professional providing mediation services focus on the issue of the unauthorized practice of law. Indeed, this may become a real stumbling block as divorce mediation grows in practice and includes the settlement of financial and property issues, typically the purview of the legal profession. It is incumbent on the mental health mediator to be knowledgeable of the law and possess the necessary technical knowledge related to divorce.

In an effort to meet this issue many mental health professionals make it a practice either to include an advisory attorney in the final stages of mediation, refer the parties to independent legal counsel on the conclusion of mediation, or co-mediate with an attorney using a team mediation approach. The team mediation model is also problematic because of legal prohibitions regarding partnerships, use of a trade name, fee splitting, and the unauthorized practice of law (Silberman, 1981, 1982).

The Nature of the Agreement

Although some writers state that mediation provides for a fair resolution of the issues (Haynes, 1981; Lohman, 1981), the issue of fairness has been cited as a professional issue. Concerns include parties reaching agreements that provide for less than the law allows or reaching agreements that are not viewed as being in their individual best interests or the best interests of the children. This then calls into question the responsibility of the mediator for the nature and content of the final agreement. It has been suggested that the mediator could address the issue of fairness directly with the parties, could refuse to participate in unconscionable agreements, could refer the parties to legal counsel for an independent review, and could report to the court any objections and nonconcurrence with the agreement.

Divorce mediation is different from the mediation of a labor dispute, where lion-and-lamb agreements may be an acceptable result. Labor and management rely on representatives who are knowledgeable about the issues to negotiate for them. Divorcing couples are often naive negotiators and may not possess sufficient knowledge about property, finances, or the effects of divorce on children. What is the responsibility of the mediator when parties reach an agreement that is financially unrealistic or dramatically favors the interests of one spouse? Additionally, divorce mediation includes agreements about children—often unrepresented third parties in the mediation process. Is it the responsibility of the mediator to assure that agreements are reached in the best interests of the children? The issue of mediator responsibility for the nature of the agreement will continue to be a knotty problem.

Mediator Qualifications

The need to determine professional qualifications for divorce mediators, the establishment of a code of ethics, and the establishment of some form of regulatory control over the practice have been noted by several authors (Coogler, 1978; Harbinson, 1981; Haynes, 1981; Silberman, 1981, 1982; Crouch, 1982; Elkin, 1982; Margulies, 1982; and Milne, 1983a,b). These concerns center on the need to establish some form of quality control to protect both the consumer and the credibility of a developing profession (Milne, 1983a,b).

The development of a system to sanction the providers of mediation services would provide a means of establishing divorce mediation as distinct from that of legal services and divorce and family counseling. Depending on the degree of restrictiveness, sanctions may assure a minimum of training and experience in the field and allow for referrals to individuals who have met a standard of practice. A system of sanctions may provide some assurance for the public against the fraudulent practice of mediation by unqualified individuals and may allow for the establishment of a uniformity of service (Milne, 1983a,b). On the other hand, to establish a set of criteria for a practice, said criteria need to be defined and in place. At this stage in the developmental process of divorce mediation, it is unlikely that a significant number of practitioners would agree on a single format or model of practice.

The ingredients of successful mediation are not yet clearly defined, nor has the research been sufficiently broad based or longitudinal in nature to establish what is effective and what provides for agreement making that holds up over time. Training programs, typically 1- to 5-day workshops, are limited by the lack of clear evidence concerning effective mediation techniques. Academic programs encompassing the legal, psychological, economic, and communication aspects of divorce mediation are still in the formative stages.[8]

Then there is the question of who will provide the certification of proficiency. Should the certifying body be a professional organization providing divorce mediation training or an independent interprofessional organization that reflects the multidisciplinary practice of divorce mediation?

---

8. Academic programs offering a certificate or speciality in family and/or divorce mediation include the University of Illinois–Urbana and Catholic University of America, Washington, DC. In addition, graduate-level courses in family and/or divorce mediation are taught at Harvard Law School, University of Maryland, University of Iowa, and San Francisco State University, among others.

It seems clear that these questions point to the difficulties that exist within a discipline that has attempted to define a set of standards to assure proficient service. The public is entitled to quality and experience; the resolution of divorce-related disputes can have long-term implications for families and individuals. How best to assure quality is problematic in a field that is still developing.

The attempt to develop parameters of practice by consensus of the professional groups that constitute the present field of divorce mediators will extend the horizon of mediation even further. As theory catches up with practice, and as enthusiasm for the practice is supported by the pragmatism of research, divorce mediation will no longer be an "emerging" model of marital intervention; it will be eminent.

CONCLUSION

Gerald Manus in his 1966 article "Marriage Counseling: A Technique in Search of a Theory" described marriage counseling as a field in which "there is a clear picture of inconsistency, contradiction and lack of a coherent theory." Mediation is not a new technique. Its history is global and long. A conceptual and theoretical body of knowledge exists. What is new is the application of mediation to the resolution of family- and divorce-related disputes. In this application, the practice of mediation is also a picture of inconsistency, lacking a coherent theory. Drawing from the disciplines of law and the social sciences, divorce mediation has emerged as a practice in search of an identity.

Psychotherapy has expanded from a psychodynamic focus on conflict within an individual to a systems theory focusing on conflict within the family. Behaviorists and therapists who specialize in divorce have taken us one step further by addressing the needs of the divorcing family through the resolution of relationship issues. The emergence of divorce mediation continues this evolutionary process as it addresses the topical issues of the divorce process.

The practice of divorce mediation has emerged to the acclaim of some and the skepticism of others. Not unlike the practice and development of marriage and family therapies, divorce mediation will now begin to build a unique body of theory accompanied by research efforts to substantiate or disprove its application. Training programs will increase as the body of knowledge grows and will eventually encompass an academic program. Interdisciplinary conflicts over turf and territory will increase but eventually dissolve as a new generation of professionals define themselves as divorce mediators and display certification of their practice and training.

Self-definition and self-determination are the precepts of the mediation process. Disputing parties agree to take responsibility for defining the conflicts and determining the solutions. The elements of self-definition and self-determination also apply to the emergence of divorce mediation as a field of practice. Divorce mediation will continue to define itself as it determines its place in the overall system of psycholegal services.

REFERENCES

Bohannan, P. (Ed.) (1970). *Divorce and after: An analysis of the emotional and social problems of divorce.* New York: Doubleday.

Brown, D. (1982, December). Divorce and family mediation: History, review, future directions. *Conciliation Courts Review,* 20(2), 1–44.

Brown, E. (1976, December). A model of the divorce process. *Conciliation Courts Review,* 14(2), 1–11.

Coogler, O. J. (1978). *Structured mediation in divorce settlement: A handbook for marital mediators.* Lexington, MA: D. C. Heath.

Crouch, R. (1982). Mediation and divorce: The dark side is still unexplored. *Family Advocate,* 4(27), 33–35.

Deutsch, M. (1973). *The resolution of conflict.* New Haven: Yale University Press.

Elkin, M. (1982, June). Divorce mediation: An alternative process for helping families to close the book gently. *Conciliation Courts Review,* 20(1), iii–iv.

Elson, H. (1982). Setting up a private mediation practice. In J. Davidson, L. Ray, & R. Horowitz (Eds.), *Alternative means of family dispute resolution* (pp. 173–203). Washington, DC: American Bar Association.

Federico, J. (1979). The marital termination period of the divorce adjustment process. *Journal of Divorce,* 3(2), 93–106.

Fisher, R., & Ury, W. (1981). *Getting to yes: Negotiating agreement without giving in.* Boston: Houghton Mifflin.

Folberg, H. J. (1982). Divorce mediation—a workable alternative. In J. Davidson, L. Ray, & R. Horowitz (Eds.), *Alternative means of family dispute resolution* (pp. 11–41). Washington, DC: American Bar Association.

Folberg, H. J. (1983, September). A mediation overview: History and dimensions of practice. *Mediation Quarterly,* 3–13.

Folberg, H. J., & Milne, A. (Eds.). (In press). *Divorce mediation: Theory and practice.* New York: Guilford Press.

Folberg, H. J., & Taylor, A. (1984). *Mediation: A comprehensive guide to resolving conflicts without litigation.* San Francisco: Jossey-Bass.

Framo, J. L. (1978, February). The friendly divorce. *Psychology Today,* 77–79, 100–102.

Gulliver, P. (1979). *Disputes and negotiations: A cross cultural perspective.* New York: Academic Press.

Harbinson, K. (1981). Family law—attorney mediation of marital disputes and conflict of interest considerations. *North Carolina Law Review,* 60, 171–184.

Haynes, J. (1978, January). Divorce mediator: A new role. *Social Work,* 5–9.

Haynes, J. (1981). *Divorce mediation: A practical guide for therapists and counselors.* New York: Springer.

Hunt, M., & Hunt, B. (1977). *The divorce experience.* New York: McGraw-Hill.

Irving, H. (1980). *Divorce mediation: The rational alternative.* Toronto: Personal Library.

Kaslow, F. (1979–1980). Stages of divorce: A psychological perspective. *Villanova Law Review,* 25 (4/5), 718–751.

Kessler, S. (1975). *The American way of divorce.* Chicago: Nelson-Hall.

Kessler, S. (1978). *Creative conflict resolution: Mediation.* Atlanta: National Institute for Professional Training.

Kressel, K., Jaffee, M., Tuchman, B., Watson, C., & Deutsch, M. (1980, June). A typology of divorcing couples: Implications for mediation and the divorce process. *Family Process,* 9, 101–116.

Kressel, K., Lopez-Morrilas, M., Weinglass, J., & Deutsch, M. (1978, Winter). Professional intervention in divorce: A summary of the view of lawyers, psychotherapists and clergy. *Journal of Divorce*, 119–155.

Lohman, M. (1981). *Comprehensive mediation: A new approach to settlement of divorce disputes.* Unpublished paper.

Manus, G. I. (1966). Marriage counseling: A technique in search of a theory. *Journal of Marriage and the Family, 28*, 449–453.

Margulies, S. (1982). Ethical principles of divorce mediation. Unpublished paper of the New Jersey Council on Divorce Mediation, Upper Montclair, NJ.

Milne, A. (1978, September). Custody of children in a divorce process: A family self-determination model. *Conciliation Courts Review, 16*(2), 1–10.

Milne, A. (1981, December). Family self-determination: An alternative to the adversarial system in custody disputes. *Divorce mediation: Theory and practice* (pp. 1–19). Association of Family and Conciliation Courts Conference Proceedings, Ft. Lauderdale, FL.

Milne, A. (1982, December). Divorce mediation—an idea whose time has come? *Wisconsin Journal of Family Law, 2*(2), 1–10.

Milne, A. (1983a, June). Divorce Mediation—shall we sanction the practice? *Family Dispute Resolution: Exploring the Alternatives* (pp. 1–8). American Bar Association Special Committee on Alternative Dispute Resolution Conference Proceedings.

Milne, A. (1983b). Divorce mediation: The state of the art. *Mediation Quarterly,* 15–31.

Milne, A. (1984, June). The development of parameters of practice for divorce mediation. *Mediation Quarterly.*

Moore, C. (1982). Mediation. *Natural resource conflict management.* ROMCOE Center for Environmental Problem Solving, Boulder, CO.

Moore, C. (1983). *A general theory of mediation: Dynamics, strategies and moves.* Unpublished dissertation.

Moore, C. (in press). Obstacles to effective divorce mediation. In J. Folberg & A. Milne (Eds.), *Divorce mediation: Theory and Practice.* New York: Guilford Press.

Pearson, J. (1983). The divorce mediation research project. Progress Report No. 12. Unpublished paper.

Rubin, J., & Brown, B. (1975). *The social psychology of bargaining and negotiation.* New York: Academic Press.

Salius, A. (1978). *The use of mediation in contested custody and visitation cases in the family relations court.* Unpublished paper.

Silberman, L. (1981). Professional responsibility problems of divorce mediation. *Family Law Reporter, 7*, 4001–4012.

Silberman, L. (1982). Professional Responsibility problems of divorce mediation. In J. Davidson, L. Ray, & R. Horowitz (Eds.), *Alternative means of family dispute resolution* (pp. 239–319). Washington, DC: American Bar Association.

Weiss, R. (1975). *Marital separation.* New York: Basic Books.

Wisemann, R. (1975). Crisis theory and the process of divorce. *Social Case Work, 56*(4), 205–212.

Marital Therapy and Family Medicine

WILLIAM J. DOHERTY

As recently as the mid-1970s, it probably would not have occurred to the editors of a handbook of marital therapy to include a chapter on family medicine. If one regards marital therapy as a specialty field for persons trained in treating serious marital dysfunction, then family medicine has no place in it. If the field of marital therapy is defined more broadly, however, to embrace all professional treatment of marital problems, then a discussion of family medicine is not only appropriate but perhaps even essential for understanding the scope of marital treatment as practiced in North America.

As most readers probably know, family medicine is the newest medical specialty, replacing general practice in 1969 with a 3 year residency and a philosophy that emphasizes comprehensive, ongoing primary-care treatment for individual patients and their families (Rakel, 1977). The mission of family medicine involves integrating biomedical and psychosocial dimensions of care, although family practice training in biomedical treatment tends to be much more rigorous than the training in psychosocial treatment. According to a national survey, over 90% of family practice residency programs provide behavioral science and psychiatric curriculum during the 3 years of training (Jones, Budger, Parlour, & Coggins, 1982). It is not known how many programs emphasize marital or family treatment, but articles on this topic have appeared regularly in family medicine journals (Bauman & Grace, 1977; Bullock & Thompson, 1979: Candib & Glenn, 1983; Christie-Seely, 1981; Dayringer, 1978; Epstein, Levin, & Bishop, 1976; Ransom & Grace,

William J. Doherty. Department of Family Medicine, University of Oklahoma Health Sciences Center, Oklahoma City, Oklahoma.

1980). In addition, book-length discussions of family treatment in family medicine have begun to surface (Christie-Seely, 1984; Doherty & Baird, 1983; Huygen, 1982). The goal of this chapter is to provide marital therapists with a way to understand the unique role of family physicians and family medical settings in the prevention and treatment of marital dysfunction. Many of the ideas discussed here come from my collaborative work with Macaran Baird, MD, a family physician–family therapist (Doherty & Baird, 1983).

In this chapter I begin with a discussion of how family physicians are involved (sometimes inadvertently) in marital treatment. Next, I describe family medicine as a primary-care marital treatment area, as distinguished from specialized marital therapy. In the third section, I discuss assessment and treatment techniques that pertain uniquely to primary-care providers. Finally, I describe ways in which family physicians and marital therapists can collaborate in a network of professionals who treat marital distress.

FAMILY PHYSICIANS AS *DE FACTO* MARITAL THERAPISTS

Although no reliable data document the extent to which marital treatment is provided by family physicians, Regier, Goldberg, and Taube (1978) present solid evidence that most treatment for mental health disorders is provided in the primary-care medical sector, the largest component of which is family medicine. Using epidemiological data and mental health services research findings, the authors concluded that in 1975 only one-fifth of patients with mental disorders were treated in the specialty mental health sector, whereas about three-fifths were treated in the general medical (primary care) sector. Although marital dysfunction was not included as a mental health disorder in this study, I think two reasonable extensions of the findings can be made: First, a majority of mental disorders involve significant marital distress as a consequence, cause, or reciprocal determinant; second, the proportion of marital problems presented to family physicians versus marital therapists (or psychotherapists) may be roughly similar to the figures offered by Regier and colleagues. In other words, family physicians may be the *de facto* source of marital treatment for most Americans.

More direct evidence for the widespread presence, if not treatment, of marital problems in family practice settings comes from Cassata and Kirkman-Liff's 1981 random survey of 207 general practitioners and residency-trained family physicians in North Carolina and Ohio. The physician respondents reported that one-third of their diagnoses were "behavioral–psychological" in nature, with the four most common problems being depression, anxiety, obesity, and marital discord. Given the tendency of nonpsychiatrist physicians to focus more on biomedical issues than on psychosocial issues, these findings may be a conservative estimate of the extent to which marital problems are significant components of patients' distress. Interestingly, Cassata and Kirkman-

Liff found that although 33% of diagnoses were behavioral–psychological, only 2–4% of patient encounters were reported as counseling or referral-making sessions. The authors concluded that there is a wide gap between the respondents' awareness of psychosocial problems and their ability to address these issues.

Why would so many people bring their marital and other psychosocial problems to a family physician with limited psychosocial training instead of directly to a trained therapist? In the absence of good research on this question, I suggest the following reasons: First, since many people have an ongoing trusting relationship with family physicians, they find it easier to bring problems to them than to a "stranger" therapist; second, physical complaints are a ready ticket to a physician's office, whereas a person generally must admit the presence of a marital problem before seeking out a marital therapist; third, some marital problems are associated with life-cycle transitions, such as the birth of a first child (Waldron & Routh, 1981), occasions when the family physician is a prominent part of the couple's life; and fourth, marital problems may be created or exacerbated by a serious acute or chronic illness that is being treated by a family physician (Pattison & Anderson, 1978). Finally, with the average American visiting a physician 4.9 times a year (Wolinsky, 1980), there are many opportunities for involving a physician in one's marital difficulties. With these ongoing contacts with individuals and families, family physicians are well situated to provide preventive and early intervention services to couples before major dysfunction arises.

I am arguing here that family physicians are involved, for better or worse, with many more distressed couples than the limited supply of trained marital therapists could ever treat. If this is true, then the following remarks by Regier et al. (1978) apply to marital dysfunction as well as to mental disorders:

> A principal implication of these findings is that mental disorder represents a major U.S. health problem, which, although requiring active specialist attention, is beyond that which can be managed by the specialty mental health sector alone. Hence, there is need for both further integration of the general health and mental health care sectors and for a greater attention to an appropriate division of responsibility that will maximize the availability and appropriateness of services for persons with mental disorder. Given the limitations of specialty resources, improvements in the mental health training of primary care providers are needed to maximize the quality of mental health services for those fully or partially dependent on the general medical practice sectors. (p. 693)

PRIMARY CARE VERSUS SPECIALIZED CARE FOR MARITAL PROBLEMS

Part of the difficulty in conceptualizing the role of family physicians in marital or family treatment lies in how to distinguish their role from that of persons trained in marital and family therapy as a specialty. On the one extreme would be an absolute distinction between the two roles: Physicians should treat biomedical problems and refer marital and other psychosocial problems, leaving such treatment to specialists. In addition to the questionable assumption about the available supply of therapists in all communities, this approach ignores the reality that many people expect their family physician to help with their marital distress. Not everyone needs a referral, especially if the problem is mild or of recent onset, nor will everyone accept a referral to a therapist. Moreover, patients' problems cannot be sorted neatly into biomedical and psychosocial categories. Since most family physicians view themselves as professionals who can attend to the whole person and the whole family, they reject the view that they should (or can) confine themselves to biomedical matters alone.

On the other extreme would be the position that family physicians should be expected to provide definitive treatment for the same kinds of couples that marital therapists spend years learning to treat. This is the discredited "superdoc" model. Family practice training will never offer the level of training and supervision provided in graduate programs in marital and family therapy. (Similarly, family physicians will never know as much about the heart as a cardiologist or about the brain as a neurologist.) In order to bring more clarity to the family physician's role in marital (and other psychosocial) treatment, Doherty and Baird (1983) have posed the same distinction made in the biomedical aspects of treatment, that is, between primary care and specialized care. Each area has unique and important contributions to make, and both areas are more effective when they work collaboratively.

In the model Baird and I have developed, marital or family treatment can be viewed on a continuum from primary care to specialized care (Figure 9-1). In a general sense, primary-care marital or family counseling has functions different from those of specialized therapy. (In order to use terms that are congruent with most family physicians' modest image of themselves in treating couples, we use the expression "counseling" instead of "therapy" in describing primary-care treatment.) We propose that primary-care marital counseling centers on providing education, prevention, support, and challenge to couples, whereas specialized marital therapy focus more on restructuring chronically dysfunctional relationships. *Education* refers to teaching and

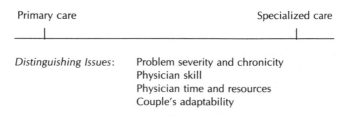

Primary care   Specialized care

Distinguishing Issues: Problem severity and chronicity
                             Physician skill
                             Physician time and resources
                             Couple's adaptability

FIGURE 9-1. The marital treatment continuum.

coaching couples about matters such as stress, coping with illness, handling a child, and communicating with each other. *Prevention* refers to family physician's unique role in providing anticipatory help before problems arise, such as during pregnancy or the dying process; this function of primary-care treatment is nearly inaccessible to specialized therapists. *Support* refers to efforts to help couples emotionally and medically through difficult times, such as might occur after a job loss or an illness. *Challenge* refers to confronting couples to mobilize themselves to make changes or to accept a referral to a therapist. Naturally, there is overlap between these primary-care tasks and what specialized therapists do; for example, many therapists begin treatment with fairly straightforward educational and supportive interventions. The difference lies more in the other direction: Primary-care treatment approaches are not sophisticated or powerful enough to deal with highly resistive couples or with chronic, rigid marital patterns that require a wide range of therapeutic interventions.

The model of primary care versus specialized care for marital treatment represents a continuum rather than a dichotomy. Some brief, uncomplicated treatment provided by marital therapists may fall in the primary-care domain (just as neurologists treating mild concussions may do nothing more than primary-care physicians would do). In like manner, a family physician struggling with a chemically dependent couple to get them to face their problems might be involved in a major effort at structural change in the marriage (therapy), even though the physician may not provide definitive treatment for the couple once they face the problem. Moreover, a family physician who receives special intensive training in marital or family therapy might move up and down the family treatment continuum depending on the nature of the presenting problem. Since specialized marital therapists may sometimes do primary-care treatment and some family physicians may engage in specialized therapy, what are the parameters that distinguish the approaches? The next sections describe how Baird and I address this question.

Problem Severity and Chronicity

In general, the more serious the marital dysfunction or accompanying problems such as depression or chemical dependency, the more likely that definitive treatment will require specialized therapy rather than primary-care counseling. Recurring marital violence, for example, taxes the resources of highly trained marital therapists; most family physicians would find themselves quickly over their heads (the same position, it should be noted, in which most marital therapists would find themselves if one of the spouses suddenly developed chest pains during a session). Similarly, a couple with long-standing difficulties in solving problems without mutual verbal recrimination is likely to require specialized therapeutic interventions. Although *definitive treatment* for severe chronic marital dysfunction usually belongs in the specialized domain, the family physician has an important *initial primary-*

care role in assessing the problem, facilitating a referral to a therapist, communicating with the therapist, and providing ongoing supportive care after the therapy is completed.

Which kinds of problems lend themselves to definitive treatment in the primary-care domain? Doherty and Baird (1983) propose that three kinds of problems are possible candidates for primary-care marital counseling by the family physician: (*a*) illness-related events; (*b*) life-cycle transitions; and (*c*) recent-onset problems that do not reflect long-standing marital dysfunction. *Illness-related events* (e.g., new and serious diagnoses, heart attack, mastectomy, extended hospitalization) may exacerbate marital stress. In these situations the family physician is on the scene as a (probably) trusted professional who can provide support and guidance for both medical and psychosocial issures. Consider the following case illustration:

> *A 26-year-old woman presented with an uncontrolled seizure disorder. During the interview with the family physician, she spontaneously volunteered complaints about her husband. Her chief complaint was that he nagged her all the time about not taking care of herself (eating well, getting enough sleep) and made her feel stupid and incompetent. She said she was taking her Dilantin faithfully, and in fact she demonstrated an adequate blood level of the medication. The physician asked her to bring her husband to the next appointment.*
>
> *When the couple was seen together, the underlying interactional power struggle over her health became apparent. He was in the role of a stern parent in their relationship, and she was in the role of an admiring but uncooperative child. He felt frustrated and scared by her seizures, and continually nagged her about taking better care of herself. She agreed with his criticisms, but would get angry at him for putting her down. After they fought, she would apologize for acting irresponsibly, but nothing would change.*
>
> *During the marital counseling session, the physician pointed out some of these interaction patterns and empathized with the frustration that each partner felt. After these and other issues were explored, the physician helped them negotiate a behavioral contract. The husband volunteered that one thing he could do would be not to nag her about her health; the wife agreed that she would let him know if she felt his comments sounded like nagging. When asked what kind of support she would like from her husband, the wife asked him to listen to her more when she talked about her frustration at work. He promised to do this as long as he could stop her when she discussed the technical aspects of her job too much. She agreed to this, commenting that such technical talk was probably something she used to sound smarter than her husband. Thus the final behavior contract called for diminishing a negative interaction pattern and enhancing a positive one. The wife could "own" her health behaviors, but could still ask for support from her husband; he could support her without becoming a frustrated parent.*
>
> *Two follow-up sessions over the next 3 months revealed that the couple had followed through on their contract. The wife had experienced no further*

seizures, marital satisfaction had improved, and the husband was acknowl-
edging that he was now more able to work on some of his own career decisions.
Six months later, this couple were continuing to do well.

Life-cycle transitions (e.g., the birth of a new baby, the redefinition of
marital roles after the children leave home, the increasing dependency of
aged parents) may generate marital stress. The family physician's unique
relationship with the family over time provides the opportunity for early
intervention at these stress points when dysfunctional patterns are not yet
set and animosities not yet high. Consider the following case illustration:

Carlos and Maria had recently arrived in the United States in order that
Carlos might attend graduate school. Both Carlos and Maria had under-
graduate degrees in an engineering field from a university in their Latin
American country. They were married several months before leaving their
country; Maria became pregnant almost immediately. The pregnancy forced
them to cancel plans for Maria to attend graduate school along with Carlos,
a frustrating development for Maria. She went to a family physician for
prenatal care shortly after arriving in the United States. She seemed to
enjoy the pregnancy, and Carlos was involved in the labor and delivery.
Maria's only complaints at this time were that Carlos was very busy and
that she didn't have many friends.

After the normal birth, Maria began to complain bitterly to her physician
that her husband was never home and that they argued all the time. The
physician invited her to ask Carlos to come to the office to discuss these
matters, but Maria said she did not think Carlos would come because Latin
men do not like to talk about personal things around strangers. The physician
set up a 45-minute appointment anyway, and Carlos came. The physician
first attempted to normalize the stress that the couple were having by
teaching them about the difficulties many couples face when having a new
baby and by emphasizing the lack of normal support from their families
and close friends. They relaxed noticeably during this discussion. The physician
then helped them make some day-to-day decisions about which they had
become stuck: Maria's getting out during the day (which required that they
both agree to use a babysitter), and their companionship time in the evenings.
Carlos also agreed to withdraw his request that they take in a boarder—a
Latin friend—in their one-room apartment.

The couple returned in 2 weeks for follow-up and reported that their
fighting had diminished greatly and that they felt more confident about
handling the stress of their difficult situation. Still pending for the future
was a decision about Maria's attending graduate school. No more couple
sessions were scheduled, but the physician monitored their progress during
routine well-child checkups.

If this couple had not responded so well to the primary-care marital
counseling, the physician was prepared to refer them to a marital therapist,
and this option was still available in the future. However, this brief intervention
appeared to help for now and was probably more acceptable to both spouses
at this early point in their problems than a referral to a marital therapist.

Recent-onset problems that do not reflect long-standing marital dysfunction is a category that overlaps with the first two, since many illness-related and life-cycle difficulties are apt to present novel challenges for couples. Even problems that are serious but unprecedented in the couple's relationship may respond to an educational and supportive primary-care intervention. Examples would include recent marital conflict precipitated by external stressful events, the first incident of marital violence, the first extramarital affair, the first drinking episode following a major argument. Couples who would not accept a referral to a marital therapist at this early stage in their problem might be open to help at the primary-care level, thereby forestalling more enduring difficulties that later would require specialized therapy.

Consider the following case illustration:

> *Within the space of a year, a husband and wife in their early 20s moved a long distance from their families and had a first baby. The wife quit work to care for the baby, who turned out to be quite irritable. The husband took an extra job to support the family, but his income from the first job plummeted because of poor sales. He then increased his hours at the second job, which kept him away from home from early morning till late night. The wife, without friends or family in the community, became more anxious at home with the fussy baby. Finally, the couple lost their recently purchased house in a mud slide and their car in an automobile accident. The wife presented to the family practice office with symptoms of anxiety and complaints about her marriage. The family physician asked her to bring her husband back for a joint session.*
>
> *The couple reported a good relationship before making the move and having the baby. Supportive counseling focused on allowing the couple to "ventilate" their feelings about the events in their lives, and on helping them plan together what steps to take to get themselves out of their difficulties. Their morale and confidence improved considerably after two sessions of such primary-care counseling.*

Physician Skill

As with biomedical illness, such as diabetes or hypertension, a key element in the decision to treat or refer a marital problem is the family physician's level of competence in treating couples. Although an unusually highly trained family physician might be able to handle most cases that marital therapists treat, the skill level of most family physicians would keep them more on the primary-care end of the continuum. Some family physicians indeed are comfortable only with a brief preliminary assessment of marital dysfunction—made with an individual patient—and then a referral to a marital therapist. While this might sound like an ideal scenario to an underutilized marital therapist, I believe that such minimal involvement by family physicians actually would lead to fewer referrals than would a more active primary-care posture of assembling couples in the office for assessment, followed by primary-care counseling or referral. My own experience has been that the stronger the primary-care skills of the family physician, the more successful referrals that physician is likely to make to me and other therapists.

Family physicians historically have not been trained adequately to provide primary-care psychosocial counseling of any sort, let alone marital counseling. This situation is changing with the advent of behavioral science training in residencies. Part of the recent difficulty in training family physicians has been the lack of models for the legitimate role of family physicians in psychosocial treatment. Now that these models are being delineated with more clarity (Christie-Seely, 1984; Doherty & Baird, 1983), progress may be forthcoming in the training area.

Physician Time and Resources

The decisions to assess the marriage briefly with an individual spouse, to assess the couple together in a conjoint session, to treat the couple in a primary-care mode, or to refer all hinge on the family physician's time constraints and office and community resources. After a night on call and faced with a bulging waiting room, the physician may elect to postpone dealing with any but the most emergent marital problems. An overwhelming practice load in a rural community may relegate the family physician to attempting quick assessments and referrals. On the other hand, the projected oversupply of physicians in many urban and suburban areas may lead to increased time for psychosocial counseling in family practice offices. In my observation, when busy family physicians view themselves as having basic skills in psychosocial counseling and want to include this activity in their practice, they find the time during the day for one or two 30- to 45-minute counseling sessions.

Time and outside resources are intertwined in the physician's decision to treat or refer. A busy physician who can send couples to trusted therapists, whether in-house or community therapists, will more readily refer couples. Fewer referral options and a slower practice might lead to a decision to treat the couple in a primary-care mode. At the same time, if referral therapists are available to consult with the family physician, then that physician might use this support to try more primary-care marital counseling. In general, I believe that the family physician who sets aside time for marital counseling and who has strong therapist resources will become most active in working with couples.

The Couple's Adaptability

Doherty and Baird (1983) have proposed that the core quality of the couple or family that determines their place on the continuum between primary care and specialized care is their level of adaptability versus rigidity. Adaptability is used here in Minuchin's 1974 sense as the couple's ability to modify their interaction patterns in the face of challenge. In Doherty and Baird's model, the more adaptable the couple, the more likely that they will respond to a supportive, educational, or mildly challenging primary-care intervention. The more rigid the couple's interaction patterns, the more they will need a rigorous therapeutic approach. The analogy to other aspects of primary-care medicine is clear: Family physicians generally provide definitive treatment for chronic conditions such as diabetes and hypertension when these conditions respond readily to standard medical treatment protocols. Cases considered more complicated—usually meaning that they do not respond to standard treatment protocols—typically are referred to physicians who specialize in those diseases. In the same way, flexible couples would be expected to respond more readily to primary-care counseling than would couples whose patterns are more resistive to change. In fact, one could argue that the therapist's specialized training comes into play most clearly in treating couples who have chronic difficulty in modifying their interaction patterns and engaging with outside help.

How can the family physician assess the couple's degree of adaptability and thereby know whether to pursue primary-care treatment or work toward a referral? Doherty and Baird (1983) propose two main ways: First, determine if the couple's history indicates chronic problems; chronicity suggests poor adaptability. Second, engage the couple in assessment and initial primary-care intervention; if they are difficult to treat or do not begin to make constructive changes after a few sessions, then their level of rigidity may be beyond the skills of the family physician to handle. Just as response to treatment is part of the diagnosis for some medical problems of uncertain etiology, marital adaptability sometimes can be assessed only by engaging the couple in initial primary-care treatment.

In summary, the appropriate place of a particular case on the primary–specialty care continuum involves a number of issues concerning the couple's specific problems, their adaptability, the physician's skill and time, and the presence of resources in the community. At present I think that the physician's skill level is the most troublesome part of the treatment equation. But I hope that appropriate training of family physicians will be more feasible (and politically acceptable) now that we are clarifying a domain in which family physicians are viewed, not as junior therapists messing where they do not belong, but as important providers of primary-care treatment for individuals, couples, and families in need of help.

SPECIAL ISSUES IN PRIMARY-CARE MARITAL TREATMENT

This section concentrates on aspects of working with couples that are unique to the primary health care domain. Although the emphasis is on family physicians, much of the discussion also applies to nurses, physician assistants, and other primary-care physicians. Features include early assessment of marital discord before it presents as a clearly defined problem; moving from helping the individual patient to helping the marital dyad; preventive, educational, and supportive interventions; and practical concerns about doing primary-care marital counseling in family practice settings.

Clinical "Red Flags"

Although there is little useful research to guide clinical judgment here, Doherty and Baird (1983) have suggested that several common clinical presentations in family practice may be associated with disturbed marital or family functioning. These are clinical "red flags" that can guide the family physician to consider relationship disorder in the differential diagnosis. This list is based mostly on Baird's clinical experience as a family physician:

1. *Atypical migraine headaches* of long-standing duration that have been evaluated and treated unsuccessfully by a string of specialists. Frequently the patient is aware of family stress as a "trigger" for these headaches but has never been asked about this by a physician. Incorporating the spouse and other family members into the diagnosis and management of this medical problem may provide the key to the role of marital or family problems.

2. *Chronic depression* that has not responded to any long-term individual therapy, either medical or electroconvulsive. If the patient also has been treated with antianxiety agents for a long time, the diagnosis might involve chemical dependency as well as marital dysfunction.

3. *Diffuse anxiety* presented over many office visits without sufficient diagnostic evidence of "organic" disease. If the patient has been taking antianxiety agents for years, there may be an important interaction between the marital dysfunction and medication use.

4. *Chronic fatigue* that has no medical explanation. Depression appears to be common among these patients, who often have assumed a chronically dissatisfying and dysfunctional role within the family.

5. *Minor pediatric complaints* for which educating the parents has not been effective. Typically these complaints are seen by the parents as serious medical problems, and no amount of explanation from the physician will dissuade them. Examples include enuresis in a child below age 2 and fussiness in the first year of life. These complaints from the parent may mask underlying difficulties that the couple are having with their marital and parental roles.

6. *Insomnia* in certain patients. In the face of no medical problem, insomnia can reflect underlying stress in the patient's family situation, along with the possibility of alcohol or chemical abuse.

In general, consistent complaints that defy medical explanation after repeated investigations by the family physician (and perhaps by consultants) are candidates for the differential diagnosis of marital or family dysfunction.

Of course, the physician must leave open the possibility of further investigation of the medical symptoms, but an adequate primary-care assessment in these cases should involve a marital or family interview to explore the possibility that family stress might be involved. Even if the physician ultimately refers couples whose problems have been identified through clinical "red flags," an important primary-care service has been provided.

Involving Both Spouses in Assessment or Treatment

Whereas marital therapists usually begin therapy with both partners present, the family physician's initial contact usually occurs through an individual meeting about medical complaints. The physician's first task, after sorting out the biomedical issues and psychosocial issues, is to form a therapeutic contract with the patient that will allow participation of the spouse. Reaching this agreement may take time, especially for patients who have not yet connected their physical and psychosocial problems. A unique aspect of primary-care treatment for marital dysfunction, then, comes in the physician's efforts to help the patient view the entire biopsychosocial context of the presenting complaint. Appreciating this context will allow the patient to understand the value of a conjoint session to further explore the problems. Once this therapeutic contract has been developed with the patient, the next step is for the patient to convince the spouse to come in for an interview. If the family physician already has a trusting relationship with the spouse, there may be little difficulty in getting the couple together. In other circumstances, this may be the most difficult part of primary-care treatment. Doherty and Baird (1983) have articulated a number of strategies used by family physicians to involve a reluctant spouse (and sometimes a reluctant patient).

1. *Confidently indicate that the spouse is expected to come.* Physicians frequently express timidity about the subject by questions such as, "Do you think your husband would be willing to come in?"

2. *Communicate a sense of urgency* to the patient about holding a conjoint interview. Physicians can use the same urgent tones that they would use to indicate the importance of diagnostic X rays or surgery.

3. *Ask for the spouse's help* to help you understand the patient's problem more fully. The couple can be brought together for the initial purpose of exploring why the patient is feeling ill, rather than work from the outset on marital problems that the spouse may not recognize or admit. The spouse can be invited to help the physician's understanding of the problem.

4. *Use the hospital as a setting* for meeting with the couple. The family physician is nowhere more powerful than in the hospital. Rarely will a married couple decline the physician's request for a conference with both of them when one is hospitalized, or when a child is hospitalized.

5. *Contact the reluctant partner* to assure him or her that you are not looking for villains. This may be especially helpful when the family physician

has a long-standing relationship with a patient but little relationship with the partner.

6. *Be patient and persistent*. At the primary-care level of treatment, patients frequently are only dimly aware of the nature of their problems, often clinging to a narrowly biomedical understanding of their difficulties. The physician may have to exhaust medical diagnostic procedures before the patient will be willing to face the marital problem. The patient may be offended by a too-soon or too-vigorous confrontation of marital problems by the physician.

7. *Declare the limits of one's ability* to help the marital problem without a conjoint session. When the patient wants to complain about the marriage but will not invite the spouse or accept a referral for marital therapy, the physician can offer to back away from the individual counseling relationship because such counseling will not help but may hurt the marriage (Gurman & Kniskern, 1978).

The experience of family-oriented physicians like Baird is that when the family physician makes family conferences a normal part of the management of a range of medical problems, patients will not think it so strange to be invited to bring in their spouse to explore how marital issues might be affecting their health or how their health is affecting their marriage. There are three major advantages to such conjoint sessions in primary-care settings: First, the physician will be able to make a more accurate assessment of the problems; second, when appropriate, the physician can initiate primary-care counseling with both partners together rather than continue to treat only one spouse; third, referral to a marital therapist should be easier if the physician first meets with the couple together to help them understand the nature of their problems and the availability of specialized help.

Consider the following case illustration of involving both spouses:

Mrs. J., a 50-year-old woman, came to a family physician's office with complaints of nervousness and fatigue. A medical examination yielded no evident physical cause for her complaints. During the interview and exam, however, the physician asked about Mrs. J.'s home and work situations. With little prodding she started to complain about her husband's busyness and lack of attention to her. The physician also discovered that she was providing much of the day-to-day support for her husband's frail mother, a role for which she felt unappreciated by her husband. The physician helped her to see that her physical complaints were possibly related to her stress at home. She appeared to be relieved to be discussing her concerns.

The physician then suggested that Mrs. J. invite her husband to return with her for a follow-up visit in order to gather more information about the stress she was under and possibly to help the couple get along better. The physician also said that he might want to conduct further diagnostic work on her physical symptoms. She replied that her husband would never agree and that, anyway, the problems were not so bad. The physician gently reiterated the symptoms Mrs. J. was experiencing and the list of marital and family complaints she had just shared. The physician then said, "It seems to me that you are in a lot of pain because of what is happening between you and your husband. Am I right?" She cried and agreed. Once again the physician explained that the best way he could help was to sit down together with the couple and help them talk things out.

This time, Mrs. J. appeared more responsive to the invitation. She said, "I would like to come back with my husband, but I'm not sure he will come with me." The physician replied, "I'll bet that your husband is feeling pain in this situation and that he might see some good for himself to be gained from talking things over. Why don't you ask him?" Mrs. J. said, "How will I bring it up to him?" The physician responded, "You know your husband better than I do, but you could try telling him that your doctor wants to have a meeting with both of you to discuss some of the stresses in your life that are giving you health problems. And that you need his help. As your doctor, I certainly feel like I need his help to help you with the concerns you brought to me today. We could go on talking between ourselves, but that wouldn't help as much as if your husband comes back with you."

Mrs. J. agreed to talk with her husband, and the physician scheduled a 45-minute appointment at the end of the office day a week later. The physician was prepared to conduct an initial assessment and determine whether brief supportive and educational counseling would help this couple or whether they would require a referral to a marital therapist. The key to bringing about the initial couple session was the physician's gentle persistence in maintaining that such a meeting was the best way he knew to help Mrs. J. If this approach was not successful, and her symptoms persisted, the physician would have considered a personal telephone call inviting the husband to participate.

Primary-Care Marital Counseling Approaches

Table 9-1 lists 14 basic marital therapy techniques that constitute a core set of techniques for primary-care treatment. These skills are learned by most marital therapists in the early stages of their training, and no discussion of them seems necessary here (see Doherty & Baird, 1983, Chap. 7). More difficult, time-consuming, and high-risk techniques are not included in the primary-care list, for example, allying with one partner to unbalance the marital system, extensive exploration of family-of-origin and intrapsychic issues, and paradoxical interventions. Similarly, dealing with major resistance to change requires skills outside the primary-care realm, although an individual family physician might have received training in such skills and be equipped to use them.

In addition to outlining these "micro" primary care techniques, I want to address in more detail some general approaches or strategies for preventing and alleviating marital dysfunction in a primary-care setting.

PREVENTION

Anticipatory guidance for couples is available uniquely in primary-care settings. Some marital stresses are predictable, as when a couple faces major

TABLE 9-1
Basic Primary-Care Marital Counseling Techniques

1. Engaging the couple
2. Initiating discussion of the problem
3. Structuring the session
4. Defining the problem
5. History taking
6. Remaining neutral
7. Encouraging a collaborative set
8. Facilitating partner discussion
9. Giving support
10. Teaching
11. Challenging
12. Dealing with mild or moderate resistance
13. Helping couples make behavioral contracts
14. Assigning homework

life-cycle changes, illness, unemployment, or relocation. Routine office visits can provide a forum for preventive marital counseling in the form of helping the patient anticipate marital stress or by normalizing problems that have already occurred. For example, a husband told me once that the anticipatory warning of his family physician concerning the first child's unsettling impact on marital equilibrium helped both spouses understand afterward that their adjustment difficulties were normal and expectable.

EDUCATION

The family physician is especially well placed to teach couples about sexual functioning before their ignorance gets them into trouble. In addition, the physician's teaching about how to cope with illness and disability can provide an important resource for couples. For example, family stress associated with senile dementia requires ongoing education from the physician about the nature of the disease, about what family members can expect in the future, and about how family members can continue leading their own lives while caring for their demented relative.

SUPPORT

Since family physicians frequently relate to couples at times of family crisis, particularly when serious illness occurs and when major environmental stressors lead someone in the family to develop physical symptoms, the family physician is well situated to provide supportive counseling in a primary-care mode. Support can come in several ways: by listening empathically to the couple, by encouraging them to persevere and face their difficulties collaboratively, and by helping them locate other sources of help and support. I know one physician who meets monthly for a year or more with couples who have lost a baby at childbirth to provide support through their grieving process and their readjustment. Supportive primary-care counseling often can be confined to brief office visits; couples who require heavy time commitments from the physician should be candidates for referral.

CHALLENGE

A competent primary-care marriage counselor must be able to challenge couples in a number of situations. Sometimes the couple will need a push to get them into specialized marital therapy. Sometimes they must be confronted about not cooperating with the structure of treatment (e.g., coming late or missing appointments). In addition, during the course of primary-care marriage counseling, several other challenges can be useful: (a) challenging unrealistic expectations about family life; (b) challenging the partners to act collaboratively; (c) challenging the partners to change dysfunctional interaction patterns; and (d) challenging the partners to take responsibility for solving their own problems instead of asking the physician to do the problem solving. In general, when such challenges are not successful, the family physician should consider making a referral to a marital therapist.

Making Referrals

The daily nemesis of the primary-care physician is the decision to treat or refer. In the psychosocial area, the twin dangers are that the family physician will fail to offer immediate help by making inappropriate or premature referrals to the specialized mental health sector, or will treat ineffectively those psychosocial problems that should be referred. The model presented here attempts to avoid these dangers by involving the family physician in the early assessment and treatment decisions regarding the problem—thereby setting the stage for an immediate referral where appropriate—and by offering the ground rule that a referral should be made if the problem is not ameliorated through primary-care counseling.

The initial criteria for referral are the same as those for distinguishing whether the case falls in the primary-care domain or the marital therapy domain: the nature of the problem; the physician's skill, time, and resources; and the couple's adaptability. An additional criterion is whether the primary-care counseling is achieving the benefits desired by the couple and the physician. Doherty and Baird (1983) suggest that family physicians explicitly address the possibility of a referral to a therapist at the outset of primary-care counseling. One approach is to propose meeting for three or four sessions and then to evaluate whether sufficient progress is being made or whether a referral would be indicated.

Sometimes therapists say that primary-care physicians should stay out of the business of counseling or therapy and should "simply" make referrals. Such an opinion tends to underestimate not only the potential contributions of primary-care counseling but also the difficulties involved in making helpful referrals. One difficulty occurs in knowing how far to explore the problem with the patient before attempting a referral. If the physician and patient (or couple) have not established a trusting relationship through serious discussion of the marital problem, then the patient may experience the referral attempt as a brush-off or as an invasion of privacy. It would be like referring a patient to a surgeon without an in-depth discussion of why surgery might be needed. The opposite difficulty stems from physician enmeshment with patients and their problems. If the physician has been drawn into an extended counseling relationship with the patient or couple, then both sides might feel ambivalent about the referral. Selvini-Palazzoli, Boscolo, Cecchin, and Prata (1980) have described the treacherous waters encountered by therapists when treating a family referred by a physician who has become part of the family. Both the family and the physician may be unconsciously relieved when the therapy fails and they can go back to treading water on their own.

When a family physician refers a couple to a marital therapist, a new triangle is created—for better or worse. Some of the burden of the referral's success lies with the referring physician, who communicates a number of expectations to each party about the other and who serves as an ongoing contact person for the couple after the referral is made. The physician can either support or undermine the therapist's efforts; for example, *supporting* by encouraging the couple to stay with the therapy or share their concerns about the treatment with the therapist, or *undermining* by suggesting that the "real" problem lies in an individual spouse and then prescribing an antianxiety agent without telling the therapist. On the physician's side, the referral becomes problematical when the therapist will not communicate with the physician, even though the patients have given appropriate permission. Another difficulty for family physicians lies in choosing therapists for referral. Medical school and residency training until recent years have prepared family physicians to refer psychosocial problems only to psychiatrists, many of whom are not trained in marital therapy. The answer seems to lie in more professional interaction between family physicians and marital and family therapists so that referrals can work well from all sides.

Practical Issues

Doherty and Baird (1983) discuss the importance of logistical issues for successful primary-care marital or family counseling. The physician must have a room large enough to hold three or more people. Some simple conferences with couples can be held during a regular 20-minute office visit, while others must be scheduled for 30–45 minutes during times when the physician is unlikely to be interrupted. One or two of these extended visits will be all that busy family physicians can handle during a day's office hours; other contact with couples can occur during hospital rounds or at the emergency room. Doherty and Baird (1983) urge family physicians to charge what they feel their time is worth, lest they fall into the trap of trying to subsidize their primary-care counseling by charges for medical procedures. Insurance often will cover the counseling if a biomedical or psychiatric diagnosis can be made. Furthermore, since primary-care counseling is not likely to involve a large number of sessions, the total cost to the couple is not apt to be high, even if the family physician is charging high fees per session. Finally, preventive and educational counseling that accompanies routine medical care should result in only minor additional charges for the patient and only a modest increment in the family physician's time commitment. In general, I believe that none of the practical obstacles to primary-care marriage counseling are unmanageable for a motivated family physician.

THE NETWORK OF PROVIDERS OF MARITAL TREATMENT

Primary-care treatment for any problem cannot be effective unless it is tied into a larger network that includes specialty care. An old country family physician I know says that he could not practice medicine without constant contact with his consultants (specialists who give him advice and to whom he refers patients). Unfortunately, in the prevention and treatment of marital dysfunction, the network of providers lacks the ongoing mutual support and feedback available in the treatment of biomedical disorders. Part of the problem has been the lack of a clearly defined primary-care role for assessing and treating psychosocial problems. Moreover, nonpsychiatrist therapists do not share the same educational and professional socialization experiences with family physicians. To some extent, I think that therapists have accepted the same mind–body dichotomy that dominates much of contemporary medicine (Engel, 1977). To exaggerate a bit, we end up with two groups with nonoverlapping training and skills: primary care physicians with little training in psychosocial treatment but who cannot avoid doing it because their patients are psychosocial as well as biological creatures, and therapists with little knowledge of medical issues but with extensive training in treating psychosocial problems outside their biological context.

The result of this bifurcation is a therapeutic network for psychosocial problems that is top-heavy and unbalanced: narrowly trained specialists and inadequately trained primary-care providers. The result, in my opinion, is not enough referrals for marital therapy because family physicians are not well equipped to address psychosocial issues, and not enough education and support for family physicians who want to improve their primary-care assessment and counseling skills.

The development of primary-care psychosocial counseling in family practice settings, then, will depend on the development of linkages between family medicine and the specialized therapy community—in this case, between family physicians and marital therapists. Primary care by definition requires a complementary level of care. In most settings, this will involve the local marital therapists, while in areas where major family therapy training centers exist, there will be a tertiary level of care to supplement the primary-care providers and the community-based (secondary level) therapists. In addition, the family physician can work collaboratively with other primary-care professionals, such as nurses and physician assistants.

Concretely, a collaborative network will involve ongoing dialogue, consultation, referral, feedback after referral, and occasional co-therapy opportunities. An ideal way for this process to germinate is for a family physician to employ a therapist part time to provide in-house consultation and therapy, and to help the physician with linkages to community resources. Another approach is for the family physician to team up informally with therapists for consultations about assessment and primary-care treatment and for referrals. Both groups can profit from the arrangement, and the community is provided with levels of care that mesh rather than compete with or ignore each other.

CONCLUSION

If one accepts a biopsychosocial understanding of human beings—that the biological, psychological, and social threads of life are wound together in a single cloth—then professional territoriality reflects an inaccurate picture of the world. From the biopsychosocial perspective, marital therapists inevitably are dealing with physical health because they are dealing with persons and relationships, just as medical physicians inevitably are involved with psychological and social issues because they are involved with biological persons. Since many people experience relationship problems first in physical manifestations, and since ongoing contact with family physicians provides a ready pathway for seeking help, family medicine is the ideal bridge between the three dimensions of biopsychosocial care. Family medicine's task is to promote biopsychosocial health, to provide primary-care treatment for uncomplicated but common biopsychosocial problems, and to refer and coordinate care for the full gamut of such problems from cancer to marital dysfunction. More training for family physicians in assessing and treating psychosocial problems, coupled with more collaboration between therapists and physicians, offers the possibility of far-reaching benefits for the prevention and treatment of marital dysfunction and a wide range of related psychosocial problems.

REFERENCES

Bauman, M. H., & Grace, N. T. (1977). Family process and family practice. *Journal of Family Practice*, 4, 1135–1137.

Bullock, D., & Thompson, B. (1979). Guidelines for family interviewing and brief therapy by the family physician. *Journal of Family Practice*, 9, 837–841.

Candib, L., & Glenn, M. (1983). Family medicine and family therapy: Comparative development, methods and roles. *Journal of Family Practice*, 16, 773–779.

Cassata, D. M., & Kirkham-Liff, B. (1981). Mental health activities of family physicians. *Journal of Family Practice*, 12, 683–692.

Christie-Seely, J. (1981). Teaching the family system concept in family medicine. *Journal of Family Practice, 13,* 391–401.

Christie-Seely, J. (1984). *Working with the family in primary care: A systems approach to health and illness.* New York: Praeger.

Dayringer, R. (1978). Family therapy techniques for the family physician. *Journal of Family Practice, 6,* 303–307.

Doherty, W. J., & Baird, M. A. (1983). *Family therapy and family medicine: Toward the primary care of families.* New York: Guilford Press.

Engel, G. L. (1977). The need for a new medical model: A challenge for biomedicine. *Science, 196,* 129–136.

Epstein, N. B., Levin, S., & Bishop, D. S. (1976). The family as a social unit. *Canadian Family Physician, 22,* 53–55.

Gurman, A. S., & Kniskern, D. P. (1978). Deterioration in marital and family therapy: Clinical, conceptual and empirical issues. *Family Process, 17,* 3–20.

Huygen, F. J. (1982). *A family medicine: The medical life history of families.* New York: Brunner/Mazel.

Jones, L. R., Badger, L. W., Parlour, R. R., & Coggins, D. R. (1982). Mental health training in family practice residency programs. *Journal of Family Practice, 15,* 329–335.

Minuchin, S. (1974). *Family and family therapy.* Cambridge, MA: Harvard University Press.

Pattison, E. M., & Anderson, R. C. (1978). Family health care. *Public Health Review, 7,* 83–134.

Rakel, R. E. (1977). *Principles of family medicine.* Philadelphia: Saunders.

Ransom, D. C., & Grace, N. T. (1980). Family Therapy. In G. M. Rosen, J. P. Beyman, & R. H. Layton (Eds.), *Behavioral science in family practice.* New York: Appleton-Century-Crofts.

Regier, D. A., Goldberg, I. D., & Taube, C. A. (1978). The de facto U. S. mental health services system. *Archives of General Psychiatry, 35,* 685–693.

Selvini-Palazzoli, M., Boscolo, L., Cecchin, G., & Prata, G. (1980). The problem of the referring person. *Journal of Marital and Family Therapy, 6,* 3–9.

Waldron, H., & Routh, D. K. (1981). The effect of the first child on the marital relationship. *Journal of Marriage and the Family, 43,* 785–788.

Wolinsky, F. D. (1980). *The sociology of health.* Boston: Little, Brown.

Couples Group Therapy

10

E. JAMES LIEBERMAN
SUSAN B. LIEBERMAN

Marriage is a group situation and, as such,
shows the general characteristics of group life.
—Kurt Lewin

To use a musical analogy, group therapy is to individual therapy as a small orchestra is to a duet. If the orchestra is made up of established duos, we have a likeness of couples group therapy. The larger ensemble, a truly mixed blessing, has the richness and limitations of size and complexity. There is no need to rank different modalities, only to know the place of various forms in a general therapeutic repertoire. Just as a good musician knows the literature of solo, chamber, and orchestral works for a given instrument, so the complete therapist knows the range of therapeutic modes. To extend the musical comparison, we may say that multiple-family group therapy may be likened to the full orchestra with (children's) chorus. Couples group is a minimal version of multiple-family group therapy.

Family therapists, like other conductors, will specialize; the former cannot be at home in all modalities any more than the latter can do equally well with Mozart and Wagner. The broadly experienced therapist will usually better serve any clientele, while developing his or her specialty in depth.

Couples meet in groups in various helping contexts. Premarital counseling under church auspices is perhaps the commonest and oldest form. Marital enrichment is a recent development that engages large numbers of couples in structured short-term learning situations that, although not defined as

E. James Lieberman and Susan B. Lieberman. The Family Institute, Washington, D.C.

therapy, involve some of the same principles. Parent groups in PTA, child guidance, or drug–alcohol programs present another category; many of these are not strictly couple situations but include single parents. Mace (1974) remarks that his introduction to couples group as a co-therapist in 1959 impressed him greatly, despite his assumption "that marital problems were so personal that a group of couples would have difficulty in openly communicating." Our experience with couples group work began at the Putnam Children's Center, Boston, in 1962, where members were parents of emotionally disturbed young children.

Since then, we have led short- and longer-term couples groups together, separately, and with other co-therapists. We have participated in a long-term (3-year) couples group led by Dr. Herbert Cohen of Washington, D.C. His model remains our most influential guide in theory and practice. In Cohen's 1977 view, group therapy is the treatment of choice for people who have a fundamentally sound marriage that needs improvement. "In a group," he has said, "good marriages get better slowly, bad ones get worse in a hurry." Our model may be called *existential*. It aims to foster individual and couple growth through participation in a minimally structured group; honesty, spontaneous yet considerate emotional involvement, and introspection are valued. Relationships across (rather than within) couples are cultivated so that individuals develop in the presence of, but not only in tandem with, their spouses. This helps break up collusive, stifling neurotic bonds. Meaning, and therefore therapeutic impact, derives from current experience more than from analysis of the past, from feeling more than intellectual (genetic) understanding, and from grappling with universal issues of age and stage of life, not just pathology (Whitaker, Greenberg, & Greenberg, 1981; Yalom, 1980). We might also label the approach "integrative," after Gurman (1981), in that it uses an expedient mix of psychodynamic, behavioral, and structural–strategic ideas, and strives to meld rather than isolate introspective and interpersonal phenomena.

RATIONALE AND SELECTION CRITERIA
FOR GROUP THERAPY

Grunebaum and Crist (1968) make a point slightly different from that of Cohen, saying they find that couples either progress rapidly or soon show that they are not likely to do so. In our individual and marital therapy sessions with spouses we are often able to reach a conclusion early on about the prospects for a particular marriage, allowing for the possibility that we may be surprised. We exclude those with poor prognosis from couples groups. Constant conflict impedes progress for all members, and the group leader bears responsibility for creating a situation in which the greatest good flows to the greatest number. Alternatives for couples not ready for couples group would be continuing individual and marital sessions, and separate groups for the spouses. This would be our recommendation also in most cases where an extramarital affair is active (known or unknown to the spouse) or, although ended, has been disclosed and remains a bone of chronic contention.

Given that a treatment powerful enough to help can also do harm, leaders are above all responsible for minimizing negative effects of therapy: *primum non nocere*. Whereas individual therapy permits completely uncensored expression by patients, constraints exist in group. Some people will leave rather than endure monopolizing, attacking, or seductive behavior on the part of fellow group members. Contrary to some rather widespread assumptions, group therapy is not a dumping place for whatever comes into someone's mind. The leader must be sensitive to the ability of all members to hear and respond to the others; this means being aware of what might hurt or alienate someone, and being aware of what might lie unexpressed because of the fear of hurting or being hurt. We are not surprised by the research finding of Gurman and Kniskern (1978) that negative effects in marital and family therapy were associated with passive leadership and the therapist's failure to moderate group feedback to members with little ego strength.

Group therapy is an exercise in the expression of real feeling, a nonviolent encounter without kid gloves. Members learn to articulate issues that, in other circumstances, might be too explosive. The leader guides the communicants between the twin perils of destructive outburst and equally damaging silence or dissembling. The words "explosive" and "destructive" suggest anger, but other emotions are included as well, for example, love, lust, sadness, elation. The leader sometimes acts as a demolition expert teaching recruits how to open a ticking package. At other times, he or she acts as a nurse or doctor who must teach a student how to examine the private anatomy of a patient in a thorough yet dignified way.

By definition, there are many "therapists" in a group. No one should be admitted who lacks the potential or the desire to help others. And since trust is essential, all members must be able and willing to keep confidences. The leader relies on members to assist the therapeutic process—starting, but not ending, with careful listening. The members learn from the therapist how to defuse bombs, or lengthen short fuses, and how to cope with increasingly direct, or "naked," emotion.

In setting up a group, therapists should interview candidates both as individuals and as couples. Because it is impossible to predict how any couple will perform in a group setting, a brief group experience may be useful as a testing ground before starting a long-term group (Budman, Bennett, & Wisneski, 1981). Ideally, prospective members will have had some prior individual therapy experience so that they know the limits and possibilities of each modality. In presenting our rationale, we emphasize that group is a setting for improvement of the marriage based on individual development in the presence of one's spouse.

> But let there be spaces in your togetherness,
> And let the winds of the heavens dance between you.
> —KAHLIL GIBRAN

While diversity is inevitable and welcome, the organizer of a couples group should look for common ground in regard to stage of marriage and parenting. We would not mix parents and nonparents. On the other hand, differences in symptoms, education, ethnicity, religion, and economic status might enhance rather than impede a group if age and developmental stage are not too disparate (Budman *et al.*, 1981) and if no two individuals or couples are egregiously incompatible. As Yalom (1975) has noted, "it is only in a cohesive group that conflict can be tolerated and transformed into productive work" (p. 271). Couples must have a stable foundation; it is not fair to the group to include marriages on the brink of catastrophe, though some reach that state despite our predictions and our therapy. Members can tolerate a wide range of life-style differences, but we draw the line at violence, major drug and alcohol problems, and extramarital sex. Group therapy can help with such problems, but they are likely to overburden the typical couples group.

Framo (1973) uses a couples group format that permits a more diverse clientele, but his model virtually eliminates spontaneous cross-couple interaction: Three couples meet together weekly, and 30 minutes are allocated for the problems of each. This approach emphasizes intrafamily issues, but it does permit cross-stage sharing, learning, and modeling. It may be a useful alternative to our approach, especially when recruitment of several appropriate couples of comparable age and stage is not feasible.

We view commitment to the marriage as a precondition for couples therapy, and this means sexual exclusivity. While we respect a spouse's right to privacy, and do not encourage disclosure of affairs, we insist that couples therapy cannot be conducted while there is an ongoing affair. This stipulation may eliminate a few clients at first, but some return later; it assures everyone that, to our knowledge, there is no current extramarital sexual involvement. This is an effective way to deal with chronic suspicion and mistrust.

LOGISTICS

Group therapy fees should be much lower than those of individual, couple, or family sessions, since the cost is shared by three or four couples. The presence of a co-therapist of the opposite sex increases the cost but is worthwhile when affordable. Ninety-minute, weekly sessions are the rule. There are no telephone or other interruptions. We do not use surnames, and we allow members to use discretion on identifying persons and places. If such details emerge, members are expected to keep absolute confidence. Such exaggerated scrupulosity has its place in therapy today, not only because of job sensitivity but also because of the "small world" phenomenon; for example, it is better for members not to know that Alice teaches at the school attended by Joe's nieces. A session may be canceled if half or more of the members will be absent. Refreshments sometimes appear spontaneously or for a birthday or anniversary. We discourage leaderless sessions or outside socializing; as Neiberg (1976) says, any contact "that affects how persons feel in the group is group business" (p. 405). Members are expected to attend if possible when the spouse has to miss a session. We allow three misses a year without charge for members; similarly, each co-leader may be excused three times.

Our groups are open-ended in process, within firm boundaries of time and rules. Whoever has an issue launches the session. The members must learn to regulate the flow to avoid monopolizing and to engage the shyer participants. The rules include the following, which are appropriate for all groups: coming and leaving on time; calling in advance, when possible, to explain lateness or absence; announcing a forthcoming absence as soon as possible (e.g., at the beginning of a session rather than at the end); giving several weeks' notice of intention to terminate.

In couples group therapy there are additional rules related to the fact that subgroups of two go home together. A group cannot function if spouses engage in censorship, recrimination, or threats at home. While the group often stimulates constructive communication outside the sessions, it can also lead to destructive turmoil. The leader should anticipate when spousal conflict aired in group needs resolution. Our operating rule is that a member should speak up about strong feelings within the session, not go out "gunning" for the partner. If hurt or angry feelings surface only after a session is over, spouses should express them constructively or hold the matter for the next session if the group's support and control is needed to prevent damage. Of course, members can and should contact the leader between sessions if they cannot control a destructive process.

We guide couples away from telling "the week that was" story of their lives; instead, we encourage individual expression of current and past emotional issues and cross-couple interaction. This is more principle than rule, but serves to indicate the group's maturity. At first, members tend to focus on intracouple issues, at home and in the group. Individuals remain subordinate to marriages. In time, members begin to feel as close to one another as they do to their siblings and friends. As Leichter (1975) put it, the group becomes a "third family." Then, relationships of members with each other gain strength and influence, which is the whole purpose of group therapy. Repetitive focus on intracouple dynamics delays this opening process, keeps the leaders in position as frustrated referees, and avoids the anxious pleasure that signals vulnerability in new relationships.

Papanek (1971) supports this argument, pointing out that the group process begins in earnest when members allow their attention to shift away from their spouses, and they begin to regard the other group members as something more than an audience or jury. We also stress the development of *new relationships*; unless the focus can be drawn away from the spouse, the rigid patterns of the marriage are likely to prevail against the efforts of the therapist.

As Grunebaum and Crist (1968) argue, the classic transference model hardly applies in couples and family work because the actual relationships are being lived out in the therapy milieu. While not dismissing transference entirely, the therapist deals with "live" issues, not their purported representation on a neutral screen. As the authors point out, countertransference is not the same, either:

> How different is the case when the feelings being expressed are directed, not toward outsiders, but toward individuals who are present in the therapy, and when these feelings are not the reawakenings of past experiences but rather the expression of love and hate in the here and now. It has been noted that when the therapist is unmoved by his experiences in family therapy, his diagnostic assessment of the family suffers correspondingly. . . . The same is true of work with couples. . . ." (pp. 501–502)

To have the constructively critical support of six or eight involved people is well worth giving up the transference theory and the relative detachment it provides the therapist.

Peter Martin (1983) reinforces this point in saying that the therapist in couples groups changes, that no two groups are alike, and that differences between them are as important as similarities. This conclusion may distress the student who needs a formula, but indispensable as the scientific method is, it does not provide more than an outline of procedure. One sign of therapeutic maturity is the ability to use anxiety constructively, that is, to tolerate uncertainty in the clinical situation while pursuing an inquiry to reduce both uncertainty and anxiety to manageable proportions for all concerned.

Anxiety is the leading edge of change. There can scarcely be a therapeutic process without anxiety. Our purpose is to build a supportive context in which anxiety can be borne well enough to permit constructive change. The climate can be prepared by pointing out what is true in all psychotherapy: Hurt feelings usually precede anger. When anger arises, try to express the matter in terms of the immediately preceding vulnerability, which, of course, means anxiety. While many people are afraid of anger and will go to great lengths to avoid it in themselves and others, some people use anger very effectively to escape anxiety. Covert anxiety lurks not only behind anger but also around love and other uncontrollable emotions. As closeness develops in the group, the attraction of members to one another becomes a challenging issue, another potent and potentially hazardous therapeutic factor.

Some therapists structure sessions, even to the extent of dividing the group time into three equal parts, each devoted to the issues of one couple (Framo, 1973). Many paths lead to the same destination, and all successful therapy experiences, group as well as individual, share some essential characteristics. Yalom (1975) found that in groups with many tasks and structured interactions, members rate the leaders more favorably, but the group outcomes are less impressive than when members are left to structure the time themselves. Since we combine individual and marital therapy with couples group therapy, to isolate the group experience for evaluation is difficult. We are client oriented in all phases of work, and advise our patients that results should be felt before long; 3 months is a reasonable interval for assessment, and we ask new group members to take that much time to decide whether the experience helps. If patients choose to continue, and we feel that the treatment is productive, that constitutes minimal ongoing evaluation in a private practice setting. We would like to see more rigorous evaluation of a kind that would command the respect of experienced clinicians and researchers (Gurman, 1975; Williams & Miller, 1981; Kaslow & Lieberman, 1981).

A CLINICAL EXAMPLE

Although we have done some short-term (10 or 12 session) groups, we advise couples that the fullest benefits derive from a year or more of group experience. In the present case, three couples (the A.'s, B.'s, and C.'s) were parents in their mid-30s to late 40s, with a total of eight children ranging from grammar school to college age. All were in first marriages (average duration 21 years), and all were college graduates. These were dual-career marriages, although the wives took major time out for childrearing responsibilities. Each member had had some prior individual therapy (most with one of us, two with other therapists); this individual work continued or tapered down as the group experience progressed. The members, described succinctly, were:

Al A.: intellectual, aggressive, demanding, compulsive.
Amy A.: poised, gentle, reserved, sad.
Bob B.: controlled, competitive, jealous, eager.
Betty B.: shy, compassionate, conscientious, depressed.
Chuck C.: silent, depressed, endearing, stubborn.
Carol C.: caustic, hysterical, bright, self-pitying.

The A.'s marriage was marked by Al's explosive temper and Amy's attempts to protect her children and herself from it. Al would be contrite after an outburst, then freely express his genuine love. Their sex life was very good. Al was a highly effective, compulsive worker; his anger burst through easily when things got beyond his control at the office or at home. Amy bore this with a long-suffering patience periodically broken by an outburst of her own.

The B.'s were rather estranged, though quietly so. Bob was critical and demanding, while Betty felt inadequate even to defend herself; she retreated into silence. Sex was unsatisfactory, as neither one had much affection to express; even when things were good, they tended not be be effusive. Bob worried about work, Betty worried about the children. Bob was jealous not only of men but of Betty's women friends, with whom she seemed more animated than she was with him.

The C.'s presented with Carol the irresistible force and Chuck the immovable object. He would hunker down for days in response to her caustic, articulate barrages. She pursued him more angrily all the while, in a typical Brer Rabbit attack on the Tar Baby. Chuck could pull out of his funk in company, creating a combination of relief and bitterness in Carol. Their passion led to good sex when positive moods emerged between estrangements.

Our basic approach to marital problems holds the partners equally responsible for the good and the bad in the relationship until proven otherwise. This "50-50 principle," which has never been faulted in practice, reduces blaming and encourages taking responsibility for one's own need to change. It teaches couples something about system dynamics and allows them to see this phenomenon in others at close range, a more palatable option than introspection! But soon each couple has its turn in the limelight, each spouse confronts the persuasive comments of peers about how he or she acts in the group, evidence that cannot be denied. This is the power of group therapy: to realize and study relationships in a protected context. Understandably, we prefer present interaction to reports of what went on at home, because the latter are subject to distortion and wrangling that the group cannot resolve.

As this group got under way, Chuck spoke simply but with feeling, winning the sympathy of others with his droll, self-critical tales. Carol was beside herself, insisting that we could not possibly appreciate her suffering because Chuck was performing in a way that belied his silent stubbornness at home. Many evenings after group, she went home enraged.

Carol found a partial ally in Bob, whose spouse also withdrew from him in silence; the two silent partners, Chuck and Betty, formed a sympathetic bond. There appeared to be two problem pairs—bullies and bullied, or askers and deniers. Fortunately, the traits in question were not gender specific, and progress resulted from the new perspective on old, entrenched patterns.

Meanwhile, the group took Al to task for his high-flown intellectual comments and his inability to come forward with feelings. At first Amy won some sympathy, but then she lost it by remaining aloof, above the fray, as it were. Before long, the group accepted the simple but challenging idea that the balance of two-person systems depends about equally on both members.

While our approach is egalitarian, there are inequalities. It is easier for a man to leave a difficult marriage than it is for his wife; his income is usually greater, and he has more chance of finding a desirable partner. In this group, the dismal conflict between Chuck and Carol escalated to such a degree that we recommended separation. Chuck was depressed, unable to say he loved Carol; she could not resist grilling him, and distorted his response to the point of claiming, "He said he did not love me!" In a rare burst of anger, the male leader accused Carol of setting up a straw man. Since she was his devoted patient in individual therapy, the criticism was hard for her to take, although it should not have come as a surprise; indeed, one could say she provoked it. It actually did wonders for the couple, since Chuck saw that Carol could deal with anger from an admired man. His reclusiveness derived in large part from his fear of his own anger. Soon, the female leader asked Chuck what it would take for her to get close to him. He was incredulous, but finally answered that it would take a lot of convincing; he would like to believe she really wanted to be close, but couldn't be sure that he would welcome it. She replied that she would be patient and persistent "for as long as it takes," a promise that he cautiously believed and that left Carol constructively nonplussed.

For several months, Chuck and Carol lived separately, meeting regularly at the group (their children were away at college). It disturbed the other members, of course, and as noted earlier, we would not have chosen a couple for group that we expected to separate. But we felt that the integrity of the individuals and prevention of further and perhaps permanent destruction of the relationship dictated that painful step. When they reestablished the marriage, it became a meaningful choice, not just the habit of people too afraid to live alone.

A phenomenon of particular moment is the participation of one spouse without the other. At some point during the 18-month duration of the group, each of the six spouses attended at least once without the partner. Usually something newly significant emerged, as though released by the absence of spousal constraint. The members always respected the delicate boundary line that therapists maintain: Not everything should be shared with one's spouse; the decision about what, how, and when to share belongs to each individual and must not be usurped by therapist or other group members.

For example, when her husband was absent, Betty told about her battle with colitis. Of course he knew about it, but she felt it was her issue, and despite several reminders to the contrary, she had resisted bringing up anything that was not a "marital" issue. Yet to be ignorant of her physical illness meant not to know her. The others immediately warmed to her, and her story began a round of individual disclosures that made each member more real as a separate individual.

A different issue was joined when Amy came alone one night and revealed that her husband had effectively censored discussion of an important area: his job. He did it on grounds of his privacy and his inability to trust (people might be able to identify his work setting). But we saw this as his ability to control her, and dealt with her collusion in this, which was more important than the problem of the job itself. Later he was able to confide quite openly about those matters, and both her fear of him and her anger subsided, as did her aloofness from group. His temper outbursts at home became quite rare.

Termination became the issue after a year. The members decided to continue another 3 months and then make a longer commitment or end. Chuck went along passively, unable to say what he wanted. Carol began to have more pleasant than unpleasant evenings after each group. Everyone was surprised that, after the next 12 sessions, Chuck and Carol most eagerly supported continuation. But it was too late. The other four members were inclined to end, although there was still much room for improvement, as Chuck was suddenly keen to point out. The leaders felt there was merit on both sides of the question, but did not want to press reluctant members to continue. We said we would be glad to hear from any who wished to be in a group in the future. A year later, all three couples reported continuing improvement in their individual and marital development.

DYNAMICS AND PRINCIPLES

Despite an increasing openness about personal and marital life in our society, few people other than therapists are privy to the interior of others' marriages. Women are likely to know more of this than men, whose discourse with one another tends to be less family centered. In couples group, husbands are likely to feel, and be, more vulnerable than their wives, who are used to discussing emotions and personal relations. As a rule, women gladly support a man's emotional risk taking. In the public world men have to impress people that they do not know; in group therapy, as at home, men get to know people that they do not impress.

In our group, Carol was dismayed by Chuck's openness because she got so little of it at home. Was he genuine in risking, or merely performing? Was she really supporting his vulnerability, or did it frighten her to the point that *she* distanced *him* at home? This complex matter could be teased apart effectively in the couples group format.

The group found Al doubly tough because of his intellectualizing and his censorship of topics: work and probably others. He made some progress, but not as much as Bob, who evolved from tight-lipped, insecure arrogance to be an egalitarian husband and venturesome participant in group.

In couples group therapy, people discover for themselves what experienced therapists have learned about how marriages work, fail, or just muddle along. The purpose of couples group is to cultivate individual growth in the presence of one's spouse, aided by peers and therapists. This experience, and the formation of strong new relationships, concerns us more than the analysis of group dynamics. Because spouses are often locked in stifling psychological embrace, we look to cross-couple dyads to spur and nurture change in individuals first, and then their marriage systems. Outcome research supports the idea that improvement in couples group is double-or-nothing: "Positive evaluation of the group marital therapy experience by participants or by independent evaluators rests upon the presence of an improved marital *interaction*" and not only individual change (Gurman, 1975, p. 200).

We do not emphasize dominance, scapegoats, or group moods. In traditional fashion, we note absences and strong feelings about the leaders. We feel responsible for group morale, including cohesiveness, and for protecting members against harm. We as leaders represent structure, rules, and general guidance. We urge members to address issues other than the patently marital, and to engage with other group members as individuals. At first, these themes or tasks seem somewhat paradoxical in *couples* therapy. But when individuals emerge from the shadow of the couple each belongs to, and the marriage clearly benefits, a telling point has been made, and the group enters a mature and exciting second stage.

We encourage, and try to model, a combination of direct emotional expression and constructive, thoughtful communication. "Truth with tact," as Thoreau put it. In so doing, we walk a sometimes narrow line between "dumping" and hiding feelings. We acknowledge and deal with the paradoxes found in most forms of psychotherapy: Emotional freedom and spontaneity of expression develop within strict limits; healthy self-disclosure depends on privacy and the right to have secrets; trust builds in situations of potential harm (emotional risk).

Because it is real, couples group holds more fascination than any staged drama. Although Carol and Chuck often went home from group sessions angry and miserable, Amy and Al looked forward to group as their best evening of the week, a pump priming for private conversation afterward. The real drama and excitement lead members from a formal commitment to a more emotional one: the "third family." In time, members learn the techniques and ideology (or philosophy) of the leaders, who, among other things, differ from one another nonviolently, if not always lovingly. From the start, members see and express things as well or better than the leaders; becoming therapeutic with others is just as important for members as is taking help from others. The leaders encourage this development and freely acknowledge their need and appreciation for this help.

Professionalism and prudence bar therapists from using sessions for personal help, for example, with marital conflict. People pay us to focus on their needs. Those who advocate blurring the lines between patient and therapist may consider us aloof and defensive; we think they are insensitive and selfish. Therapists may refer to relevant personal problems that are under control if it seems helpful to the group. This is not to say that we avoid conflict altogether; disagreement in the group process can be very enlightening if handled appropriately. Revealing a major event such as the death of a parent may be essential for a therapist in this other "family," and valuable to it. But self-disclosure can become a fetish, a mindless indulgence for patients and therapists alike, as bad in its way as withholding or dissembling. The leaders' own vulnerability can be revealed and used, but is always subordinate to the needs of those we serve.

Another facet of therapist responsibility is keeping confidences, so that no material from individual sessions is "leaked" into the group (or into any couples session). We know of cases in which this basic ethical principle was breached, causing havoc in groups, departure of couples, and irreparable loss of confidence in the leadership. Some therapists argue that it is too difficult for them to compartmentalize material obtained in different settings. Others feel that all secrets are pathogenic, an intriguing but simplistic conclusion. Some therapists argue that keeping patients' secrets amounts to collusion with the illness or defenses. But passing secrets on, or denying a truly private forum, seems worse to us. Secrets are not magic; some of them are powerful, but the analysis of that power and import cannot be swept aside with a "tell all" reflex. We have kept secrets about affairs, jobs, fame and fortune, mastectomy, homosexual adventures, etc. Some such matters have been revealed in group by the people concerned, usually with our encouragement but never by our usurping the responsibility for telling. We will not even be lured into revealing something by an assurance that "my spouse knows everthing I've told you—you can bring it up if you want to." We find that people who deny secrets or seem "allergic" to them are using disclosure to control feelings or behavior, their own or the partner's.

We are surprised and distressed by the cavalier treatment of this topic by a number of professionals, reminiscent of the cavalier dismissal of jealousy as a legitimate emotion in the heyday of "open marriage." Therapists cannot escape the burden of keeping other people's secrets. We do it willy-nilly; for example, when secrets about neighbors, friends, colleagues or celebrities are told us in privileged communication. After the novelty wears off, we must develop compartments for things we wish we did not know, and for things we want to know but cannot use overtly. In handling confidential material regarding our couples, we model an essential group function: holding privileged information in confidence. If members cannot do this for one another, they do not belong in group therapy. Trust is slow to build and quick to collapse. Openness cannot endure without trust; where openness threatens trust, the leader should support limited disclosure. The underlying value assumption is that relationship outweights "truth" when the two are incompatible.

Unlike other group therapies, this one has specific subgroups meeting between sessions. Barring separations, spouse pairs go home together. The process of "home fermentation" probably accelerates progress in group therapy, but at times it can reinforce resistance. There is no way to prevent spouses from discussing group sessions, opinions about other couples, and the like, and some of this material may remain inaccessible. The leaders should be alert to intentional or unwitting collusion, evidenced at times by guilty glances toward a spouse when certain subjects come up.

Couple-led couples group therapy provides unique therapeutic symmetry. Each member relates to both same-sex and opposite-sex leaders. We postulate four different therapeutic dyads:

Therapist

Patient		Male	Female
	M	M–m	M–f
	F	F–m	F–f

Much has been written recently about the fact that most psychiatrists and psychologists are men, while a majority of their patients are women. We believe that the gender of therapist and patient are relevant considerations in treatment, although a well-qualified therapist of either sex can be helpful in most situations. We go so far as to say that men and women need and seek different things in relationships, including therapy. The recent work of Gilligan (1982) suggests that men thrive on autonomy and fear intimacy, while women thrive on connectedness and fear isolation. Extrapolating to therapy, we might say that the chief task for women is to develop autonomy without sacrificing relationship; the task for men is to develop intimacy without losing the sense of autonomy. Women's need for relationship and their sensitivity to others' needs often masks their own independent values. Women become compliant for the sake of relationship, while men may move in the opposite direction, asserting difference in order to prove their autonomy.

These interesting and complex dynamics figure in therapeutic work, whether or not labeled "transference," to a degree that is only beginning to be appreciated. Men's autonomy may be threatened when they are in the patient role, and this may explain in part their reluctance to enter therapy before they are desperate. Women more easily yield autonomy in the service of relationship, and they readily use the structured, intense, process regardless of the sex of the therapist. Because of the sexual element, the experience of intimacy with a trusted male may make a woman patient feel comfortably adult. The male patient with a female therapist might be inclined to feel boyish rather than adult, since she is the leader, the authority. Following the paradigm logically, we suppose that intimacy develops most easily in the two-woman dyad, least in the two-man situation. Other factors play a part, of course, including the ages of therapist and patient, and the personal history and current relationships of each person.

Couples group therapy is one modality that embraces all four permutations of therapist–client dyad. Just as we encourage cross-couple interaction among members, so we relate as therapists on an individual basis to members; we do not feel the need to provide a "united front" on every issue. A flexible approach to individual sessions allows the most effective combinations to be reinforced, the difficult or resistant ones to be balanced. For example, a wife who relates especially well to the female therapist but is having a hard time in the group can be seen individually for a few sessions to work on issues in a more concentrated or supportive context. On occasion it may be useful to discuss or interpret the different relationship issues (transference or other) manifest in the group to illustrate the qualities of different dyads. As in individual therapy, however, we are inclined to leave well enough alone, not making interpretation an end in itself. We prefer to let relationships develop and intensify, using interpretation judiciously to clear difficulties from the path.

Just as the need for individual or family sessions is handled flexibly, so is the need for medication. For example, when a member is too depressed or anxious to function adequately, medication will be considered on an individual basis. We are primarily psychotherapists, and medication is resorted to only when suffering or disability seriously limits participation in psycho-therapy, the living situation, or both.

As a couple leading couples group therapy, we provide a marital model, for better or worse. We can joke about how the sessions cause us to shape up our relationship at least every Thursday night! Members have not been averse to challenging us, notably when the more experienced therapist made a statement of respect for the equal merit of his colleague and spouse. Some members found the comment patronizing because they had long since taken the matter for granted. The co-therapist found her spouse's comment welcome, and everyone enjoyed and learned from the complex interplay of marriage and therapy.

Recent literature brings marriage to the fore as both cause and effect in psychiatric illness and social pathology (Merikangas, 1984; Bird, Schuham, & Martin, 1984). Conjoint treatment cannot be slighted as a treatment modality, despite its refusal to fit the medical model. Couples group therapy imposes certain limits of time and freedom to speak, but it provides advantages of scale and, with couple leadership, gender symmetry with parental and peer models. It should enjoy an important place in the repertoire of every marital therapist.

REFERENCES

Bird, H. W., Schuham, A., & Martin, P. A. (1984). Reply to James E. Miles on "The marriage of the collapsible man of prominence." American Journal of Psychiatry, 141, 153–154.

Budman, S. H., Bennett, M. J., & Wisneski, M. J. (1981). An adult developmental model of short-term group psychotherapy. In S. H. Budman (Ed.), Forms of brief therapy. New York: Guilford Press.

Cohen, H. (1977, February 2). Family counsel. Interview with Susan B. Lieberman, broadcast and tape recorded, WAMU-FM, Washington, DC.

Framo, J. L. (1973). Marriage therapy in a couples group. In D. Bloch (Ed.), Techniques of family psychotherapy: A primer. New York: Grune & Stratton.

Gibran, K. (1923). The prophet. New York: Knopf.

Gilligan, C. (1982). In a different voice. Cambridge, MA: Harvard University Press.

Grunebaum, H., & Crist, J. (1968). Interpretation and the task of the therapist with couples and families. International Journal of Group Psychotherapy, 18, 495–503.

Gurman, A. S. (1975). Some therapeutic implications of marital therapy research. In A. S. Gurman & D. G. Rice (Eds.), *Couples in conflict*. New York: Jason Aronson.

Gurman, A. S. (1981). Integrative marital therapy: Toward the development of an interpersonal approach. In S. H. Budman (Ed.), *Forms of brief therapy*. New York: Guilford Press.

Gurman, A. S., & Kniskern, D. P. (1978). Deterioration in marital and family therapy. *Family Process*, 17, 3–20.

Kaslow, F., & Lieberman, E. J. (1981). Couples group therapy: Rationale, dynamics and process. In G. P. Sholevar (Ed.), *The handbook of marriage and marital therapy*. New York: Specturm.

Leichter, E. (1975). Treatment of married couples groups. In A. S. Gurman & D. G. Rice (Eds.), *Couples in conflict*. New York: Jason Aronson.

Lewin, K. (1948). The background of conflict in marriage. In K. Lewin, *Resolving social conflicts*. New York: Harper & Row.

Mace, D. (1974). Marital and sexual counseling: The state of the art. In D. W. Abse, E. M. Nash, & L. M. R. Louden (Eds.), *Marital and sexual counseling in medical practice*, 2nd ed. Hagerstown, MD: Harper & Row.

Martin, P. (1983). Group psycotherapy with couples. In H. I. Kaplan & B. J. Sadock (Eds.), *Comprehensive group psychotherapy* (2d ed.). Baltimore: Williams & Wilkins.

Merikangas, K. R. (1984). Divorce and assortative mating among depressed patients. *American Journal of Psychiatry*, 141, 74–76.

Neiberg, N. A. (1976). The group psychotherapy of married couples. In H. Grunebaum & J. Christ (Eds.), *Contemporary marriage: Structure, dynamics and therapy*. Boston: Little, Brown.

Papanek, H. (1971). Group therapy with married couples. In H. I. Kaplan & B. J. Sadock (Eds.), *Comprehensive group psychotherapy*. Baltimore: Williams & Wilkins.

Whitaker, C. A., Greenberg, A., & Greenberg, M. L. (1981). Existential marital therapy: A synthesis. In G. P. Sholevar (Ed.), *The handbook of marriage and marital therapy*. New York: Spectrum.

Williams, A. M., & Miller, W. R. (1981). Evaluation and research on marital therapy. In G. P. Sholevar (Ed.), *The handbook of marriage and marital therapy*. New York: Spectrum.

Yalom, I. D. (1975). *The theory and practice of group psychotherapy* (2d ed.). New York: Basic Books.

Yalom, I. D. (1980). *Existential psychotherapy*. New York: Basic Books.

Emotionally Focused
Couples Therapy

LESLIE S. GREENBERG
SUSAN M. JOHNSON

THEORETICAL BACKGROUND

This approach to marital therapy is based on an experiential tradition in psychotherapy, which emphasizes the role of affect in change (Greenberg & Safran, 1984a; Perls, Hefferline, & Goodman, 1951; Satir, 1967), and on the systemic tradition, which emphasizes the role of communication and interactional cycles in maintaining problem states (Hoffman, 1982; Sluzki, 1978; Watzlawick, Beavin, & Jackson, 1967).

Experiential Theory

Experiential therapy is an outgrowth of humanistic-existential theory. Gestalt therapy, one of the major experiential therapies, although developed and applied in the context of individual therapy, particularly lends itself to thinking about organism–environment interactions (Greenberg, 1983; Kaplan & Kaplan, 1982; Perls, 1973). Gestalt is wholistic in its philosophy and attempts to overcome both organism–environment and mind–body dualities by adopting a field conception of human functioning that leads to focusing on what is occurring between the organism and the environment at the contact boundary. Gestalt views thus lend themselves to an integration with systemic perspectives in which context is regarded as an important determinant of behavior. Perls's concept of field, drawn from Lewin (1935), emphasizes that at every moment the individual is a part of some field and that it is the

Leslie S. Greenberg and Susan M. Johnson. Department of Counseling Psychology, University of British Columbia, Vancouver, British Columbia, Canada.

nature of the relationship between the individual and the environment that determines behavior. Neither creates the other; rather, each stands in a relationship of mutuality to the other. In this view, both perception and context are important determinants of human behavior. However, in its work with individuals, Gestalt therapy has focused primarily on individual awareness, to the neglect of environmental context. With this emphasis on awareness, the person's current organization of the world and the figure–background formation process have been the focus of therapy. Blocks to awareness and experiencing, such as restrictions of awareness, avoidance, and the disowning of aspects of current experience, have been seen as central to individual dysfunction.

In an experiential view of human functioning (Rogers, 1951; Perls, Hefferline, & Goodman, 1951), experiencing is regarded as a primary referent or datum. According to this view, people are not purely rational or cognitive but also respond wholistically to situations in adaptive ways. People are regarded as wiser than their intellects alone and as functioning more effectively when they pay attention to all of their internal experiences. In addition, people are seen as active organizers of their perceptual world, and it is these perceptions that determine their behavior. The therapist in this approach attempts to enter the person's frame of reference to explore the reality of the world as it appears to that person. Acceptance of "what is," by both therapist and client, is a cornerstone of this phenomenological approach. As blocks to experiencing and restrictions of awareness are encountered, the client is helped to identify with and integrate these aspects of functioning, thereby expanding the scope of experience and making available potentially adaptive organismic feelings and needs.

Individuals are viewed as having inherent tendencies to survive and grow and develop their capabilities in ways that will serve to maintain or enhance the organism. All behavior, therefore, derives from individuals' quests to actualize themselves. As such, it can be assumed that at any moment, people's behaviors are their optimal means of actualizing themselves in their current contexts, as they perceive them. For example, a woman may be feeling very hurt and in need of support, but in her life experience a person who expressed hurt was regarded as weak and was either depreciated or ignored. Therefore, when she is hurt, she believes it is important to be strong. When hurt by her husband, she defends by attacking verbally—by blaming him and telling him he does not appreciate her. These behaviors bring her neither the comfort nor the support she needs; rather, they serve to distance her husband. What she is striving for is to have her husband accept her and provide comfort and support. Her underlying need for support and comfort is an organismically important one; however, her method of communicating this need is dysfunctional and is based both on her perceptions and on the contextual conditions that seem to support these perceptions. She blames her spouse, and he, in turn, having learned that it is important to be right, defends his actions, which she then experiences as unsupportive.

This interaction is organized in a reciprocally determined way in which she and her husband each act according to his or her perceptions of the situation and mutually alienate one another. In this way, expressions of basically adaptive human needs for support and self-esteem can result in negative interactional cycles.

In our view, people are active perceivers who construct meanings and organize what they see or hear on the basis of their current emotional states and experiential organizations (Kaplan & Kaplan, 1982). The person's current experiential organization determines perception and action. Emotions, thoughts, bodily sensations, and images are all aspects of the ongoing experiential process, the organization of which determines the person's behavior. What is significant about a person's experiential process is that at any one moment more is going on than is available to awareness or observation. A person's current organization of experience utilizes only some of the information available to the person and structures this into only one of a number of possible self-organizations. At any moment, there are a large number of internal processes out of which an individual's conscious experience emerges. Greenberg and Safran (1984a, 1984b, in press) have elaborated an information-processing model of emotion in which emotional experience is constructed by integrating information from a set of expressive motor reactions, schematic emotional memories, and self-schemas, plus a set of conceptual rules about emotional expression. These components are all aspects of a person's current process, many of which are out of awareness and all of which are continually being integrated to form some final conscious emotional experience.

According to this view, a person can, at one point, be organized as "vulnerable" and at another time be "assertive." At any one time, a particular organization dominates, while other organizations and aspects of experience are not in focal awareness. In this manner, people's immediate organization of experience dominates focal awareness and governs their functioning. A person who chronically organizes experience in terms of feelings of hurt and rejection is inclined to perceive a spouse's actions as directed against him or her, whereas when this same person organizes his or her experience as feeling loved, he or she may perceive the spouse's same actions as unrelated to him or her. In addition, when individuals' dominant self-organizations are restricted, their response alternatives are limited.

Kaplan and Kaplan (1982), in a paper on Gestalt family therapy, have argued that internal experience can be viewed as determined by field factors as well as by intrapsychic processes. They suggest that by focusing on processes between the individual and the environment, field processes that determine individual experience can be identified in the here and now of the interactional field. Just as a person may be viewed as disowning aspects of the experience, such as sadness or anger, because of internal blocks or splits, so too can these experiences be viewed as discordant with, or disallowed by, particular relationship rules or contexts. The experience and expression of a particular emotion implies a certain relationship definition that may be threatening or disallowed, and so experience and disclosure is avoided. The experience and expression of certain emotions may be disallowed because they are a threat to a definition of the self-in-relationship and to the relationship rules. What people attend to in themselves and their partner is determined by a set of internal categories or schemas that have their origins in the relationship itself. Each interaction is a current reminder of these categories, implying as it does rules such as, "Don't attend to your anger." In addition, people's concepts of themselves in a marriage are influenced by the manner in which they are treated by their spouses. The current functioning of an individual can therefore be viewed as being reflexively organized by both internal and field forces.

A person's experience is always organized so that some processes are relatively dominant and more focally in awareness. This concept is basic to a Gestalt view of human functioning. If individual or contextual factors act to interfere with the individual's most dominant experience rising to awareness, individual system dysfunction occurs and restricted awareness results. The person begins selectively to attend to a restricted subset of experience and avoids other experience. The result is that some aspects of experience fail to be integrated and are disowned or disallowed. People, therefore, become organized in terms of a limited set of contact possibilities permissible within a particular relationship context. In couples therapy, change can occur by changing the conditions that organize a particular form of contact between people, be it by changing one person's experience and perception, by changing the context (i.e., the other partner's position and pattern of responses), or most likely, by changing both simultaneously and in a reciprocally determining fashion.

Within an experiential framework that emphasized individual awareness, Satir (1967) added a much-needed focus on the importance of congruent communication and closeness in relationships. The affective systemic approach presented here clearly shows her influence and shares some of her goals in working with systems. According to Satir (1967), a mature person is (a) able to be in touch with feelings and needs; (b) can communicate these clearly; and (c) can accept others as different. This is what is needed for good communication in couples. Communication dysfunction within a couple is seen as reciprocally related to the self-concepts and self-esteem of the individuals. Satir believes that the family functions as a system and regards the feeling or emotional system of the family as of primary importance. This system is being expressed through communication, and she strives to have people communicate congruently in order to clarify interactions. Her practice is characterized by responding tenderly and empathically to people's pain. The giving and receiving of support and nurturance are central in her practice. This supportive emphasis helps people experience and express feelings congruently. Communication lies in the affective domain. This emphasis on affect places her approach in an experiential framework while the emphasis on the communicative aspect of affect and on the interrelatedness of people's behavior places her approach in a communication–systems framework.

AN INTEGRATED APPROACH

In the affective systematic approach presented here, the focus of treatment is to change both the interactional cycle and each person's experience of the relationship. Negative interaction cycles in couples have been observed repeatedly to evolve in dealing with issues concerning closeness and distance and dominance and submission. Once a negative interaction cycle is in place, it seems to become its own reason for existence and is extremely difficult to dislodge by behavioral training. The focus in this approach is, first, on clearly identifying repetitive interactional sequences of behavior around these issues and assessing the positions that people adopt in these interactions; and, second, on reframing their positions and redefining the problem in terms of their underlying feelings. In this view of marital interaction, communication is seen as an attempt at establishing a relationship definition that in turn maintains a particular self-definition.

In an integrated experiential–systemic view, organization of both the individual subsystems and the whole, the couple system can be seen as interdependent and as varying simultaneously and reflexively. For example, when the interaction is organized in a complementary fashion, such as "pursue–distance" or "attack–withdraw," the individuals can be seen as organized so that pursue and attack, or distance and withdrawal, are the dominant aspects of their individual organization. This organization is maintained simultaneously and is supported by both (a) *the negative interaction cycle* (i.e., couple system functioning) and (b) *some individual processes being more dominant in focal awareness* (i.e., individual subsystem functioning). Change in interaction is brought about by reframing negative interactional cycles in terms of underlying or subdominant emotional experiences in each partner.

This approach to therapy with couples involves attention to the current interaction and the current experiential process within the individual. Change occurs both by change in people's view of themselves and by change in their context (i.e., in the partner's communication). Insight in this approach is not enough to bring about change in people's views of themselves. Rather, clients must experience, on an emotionally meaningful level, new aspects of themselves and new interactions. Partners must encounter each other in the session and participate in a "corrective emotional experience," which reestablishes the possibility of having a positive human relationship with each other.

This approach is predicated on the assumption that the members of the couple have healthy feelings, needs, and wants that will emerge with the help of the therapist. A major hypothesis of this approach is that accessing and expressing primary feelings, needs, and wants by the spouses can aid adaptive problem solving and produce intimacy. It is not people's feelings and wants that cause problems in marriage (Wile, 1981), but the disowning or disallowing of these feelings and wants that leads to ineffective communication and escalating interactional cycles. Some of the major needs in couples are needs for closeness, contact–comfort, and intimacy. Intrapsychic fears of closeness and interactional patterns that prevent closeness are therefore major targets of change.

This approach involves encouraging people to make explicit statements to their spouses of currently experienced feelings and needs. A strong distinction is made between "talking about" feelings versus involvement in the current moment and congruent expression of experience. Experience and communication of currently experienced feeling are far more likely to produce change than intellectual insight or discussion about feelings. The use of the basic skills of good communication is seen as emerging more as a result of change than bringing about change. Affectively oriented encounters create change in communication style as partners experience themselves and their partner differently. The experiencing of new feelings helps motivate problem solving and good communication practices. The perception of the partner as more accessible and responsive also motivates and facilitates open communication. Poor communication skills often reflect a relationship definition that disallows congruent disclosures and open dialogue. When partners witness the disclosure of fears, for example, rather than defensive reactions, such as aloofness, new responses are often elicited by their new perception of their partner's vulnerability. This sets a new interactional cycle in process.

THE PROCESS OF CHANGE

How do the experience and expression of emotion bring about change in couple interaction? It seems that affective expression is involved in change at two levels in couples therapy, for affect is both a means of communication and a motivator of individual action.

In interpersonal interaction, affect is a primary signaling system that serves a communicative function from birth. Infants are equipped with a set of adaptive expressive patterns long before their capacities for exclusively human cognitive operations are developed. Through certain organized behavior patterns, infants communicate their needs, wants, and distress. Their ability to communicate through the facial musculature is highly developed and serves as a nonverbal system of affective communication. This affective behavior is not a release but a form of communication that is either understood or misunderstood by the parent.

Affective expression, therefore, is a crucial form of communication, and expression of particular emotions have particular significance in human interaction. For example, vulnerability tends to "disarm," while anger creates "distance." The expression of fear and vulnerability, besides evoking compassion, also communicates analogically that "this is not an attack" and often represents a major change in position in the interaction by that person, especially if the prior position was either blaming or withdrawing. Similarly, expressions of sadness and pain communicate a need for support, while newly recognized or expressed anger and resentment help define differences, delineate individual boundaries in the relationship, and can represent major changes in position in an interaction. All are complex means of analogic communication.

The degree of closeness–distance and dominance–submission, the two indices of greatest importance in assessing couple interaction, can be modified effectively by appropriate changes in affective expression. The expression of fear or sadness tends to evoke protection and compassion in the other, and this can result in closeness; anger or disgust produces clear personal and interactional boundaries and can result in greater independence, appropriate separateness, and recognition by the other of one's rights. For example, the statement by a dominant member of his or her fear of rejection and need for acceptance can generate closeness, while the expression of resentment by a withdrawn partner or a statement of dislike by a placating partner helps establish boundaries and appropriate distance. The emergence of emotions in the session as both a currently "lived" experience and a change in expression is important in providing *new information* in the relationship. Information is derived both from the *analogic* level of communication and from the *difference* between the new and the earlier expressions. Thus it is not the oft-repeated litany of resentments or the continually expressed sadness that is sought after in this therapy but the previously unexpressed resentment or the buried sadness.

Although expressions of love and intimacy can be inherently reparative in intimate relationships, these expressions are often more the result than the process of an affectively oriented couples therapy. The primary emotions expressed most often as part of an affective therapy are fear and vulnerability, sadness and pain, and anger and resentment. Major changes in interactional sequence can be brought about by reframing a negative interactional cycle in terms of the unexpressed aspect of the person's feeling. A "pursue–distance" interaction can therefore be reframed in terms of the pursuer's caring or fear and the distancer's fear or unexpressed resentment. *The reframe is much more likely to be experienced as valid when these previously unacknowledged feelings are experienced and expressed during therapy.* The deeper the experience and expression of these feelings, the stronger the reframe and the change in meaning of the interaction. The new expressions are also themselves changes in the interactional sequence, which promotes further changes in the interaction in a mutually causal circular process.

In discussing how change in individuals' experience of themselves comes about, Greenberg and Safran (1984a, in press) argue that affect and cognition are not related linearly but are essentially interdependent; and it is misleading to focus on one to the exclusion of the other. The experience of emotion is rather the end product of a set of automatic or unconscious information processing activities. A recent network analysis of emotion (Leventhal, 1979) in which emotion is shown to be a *construction* of expressive-motor reactions, emotional schemas or memories, and ideas, rather than an *inference,* or product of thought, show that activation of any one of the components can evoke other parts of the network. In this view, activation of one component automatically spreads to other components of the network, increasing their probability of becoming conscious or producing a conscious emotional experience.

Emotional experience is therefore as much a function of information processing that takes place at preconceptual, expressive motor and schematic memory levels as it is a function of conceptual cognition (Greenberg & Safran, 1984a, 1984b). Purely conscious conceptual change involving a change in people's reasoning or attributions does not necessarily produce a change at an emotional level. What is needed for emotional experience and change of this experience is the evocation of all three levels of processing.

Affect is very important in changing attitudes because affectively laden internal information appears to be closely linked to people's self-schemas and tends to override other cues and dominate the formation of meaning. Greenberg and Safran (1984a, in press) have noted a number of intrapsychic change processes in which affect plays an important role, two of which are highly relevant to couples therapy. The first is the process of *acknowledging previously unacknowledged biologically adaptive primary emotions* that aid problem solving. The second is *the modification of state-dependent cognitions* that emerge for therapeutic consideration only when the person is in the aroused affective state. These affective change processes occur in each individual during the process of successful couples therapy. Accessing biologically adaptive primary emotions, previously not dominant in individuals' organization of their experience, provides information that helps people define themselves better, increases motivation for and enhances problem solving, and helps spouses communicate their needs more clearly. Greenberg and Safran (1984b, in press) emphasize that not all emotional experiences are adaptive and that it is necessary to assess emotional expression in therapy as being expressions of either facilitative primary adaptive emotions or disruptive, secondary reactive, or instrumental emotions. Secondary reactive emotions, such as defensive anger, are secondary to more primary underlying biologically adaptive experience such as fear, whereas instrumental emotions, such as manipulative crying to get help, are expressed *in order* to make impacts on others. These latter emotions can disrupt problem solving and are not encouraged in an emotionally focused treatment. Rather, the experience and expression of primary emotions such as fear, pain, anger, and joy are in themselves biologically adaptive responses to a situation and are encouraged.

These emotions are action tendencies (Arnold, 1968) and provide a disposition to respond in a particular way that can aid problem solving.

In addition to affect leading to change by enhancing problem solving motivation, it has become clear that arousal of currently experienced emotions can provide access to certain state-dependent learnings. Certain core cognitions, cognitive–affective sequences, and complex meanings learned originally in particular affective states are much more accessible when that state is revived. Accessing these "hot cognitions" (Safran & Greenberg, 1982) can be particularly important in clarifying couples' interactions because often momentary construals that induce certain key behaviors in the interaction are not readily available for recall when the problem is being discussed coolly, after the fact, in therapy. Helping couples re-create the situation and relive the emotions in therapy often makes the cognitions governing these behaviors more available for inspection, clarification, and modification.

In summary, change occurs in this approach by a deepening of experience that brings new aspects of self into focal awareness and into the interaction. Specific interactional behaviors are positively reframed in terms of these unlerlying emotional states, which then lead to change in the sequence of interactions. At least five processes of change appear to occur in the emotionally focused treatment of couples:

1. An individual perceives himself or herself differently by bringing into focal awareness experiences not previously dominant in this person's view of self. For example, "I see and accept my vulnerability."
2. The spouse, upon witnessing the partner's new affective expressions, perceives the partner in a new way. For example, "I see your need for caring and contact rather than your hostility."
3. The individual's personal reorganization leads to different behavior in the interaction with the spouses. For example, "I now ask you for reassurance from a position of vulnerability."
4. The spouse's new perceptions of the partner leads to different responses. For example, "I comfort you rather than withdraw."
5. As a function of their partner's new behaviors, individuals come to see themselves in a new way. For example, "Since I can fulfill your needs, I see myself as valuable and necessary to you."

The combination of the above processes leads to a redefinition of the self in the relationship for both partners. Different aspects of the self are accepted in the relationship and expression of these leads to a change in the interactional sequences. The partners' views of each other are framed in new terms, and so their responses to their partners are different, and they are more able to accept certain behaviors in their spouses that were previously unacceptable. Because of the high demand for disclosure, this whole process is conducive to the building of intimacy and emotional bonds, both of which are key aspects of marital satisfaction (Tolstedt & Stokes, 1983).

THE PROCESS OF THERAPY

The treatment manual for training in this approach contains the nine steps outlined below:

1. Delineate conflict issues in the core struggle.
2. Identify the negative interaction cycle.
3. Access unacknowledged feelings.
4. Reframe the problem in terms of underlying feelings.
5. Promote identification with disowned needs.
6. Promote acceptance of partner's experience.
7. Facilitate expression of needs and wants.
8. Establish the emergence of new solutions.
9. Consolidate new positions.

Although the process of therapy is delineated here in terms of a linear sequence of steps, therapy actually progresses in a circular rather than a linear manner. A deepening and development occur over the sessions as new, previously unacknowledged emotional responses slowly become accessed, acknowledged, and communicated in the relationship.

Step 1: The Delineation of Conflict Issues and Themes in the Core Struggle

The therapist begins by helping the couple delineate conflict issues and describe attempted solutions. Each partner's perception of the relationship problem is explored and validated. The therapist also begins to identify themes in the struggle between the spouses; often such themes will center on control and the issues of separateness and connectedness, which Rausch, Barry, Hertel, and Swain (1974) suggest represent the core issues in the majority of marital conflicts. The focus of the initial exploration is on how partners view themselves in relation to each other and the positions each partner takes in the process of interaction. The therapist also enquires about the history of the relationship, the developmental stage of the relationship, the tasks implied by that stage, and the level of present commitment. The therapist begins to identify and clarify the positions each partner takes by first observing the couple's interaction during the session and identifying sequences of problematic reactions as the couple narrates them. The therapist begins as soon as possible to relate the behavior of each spouse to the stimulus provided by the other's behavior, and their perceptions of each other's intentions and motivations. The therapist begins to frame the relationship problems in terms of deprivation and unmet needs (Wile, 1981), and in terms of repetitious circular escalating interactions that alienate the partners from each other (Guerin, 1982; Watzlawick, Beavin, & Jackson, 1967). The partners are portrayed as equal participants in the creation of such repetitious interactions and equally imprisoned by them.

The therapist is working constantly in the first few sessions to join with both partners and maintain balanced coalitions by validating both partners. The goal is the establishment of a positive therapeutic alliance with each partner (Bordin, 1979), to create trust, to convey hope regarding positive treatment outcomes, to establish shared goals, and to agree on therapeutic tasks that will attain these goals. The therapist attempts to validate each client's perspective even if partners present opposing realities, and takes the position that both clients are entitled to their feelings and point of view.

Step 2: The Identification of the Negative Interaction Cycle

Once the therapist is clear about how each partner perceives the problem and has begun to explore the positions each takes in the process of interaction, the negative interaction cycle is identified and the resulting alienation experienced by the couple highlighted. An example of such a cycle might be, "When you seek attention in this way, he withdraws and becomes more silent. You become upset and try harder to get his attention and the cycle repeats itself. You finally give up and withdraw." In such cycles, both partners attempt to protect themselves, and each attempt intensifies the problem for the other. Such cycles may be talked about and reconstructed, or they may occur in the therapy session where the therapist identifies and comments on them as they happen. The identification of the cycle as it is occurring makes it easier to establish it vividly and access the underlying experience.

Negative communication practices in these cycles, such as accusing, interrupting, or mindreading, begin to be explored in terms of underlying feelings and needs, usually feelings of fear or loneliness and need for contact or reassurance. A pursue–distance cycle seems to be the most basic and most frequently occurring interactional pattern in distressed couples. This cycle is focused on as the core negative cycle. The framing of behavior in terms of this interactional cycle fosters a perspective of mutual responsibility and allows the partners to see how they each perpetuate the deprivation that they both find so distressing.

Step 3: The Accessing of Unacknowledged Feelings

Having identified the cycle, the therapist focuses on accessing and validating the unacknowledged feelings underlying the interactional positions in the problematic cycle. For example, a husband's tendency toward self-denigration and passive withdrawal, especially when confronted by his wife, might be explored in terms of his feelings of personal inadequacy in relation to her and his ensuing need for distance in the relationship.

Emotional responses at the periphery of awareness are attended to by focusing inward; they are heightened and linked to self-perceptions. Particular attention is paid to vulnerabilities, fears, and unexpressed resentments. Significant relationship events arousing strong emotion are reconstructed or enacted in the session to reveal underlying emotion. Clients are thus exposed to new aspects of self in the presence of the other spouse. The experience and expression of emotion are to be distinguished from the ventilation of superficial and/or defensive reactions; rather than a reactive response, what is occurring is the synthesis of a new emotional experience in the present. An example of a superficial reaction would be an angry or blaming reaction expressed with no awareness of the sense of threat or underlying fear. Such a reaction is expanded by exploring the underlying experience of fear.

Many of the basic methods used by the therapist to facilitate the accessing of emotional responses come from Gestalt therapy (Perls, Hefferline, & Goodman, 1951) and from developments in client-centered therapy, such as evocative responding (Rice, 1974; Rice & Saperia, 1984). In the Gestalt approach, questions, suggestions, and attention to nonverbal expression are used to increase present awareness and deepen experience. Questions, such as, "What do you experience as you say this?" or suggestions, such as, "Tell this to your wife—I feel frightened when you don't respond," are used to heighten emotional experience and contact. Evocative responding attempts to re-create experiences by vividly evoking the stimulus situation and the subjective response to it and then to explore the client's idiosyncratic experience of the situations. For example, if the therapist wishes to evoke a situation, either the stimulus or the client's response can be focused on to help bring the situation alive again. The therapist may make the stimulus more clear, specific or alive, by focusing on cues in the situation and the meaning of the cues to the individual so as to differentiate the impact of a particular stimulus.

Consider the following example:

THERAPIST: What is it that sparks off your cynicism and makes it hard for you to listen to him?
WIFE: He's so condescending, I get hostile.
THERAPIST: What about the way he does this gets to you?
WIFE: He is so logical, never lets go, and that look on his face, looking down his nose like he is saying, "I know better."
THERAPIST: He seems to be looking down sort of cold and superior.

If the client's response in a situation is unclear, the therapist can help differentiate the response so that the couple can clarify and elaborate their interactions in terms of emotion, cognition, and behavior.

Consider the following example:

THERAPIST: So what happens when Pat tells you that she doesn't want to make love, and turns away?
HUSBAND: Nothing, I accept it, might ask her why.
THERAPIST: I'm wondering if you don't feel hurt or feel that need to get back at her?
HUSBAND: Yeah, I do feel hurt, sort of deserted and helpless.

THERAPIST: And what do you do when you are feeling this way?

HUSBAND: Well, I lie quietly for a while, but I am smoldering inside.

THERAPIST *(to wife)*: What is happening for you as he lies there in silence, smoldering inside?

The therapist continues in this way to differentiate both partners' internal responses in order to deepen their experience and identify the sequences.

More interpretation of inner states is used in couples therapy than in individual experiential therapy because with both partners present and their emotional reactions to each other occurring more visibly in the session, checks on the validity of the interpretations are more easily available. In general, then, the therapist may attempt to supply missing feelings, or supply sentences for a client to finish. The therapist also attends to bodily sensations the client is experiencing in the present and pays special attention to nonverbal behavior in general. Images and metaphors, such as feeling like a trapped animal, may also be used to heighten and clarify emotional responses. The focus in on looking at, and owning, each inner experience. This experience is then validated by the therapist. There is a continuing focus on the emotional experience occurring in the present. This focus results in spouses' becoming aware of the primary emotional responses that underlie their patterns of interaction and communication.

An example is presented below of an episode of accessing feelings in one member of a couple. The couple came into therapy with problems of alienation and the cessation of their sexual relationship. The relationship had been characterized in the early sessions as one in which she pursued him for more emotional communication, and he withdrew. Then, unable to have the contact she wanted, she withdrew, and they became alienated from each other.

This excerpt occurs toward the end of the fifth session and begins with the therapist focusing in on the wife's experience after having had the husband, in the earlier part of the session, look at his wife and express some of his feelings to her.

THERAPIST: What's happening?

HUSBAND: I, I—uh. *(Pause of 10 seconds.)*

THERAPIST: You experience some pain?

HUSBAND: I recognize this is the same situation, when I tell you something a lot of the time, you never quite accept it a lot of the time.

THERAPIST: It's difficult to touch her.

HUSBAND: You're pleased when I tell you something, but you never quite believe it.

THERAPIST *(to wife)*: What do you experience?

WIFE: *(she sighs.)*

THERAPIST: Would you like to believe him? Can you say this?

WIFE: It's very hard for me to believe you.

THERAPIST: You seem so convinced?

WIFE: Uh, hum.

THERAPIST: Can you tell him this, something about "I don't know how you could convince me?"

WIFE: I don't know how you could convince me. I've been feeling really ugly, especially the last few days.

THERAPIST: What do you want from him when you're feeling this way? Is there anything he could do for you?

WIFE: I don't know.

THERAPIST: Do you tell him, "I'm feeling bad, I'm feeling ugly?"

WIFE: No—maybe, sometimes (quietly).

THERAPIST: You're saying that's symbolic of how you're feeling inside?

WIFE: Uh-huh—that's how I've been feeling the last few days, really angry, pushed out of sorts, and when I get like that, the message I got that was always fed to me was you're bad if you feel that way, therefore you're ugly.

THERAPIST: From him?

WIFE: No, from long ago.

THERAPIST: So, inside you feel—you're getting this message you're bad, you're ugly for feeling angry. What do you want when you feel this way?

WIFE (sighs and looks down): What do I want? I usually want privacy.

THERAPIST: Somehow because you've never known that anybody could help you with that, the best thing is to be alone.

WIFE: Uh-huh. (Pause of 20 seconds.)

THERAPIST: I imagine I would want someone to hold me and tell me I was valuable. I don't want to impose that on you as I don't know, but somehow from all you say to me, it sounds like you really want to be loved.

WIFE: Uh-huh.

THERAPIST: But when you fear or decide that you can't get it, you take space?

WIFE: Uh-huh. (She looks down.)

THERAPIST: Somehow you're not sure he can give you this nurturing that you want so much. I don't think he knows that's what you really want, or he doesn't know he could really get to you because he gets so many messages of "leave me alone." (Pause of 20 seconds.) Can you tell me what's happening for you right now?

WIFE: Fear.

THERAPIST: Can you try to give a name to that fear. I'm afraid—

WIFE: (She looks down, pause of 15 seconds.)

THERAPIST: You're afraid that if he gets close to you, or if you let him get close, something bad might happen?

WIFE (after pause of 15 seconds): Yeah! (She looks up.) I guess I'm afraid to reach out.

THERAPIST: What might happen if you reach out that's bad? (Pause of 20 seconds.) Somehow you've had a strong learning that if you reach out, you don't get the acceptance you wanted so much. So it's difficult to risk that.

WIFE: (Cries quietly for 35 seconds then reaches for Kleenex.)

THERAPIST: Yuh! Where does this rejection come from initially?

WIFE: Parents.

THERAPIST: Uh-huh. Who particularly?

WIFE: I think both of them.

THERAPIST: Uh-huh. As you go into this—sad space—does any particular thing emerge for you, what's this feeling? I know it's a difficult tight knot.

WIFE: (She looks up and then down and cries.)

THERAPIST: Just some feeling like you can't get what you need?

WIFE: Uh-huh.

THERAPIST: You just want to be taken for who you are. What's it like for you in that experience?

WIFE (*after pause of 25 seconds*): I don't know.

THERAPIST: Are you beginning to withdraw now?

WIFE: Uh-huh.

THERAPIST: I see you sit there—I don't know if I said something that didn't fit. I know you're inside there wanting something?

WIFE: (*Cries for 20 seconds.*)

THERAPIST: But it's so difficult to come out?

WIFE: Uh-huh (*She breathes.*)

THERAPIST: I guess you're saying it's easier to close off that part and nurture it yourself, because bringing it out would be so confusing and painful and difficult?

WIFE: Yeah!

THERAPIST: So you kind of go in there and manage it all yourself?

WIFE: Uh-huh.

THERAPIST: And I think you're saying it kind of leaves you feeling lonely?

WIFE: Yeah.

THERAPIST: And out of contact?

WIFE: Yeah.

THERAPIST: Yeah. So what is it you would like, as I know you can't be rushed too quickly or be rushed in on too quickly? So what would you like from Michael in these situations? Would you like him to come in after you or give him a signal, or you just don't know?

WIFE: (*Cries, shakes head, and nods.*)

THERAPIST: I'm going to push you a little, right, as not knowing keeps you there. What would you like? What would make it easier for you so you could get more of what you want? (*Pause of 20 seconds.*) I'm going to ask you to do something difficult. Will you look at Michael and tell him you feel pain and hurt.

WIFE (*looks up*): Yeah, I feel hurt. (*She sobs loudly.*)

THERAPIST: Stay with that—it's painful. (*Pause of 20 seconds.*) What would you like? Can you hear me?

WIFE: Yes. (*She cries.*)

THERAPIST: What would you like from Michael? (*Pause of 15 seconds*) I do know that even if you want something without asking for it, you have to know what you want. What do you want?

WIFE (*looks up*): I don't know. Not to judge me. I don't know if he does, or it's just myself.

THERAPIST: Check with him.

WIFE: Do you judge me or is it just myself?

HUSBAND: I don't think so. When you're just saying what you feel.

THERAPIST: Will you tell her now as you see her cry what you experience.

HUSBAND: I share your pain. I want to put my arms around you, I want you not to hurt and I don't want to stop you hurting, but I just want to be with you.

THERAPIST: Do you know if she wants you to put your arms around her?

HUSBAND: There are many times you haven't wanted me to put my arms around you.

THERAPIST (*to wife*): Is that true?

WIFE: Yeah. (*She holds herself, rubs and then scratches her arm.*)

THERAPIST: Is that what you wanted then?

WIFE: Maybe. (*She rubs her arm.*)

THERAPIST: Try it, will you? Ask him, "I want you to hold me." I think you need to reach

out when you feel bad. I believe you can do it.
WIFE: Will you hold me?
HUSBAND: (*Moves over and hugs her.*)

This experience was then briefly discussed by the therapist and the major themes summarized. An agreement was established with them that the wife would reach out to her husband during the week when she felt vulnerable.

Step 4: Reframing the Problem

The problem is reframed in terms of newly synthesized underlying emotional experiences and related to legitimate unmet needs. Individual vulnerabilities are explored and interpreted, and individual experience is translated into the meaning carried for the other spouse and the relationship.

New perspectives on the relationship and the partner's behavior are created by the newly acknowledged feelings. For example, withdrawal may be seen as a fear response instead of as an attempt to punish or hurt. Attempts are made to capture these new feelings as they occur in interactions during the session. The clients are encouraged to interact with each other in the sessions and to share their underlying feelings as they emerge in the session in reaction to their partners. There is a strong focus on what is occurring in the present between the partners. These feelings are explored fully, both in terms of their personal meanings and their meaning to the partner. The experience of strong and significant emotion is a powerful modifier of the perceived meaning of behaviors, both for the experiencer and the observing spouse.

Step 5: Identifying with Disowned Feelings and Needs

Each partners position in the cycle, redefined in terms of underlying emotional experience and needs, is enacted deliberately in order for the partners to become more aware of their underlying needs and gain a sense of control of these previously automatic responses. For example, the withdrawer and the pursuer are both encouraged to experience more fully their underlying feelings and needs, which were previously disowned. Aspects of experience, such as the withdrawer's fear of being overwhelmed and the need to engage in protection, are fully explored and validated. Each person is asked to identify with disowned aspects of their experience, and to deliberately engage in some of the behaviors associated with their previously disowned feelings and needs. This is an intrapsychically oriented intervention focusing on enacting disowned parts (Perls, Hefferline, & Goodman, 1951). A distancing husband, for example, may be asked in the session deliberately to protect himself as a way of becoming more aware of and gaining control over this aspect of his behavior. This behavior is validated as being important to him in that it prevents him from feeling overwhelmed. Once partners have identified with disowned aspects of their experience in the session, it is helpful to give them homework to identify with disowned aspects of their experiences. This man would be asked deliberately to protect himself during the week whenever he began to feel a fear of being intruded on or overwhelmed. Having explored the underlying feelings of worthlessness or helplessness of the wife, which results in her pushing or criticizing her husband, she is asked for homework at least twice during the week to talk to her husband about her underlying feelings of being flawed and her basic vulnerabilities. This helps them to integrate these aspects both intrapsychically and inter-personally. The focus is on having people changing to be more fully what they are rather than what they are not, and to do this with full awareness and responsibility in order to create awareness and choice in the place of automaticity.

Step 6: Acceptance of the Partner's Experience

The focus is now on the communication to the spouse of the newly experienced emotional responses, and on facilitating the partner's acceptance of these responses. The therapist encourages the disclosure of vulnerability and the acceptance of the other's needs on the part of each spouse, primarily by encouraging interactions and blocking or exploring rejecting responses. The phobic avoidance of the expression of vulnerability in the relationship and the risks involved in exposing the self to the partner generally are confronted in this process. This part of the process is not directed toward the teaching of the skill of empathic listening but toward helping partners reveal new aspects of themselves to their mates in such a way as to evoke responsiveness and contact between the partners. Blocks to one partner's ability to hear and accept the other's experience (Pinsof, 1983) are explored and interpreted in terms of that partner's view of self, past learning in family of origin, and catastrophic fears. This serves to validate the person in terms of understanding the block and leads to change in the interaction. The therapist facilitates acceptance of self and others in contrast to the usual pattern of reciprocal disqualification that occurs in distressed relationships.

Step 7: Facilitating the Expression of Needs and Wants

The emotional synthesis of issues in terms of intra-individual and interpersonal experience leads to a clarification of needs and wants in the relationship. Partners can now directly ask for what they want or need from each other, and the implications of these desires for individuals and the relationship can be examined.

Step 8: The Emergence of New Solutions

The statement of needs and wants, accessed, integrated, and accepted by the spouse, leads to the creation of new alternative responses that constitute new solutions to the couple's struggle. The therapist draws attention to and highlights new positions and patterns of interaction. These new responses constitute a redefinition of the relationship. For example, a relationship may change so that one person can state needs and the other can give support, rather than have a relationship in which one partner defines reality or coerces and bullies the other into seeing and responding in a certain way. This process is not one of bargaining or compromise; it is more the creation of a context for *possible new responses*, responses evoked by the increased clarity of the other's needs. A withdrawing husband, for example, may find himself reaching out to his wife when she is able to disclose her desperate need to be taken care of.

Step 9: The Consolidation of New Positions

The therapist helps the couple create a new image for the relationship. The couple is encouraged to develop a meta-view of their problem cycle and of the present, more functional positions in the relationship. Not until partners agree that neither benefits from the cycle and that they should fight to "draw" rather than "win" is change consolidated. They need to know their cycle sufficiently well to know that it will not help them meet their needs.

Summary

The process of therapy involves a reciprocal redefinition of self and the relationship. Both partners access key emotional responses that underlie their reactions to each other; they are then able to view themselves and the actions of their spouse differently and with more acceptance and compassion. This results in partners presenting a new view of self in the relationship, which evokes new responses from the other. These new responses in turn affect the self-definition of the respondent; for example, when a hostile wife experiences her fragility and need for contact with her husband and begins to see his withdrawal as self-protection rather than as rejection of her, she is able to present her needs to him in such a way as to evoke a caring response from him. He experiences his wife then as vulnerable and in need of his care; this perspective and his ability to respond to her both sustains her new stance toward him and enhances his view of himself as a caring husband whose response is essential to his wife's sense of well-being. Inherent in this process is the creation of trust and intimacy facilitated by the reciprocal disclosure of self and the responsiveness of another to the self. The process evokes a giving, receptive, rather than a *quid pro quo*, or self-protecting, stance toward the partner on the part of both spouses.

THE ROLE OF THE THERAPIST

The therapist essentially fulfills three roles within this model. First, the therapist must establish a therapeutic alliance that allows a new experience to be explored with confidence; second, the therapist facilitates the accessing of emotional experience; and third, the therapist reframes the interaction and helps the clients to symbolize and integrate new experience, to create new meanings that enhance the couple's responsiveness to each other.

The creation of a safe environment is particularly pertinent when the accessing of emotional experience is an essential part of a therapy process. The therapist must be seen as equally accepting of the realities of both partners and as legitimizing the responses of each partner by placing seemingly unacceptable behaviors in the context of universal human needs. The reframing of the negative interaction cycle in terms of such needs helps build a therapeutic alliance and furthers the progress of therapy.

Emotionally focused therapists need to feel comfortable with the expression and exploration of emotional experience. They need to have sufficient experience in working with emotions to be able to promote the processes of experiencing and expressing emotion so that they are carried through to completion rather than impeded by defenses or anxiety. Inexperienced therapists or those uncomfortable with emotional experience and expression can become frightened by the emergence of their client's deeper feelings. Communication of this fear or indirect attempts to move the exploration to a more conceptual level tend to heighten the client's own fears and interfere with the experiencing process, resulting in the person's feeling incomplete. Experienced emotional therapists are better able to help clients discover the action tendencies implied by their emotions and thus help them find a sense of direction.

Working to deepen people's experience in therapy requires a particular style of intervention in which the therapist helps clients *focus attention* on internal experience and deepen this experience. The therapist works with clients to bring into awareness certain feelings and needs and continually directs them to pay attention to any inner information that might increase awareness of internal experience. A characteristic of good emotionally focused therapists is that they continually *refocus clients' attention inward* when clients deflect away from experiencing. Reorganization of experience takes place in the present so that it is important continually to focus attention on *what is occurring right now*. The therapist pays particular attention to the manner of nonverbal expression, for this contains important information about the person's affective state. Facial, postural, and gestural expressions convey a great deal about what the person is feeling and about the nature of the interactions in the room. Voice tone, sighs, and glances are all important signals of affective states and relationship statements. These are often intensified in order to heighten the person's experience and make the expressions clear. Finally, in this approach, experience must be *symbolized in awareness*, a process in which new verbal symbols, such as "I feel lonely when you are silent," represent the end product of an experiential reorganization process.

As mentioned, the therapist also facilitates the accessing and exploration of emotional responses by evoking problematic relationship events using evocative responding. These interventions consist of probes or reflections that attempt to re-evoke and heighten the client's emotional experience of that situation in therapy and make these automatic experiences a focus of conscious awareness. Intrapsychic experience is always related back to the interaction, and vice versa. Interactions are explored in terms of the feelings they produce and maintain, while feelings as they are accessed are communicated and used to change interactions. This process is aided by asking partners, in turn, the following questions:

1. When your partner does this, how do you perceive or interpret it?
2. When you see this, what do you experience, feel, and think?
3. What do you do when you feel or think this?

When these questions are answered, the therapist then asks the other spouse the same questions concerning his or her responses to the party's action disclosed in the previous questioning.

The therapist also guides the formulation of meanings as new experiences occur. The task is to reframe hostility as desperation or distance as fear in such a way that this reconstruction remains true to the client's present experience. The new framing or interpretation is always chosen to evoke acceptance from both the experiencer and the observing spouse, and to promote contact between the partners.

CLINICAL ISSUES

This approach to marital therapy has been tested empirically and found to be effective in increasing marital adjustment and intimacy and in facilitating improvement in target complaints and the attainment of relationship goals (Johnson & Greenberg, 1984). The strengths of this approach would appear to be that it addresses the emotional pain, the "hurt," which is the immediate and salient experience that brings couples into therapy, and uses the power of affect to change meanings and increase intimacy. However, certain important conditions must be met for successful implementation of treatment.

First, it is necessary to distinguish between "talking about" emotions and exploring emotional experience. Intense experience is often easier to elicit in couples therapy than in individual therapy because the stimulus environment eliciting the emotional response (i.e., the other partner) is immediately present. "Talking about" gives the couple some intellectual insight but seems to create little change in terms of positions, interaction patterns, and view of self and the other.

Purely cognitive change (i.e., change in conscious conceptual-level processing) is not in itself sufficient for change unless it evokes the whole network of schematic and expressive components that affords the subjective meaning to an experience. For example, if a therapist interprets to a client that he or she feels hurt, and the client agrees but does not experience the hurt, no lasting change will take place. Even if the client conceptually believes that he or she feels hurt, and the partner thinks that he or she should feel more compassionate (i.e., they both attribute a different meaning to the situation), the degree of conviction to this belief is greatly enhanced by the actual experience and expression of both the hurt and the compassion. We are suggesting that it is the complete emotional experience that helps access the unconscious processing involved and provides the appropriate context for lasting alterations in attributions and beliefs. Although purely conceptual reframes of underlying emotions may be initially helpful in this therapy as advanced organizers of experience or as educational interventions, it is only when the person fully experiences what was previously simply "talked about" that change is achieved.

Characteristics of bad emotional therapy are either "talking about" emotions or, at the other extreme, working with affective experience mainly in terms of ventilation of emotion with notions that people purge themselves of their emotions by expression. Emotional discharge is not what is being suggested in this approach, and it can become potentially dangerous because it may entrench already destructive patterns of escalation. It is important to assess emotions as to whether they are primary adaptive emotions, in which case they need to be bypassed or modified, but in neither case is there any discharge or purging of emotion.

Of great clinical importance is the careful assessment of the appropriate time at which to encourge the disclosure of vulnerability. This should be done only when both partners have been prepared for such disclosure and when the observing spouse is assessed, based on content, nonverbal, and general context cues, as likely to listen sympathetically even if he or she may not be able or willing to respond in the way that the partner wishes. A scenario in which one of the partners discloses a vulnerability and is then attacked by the spouse would impede the therapy substantially and could lead to negative effects in the form of further distancing and alienation. If this occurs, the therapist focuses on the attacking spouse's inability to respond and relabels this in terms of underlying emotions. Emotion is therefore not expressed for its own sake, but to modify positions and interactions.

Inability to experience and communicate feelings is dealt with in this approach by validation and by encouraging the clients to identify with their blocks to expression as they experience them in the moment. For example, a client may be unable to express some feeling toward his or her spouse. The therapist then would legitimize the client's difficulty and view this response perhaps in terms of the fears such an expression might arouse and then explore how difficult it was for this client to be open and direct with her husband, encouraging her to make a statement to her spouse, such as, "I don't want to be open with you." Blocks to experiencing or expression thus become interaction patterns in the relationship. If one spouse's underlying feelings appear to be inaccessible in therapy—for example, if he or she maintains a position of constantly berating his or her partner in spite of therapist interventions—the therapist focuses on this spouse's underlying vulnerabilities and, if necessary, interprets the affect that is hypothesized as maintaining this behavior, seeking particularly to access the experience of pain and fear in the attacker. Attempts are always made to have people experience their underlying emotions. If this fails, an interpretation of underlying experience is given in order to reframe the interaction and provide a cognitive organization to facilitate the experience of the emotions at a later stage.

Individual symptoms such as depression or anxiety are dealt with by viewing the symptoms as functions of the individual's position in the relationship and, to a certain extent, as maintained by the interaction patterns in the relationship. However, there is also room in this model to consider the individual's problems as an intrapsychic issue that may require accommodation in the relationship or a certain kind of responsiveness from the spouse to facilitate effective coping strategies.

For example, a client with a number of long-term debilitating phobias came into marital therapy; as therapy progressed, it became clear that his withdrawal and accommodation in interactions with his wife and the general position he adopted with her, that of inferior dependent, related to the occurrence of his phobias and his very low level of self-esteem. His wife took the complementary position of the overfunctioning, strong, assertive partner. When the wife was able to access and express her fragility and need to depend on her spouse, rather than constantly exhort him to change, the husband began to support her and take a more active role in the relationship. He began to ask for her acceptance of his own fears and clarified for his spouse how her anxiety and resulting intrusiveness actually exacerbated his difficulty in dealing with his problem. His image of himself also appeared to improve as his wife's need for his support became apparent. The change in relationship definition alone did not remove this client's phobias; however, it did appear to have an impact on his evaluation of himself as a competent person who could offer something to others, and improved his ability to cope with his problems effectively. The marital relationship also became a source of support for him rather than an additional problem in his life. In this view, whether a symptom is an expression of individual problems or relationship definition is not as important as the fact that, for purposes of intervention, focusing on people in their relationship contexts creates a powerful arena for change.

Extreme individual symptoms such as suicide, psychosis, and alcoholism are contraindications for this treatment. In addition, extreme negative interaction cycles involving suicide attempts, violence, and overt indications that expressions of underlying vulnerabilities will not be respected but will be used to heap further abuse on the partner are also contraindications for this treatment. Among the positive indicators for the treatment are presenting problems of alienation and lack of intimacy, "bad communication" or too much fighting, and general statements of marital dissatisfaction.

This treatment was designed to increase intimacy; it is not divorce or separation counseling. It is important to determine that the couple is attempting to work toward the creation of intimacy before one intervenes to access underlying experience and express emotions and needs. If it seems that the goal is separation, then more of a problem-solving orientation is indicated, in which the therapist does not attempt to have people access and share their pain but negotiate around problems or issues of separation. If one partner is already in a state of emotional divorce, emotionally oriented interventions may not be appropriate; however, if partners are feeling attacked but unsure as to their investment in the relationship, emotionally focused interventions can be helpful in clarifying the relationship.

The therapy outlined here was designed to be brief, 8 to 15 sessions, in line with recognition of the need for brief treatment (Budman, 1981) and prompted by the demonstrated efficacy of brief marital treatment (Jacobson & Margolin, 1979). In line with the brevity of treatment, the use of homework in accord with the goals of the treatment is encouraged. Different homework exercises to promote awareness of the negative interaction cycles and of underlying feelings and needs have proved useful. They provide a focus for the next session and help speed up the therapy. In addition, homework designed to have partners identify with disowned aspects of experience, after they have been accessed in therapy, are most helpful in promoting the taking of responsibility for feelings and needs, validating these, and having the partner accept them.

REFERENCES

Arnold, M. (1968). *The nature of emotion.* Baltimore: Penguin Books.

Bordin, E. (1979). The generalizability of the concept of the psychoanalytic concept of the working alliance. *Psychotherapy: Therapy, Research and Practice, 16,* 252–259.

Budman, S. (1981). *Forms of brief therapy.* New York: Guilford Press.

Greenberg, L. (1983). The relationship in Gestalt therapy. In M. Lambert, *Psychotherapy and patient relationships.* Homewood, IL: Dow Jones–Irwin.

Greenberg, L., & Safran, J. (in press) *Affect, cognition and action: The process of therapeutic change.* New York: Guilford Press.

Greenberg, L., & Safran, J. (1984a). *Integrating affect and cognition: A perspective on the process of therapeutic change. Cognitive Therapy and Research.*

Greenberg, L., & Safran, J. (1984b). Hot cognitions: Emotion coming in from the cold. *Cognitive Therapy and Research.*

Guerin, P. J. (1982). The stages of marital conflict. *Family Journal, 10,* 15–26.

Hoffman, L. (1982). *Foundation of family therapy.* New York: Basic Books.

Jacobson, N. S., & Margolin, G. (1979). *Marital therapy: Strategies based on social learning and behaviour exchange principles.* New York: Brunner/Mazel.

Johnson, S., & Greenberg, L. (1984). The differential effects of cognitive behavioral and experiential interventions in marital therapy. Submitted to *Journal of Consulting and Clinical Psychology, 53*, 175–184.

Kaplan, M. L., & Kaplan, N. R. (1982). Organization of experience among family members. In the immediate present: A Gestalt/systems integration. *Journal of Marital and Family Therapy, 8*(1), 5–14.

Leventhal, H. (1979). A perceptual motor processing model of emotion. In P. Pliner, K. R. Blankstein, & I. M. Spigel (Eds.), *Advances in the study of communication and affect*, (Vol. 5., *Perception of emotions in self and others* (pp. 1–46). New York: Plenum Press.

Lewin, K. (1935). *Dynamic theory of personality*. New York: McGraw-Hill.

Perls, F., Hefferline, R., & Goodman, P. (1951). *Gestalt therapy*. New York: Julian Press.

Perls, F. (1973). *The Gestalt approach and eyewitness to therapy*. San Francisco: Science and Behavior Books.

Pinsof, W. (1983). Integrative problem centered therapy: Toward the synthesis of family and individual psychotherapies. *Journal of Marital and Family Therapy, 9*, 19–35.

Rausch, H. L., Barry, W. A., Hertel, R. K., & Swain, M. A. (1974) *Communication conflict and marriage*. San Francisco: Jossey-Bass.

Rice, L. (1974). The evocative function of the therapist. In D. Wexler & L. Rice (Eds.), *Innovation in client centered therapy*. Wiley Interscience.

Rice, L., & Saperia, E. (1984). Task analysis of the resolution of problematic reactions. In L. Rice & L. Greenberg (Eds.), *Patterns of change: Intensive analysis of psychotherapy process*. New York: Guilford Press.

Rogers, C. R. (1951). *Client-centered therapy*. Boston: Houghton Mifflin.

Safran, J., & Greenberg, L. (1982). Cognitive appraisal and reappraisal: Implications for clinical practice. *Cognitive Therapy and Research, 6*, 251–255.

Satir, V. (1967). *Conjoint family therapy*. Palo Alto, CA: Science and Behavior Books.

Sluzki, C. (1978). Marital therapy from a systems theory perspective. In T. Paolino & B. McCrady (Eds.), *Marriage and marital therapy*. New York: Brunner/Mazel.

Tolstedt, B. E., & Stokes, J. P. (1983). Relation of verbal, affective and physical intimacy to marital satisfaction. *Journal of Counseling Psychology, 30* (4), 573–580.

Watzlawick, P., Beavin, J. H., & Jackson, D. D. (1967). Pragmatics of human communication: A study of interactional patterns. In *Pathologies and paradoxes*. New York: Norton.

Wile, D. E. (1981). *Couples therapy: A non-traditional approach*. New York: Wiley.

III

INTERVENTIONS WITH VARIOUS POPULATIONS AND RELATIONALLY DEFINED PROBLEMS

Separation and Divorce Therapy

DAVID G. RICE
JOY K. RICE

After having increased for approximately 20 years, the annual divorce rate in the United States has begun to level off (National Center for Health Statistics, 1982). Still, two of every five couples who reach their fifth anniversary will ultimately divorce, and it is highly probable that the marital therapist will continue to see a large number of couples who seek help with the dissolution of their relationship.

In some ways, working with separated or divorcing couples represents one of the most frustrating areas of marital therapy practice. The therapist is likely to feel that she or he is intervening when it is too late for optimal therapeutic input into the marital system. Much of the therapist's usual source of satisfaction in helping spouses improve their interaction and ultimate marital happiness is missing when one deals with separation and divorce. Perhaps for this reason, many therapists have looked to a theoretical model that stresses "positive" crisis intervention and resolution in the dissolution process (Framo, 1978; Kaffman & Talmon, 1982; Kaslow & Hyatt, 1982; Kraus, 1979; Singer, 1975). Krantzler's 1975 book, *Creative Divorce*, was the first and the most popular of many writings during the past decade to emphasize the psychological growth that can come out of the pain of marital separation and divorce.

A developmental theoretical model and therapeutic framework are favored by the present authors for helping couples and individuals in the dissolution

David G. Rice. Department of Psychiatry, University of Wisconsin Medical School, Madison, Wisconsin.
Joy K. Rice. Departments of Educational Policy Studies and Women's Studies, University of Wisconsin–Madison, Madison, Wisconsin.

phase of their relationship (Rice & Rice, 1985). Such a model emphasizes the substantial normative change that almost all individuals undergo during the developmental life cycle and the necessity for the marital relationship to change correspondingly and accommodate over time. Berman and Leif (1975) have provided a useful summary of marital issues and expected stresses that parallel the different periods of adult development.

The healthy marriage is able, flexibly and even synergistically, to adapt to the individual growth of each partner. In contrast, a dysfunctional marriage is likely to be strained by the inevitable developmental changes of the spouses. Such individuals literally grow apart, although along the way there may be resented accommodation to the spouse, self-denial of opportunities for each spouse's individual growth, or both. Such attempted compromises often work against the relationship over time, stifling the growth of the marriage and leaving the individuals unfulfilled. Eventually many couples in this situation seek marital therapy. Through therapy or through one's own painful introspection, it may become clear that the personal costs of maintaining the marriage are too great. After a period that is marked commonly by much ambivalence and wavering about whether to stay in the relationship, one spouse typically makes the decision to separate. Many psychic scars can remain as sequelae to a dissolved marital relationship. A therapist may be called on to work at any point along the dissolution continuum, dealing with pre- and postseparation issues, eventually seeing one or both spouses in divorce therapy, or both.

The developmental model leads the therapist to attend especially to issues of identity and self-esteem in the divorce process. Many people believe that "being married" somehow confers an identity on them as individuals. Marriage is perceived as a sign of personal maturity, as a significant part of becoming an adult. In many cases, however, the decision to get married was made before the individual had truly been on his or her own. Premarital development is often characterized by a series of essentially dependent relationships, first on one's parents, then on school, the armed service, or another institution, and subsequently on one's spouse. In this process, personal identity becomes closely tied to, and shaped by, the actions, needs, and demands of others.

The process of submerging one's self into a marital relationship is often done willingly. The lack of felt personal identity is usually not perceived as problematic if the marriage is functioning smoothly. When the bond is more tenuous, a struggle begins around the issue of whether one could make it on his or her own. Among other things, the perception that the marriage may not work out can precipitate an identity crisis. Individuals in this situation typically feel very unprepared for, and anxious about, the prospect of life as a single person. Yet the choice of continuing to stay in an unfulfilling relationship may seem equally unsatisfactory. Ultimately this conflict results in many individuals choosing to leave or feeling forced to do so by the actions of their spouse. Developmentally, the ending of a marriage can provide both a marked threat to one's identity and an opportunity for resolution and consolidation. Therapy can be helpful in this process.

A second major area for therapeutic focus with separated and divorcing couples concerns feelings of lowered self-esteem. The perceived inability to work out marital problems after one invested so much time and resources leads to a sense of personal failure. Such feelings are usually present even when there is much justification for ending the marriage (e.g., in the case of physical abuse). Even with the confidence that leaving is the "right" thing to do, and despite a sense of relief at having made a decision, one must still struggle against perceived narcissistic injury and doubts about ever being able to achieve and maintain a satisfying marriage.

Marital therapy during the separation period or following divorce can be very helpful in dealing with issues of self-esteem (Rice, 1977). The working through of guilt, self-blame, and self-doubt needs to be accomplished if one is to complete the necessary development process of emotional or psychic divorce (Bohannan, 1971). Individuals who have not been able to resolve emotional issues from a prior marriage have a greater likelihood of reproducing such conflicts in future intimate relationships, subsequently impeding their personal development. Restoration of self-esteem and resolution of personal identity can thus go hand in hand.

Individual and couple issues must be dealt with following separation. Couple issues include financial arrangements, providing for visitation and custody of children, and setting up two separate households. Individual issues have to do with being on one's own, perhaps for the first time, and coping with the many mixed feelings about the marriage's not working out. The therapist usually needs to attend to both issues. A combination of individual and couples therapy can be most efficacious. One should be prepared to shift back and forth between these formats, as the couple desires and clinical issues warrant. Therapists who insist on seeing only the couple or only one spouse in individual therapy, once a decision to separate has been made, are likely to be of less than optimal benefit to the parties involved.

A developmental model predicts that one can grow psychologically as a result of facing and working through the personal issues surrounding divorce successfully. Such growth is a necessary precursor to ultimate personal happiness and achieving sustaining intimate relationships. Emotional resolution takes time. Both therapist and client should be cautioned not to rush or truncate the process. The therapist should be prepared to be available to the client over a longer period of time, beyond the initial crisis period occasioned by separation. Individuals complete the process of emotional divorce at varying paces. An individualized schedule of therapy takes this into account. Some people want to struggle with, and resolve, the issues immediately. Others want a breathing period, returning to therapy after some time has elapsed. The therapist must be respectful of the individual's need to maintain existing coping defenses and the variable pattern of psychic resolution following divorce (Toomim, 1972). In this manner, the course of therapy in separation and divorce can be anticipated or prescribed only to a limited degree. This caveat should be kept in mind in regard to outlining the therapy process in the material that follows.

This chapter is not intended as a comprehensive review of the literature on divorce and divorce therapy. For such broad overviews, the interested reader is referred to Bloom, Asher, and White (1978), Brown (1976), Goetting (1981), Kaslow (1981), Kitson and Raschke (1981), Kressel and Deutsch (1977), Levinger (1965), Rice and Rice (1985), and Sprenkle and Storm (1983).

A THEORY OF THERAPEUTIC CHANGE

The following therapeutic assumptions are based on a developmental model for the treatment of individuals and couples in marital separation and divorce:

1. Separation leads to a perception of personal crisis, at least on the part of the individual who is being "left," and frequently for both. Therefore, knowledge of crisis theory and crisis intervention techniques are important for the therapist.

2. Dealing with the crisis of separation leads to both perceived emotional pain and the opportunity for psychological growth. It is important to create a therapeutic climate in which both experiences can be facilitated.

3. Dealing with the reality of divorce can precipitate an identity crisis, particularly for individuals who have been in a series of essentially dependent relationships and never truly on their own. Issues of personal identity need to be addressed in therapy. A resolution of identity issues may be precluded if the individual moves too quickly into another (transitional) relationship. The therapist should help clients realistically appraise the potential for personal growth and happiness in such relationships.

4. One of the emotional concomitants of divorce is perceived narcissistic injury and loss of self-esteem. Both partners are hurt by the "failure" of their relationship and may question their capability to find fulfillment in marriage. In therapy, the process of divorce is likely to reactivate the pain of former experiences that led to a sense of diminished self-confidence. Patterns of dysfunctional behavior revealed in this process need to be addressed in therapy and worked through to prevent their reemergence in future meaningful relationships.

5. The temporal process of emotional divorce varies among individuals, based in part on developmental considerations, for example, the degree of previously achieved personal identity, autonomy, and individuation. A flexible course of therapy is needed. The therapist should be prepared to see the individuals, the couple, the nuclear family, and even both families of origin as may be needed over the course of treatment.

6. Support from a variety of individuals is especially important when one is dealing with the loss of a significant other. Therefore, group therapy

with other individuals in the process of divorce can be a helpful supplement to individual therapy. It is preferable that the client not be in both kinds of treatment at the same time, as a splitting of the two therapists can occur, to the detriment of both treatments.

7. The therapist should be prepared to deal with the practical concerns that accompany marital dissolution, such as talking about financial arrangements, visitation and child-custody arrangements, setting up separate households, and facilitating the legal process. The knowledge and use of mediation techniques can be helpful in dealing with issues that prove difficult to resolve.

The above assumptions form the basic tenets of a theoretical framework in which the treatment goal is ultimately to help promote growth and healthy developmental change out of the crisis of marital separation and divorce. The next section focuses on the therapeutic implementation for achieving such changes.

Assessment Issues

One of the most important considerations for the therapist is at what point she or he first intervenes in the separation–divorce process. It is increasingly common and therapeutically desirable to begin seeing the couple as a dyad before the actual decision to separate has been made. This gives the therapist a firsthand look at the partners' marital interaction patterns. Couples frequently enter marital therapy as a last-ditch attempt to salvage a marriage that one or both spouses feel pessimistic about continuing. Thus the initially stated goal may be to work through the marital problems, not to help with the marital dissolution. The inevitability of eventual separation may become clearer to one or both individuals before it is perceived by the therapist, who lacks the historical perspective and experience of the partners. Most marital therapists struggle to leave no stone unturned in their efforts to help the couple stay together. As we discuss later, this may reflect the therapist's need to avoid a sense of failure rather than the couple's desire to continue the marriage against insurmountable odds.

For many couples, the emotional pain and anxiety aroused by the consideration of separation or divorce leads to strong defensive maneuvers (e.g., denial) that result in a prolonged period of ambivalence and wavering in regard to the decision. Much of this seesaw process may have taken place before the couple enters therapy.

A central assumption of most approaches to marital therapy is that one needs to see both spouses in order to facilitate therapeutic change (Gurman & Kniskern, 1978). This format can also apply in divorce therapy; for example, even if a separated spouse presents alone, it is often useful to see the other spouse for at least one session. Hearing both sides of the story can greatly aid the therapist in thoroughly assessing the state of the marriage. It is important to take a careful marital history and at least a brief developmental history of each spouse. For individuals who have been married previously, it is valuable to review the chronology of the earlier marriage(s). The therapist needs to get a sense of dysfunctional interaction patterns and the contribution of each partner's personality structure and dynamics. One looks also for repetition of previous dysfunctional marital interaction patterns, either modeled in the families of origin or manifest in the partners' prior intimate relationships.

Having the time to take a careful and useful history is often seen as a luxury by the therapist. Couples who are considering or are already in the process of separation frequently come in a state of extreme distress. It may be necessary to employ crisis-intervention techniques, for example, setting up a structured separation with counseling (Granvold & Tarrant, 1983; Toomim, 1972). The urgency of beginning the therapeutic process quickly should not preclude some history taking, although of necessity this may be put off until a second session. Many of the goals and much of the process of divorce therapy is dictated by the developmental status of the marriage as well as of the two individuals. A "young" marriage, one of approximately 2 years or less, is likely to dissolve more easily than one of longer duration, and this is particularly true if the couple does not have children. The developmental model predicts that the more cohesive the individuals' sense of personal identity, the more individuated each partner was from his or her family or origin, and the fewer self-esteem injuries, either from the marriage or from previous intimate relationships, the easier the process of psychic divorce.

The Structure of the Therapy Sessions

Who is seen in therapy, and when, will be dictated by when in the separation–divorce process the therapist intervenes. Usually the decision to begin dissolution of the marriage is made after a period of couples therapy, during which both partners have been seen together. The authors believe that the format of the therapy sessions should mirror the reality of the relationship at any given point in the divorce process. Thus, when the couple separates, a combination of individual and couple sessions is usually desirable, in view of the fact that the partners are not still together (i.e., they are separated) but not yet apart (i.e., they are not divorced). It is important to preserve options during a separation and not do anything therapeutically that might hinder either reconciliation or eventual divorce. Forming a strong individual therapy bond with one spouse can sometimes work to alienate the other, with therapy partly taking care of that vulnerable partner's emotional needs and decreasing the motivation to work things out with the other spouse (Whitaker & Miller, 1969).

If the therapist is uncomfortable seeing both partners in individual therapy during a separation period, a co-therapy format can be utilized. Ideally the co-therapists would have seen the couple together in marital therapy before the decision to separate had been made. During the separation, individual and couple sessions can be alternated, with one therapist seeing the husband individually and the other therapist seeing the wife. For this procedure to work in everyone's best interests, it is important that two competing therapies not be set up. This is also a risk if the same therapist sees both spouses individually and comes to be perceived as favoring one spouse over the other. Co-therapists need to talk frequently and regularly, and be alert for signs that they are being "split" by the couple (e.g., one therapist being seen as "nurturing," the other as "demanding"), either in the conjoint or the individual sessions.

Once a decision to divorce has been made, the opportunity to continue in individual therapy can be extended to the partners. It is unusual for both individuals to wish to continue therapy. It is not uncommon for one spouse to express a desire to continue treatment, and often this is the individual who perceives that he or she has been "left" by the other or the individual who is more open and ready for developmental change. The advantages of continuing to work with the same therapist would appear to outweigh the disadvantages (Rice, 1981).

THERAPEUTIC PROCEDURES AND TECHNIQUES

A most helpful technique in treating couples who wish help with the decision to remain in, or dissolve, a conflicted relationship involves a structured separation with counseling (Granvold & Tarrant, 1983; Toomim, 1972). A variation of this procedure is the transient structured distancing maneuver (Green, Lee, & Lustig, 1973) in which the spouses continue to live under the same roof but primarily in defined, separate areas.

In a structured separation with counseling, the partners agree to separate physically for a defined period and to work on resolving the question of whether they will stay together or proceed toward divorce. On the average, a 3-month separation period is recommended, although extenuating circumstances may dictate a shorter or longer period. From a phenomenological standpoint, the main purpose of the separation is to put a sense of choice back into a relationship in which the individuals feel "stuck" or paralyzed in terms of freely choosing either to be together or to be apart. The principle of choice determines the nature of the couple's interaction during the separation period. They can see each other as frequently as they like, but only if *both* individuals choose to do so. Similarly, continuing the sexual relationship is appropriate if mutually desired, but each partner can choose to decline the other's invitation for a sexual encounter.

The couple usually needs to negotiate a variety of issues in regard to the logistics of the structured separation. The more important of these issues include (*a*) financial support (e.g., the need for a temporary maintenance agreement); (*b*) child care and living arrangements (e.g., who will the children stay with, where, and for how long?); (*c*) how frequently the partners will see each other, as well as the nature and location (e.g., whether any meetings will take place in the home, thus possibly creating for the children an illusory sense that "Mommy and Daddy are now back together"); and (d) the issue of relationships with other people during the separation period. Granvold and Tarrant (1983) discuss these and other issues likely to require negotiated discussions.

Toomim (1972) encourages the exploration of other relationships during separation, feeling that eventually one is in a better position of choosing either to return to the marriage *or* to divorce if he or she has tested out whether "things would be different with someone else." It is important that a single standard be negotiated; that is, both partners agree to have, or not to have, other relationships, that these can be sexual or nonsexual, and that they will either tell or not tell the other spouse about such relationships. The therapist should be alert to one spouse's agreeing to a common standard but actually adhering to a different one as a way of gaining power in the relationship by attempting to make the other feel guilty. One wishes to prevent statements such as, "Well, I've remained faithful to you during the separation; if you really cared about me, you would have chosen the same, even if we did agree originally that it was O.K. to see other people."

The general goal in helping the couple negotiate a structured separation is to give both partners a sense of equity and fairness in the agreements. If one individual, out of generosity or guilt, agrees initially to a disadvantaged arrangement, feelings of resentment usually surface over time and can undermine the most carefully negotiated agreement. Thus the therapist and the individuals need to be alert to the need for possible renegotiation and fine tuning. Granvold (1983) gives an illustration of the behavioral contracting steps and the process required in negotiating a more formal structured separation agreement.

In terms of therapy format, a sequence of individual and couple sessions or couple-only sessions can be employed. The therapist could see the couple conjointly one week and then each spouse separately the following week, followed by a conjoint session the third week, individual sessions the fourth, and so on. The therapist needs to remain flexible in this regard, as the clinical situation dictates. The number of individual sessions with each spouse should be roughly equal over the structured separation period so that one person does not feel that the therapist is favoring the other.

A structured separation is not a useful therapeutic tool if one spouse clearly has made a decision to end the marriage. It is more honest for this fact to be stated openly rather than camouflaging the reality of such a decision by "going along" with a separation and therapy and pretending there is a possibility of reconciliation. A structured separation is not a panacea for preventing divorce. In Toomim's 1972 study, approximately two-thirds of the couples who went through a structured separation with counseling decided to proceed toward divorce. However, there were remarkably few difficulties in reaching a settlement and working through the potentially difficult issues in this regard.

Case Illustration

(Composite of several cases, altered to preserve confidentiality)

At the time they initiated therapy, John, age 33, and Judy, age 32, had been married for 10 years. They had two daughters, Allison, age 6, and Carrie, age 3. Judy had attempted to discuss with John her increasing dissatisfaction with the marital relationship, but he would either divert the conversation or rationalize her complaints along the lines of "Well, everybody that's married has those kind of problems, Judy." She turned to her women friends, seeking justification for her feelings of frustration at John's long work hours, his inability to share his deeper feelings with her, and the lack of shared responsibility for domestic tasks and child care in the marriage. Sensing Judy's frustration, a close friend asked if she had ever "considered a separation," since it appeared that her repeated efforts to make John aware of her dissatisfaction had resulted in few sustained, constructive changes. The suggestion shocked Judy, who replied to her friend, "Am I that unhappy?" She mulled over the idea for several weeks, at the same time telling herself (but not John) that she was "giving him one more chance." During this time, Judy did not see evidence that John really wished to change, and she finally summoned the courage to tell him that she wanted a separation. He was stunned by her request, feeling it "came out of the blue." John agreed to think about it, and 2 days later suggested an alternative proposal, namely, that they seek marital therapy. Judy agreed, although she could not resist pointing out that she had suggested therapy on several occasions, only to perceive that the request "fell on deaf ears." John obtained the name of a marital therapist from a co-worker he knew who had had marital problems and had been in therapy.

The couple was seen for the first session approximately 10 days after Judy's revelation. She appeared somewhat reserved; John seemed eager to talk. The session was spent primarily in taking a marital history, getting some idea of the functional and dysfunctional areas of their present interaction, and beginning an inquiry about their families of origin.

John and Judy met midway through their freshman year at a small state college in the Midwest. They were introduced by John's dormitory roommate, who had gone to high school with Judy. Both had been feeling lonely, John because he was away from home for an extended period for the first time in his life and Judy because she missed a high school boyfriend, who had chosen to attend another, distant college. They felt a strong initial attraction and began dating regularly. Judy was attracted to John "because he was serious about important things, such as social values. I mean he seemed to want to make the world better . . . That sounds a little corny, but he could also have fun and get me away from studying so hard." John indicated about Judy: "Well, she was more sophisticated than the girls I was used to. She came from a big city and her family was involved politically, which I liked. There was a physical attraction, too; she was short and cute and cuddly." Judy interjected, "You make me sound like a teddy bear!" When asked about any perceived differences, John mentioned religion: "Judy is Jewish, and I was raised Catholic. I even thought about the priesthood at one point. But religion didn't seem like the most important thing then. We later talked about children, and I said I didn't care if they were Jewish."

John had been raised in a small town where his father was the postmaster. His mother worked part-time as a teacher's aide at the local elementary school. He was the middle of three boys; his older brother, age 34, was married, had one child, and worked as an engineer in a large city about 50 miles from where the family grew up. His younger brother, age 29, was a high school history teacher, had recently gotten married, and lived in a nearby state. John described his family: "We got along O.K. My father was pretty strict, and Mom had her hands full with three boys. What else would you like to know?"

Judy was the older of two children. She had a brother, age 30, who was unmarried and a lawyer with an agency of the federal government. Her father was a successful CPA. Judy's mother was not employed outside the home but was active in several clubs and was a volunteer at one of the city hospitals. Asked what her family was like, Judy replied: "Well, everything got discussed. I was—I am—close to my dad. We used to have long talks. Growing up in the 1960s, there were a lot of things to discuss, and we didn't always agree. He and I thought more alike. Mom tended to be shocked at the things kids were doing—she's a little 'straighter' than he is."

Growing up was relatively uneventful for both John and Judy. They were both good students, and Judy almost went to the expensive private college where her boyfriend had matriculated, but he discouraged that and she ended up making a late decision to attend the state college where she eventually met John. This prior relationship had been Judy's "only serious one" and had lasted for almost 3 years. John had had limited dating experience and reported "no really serious relationships" before his involvement with Judy.

John majored in sociology and did graduate work, receiving a master's degree in urban planning. They married after John graduated, before Judy's senior year. Judy received a BA in social work, toyed with the idea of getting a MSW, but decided to go to work in a social service agency "to earn money to help John out with graduate school." After graduating, he got a job with the local Department of City Planning, and Judy stopped working in anticipation of starting a family. Allison was born approximately 18 months later.

The therapist indicated that he would like to see the whole family for at least part of the second session, to get some idea how the marital tensions might be affecting the children. Judy wondered "whether it's necessary to bring them into this?" but acceded to John's insightful observation that "they're already in it."

The family interaction was the focus during the first half of the second session; the children appeared asymptomatic and generally looked at Judy for reassurance as to how they should act (e.g., whether it was O.K. to accept the therapist's offer of paper and magic markers if they wished to draw a picture). John kept exhorting his older daughter to "say what you feel about that." The rest of the second session was spent in completing history taking. Toward the end, after both had acknowledged a need to work on their "communication," the therapist suggested they practice a communication exercise between sessions that was aimed at enhancing listening and empathy skills. He suggested they find a half-hour period when both individuals would be generally free of other distractions (e.g., when the children were asleep or not at home). They were instructed either to agree between themselves or to flip a coin to decide who would go first. In this procedure, the half-hour period is divided into six 5-minute segments. To begin, one individual speaks for 5 minutes on a topic or issue about which she or he does not believe her or his feelings have been heard or understood by the other. The partner listens, without comment. Then, during the second 5-minute segment, the "listener" tells what she or he heard both cognitively and affectively. During the third segment, the "speaker" gives feedback to the "listener" in regard to whether there seemed to be accurate perceptions of what was being communicated. Then the process is reversed for the last three segments, with the original "speaker" becoming the "listener." The emphasis throughout is on "I statements" (e.g., "I feel that—" or "I have a sense that—" or "I heard you say that—") rather than accusatory-sounding "you statements" (e.g., "You never—" or "You wouldn't—" or "You should—").

Judy reported at the third session a week later: "We tried what you suggested last night [the therapist had suggested a half-hour period three times a week]. We were both tired, after getting the girls to bed . . . and I guess it helped, although I don't think John heard anything new." John nodded agreement, but indicated: "I felt she was blaming me again, like I can't do anything right." Judy's affect and manner carried an air of resignation, as if she had indeed already made up her mind that she wished to leave the marriage. When the therapist reflected this back to her, she agreed, saying: "Yes, I think you're right. I am feeling guilty . . . and I've been telling myself I'm only doing this for him [John]." Her perceived lack of caring on John's part, particularly over the past 2½ years (since shortly after Carrie's birth), appeared to have left Judy with deep self-esteem wounds. She seemed to be saying that the only way to heal was to "declare her independence" (i.e., separate). John agreed that it appeared as though she had made up her mind and added, "It runs in her family. . . . I mean they're all strong willed. Once they make up their mind to do something, brother, that's it."

The therapist asked Judy if separating basically meant getting a divorce or if, indeed, what she desired was a "separation." She indicated the latter, saying, "I haven't made up my mind about anything that final. I just feel like we—maybe I better say I—I need to get away from John for a while—to sort things out. Be more on my own." The therapist acknowledged John's pain at the clarity with which Judy stated her intentions. He then suggested that the couple consider a structured separation with counseling, proposed for discussion a 3-month period, talked about the parameters of such a procedure, and suggested they discuss it on their own during the coming week. The therapist answered a few questions about the suggested procedure and after a short silence, which felt something like a period of mourning, the session ended.

The fourth session began with the couple's indicating they had "done a lot of work" during the week. They had, indeed, decided to follow through on the structured separation plan. During the coming weekend John had arranged to move in with a single male friend whom he had met at their athletic club. John and Judy had agreed that he would see the girls on Wednesday nights and during the day on Sunday, at the house, and Judy would arrange to be out. They had "talked" (Judy's word) or "argued" (John's version) about finances, soon realizing that any new arrangements would strain an already tight budget. However, they had negotiated a plan for allocation of income, subject to modification.

The therapist praised the couple for working out some difficult issues and commented that the tension seemed to be lessened this week. Both spouses acknowledged some relief that a decision had been made, although John said, "I still have a lot of mixed feelings about whether this is really the right thing to do." Judy asked him: "Do you see any alternative? I don't think we can go on—the way I've been feeling—and the kids know something's up. Allison's been more 'squirrely' lately." John said resignedly that he did not "really see any other alternative, short of divorce, and I don't want that."

The therapist inquired whether the couple had talked about the issue of relationships with other people during the separation period.

JOHN: Yes, we *talked* about it. But that was about all—I don't think we resolved anything (*sarcastically*). It's a little late for Judy to go back and see Mike [her old boyfriend], isn't it?

JUDY (*half playing along*): I'm not sure I know where he is.

THERAPIST: This is an area where it's pretty important to spell out the rules, and they should be mutual. Do you feel like it would eventually help you decide what to do about the marriage, if you saw other people?

JUDY: I—uh—I don't want to set any limits on that—but (*looks concernedly at John*) I don't have anybody in mind.

JOHN (*half sarcastically*): She needs to be able to do whatever she needs to do.

THERAPIST (*to John*): How about you?

JOHN: It would be nice to be with someone who wanted me. (*Judy looks guilty, as John probably intended.*)

THERAPIST: Do you want the prerogative of having sexual relationships? And do you want to know about them—if something happens?

JOHN: I wouldn't want to know.

JUDY: Nor I.

THERAPIST: Again, the guideline could be if you think it will help you decide what to do about the marriage.

JUDY: I want the freedom to decide, whatever I choose to do. I suppose that could mean sleeping with someone. (*She pauses; John looks pained.*)

THERAPIST: John?

JOHN: I guess that's O.K. by me, but I don't want to know.

THERAPIST: Are we agreed then? (*Both nod.*) Maybe we should have done this first, but how about the issue of seeing one another during those three months? Did you talk about that?

JUDY: Uh—remembering what you said last time about both of us being able to have a choice—if we wanted to be together. I think I would like to see John, some.

JOHN: I'd still like to get together, not just to see Carrie and Allison.

THERAPIST: It sounds like you need to talk more about this aspect of things and make sure you come to some agreement about your preferences and expectations.

The session ended shortly thereafter, and the therapist indicated he would like to see each partner separately toward the end of the following week. During the fifth session, John, seen alone, said his new living arrangement was "working out O.K., but it's not like being at home." The therapist explored the issue of whether he had any better appreciation of why Judy had come to be so unhappy in the relationship. John acknowledged his perplexity, adding, "I think I just expected to get married and that was that. My parents have stayed married, after all. It's not just being Catholic— at least, I don't think that's all there is to it. They've had ups and downs— yet they've stuck it out." John thus acknowledged that he had very little preparation from his primary role models for the possible dissolution of a marriage. Nor did he seem fully cognizant of the psychological pressures on marriage these days, compared to his parents' generation. Thus, Judy's strong belief, supported by her friends, that she had a right to expect emotional fulfillment in marriage had been somewhat puzzling to John. He seemed to be starting to get in touch with his own needs in this regard, as indicated by his statement during the previous session that "it would be nice to be with someone who wanted me."

During the individual (sixth) session with Judy, she expressed a surprised sense of relief, saying, "This week has not been nearly as bad as I expected. I think I may have been preparing for this for some time." Judy illustrated in her statement that she may have begun to do some of the work of "emotional divorce" (Bohannan, 1971) even before deciding on a separation. In the authors' experience, such acknowledgments are often prognostic, diminishing the possibility of later reconciliation. Judy continued: "The worst times have been at night. I don't like to sleep in an empty bed. I never have—even when John was gone for a night, I didn't like it. Not that there was all that much touching, or making love, when he was there. It was just having someone next to me. I don't know, maybe I felt safer." From a psychodynamic standpoint, Judy's statement that her own presence in the bed (without John) still left it "empty" is a possible indication of her own lowered self-regard. This is but one of several signs of the narcissistic injury that she had suffered, in part as the result of disillusionment in the marriage. As we illustrate later, this theme, along with her lack of a clear personal identity apart from being a "married person," were the focus of a period of individual therapy postdivorce.

The following (seventh) session occurred a week later, with both spouses present. Judy felt less elated, and John began to express his anger more openly, particularly his sense of being "abandoned" by Judy. The couple wanted to focus on their daughters and how they were dealing with the separation, although there was no indication from the parents' verbal report that the children were suffering seriously. Instead, the focus on the children seemed a ploy, especially on John's part, to manipulate Judy with guilt. His implication that she was "hurting" the children seemed to be a displacement of his own hurt and anger at his wife for leaving. The therapist attempted to focus more directly on John's feelings about the separation, trying to get him to "own" his anger. This strategy was dictated in part by the therapist's perception that Judy was indeed leaving the marriage. John's anger was, at least potentially, a double-edged sword. It could continue to bind him into the marriage long after a divorce (i.e., "hating is a relationship") (Framo, 1978). On the other hand, "letting go" honestly by expressing angry feelings might provide some impetus that could begin the process of personal reconstruction after the marriage had ended. Working on the themes of anger, guilt, and hurt, and how they were expressed in experiences with their families of origin, formed the bulk of the therapeutic process for the rest of the structured separation period.

The couple realized after about 2 months of separation, with some essentially disappointing attempts to "date" and rekindle romantic and sexual feelings, that divorce was probably inevitable. By this time, John had invested more in his job and was enjoying his daily routine of working out physically. He indicated that "Judy always seemed to resent the time I took for this." He reported in one of the individual sessions that he had begun to fantasize having a relationship with a younger woman who worked at his athletic club. John was struggling with the issue of whether to ask her out, although this seemed like a good bet, since she appeared to have indicated some interest in him. At this point, Judy had not yet begun to deal with the issue of seeing other men.

In the last session (the fifteenth), with the couple already having decided to file for divorce and seek joint custody of their daughters, the therapist inquired whether either or both individuals wished to continue working in individual therapy. John declined, but Judy accepted the offer, saying, "I don't think I'm really dealing with some things—I still wake up and feel depressed too often. And it's getting clearer I'm going to have to go out and get a job, if we're going to hang in there financially." Her initial relief and mild euphoria following the separation clearly had passed, and Judy was starting to struggle with identity issues. These were worked on throughout the following year as she met with the therapist for approximately 20 more sessions.

Judy came to understand that she had defined her personal identity too much in terms of others' expressed liking and acceptance. Always orienting her responses too much to the wishes and needs of others (particularly her father, John, and her daughters) had left her vulnerable to their actions and without a firm sense of herself. When others did not meet her expectations, her self-esteem plummeted. During the first year of her divorce, Judy began a job, working part-time for the city welfare department. She had an intense "fling" (her word) with one of her supervisors, who had been divorced for about 3 years. At first, she convinced herself that she was in love with this man, but began to realize "that must have been necessary for me to feel O.K. again." She recognized eventually that this was basically a transitional relationship. Her attraction seemed to be primarily the result of a need to heal quickly the self-esteem wounds inflicted in part by the lack of passion and desire that had characterized the middle and later stages of her marriage. She exited the relationship gracefully but somewhat ambivalently after about 6 months and began to date several people, though none "seriously."

At this point in therapy, Judy indicated, "I think I'm finally ready to go out on my own—it feels like I've grown up—finally, don't you think?" Asked about her feelings toward John, she replied, "We still talk, mostly about the children. He tells me a little about his life, and I'm interested— but from a distance, like I'm not really involved anymore. But if he has a special experience, like a nice trip South to a conference, that he gets paid for, I can still get jealous." The therapist replied, "That sounds pretty human. I think I'd be jealous, too. I like what I'm hearing from you; it sounds like maybe we are getting ready to stop." Therapy ended after one more session. Judy came back to therapy approximately 9 months later, to talk about a serious relationship she was having, in which she was afraid she was repeating dysfunctional patterns from her marriage. After three sessions, she apparently gained the support, insight, or reassurance she needed, and has not returned to therapy since that time.

Obstacles to Successful Treatment

The primary obstacle in working with separating and divorcing couples is the intense ambivalence that can characterize this period of decision making (Bloom, Asher, & White, 1978; Goode, 1956; Weiss, 1975). The threat of divorce is used frequently by one spouse as a weapon, perhaps the only one in the communication arsenal loud enough to be heard through defensive "armor." Thus, although couples may come to therapy saying they want help with separating, this may or may not be the case. The therapist needs to ascertain carefully what such a request actually means. It may be a disguised challenge to the therapist to try to get the spouses back together by convincing them that the marriage is worthwhile, that is, "tipping" the ambivalence in a positive direction.

It is important to assess early in therapy whether *both* partners truly wish to be there. One spouse may have decided that he or she wants out of the relationship and may have someone else "waiting in the wings." Primarily out of guilt, such an individual may have come to therapy basically to turn over the spouse to the therapist. Thus, one spouse's hidden agenda may be to get out of therapy as quickly as possible and get on with his or her (other) life. To set up a therapeutic contract to work together (e.g., in a structured separation with counseling) is likely to be unproductive in such circumstances. Hidden agendas of one or both individuals should be brought out into the open as soon as psychologically feasible in therapy, while taking into account what may be the defensive purpose of such behaviors.

The intense ambivalence felt by couples approaching the issue of separation or divorce also means that they may have a good deal of difficulty in actually making the decision to separate. Much patience may be required on the therapist's part as the couple struggles with this usually painful decision. One or both individuals may want the therapist to make the decision, thereby relieving further guilt feelings related to perceived abandonment and failure. Frustrated by the back and forth, "in" and "out," character of the partners' behavior, the therapist may indeed be tempted to "play God" and tell the couple that they should, or should not, stay together. Most therapists are understandably and appropriately uncomfortable with such decision making (Kressel & Deutsch, 1977). Instead, the authors recommend something like the following approach. Such a response is usually communicated to the couple by the therapist after a course of marital therapy during which the spouses have been unable to decide whether to stay together or not.

> It appears as if we've worked on all the important relationship issues. It's probably time to make some decision, either to separate or to really make a commitment to making the marriage work. Either way, I'm willing to continue working with one or both of you, either on an individual basis or together, whatever you like. Why don't the two of you talk things over and let me know next time what you've decided?

Such an approach makes clear that it is the couple's decision. By his or her willingness to continue working with the individuals, the therapist mutes a further sense of abandonment, already salient because of the possibility that the marriage may dissolve.

Another obstacle to working with couples in the process of divorce has to do with any concurrent legal intervention. Kressel and Deutsch (1977) discuss the problems for therapy of the necessarily adversarial nature of legal divorce. There is an increasing recognition in the literature that lawyers and therapists need to work together for the mutual benefit of client and professional(s). A good discussion of issues and proposals along these lines can be found in Fisher and Fisher (1982).

Limitations of the Structured Separation Approach

The primary limitation of the structured separation approach is that it requires continued cooperation and collaboration of the spouses. There must be open and honest communication and negotiation (e.g., about the choice to see one another); how to handle issues about the children, finances, and housing; whether to maintain an intimate relationship; and the question of seeing other people. At such a vulnerable time in the relationship, with the accompanying frustrations, felt failures at communication, and ego wounds, the degree of psychological health required to implement the structured separation approach may be too great for many individuals. The desire to hurt, to seek revenge, and/or to gain a power advantage (e.g., by introducing a third party primarily to stir up jealousy, or by sabotaging access to children) may outweigh the benefits of reintroducing the feeling of choice into an ambivalent, conflicted relationship.

Another major limitation of the structured separation approach (A. S. Gurman, personal communication, 1984) is that the opportunity for working on behavior change is usually severely limited by the restricted amount of husband–wife time together, during which there is likely more focus on issues than on concrete behavioral changes. This limitation may unwittingly reinforce one spouse's sense that his or her mate is "saying all the right things during this separation, but not really acting any differently."

Furthermore, both individuals are unlikely to be at the same place in terms of their cathexis to the relationship during the separation. This inequity can lead to frustrated hopes for early reconciliation, disappointment, and bitterness over differing agendas (e.g., one party wanting out, the other wanting to stay in the relationship.) One spouse may need to be patient while the other catches up psychologically with the help of the therapy and the process of exploring highly ambivalent feelings.

THE ROLE OF THE THERAPIST

In working with separating and divorcing couples, a primary function of the therapist is to serve as a catalyst for decision making. This is not just a "cognitive" role (i.e., a negotiator). Emotional sensitivity is required, given the high degree of personal stress, felt ego wounds, and impact of decision making on others (i.e., children, relatives, and friends). Personal as well as therapeutic maturity is required for successful therapy with such couples. The couple may take out their frustration on the therapist, for example, becoming angry that he or she did not provide early clarity and resolution to a complicated relationship, characterized by conflict of some duration.

The level of anger is likely to be very high; anger over the present situation for the partner who is left, and hostile feelings from past incidents on the part of the one who is leaving. This degree of hostility may be disturbing to one or both spouses and dealt with defensively via projection of such feelings onto the therapist. A common example of this process is the feeling or accusation that the therapist is "taking sides" (i.e., favoring the views or wishes of one spouse over the other). This accusation can serve several defensive purposes, among them justifying the wish to leave therapy prematurely and/or indirectly attacking the other spouse, now identified as "being with" the therapist.

In many ways, dealing with separation and divorce can be as problematic for the therapist as for the clients. The therapist needs to examine carefully his or her attitudes toward divorce. Marital therapists are likely to have difficulty if they measure their success as clinicians by how many couples they see stay together. Indeed, unless one is initially highly selective in terms of referrals, many of the couples seen in a general marital therapy practice will go on to divorce.

The therapist who feels that he or she has failed when a couple decides to separate, after originally seeking therapy to save the marriage, is likely to communicate such feelings in subtle ways to the clients, thus compounding the negative self-evaluation they may be feeling. A therapist who has not dealt with his or her own personal separation anxiety, or has not worked through emotionally a personal separation or divorce, is likely to be less effective in working professionally with such couples. Thus, the therapist must carefully examine his or her attitudes toward divorce, making sure that the client(s) will be guaranteed a freedom of choice. If the therapist has definite biases pro or con divorce, these should be stated openly and directly early in therapy, in the spirit of *caveat emptor*.

A common omission in working with separating and divorcing couples is to lose touch with the impact of the couple's decision on significant others. This applies particularly to children. Many couples do not wish to include their children in sessions where the goal is to make a decision regarding the continuance or termination of the marriage. The myth that children are unaware of the tensions in the marriage is still believed by many couples. On the other hand, insisting on doing only family therapy, requiring all or almost all family members to be present, can both inhibit the parents in their decision making and hold out false hopes for the children, who may believe "the family that goes to therapy together, stays together." If the therapist decides not to include the children regularly in the therapy sessions, she or he should inquire frequently about the children and whether they appear to be reacting symptomatically to the marital problems and stress. Common indicants would be signs of school refusal, increase in health problems that require the child to stay home, decline in school performance, social withdrawal, and increase in aggressive or sexual acting out, all beyond age norms and expectations. The continued appearance of any of the these symptoms would signal the need to bring the children into the treatment sessions.

The therapist should be alert that children can be used as pawns in a contested divorce, with the threat of a "custody fight" held up to the spouse who is not capitulating to the other's wishes. Pointing out the potential emotional and financial costs of a custody battle, and raising the issue of whether such a procedure would truly serve the child's best interests, can be an important part of the therapy. Many therapists favor the couple's attempting to work toward a joint or shared custody arrangement. A discussion of the issues in this area can be found in Abarbanel (1979), Clingempeel and Rapucci (1982), and Grote and Weinstein (1977).

ADDITIONAL CLINICAL ISSUES

A primary form of resistance encountered with separating and divorcing couples has to do with getting *both* spouses into therapy. In this way, such couples are similar to others who experience marital problems but are not yet at the point of seriously considering a separation. Seeing only one spouse and attempting to help that individual come to some decision about continuance or dissolution of the marriage is likely to result in misperceptions. There are clearly two sides to every issue in marital dysfunction. The therapist needs to help each partner gain a more dispassionate appreciation of the other's viewpoint. To see only one person is likely simply to reinforce that person's idiographic conception of the marital problems. Such a therapeutic tack also does not prepare a couple for the give and take required in negotiating the difficult issues of separation and divorce, although the client may draw support and comfort from seeing the therapist on a one-to-one basis.

A more efficacious position is for the therapist to make an earnest attempt to see both spouses, for at least one of the sessions, especially early in the therapy process. If one spouse's exhortations do not succeed in bringing the other into therapy, the therapist may wish to try to contact the nonattending spouse directly, explaining the rationale for wanting to see both partners. Occasionally, clients may seek individual therapy after they and their partner have clearly made a decision to divorce, and the legal process may be well under way. In such instances it is still useful therapeutically to see both individuals together for at least one session, although this is not mandatory from a strategic standpoint. In such cases, the therapy takes on a postdivorce stance with the objective being one of trying to help the client adjust to the decision and its consequences and to move on developmentally.

Another common form of resistance relates to the previously mentioned fact that one spouse is usually more certain than the other about the advisability of separating or divorcing. Holding back participation in therapy or resisting the therapist's suggestions aimed at helping to move the decision-making process along may represent an indirect attempt to hold on to or prolong the marriage, thereby delaying its feared termination. Such behavior is generally self-defeating, and gentle efforts on the therapist's part can help point out how one is accepting or holding on to less than they rightfully deserve. For example, the therapist might say, "It seems to me that you basically want someone who clearly cares about you, and is able to show that pretty directly, rather than staying with someone whose feelings about you are so unsure." Developmentally, the emphasis is on helping the client "get on" with his or her life, and pointing out that while separation is an ending, it also symbolizes a new beginning and a chance to start over again personally and eventually in another relationship.

A useful treatment procedure for either the postseparation or postdivorce periods is group therapy with others in the process of separation and divorce (Granvold & Welch, 1979; Kessler, 1978). Many individuals feel very uncertain about their relationship skills and social acceptability following the breakup of a marriage. At the same time, they feel lonely and need to share experiences and feelings with others in similar circumstances. Useful descriptions of the personal reactions during this period can be found in Hunt and Hunt (1977) and Krantzler (1975). Group therapy can provide helpful emotional support, practical information, and a springboard for social reentry.

SUMMARY

This chapter has outlined a developmental approach for treating couples and individuals who are dealing with separation and divorce. The basic tenet of this framework is that separation and divorce are life events and processes involving not only psychic pain and loss of self-esteem but also the opportunity for growth and establishment of a stronger personal identity. A structured separation with counseling procedure is advocated for helping couples decide whether to remain in a conflicted relationship or proceed toward divorce. An illustrative case study utilizing this approach was presented. Postdivorce individual therapy was discussed, particularly for dealing with perceived narcissistic injury and for understanding dysfunctional interaction patterns in the marriage, hopefully preventing their reoccurrence in future relationships.

REFERENCES

Arbarbanel, A. (1979). Shared parenting after separation: A study of joint custody. *American Journal of Orthopsychiatry, 49,* 320–329.

Berman, E. M., & Leif, H. I. (1975). Marital therapy from a psychiatric perspective: An overview. *American Journal of Psychiatry, 132,* 583–592.

Bloom, B. L., Asher, S. J., & White, S. W. (1978). Marital disruption as a stressor: A review and analysis. *Psychological Bulletin, 85,* 867–894.

Bohannan, P. (1971). The six stations of divorce. In P. Bohannan (Ed.), *Divorce and after.* New York: Anchor.

Brown, E. M. (1976). Divorce counseling. In D. H. L. Olson (Ed.), *Treating relationships.* Lake Mills, IA: Graphic Press.

Clingempeel, W. G., & Repucci, N. D. (1982). Joint custody after divorce: Major issues and goals for research. *Psychological Bulletin, 91,* 102–127.

Fisher, E. O., & Fisher, M. S. (Eds.). (1982). Therapists, lawyers, and divorcing spouses. *Journal of Divorce, 6,* 1–138.

Framo, J. L. (1978). The friendly divorce. *Psychology Today, 12,* 77–79, 100–102.

Goetting, A. (1981). Divorce outcome research: Issues and perspectives. *Journal of Family Issues, 2,* 350–378.

Goode, W. (1956). *Women in divorce*. New York: Free Press.

Granvold, D. K. (1983). Structured separation for marital treatment and decision-making. *Journal of Marital and Family Therapy, 9*, 403–412.

Granvold, D. K., & Tarrant, R. (1983). Structured marital separation as a marital treatment method. *Journal of Marital and Family Therapy, 9*, 189–198.

Granvold, D. K., & Welch, G. J. (1979). Structured, short term group treatment of postdivorce adjustment. *International Journal of Group Psychotherapy, 29*, 347–358.

Greene, B. L., Lee, R. R., & Lustig, N. (1973). Transient structured distance as a maneuver in marital therapy. *Family Coordinator. 22*, 15–22.

Grote, D. F., & Weinstein, J. P. (1977). Joint custody: A viable and ideal alternative. *Journal of Divorce, 1*, 43–53.

Gurman, A. S., & Kniskern, D. P. (1978). Research on marital and family therapy: Progress, perspective and prospect. In S. Garfield & A. Bergin (Eds.), *Handbook of psychotherapy and behavior change* (2d ed.). New York: Wiley.

Hunt, M., & Hunt, B. (1977). *The divorce experience*. New York: McGraw-Hill.

Kaffman, M., & Talmon, M. (1982). The crisis of divorce: An opportunity for constructive change. *International Journal of Family Therapy, 4*, 220–233.

Kaslow, F. W. (1981). Divorce and divorce therapy. In A. S. Gurman & D. P. Kniskern (Eds.), *Handbook of family therapy*. New York: Brunner/Mazel.

Kaslow, F. W., & Hyatt, R. (1982). Divorce: A potential growth experience for the extended family. *Journal of Divorce, 6*, 115–126.

Kessler, S. (1978). Building skills in divorce adjustment groups. *Journal of Divorce, 2*, 209–216.

Kitson, D. C., & Raschke, H. J. (1981). Divorce research: What we know; what we need to know. *Journal of Divorce, 4*, 1–37.

Krantzler, M. (1975). *Creative divorce: A new opportunity for personal growth*. New York: Signet/New American Library.

Kraus, S. (1979). The crisis of divorce: Growth promoting or pathogenic. *Journal of Divorce, 3*, 107–119.

Kressel, K., & Deutsch, M. (1977). Divorce therapy: An in-depth survey of therapists' views. *Family Process, 16*, 413–443.

Levinger, D. (1965). Marital cohesiveness and dissolution: An integrative review. *Journal of Marriage and the Family, 27*, 19–28.

National Center for Health Statistics. (1982). Provisional statistics, 1981. *Monthly Vital Statistics Report, 30* (112). Washington, DC: Government Printing Office.

Rice, D. G. (1977). Psychotherapeutic treatment of narcissistic injury in marital separation and divorce. *Journal of Divorce, 1*, 119–128.

Rice, D. G. (1981). Transition from marital/family therapy to individual therapy following separation or divorce. In A. S. Gurman (Ed.), *Questions and answers in the practice of family therapy*. New York: Brunner/Mazel.

Rice, J. K., & Rice, D. G. (1985). *Living through divorce: A developmental approach to divorce therapy*. New York: Guilford Press.

Singer, L. J. (1975). Divorce and the single life: Divorce as development. *Journal of Sex and Marital Therapy, 1*, 254–262.

Sprenkle, D. H., & Storm, D. A. (1983). Divorce therapy outcome research: A substantive and methodological review. *Journal of Marital and Family Therapy, 9*, 239–257.

Toomim, M. K. (1972). Structured separation with counseling: A therapeutic approach for couples in conflict. *Family Process, 11*, 299–310.

Weiss, R. S. (1975). *Martial separation*. New York: Basic Books.

Whitaker, C. A., & Miller, M. H. (1969). A reevaluation of "psychiatric help" when divorce impends. *American Journal of Psychiatry, 126*, 57–62.

Therapy with Unmarried Couples

ELLEN M. BERMAN
MARTIN GOLDBERG

13

It is generally considered that marital therapy (or "marriage counseling") had its origins in post–World War I Germany in the 1920s (Broderick & Schrader, 1981). Various clinics were established at that time to deal with the problems of venereal disease and illegitimate or unwanted pregnancies, which were rampant in the permissive and turbulent society of the Wiemar Republic, as they were in Jazz Age America and in the rest of Europe. Sex education and the providing of contraceptive information were primary purposes for the early marriage counseling centers, and even 50 or 60 years ago, many couples who were seen in "marriage counseling" were not actually married, either legally or in common law. The modal "premarital" case, as described in the early papers at Marriage Council of Philadelphia (Mudd, 1941) was a young woman, generally inexperienced, seeking sexual and contraceptive information prior to her wedding.

The Great Depression and World War II and its aftermath ushered in a period of conservatism. In the last 15 or 20 years, however, there has been another extended period of social permissiveness in the United States and Europe, and marked cultural changes have taken place. Love and marriage no longer "go together like a horse and carriage," as the song suggested. A wide variety of nonmarital love relationships are acceptable, even encouraged, and sexual ignorance is a less frequent problem than relationship-centered concerns.

From a statistical viewpoint, it may be noted that the number of unmarried couples living together tripled between 1970 and 1980 (Spanier, 1983) to

Ellen M. Berman and Martin Goldberg. Department of Psychiatry, University of Pennsylvania, Philadelphia, Pennsylvania and Marriage Council of Philadelphia, Philadelphia, Pennsylvania.

approximately 4% of all cohabiting couples. In actuality, this figure is a minimal estimate, and the number is probably considerably higher. When this figure is considered along with the huge pool of noncohabiting couples, it is not surprising that at Marriage Council of Philadelphia, 13% of all couples seeking therapy are unmarried. A similar percentage has been noted in the private practice of the second author.

Unmarried couples present with a broad range of problems. Such couples range from college students with a sexual problem, clear that this is a transient relationship, to the couple living together for several years and undecided whether to marry or split up, to the common-law marriage of many years. Even the premarital couples presenting at clinics do not look like the premarital couples of earlier decades. Except in settings with active outreach programs for young couples (often religious or educational institutions), the average premarital case is a couple in their late 30s, with one or both having been previously married, and with children from the former marriages.

Although any couple, married or not, has a relationship with stable rules that can be examined systemically, the fact of their unmarried state in some ways changes the character of the relationship and, therefore, the issues involved in counseling. For the majority of people, unmarried means "uncertain" and marriage means "forever," although divorce statistics suggest otherwise. In addition, the concept of marriage also has strong, and sometimes idiosyncratic, personal symbolism. For example, if a person sees "being married" as "being controlled," this affects not only that person's choices, but also the interpretation of others' behavior. He or she is likely to see any proposal of marriage as an attempt at domination; being unmarried, even if living together and pooling resources, is seen as safety. The fact that a yes–no decision is inherent in the situation and that the results of that decision are, by definition, public may concern people who are uneasy with decisions or concerned with public opinion. Not only the partners, but the family of origin as well, and often friends or colleagues, may have a stake in the decision and feelings about it; the pressure they place on the participants may also affect the system.

For therapists, too, deeply held beliefs and values about marriage and the family may affect their perception of the couple, regardless of professional training and experience. The wide range of presentations requires a range of therapist skills and a careful examination of the therapists' own value system.

> A couple entered therapy because of constant arguing about whether or not to marry. Both were in their early 30s, with previous marriages; both had children, and neither wanted more. They were bright, well-educated professionals from middle-class backgrounds. They had been living together for 2 years; had stable, separate incomes; and were behaving as a married couple in many ways (e.g., monogamy, child discipline). Both knew that promises of "forever" could be broken.

Why was this couple arguing about marriage? What functions was the unmarried state serving, and what would be changed by their marriage? The answers to these questions occupied a considerable part of the therapy and highlight the changing functions of marriage in today's world and its interface with individual and system dynamics.

THE HISTORICAL FUNCTIONS OF MARRIAGE

Attitudes toward marriage are developed from an amalgam of familial and cultural norms. Changing cultural expectations of marriage and its functions may greatly influence individual perception and behavior. Therefore, an understanding of individual issues should include some sense of social norms and values for the people involved.

Marriage has been defined as "a socially legitimate sexual union, begun with a public announcement and undertaken with some idea of permanence; it is assumed with a more or less explicit marriage contract, which spells out reciprocal rights and obligations between spouses, and between the spouses and their future children" (Stephens, 1963, p. 5). Marriage is fundamentally a social institution, part of the web of patterned social behavior that allows for predictability of behavior, and permitting groups to get on with the business of survival. All societies have needed to define lineage and kinship systems in order to arrange for inheritance and responsibility for care of children.

Humans also have certain biological needs for some form of contact and closeness with others, a sexual outlet, and enough pattern in daily behavior with others to allow for some consistency in life. These needs can be satisfied in many ways. Marriage provides one possible regular and predictable method. The spouses' expectations of marriage, *per se*, at the emotional level are determined by the role of the marital pair in the community and the outlets available for the satisfaction of bonding needs.

Murstein (1974) points out that marriage was a firmly established institution when recorded history began, so we can only speculate as to its origins. Indeed, it is not even known whether the first marriages were monogamous. Anthropologists have described promiscuity among tribal members, matriarchy, and polygamy as earlier marital forms. In Murdock's 1949 classification of societies, 193 were described as polygamous and 43 as monogamous. Polygamy tends to be found primarily in cultures of scarcity, however, and then only among the rich of the culture. In sheer numbers, the bulk of the world's population has chosen the dyad as the central family building block, and has developed some form of ceremony defining the social legitimacy of the relationship. Around this dyad, kinship lines are traced in a more or less elaborated manner. In tightly knit kin structures, the larger system defines the form of the marriage and often chooses the marital partner.

Western European culture in the Middle Ages was, at least among the rich, focused on a patriarchal, extended-family model. In such a society, where the primary bonds are between blood kin, and extended families are the rule, individual needs are subordinated to the group, and emotional ties to kin are often more powerful than marital bonds. (Such societies are most likely to flourish in nonindustrialized areas where survival of all depends on the ability of groups of people to work together, and where parents can bequeath much of real value, such as land, which is not easily acquired by individual labor.) In such a system, the function of marriage is to provide "new blood" for the system, that is, the joining of lands or money or title, as well as procreation of children. The satisfaction of psychological and biological needs of the participant is of secondary concern. Marriage is very important in such a system, but for very different reasons than in our current system. What is gained by the individual in an extended family is a broad range of people directly involved with one's welfare and life. It provides a very different and strong sense of security, at the expense, of course, of much freedom. It should be added that poor families, with little money or land to pass on, never had as much control of their offspring. The pattern among the peasants of Western Europe was generally that of some attempts by parents and the cultural milieu to control the range of eligibles, slightly more of the choice being left to the partners (Shorter, 1975). Nevertheless, it was perfectly clear to the participants that marriage was still more a survival mechanism than a chance for self-enhancement. In many cases, life in lower socioeconomic groups was lived 10 or 12 people (children, parents, farmhands) to a single room, and "family" as a private place did not exist. Many people remained unmarried for their entire lives. They generally lived as boarders, or hired hands. They did not, however, set up housekeeping with other unmarried young people.

The 1700s in the West saw the decrease in power of the extended-kin group. Both Protestantism and capitalism promoted individualism rather than extended-family cohesion. The Industrial Revolution provided increased rewards for mobile and independent people, and allowed for acquisition of resources by individuals rather than families. The increasing economic independence of young people, plus increasing ideals of autonomy, allowed for free choice of mate and the idea of marriage for love, plus decreased interdependence with older generations. In America, the nuclear family model arrived with the original settlers, who left behind their extended families and found a situation conducive to independent family living— enough land for everyone (Blumstein & Schwartz, 1983).

The last century and a half has seen a major shift in the functions of marriage, and it now carries alone the primary, almost total responsibility for the emotional and often economic well-being of its members. This is not limited to Western Europe—cross-culturally, the world is moving toward more free-choice marriage and lessened ties with the extended family. The rate of change seems to be related to the rate of industrialization. Couples who manifest a free-choice pattern in any culture show later age at marriage, higher educational level, higher socioeconomic state, and urbanization (Murstein, 1980).

This is not to say that all connections with the extended family have vanished. Children are still concerned about their parents' approval, and parental blessings or curses can be powerful psychological forces in their marriage. Parents' economic or social control is in most cases gone, however, and the ideal of many young people (seldom realized) is to make a decision regarding a mate without considering their parents' opinions.

The need for marriage as a legal institution can also be altered by changing cultural patterns. In Scandinavia, for example, a drastic decrease in marriage has occurred, presumably because of the acceptance of cohabitation and parental support or state support for children born out of wedlock (Murstein, 1980). This has not decreased the need for pairing, but only for marriage *per se*. Emotional needs are still met by members of the cohabiting dyad.

The current American trend of individualism promotes the individuality and separateness of each person. The 1970s pushed this ideal to its extreme. This arrangement, with its goal of self-sufficiency, paradoxically increases loneliness because one is freed of the obligations and ties that produce a feeling of connectedness along with constriction. Accompanying this trend has been a pattern of later and fewer children, further reducing the need for a secure family setting. In large urban centers, once seemingly secure ties to work, religion, and extended family are also attenuated, leaving love relationships almost the only binding relationships left.

In this setting, marriage is seen as a promise of intimacy and security, and as an attempt at, if not a guarantee of, permanence. (This, obviously, is a mixed blessing to a person seeking space and new experiences.) It also represents a mark of great valuing of the other. Both the ceremony and the consequences bind the couple into the extended family in one of the few ways left, as well as providing some legal safeguards for chidren.

If the central conflict today is between the need for autonomy and the need for roots and connectedness, and if love–sexual dyadic relationships are seen as the primary available source of connectedness, cohabiting or long-term noncohabiting love relationships provide a set of "medium-range" solutions. Nonmarital relationships run the gamut from temporary and nonbinding connections to couples who function in a marriage-like manner, economically and emotionally dependent (Macklin, 1978). For most couples, however, the lack of the "public announcement" implies to self and world the potential of availability and lessened interdependence. Even long-term cohabitors are less likely than married couples to pool incomes, and almost all in the middle class are two-career couples, with each person having clearly defined separate goals and interests (Blumstein & Schwartz, 1983). The current relationship can be defined as an experiment. (It is worth remembering, unfortunately, that there is no evidence that premarital cohabitation decreases the divorce rate.) For some, the unmarried state allows participants to avoid role behavior from their families of origin that they associate with being a "husband" or a "wife." For some couples, the legal state of being unmarried provides the illusion of freedom in what is actually a fused and tightly dependent relationship.

From the clinician's point of view, a medium-range solution is not necessarily a problem. A society of long-lived and independent people probably requires a variety of solutions other than the single option proposed by the 1950s—an early marriage, preferably between two virgins, who would remain together for their entire lives. The uncertainty and societal challenge built into these new relationships can be useful for allowing people time to grow up, to learn about themselves and others, and to make a statement of independence to family, lover, or self. They do not necessarily imply a lack of commitment, but may be chosen out of a wish to avoid what are seen as prescribed marital roles. Such relationships can, however, be used defensively to avoid intimacy and interdependence, although marriage, of course, does not guarantee these either. Long-term intense nonmarital relationships are particularly difficult for the children of each partner, who need clarity of roles and permanence from their caretakers.

From the point of view of the wider community, relationships with known rules and obligations are needed for society to function smoothly. If a variant pattern becomes widespread enough, rules and patterns will be constructed around it. Common-law marriage and palimony are examples of such rules already in force. When there is cultural agreement for the term describing "the person who is living with me and is my sex partner," the pattern and roles will probably be complete, and people will have to find other ways to be outrageous.

Couples who choose to present to a therapist are in disagreement about the rules of their relationship or have been unable to make it work. The rest of this chapter describes the problems that can occur in nonmarried relationships and how the marital therapist can respond to them.

CLINICAL ISSUES WITH DIFFERENT COUPLES

Dyads vary greatly in whether they define their state as "premarital," and very often they disagree between themselves. For many couples, there is no coherent plan to marry (or to stay unmarried). For young couples, especially, such pairings, moving in an unplanned way, "drift" (Jackson, 1983) toward marriage, and the final decision is made at the conscious level because of pressure from in-laws, job moves, and so on. This type of decision is particularly susceptible to cultural norms of the "right time" to marry. For other couples, one or both partners has very clear ideas about the direction the relationship should take, emotionally and legally.

Therefore, when seeing unmarried couples, the therapist must consider the following issues: the goals of the relationship for each partner; the current relationship contract (extent of availability to others desired by each); and the functions, legal, emotional, and cognitive, of the present unmarried state.

Couples presenting to a therapist are most likely to have at least one previously married member and to present with relatively complicated content issues. Probably the most common presenting style is a major difference in commitment level, with one partner, more often the woman, wanting marriage and the other uncertain. Other frequent presenting complaints involve couples where both, overtly, at least, wish to remain together but are experiencing relationship distress; and truly "premarital" couples, with the date set, who wish either education and enrichment or are having severe problems, often related to previous marriage and children. In addition, some unmarried couples enter therapy with marriage *per se* not being an issue—either young, basically uncommitted, couples wishing sex therapy or couples with children who are legally unmarried and have agreed to remain so. Homosexual couples also, of course, are unmarried. Their specific issues are considered elsewhere in this volume. The inability to use the symbols and legal sanctions of marriage are often part of the stress these couples experience.

Presenting couples vary in the length of time they have been together, whether they are cohabiting or not, and what the rules of the relationship are. Nevertheless, they present with the same systemic issues as married couples: overcompetent–undercompetent pairs, family-of-origin issues, etc. In the following section, examples of common presenting problems are given. They are classified by how marriage, as an issue, interrelates with other presenting problems.

Premarital Couples, First Marriage, and Enrichment

Fran and Bill were classmates in medical school, involved for 6 months but not cohabiting, who planned to get married the following year. Their relationship, while brief in duration, had been unmarred by any severe clashes. They appeared to be equally devoted to each other and well matched in personality type, interests, and family backgrounds.

Fran and Bill came for counseling primarily at the suggestion and mild urging of Bill's father, a family physician who had had some training in marital–family therapy. That training had led him to believe that any couple contemplating marriage was well advised to have at least a brief experience in conjoint therapy. Even though this suggestion came from outside the dyad, Fran and Bill responded to it with some degree of enthusiasm. Both were intelligent and sophisticated enough to realize that conjoint therapy might be helpful, even though they had not yet encountered problems in the relationship.

The couple contracted for three conjoint sessions. In these sessions, much of the discussion was about the problems that may develop in a two-career marriage, specifically in marriages in which both spouses are in the same profession. Both Fran and Bill recognized that, like most medical students in our society, they were highly competitive, and consideration was given to ways that they could develop more cooperative attitudes in their relationship. The three conjoint sessions went so well and there was such lively discussion that it was decided to extend the therapy for another three sessions. In these, consideration of cooperative versus competitive interaction continued, and there was some discussion of the two families of origin. Particular attention was focused on Bill's father, who was the strongest person in the cast of characters. Bill and Fran recognized that he was also a very benevolent and positive force in their lives, but they discussed ways to deal with his strength so that it would not be overwhelming or intrusive in their relationship. At the end of six conjoint sessions, the counseling was terminated by mutual agreement. All felt that it had been a positive experience, even though no issues of great complexity or depth had emerged.

In urban clinic therapy settings, couples such as Fran and Bill—never married, equally committed, generally well functioning—are rare. The senior author, in fact, cannot recall a similar case in all the years of her practice. Couples such as this are more likely to present to their minister, or family doctor, or one of the many group experiences now available. Such educational groups have proliferated in this country, and reviews of such programs are available (e.g., Bagarozzi & Rauen, 1981). If such couples request help from an individual practitioner, they should be enjoyed fully. Usual areas of review include communication training, conflict negotiation, consideration of issues and people from family of origin, and sex. Therapists vary in their concern for content issues such as money, religion, and children. Obviously, each couple will have its own specific issues, such as, in the case above, dual-career questions and boundary problems with in-laws.

Many such cases who appear in the therapist's office, however, are likely to have a hidden agenda that moves them into the next category.

Couples with Problems of Commitment

Al, a 32-year-old attorney, and Sharon, a 30-year-old schoolteacher, had been living together for 2 years. Neither had been married previously. They had known each other for 4 years. They sought conjoint therapy primarily at Sharon's insistence. Their chief complaint was a lack of good communication, but it was soon evident that the real difficulties lay elsewhere. Al described himself as basically satisfied with the relationship as it was. He indicated that he and Sharon would, in all likelihood, get married sometime in the future, but he was quite vague about when that might be. Meanwhile, he had a roving eye and occasionally got involved in brief sexual alliances with other women. He felt that these were of little or no significance and that Sharon should not worry about them. Additionally, he protested (perhaps a bit too much) that Sharon was perfectly free to have such extracurricular affairs also, and that it would not trouble him in the least.

For her part, Sharon said she was deeply in love with Al. After 2 years of living together, she felt they cared deeply for each other, and generally got along very well. She wanted to marry in the very near future. She failed to comprehend why Al would not agree to setting a date. Moreover, Al's sexual affairs, which she initially regarded with some real or feigned tolerance, were now becoming quite objectionable to her. She felt they were somehow wrong, but since she and Al had never adopted a code of strict sexual fidelity, she did not have a peg on which to hang her objections. Intellectually, she agreed with Al that the affairs were acceptable, but more and more her gut reaction to them was negative and she was coming to feel somehow degraded and exploited.

During the first three or four conjoint sessions, the therapist asked each of them to spell out goals, and it quickly became evident that Al wished to maintain the status quo, while Sharon wanted to plan for an imminent marriage. The therapist aligned himself with neither goal. He suggested that Sharon work intensively on the question why she was not content with the status quo and that she accept as an assignment the delineation of reasons why marriage to Al would not be desirable at the present time. Al was given an assignment of considering why he balked at the idea of an imminent marriage to Sharon and was asked to delineate all the reasons why it might be desirable.

In the fourth conjoint session, Sharon demanded that Al agree to abstain from any sexual affairs while therapy was in progress. Al flatly refused. The therapist suggested that they do something they had never done, that is, negotiate a clearly spelled out agreement on their sexual and dating behavior while they were living together. This process revealed serious conflicts in both areas of power and intimacy. Sharon clearly wanted a deeper degree of intimacy than Al opted for. If she could obtain this, or something approximating it, she was willing to continue to live with Al without marriage. On the other hand, if Al would not increase the amount of genuine intimacy in their relationship, she was still willing to continue it, providing he married her immediately. In effect, Sharon was willing to settle for either the form or the substance of an intimate relationship. Al wanted neither, and resented Sharon's attempts to influence him in this direction. He saw this as an incursion on his freedom.

By the tenth conjoint session, it was clear that neither would move from their position. Al needed the distance he had maintained by refusing both marriage and a more intimate and committed emotional stance. Sharon refused to continue as is, and was willing to leave the relationship if no change was forthcoming. The couple thus came to a decision to end the relationship. Al dragged his feet on this, still hoping for a continuation of the status quo, but Sharon maintained the impetus to move and, indeed, found another apartment and moved out of their joint residence and out of the relationship. Sharon subsequently asked the therapist to continue to see her individually, but at his suggestion accepted a referral to another therapist for the work of trying to understand herself better.

At the end of the conjoint therapy, Sharon was sad at the termination of the relationship with Al, but felt that the therapy had been very helpful in getting her to confront the reality of an unrewarding involvement and to move along. Al, despite his inertia concerning change, also expressed the feeling that the therapy was very helpful. The therapist was left feeling that *both people had some complex issues to deal with: Sharon, in terms of her willingness to settle for the mere form of what she ostensibly desired so deeply; and Al, in terms of his unwillingness to consider another person's needs or yield any control to someone with whom he was involved in a relationship. (It seemed unlikely, however, that Al would change these characteristics, since he was not really unhappy about them.)*

Couples with commitment disputes may vary greatly and require different approaches. They may be apparently polarized, as were Al and Sharon, or may both be very ambivalent. It is remarkable how long some of these relationships may continue because of the comfort of the status quo and the fear of being alone. Many of those entering therapy are 4- to even 8-year relationships that are finally pushed to a decision by some external factor, such as a job offer in another city or the ticking of the woman's biological clock and her increasing desire to become a mother. Some of these cases are short term, and the fact of the therapy allows for confrontation with previously avoided issues and precipitates a decision. Some people, however, can use being in therapy as a way of avoiding decision making, that is, as long as they are "trying," or "struggling with the issues" in therapy, a real decision can be put off.

For the latter couples, especially, the task of the therapist is to produce some movement to help the couple get off dead center. This may take the form of providing insight, offering a challenge, or setting forth a strategically planned task. Long-term, ambivalent couples are often more amenable to a strategic solution. An excellent example of such an approach is described by Stanton (1981).

Complex Problems Related to Previous Marriages in an Ongoing Couple

Ben, a 46-year-old college professor, and Kris, a 25-year-old college instructor in the same department, requested couples therapy for help with the complexities of their current relationship. Ben had been married for 20 years to Bertha, a woman he convincingly described as domineering, unstable, and non-nurturing. There were three sons from their marriage, ages 18, 16, and 13. Ostensibly "because of the children," Ben stayed with his marriage for many years, despite his discontent. Bertha adamantly refused to accept any professional help for their relationship or for herself, and Ben finally sought individual therapy. Largely as a result of this therapy, he eventually moved out of the house. It took many years of legal battling, however, before he was finally granted a divorce. During that time, he met Kris, 20 years his junior, who was at that time a graduate student in romance languages attending the university and department that Ben chaired. He was immensely impressed with her intellectual brilliance, her genuine desire to learn, and her emotional warmth. What was originally a protégé–mentor relationship quickly deepened into an intense emotional interaction. Kris was sensitive, receptive, and empathic and exhibited a personal interest in Ben that was quickly reciprocated. Ben was at first uncomfortable about the sizable age difference and the implications of developing a personal relationship with one of his students. Nonetheless, he had been experiencing a long period of emotional starvation in his marriage and was all too vulnerable to developing another relationship. Kris, for her part, had experienced several unrewarding and disappointing relationships with men her own age who were not her intellectual equals, and she was strongly attracted to Ben, who offered much more in terms of compatibility and capacity to stimulate and interest her.

In a fairly short time, Kris and Ben were deeply in love, and she moved in to share his apartment. When Bertha, who was still legally married to Ben at the time, heard of their affair, she was infuriated and told Ben that he could no longer visit his sons or spend time with them in any way. Much battling over these ultimatums ensued, and eventually Bertha found that she could not enforce them and that Ben had the legal right to see his sons. Even more to the point, the boys quickly made it clear that they had no intention of allowing their mother to dictate to them on this matter. However, Ben was unpleasantly surprised and somewhat hurt to find that while his sons had every intention of continuing to see him, they did not embrace their father's new-found friend with great warmth. In varying degrees, each of them was upset at the emergence of this young woman as someone who was very actively and romantically involved with their father. The middle son in particular took a violent dislike to Kris and refused to see her or have anything to do with her. Thus, Ben was confronted with situations such as his son's announcement that he would be happy to spend time with his father but only in the absence of Kris, and the son's refusal to come to Ben's apartment since Kris was living there.

All of this created a dilemma for Ben. He was very aware that he had not been particularly close or attentive to his boys during the years of his marriage, and he felt considerable guilt about this. After leaving his wife, he had vowed that his freedom would enable him to be a better father. Now, he was caught in a severe conflict between his feelings of attachment and obligations to his sons and his love for Kris. To add to the problem, Ben's elderly and deeply religious parents took a position strongly opposing his new relationship. Their upset over the matter was sufficiently great that, after making a number of attempts to persuade Ben to drop Kris, they officially renounced him by writing him out of their will.

Kris began to complain that Ben was often too preoccupied with his family troubles to pay sufficient attention to their relationship. Kris also harbored the strong feeling that Bertha, whom she had never met, was a constant presence in their home.

In the midst of all these conflicts, Bertha made a legal move. Even though the divorce had long since been granted and her alimony and child support fixed, she filed suit, charging that Ben had concealed important financial aspects at the time of the divorce settlement and claiming that she was entitled to larger amounts of money.

At this juncture, Ben and Kris sought conjoint therapy. They presented themselves to the therapist as deeply in love but needing help with their relationship. Ben tended to minimize their difficulties and felt certain *"everything would work out fine." Kris was much more realistic about matters. She felt their communication was deteriorating and gave the general impression of being fed up with the complexities of their life. An example, she indicated, was that Ben had still not brought their relationship "out of the closet." Although some people may have suspected it, nobody in their academic department had been told that they were "an item," let alone that they were living together. (Kris had long since finished her studies in the department and was now employed as an instructor in the department that Ben headed.) Also, Ben's sons had continued to ignore her.*

The early therapy sessions were filled with discussion of such matters. Both Kris and Ben made it very evident that they regarded their relationship as a permanent one, but neither of them ever mentioned marriage. After three sessions, the therapist was quite curious and asked, "Have you thought of getting married in the near future?" Was it possible that some of the objections, from Ben's children, parents, and others, could have been mitigated if their relationship took on a legal status and showed more obvious signs of permanency? At the next therapy session, Ben revealed that Kris was quite angry about the therapist's intervention. Typically, Kris did not express this directly to the therapist, but with some encouragement she said there were additional facts that needed considerations. Her initially stated concern (perhaps not unfounded), that if she and Ben were to marry before Bertha's suit for a larger divorce and support settlement was heard, Kris might wind up having to contribute some of her income to support Ben's ex-wife and children, was prominent among these concerns.

In the next few sessions, their financial complications were thoroughly considered. Ben felt they could be worked out, and took a low-key but definite stance, indicating that he was really ready to marry Kris. What then emerged was a good deal of old emotional baggage that Kris had not previously revealed and that prejudiced her against marriage. She discussed her parents' marriage and her siblings' marriages—all extremely unhappy and unrewarding. A good bit of unfinished business pertaining to her family of origin emerged and was worked with in a series of sessions. (It is, of course, not uncommon to see one partner's ambivalence emerge when the other makes a decision.)

These sessions were not limited to considerations of Kris's problems. Throughout this process, equal therapeutic time was spent considering Ben's problems. Why was he so slow and so reluctant to make the emotional moves out of his former marriage and into the present relationship? Considerable guilt and shame were dealt with. It became apparent that Ben had stayed in his marriage for years, not "because of the children," as he originally insisted, but because his self-esteem was so low that he felt he deserved nothing better.

After about 30 sessions, Ben and Kris both felt that their relationship had solidified, their communication had been greatly improved, and that they were now able to continue on their own. Bertha's suit against Ben— often postponed—was still pending. He and Kris had not decided to marry but gradually their relationship had "gone public." Everyone in their academic department knew of it. Ben's sons had slowly but steadily become more accepting of Kris. Progress was clear.

The example of Ben and Kris indicates how complex the issues may be for a couple wherein one partner has been previously married. Despite its complexity, the case is not at all atypical. Issues from previous marriages interact with issues from early life and from the family of origin to contribute to the current communication issues.

This case highlights problems that may develop around children from such previous marriages. About 28% of unmarried cohabitors have one or more children present in the household (Spanier, 1983), and the majority of older dating couples have children involved with them. Children are often deeply involved with the new relationship and are seldom, if ever, unambivalently pleased by it. Issues of loyalty, money, and time with the parent (already seen as a scarce commodity even without the new "interloper") are common. Many therapists, at some point, if possible conduct a "family" session with the couple in therapy plus the children from one or both previous marriages. In this case, the therapy was conducted only with the adults because Bertha refused to have Kris and the boys meet. This was unfortunate but not unusual. In these cases, a session with the parent and children alone should be considered. When children are brought into therapy in such cases, adult expectations of the children must be clearly delineated. Since the couple is unmarried, which to the children suggests uncertainty about the relationship, the parent must make clear as possible to the child what the status of the relationship is and what is expected of the children in their dealings with the new partner. Discipline, in particular, is a difficult issue. Most couples do not involve a nonmarital partner in major rule making and discipline unless they are clearly planning marriage or are in a marriage-like cohabiting relationship. However, the partner needs some rights in the situation to avoid being treated as second-class citizen. If the relationship is clearly uncertain, it is important not to expect much emotional involvement from the children, who would be hurt again if the relationship were to break up. Some therapists (e.g., Sager, Brown, Crohn, Engel, Rodstein, & Walker, 1983) involve the former spouse in the session, particularly if the children are symptomatic. The decision as to who attends must be carefully discussed.

Dealing with families of origin can also be a real stress for unmarried couples. Although parents may not be as upset as Ben's, often they do not look kindly on such arrangements (Jackson, 1983). Even if they are not upset at a moral level, they may fear that their child is being used in some way. At the least, they are reluctant to make an emotional investment in someone who is, by definition, a possibly less permanent addition to their child's life. This may upset or anger the couple, as it did with Ben and Kris. The couple must think carefully with the therapist about what behavior they want from each family. Each person should remain the expert on their own family and should be the primary communicator, at least in the beginning. Family-of-origin sessions can be useful here. It is probably best to have the initial sessions kept within the biological family, to allow parents and child to deal more easily with one another. The job of the therapist is to help the system clarify its issues and to avoid developing emotional cutoffs (Bowen, 1978).

Additionally, changes in social norms are evident in the case of Ben and Kris. The fact that they, former teacher and student and now members of the same department, can cohabit openly is an option that would have been unavailable 20 years ago. This allowed them the choice of proceeding slowly with the relationship rather than marrying in haste or keeping the arrangement secret.

Unmarried Couples Living a Married Life Style

Frank and Carole have been living together for 3 years in a house they mutually purchased. In the house with them are Carole's three children, ages 14, 12, and 9. Frank, who has been married twice, has four children of his own who are living with their respective mothers. Both Frank and Carole are in their late 30s and both have active careers, although Frank's income is considerably higher.

This couple originally presented themselves for conjoint therapy at Frank's insistence. The immediate matter that was making him unhappy was their sex life. Frank felt that Carole had been doling sex out to him for the last several years and that she was using it as a ploy to exert power in a relationship that he might otherwise have dominated because of his greater financial contribution.

In their early interviews they presented their dilemma in a classic fashion: Frank complained of sexual deprivation, while Carole complained that he was not loving and attentive to her. Frank insisted that if they had a better sexual relationship, he would feel more loving and attentive. Carole answered that if Frank were more loving and attentive, she would feel sexually stimulated more often.

Carole complained that Frank was unloving and unattentive to her children as well, and that he did not act fatherly. Frank countered that he could not feel fatherly because he was not allowed to participate in establishing some rules and discipline for the children. (This is a common theme in remarried households—and even more so when the symbolic joining of marriage has not occurred.)

In subsequent interviews, it developed that Carole's husband left her for another woman, as a result of which she suffered through a deep and lengthy depression. In her marriage, she had lived by a rule of never refusing her husband's sexual request or demand. She felt now that she suffered for this and had vowed never to leave herself vulnerable again.

Frank, in his two marriages, experienced infidelity on the part of both wives. He was reluctant to say so, but finally admitted that Carole's sexual refusals made him fear that she may have been contemplating other affairs or may have already been straying sexually.

As the interviews progressed, various matters besides sex, affection, and the children were discussed, but they all had a common theme: Each partner was afraid to stick his or her neck out for fear they would get hurt, reflecting the deep suffering they each had incurred in their previous relationships. Therapy proceeded quite slowly, and only after a year of regular weekly sessions did the games begin to lessen and trust start to build.

Needless to say, the complaints that this couple present are common to married couples as well as unmarried ones. This couple is, in fact, living a marital, interdependent life style, and the refusal to choose the official commitment of legal marriage is a way of promising themselves that they will be less hurt, this time, if things go poorly. With people who have had previous divorces, there is sometimes an almost superstitious sense that marriage itself is the cause of the problems, and refusing to marry will somehow make things safe. Of course, each partner may see the other's fear of marriage as a personal statement about them, making it even harder for each to reach out. In the case above, marriage became a topic for discussion only after many other issues had been worked out, and became a recognition of a commitment already made.

Ray, a lawyer, and Ellen, a physician, had been living together for 3 years and had an 18-month-old boy. They were living in a monogamous, inter-dependent life style, had joint bank accounts, and so on. Ellen, however, had refused to marry Ray, saying that she was afraid of marriage. She was unable to give much more of an explanation, although her unhappy childhood and difficult previous marriage were enough to make her anxious. Ray would have much preferred to marry, but had chosen not to press her. They entered therapy because of severe arguments, and were trying to decide whether to stay together, which they eventually decided to do. The legal issue of marriage was not brought up by either of them as a problem.

What is intriguing about this couple was that the woman was the one refusing marriage. This had been true before the arguments began, and continued after the dispute was settled and they had decided to stay together. The authors have seen two similar cases in two professional couples. It is possible that this stance, traditionally the man's choice, may become more common as professional women who are economically self-sufficient see marriage as a choice and do not need the protection of marriage on financial grounds. Interestingly, these women, one of them a lawyer, were not at all concerned overtly about the legal status of their children.

Nonpermanent Couples Presenting for Sex Therapy

Ann and Lou were law students, not formally cohabiting but spending a good deal of time at each other's apartments. They had chosen not to define their relationship at this time, and were uncertain as to whether or not they would move to the same city after law school. They presented with Lou's premature ejaculation as the central issue. The therapist accepted at face value the couple's insistence that commitment was not an issue and proceeded with simple communication training and sexual tasks. The problem remitted over a period of some weeks.

Such cases are usually treated with standard behavioral therapy techniques and sex education. The therapist, however, must consider the question of whether the uncertainty of the relationship is contributing to the problems. It is important not to assume this, but to do the simplest things first. The same issues surface when a sexually dysfunctional person brings in a companion who is a friend or a new relationship, specifically for help with the sexual problem.

THERAPIST ISSUES WITH UNMARRIED COUPLES

It is impossible for a therapist to avoid having a personal set of values and beliefs regarding marriage that may affect therapeutic judgment and may have particular salience with unmarried couples. Some common clashes between therapist and client concerns are described in this section. Obviously they have major ethical implications.

Should People Get Married?

Although therapist discomfort with premarital sex or cohabitation is, in the main, a thing of the past, therapists vary in their valuation of marriage. This valuation tends to be related primarily to their own experiences, together with their wishes and fantasies regarding marriage. A therapist who is pleased with his or her life solution will probably have some mild bias toward that solution, whatever it was. A person dissatisfied with his or her choices may encourage in others what he or she has not had the courage to do. For example, a therapist who married early to his first girlfriend may find himself encouraging a male client to keep his options open.

The therapist's gender and age may affect treatment planning. The life stage of the couple may interact with the life stage of the therapist to affect treatment. For example, a 50-year-old therapist, familiar with the developmental transitions of adult life at first hand, may have more concerns about the marriage of two 21-year-olds than will his 27-year-old colleague. A young therapist may wonder why a couple in their 60s is worrying about marriage. Women therapists dealing with couples in their 30s, where the woman client has never been married and is near the end of her childbearing years, may have strong feelings about "getting things moving."

Should the Couple I Am Treating Get Married?

Most therapists cannot help making personal judgments about partners' suitability for each other and about the system's ability to function without causing injury to the partners. (Of course, after a few years of practice, one learns that one's predictive powers are often lacking.) Certain couples may cause a reaction in the therapist strong enough to impair his or her ability to maintain enough distance to consider the couple's wishes and needs. Examples are interracial or interreligious couples, or dyads where there is a sharp divergence from cultural norms (e.g., the husband is much younger, or the wife makes much more money). Even more troubling are couples in which one member appears schizophrenic or sociopathic, and there is evidence that this condition predates the relationship.

The therapist here has a choice of behaviors regarding how much she or he will overtly share concerns with the couple or covertly move the therapy in the way he or she thinks it should go. Most therapists in this predicament prefer a combination of watchful waiting, and reflecting back to the couple what they see of the process. This open-minded stance can be often difficult, particularly since, if a marriage does result, the couple is likely to have children, who would be born into a situation that the therapist sees as potentially damaging. The authors feel that a therapist who experiences a personal bias as unmanageable is best to explain to the clients what his or her concerns are, and recommend a second opinion or referral to another therapist.

Couples whom the therapist feels would be "good together" may also be problematic, for the same reasons. The therapist may be impatient with the laggard party.

John, 36, and Susan, 35, both previously married professionals, had been living together for a year and came in unable to resolve a dispute about whether or not to have children. John, with children from a previous marriage, wanted no more children; Susan, childless, wanted a baby very much. It was soon evident, however, that they disagreed at a more basic level—Susan had assumed they would be married after living together for some time; John, confronted with this, said he had never agreed to it. Susan presented herself as certain of her investment in marriage and children. John admitted that Susan was an excellent match for him, wanted very much to remain in the relationship, but was unwilling to marry and unable to explain why. The therapist saw the couple as well matched and well functioning, and personally liked them a good deal. In addition, she had just had a baby, was feeling very "pro-baby," and was uncertain about her ability to keep this bias under control. She chose to share this with the couple. The couple insisted that they wanted to see her, so a contract was made that all three participants would watch for evidence of a coalition. After several weeks of reviewing various issues, such as communication and relationships with John's children from his previous marriage, John reported feeling pushed by both Susan and the therapist. The decision was made that John was truly outnumbered by two professional and pro-baby females and a male co-therapist was added to the therapy.

When Is a Couple a Couple?

Seeing two people as a couple implicitly accepts the relationship as defined. Therefore, the therapist must choose whether or not he or she wishes to convey such a view of the relationship.

> A separated but not divorced man called his previous therapist (who had seen him with his wife 3 years before) and requested therapy for himself and his girlfriend. He stated that the current relationship was the one of interest. However, he still maintained frequent contact with his wife, and during the phone conversation with the therapist it became clear that he had been holding out to his wife the possibility of reconciliation.

At what point does the therapist validate the new relationship by seeing them as a couple? With this couple, the possibilities included seeing the man with his girlfriend, asking the man to come in with his wife, sending the new couple to another therapist, or defining the problem as that of ambivalence and recommending an individual session to the husband. The authors prefer the last option, at least initially. If therapy with the new dyad seems indicated, they will probably refer the couple to another therapist.

> A young, never-married, noncohabiting couple requested therapy. They had been involved with each other for 9 weeks. The evaluation revealed that the man, who had pressed for the therapy, was someone who had been in therapy for 9 years and seemed to use it as a major way of getting through life.

Would accepting this couple in therapy define them as a couple? Should a couple that is having trouble so soon in the relationship be encouraged "to let the relationship be" for a while, either to develop or to die a natural death, rather than use a therapist to stabilize it? Or do we have an obligation to help anyone who asks for help?

In this case, the couple was accepted for therapy, since they seemed determined and since the woman had issues of her own that seemed very workable in that setting. However, they were unable to find a therapist whom both of them liked. The final outcome was that the woman began individual therapy. The relationship at present is uncertain.

CONCLUSION

The choice of an unmarried but intense relationship can be an experiment, a transitional state, a long-term statement to society, or a way of preserving emotional and financial separateness to avoid vulnerability. Such relationships are not, in and of themselves, problematic, but many are problematic. Common difficulties presented to a therapist include differences in commitment level, or standard relationship issues (communication, parenting, sex) that may or may not be related to the unmarried state. Treatment may be done in a variety of styles, depending on the presenting issues. Therapist bias about marriage may intrude into the therapy and must be taken into account.

REFERENCES

Bagarozzi, D., & Rauen, P. (1981). Premarital counseling: Appraisal and status. *American Journal of Family Therapy*, 9, 13–30.
Blumstein, P., & Schwartz, P. (1983). *American couples*. New York: Morrow.
Bowen, M. (1978). *Family therapy in clinical practice*. New York: Jason Aronson.
Broderick, C. B., & Schrader, S. S. (1981). The history of professional marriage and family therapy. In A. Gurman & D. Kniskern (Eds.), *Handbook of family therapy*. New York: Brunner/Mazel.
Jackson, P. (1983, May). On living together unmarried. *Journal of Family Issues*, 35–59.
Macklin, E. (1978). Non-marital heterosexual cohabitation. *Marriage and Family Review*, 1, 1–72.
Mudd, E. (1941). Premarital counseling in the Philadelphia Marriage Council. *Mental Hygiene*, 25, 98–119.
Murdock, G. (1949). *Social structure*. New York: Macmillan.
Murstein, B. (1974). *Love, sex and marriage through the ages*. New York: Springer.
Murstein, B. (1980, November). Mate selection in the 1970's. *Journal of Marriage and the Family*, 777–791.
Sager, C. J., Brown, H. S., Crohn, H., Engel, T., Rodstein, E., & Walker, L. (1983). *Treating the remarried family*. New York: Brunner/Mazel.
Shorter, E. (1975). *The making of the modern family*. New York: Basic Books.
Spanier, G. (1983, May). Married and unmarried cohabitation in the United States: 1980. *Journal of Marriage and the Family*, 277–288.
Stanton, M. D. (1981). An integrated structural/strategic approach to family therapy. *Journal of Marriage and Family Therapy*, 7, 427–441.
Stephens, W. (1963). *The family in cross-cultural perspective*. New York: Holt, Rinehart and Winston.

Therapy with Remarried Couples

14

CLIFFORD J. SAGER

Remarried (Rem) couples constitute a group worthy of special attention differentiated from couples married for the first time. Currently, 75% of divorced women and 83% of divorced men remarry. The theory and techniques for treating Rem couples do not differ basically from those dealing with troubled first-marriage couples. But several additional factors make the situation more complex; the Rem family has structural and historical aspects that are not present in the intact, nuclear family and hence make them different in some important ways.

Our focus is on the problems and advantages that are the result of these additional structural and historical factors. The most important are these:

1. Either one or both partners has been married previously. The ending of that marriage leaves scars, caveats, and bonds that affect the second couple relationship.

2. More likely than not, the couple start their married life with an *instant family*: the children of either one or both. The spouses have little time to consolidate their marriage before having to cope with the immediate presence of children and their care.

3. There may be no children from previous marriages. Research of Pasley and Ihinger-Tallman (1982) on a nonclinic population confirms that serious marital relationship problems for this group are much fewer than those with children. Remarriage with stepchildren is a more difficult undertaking.

Clifford J. Sager. Jewish Board of Family and Children's Services, New York, New York.

4. Motivations for marriage (e.g., love, companionship, child rearing, to have a family) may not be as important to one partner as the other, and some motivations may exist that are not present in first marriages.

5. Where "emotional divorce" is incomplete, the former spouse may present problems for the newly remarried couple that do not exist for the first-married. Former lovers rarely seem to have the same carryover impact as a former spouse of several years with whom one has produced children.

6. Children have only one biological parent in the Rem family. They have not had a lifelong history with the stepparent, whose entry onto the child's scene disturbs the adaptation established during the dual single-parent stage between the child with his two bioparents.

7. Spouses' life-cycle position is a factor. In second marriages, each spouse's life-cycle position and hence needs and desires are more likely to be disparate than in first marriages.

8. Finances are a factor. In a first marriage couple income is spent for the family unit and planned for by two spouses. In Rem, money decisions have been made by courts and/or agreements with a previous spouse and are often determined by one's guilt or ambivalence. This limits the money at the disposal of the Rem couple for their unit. As a corollary, the child support to a mother may be insufficient and the source of problems between her and her new spouse.

A THEORETICAL MODEL

A working theoretical model for evaluation and therapy should provide a matrix for understanding the couple and the sources of their dysfunction and then make evident salient points for therapeutic entry. Based on the marriage contract concept (Sager 1976, pp. 4–22; 1981; Sager et al., 1983, pp. 74–83), we are concerned with (a) the couple as a system and those other social, family and internal systems that impinge on the marital system; (b) the life cycles of each partner and how this affects the Rem marital and family life cycles; and (c) the individual psychodynamic strengths and frailties of each spouse. This can be summarized as systems–cycles–psyche (Sager et al., 1983, pp. 130–153).

These theoretical constructs provide a systemic basis for understanding the dynamics of intimate relationships. In addition, they provide a descriptive diagnosis of the interactional pattern of the couple. Additional factors, not included in this schema, also contribute to the total picture, but what is included does provide an excellent working basis. The marriage contract reminder list for couples has been adapted for Rem (Sager et al., 1983, pp. 355–361). "Marriage contract" is a premeditated misnomer as the term is used here. These are not legally written contracts that both mates write out and subscribe to openly. Each has his or her own "contract," which probably differs from that of the other partner. The contracts deal with emotional and psychological factors, as well as the nuts and bolts of marriage. Both partners act as if the contract had been known to himself or herself as well as to the spouse. The operational impact on the relationship is *as if* a legal and spiritual contract had been violated.

The three concepts that describe a couple's marriage and its dynamics are the partners' two individual marriage contracts, their interactional contract or script, and the behavioral profile that each displays in the marriage. Their marital system, where both partners are in their own life cycle, and the intrapsychic dynamics of each spouse interrelate with the individual contracts and contribute further to the quality of the relationship.

Much of therapy consists of making the interactional contract and the partners' behavior in it more conscious, working toward a new single contract, the terms of which both partners are aware. Even if they are not in complete accord, they are to try to respect one another's position. Goals of therapy are established rapidly among the two mates and the therapist. To accomplish these goals requires all the skills of the therapist, who utilizes her or his knowledge of marital, family, individual, group, psychoanalytic, behavioral, and systemic approaches to treatment. Therapists will find that the biases of technique and theory that they bring to their work can fit in with the conceptual system proposed. For further details of the more comprehensive work in this area, see Sager (1976) and Sager, Brown, Crohn, Engel, Rodstein, and Walker (1983).

MOTIVATIONS TO REMARRY

Divorce, in contrast to widowhood, is a volitionally created state. It is an act on the part of one or both spouses to terminate a marriage and seek a better life. To seek a better life may or may not include a new partner at first, but for most formerly married persons, it eventually does. The majority of those who remarry do so within 5 years of divorce.

Many of the motivations to marry again are similar to those that move people to marry the first time. We focus on motivations that are more particular for the person who remarries and for the never-before-married person who selects a divorced or widowed mate.

The pain of separation and divorce, and of not being connected to a mate, often causes extreme disequilibrium. A large number of formerly married persons experience the loss of their partner as a threat to themselves that may lead to a state of disintegration, with accompanying rage, frag-mentation, frustration, abandonment, and/or depression. They may fear being alone, fail to take care of themselves and their living quarters, or go to irrational extremes to try to get back their former mate. The vacuum left by a departed mate can be devastating, as it also can be for the person who has elected to leave. Divorce is often the most stress-producing event in one's life. The promise of a caring and loving relationship is the prime motivation for remarriage.

Other motivations may flow from utopian dreams: The recently divorced mate was a horror—this one will be loving, kind, considerate, understanding, sexually giving (or have a lower or higher level of sexual desire); the new mate will be the perfect, loving person and "we will have a perfect family with our two sets of children."

Motivations to remarry may include the desire to have a family. To be a parent to someone else's children may not only be acceptable but desirable. This "cuckoo's nest syndrome" among those not married previously may be found in men or women. Others may, unconsciously, see their new spouse (the child's bioparent) as a strong and able person who will be their own good parent as well as their spouse.

An older person may be motivated to seek out an appreciably younger mate—someone they can teach and guide, and whose freshness and discovery of the world will revitalize them. This was almost solely a male motivation until recently. Now that an increasing proportion of women have money and power, the youthful qualities of a younger man may be a motivation for second marriages among older women. Still, for others, the second marriage becomes an opportunity to fulfill what they had not done or had up to now—a different life style, work, fun, or security.

Another group can be characterized as seeking to escape the parental home. For example, a younger, never-married woman may marry an older man with children to escape her dependency on her parents. The older person is seen as a "good" parental figure who will fulfill deep emotional needs in a socially acceptable fashion and will provide prestige, financial security, and power.

ASSESSMENT

Whether the Rem couple requests help with a child-centered problem (as 56% do) or places the difficulty within their own relationship (27%) (Sager & Santealla, 1977), it is usually essential to evaluate the marital relationship.

Marital stress is often present even when it has not been mentioned as a presenting complaint. The therapist has to be sensitive to the spouses' reluctance to perceive a flaw in their relationship, as they are fearful of another marital failure. Scapegoating a child or a former spouse supports their denial and preserves their whistling-in-the-dark pseudo-mutuality. One finds that these fears may lead couples to conceal information about previous relationships from the therapist and/or from other family members. Developing a genogram with the therapist may bring awareness of prior relationships into the open and disclose intergenerational problems and events.

When couples present a marital difficulty, the clinician can begin to work with them more directly. However, the therapist may elect to have at least one family session to assess the total family interaction and dynamics. It is usually contraindicated to involve former spouses in the assessment or early phase of the treatment program if complaints focus on the present couple's interaction and not on children. While the reminder list of contractual terms may not be appropriate for every couple in the evaluation stage, the parameters of the contract can be kept in mind by the clinician.

The reminder list can be given to a couple to take home and talk through or write out together. They then write down the significant items and detail their differences without necessarily trying to resolve them. For others, particularly those who cannot discuss their contract without ending in a pitched battle, it is wiser to ask them to write out their responses separately and discuss them in the conjoint sessions.

In understanding the Rem couple, the "contractual" parameters that are particularly pertinent follow (see Sager *et al.*, 1983, pp. 355–361, for the complete reminder list):

1. Expectations regarding the spouse's relation to one another's children. Stepparent roles, stepchild roles, and what bioparents and child's roles, responsibilities, and duties are to one another.
2. Expectations about decision-making processes, duties, responsibilities, and tasks of the family and/or how these will be guided by the couple.
3. Expectations regarding the handling of money and responsibilities for financial support.
4. Expectations regarding the extent of inclusion or exclusion of members of the Rem family suprasystem (ex-spouses, in-laws, etc.) and the inclusion or exclusion of the noncustodial children.
5. Expectations regarding closeness–distance, autonomy–dependence, inclusion–exclusion of others, power and control.
6. Differences relevant to where each spouse is in his or her individual life cycle and in his or her willingness and ability to fulfill the appropriate marital or family-cycle role (Carter & McGoldrick 1980; Sager *et al.*, 1983).
7. Anxieties about another marital failure and how these are handled or denied. How the partner reacts to these fears.
8. Fears of loneliness or abandonment.
9. How the former relationship impedes on the present; transferential-like reactions from the former spouse to the present one.

In the process of evaluating the Rem couple, the therapist can verbally elicit significant marital contract terms during sessions or can have the couple talk through the items on the reminder list. In doing this, the clinician highlights the positive (complementarity and concordant, acceptable difference) and negative (mutually exclusive, unrealistic, conflictual, ambivalent) terms.

The interactional script can be deduced from the couple's description of their dyadic dynamics and how they relate together. Here the therapist depends not only on their accountings but on what he or she observes in session. The behavioral profiles, similarly, are deduced from history of their relationship and complaints, scripts, and direct observation. When the therapist helps the two spouses see the patterns of their script and profiles, it demystifies their behavior. They feel taken into the therapeutic process, which then makes sense to them.

Essential data to be gathered in the assessment phase include each spouse's past marital or love relationship history; the patterns of those relationships; why and how they terminated; current feelings and relationship with the former spouse or lover and any financial or moral obligations to these people or their joint progeny; current relationship and visitation or custody of children, their sex, ages, and quality of relationship with each. Briefly, how each partner viewed the quality of their parents' relationship when they were young, how they related to each, their ordinal order among siblings and current status of parents' marriage and their relationship with nuclear family members today, the couple's physical status and history, and their use of alcohol and prescribed and street drugs.

It is important not to structure the assessment sessions fully, but to allow time for each spouse to unload what they wish to state. Therapists should halt circular, negative interactions once they perceive the pattern of such behavior. At all times the therapist maintains control of the session. If it is obvious that both spouses cannot deal at this point with discussing the reminder list at home, it might be harmful for the therapeutic relationship to force the issue. The therapist can then address the most salient areas of their contracts by bringing those subjects up for discussion. If the marriage contracts are to be written out, the material of one partner should not be used in session until both have submitted their responses. To do otherwise is unfair to the more cooperative spouse, who would then be vulnerable to the less open partner.

It is important not to be rigid in pursuing any area. Keeping an eye on the triangular relationship among spouses and therapist at all times is imperative.

THERAPEUTIC PRINCIPLES AND TECHNIQUES

The therapist who has had experience and is at ease in individual, group, marital, family, and sex therapy modalities is at an advantage when working with Rem couples. Knowledge and experience with a variety of theoretical approaches also is most helpful. Those broad theoretical approaches that can be most useful are (a) a general systems theory approach to understand family structure and dynamics; (b) the psychoanalytic concept of various psychoanalytic schools, as well as Gestalt and transactional analysis and other theories of insight production to help understand individual dynamics and their reciprocating relationship with family dynamics; and (c) learning theory with its therapeutic application, behavior therapy.

Use of Marriage Contracts, Interactional Script, and Behavior Profile

When the *dual marriage contracts* are combined with the couple's interactional script and their behavior profiles, these three descriptive constructs help therapists make sense out of confusion and leave them free to choose more intelligently from among the techniques and theories with which they are most comfortable. Rem contracts should take cognizance of the fact that Rem partners live out aspects of their lives in two marital and two family cycles simultaneously.

The *interactional script* is the "rules of the game" that couples have evolved for themselves in their daily relating. In the practice of living together partners automatically evolve rules of how far, and in what way, each can push to attempt to achieve the terms of his or her own "contract." It includes their style of discussion; methods of fighting, giving, taking, loving, caring, compromising; *quid pro quos*; what is fair, and what is off limits. Where, in an interaction, do situations cease to be positive or neutral and become negative? What are the flash points and loops? What do they do to escalate, deescalate, reach resolution, make up, cool off, or spiral down to ongoing warfare or up to new reaches of love and fulfillment? The therapist must question the couple carefully to see where and how they "fall" into a negative interaction and then may elect to try to interrupt the pattern by modifying behavior before the negative feedback loop starts, trusting that the couple will then find a new *modus operandi*. Or therapists may assign different tasks to each partner (restructuring aspects of their dyadic system—a mixture of systemic and behavioral approaches); or may offer interpretations of each partner's behavior, possibly relating the behavior to intrapsychic mechanisms or earlier modes of adaptive behavior that no longer can serve to accomplish today's objective.

> A Rem couple without children sought help because each spouse recognized that the marriage was following the path of his and her previous marriages. Each felt unloved and exploited by the other. The woman had been raised in a family where love was demonstrated by the frequency and cost of material gifts. In courtship and marriage, she had been insistent on receiving gifts. She married a man brought up by withdrawn and isolated parents, who as long as he could remember, were always fighting and bickering. He had developed a counterphobic reaction to his fear of abandonment by surrounding himself at all times with friends. Each mate was angered and hurt by the other's defense against their common fear of abandonment. He came to feel she did not love him and wanted him only for the expensive gifts he could provide; and she was angered by the fact that they were rarely alone together, concluding that her husband didn't find her sufficiently

interesting. When it was pointed out to them that each had the same fear of not being loved and of being abandoned, but had developed different defenses against the same underlying source of anxiety, they were able to understand and to change the rules of their game, rekindling their love again on a sounder basis.

The *behavioral profiles* are a particular subdivision of the interactional script. The behavioral profile is the characteristic way in which each partner behaves with the other in order to attempt to get her or his marriage contract fulfilled. In this area we often observe the complementarity (positive or negative) of partners. Behavioral profiles of partners differ from how they behave with other people or situations in their current lives. Profiles for any individual may vary markedly with different mates or at different times in their marital life cycle. In about 65% of remarriages, the Rem partner's profile will differ with the second spouse from what it was with the first.

There are seven major profiles. All fall within "normal" and socially acceptable behavior. When extrapolated beyond a certain point, however, any of them can become pathological. The seven are the equal, romantic, parental, childlike, rational, compassionate, and parallel partners. Using the male's designation first, we then have a handy descriptive typology of the couple's interaction. For example, a romantic–equal couple would be one in which the husband conducts himself as a romantic and the wife as an equal partner.

Early in treatment I usually start to orient spouses to work toward a *single contract*. At first this is often done implicitly, as the couple and therapist compare the terms of the two separate contracts that have been verbalized or written out. Respect for each other's terms and working out *quid pro quos* are important. In its broadest sense, the road we travel along toward the goal of a single contract *is* the work of therapy. The terms of the contract must be the choice of the two spouses, not of the therapist. The clinician tries to be a guide, a facilitator, a remover of roadblocks, drawing the couple's attention to the problem areas as well as to those that are congruent and complementary. The therapist devises tasks to change their behavior toward each other and interprets their intrapsychic and system dynamics to them when that will help. The present is related to the past, to their parents' marriage and their relationships with their parents, to their role assignments in their families of origin, to their relationships with siblings, and to other life experiences. The therapist manipulates their system on their behalf, with their consent and cooperation.

The therapist first does this by clarifying the major items of each partner's contract. The therapist may point out that some of their items are unrealistic; others are compatible with their spouses'; some perhaps, although reasonable, may be something that the other partner cannot or does not want to fulfill.

A 78-year-old man with two married daughters came for help with his 67-year-old wife of 5 years, who had not been married previously. She had had a successful career and took pride in her independence. The man had a rigid picture of what marriage should be like, and he wanted his wife to merge with him on his terms. Clarification of this expectation and working out a series of quid pro quos in this otherwise compatible and caring relationship set the marriage on a happier course. Both partners were intelligent and had a sense of humor. By means of humor, their goodwill, and the threat of possible dissolution of the marriage if they did not change, the therapist was able to stimulate sufficient insight in the husband so that he found the flexibility to change sufficiently to keep the relationship for his independent, nonmerging wife.

Therapists may elect not to verbalize the marriage contract with the couple, but may use it as a framework to help them organize data and understand motivations. With some couples, the concept may be utilized in sessions with the therapist raising questions from the reminder list that she or he suspects may be seminal sources of couple dysfunction. For others, the therapist may give the reminder list to the couple or develop her or his own (briefer, perhaps) list. The contract is a flexible concept that can be employed in many ways by therapist and patient.

When the spouses have written their individual contracts or have talked through their responses at home, the therapist should use this material the day it is brought back to the session. It is the therapist's responsibility to ask for it if it is not volunteered. Reasons for noncompliance are discussed. The easiest way to continue the process on the return session (the therapist not being able to take time to read the material during the hour) is to ask each partner what he or she felt was the most important item. Between sessions, the therapist reviews the material, noting problems, ambivalence, congruences, complementarity, and conflict. When doing this, the therapist builds hypotheses to attempt to structure a unity among his observations, the dual contracts, interactional script, and each mate's intrapsychic dynamics. He then can think of how to clarify goals and how best to intervene therapeutically. A therapeutic plan is necessary, albeit one must always be ready to change it.

Poor therapy at this point would be not to use the material immediately. Reward by the therapist for the couple's effort is important. Similarly, acknowledgment of the positive aspects of the relationship is necessary. Total emphasis on the negative is discouraging and serves to convey an inaccurate picture of most relationships. Not to think through the material, organize it, and use it as a basis for arriving at a treatment plan is not to be a responsible professional.

Although not all the elements in the new single contract may please each spouse, the single contract is based on *quid pro quos* that the spouses agree on and find acceptable without either feeling defeated or overwhelmed by the other or the therapist. The agreements they develop are ones they have to have the capacity to fulfill. "Contractual" terms should be examined and renegotiated periodically. When couples present the clinician with typical complaints over poor communication, money, sex, past injuries, child rearing, former spouses, friends, etc., the contract concept makes it possible for the therapist to go beyond these complaints to the more basic issues that underlie them. These may include power, inclusion–exclusion, closeness–distance, and passive–assertive parameters, absence of love or caring, sexual problems, and others. The therapist is in a better position to determine whether to deal with the symptom directly or with the common etiological factor that may cause several symptoms to surface. It is up to him to translate the singular to the generic and to point out patterns and underlying forces.

> A man who had not married before came for treatment with his wife bearing a long list of complaints. Money for the couple was inadequate, he felt, because so much of his income had to go to support his wife's children. His wife consistently resisted his urgings that she reopen the child-support subject with her former spouse. Although it was largely his money that bought their home shortly after marriage, he felt he had no authority in the house, either with his stepchildren or his wife. He claimed vacations were determined by the children's desires, not his. Rather than attempt to deal with each issue, the therapist connected them all as evidence of the husband's feelings that he lacked power in every area of his home life as contrasted to his life outside the home. It was difficult for his wife not to see this, yet she felt unable to change her behavior. Once redefined and explored, structural changes were made that caused her to refrain from undermining his co-parenting role with her children. This was done by assigning him prime responsibility for final decision making within the family after consultation with his wife on the particular issue. The wife's anxiety about relinquishing control was related to her perception of her father and first husband as weak and irresponsible men who were indecisive or mismanaged their affairs. She had loved her husband's good judgment and abilities prior to marriage, but then, unwittingly, she had struggled to force him into following the pattern of the other men who had been influential in her life. Restructuring tasks and insight were the two prime underlying concepts and techniques used to change the marital system. The wife and husband evolved a good collaborative sharing relationship; she could now trust him to follow through so that she was able to relax her hand on the tiller. The couple, on their own, by the end of treatment had arrived at an equitable sharing of power that reflected an equal–equal partnership.

The interactional scripts provide a rich focal area for intervention where communication, strategic, and structural interventions are most useful.

EIGHT FACTORS PECULIAR TO REM COUPLES

At the beginning of this chapter I stated that the theory and techniques underlying the treatment of Rem couples are essentially the same as for first-married couples. However, eight additional factors that exist for Rem couples were listed that require consideration because Rem couples differ historically and structurally from first-marrieds. These factors are the previous marriage, instant family or children, no children, motivations for second marriage, incomplete emotional divorce, only one bioparent in Rem family, life-cycle problems, and financial problems resulting from the Rem state.

One or Both Partners Married Previously

Scars, caveats, and bonds related to the first marriage often impinge on the second: Whether the partner in question had desired the divorce or not, a deep injury and dislocation occurred. Previously married people tend not to function as well when they become single. Upset emotions, status change, and a sense of loss of attachment take their toll. This commonly leads to a defensive depression, loss of ego, and fear of being close to someone again. After the immediate shock is over, one is likely to be fearful of closeness for 1 to 5 years, or even longer. Vulnerability to physical and mental illness is greatly increased among the recent formerly married (Seagrave, 1980).

> A man who went through a bitter divorce, initiated by his wife, spent the next 2 years having a string of brief affairs to reestablish his confidence that he could be desirable to women. During this period he felt detached, alone, and depressed. In the third postdivorce year he met a woman, also divorced, who appeared to be his ideal and who, after several months, proclaimed her love for him. He resisted a monogamous relationship but then, cautiously, over the next year, agreed to live together. For the next 2 years he fought his deeper feelings of love for this woman and refused to marry. He observed her a thousand different ways. At first he would see some of his former wife's negative traits in her, and then he gradually gave that up. His woman friend had a cancer scare. During the few days it took to determine that she did not have a life-threatening illness, he faced himself and knew that if she were ill, he wanted to stay with her to see her through it. With that awareness, he was willing to set a marriage date with her.
>
> This couple had come to me premaritally to talk through some possible remaining problems that the man thought might cause trouble in the future. As is customary with such couples, we had talked through and clarified each partner's marriage contract and possible source of problems. The major problem seemed to be the man's discomfort over the fact that after a divorce that had stripped him of assets, he alone could not afford to maintain a living standard for himself and his wife at a level to which she and he had previously been accustomed. By pooling income equally and using some of her assets to buy a house, as his fiancée had offered to do, they could have a fine standard of living. He had fallen back on a male supremacist attitude as his last holdout against his anxiety to marry. We established that he did want to risk love and commitment again, as did she, but wondered if he could be comfortable if she supplied more funds than he could. The three of us worked out a financial arrangement that he realized he would have

accepted if he were the spouse with the assets. His "guilt" at accepting the situation was worked through when he realized he would not be failing his bride or his own image of a mature person (man).

It would have been poor therapy to ride roughshod over his doubts and anxieties. A thesis, which I firmly believe, is that if we take the risk of loving again and being loved, it is true that we may be hurt. No one can guarantee that love will last forever. But if we do not take that risk, we lose out on the most important things in life. As therapists, we can help those who want to be helped in these matters. Part of our obligation is to help, as best we can, to keep women and men from not making the mistakes they most fear, and had made before.

Bonds to a former mate can be a powerful negative factor affecting the new marriage. Continued intense hostility is itself an evidence of an overly cathected bond. The most ubiquitous problem stems from still having a love attachment, particularly when it is denied. It is important for the therapist not to brush aside a new mate's complaint of partner overattachment to an ex-spouse. The jealousy may be well founded, as in the following situation:

One spouse complained of her husband's calling his former wife "darling" and "dearest" on the phone. He haltingly explained, "If I'm not nice to her, she gives me a rough time with the kids." Reassured that it was O.K. to still have warm feelings toward the mother of his children, I asked him to ask his wife to role-play the same scene, but reversing roles so that he would overhear his present wife calling her former husband "darling" and "dearest." He got the point when he felt his ire mount as she role-played his words.

It would have been poor therapy to assume that this one intervention would permanently halt his inappropriate feelings toward his first wife. It was necessary, a few weeks later, with his present wife's understanding and approval, to have the husband and his former wife meet with me to help them effect the rest of their emotional divorce. They were encouraged to talk about their residual warm feelings and redefine their relationship as "friends but lovers no more," as the woman stated. Both recognized that they had grown apart and required different life styles and mates.

Triangulating the ex-spouse in with the current one is a common unconscious game of mates, as is scapegoating the ex-mate to avoid dealing with their own marital problems. The therapist who is alert to those possibilities can be very effective. These call for techniques analogous to those we use to deal with parental triangulation in a marriage.

Instant Family

When there are custodial or visiting children from a previous marriage, the couple often do not have time to consolidate their own marriage before they are caught up in a morass of child-care problems, ill-defined roles, and triangulation issues in the Rem family. Any number of techniques can be used to effect de-triangulation. My preference is to help couples first perceive what they are doing and then help them extricate from the triangle. If necessary de-triangulation is not accomplished this simply, then further intervention is necessary on the therapist's part. This can be done by strategic or restructuring maneuvers. I find the perception stage to be important because it makes it easier for spouses to cooperate in whatever might be the next therapeutic approach to effect the de-triangulation. The latter is usually determined by one's therapeutic bias and ingenuity once the situation is correctly perceived by all three of us. Enlisting the couple's suggestions of how to effect the desired result is most constructive.

Often the major problems of working with couples who see children as the source of their marital and family difficulty is to get the marital pair to focus on themselves. To do this often requires bold direction, for example, to help the couple develop a support system so they can get time alone together. I take steps to normalize their feelings toward the child's presenting problems. On the other hand, to tell them that they should have realized what they were getting into by marrying someone with children is a most destructive therapeutic mistake. Help them get breathing space, to have time together without the kids. Then they can begin to work on role problems and begin to act in ways that help the children be less reactive to this new and formerly undefined marriage of their bioparent.

Sabotage of therapeutic tasks may be based on a high level of parental guilt that is generated as the bioparent–spouse feels anxious about moving closer to his or her new spouse. The therapist can first prescribe stepwise tasks (to desensitize the cathected situation and so bypass the source of the anxiety). This may be as simple as helping the couple arrive at how to arrange for a babysitter so that they can go out together for an evening. Resistance to carrying out structured tasks is dealt with as it arises. When the behavioral techniques do not work, it becomes necessary to determine whether something in the interaction of the spouses frustrates the objective, or whether one spouse is not motivated to pursue the goal of a closer love relationship and commitment to the marriage.

A couple were at one another's throats in an 8-month-old marriage in which the man had moved into the home of his wife and her two custodial children. They had no time alone together (the children were 5 and 8). The wife felt it would be too upsetting to the children (possibly her own guilt and anxiety) if a competent teenager or adult babysat. The children habitually walked into the adults' bedroom so that the latter had no privacy; the wife refused sex because "the children might wake up and come into our room." The husband had become increasingly exasperated with the children and his wife, feeling he had married for romantic and love reasons and was willing to be a co-parent, but now had no time to be alone with his wife. Further, his wife did not allow him to play a meaningful role with the children. The children were seen by him as the cause of their problems. The mother said that she, too, wanted privacy, and at the therapist's suggestion agreed to tell the children that when the bedroom door was closed, the children were to knock and wait for permission to enter. In the next session the mother stated that she had been unable to carry out the task because she would be pushing her children away.

I split the session at this point, saying I wished to speak to each of the adults alone. I questioned the mother, and she reported feeling guilty and fearful of the emotional injury she would be causing her children. She liked and maybe loved her husband, but she had married him mostly for financial security, and she could not bring herself to "let him into the family." I suggested that she speak to her husband about her feelings—I suspected he already knew her "secret" but loved her anyway. She did this in front of me when he came back into the consultation room. This began the change that shifted the couple into a warm, loving marriage and a good stepfamily situation. In subsequent sessions, parent, stepparent, and marital roles were clarified and seen as not mutually exclusive. With the couple's relationship improved, the stepfather willingly and naturally developed his stepfather role with the children. After the initial evaluation period, the adults were seen alone for 10 sessions, and the last session was a family session with the children included in order to evaluate progress.

In their marital sessions the adults agreed on steps to consolidate their relationship, worked out their basic problems, and were able to expand into a family unit that fulfilled adult and child needs, as well as marital and family-cycle responsibilities and needs.

The Rem Couple with No Children

Childless couples are essentially on their own; they have no children to be sources of problems or whom they can scapegoat. Both partners usually see their mate's negative role more readily than their own contribution.

Persons who are locked into neurotically based object choices and behavior with their spouses are less likely to be capable of sustaining a gratifying relationship. Even without having worked through underlying problems, however, the difference that a new mate contributes to the interaction can be decisive in establishing a viable marriage as compared to the relationship with the first-spouse. I learned a great deal from the following case. It is one of my most successful outcomes, due to serendipitous events, not my interventions.

A woman, herself somewhat of a parallel partner who could not tolerate great intimacy, had been married previously to a romantic partner who was most insistent that she be more emotionally and intimately communicative. Her flight from his demands led to their divorce. Her ego injured by divorce, and carrying the burden of her "failure" to please her husband, she resolved to be more open and intimate. The second time, she married a man who also professed he wanted intimacy, and she tried to outdo him at the intimacy game. They began, after a while, to be edgy, to avoid one another, and to quarrel.

Between the first and second interviews, the wife, who had an expanding career, was offered a job in a city about 2 hours' train travel from New York. Their relationship improved as they slipped into a comfortable weekend marriage. Eventually they bought a house situated between New York and the other city. Apparently the woman's new husband was also a parallel partner, who also had been making an heroic effort to be more intimate. When circumstances caused them to spend only 2 of 7 days and 3 nights a week together, they evolved a beautiful relationship that was loving, caring, and gratifying for both. Circumstances had forced this couple to live with the correct equation of intimacy, contact, independence, and distance they required.

Therapists should look carefully at demands for intimacy. Some of the unconscious factors that contribute to mate selection sometimes cause some to choose mates who cannot be as intimate as they believe they want, whereas on the unconscious level they may have made a good choice for their needs. Instead of rushing to change the "more distant" partner, I move first to help each partner understand the other's style of showing love and caring. It is fascinating to see how often the "intimate" spouse is blind to perceiving the love that is offered.

Motivations for Remarriage

Motivations for remarriage that are not realized by a spouse become common sources of marital problems. To believe that one's new mate will automatically fulfill all one's expectations (especially when one does not know what some of them are) sets up an impossible situation. Many motivations or expectations are inappropriate; some mates are able to correct an unrealistic expectation when the therapist makes them aware of it. Others may not respond to a cognitive or behavioral approach and may require individual therapeutic attention.

We need to differentiate between current etiological factors that produce marital conflicts from outside stress and those resulting from the couple's interactional malfunctions and those that are more etiologically remote and are often rooted in childhood. It is worthwhile for the therapist to make the effort to see if even a remote etiological factor that contributes to a negative interaction can be bypassed by a task that alters the structure or strategy of the couple system. Bypassing frequently does work; in which case, there is no need for prolonged, individual therapy.

A partner was eliciting negative reactions from his wife because of his clinging behavior, which was touched off by anxiety generated by his wife's continuing to work, even though his business provided them with all of the material things and financial security they needed. He had an underlying fear of being deserted. This was clearly related to early life experiences that had been reinforced by his first wife's leaving him when her career began to prosper. Now that his second wife insisted on continuing to work, his behavior, despite her love for him, was moving them along a path that could make his fear of losing her a self-fulfilling prophecy.

I made connections between the man's earlier experience and the reasons for his behavior, which increased his insight slightly but did not affect his behavior. In the evaluation sessions I had noted that the couple had decided premaritally, at the husband's request, not to have children. The wife, with reluctance, had agreed and had then thrown herself whole-heartedly into her career. I suggested that, since they had been married for 4 years, they might consider reopening the question of children. The wife immediately said that she always had wanted children, that she resented her husband's decision not to have them. He responded less eagerly, but agreed to reopen the matter. I instructed them to discuss it together at home. Because of their recent history of escalating quarrels and not listening to each other, I gave them simple rules for conducting discussions (Bach & Wyden, 1969). We would then talk about their discussion next time.

In the next session they reported that the wife had agreed 4½ years ago to forego having children because she loved her husband. He had said his own childhood was such a mess because his mother had deserted the family. In this session he recognized that he wanted her "all for myself—I didn't want to share her." Within a few weeks the couple decided to become a family. Follow-up 3 years later found that the couple had an 18-month-old girl. Mother was working part-time, and they had decided to try for a second child.

In this case we bypassed dealing with the remote causes of his fear of abandonment, which would have required lengthy treatment. Instead, I took advantage of the wife's desire to have children. A contributory factor to the husband's change of mind was his belief that this might tie her to him better than would her advancing career. We discussed this, and I'm sure it was a factor, but more healthy ones were present too—including a greater sense of his own worth and lovability. His wife's willingness to give up the opportunity to advance her career in order to have a family with him was an important reaffirmation to him of her love.

Incomplete Emotional Divorce

Continued hatred and anger toward the former spouse that is as fresh as the day of separation is an important sign of overattachment. An equally reliable sign of overattachment is the ex-spouse who still carries a torch, extols the virtues of the divorced spouse, and makes invidious comparisons to the present spouse.

The therapist's first step is to attempt to get through the defensive denial of the continuing overattachment. After accumulating a few examples with the help of the current spouse, if there is no true recognition of the problem,

I generally see the overattached partner a few times alone. Often without the presence of the current spouse it is easier for someone to be in better touch with feelings.

A man was excessively generous to his former wife because she would "get upset" if he did not give her sizable sums of money beyond their agreement for "emergencies." He couldn't stand the idea that she would be angry with him. He had left her for his current wife and felt guilty that the latter and he had a much better relationship. His current wife was upset over the attention and extra money he gave to his first wife. His wife had mentioned how recent photographs of his former wife and him had been taken by their son (her stepson) on a recent visit and sent to him by his former wife with a note replete with some loving comments. He had made no mention of these pictures but had left them in an open envelope in a drawer that he and his wife both used. The husband grudgingly began to perceive his provocations. He recognized that although he had made the decision to leave his former marriage, he blamed his present wife for this because he loved her and she had refused to have an affair with him unless he left his marriage. His unconscious attachment and guilt toward his former wife and his blaming of his current mate led to the provocative behavior that infuriated his second wife.

His behavior had been preconscious and readily seen by him with my help after two individual sessions. We then resumed conjoint sessions, which ended shortly thereafter. Altogether there were 12 sessions. He had completed his emotional divorce and was now more fully able to accept his wife.

Children with One Bioparent and One Stepparent

This situation can be a source of friction between the two adults. A good starting therapeutic approach is to try to normalize the situation with all its attendant difficulties for the bio- and stepparent as well as the child. The therapist should help to define the problem and get it out in the open; should explore superego factors related to guilt of the bioparent and relieve them if it is appropriate to do so. (For example, the need to change an overly cathected mother–child relationship that served useful functions during the single-parent phase while being careful not to blame the parent for its understandable origin.) Elicit the plausible positive effects the Rem situation can now offer to all concerned. Help the bioparent to allow the child and stepparent to develop their own relationship. The bioparent is not to ask the stepparent to intervene or discipline the child and then interfere by undermining his or her efforts. The bioparent is to allow the stepparent slowly to take on a more disciplinary role as the relationship, role definition, and trust grow. Stepparents cannot expect instant love or obedience from a child. Stepparents must accept that the child has a father or mother in another household.

Help the couple minimize the child's potential for loyalty conflict by not forcing choices and by respecting the child's need and feeling for her or his other bioparent.

> A stepmother vented her anger in a conjoint session about her stepdaughter and her husband because she felt rejected by the child. After spending a delightful day, later at the dinner table the child suddenly withdrew, refused to eat, and asked when she could go home. I wondered out loud if the child suddenly had thought about her biomother and felt guilty because she had had such a good time with her stepmother. The stepmother thought it was a good possibility. We then discussed ways in which she could be alert to situations like this. I suggested that she tell the child that it's O.K. if she likes her stepmother too, but of course her mother is someone very special whom she has special love for, etc.

With a remarriage there is a new release of sexual activity, and an aura of sex often permeates the household. This can be particularly stimulating and/or upsetting to adolescent children. It can stimulate defensive feelings as children's sexual awareness is heightened. In our Rem clinic we had several boys and girls who embarked on an active sexual life coincident with a parent's remarriage.

A number of factors make the likelihood of household sex abuse greater in Rem families than in intact families.[1] Certainly the abuse ("incest") barrier between stepfather–stepdaughter and stepsiblings is appreciably lower than in consanguinous relationships. Parents and stepparents should be alerted to these possibilities. It is particularly important for bioparents to take seriously any attempt on their child's part to discuss possible abuse with them, be it heterosexual or homosexual.

Spouses' Life-Cycle Position

Spouses may be in different life-cycle positions. Conflict arises, for example, when a woman embarks on a career at the time her husband has made it in his. He now wants a companion, lover, and playmate, and he finds it difficult to accept the time and preoccupation his wife may put into her career instead of with him. On the average, remarried couples have a greater age spread than do first marrieds and are therefore more likely to have different life-cycle and family-cycle needs and desires.

Life-cycle and marital-cycle needs may be consonant for the two partners, but the stepparent may not accept or be able to fulfill family-cycle roles. This is particularly so in regard to co-parenting and its attendant responsibilities. An awareness of where the problem lies and bringing the problem to full awareness of both spouses is a prerequisite step for resolution. The therapist

---

1. Household sexual abuse in remarried families is discussed more fully in Perlmutter et al. (1982) and Sager et al. (1983).

in these situations often has to help the bioparent accept that his or her spouse will not share the responsibility for child care. Possibly the spouse is not an effective co-parent because he or she is like another child and competes with the children for the attention of the wife or husband. As in intact families, it is sometimes necessary to accept a partner's limitations and work within that framework. If it is not possible to do so, the marriage is not likely to survive, or if it does, it survives with a large degree of malfunction or dissatisfaction.

Finances

Men who remarry are often not in a position to finance the endeavor, can do so only marginally, or the couple cannot make peace with relying on the wife's contribution. If there is not full disclosure of income and obligations by both partners, the marriage may have been founded on false premises. The therapist may have to play a mediating role in such situations and help the couple explore motivations for marriage and whether they feel duped, exploited, or taken advantage of in other ways as well.

Young couples starting out in marriage most often accumulate together. In remarriage there is more of a tendency to try to hold on to and control the assets each has brought to the marriage. Those who have children wish to protect the financial future or inheritance of their children. These questions have led to the common practice of prenuptial agreements, which at times can be very destructive as well as have a positive effect. Aware of the frailty of marriage, many prenuptial agreements that start out severely limiting inheritance rights to the new spouse may also include increasing amounts of more equitable distribution after varying years of continued marriage. It is important that mates-to-be discuss financial matters in advance. Not to do so can effectively and rapidly destroy Cupid's work.

Those who remarry are an older group than the first time around. They have obligations to children and/or former spouses. They literally bring with them the baggage of former marriages and homes in terms of life styles, furniture, and customs to which they have been committed. It is necessary to accept that life with someone else they love will have to be different from what it had been previously. Therapists are most helpful in normalizing these factors in terms of being common problems that can be improved. Having mates reverse positions in role playing and the use of *quid pro quos* and compromise can be effective therapeutic techniques when the spouses have a reasonable measure of affection and caring for one another on which to build.

THE THERAPIST

The potential for counterproductive emotional and cognitive reactions in therapists varies with their ability to be nonjudgmental, to know themselves well, and the amount of stimulation (causing anger, identification, distaste, denial etc.) the therapeutic situation provides to their emotional and value systems. No one can be completely free of countertransference, but we all must be alert to the signs of its evidence. Working with Rem couples and families probably provides more such stimulation than other treatment situations. Early warning signs help us to convert our reactions to therapeutic advantage, or at least help us to avoid damage.

The first areas of emotional assault on the therapist are those that relate to values, particularly male–female relations, divorce, remarriage, and child care. The therapist may have values markedly different from those that have allowed Rem adults to divorce and remarry, live with someone, not maintain child support or alimony, and so forth. The actions, attitudes, and feelings of various Rem family members touch off emotional reactions based on experiences and values that the therapist has had, has feared will happen, or has not dared to bring about in his or her own life because of guilt, anxiety, or culturally determined constraints. More narrowly defined countertransferential reactions may also occur wherein patients and/or their systems enmesh the therapist so that she or he reacts the way the family system unconsciously set her or him up to react.

The complexities of Rem family systems, the sense of despair, hopelessness, and loss that may be present, and the chaos and crises that are at work may spill over into the therapist's personal life. My colleagues and I in the Remarriage Consultation Service found ourselves postponing our personal commitments to others. Depression and despair were common reactions, without our having clarity about the source of these feelings.

These reactions can best be dealt with through the use of a trusted and supportive group of peers. Consultation, supervision, and the use of the group to help individual therapists resolve personal reactions mitigate some of the anxiety and pain that seems built into work with Rem systems. Specific areas of vulnerability for therapists working with Rem systems can be outlined (see Sager et al., 1983).

Unrealistic Expectations

Many Rem couples marry with the hope that the marriage will right all previous relationship disappointments, including both parental and past marital "failures," and that this time their marriage contract and expectations, even if unrealistic and magical, will be fulfilled. Other family members may also expect that their unmet needs will now be gratified. If therapists accept the unrealistic expectations, they too may be drawn into experiencing the feelings of hopelessness that so often characterize the clinic population of Rem. To accept the client's unrealistic expectations leads the clinician into becoming enmeshed in disappointment and disillusionment and will lead to therapeutic paralysis and despair.

Denial

If the adult partners are pseudo-mutual and deny their differences, conflicts, and disappointments, they are likely to focus their problems on a child, a former spouse, or someone other than themselves who is scapegoated. The therapist, sensing that certain material is forbidden, may join the denial and also displace to the child, thereby encouraging the pseudo-mutuality and scapegoating. Therapists may also collude with the family in their denial of the importance of their history and the suprasystem as relevant to the present problem. All too often, children are told by the remarrying parent that the marriage is for the child's benefit or welfare, the parent denying his or her own needs to the child. This type of denial may arouse critical feelings within the therapist that are also denied, only to emerge indirectly. The key is knowledge; the more therapists know about Rem, the less likely they are to join family members in their resistance and obfuscation.

Abandonment Fears

Loss and abandonment are prime issues for adults in Rem, and may trigger therapists' own abandonment anxieties.

Control Issues

Therapists may attempt to allay their anxiety by becoming over controlling, as do some harried stepparents, or by taking impulsive therapeutic action. They may rush too soon to try to impose order, and consequently push the couple away. They are likely to despair when the chaos does not right itself quickly in response to their interventions, and they may consciously or unconsciously dismiss the family at the first sign of any slight, immediate change for the better. The ability to tolerate ambiguity and chaos is required along with the patience and awareness of the process that needs to take place during treatment.

Value Issues

Value issues may affect never-married, once-married, formerly married, and remarried therapists. For the unmarried and the once-married, working with Rem situations can stimulate fears of what might happen to them or what they might fear to do themselves. Often such fears become expressed defensively as value judgments that bind the therapist's anxiety. This occurred in the following situation brought to the Remarried Consultation Service by a senior staff member in one of the community clinics.

> The therapist was a 55-year-old male who reported that he was not being very helpful with a Rem couple composed of an older man who had left his

wife and his appreciably younger bride. He felt that there were signs that he might lose the couple soon and wondered what he was doing wrong or "should" be doing. He went into some detail about the case.

After he finished his presentation and responded to a few questions from the staff, I told him that we approached problems of this nature by role-playing parts of the session. If he wished to cooperate in doing this, we might touch on some personal reactions that he may experience. Our staff was experienced in doing this among ourselves and maintained strict confidentiality. Could we feel free to proceed this way with him? He agreed.

In role playing an issue in the session it was apparent that he was hostile to his male client. One of the staff asked him how he felt toward the man at the moment (played by the staff member, who felt his hostility directly). He replied: "I feel he deserves the trouble he's having for marrying this [younger] woman." He said this with great righteousness and certainty. He was then asked by another staff member if he was married. Another question revealed that he had not been happy in his marriage for a long time, frequently fantasized leaving his wife, but considered it to be morally wrong. As someone started phrasing the question to him: "I wonder if you see any connection between—"He saw it! He said he realized that he secretly relished the couple's marital problems, saying to himself, "He deserves what he got." He was reassured that we all had experiences in working with Rem couples that touched our own values and personal lives most deeply and interfered with our professionalism. Recognizing his negative feelings, and their source, we were able to go on to discuss therapeutic measures.

Misdiagnosis

Because of the heightened emotionality manifested by some Rem couples as they see their "second chance" for a happy marriage and family life disappearing, the stress may cause them to react in ways that appear to be disproportionately abnormal. It is easy for therapists to misdiagnosis individual psychopathology and hence to designate a more serious diagnosis than is accurate. In these situations, relief of stress may be the first priority of marital therapy (e.g., consolidation of the marital relationship, time away for the couple without the kids, or relief of guilt about not loving a stepchild). Poor therapy would result if one did not move carefully or check out the impulse toward the more serious diagnosis that might lead to a course of treatment (e.g., pharmaceutical intervention) that would encourage avoidance of dealing with the stress.

Support Groups for Therapists

All too few mental health facilities, under the financial pressure to increase "productivity," allow time or encourage staff who work with Rem couples to arrange for regular conferences or staff meetings that can also serve as a support group for the staff. In such staff groups there must be security of confidentiality and separation from administrative censure of any form for what self-exposure may reveal in these groups if therapists are to be able to deal properly with the emotional fallout of their work. We all support protective health measures for individual workers, but do nothing to protect ourselves and our staffs in the mental health field.

For all therapists in private practice who have completed formal training, it is important to have a place where cases, feelings, and new ideas can be discussed. For most of us, this is best done in a peer group. Attending classes, workshops, and meetings, as well as reading, is helpful but does not provide what is available in mutual peer review. Peer groups, as the name implies, do not follow a guru or have a leader; no money changes hands. One or more members during the course of a session may temporarily assume the role of group leader with the tacit or expressed consent of the others. The participants are bound together by mutual respect and trust. A diversity of disciplines and theoretical positions helps to keep a group from getting lost in the dogma or shibboleths of any monolithic approach. This diversity encourages openness, curiosity, and creativity. Peer supervision, where countertransferential matters can be brought to one's attention in a constructive fashion, where new ideas can be discussed, and even where some therapy is done (as long as the last is an agreed-on function of the group), is essential for the continued excellence of work and personal well-being of therapists.

The approach to treating the Rem couple described in this chapter is not the final word by any means. It is a flexible approach providing a theoretical system and methodology that allows a great deal of individual initiative for therapists to follow their own choice of theoretical and technique proclivities. It is a system of therapy that usually calls for one therapist. As in all therapy, however, therapists require the support of their colleagues in some form of supervision in a peer group. The more diverse the professional, theoretical, and experiential backgrounds of the group, the more likely it is that therapists will constantly review their work and continue to improve the quality of their endeavors.

We have focused on the marital couple in this chapter. However, it is important to remember that children, ex-spouses, and other subsystems of the Rem suprafamily system often have to be seen in the assessment phase and/or at various times during the course of treatment.

ACKNOWLEDGMENT

This chapter is based on studies conducted by the Remarried Consultation Service of the Jewish Board of Family and Children's Services, New York City. The complete report of the study is titled *Treating the Remarried Family*, coauthored by C. J. Sager, H. S., Brown, H. Crohn, T. Engel, E. Rodstein and L. Walker, published by Brunner/Mazel, New York, 1983.

REFERENCES

Bach, G. R., & Wyden, P. (1969). *The intimate enemy:* How to fight fair in love and marriage. New York: Morrow.

Carter, E. A., & McGoldrick, M. (1980). *The family life cycle—A framework for family therapy* (pp. 265–294). New York: Gardner Press.

Pasley, K., & Ihinger-Tallman, M. (1982). Remarried family life supports and constraints. In N. Stinnett *et al.* (Eds.), *Family strengths*, Vol. 4, *Positive support systems*. Lincoln, NE: University of Nebraska Press.

Perlmutter, L. H., Engel, T., & Sager, C. J. (1982). The incest taboo: Loosened sexual boundaries in remarried families. *Journal of Sex and Marital Therapy*, 83–106.

Sager, C. J. (1976). *Marriage contracts and couple therapy: Hidden forces in intimate relationships.* New York: Brunner/Mazel.

Sager, C. J. (1981). Couples therapy and marriage contracts. In A. S. Gurman & D. P. Kniskern, *Handbook of family therapy*. New York: Brunner/Mazel.

Sager, C. J., Brown, H. S., Crohn, H., Engel, T., Rodstein, R., & Walker, L. (1983). *Treating the remarried family*. New York: Brunner/Mazel..

Sager, C. J., & Santaella, W. (1977). Survey of remarried couples and their children in treatment at the Jewish Family Service, New York City. Unpublished paper.

Seagrave, R. I. (1980). Marriage and mental health. *Journal of Sex and Marital Therapy*, 6, 187–198.

15

Sex-Role Issues in Marital Therapy

LARRY B. FELDMAN

Sex roles are culturally defined norms that delineate "appropriate" (desirable or acceptable) and "inappropriate" (undesirable or unacceptable) behaviors, thoughts, and feelings for males and females. These norms are enforced by interpersonal and intrapsychic sanctions—positive sanctions (rewards) for role conformity and negative sanctions (punishments) for role deviation (Feldman, 1982a).

Sex roles have a sociological and a psychological dimension. The sociological dimension consists of gender-specific norms for the allocation of work and family responsibilities; the psychological dimension consists of gender-specific norms regarding interpersonal and intrapsychic aspects of psychological functioning. Sociologically, traditional sex roles have defined income-producing work as primarily a male responsibility and housework and child care as primarily female responsibilities. In recent years, as a steadily increasing number of women have begun working outside their homes, some shifting has taken place in these expectations. Nevertheless, there is considerable evidence to suggest that, in general, the prevailing norm continues to be the traditional one, even when both spouses are employed outside the home (Nye, 1976; Pleck, 1977; Tomeh, 1978). Psychologically, traditional sex roles have prescribed independence, rationality, strength, and dominance for males and dependence, emotionality, weakness, and submissiveness for females. Again, while there has been some shifting in regard to these expectations, they continue to be the predominant norms (Bem, 1974; Dowling, 1981; Goldberg, 1983; Williams & Bennett, 1975).

Larry B. Feldman. Department of Psychiatry, Loyola University Medical School, Maywood, Illinois.

The sociological and psychological aspects of sex-role conditioning are characterized by narrowness, rigidity, and irrational stereotyping. Males and females are systematically conditioned to behave, think, and feel in stereotypically "masculine" or "feminine" ways and to label themselves as inadequate or inferior if their behaviors, thoughts, or feelings deviate from the stereotype. This form of socialization is dysfunctional for both women and men, and for the intimate relationships that they attempt to create. The problems that cause distressed couples to seek marital therapy are often a result, in whole or in part, of dysfunctional sex-role conditioning (Feldman, 1982a).

From a behavioral perspective, sex-role conditioning contributes to relationship distress in two major ways: (a) It inhibits the development and expression of functional relationship behaviors; and (b) it stimulates the development and expression of dysfunctional relationship behaviors. Male role conditioning inhibits the development of emotional expressiveness and mature dependency and stimulates the development of intellectualization, passive–aggressive behavior (e.g., ignoring spouse, forgetting important dates), and physical aggression. Female conditioning inhibits the development of cognitive expressiveness and mature independence and stimulates the development of excessive emotionality, excessive dependency, and verbal aggression (e.g., nagging, complaining, criticizing) (Feldman, 1982a).

From a cognitive perspective, sex-role conditioning contributes to relationship distress by stimulating the development of irrational beliefs and dysfunctional expectations. Sex-role-conditioned beliefs ("men should/should not"; "women should/should not") are irrational in that they are arbitrary and absolutist (Beck, 1976; Ellis, 1977). In relationships, they lead to the development of dysfunctional expectations. Men are conditioned to expect their wives to be dependent, submissive, and admiring. Women are conditioned to expect their husbands to be protective, supportive, and attentive. These role-conditioned expectations have the quality of intrapsychic "contracts" (Sager, 1976) that, when violated, lead to feelings of resentment and betrayal. Thus, men are sensitized to overreact to any signs of disagreement or disapproval from their wives, while women are sensitized to overreact to any signs of inattention or lack of support from their husbands.

From an emotional perspective, sex-role conditioning stimulates feelings of narcissistic vulnerability (insecure self-esteem) in men and women. Because of the narrow and rigid standards by which males and females learn to evaluate themselves, both sexes are highly vulnerable to feelings of diminished self-esteem in response to experienced threats to their masculine or feminine self-image. These feelings play a major role in the maintenance of role-conditioned behaviors, acting as negative feedback signals in response to actual or anticipated change (Feldman, 1982a). They also play a major role in the initiation and escalation of dysfunctional relationship conflict (Feldman, 1982b). When role-conditioned expectations are violated, each spouse's sense of self-esteem is threatened. To defend against this emotional threat, the spouses attack and blame each other. This, in turn, further threatens each person's self-esteem, and an escalating spiral of dysfunctional conflict is triggered.

In clinical work with distressed couples, sex-role issues appear in a number of different forms. In *traditional* relationships, work and family responsibilities are allocated along traditional lines, with the husband primarily responsible for earning income and the wife primarily responsible for housework and child care. Relationship distress in such couples may be related to this role allocation (e.g., wife wants to work outside the home, but husband objects; husband wants to work less and be at home more, but wife objects), or it may be limited to psychological aspects of role conditioning (e.g., wife complains about husband's lack of emotional expressiveness, and husband complains about wife's excessive emotionality). In *transitional* relationships, both spouses work outside the home and both participate (though not necessarily equally) in housework and child care. Distress in these relationships often stems from discrepancies between spouses' expressed wishes and their more deeply rooted feelings and beliefs. For example, consider the wife who says she wants her husband to share the housework equally but then disparages his efforts when he attempts to do so; or, the husband who says he wants to share child care but then is always "too busy" to be with his children. In addition to such conflict in regard to social roles, these couples also manifest the same kinds of conflict as more traditional couples in regard to interactional issues (emotional expressiveness, nagging, etc.). Sex-role conditioned blocks to effective relating are deeply rooted in each spouse's psychological development; they do not simply disappear when social roles are rearranged.

A THEORY OF THERAPEUTIC CHANGE

Goals

Based on the preceding analysis, therapeutic efforts are directed toward helping distressed couples overcome the dysfunctional effects of stereotyped sex-role conditioning. The *behavioral* goals are to facilitate a decrease in the dysfunctional behaviors promoted by such conditioning (intellectualization, passive–aggressive behavior, and physical aggression for men; excessive emotionality, excessive dependency, and verbal aggression for women) and an increase in the functional behaviors inhibited by such conditioning (emotional expressiveness and mature dependency for men; cognitive expressiveness and mature independence for women). The *cognitive* goals are to facilitate a decrease in the dysfunctional expectations promoted by sex-role conditioning and an increase in functional expectations, free from sex-role rigidity. The *emotional* goals are to facilitate a decrease in sex-role-conditioned narcissistic vulnerabilities and an increase in emotional tolerance for nonstereotyped behavior by self and other.

Structure

In order accurately to assess and effectively to promote changes in the behavioral and intrapsychic dimensions of sex-role conditioning, an integrated combination of conjoint and concurrent (individual) interviews is utilized. Concurrent interviews are important for three major reasons: (a) Information about spouses' sex-role-conditioned attitudes and feelings is often most easily obtained in individual interviews; (b) cognitive and emotional changes can often be most effectively promoted in individual interviews; and (c) behavioral changes can often be most effectively stimulated when they are discussed and/or rehearsed with the therapist in an individual interview before they are attempted with the spouse in a conjoint interview. In practice, conjoint and concurrent interviews are synergistic, that is, knowledge gained and changes produced in each format are complementary and mutually reinforcing (Feldman, 1985).

Assessment

Assessment is directed toward identifying the behavioral, cognitive, and emotional effects of sex-role conditioning for each spouse and how these effects are contributing to their relationship distress. Both self-report and observational procedures are utilized.

BEHAVIORAL ASSESSMENT

Behavioral assessment begins with the Relationship Problems Assessment (RPA) instrument (Feldman, 1983), which both spouses complete before the initial conjoint interview. This instrument assesses the spouses' perceptions of the major problems in their relationship. The identified problems are then utilized to develop diagnostic hypotheses about each spouse's sex-role-conditioned behavioral excesses and deficits. For example, Mr. A. identified the major problems in his marriage as (a) his wife's excessive emotionality ("She explodes in anger"); and (b) his wife's excessive dependency ("When I'm not around, she becomes depressed"). Mrs. A. identified the major problems as (a) her husband's lack of emotional expressiveness ("He never talks to me about his feelings"); and (b) her husband's lack of availability because of his frequent out-of-town business trips.

Hypotheses: These problem statements suggest the presence of sex-role-conditioned emotional inexpressiveness and lack of mature dependency in Mr. A.'s behavior and sex-role-conditioned overexpressiveness and lack of mature independence in Mrs. A.'s behavior.

The hypotheses formulated on the basis of the identified problems are evaluated in the ensuing conjoint interview. As the therapist directly observes the interactions between the spouses, the initial hypotheses are strengthened or weakened, and new hypotheses may be formulated. In the case of Mr. and Mrs. A., the initial hypotheses were strengthened by the behavioral observations. Mr. A. related to his wife in a tightly controlled, unemotional way that was highly congruent with stereotyped masculine socialization. Mrs. A. related to her husband in a volatile, overly emotional way that was highly congruent with stereotyped feminine socialization. In their interactions, it was clear that these stereotyped behavior patterns were contributing significantly to their relationship distress.

EMOTIONAL ASSESSMENT

Emotional assessment is directed toward identification of each spouse's sex-role-conditioned narcissistic vulnerabilities and the effects of these vulnerabilities on (a) each person's behavior in the relationship; and (b) each person's emotional reactions to the other's behavior in the relationship.

Clarification of each spouse's emotional reactions to the other's behavior is a central focus of both the initial conjoint and concurrent interviews. Of particular importance is the identification of hurt feelings (narcissistic injuries), which are often covered over by anger. Initially, an open-ended question is asked, such as, "When (s)he does that, what feelings do you start to feel?" This can be followed up with a more specific question about hurt feelings: "When (s)he does that, are you aware of feeling hurt?" In regard to sex-role issues, the goal of emotional clarification is to heighten each spouse's awareness of his or her feelings of narcissistic vulnerability in response to frustrations in the relationship that violate role-conditioned expectations. For example:

MR. A.: The biggest problem for me is when Ann gets angry with me and starts yelling at me.
THERAPIST: When she does that, what feelings do you start to feel?
MR. A.: I feel mad, like I want to punch her in the nose to shut her up.
THERAPIST: What about before you get mad. What do you feel before you start to feel mad?
MR. A.: I don't know.
THERAPIST: Is there a feeling of being hurt that comes first?
MR. A.: Yes, now that you mention it, there is. I do feel hurt, like a little boy who's being insulted by a bully. I can almost hear a voice inside my head saying things like, "Are you going to let her talk to you that way?" "What are you, a man or a mouse?"

In addition to assessing each spouse's emotional reactions to the other's behavior, it is important to assess the emotional factors underlying each spouse's own behavior. Here, the major focus is on the anxieties (feelings of narcissistic vulnerability) that serve as negative feedback signals maintaining behavior within sex-role-determined limits. Again, assessment begins with the presenting problems, especially those problems accepted as such by both spouses but that nonetheless persist. For example:

MRS. A.: Whenever Art is out of town, I go completely to pieces. I know it's a problem, but I can't stop doing it.
THERAPIST: During those times, what feelings are you aware of feeling?

MRS. A.: Helpless, completely helpless. As if I am totally unable to handle things without him.

THERAPIST: Where do you think that feeling comes from?

MRS. A.: Well, there is definitely a part of me that feels a very strong need for a man to protect me and take care of me. On my own, I feel weak and helpless.

COGNITIVE ASSESSMENT

Cognitive assessment is directed toward identification of each spouse's sex-role-conditioned expectations of self and other in the relationship. As with the behavioral and emotional assessments, cognitive assessment begins with an examination of the presenting problems. From a cognitive perspective, the problems that the spouses identify can be viewed as data for the construction of hypotheses about their dysfunctional expectations. For example, Mr. A.'s identification of his wife's critical behavior as a problem suggests the possibility that he may be consciously or unconsciously expecting her to relate to him in a passive, obedient, and uniformly admiring way. Similarly, Mrs. A.'s identification of her husband's lack of involvement in the relationship as a problem suggests the possibility that she may be consciously or unconsciously expecting him to be constantly attentive to and involved with her, to the exclusion of everything else. These cognitive hypotheses are in no way seen as alternatives to the behavioral hypotheses. Rather, both dysfunctional behaviors *and* dysfunctional cognitions are viewed as important causes of relationship distress.

More direct data about spouses' dysfunctional expectations are collected by asking each spouse to keep a journal of their relationship problems. In this journal they record all incidents in which they felt frustrated, angry, or hurt by the other and use these feelings as signals to begin an introspective search for dysfunctional expectations. The therapist explains that both spouses have functional and dysfunctional expectations and that both are important. The reason for focusing on their dysfunctional expectations is that they are the ones that are contributing to the problems between them. The therapist then explains how the lessons that the spouses have learned about how men, women, and their relationships should or ought to be are helping to create their dysfunctional expectations.

On the basis of the identified problems and the journal entries, each spouse's "individual contract" (Sager, 1976) is delineated. In the case of Mr. and Mrs. A., it soon became clear that Mr. A. expected his wife to admire his accomplishments in the world of work and relate to him in a totally accepting and admiring way. He also expected her to be the "emotional one" in the relationship, while he would be the "strong, silent one." Mrs. A., on the other hand, expected her husband to be intensely involved with her and with their relationship and to put everything else, including his work, second. She also expected him to be protective toward her and to cheer her up when she felt depressed.

SPECIFIC TECHNIQUES

In attempting to help distressed couples overcome the dysfunctional effects of stereotyped sex-role conditioning, I have found an integrative interpersonal–intrapsychic approach to be most useful. In addition to the previously mentioned integration of concurrent and conjoint interviews, this approach integrates techniques from the behavioral, cognitive, and psychodynamic perspectives. In this section, these techniques are described and illustrated with clinical examples.

Behavioral Techniques

COMMUNICATION TRAINING

Sex-role conditioning exerts an inhibitory effect on the development of important communication skills in men and women. Specifically, such conditioning inhibits the development of emotional expressiveness in men and cognitive expressiveness in women. The behavioral technique of communication training can help spouses overcome this dysfunctional conditioning.

Behavioral communication training (Jacobson, 1981; Jacobson & Margolin, 1979) is composed of three interrelated components: (a) feedback—the therapist provides information to spouses about positive and negative aspects of their communication; (b) instructions—the therapist suggests and/or models constructive alternatives to dysfunctional communication; and (c) behavior rehearsal—the spouses practice constructive communication, with coaching from the therapist. In working with sex-role issues, these components are applied in both conjoint and concurrent interviews. In conjoint interviews, spouses are given feedback about their dysfunctional communication, and constructive alternative behavior is suggested and modeled. Then, behavior rehearsal takes place in both conjoint and concurrent interviews. The latter is an essential part of the process because spouses are often very resistant to "trying out" role-incongruent behavior in a conjoint interview but quite willing to do so in an individual interview. Once they have had the experience of rehearsing "in private" with the therapist, they are then willing to try it with the spouse in a conjoint interview.

> Mr. and Mrs. A. exhibited a stereotype-congruent pattern of male emotional underexpressiveness and female emotional overexpressiveness in their relationship. In their first conjoint interview, the therapist gave them feedback about this pattern and suggested that their relationship was in need of more emotional expressiveness by Mr. A. and more emotionally neutral cognitive expressiveness by Mrs. A. They agreed to work on these issues. In their next (concurrent) interviews, each spouse began practicing the new behavior by means of role playing, with the therapist alternating between taking the

role of the partner and modeling the new behavior by taking the role of the participating spouse. Subsequently, conjoint behavior rehearsal was introduced and then utilized in an alternating format with concurrent behavior rehearsal (i.e., conjoint one week, concurrent the next). During the course of their 6-month therapy, Mr. A. was able to greatly increase the frequency of his emotionally expressive communication, and Mrs. A. was able to greatly increase the frequency of her emotionally neutral cognitive communication. Both spouses reported increased marital and personal satisfaction.

PROBLEM-SOLVING TRAINING

The behavioral technique of problem-solving training (Jacobson, 1981; Jacobson & Margolin, 1979) is designed to teach couples to define relationship problems constructively, make specific requests for behavioral change, and constructively negotiate behavior-change agreements. The process begins with problem definition and the formulation of behavior-change requests. As Jacobson (1983) and Margolin, Fernandez, Talovic, and Onorato (1983) have noted, the Behavioral Marital Therapy (BMT) literature has emphasized the form of these behavior-change requests (clear, specific, limited, etc.) but neglected their content. Essentially, the BMT position has been that the therapist is not to question the validity of spouses' behavior-change requests. Unfortunately, however, these requests are often stimulated, in whole or in part, by dysfunctional sex-role expectations. When this is the case, the therapist is in a position to help spouses confront and change such expectations, rather than implicitly reinforce them by saying nothing. For example, Mr. B. identified his wife's "unreasonable" objections to his authoritarian directives (e.g., "Betty, make me a sandwich" or "Betty, call my office and see if I've had any messages") as a major relationship problem. Therapeutic intervention took the following form:

THERAPIST: Bill, I agree with you that Betty's yelling and name-calling are not constructive ways for her to react to your behavior. However, I disagree with you when you say it is unreasonable for her to object to the behavior.

MR. B.: What's reasonable about it?

THERAPIST: What's reasonable is that sometimes you talk to Betty as if she were your employee, not your wife.

MR. B.: I'm just used to giving orders. What can I do?

THERAPIST: Well, what you could do is change your behavior so that you consistently relate to your wife as a partner, not an employee. If you were to do that, I think you would find that your marriage would be a lot more enjoyable.

In making such an intervention, the therapist needs to balance the confrontation with an initial validation. In the example, Bill's complaint about Betty's yelling and name-calling is validated before he is confronted about his role-conditioned dysfunctional behavior. Also, the rationale for recommending a behavior change is a pragmatic one—his marriage will be more enjoyable if he changes. Such a rationale is more likely to be accepted than one based either on egalitarian ethics or altruism. One further consideration is the need to balance a confrontation with one spouse with a similar confrontation with the other spouse at the earliest opportunity. In that way, the therapeutic system remains in balance, and both spouses are helped to rework their stereotyped sex-role conditioning.

After a problem has been defined and a behavior-change request formulated, problem-solving training moves on to its next phase, the negotiation of a behavior-change agreement. Here, sex-role issues emerge primarily in regard to spouses' responses to their partner's requests. For example, Mr. C. identified his wife's sexual passivity as a problem and made a specific request that she make a sexual advance at least once a week. She would not agree to that because, she said, it "just doesn't feel right for me to make the first move." Therapeutic intervention was as follows:

THERAPIST: In what way doesn't it feel right?

MRS. C.: Well, I was always taught that the man should approach the woman. It doesn't feel right to have it be the other way around.

THERAPIST: I can understand that. Old lessons are hard to unlearn. The problem, though, is that sometimes those lessons make it hard for people to have relationships that they both feel good about. Would you be willing to try to unlearn some of your old lessons in the interest of improving your marriage?

MRS. C.: I guess I'd be willing to try, but it still doesn't feel right.

THERAPIST: I think you'll find that if you do make some initiatives, and if Charley responds in a positive way, your feelings about making initiatives will begin to change.

Cognitive Techniques

Cognitive techniques for monitoring and changing dysfunctional expectations and beliefs (Beck, 1976; Ellis, 1977; Epstein, 1982; Meichenbaum, 1977; Novaco, 1975) are of central importance in working with sex-role issues in couples therapy. As noted, *cognitive monitoring* begins with an explanation by the therapist of how dysfunctional expectations contribute to relationship distress and how stereotyped sex-role conditioning contributes to the creation of dysfunctional expectations. Then the therapist asks each partner to monitor his or her dysfunctional expectations by focusing on the preconscious "automatic thoughts" (Beck, 1976) that accompany their dysfunctional interactions. In therapy sessions (conjoint and concurrent), these interactions are reviewed, and dysfunctional expectations are clarified.

MR. D: Last Thursday, we got into a big argument about which of us was going to drive our daughter to her dentist appointment.

THERAPIST: How did the argument begin?

MR. D.: Well, I had been assuming that Diane would take her because I had appointments at the office. I told her that and she got mad. Then I got mad at her for getting mad at me, and we got into a shouting match.

THERAPIST: When you got mad, what thoughts were you thinking?

MR. D.: I was thinking: "She is being completely irrational—there is absolutely no reason for her to be getting angry with me."

THERAPIST: What do you think about that now, looking back on it?

MR. D.: Well, she said she got mad because I had assumed that she would take care of our daughter, even though we agreed to share that responsibility equally since we're both working full-time. I guess it is true that when things get tight, I do expect her to take care of the child care. I don't like to admit that, but I can see that it is sometimes true.

THERAPIST: It sounds like one part of you really wants to share things equally, but another part still expects Diane to take primary responsibility.

MR. D.: Yes, that's true. Logically, I can see that sharing is the right thing to do. But, emotionally, I still expect her to take the major responsibility.

Once spouses have learned to monitor their dysfunctional role-conditioned expectations, the next step in the cognitive restructuring process is for each person actively to question those expectations. For example, Mr. E. felt hurt and angry whenever his wife rejected a sexual overture from him. By focusing on his cognitive reactions to such rejections, he became aware of the fact that, preconsciously, he had been telling himself that it was his husbandly "right" to have sex with his wife whenever he wanted to and that it was her wifely "duty" to be available for sex whenever he was interested. In therapy, he learned actively to question these stereotyped expectations by asking himself such questions as: "Do I really have a *right* to sex with Elaine?" and, "Doesn't she have the right to say no if she's not in the mood?" By asking such questions, spouses learn to distance themselves from their stereotyped expectations. This prepares the way for the replacement of stereotyped expectations with nonstereotyped ones.

The therapist stimulates the substitution of flexible, nonstereotyped expectations for rigid, stereotyped ones in two major ways. First, she or he is an open advocate of nonstereotyped relating. The rationale for this advocacy is a pragmatic one, that is, the relationship is likely to be more satisfying and more growth-promoting for each spouse if their expectations are flexible and nonstereotyped than if they are rigid and stereotyped. Second, the therapist encourages spouses to practice nonstereotyped behavior as a way of changing stereotyped expectations and beliefs. For example, Mr. E. was encouraged to stop making sexual initiatives, and Mrs. E. was encouraged to take responsibility for making sexual initiatives when she was in the mood for sex. This suggestion violated both spouses' stereotyped expectations of how things ought to be, but they agreed to give it a try. After a halting start, they were able to reverse roles in regard to making sexual initiatives, and both reported an increase in marital and sexual satisfaction. Over time, they learned to share sexual initiating on an equal basis, and their relationship continued to improve.

Psychodynamic Techniques

Psychodynamic techniques are utilized to increase each spouse's conscious awareness of his or her sex-role-conditioned anxieties and conflicts and the role they play in stimulating and maintaining relationship problems. The main forms of psychodynamic intervention are confrontational interpretations, explorational interpretations, and dream interpretations.

Confrontational interpretations are statements by the therapist that suggest that overt behaviors or behavioral inhibitions are motivated, at least in part, by intrapsychic anxieties and conflicts. In making such interpretations it is important to acknowledge that interpersonal factors (i.e., the spouse's behavior) are also very important. For example:

WIFE: The reason that I'm not pursuing my career is that Frank doesn't want me to work.
THERAPIST: Felice, I agree that Frank's opposition is part of the explanation for why you're not pursuing your career. However, I don't think that's the whole story. I suspect that part of what's holding you back is that you have some feelings about this that don't have much to do with Frank.
WIFE: Well, I am a little uneasy about leaving the security of my nest and trying to make it in the work world. In some ways it's easier to stay home and complain.

Explorational interpretations are statements by the therapist that suggest connections between conscious thoughts and feelings and preconscious anxieties and conflicts. These interpretations may include exploration of the historical roots of particular conflicts. For example:

WIFE: I would like to be more active in our sexual relationship, but whenever I start to make an advance, I get all tensed up. I feel like there's a big rock on my chest, holding me back.
THERAPIST: It sounds like there is one part of you that wants to make the sexual advance, but another part that says, *Don't do it!*
WIFE: That's right. It's like there's a voice inside telling me that it's O.K. to respond when Sam wants sex, but it's not O.K. to want it for myself.
THERAPIST: Where do you think that voice comes from?
WIFE: My mother, mainly. I can remember so vividly how she used to stress to me that "good girls" are not interested in sex and how "improper" it is for a girl to "throw herself" at a boy by making any kind of advance.

Dream interpretations are statements by the therapist that suggest connections between a dream, the dreamer's associations to the dream, and his or her preconscious anxieties and conflicts. Dream work is generally done in concurrent interviews, although with some couples conjoint dream work can be very beneficial. The following example illustrates the use of dream interpretation in working with sex-role issues in couples therapy:

Mr. H. was a tense, emotionally inhibited man who came for marital therapy with his wife because of frequent arguments, during some of which Mr. H. became physically violent (slaps across the face). In therapy, he reported the following dream: He and his wife were being chased by a gangster. They hid in an abandoned house, but the gangster found them. When he did, he told Mrs. H. to stand up, and then he prepared to beat her up. At that point, Mr. H. awoke, feeling intensely guilty and ashamed because he had made no effort in the dream to rescue his wife. In his associations to the dream, Mr. H. realized that he had two sets of feelings about the gangster. On one hand, he found him frightening and repulsive; on the other, he admired his "manly" air of decisiveness and self-confidence.

My interpretation was as follows:

THERAPIST: It sounds like we're dealing with two different parts of you in this dream. One part you experience as weak, cowardly, unmanly. The other part, the gangster part, you experience as strong, decisive, and manly.

MR. H.: I guess that's true, although I don't like to think of myself in either of those ways.

THERAPIST: I understand. But what the dream tells us is that both those images are present in you and therefore your conscious feelings, thoughts, and actions are being affected by them. I would guess that one of the things that happens when you and Harriet get into an argument is that the "I am a weak, cowardly, unmanly person" part gets set off and you react to that by starting to behave like the "manly" gangster.

Integration of Behavioral, Cognitive, and Psychodynamic Techniques

Behaviorally oriented techniques and intrapsychically oriented techniques are both of central importance in the therapeutic effort to help spouses overcome the dysfunctional effects of stereotyped sex-role conditioning. In practice, the two groups of techniques are mutually reinforcing. Cognitive and psychodynamic techniques weaken intrapsychic blocks to effective implementation of the behavioral techniques. The latter provide a vehicle for translating cognitive and emotional insights about stereotyped expectations and role-conditioned narcissistic vulnerabilities into specific behavioral changes. By utilizing an integrated combination of behavioral, cognitive, and psychodynamic techniques, the therapist is in a stronger position to help spouses overcome the dysfunctional consequences of sex-role conditioning than if she or he were to use either group of techniques without the others.

OBSTACLES TO SUCCESSFUL TREATMENT

Obstacles to successful treatment can arise from four major sources: (*a*) each spouse's resistance to changing his or her own sex-role conditioned behavior; (*b*) each spouse's resistance to changes in the other's sex-role-conditioned behavior; (*c*) the therapist's failure to perceive the relationship between marital dysfunction and sex-role conditioning; and (*d*) the therapist's failure to empathize with the anxieties that underlie spouses' resistance to changing their sex-role-conditioned behaviors, attitudes, and feelings.

Spouse-Centered Obstacles

Each spouse is resistant to changing his or her sex-role-conditioned behavior because to do so would arouse feelings of narcissistic vulnerability. Both spouses have been conditioned to associate role-incongruent behavior with feelings of inadequacy and inferiority. These feelings function as negative feedback signals to counteract actual or anticipated changes. In order for the therapist to help spouses effectively overcome their resistances, she or he must be empathically sensitive to the anxieties that underlie them. By demonstrating an empathic understanding of the spouses' role-conditioned anxieties, the therapist creates an atmosphere of trust in which change-promoting confrontations and directives are experienced as helpful, rather than traumatic.

In addition to being resistant to changing their own role-conditioned behavior, spouses are likely to be resistant to changes in the other's role-conditioned behavior. Again, the basic cause of resistance is narcissistic vulnerability. Stereotyped sex roles are complementary. Not only does a person have to behave in an appropriately "masculine" or "feminine" way in order to feel good about self, but his or her partner also has to behave in a complementarily appropriate way. For example, the husband who says he wants his wife to be more sexually initiating may find that his sense of masculinity is threatened when she actually begins to do so. Similarly, the wife who says she wants her husband to share housework and child care equally may find that her sense of femininity is threatened when he does begin to change. The therapist's task in such an event is to communicate empathic understanding of the spouses' anxieties and at the same time emphasize the importance of overcoming those anxieties in order for relationship change to occur.

Therapist-Centered Obstacles

From the therapist's side, the first obstacle to successful treatment is failure to recognize the relationship between marital dysfunction and sex-role conditioning. Therapists fail to recognize this relationship for two major reasons: (a) lack of understanding of the dysfunctional effects of sex-role conditioning; and (b) anxiety related to their own sex-role conditioning. In order for therapists to be able to recognize the effects of sex-role conditioning in others, they need to be able to confront those effects in themselves. Lack of awareness of their own sex-role conditioned behaviors, attitudes, and feelings creates a serious block to therapists' ability to recognize these phenomena in the couples with whom they work.

The second major therapist-centered obstacle to successful treatment is failure to be empathically sensitive to the narcissistic vulnerabilities that underlie spouses' resistance to changing their sex-role-conditioned behaviors, attitudes, and feelings. Such empathic failures lead to interventions experienced as attacks rather than helpful confrontations. For example:

HUSBAND: I don't want my wife going out to work. It may be old-fashioned, but I still believe a woman's place is in the home.

THERAPIST: Don't you think it's about time you gave up such sexist ideas and joined the twentieth century? You're probably just afraid to have an equal relationship with your wife.

CONCLUSION

Sex-role issues are a major source of marital distress and a major source of resistance to change in marital therapy. A clear understanding of the dysfunctional effects of sex-role conditioning greatly facilitates both clinical assessment and therapeutic intervention with distressed couples. While some couples and/or individual spouses are extremely resistant to examining and changing their sex-role-conditioned behaviors, attitudes, and feelings, most are willing to do so if they are confronted by the therapist in an empathic and validating way.

REFERENCES

Beck, A. T. (1976). *Cognitive therapy and the emotional disorders*. New York: International Universities Press.

Bem, S. L. (1974). The measurement of psychological androgyny. *Journal of Consulting and Clinical Psychology, 42*, 155–162.

Dowling, C. (1981). *The cinderella complex: Women's hidden fear of independence*. New York: Summit Books.

Ellis, A. (1977). *How to live with—and without—anger*. New York: Reader's Digest Press.

Epstein, N. (1982). Cognitive therapy with couples. *American Journal of Family Therapy, 10*, 5–16.

Feldman, L. B. (1982a). Sex roles and family dynamics. In F. Walsh (Ed.), *Normal family processes*. New York: Guilford Press.

Feldman, L. B. (1982b) Dysfunctional marital conflict: An integrative interpersonal–intrapsychic model. *Journal of Marital and Family Therapy, 8*, 417–428.

Feldman, L. B. (1983). *Relationship problems assessment*. Unpublished manuscript, Center for Family Studies, Chicago, IL.

Feldman, L. B. (1985). Integrative multi-level therapy: a comprehensive interpersonal and intrapsychic approach. *Journal of Marital and Family Therapy*, in press.

Goldberg, H. (1983). *The new male–female relationship*. New York: Morrow.

Jacobson, N. S. (1981). Behavioral marital therapy. In A. S. Gurman & D. P. Kniskern (Eds.), *Handbook of family therapy*. New York: Brunner/Mazel.

Jacobson, N. S. (1983). Beyond empiricism: The politics of marital therapy. *American Journal of Family Therapy, 11*, 11–24.

Jacobson, N. S., & Margolin, G. (1979). *Marital therapy: Strategies based on social learning and behavior exchange principles*. New York: Brunner/Mazel.

Margolin, G., Fernandez, V., Talovic, S., & Onorato, R. (1983). Sex role considerations and behavioral marital therapy: Equal does not mean identical. *Journal of Marital and Family Therapy, 9*, 131–145.

Meichenbaum, D. (1977). *Cognitive behavior modification: an integrative approach*. New York: Plenum.

Novaco, R. W. (1975). *Anger control: The development and evaluation of an experimental treatment*. Lexington, MA: Heath.

Nye, F. I. (1976). *Role structure and analysis of the family.* Beverly Hills, CA: Sage.

Pleck, J. H. (1977). The work–family role system. *Social Problems, 24,* 417–427.

Sager, C. J. (1976). *Marriage contracts and couple therapy.* New York: Brunner/Mazel.

Tomeh, A. (1978). Sex-role orientation: An analysis of structural and attitudinal predictors. *Journal of Marriage and the Family, 40,* 341–354.

Williams, J. E. & Bennett, S. M. (1975). The definition of sex stereotypes via the adjective check list. *Sex Roles, 1,* 327–337.

16

Treating Sexually Distressed Marital Relationships

JULIA R. HEIMAN

Noting that confession had been Western culture's means for extracting the truth about sex for some centuries, Michel Foucault (1980) puzzled over how the ritual sexual confession came to be constituted in scientific terms in the nineteenth century. One factor was diffuse causality.

> There was scarcely a malady or physical disturbance to which the nineteenth century did not impute some degree of sexual etiology. From the bad habits of children to the phthises of adults, the apoplexies of old people, nervous maladies, and the degenerations of the race, the medical era wove an entire network of sexual causality to explain them. (p. 65)

Professionals are continually "weaving networks" to explain the meaning of sex—especially as sex relates to (normal and pathological) individual development, and (healthy and unhealthy) marital relationships. Currently, sex is not seen as *the* etiological factor in illnesses and bad habits. To the contrary, in the marital and family therapy field, sex is more likely to be seen as a superficial problem, or a distracting symptom. This is especially interesting in the light of the previous century's views and considering the fact that marital sex is so special—or perhaps so peculiar—that only in the marital institution is sex formally sanctioned.

Therefore, the purpose of this chapter is to focus on the description, understanding, and general treatment approach for those sexual problems that are the most common complaints of ongoing, marital relationships. Minimal attention is given to the problems of arousal and orgasm, as these

Julia R. Heiman. Psychiatry and Behavioral Sciences, Harborview Community Mental Health Center, University of Washington School of Medicine, Seattle, Washington.

dysfunctions have been discussed extensively in the clinical literature (e.g., Arentewicz & Schmidt, 1983; Kaplan, 1974, 1979; Leiblum & Pervin, 1980; LoPiccolo & LoPiccolo, 1978; Masters & Johnson, 1970). Instead the emphasis will be on problems of sexual desire, including low interest and the more vague frequency dissatisfaction complaints, as these areas seem to be especially frequent in couples with a significant past or planned future marital commitment (Kaplan, 1979).

THEORETICAL MODELS

The basis of understanding and treating sexual problems can be summarized by Figure 16-1. Etiological explanations and treatment need to address a combination of the individual, interactional and sociocultural patterns, the importance of each changing throughout one's life (visually, one can imagine the cubes changing relative size). The figure concisely states that (a) all levels have some degree of interdependence or, in fact, there is *automatically* some interaction among the three levels; (b) one can see each of the cubes as having a "current" face and "past" layers behind the face; and (c) therapists also come to the session with each of these levels operating on their ability to conceptualize the client's problems in different ways. The therapist needs a conceptualization that is thorough, flexible, and imperfectly matched to the client's own conceptualization. Therapist and clients must come to an understanding of the problem that is sufficiently similar, so clients may assimilate it, and is sufficiently different so that clients' views must shift slightly in order to accommodate it. Therapy is then underway.

Three major theoretical orientations are currently used to treat sexual dysfunctions: cognitive–behavioral, psychoanalytic, and systems theories. If we try and locate these on Figure 16-1, we see that, except for systems approaches, the focus for most interventions is on the individual and how the individual, or individuals within the couple, interpret and manage the experiences from the interactional and sociocultural levels.

For example, Masters and Johnson's 1970 program conceptualizes sexual functioning as a normal biological response that can be upset by poor learning histories, traumatic events, religious orthodoxy, and the resultant interfering emotions of fear and anxiety. Masters and Johnson's program uses a variety of techniques that can be seen as a type of *cognitive–behavioral* therapy (Heiman, LoPiccolo, & LoPiccolo, 1981). They work with the couple, although less from a systems perspective than from a "getting the individuals in harmony" perspective. Furthermore, the Masters and Johnson approach, which essentially crystalizes the elements of what we now know as "sex therapy," takes the sexual problem seriously in its own right. Several hallmarks of this therapy include at-home exercises prescribed so that patients can decrease anxiety, especially performance anxiety; skill training in sexual communication and techniques; and attitude confrontation and change.

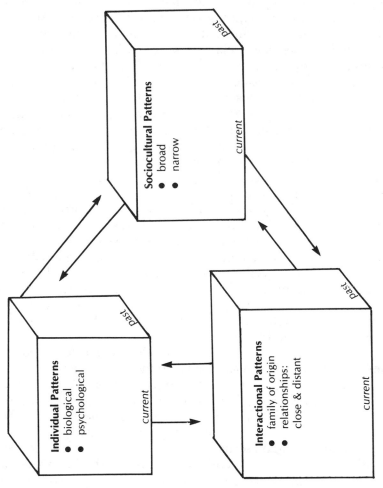

FIGURE 16-1. levels of understanding and treating sexual problems.

A significant attempt to *combine a psychoanalytic perspective with the more behavioral* interventions of Masters and Johnson sex therapy has been described by Helen Kaplan (1974, 1979) in the United States and by Arentewicz and Schmidt (1983) in Europe. Kaplan tends to use behavioral sex therapy unless deeper problems become evident through strong emotional reactions or resistance. Generally, Kaplan sees behavioral management as adequate to account for recent and superficial inadequacy, with psychoanalytic factors needed to explain the deeper (e.g., consciously inaccessible) causes. Arentewicz and Schmidt (1983) classify dysfunctions as expressions of sexual inhibitions, regardless of their manifestations, and propose several categories of behavioral and analytic etiology that direct their treatment. They theorize that although learning, anxiety defenses, relationship factors, and cognitive self-defeating cycles are the major factors that cause or maintain sexual problems, the level to which one must go to resolve superficial versus deep conflicts is variable and depends upon the case. Although not using systems orientation, these authors give significant attention to the degree to which the sexual problem may serve different functions in a relationship.

Systems theory has in fact rarely been articulated in the treatment of sexual problems, which is peculiar given the interactional nature of sexual contacts, as well as the changing role of sex in a long-term marital relationship. Perhaps one problem has been that systems theorists usually see sexuality as *only* a symptom or a metaphor put forth as a smokescreen by a troubled dyad to avoid dealing with the more essential family issues (e.g., Whitaker & Keith, 1981). The next section shows that there is some validity for this point of view. At the same time, the sexual problem can be dealt with from a systems perspective by focusing on the couple's nonsexual and sexual interaction patterns, as well as examining the stabilizing function the sexual distress serves (e.g., Verhulst & Heiman, 1979).

Several other features should be noted. One is that few theoretical approaches are pure when eventually applied to the troubled couple. (Indeed, it could be fascinating to have family therapists Andolphi, Minuchin, and Whitaker observe Masters and Johnson and describe what they see.) Second, the above approaches—all variants on what we call sex therapy—have been documented as quite successful for the remission of sexual symptoms and the increase of satisfaction on sexual function. While the data collected by Masters and Johnson have been criticized for their restricted, vague, and unrigorous methodology (Zilbergeld & Evans, 1980), people working more recently have generally documented significant improvements with a wide variety of clients, therapists, and dysfunctions (e.g., Arentewicz & Schmidt, 1983; Heiman & LoPiccolo, 1983; Marks, 1980; Wright, Perreault & Mathieu, 1977). Masters and Johnson have shown the most consistently low failure rates, in the neighborhood of 15–25%, with the longest and best-maintained follow-up. Other researchers usually reporting higher failure rates (e.g., 25–35%) with more deterioration following therapy. The explanation for these differences has been (*a*) the increasing complexity of cases (which at one time included the purely educational and sex technique areas and now include a variety of physically impaired, neurotic, and psychotic patients); (b) the expertise of Masters and Johnson combined with the demand characteristics inherent to their public image; and (c) the differences in methods of data collection and computation.

A detailed examination of these problems has been taken up elsewhere (e.g., LoPiccolo, 1978; Heiman & LoPiccolo, 1983). The factor to take note of here is that sex therapy procedures, based on a multitheoretical model, are very effective for most of the diagnoses. Almost no outcome data exist on low sexual desire and aversion. One archival study recoded previous cases and examined desire and aversion in 152 couples (Schover & LoPiccolo, 1982). With a multifaceted sex therapy program, these couples significantly increased their sexual frequency, satisfaction, initiation, and response to their mates' advances, and maintained those gains (allowing for a 50% attrition of follow-up data) for one year. However, the authors noted that the resulting absolute level of sexual satisfaction was modest, and they proposed a revision for treating desire phase disorders.

A THEORY OF THERAPEUTIC CHANGE

Change comes about coincidentally with thinking, feeling, and/or behaving differently. For a couple, this means changing how one member of the couple thinks, feels, or behaves with the other. The job of the therapeutic relationship is to arrange circumstances, in and out of therapeutic sessions, where that might occur. At what point change begins, I do not know; but the process of changing may be one of recognizing a change already occurring, permitting a change to occur, working for a change, or trying to direct the course of the change process. The processes of change are complex and at times difficult to predict. It is quite clear that "working" for change is sometimes the process least likely to result in the goal. Intense striving for improvement in arousal or orgasm can guarantee their elusiveness. In other cases, a change may not be recognized in spite of dramatic shifts in the problem. For example, one therapy outcome study noted that wives of men with erectile problems reported significant improvement in their husbands' erectile functioning, though the husbands were more likely to report minimal or no change (Heiman & LoPiccolo, 1983).

One of the most important features of therapeutic change is to recognize that, beyond the usual ambivalence, a couple may not want the change they are requesting. The most likely alternatives are that they want a change that they cannot or will not articulate (e.g., a divorce); that their presenting problem is intellectually unacceptable and thus they feel forced to take care of it, although at a deeper level they are comfortable with the status quo (e.g., thinking that they *should* want sex more often); that they want permission not to change the thing that they are asking to change, but to change something else instead (e.g., her aversion to semen vs. her lack of acceptance of sex as enjoyable). A therapist will know that these issues are prominent if there is a great deal of evasiveness (the "problem" seems to jump around and be ill defined), if there is a great deal of resistance in spite of flexibility on the part of the therapist, or if the couple terminates suddenly. Perhaps the clearest example of this was a case of one of my colleagues, where an 8-year unconsummated marital couple arrived at the therapy center for a "last chance" cure. They were both orgasmic, she had even become pregnant through interfemoral intercourse, but they never were able to have penile–vaginal penetration. After three sessions of not doing the sex therapy home assignments, it was mutually decided, though at the couple's prodding, that therapy was not necessary. They liked their current pattern after all and did not want it tampered with. They left, smiling, feeling fine about one another. Perhaps more important, the therapists permitted this to be a satisfactory outcome, rather than pure resistance, so that the couple could leave feeling a professional blessing (they were devout Catholics), or a sense of united defiance, for their pattern. The alternative temptation to call this couple stuck or individually psychically immature can be as much a moral reaction as a therapeutically based one.

This raises a final point about change: People have the right not to change. The therapist needs to be constantly watchful about coercing a couple to change in a way that seems correct to the therapist. There are landmines of values about sex and marriage that suddenly intrude on the therapy session. Some psychoanalytic and systems-oriented therapists in particular tend to accuse the stalled couple—categorizing one partner's reactions as infantile demands, or noting the couple's ploys to maintain control— while some behaviorists seem to have been surprised that a number of couples balk at the idea of exchanging sexual attention for nonsexual household chores. When a couple says no, it in fact is an excellent opportunity to see what the lack of change means to the definition of the problems between the partners *and* between the couple and the therapist. The therapist's job is to analyze the resistance to change, and my bias is to do so with them, if possible, so that its importance and value can have a therapeutic impact.

Diagnosis and Assessment

DIAGNOSIS AND DESCRIPTION

As in other psychological disorders, the diagnosis of sexual problems is based on an individual's having a particular problem. Kaplan (1974, 1979) developed a classification system, much of which was adapted by the Third Edition of the *Diagnostic and Statistical Manual of Mental Disorders* (American Psychiatric Association, 1980). The basis of classification of the DSM-III psychosexual disorders is the sexual response cycle, including *desire, excitement,* and *orgasm* disorders, plus functional dyspareunia, functional vaginismus, and "atypical psychosexual dysfunction." While this system is adequate in its inclusiveness, for clinical description the categories lack specificity. An alternative has been proposed that more precisely describes the sexual problem, although it does not attempt to imply etiology (Schover, Friedman, Weiler, Heiman, & LoPiccolo, 1982). Schover *et al.* (1982) divide the sexual dysfunctions into six axes: desire, arousal, orgasm, coital pain, satisfaction with current frequency of sex, and qualifying information. For each partner separately, each of these axes is noted as to its presence or absence, its duration (lifelong vs. not lifelong), its pervasiveness (global vs. situational), and whether the client or the therapist is noting it as a problem. Table 16-1 shows some of the categories covered and provides a quick way to behaviorally describe the problem. Overall, the value of the diagnostic system has been far greater for researchers than for the ongoing practice of therapy.

INTERVIEW

As important as the behavioral labeling of the sexual difficulties is, the most essential purpose of assessment is to get a careful and clear description of the problem, from both partners if possible. Classically, sex therapy has taken up to 8 hours to work up a history, usually separately with each individual (Masters & Johnson, 1970). This allowed for extensive rapport building between same-sexed client and therapist. However, the time and cost did not readily balance the gains, and most therapists now do a one-

TABLE 16-1
Describing Sexual Problems[a]

- *Desire phase*:   sexual desire, aversion to sex
- *Arousal phase*:   difficulty achieving and maintaining erections, decreased physiological arousal (women), decreased subjective arousal
- *Orgasm phase*:   premature ejaculation, inhibited ejaculation, orgasm with flaccid penis, anhedonic orgasm, inorgasmia, inorgasmia except for masturbation, inorgasmia except for partner manipulation, inorgasmia except for vibrator stimulation, infrequent coital orgasms
- *Pain*:   vaginismus, dyspareunia, pain on or after ejaculation or orgasm
- *Frequency dissatisfaction*:   current frequency higher or lower than current activity level
- *Qualifying information*: homosexuality, sexual deviation, sadomasochistic practices, degree of psychopathology past or current, history and current use of alcohol and other nonprescription drugs, spouse abuse past or current, sexual extramarital affair, medical conditions, medications

---

[a] Adapted from Schover, Friedman, Weiler, Heiman, & LoPiccolo, 1982. Many of the above categories can be modified with L vs. N, lifelong vs. not lifelong; G vs. S, global vs. situational; P presenting complaint of person. Each partner is meant to be evaluated in each category of this system, thus allowing for a broad behavioral description.

or two-session interview, during which a decision is reached as to whether the couple and therapists can agree on a common set of goals, which they will address. The initial interview needs to cover several *content areas*:

1. *Individual physical and psychological health.* Rule out obvious organic factors or decide to refer for physical evaluation. A medical referral is especially appropriate for certain types of low sexual desire, all pain symptoms, and many erectile failure cases. Specialized medical procedures are beyond the scope of this chapter, have been addressed elsewhere, and include the measure of penile blood pressure (Abelson, 1975), cavernosograms (Fitzpatrick & Cooper, 1975), the measurement of erections during sleep (Karacan, 1978), neurological tests, and tests of resting hormone levels (Spark, White, & Connolly, 1980).

Any system malfunction, disease, or drug that might affect the neural–vascular–endocrine pathways can influence sexual desire, arousal, and orgasm. The most frequent culprits are the long- and short-term effects of alcohol, psychotropic medications, and antihypertensives or even diuretics. Also, some people with chronic diseases may require additional rehabilitative measures. One may not be able to eliminate totally the possibility of physical etiology, but one can work within the confines of that situation. The major purpose of the review of individual health factors is to avoid missing the underlying depression, alcoholism, clinical level of anxiety, incipient diabetes, hyperprolactinemia, or other serious physical condition. A nonmedical psychotherapist will need a good referral network, as some MDs are not able, and occasionally not willing, to spend the time to do the careful assessment that may be required.

Additionally, watching for psychodynamic and intrapsychic factors that could account for the intensity, duration, or meaning of the sexual problem to each individual requires exploration. One can also examine individual histories for trauma and the early development of attitudes and values.

2. *On the interpersonal level*, it may be useful, briefly and selectively, to seek out common threads between the couple's current interactional patterns and those occuring, in their respective families of origin. Most people, incidentally, have experienced a less than optimum exposure to sexual information and education in their families of origin, so this factor alone cannot be automatically cited as a sexual factor. More significant patterns to explore are (*a*) How were physical and emotional affection expressed in the family, among all the participants? (*b*) How did family members know others loved them or were angry with them? (*c*) How, if at all, was the topic of sex treated, especially by the parents? (*d*) What was each patient's role in the family (e.g., the smart one, the black sheep, the caretaker, the peacemaker)? These questions, while not exhaustive, will sketch out a sense of the emotional interaction rules to which both partners were exposed as they were learning how to live in a family, watching and experiencing what were the rough and smooth sides of their parents' marital arrangement.

Previous romantic or sexual relationships of each person may or may not be relevant. They are often necessary to explore from the perspective of emotional experiences, previous instances of sexual problems, and the repetition of patterns. The therapist's line of probing in this sphere follows from trying to see how previous relationship themes prepared the way for the current problem they experience.

The current interactional patterns are the most important to assess, and in considerable detail. Although there are many categories one could explore, I think the most essential are the ways in which the couple manages and uses conflict, intimacy, and stress: Are conflict interactions expressed directly or indirectly; how much and when is anger permitted; is there a mutual or one-sided anger explosion; how is tension managed in the relationship; and so forth. In other words, the therapist assesses the couple's rules about conflict, and what function the conflict serves for them (e.g., to get distance, to stay involved with one another). Similarly, for intimacy, one part of which is affection and sex, what are the couple's rules for asking and securing it, and how does affection function in the system? Rules are meant in the sense of Sager's (1976) contracts—some spoken, some conscious but unspoken, and some unconscious. Stress management is less essential to evaluate, but I raise it because it allows the therapist to understand with the couple how different styles of relating to stress may individually escalate each partner's tension toward the other. Also, the therapist needs to get a sense of the effect of external stress on the couple's conflict and intimacy patterns.

Assessing the interactional level is therapeutically useful in several ways. For example, it can be used to allow the therapist to make sense out of the pattern the couple currently has, and it can do so in a nonblaming fashion; and it can give the therapist a sense of how sex fits into the major interaction patterns around affection and conflict, and should give some richer insight into how sex functions in the particular relationship. Thus this level of assessment provides the therapist and couple with an understanding of the possible value and meaning of the problem to the overall relationship. This is a good position from which to make an intervention, especially an intervention that will have an impact on the couple's interactions.

3. *Sociocultural-level assessment* gives attention to past and current religious beliefs (as they interact with sex), social class, current sex roles, current cultural emphasis on sex (e.g., more is better, multiple orgasms are superior to single orgasms, the G-spot will bring happiness, sex for fun) and ethnic or racial standards. These factors are equally important for the therapist and the client as value judgments are inseparable from sexual practices. For example, imagine that a couple came in asking to learn not to have sexual feelings (e.g., to create a lack of desire) toward each other, and to learn to be celibate. Would some therapists be "resistant" to working with such a couple? I think, at least for a heterosexual couple, the answer is yes.

MEASUREMENT

Several tools have research and clinical utility, although perhaps limited clinical utility unless one has minimal patient-contact time and maximal administrative help. The Spanier Dyadic Adjustment Scale (Spanier, 1976) permits a marital assessment with four factors (consensus, satisfaction, affectional expression, cohesion), which is the reason it can be more useful than the Locke–Wallace, although both are excellent instruments and the choice is one of personal preference. For sexual functioning, the Sexual Interaction Inventory (LoPiccolo & Steger, 1974) is still the most widely used, and is useful for giving a sense of present and ideal frequency, pleasure and perception of partner's pleasure. With couples who do not come in presenting with a sexual complaint or with extremely lower-class couples, I find the next form to be more appropriate in length and topic. The Sexual History Form from J. LoPiccolo's clinic is a very useful symptom and satisfaction questionnaire—short, direct, and with norms based on a large sample of functional middle- and lower-middle-class couples (e.g., Heiman & LoPiccolo, 1983). Finally, the measurement of interactional patterns is in its infancy, but I have used the FACES (Olson, Sprenkle, & Russell, 1979; Olson, Russell, & Sprenkle, 1983) with some interest. Although primarily appropriate for families with children, it can provide interesting additional insight into two interactional dimensions: cohesion (detached–enmeshed) and adaptability (chaotic–rigid).

Treatment Goals

Couples with desire and aversion problems usually want to decrease their conflictual feelings around having sex with each other and create a more harmonious sexual relationship. However, these goals may shift during the course of therapy, and other goals may become more important. One can therefore split the therapeutic goals into two phases. *Phase 1 goals* are centered on understanding, with the couple, how the current sexual problem functions (i.e., how it makes sense given past and current factors in the couple's lives). This is done in a way that does not blame either person by acknowledging the effort each has made to stay in the relationship while accommodating the sexual difficulty. The problem usually does have a positive function in the relationship. This needs to be recognized in part to acknowledge the problem's complexity, in part to reframe its role, and in part to decrease the tendency to protect it. Furthermore, processing this first goal will reveal a lot of information about affection, sex, and the necessity of recommending additional individual therapy for the partners. While rarer in low-desire problems (except the extreme lifetime, global low-desire individuals), individual therapy for aversion problems is somewhat more common.

   Phase 2 goals thus emerge against a view of the sexual problem that is somewhat different from the couple's initial view. Goals in this phase tend to be more intervention oriented but may extend beyond the purely sexual area. For example, some couples decide to focus only on enhancing their affectionate relationship, exclusive of sex. Other couples decide to work on the specific sexual difficulty. Still others turn their attention toward changing their overall relationship. If there are two central features of phase 2 goals, they could be seen as (*a*) the reintegration of sex into the relationship; and (*b*) the sense that the partners are collaborating. It is important to note that reintegrating sex may mean adjusting to a low frequency of sexual contact, with both feeling comfortable with that arrangement.

The Structure of Therapeutic Sessions

Other therapists have noted that desire problems require an average of 15 to 25 1-hour sessions (Kaplan, 1979; LoPiccolo & Friedman, 1985; Schover, 1981). Wherever possible, I find it useful to have 4 to 5 sessions of from 1 to 1½ hours, discontinue for a while (1 month) and then carry on additional sessions. This structure is advantageous in several ways, for example, by (*a*) increasing the intensity; (*b*) accenting the expectation that some but not necessarily all change should begin early in treatment, which the partners will then amplify on their own; (*c*) helping decrease the suction of the individual therapist into the couple's system; (*d*) permitting a way to work on multiple problems by dealing with only one or two at a time.

The therapy sessions themselves are a combination of (*a*) working with the problem's content, affect, and function by discussion and observation of the couple's behavior toward each other and toward the therapist; (*b*) using therapist reactions to process the couple's emotional distress; (*c*) encouraging clients to talk to each other in sessions; (*d*) assigning tasks, projects, and interactions at home, using the reactions to these tasks as further data on nature and flexibility of problem; and (*e*) periodically, using an educational framework to allow clients to take some distance from their problem and thereby encourage a no-blame interaction.

Active Ingredients of Therapy

Therapy for most sexual problems has included a cognitive–behavioral and occasionally psychodynamic smorgasbord of approaches, from which no studies have been able to clearly identify the active versus inert ingredients. Similarly, for recent attempts to address the problems of desire-phase disorders, a multilevel, eclectic approach has been proposed (Friedman, 1982; Kaplan, 1979; L. LoPiccolo, 1980; J. LoPiccolo & Friedman, 1985; Zilbergeld & Rinkleib, 1980). For example, Friedman (1982) proposed and is evaluating low-desire problems treated with four major elements: insight, experiential–sensory awareness, cognitive restructuring, and behavioral intervention. Earlier, L. LoPiccolo (1980) had mentioned, as needed, hormonal therapy, anxiety reduction, treatment for depression, increasing sensory awareness, relationship improvement, enhancement of sexual–sensual experience, facilitation of erotic responses, and dealing with intrapsychic conflict. Finally, Kaplan (1979) mentioned the use of psychosexual therapy, her term for a combination of behavioral (e.g., *in vivo* desensitization) and psychodynamic techniques.

If all of this seems like an eclectic's delight and reminiscent of broad-based sex and marital therapy techniques, then perhaps we can conclude that desire-phase sexual problems (and, I would argue, most sexual problems) require flexible and tailor-made interventions. Perhaps the greatest injustice in the sex therapy field has been the perception that arousal, orgasm, and low-desire problems were more alike than different among identified couples. This impression is a frequent casualty of clinical research that forces a parsimonious diagnosis, usually based on the most obvious (rather than necessarily the most salient) symptom.

There need to be a few common therapeutic, operational bases, however. Drawing from the recent literature as well as clinical work, the more essential ingredients of therapy (presuming a major psychogenic component) are these:

1. Some acceptance and understanding of structure and function of the problem for the individual and the relationship.
2. Anxiety management via hypnosis, Gestalt work, relaxation, *in vivo* exposure, sensate focus exercises.
3. Relationship adjustment, especially in the areas of affection, sex, communication, territoriality, bonding, dominance, increased flexibility in role expression, and increased tolerance.
4. Permitting or creating the context in which the couple can talk to each other in session and provide the therapist with an opportunity to work with the relationship's affective communication elements right there.
5. Assign tasks, projects, exercises for the couple to do at home, looking at both the process and outcome by which they do or do not get done. Sometimes a paradoxical instruction can be useful ("Do not have any sexual thoughts this week, but if you do, write them down") if the therapist uses it with the aim of creatively moving the system toward change. Also, paradox is most useful when a system is repeatedly "stuck," and when the therapist believes in the paradoxical intervention.

A few other factors are related to active therapeutic intervention. Sexual feelings, like other feelings, cannot be created and certainly cannot be forced by a therapist or a spouse. The only hope is to create an atmosphere in which sexual feelings are not buried under anxiety, hostility, or boredom. For example, not all clients will do the hallmark of sex therapy—sensate focus exercises. Some couples have already tried them and turned into relaxed roommates rather than interested lovers; some feel it slightly decadent (my lower economic class clients taught me about this); and others have such hostile feelings that they are unable to do the exercises. Thus these exercises may not be appropriate, but clients' feedback will be useful in creating alternatives.

SPECIFIC AND NONSPECIFIC THERAPEUTIC INTERVENTIONS

I have selected several intervention issues and examples to discuss, based on what I think are a few important elements in a therapist's interaction with a client around the topic of sex. It may be useful for the reader to keep in mind that these remarks, unless otherwise noted, are based on couples presenting at a general family and marital problems clinic, rather than specifically at a sex therapy center. Additionally, I have selected those cases of low desire–low general satisfaction that were not lifelong and were not based exclusively on physiological disturbances.

Early in Therapy

A sexual problem can be quite circumscribed with little connection to other areas of the couple's life. Sex may also be purely a metaphor expressing some broader or deeper level of discord. Therefore, the early stage of therapy draws the therapist and clients into the task of *exploring the content, context, and function of the sexual complaint.*

CONTENT AND CONTEXT

Assessing the individual, interactional, and sociocultural levels discussed earlier leads one directly into the content of therapy. Listening to content means paying attention to what people say (and do not say), getting precise details from each person on certain aspects of their interaction (e.g., their last conflict, the times they try to have sex, the therapeutic assignment). Content themes are also valuable to listen for; the repeated use of certain words or ideas such as loneliness, loss, effort, or illness may be important clues for therapeutic intervention.

The context in which the content is expressed is equally important: the verbal and nonverbal reactions of each partner to the other in the course of the session, the range of emotions discussed and expressed, and similarity or differences in the emotional investment apparent between partners. The therapist, of course, is part of the context. The therapist is a sensor of the degree of warmth, tension, anger, and hostility of the partners toward each other, and between therapist and couple.

When to use those reactions directly in the therapeutic session is a topic beyond the scope of the present chapter. As a general rule, I prefer therapists to be very aware but to underexpress their own feelings unless they are clear on ways it might be therapeutic for the couple.

It should be clear that in order to gather the content and context of a couple's situation, the therapist has to be less obtrusive and intrusive in the beginning of treatment. Let's look at two examples:

MRS A.: Our sex life is nonexistent.

THERAPIST: Non-existent?

MRS. A. We had sex—the last time—six weeks ago.

MR. A.(*interrupting*): Actually it was two weeks ago. . . . It was after I got the job change at work.

MRS. A.(*impatiently*): That wasn't really sex for me. You had been drinking.

Notice the therapist's role—letting the clients explain what they mean and what the sex problem means to them. The content here is that sex is too infrequent and unsatisfying, especially for Mrs. A. The context—irritation and conflict from both partners—suggests a shared affective investment over the relationship's future. Compare that to another couple, about the same age and with a similar complaint about one partner's sexual disinterest:

MR. B. : As soon as we got married [8 years ago] we started to grow apart. Sex became less frequent. I desire Carol [his wife] but now we seem so different (*correcting himself*) distant. (*Looks down, appears tense, while Mrs. B. appears attentive but very calm*).

THERAPIST (*to Mrs. B.*): What have you noticed?

MRS. B.: Well, in the beginning I really pushed for sex. Then . . . I just quit trying, especially after Sara [their 3-year-old] was born. I found other friends through my work, which helped me feel socially involved, and now I am not really interested in sex.

THERAPIST: Not at all?

MRS. B.: What do you mean?

THERAPIST: Are you disinterested in sex generally or just with your husband?

MRS. B.: Well, I don't know, I haven't thought about it outside of our sex together.

The content has to do with sexual distance (and difference), but the therapeutic session felt more like a near severance of the relationship. He was tense, and she was rather removed emotionally. They had repeatedly pointed out her ambitious fast life style versus his low-key approach to life. I was wondering if Mrs. B. had any comparable level of anxiety about the problems, or if she had emotionally given up.

THERAPIST: This (*intentionally vague*) sounds serious. Do you think if the sex doesn't change, your relationship will end?

MRS.B.: I want the marriage to succeed, but I am not very optimistic.

MR. B.: I doubt the sex thing alone would finish us.

The issue here has been said by the clients: differences and distance; loss of affective investment in the relationship but still a sense of duty to their child on Mrs. B.'s part; and fear of further trauma if sex were tried and failed, paralyzing Mr. B. from initiating at all. Thus the couple's apparent level of affective commitment is unbalanced, with Mrs. B. almost without feelings for her husband.

In both examples, one could simply go after the marital issues and drop sex completely. There is no single correct way to approach these themes. However, I tend not to ignore the "symptom" offered by the clients, especially if it is sex, until one has found out (*a*) what sex means to the couple (love, intimacy, a sign that the relationship has a future, a right, a duty, the essence of their roles); and (*b*) in what way sex summarizes what they want to say about themselves, their relationship and their future. In brief, the sexual problem (especially desire-phase problems) can be the couple's only way of comfortably expressing marital dissatisfaction, emotional emptiness, a power struggle, a change of feeling that they cannot *verbally* explain but only *nonverbally* (via sex) express.

A sexual problem may be "only a symptom," but it is a unique symptom, potentially rich with significant clues to the therapist who is willing to attend without too many preconceived ideas of what is or is not the most important problem.

Other strategies for addressing the content and context of the session are to ask for a comparison of a time when their sex life was better than it is currently, noting what they select as important discriminating features. The couple (each partner) needs to describe *in detail* what a good and bad sexual experience consists of, including situation, time, place, feelings, approach, type of activity, interaction, and feelings after the sexual experience. Some couples cannot do this very easily due to such long intervals between activity, or in the case of aversion, because each person avoids or feels guilty recalling what occurred. However, this material is extremely important for evoking with the therapist the content and affective material. This material often can be better revealed through a line of inquiry that includes aspects of a light hypnotic induction (J. Verhulst, personal communication, 1982), for example, creating a multisensory memory evocation so that the client can begin to reexperience the conflicting emotions felt on a previous sexual interaction. While this intervention evokes predominantly conscious material, it also will raise more unconscious themes. An obvious example was a female patient who was describing to me her last sexual contact with her husband, with whom sexual contact was extremely unpleasant and repulsive, and she called him Bob instead of Bill. Later it was revealed that her brother, Bob, had had an incestuous relationship with her as a child. Other therapists use a variety of hypnotic techniques to explore the nature and meaning of the symptom. The reader is referred to Araoz (1982) for a sensitive and skilled discussion of these possibilities and their effectiveness with over 800 patients.

FUNCTION

While content and context of the sexual symptom of low sexual desire can be assessed fairly directly, the function of the symptom—what purpose it serves to the individuals and particularly to the relationship—often proves to be more evasive. Of course, sexual problems do not always begin because they solve a problem within the relationship, but they are often maintained because they have some positive value or get incorporated into broader relationship patterns.

Major interaction patterns that impinge on the sexual life of couples have been described elsewhere (Verhulst & Heiman, 1979). If one looks at the management of stress, intimacy, and conflict in a particular couple, it becomes clear that there are interactional patterns which influence a couple's sense of togetherness–separateness. The interactional patterns that are particularly useful to examine are those of territoriality (rights of ownership), attachment (affiliation and bonding), and ranking order (status, dominance, and power).

Often in couples with low interest or desire, the sexual pattern seems to help regulate (or be synonymous with) the couple's emotional distance and interpersonal territory, though not always in the ways one would expect. Infrequent sex can be a sign that the couple is fearful of too much—or too little—closeness.

How to find the critical relationship themes is a matter of listening with interactionally predisposed ears. We are so indoctrinated to believe that sex is "in" the individual that we therapists can get trapped in our own thinking. For example, several couples I have seen have developed a ritual of sleeping in separate rooms. All other reasons aside, this is a red flag that territorial issues (personal space, time, rights) may be important. Or in a welfare couple I saw, living with their two children in a one-room-plus-kitchen apartment, sex was very infrequent and a low-priority problem, although it was mentioned. The woman would occasionally go into the closet for 20 or 30 minutes in order to have some privacy from the family. Territorial issues were paramount and aided by a move to a more spacious public housing apartment complex where the couple's fights decreased and sexual problems improved. Another example might be two male clients I recently saw who were both amateur marathon runners, running 75–150 miles per week, and noting that they had lost their interest in sex with their wives. While lowered sex drive may sometimes accompany distance running, there were psychological factors operating in these cases. One of the solutions provided by running was a means to escape a sense of being territorially confined—one's time and space being claimed by the responsibilities of a relationship.

So one function of the sexual problem may be to manage the couple's optimum intimate distance and space needs. Early in therapy, the therapist can present these observations in a rather paradoxical way, or at least in a way that amplifies the conflict between changing and not changing. Examples:

THERAPIST (*to a couple concerned because they never desire sex*): One way to look at the problem of little sexual desire is that a major value you both have is respecting one another's need for separateness and independence. This is a strong way to bond with one another in expressing that value. I wonder if you can afford to get closer sexually? Wouldn't something be lost?

THERAPIST (*to a couple where the woman wants more sex and the man says he is disinterested*): I can see how this is a problem, still I can't help but notice how it is such a good solution to the problem that you both want to feel closer but are afraid you might begin to smother one another. It is very delicate for you. In a way, it would be best to try not to change any of your sexual patterns for these first two weeks.

The latter circumstance is useful to relieve the couple of the fear that they have that the therapist will force them to be sexual, thus set up a reenactment of the problem as it exists in the relationship. It also can serve as a mildly paradoxical, symptom-amplifying intervention, which in the next session the therapist can check to see if some sexual thoughts, feelings, or even behavior were permitted to emerge under reduced pressure.

As Therapy Continues

While formulas for making interventions on the interactional levels are not possible, the following examples illustrate several basic features about the therapy approach.

> Mr. and Mrs. C. are a couple in their early 50s who have been married 25 years. Mrs. C has a 20-year psychiatric history of manic-depressive illness, with multiple hospitalizations. Currently she has been adequately maintained on psychiatric medications, except for some periods of depression. They came to therapy to address marital issues of intense conflict and periodic divorce threats from Mrs. C. After working with the couple for a month, with some improved management of conflict, the issue of affection came up. It turned out they had not had sex for several months. On that occasion, both were unclear about what had happened.

MRS. C.: He was not interested in me, just in himself.
MR. C. (*shrugging*): I don't know what she means—it seemed o.k. but afterward she blew up and told me how I did it wrong.
THERAPIST: Does that usually happen when you try to have sex?
MR. C.: Yes.
THERAPIST: Is it safer *not* to be sexual toward her?
MR. C.: (*assents with a shrug.*)
THERAPIST: Even if you want to?
MR. C.: Right.

His passivity and her domineering style cyclically maintained one another. Both felt trapped in this pattern, and their sex life suffered. A more telling example occurred during a later session. In response to the question whether Mrs. C. can ask for affection (a hug):

MRS. C.: I put up signs on the refrigerator saying, "I need a hug."
THERAPIST: What happens?
MR. C. (*trying to joke*): I hug the fridge.
MRS. C. (*continues*): I get one, but I don't think he wants to do it.
THERAPIST: So the unwritten rule is, you can't ask and if you do, it is not genuine?
MRS. C.: Right.
MR. C.: That's not the problem. I just go numb.
THERAPIST: When?
MR. C.: When I hug her, it's like I go numb.
THERAPIST: Do you have the freedom not to hug?
MR. C.: It would sure cause a lot of trouble (*not hugging*).

So, in gathering information on their last sexual encounter and their efforts to get affectionate needs met, we learned which therapeutic directions would be most valuable. First, from their marital history and current conflict level, it was clear that they were connected to one another. The interaction patterns that interfered with affection and sex had become completely entangled in the ranking-order interaction. Additionally, Mr. C. did not even perceive his body to be his own territory. They also slept in separate rooms, and Mrs. and Mr. C. agreed that she claimed and managed the entire territory of the house and yard. It should be obvious that directly intervening in the sexual–sensual with assignments for sensual contact was not addressing the core issues. In fact, several such assignments were attempted with consistent lack of cooperation. Instead, the interactional issues were addressed as follows:

1. Acknowledging the passive–domineering pattern as a residual style left over from successfully coping (standing by one another) with the numerous manic and succeeding depressive episodes. Her flamboyant (and sexual) highs and angry lows were complemented by his rocklike stability and ability to withdraw in self-defense. Their current communication style, especially during a problem, consisted of her criticism and his silence.

2. Describing the territorial and ever escalating and fruitless ranking-order interactions they engaged in, explaining how these patterns prevented them from permitting affection and sex. The quotes show that Mr. C. did not even feel his own body belonged to him. They also slept in separate rooms—a signal that territory is an issue—and both agreed that she had the psychological ownership and management of all areas of the house and yard, while his only territorial space possessions were the family cars.

The therapeutic intervention thus consisted of teaching the clients what problems were solved and what problems were created by their current pattern (i.e., the sense of the problem) in order to look for other ways to solve the problems between them (her need for his approval, his need for her to take care of him).

A very important factor was to help these clients see how they had both been fighting for the relationship all along, but their style had become antiquated for their needs. Territorial and ranking-order issues were addressed through changing several patterns—encouraging her independent management of shopping and appointments, while he occasionally had some separate time for himself (for this couple, time was easier to separate territorially than the space of the house). This was not a way just to get separateness; it was a way for both partners to take weight off of the relationship by taking care of themselves. The couple also worked in session on how to communicate about problems, complaints, and bad and good feelings. After 18 sessions over 12 months they were feeling better toward each other, laughed more, and had much improved spontaneity of affection. Their sexual contact was still infrequent, but it was more pleasant and neither spoke of it as a problem.

Decreasing the territorial or the ranking-order quality of emotional problems does not automatically lead to an increase in intimate feelings. Rather, it washes the first level so that more affiliative interactions can surface. This reminds me of another couple, Mr. and Mrs. D., both of whom were highly irritated and near separation when they arrived for couples therapy. Mrs. D. had bouts with depressed mood for which she was in individual therapy with a psychiatrist. They felt a major problem was also that they (both) almost never desired sex. Married 10 years and in their late 30s, they were sleeping in separate rooms. There are two relevant issues in our discussion here. Their fights, including screaming, wrestling, and physical fights, stopped when they learned what space meant to each person. Mrs. D. rarely liked to be touched unexpectedly. This was done by the therapists telling (a) Mr. D. to give Mrs. D. some 30 minutes of uninterrupted silent time without any physical contact when she arrived home; (b) Mrs. D. to give a clear sign when she no longer needed this breather; (c) Mr. D. not to "hover" over Mrs. D. to wonder about her mood (her depressed moods had always made him feel worried and guilty) but to ask her if she was feeling o.k. (and she would give a clear answer) and if he could do anything (and she would let him know). In other words, Mrs. D.'s personal space was shown more respect at an important time of day for her, and she agreed to be responsible for watching her own moods, which indeed were *her* territory and not Mr. D.'s. The therapist was instrumental in this process by helping Mrs. D. explain to her husband that claiming her territory was not a rejection of Mr. D., who had acted out of a sense of concern. Instead, Mr. D.'s caring was expressed as a gift—of time and space—while meanwhile decreasing his burden of worried attention. This was important, for the relationship had been characterized by a high degree of tension and explosiveness. They began sleeping together again. Sexual interest was slightly better, physical violence stopped, and cooperation was much improved. She returned to school for an advanced degree in a different field. In short, the solution they arrived at in two sessions was a more independent, more respectful, and slightly more affectionate relationship, where a high frequency of sex did not measure its value. It should be of interest that one of the earlier concerns, whether to have a child, was decided to be put aside, perhaps permanently.

These two examples summarize several features of treating these types of sexual problems. First, while there is no simple set of techniques, there is an approach or way of untangling what pieces of the puzzle are interconnected. Second, couples often will not or cannot make progress if the sexual–sensual is the direct target of the at-home experiential change. It is often only after a shift in awareness level that sexual and affectionate issues readjust. This may be far more characteristic of couples initially presenting with marital than with sexual problems. Therapists who have doubts might try sexual exercises and assess the couple's reactions both to the assignment and to the actual exercise. Third, territorial and ranking-order interactions are very common in these couples, and one sees evidence of this in how they deal with problems, structure their time and space with one another, and sometimes in their communication patterns. However, the therapist has to recognize these patterns, for the couple may come in asking for more intimacy, closeness, sex, time together, and the like when actually they would benefit from a decrease in their focus on one another. Finally, at the end of therapy, a couple's eventual objective sexual improvement may seem modest, and it probably is, especially if it is focused on frequency. Yet I am struck by how much the attitude and comfort around sex–intimacy shifts in those cases that do well (by my and their account). Satisfaction is considerably higher with respect to sex and the relationship in general. Perhaps this means that sexual desire and conduct in long-term relationships will not shift very much. Or perhaps it means that we do not know very much about the natural interaction of marital patterns and sexual intimacy (and that these clients can teach us).

Additional Therapeutic Issues

Several other therapeutic interventions deserve mention because of their frequency of use or suggested value by others.

1. *Managing anger.* The level of anger in couples with desire-phase disorders and aversion is often very high, and sometimes very indirectly expressed. Anger-management techniques, including the recognition, appreciation, resolution, and control of anger in the relationship are important.

2. *Desensitization.* Once the hostility level is at a more moderate level, some couples respond to a gradual effort at getting reacquainted with their sexual feelings. This may be several weeks of simply letting them tune into those things that allow mildly sensual and desirous feelings (e.g., wanting to touch or be touched) to emerge. Hypnotic techniques can be very helpful here, and in the case of aversion, where there may be numerous aspects to the aversion that can be better managed in a hypnotic intervention.

3. *Physical proximity.* Separated couples are cut off from physical touching without sex and spontaneous expressions of sexual–sensual feelings. Thus, if the separate sleeping arrangement does not change, I find it a less than optimal sign (barring handicaps or illness). Some couples will agree just to try sleeping together without sex for a week, especially if the therapist suggests it from an exploratory perspective. The therapist does need to watch for any changes in other interactions during that week and in session (e.g., fighting, talking, cooperating, working). However, forcing couples to sleep together is often less successful ultimately than using this pattern as a barometer while aiding other areas of the relationship enough so that the couple makes the change themselves (e.g., the cases described above).

4. *Sexual exposure.* Although other therapists have reported success with exposing persons to erotic books and films, I find this inadequate, repulsive sometimes, with the type of desire-disorder clients I have seen. This technique may be more useful with sexually discovering or naive clients. However, occasionally I will ask a couple just to have sex together, *without* trying to do anything "right," which allows everyone to assess the affective content

and context. Still, many couples balk. Sometimes an alternative is to have the couple talk in session about what would be the worst sexual experience—what could go as "wrong" as possible—if it were to occur that evening. This usually reveals enough material and affect that some degree of therapeutic movement can occur.

THE THERAPIST'S ROLE

I suppose it is obvious that the person who treats sexual problems should become comfortable raising the topic. I have seen a number of trainees become mechanistic in their language or paternalistic in their manner out of pure anxiety in asking a 63-year-old couple about their sex lives. I almost prefer that professionals have some discomfort in the beginning as it will help them to understand their patients' hesitancies. The major issue is that the therapist receive training that will permit greater comfort while respectfully asking details about a couple's sex life and prescribing things for them to do at home without feeling like an intruder.

Treating sexual problems requires a person skilled in general assessment–diagnosis and psychotherapy (Arentewicz & Schmidt, 1983; LoPiccolo, 1978). Exposure to, and use of, more than one theoretical system is useful. Experience with treating couples is essential, even if the therapist deals with only one person of the couple, as is sometimes unavoidable. Beyond the general professional degree and training, working with sexual problems requires a theoretical knowledge of human sexuality and sexual disorders and preferably co-therapy experience with advanced therapists combined with group discussion of cases.

A related issue is that therapists commonly have a tendency to locate the sexual problem in one person and get the other to adjust to it. For example, for the 45-year-old couple where he wants sex more often than she does not, and their current frequency is once per month, there is often a tendency to say that he has more right to insist "yes" than she has to insist "no." The therapist who believes that will make the problem worse.

CONCLUDING REMARKS

While touching on individual and sociocultural patterns mentioned in Figure 16-1, this chapter has been primarily devoted to assessing and working with the couple's sexual interactional patterns. This seems to be essential, perhaps more so because they are almost never discussed but usually presumed. However, several noteworthy clinical issues deserve brief mention that fall more into the individual or sociocultural categories.

1. *The unknowns of long-term relationships.* Most of our knowledge about sexuality and its meaning in people's lives comes from the early

relationship stages. Neither we nor our couples know what constitutes a satisfying long-term sexual relationship. It is unlikely to be sufficiently measured by level of frequency and desire. Some research has shown that happily married couples may include 40% sexually dysfunctional men and 60% sexually dysfunctional women (Frank, Anderson, & Rubenstein, 1978). Yet a recent survey of over 6000 American couples, heterosexual and homosexual, concluded that frequency is correlated with sexual satisfaction (Blumstein & Schwartz, 1983). However, this research also demonstrated that sex was more important as a relationship's "cement" in cohabiting nonmarried couples than married couples, and that most couples felt a woman had more rights to refuse sex than a man did, while it was a man's right and duty to ask for it (Blumstein & Schwartz, 1983). These researchers noted, relevant to the case of Mr. and Mrs. B., that the happier sex lives were couples who had equality in the rights and practice of initiating *and* refusing sex.

Even more important, there is no information on how sex changes in its value and meaning over a couple's development. One could imagine that a married couple will find different qualities of sex to be satisfying as newlyweds compared to their 20th year together when they are 50. This is a useful observation to keep in mind in therapy, for a couple is really trying to find their *own* meaning and satisfaction and the therapist is there to explore the options rather than fit them into anyone's predetermined mold.

2. *Sexually abusive histories.* If one person, most often the female, has a strong aversion to sex, or anhedonia, the possibility of a *sexually abusive history* needs to be considered. The mangement of this problem varies. A general guideline I find helpful is that if the client seems at ease discussing it in front of her partner, then that can be extremely useful to both. If not, then the client may benefit from some individual work prior to couples therapy. The reason for doing couples therapy is to help all concerned to understand that the abused client's problem is not caused by his or her partner but may be influenced by certain interactions. Also, the abused client is helped by increasingly clear discriminations between the past sexual abuse and the present sexual relationship. In terms of what we have examined in this chapter, territoriality is an important concept for the abused person: One has to feel a sense of ownership over one's own body before one can "freely" allow another person access to it. People who have been repeatedly sexually abused a children, or raped as adults, have had that sense of bodily ownership threatened or have lost it. However, *forcing* the client to come to terms with the abuse, especially in couples therapy, is ill advised, in part because it symbolically re-creates the precise problem the person has experienced—the deliberate attempt to delve into the sexual abuse against the client's will.

3. *Psychological issues around medical problems and interventions.* Briefly, much of the therapist's role in cases where the person is on prescription drugs with antisexual side effects is one of rehabilitation. For example, adjusting to lithium carbonate may be difficult because patients often report

feeling thicker, slower, lower in energy and less able to detect sensual stimulation of all kinds. They may need to learn to feel sensually receptive again. Similarly, with illnesses such as diabetes and multiple sclerosis, people may find they need far more stimulation that they once did, and if the partner is not aware of this, he or she may gradually lose sexual interest. Issues of marital intimacy can sometimes present as sexual complaints in couples where a life-threatening or serious disease is present. The collective archetype of sexual activity embodies growth, energy, rebirth, and rejuvenation. When faced with deterioration, loss, or death, a person's sexuality may indeed be the focus of his or her sense of mortality. These symbolic issues are often present in the ill and the healthy spouse, although the healthy partner is frequently the least likely to discuss or even admit to changes in intimate feelings. The healthy partner often feels guilty, especially if she or he begins to feel more distanced or less attracted to the ill partner.

In treating such couples, several general principles are important: (a) Clarify what each person would like in the sexual relationship and note the similarities or differences; (b) encourage partners to share fears, anger, misgivings, and worries to the extent that they are able; (c) maintain an attitude of adjustment, in particular what may need to be given up and what is important to nurture. Often, loss of sexual contact is not the worst fear, but it best expresses the despair of the body's failure and the apprehension over ultimate loss of intimacy. If couples can find their way to face uncertainty and loss together, some of the alienation and conflict between the partners will be decreased.

REFERENCES

Abelson, D. (1975). Diagnostic value of the penile pulse and blood pressure: A doppler study of impotence in diabetics. *Journal of Urology, 113*, 636–639.

Araoz, D. L. (1982). *Hypnosis and sex therapy.* New York: Brunner/Mazel.

Arentewicz, G., & Schmidt, G. (1983). *The treatment of sexual disorders.* New York: Basic Books.

Blumstein, P., & Schwartz, P. (1983). *American couples.* New York: Morrow.

Fitzpatrick, T. J., & Cooper, J. F. (1975). A cavernosogram study in the valvular competence of the human deep dorsal vein. *Journal of Urology, 113*, 479–499.

Foucault, M. (1980). *The history of sexuality,* Vol. 1: *An introduction.* New York: Vintage Books. Originally published in France, 1976.

Frank, E., Anderson, A., & Rubenstein, D. (1978). Frequency of sexual dysfunction in "normal" couples. *New England Journal of Medicine, 299*, 111–115.

Friedman, J. M. (1982, June). *A treatment program for low sexual desire.* Paper presented at the annual meeting of the American Society of Sex Therapy and Research, Charleston, SC.

Heiman, J. R., & LoPiccolo, J. (1983). Clinical outcome of sex therapy: Effects of daily versus weekly treatment. *Archives of General Psychiatry, 40*, 443–449.

Heiman, J. R., LoPiccolo, L., & LoPiccolo, J. (1981). The treatment of sexual dysfunction. In A. S. Gurman & D. P. Kniskern (Eds.), *Handbook of family therapy.* New York: Brunner/Mazel.

Kaplan, H. S. (1974). *The new sex therapy.* New York: Brunner/Mazel.

Kaplan, H. S. (1979). *Disorders of sexual desire.* New York: Brunner/Mazel.

Karacan, I. (1978). Advances in the psychophysiological evaluation of male erectile impotence. In J. LoPiccolo & L. LoPiccolo (Eds.), *Handbook of sex therapy*. New York: Plenum Press.

Leiblum, S. R., & Pervin, L. A. (Eds.). (1980). *Principles and practice of sex therapy*. New York: Guilford Press.

LoPiccolo, J. (1978). Methodological issues in research and treatment of sexual dysfunction. In R. Green & J. Winer (Eds.), *Methodological issues in sex research*. Washington, DC: Government Printing Office.

LoPiccolo, J., & Friedman, J. M. (1985). Sex therapy: An integrated model. In S. J. Lynn & J. P. Garske (Eds.), *Contemporary psychotherapies: Models and methods*. New York: Charles E. Merrill.

LoPiccolo, J., & LoPiccolo, L. (Eds.). (1978). *Handbook of sex therapy*. New York: Plenum Press.

LoPiccolo, J., & Steger, J. C. (1974). The Sexual Interaction Inventory: A new instrument for assessment of sexual dysfunction. *Archives of Sexual Behavior, 3*, 585–595.

LoPiccolo, L. (1980). Low sexual desire. In S. R. Leiblum & L. A. Pervin (Eds.), *Principles and practice of sex therapy*. New York: Guilford Press.

Marks, I. M. (1980). Review of behavioral psychotherapy, II: Sexual disorders. *American Journal of Psychiatry, 138*, 750–756.

Masters, W., & Johnson, V. (1970). *Human sexual inadequacy*. Boston: Little, Brown.

Olson, D. H., Russell, C., & Sprenkle, D. H. (1983). Circumplex model of marital and family systems, VI: Theoretical update. *Family Process, 22*, 69–84.

Olson, D. H., Sprenkle, D. H., & Russell, C. (1979). Circumplex model of marital and family systems, I: Cohesion and adaptability dimensions, family types and clinical applications. *Family Process, 18*, 3–28.

Sager, C. (1976). *Marriage contracts and couple therapy: Hidden forces in intimate relationships*. New York: Brunner/Mazel.

Schover, L. R. (1981). Assessment and treatment of low sexual desire (research and clinical exchange). *American Journal of Family Therapy, 9*, 89–91.

Schover, L. R., Friedman, J. M., Weiler, S. J., Heiman, J. R., & LoPiccolo, J. (1982). Multiaxial problem-oriented system for sexual dysfunctions. *Archives of General Psychiatry, 39*, 614–619.

Schover, L. R., & LoPiccolo, J. (1982). Treatment effectiveness for dysfunctions of sexual desire. *Journal of Sex and Marital Therapy, 8*, 179–197.

Spanier, G. B. (1976). Measuring dyadic adjustment: New scales for assessing quality of marriage and similar dyads. *Journal of Marriage and Family Therapy, 38*, 15–28.

Spark, R. F., White, R. A., & Connolly, P. B. (1980). Impotence is not always psychogenic: Newer insights into hypothalamic–pituitary–gonadal dysfunction. *Journal of American Medical Association, 243*, 750–755.

Verhulst, J., & Heiman, J. (1979). An interactional approach to sexual dysfunction. *American Journal of Family Therapy, 7*, 19–36.

Whitaker, C. A., & Keith, D. V. (1981). Symbolic experiential family therapy. In A. S. Gurman & D. P. Kniskern (Eds.), *Handbook of family therapy*. New York: Brunner/Mazel.

Wright, J., Perreault, R., & Mathieu, M. (1977). The treatment of sexual dysfunction. *Archives of General Psychiatry, 34*, 881–890.

Zilbergeld, B., & Evans, M. (1980). The inadequacy of Masters and Johnson. *Psychology Today, 45*, 28–43.

Zilbergeld, B., & Rinkleib, C. E. (1980). Desire discrepancies and arousal problems in sex therapy. In S. Leiblum & L. Pervin (Eds.), *Principles and practice of sex therapy*. New York: Guilford Press.

The Treatment
of Marital Violence

17

ALAN ROSENBAUM
K. DANIEL O'LEARY

Although marital violence has a history as long as marriage itself, only recently has it become recognized as a problem worthy of attention by mental health professionals and researchers. Recent estimates suggest that almost one-third of all married couples will experience violence at some time in the marital relationship (Straus, Gelles, & Steinmetz, 1980). The impact of marital violence on both the affected families and society is very substantial. Victims are often physically injured and may even be killed. Chronic physical and stress related disorders, depression, elevated suicide-attempt rates, and anxiety are common emotional correlates (Gayford, 1975). Separation, divorce, alcohol and drug use, child abuse, and a host of behavioral and emotional difficulties among witnessing children are frequently consequences of an abusive relationship. It should surprise us that this most common form of couple conflict has received so little attention from marital therapists and researchers.

The shame and stigma that traditionally have been attached to marital violence, coupled with cultural and societal acceptance and legitimacy, contributed to the invisibility of this problem and the proliferation of the myth that physical violence among married couples was rare. Therapists, ill prepared in their training programs to deal with such issues, rarely assessed specifically for marital violence. Failure to assess for abuse led to failure to find abuse, further reinforcing the myth.

The raising of our collective consciousness over the past decade, primarily through the efforts of women's groups, has increased the probability that

Alan Rosenbaum. Department of Psychology, Syracuse University, Syracuse, New York.
K. Daniel O'Leary. Department of Psychology, State University of New York at Stony Brook, Stony Brook, New York.

couples will cite violence as a presenting problem. However, it is still not uncommon for couples to be very guarded about such issues. It seems prudent for marital therapists routinely to assess for the occurrence of violence in discordant marriages. The more discordant the marriage, the higher the probability that violence is a factor (Rosenbaum & O'Leary, 1981). Although our knowledge of the factors that predispose a couple to violence is far from conclusive, research over the past decade has generated a number of promising predictors that can be profitably utilized in assessing marriages for either the existence of, or the potential for, violence.

This chapter is organized around the following topics: assessment, treatment conceptualization, treatment strategies, relationship enhancement, and therapist issues specific to marital violence.

ASSESSMENT

Marital violence is often used synonymously with wife abuse, as it was in the foregoing introduction, despite recent evidence regarding the mutuality of marital violence. Straus *et al.* (1980) suggest that about a quarter of all marital violence is husband toward wife, a quarter is wife toward husband, and about half is mutual. There is, however, general agreement that wife battering is the more serious problem because the physical damage to wives caused by husbands is usually greater than the physical damage to husbands by wives. We do not wish to diminish the effects of husband abuse by wives; however, wife abuse has received considerably more research and clinical attention, and the present chapter is concerned primarily with wife abuse, except where noted.

What constitutes marital violence is often taken for granted and seldom addressed. In an area as politically loaded as wife abuse, the position is often espoused that any violence in a marital relationship is unacceptable and constitutes abuse. Others, most notably Straus *et al.* (1980), have suggested that a certain amount of violence in marital relationships is so common as to be considered normative and that the distinction should be made between "normal violence" and "abusive violence." This chapter takes the position that, "normal" or otherwise, violence in a marital relationship is unacceptable and damaging to the entire family.

A more pertinent issue concerns identifying marital violence or the potential for such violence. Ganley (1981) describes four forms of marital violence: (*a*) physical violence; (*b*) sexual violence; (*c*) psychological abuse; and (*d*) the destruction of property and pets. Physical violence involves any form of aggression directed at the victim's body and may include punching, pushing, kicking, slapping, choking, limb twisting, scratching, biting, or the use of a knife, club, strap, stick, or gun. Sexual violence includes forced sex (marital rape) or physical attacks directed at the breasts or genitals of the victim. Psychological abuse includes threats (against the victim, the victim's children, or even against the perpetrator, such as a suicide threat), forcing the victim to do degrading things, (e.g., eat off the floor, beg), controlling the victim's life (e.g., by restricting access to the car, money, clothing, or refusing to let her work or have friends), verbal abuse and insults, and intentionally frightening the victim (e.g., by reckless driving, brandishing weapons, staring at the victim). Ganley distinguishes between this form of violence and emotional abuse by the existence of an atmosphere of physical violence in the former case. "The power of psychological battering comes directly from the physical/sexual violence that has already occurred. The offender is successful in dominating and coercing the victim by using psychological weapons, precisely because she [the victim] knows from experience that he is capable of backing up his psychological battering with physical assaults" (p. 12). The final form of battering, the destruction of property and pets, has commonalities with both physical and psychological violence. It is a physical assault, although not aimed directly at the wife, that is psychologically terrifying, reinforcing the belief that the husband is a dangerous person. The destruction of property particularly treasured by the wife is both hurtful and humiliating. All forms of violence can be psychologically devastating to the victim. Often, many or all forms may be present in a relationship. It should be noted that nonphysical forms of battering are often overlooked by therapists. The interventions discussed in this chapter are primarily directed at the control of physical violence. Nevertheless, the existence of nonphysical battering, should alert the therapist to the potential for physical violence. It may also be useful to adapt some of the strategies presented in this chapter to nonphysical forms of battering that may occur in relationships.

Although some investigators have suggested that there may be a relationship between marital violence and lower socioeconomic status (Finkelhor, 1983), there is general agreement that it occurs in every socioeconomic, racial, religious, and ethnic group. Therapists should not, therefore, be misled by the socioeconomic, occupational, ethnic, or educational status of the couple. There is some evidence that violence is more probable in either interracial or interreligious marriages (Rosenbaum & O'Leary, 1981a; Wasileski et al., 1982) and in couples where there is status incompatibility (Hornung, McCullough, & Sugimoto, 1981), such as when the wife has a higher occupational status than her husband. Violence seems to be related more to differences between spouses on these dimensions than to any specific racial, religious, socioeconomic, or educational characteristic. It is frequently asserted that violent couples grew up in families characterized by violence. It has been repeatedly demonstrated that wife-abusive husbands are significantly more likely to have both witnessed parental marital violence and to have been abused by their parents than are their nonabusive counterparts (Rosenbaum & O'Leary, 1981b; Coleman, Weinman, & Hsi, 1980). In addition, there is some suggestive evidence that women who observe parental marital violence are more likely to hit their spouses than women who did not observe marital violence (Kalmuss, 1984). It is not true, however, that women who are hit by their spouses are more likely to have observed parental marital violence than women who are not so abused (Rosenbaum & O'Leary, 1981; Curley & O'Leary, 1980; Pagelow, 1981).

Low self-esteem has been associated with both child and wife abuse (Rosenbaum, Goldstein, & O'Leary, 1980; Spinetta & Rigler, 1972), as well as with other forms of violent crime (Maurer, 1976). Husbands with low self-esteem may, therefore, be at risk for perpetrating both wife and child abuse. Abused wives have also been characterized as having defective self-concepts, and self-esteem deficiencies in either spouse may signal the existence of, or potential for, violence.

Alcohol use, especially by the husband, is frequently implicated in all forms of family violence. Abusers are frequently alcoholic (Rosenbaum & O'Leary, 1981), and even if they are not actually alcohol abusers, incidents of abuse are often associated with alcohol use. Drug abuse and gambling are other addictions commonly found in wife-abusive populations. Clinical reports suggest that pathological jealousy may be characteristic of these men. This is often manifested in an attempt to isolate the wife socially. The abused wife may not be permitted to work outside the home or engage in other outside activities. The husband closely monitors her activities, and she may not have access to either transportation or money.

Abused wives frequently present with problems of anxiety, depression, and somatic complaints (Gayford, 1975). The strong associations between marital violence and both child abuse and behavioral or emotional problems in children suggest additional factors that should alert therapists to the possible existence of, or potential for, marital violence.

If there is a suspicion of violence, care must be taken to assess in a way that protects the safety of the wife. If the couple has not volunteered such information, there is a strong possibility that the wife may be afraid to report in the husband's presence. We have found it useful to inform the couple routinely at the outset of the intake interview that the therapist will spend time alone with each spouse during the course of the intake interview. If during such an assessment the wife reports violence, ethical practice demands that the protection of the wife becomes the first priority.

The first step is to assess whether the wife feels that she is in immediate danger and if she wants referral and/or assistance in getting to a refuge (shelter or safe home). In some circumstances it may be necessary to offer (and provide) police protection from the therapist's office to such a refuge. The therapist should convey the message that abuse is unacceptable and illegal, and encourage the wife to utilize the legal remedies and protections available to her. It must also be recognized that often these so-called remedies and protections do not serve the needs of the abused wife. A frequent complaint of abused wives concerns the lack of response by police and legal agencies. Often, when an abusive husband is arrested, he is quickly released on his own recognizance and free to return to his home and the woman who has just had him arrested.

Therapists working with married couples should familiarize themselves with the facilities serving abused wives in their communities. Many communities, and most urban areas, now have shelters or agencies serving abused women. These agencies are better acquainted with the nature of enforcement and judicial process in family violence matters, and are therefore better able to advise the abused wife of her realistic options. Further, they can offer her shelter from her husband while she pursues the various options.

Thus far we have addressed the first two critical questions of the assessment process: Is violence occuring in the marital relationship, and if so, is the wife–victim safe and aware of the appropriate service-delivery agencies? The third issue concerns the selection of an appropriate treatment modality. Many people working with abused wives are of the opinion that the only successful way to resolve a violent marriage is to dissolve it. To this end, the treatment of choice is usually aimed at providing support, legal assistance, vocational counseling and/or training, child care, and advocacy through the social service system, if necessary. Many shelters operate support groups for abused wives, to help them develop the strength and independence to exit from the marital relationship. Many abused wives, however, are either unable or unwilling to leave their marriages, opting instead for marital therapy. The third decision concerns whether the couple are appropriate candidates for marital reconciliation. It may be useful to explore with the couple, particularly with the abused wife, whether the remediation of the marriage is a realistic or desirable goal. If there is substantial doubt regarding the viability of the relationship, referral to a woman's support group and/or individual or group counseling for the husband should be considered.

If the decision is to provide marital therapy for the couple, there are several options for treatment. The two forms of treatment that have received the most attention are conjoint marital therapy (Geller & Walsh, 1977–1978; Margolin, 1979) and group approaches for the husband (Purdy & Nickel, 1981; Frank & Houghton, 1982).

Margolin (1979) proposed a model of marital violence based on social learning theory. She suggests that marital violence is an interactional pattern involving both spouses, in which the violent behavior of one spouse is seen as instrumental in producing compliance from the other spouse, but also elicits reciprocal coercive counterresponses directed toward the aggressor, leading to an escalation of hostility within the relationship. This model, which is a variation of Patterson and Reid's (1970) reciprocity and coercion model, is consistent with suggestions that spouses often resort to violence because other, less violent methods of argumentation have been unsuccessful. Nye (1978), for example, has suggested that the more a spouse lacks verbal skills, the more likely he or she will be to resort to violence in order to win arguments. Similarly, Purdy and Nickle (1981) report that a basic assumption of their groups for men who batter is that violence is an addictive behavior because it is immediately effective, however destructive it might eventually become. It is also congruent with evidence regarding the mutuality of violence in abusive relationships (Straus *et al.*, 1980). The intervention strategy derived from this model involves dealing with violence as a couple problem, in the context of conjoint marital therapy.

Although conjoint marital therapy is most often seen as the treatment of choice for couples professing a desire to remain in the relationship, the nature of the therapeutic relationship in couple counseling connotes a belief in the mutuality of responsibility for the marital turmoil. This poses a conceptual dilemma for many therapists working with marital violence, since a major goal in eliminating violence involves getting the husband to accept responsibility for his violent behavior. One way of operationalizing the belief that the couple are mutually responsible for the marital discord, but the husband alone is responsible for his violent behavior, is to provide the husband with some form of intervention dealing specifically with violence control, either before or concurrent with conjoint marital therapy.

This approach is congruent with a conceptual framework, which has been articulated elsewhere (Rosenbaum, 1984) in which environmental stressors (e.g., financial difficulties, job stress), ideological differences (e.g., racial or religious differences), and personal problems (e.g., alcoholism, gambling) are seen as productive of the marital discord that sets the stage for violence. Whether or not the discord becomes violent is seen as dependent on the characteristics of the husband and on his background. If the husband comes from a background in which he witnessed or experienced violence, has low self-esteem, and/or has difficulty asserting himself with his wife, the probability of violence is increased. This model suggests that although both spouses contribute to the production of marital discord, the person doing the hitting is responsible for that behavior. It makes sense, therefore, to treat the couple in order to reduce or eliminate the discord that is often a precipitating factor in the violence, and to treat the husband alone in order to reduce the violence. If men's groups dealing specifically with wife abuse are not a realistic consideration, it is still practical to deal with the husband's responsibility for his violent behavior, in the context of marital therapy. In fact, many techniques common to most men's workshop programs are even more effective if the wife is informed and involved. Consider the following example:

> Mr. M. was a participant in one of the men's workshops conducted by the first author. After we had introduced the concept of taking a time-out (i.e., leaving a volatile situation before violence occurs), Mr. M. tried it out during a particularly intense argument with his wife. His wife, unaware that he was implementing a violence-reducing strategy, tried strenuously to prevent him from walking out on her. She blocked the door, whereupon he pushed her out of the way and got into his car. She ran out the door and jumped on the hood of his car as he was pulling out. He accelerated quickly, in reverse, throwing her off the hood onto the driveway, resulting in a serious injury to her.

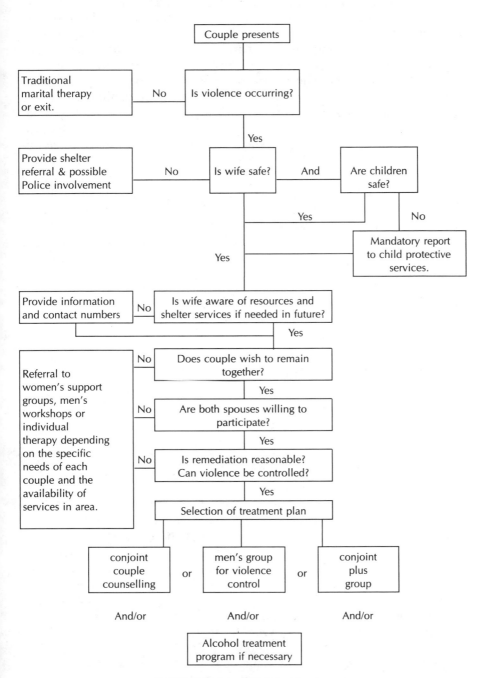

FIGURE 17-1. Assessment decision tree.

This technique is much more effective (and safe) when the wife is an informed participant, but even when the wives are informed of the husbands' need for withdrawal from an arguement, it is often very difficult to get them to refrain from pursuing their husbands to "finish the argument." The importance of this cooling-off period must be reemphasized frequently.

A word of caution: The choice of pursuing conjoint couples therapy must be tempered by the knowledge that abusive couples are volatile, and marital therapy often exposes sensitive issues that might provide an opportunity for violence. Certain forms of therapy, for example assertiveness training for the wife, may be particularly productive of violence and must be cautiously implemented. Moreover, since many couples are separated (often the wife is at a shelter or living with friends or relatives), conjoint counseling necessitates bringing them together, at least for the session, providing an opportunity for harrassment and/or violence. This is also complicated by the fact that, for safety reasons, many shelters (and wives) choose to keep their locations secret. Bringing the couple together provides an opportunity for the husband to follow his mate back to her address. Providing the husband with individual (or group) treatment prior to conjoint counseling may prevent the occurrence of these difficulties or at least give the therapist a chance to assess whether the husband is using couples counseling as a ploy to gain access to his wife.

See Figure 17-1 for a summary of the assessment process.

TREATMENT CONCEPTUALIZATION

The contents of the interventions for maritally violent couples have many elements in common, regardless of the intervention format. Although in the Syracuse program we typically put the man into a 6-week educational workshop for abusive husbands before beginning marital therapy, programs that offer only conjoint therapy cover many of the same issues as the men's group, in the conjoint context.

The foci of intervention for abusive couples are attitude change and behavior change. Marital violence is a behavioral problem in the context of a sociocultural environment that has, throughout history, endorsed its legitimacy. Until recently, a man's right to "chastise" his wife for misbehavior was protected legally. Although marital violence is covered by the same assault-and-battery statutes that apply in cases of violence between strangers, abusive husbands are seldom arrested, and if arrested, they are infrequently tried, convicted, or sentenced for their acts (Sanson, 1979–1980). Similarly, marital rape is not considered a crime in most states (Russell, 1982). Since many abusive husbands grew up in homes where they witnessed their mothers being abused by their fathers, societal acceptance is reinforced by the presence of a violent role model. It is not surprising, therefore, that many abusive husbands come into therapy professing the belief that it is not only their right, but their duty as a husband, to abuse their wives physically. A second attitudinal problem concerns another aspect of the legitimacy of violence, namely, that violence is justified if the husband is provoked. Abusive husbands most frequently explain that they wouldn't hit their wives if (a) "She'd only listen to [obey] me"; (b) "she'd take better care of the kids and house"; (c) "she'd stop nagging or yelling at me"; and (d) "she'd stop talking back to me." The underlying belief being articulated is that there are circumstances under which a wife deserves to be hit. This belief is closely related to the belief that "she makes me do it," which is one of the many forms taken by the third major attitudinal problem: that the husband is not responsible for his violent behavior.

Acceptance of responsibility for the violence is probably the most important attitudinal change the abusive husband can make. The husband's belief that he is not really responsible for his violent behavior is expressed in several ways. Since violence is often associated with alcohol use, abusive husbands frequently blame the violence on the alcohol. In fact, it has been suggested that alcohol is used primarily to provide an acceptable method of disavowing responsibility for such behavior. Even in the absence of alcohol use, abusive husbands frequently contend that violence against the wife represents a loss of control. Finally, abusive husbands resist accepting the label of wife abuser. They frequently imply the acceptability of the "less serious" forms of violence with statements such as "I don't beat her, I only slap [push] her around a little."

Attitude change is also important for the abused wife. Years of verbal and physical abuse have often left her with damaged self-esteem, while restricted access to social contacts may have impaired her reality testing, resulting in the belief that she deserves to be abused and acceptance of the husband's contention that if she were only a better wife and mother, this would not happen. She, too, has grown up in a sociocultural context that legitimizes wife abuse and may have accepted violence as part of the wife role.

Counseling maritally violent couples is somewhat more didactic than traditional marital therapy with nonviolent couples. Most of the treatment approaches in the literature identify specific concepts that are transmitted to the couple. The following list represents a compilation of the concepts most frequently cited in the treatment literature.

1. The abuser is solely responsible for the violence. The victim cannot either cause or eliminate it.
2. Violence is a learned behavior. The abuser learned to be violent, most commonly in his family of origin. If the abuser can learn to be violent, he can also learn to be nonviolent.
3. Provocation does not equal justification. There are always nonviolent alternatives. There are no circumstances under which violence between spouses is legitimate.
4. Violence is detrimental to all members of the family, including the abuser. The violence to the victim may be obvious. Less obvious,

but perhaps equally serious, are the effects on the children. Violence is illegal, and the abuser can be arrested, tried, and jailed if convicted.
5. Once violence has occurred in a relationship it will most likely continue to occur unless changes are made.

TREATMENT STRATEGIES

The first step in the therapeutic process involves establishing ground rules. In addition to those that would typically be established in marital therapy, work with violent couples requires the additional rule that violence between spouses is unacceptable under any circumstances. Margolin (1979) suggests that this ground rule be backed up by the contingency that if violence does occur, the couple will separate. Since alcohol and/or drug use is so common among abusive husbands, a second rule is that spouses cannot come to a session in any state of intoxication. If this rule is violated, the session should be terminated, and a new appointment should be made. This rule is important, since it may endanger the wife and/or therapist to continue with the session if the husband is intoxicated. It should also be noted that sending the couple away for this reason might provoke the husband. It is important that clinics (or individual therapists) working with violent couples develop contingency plans for the protection of all parties involved. These plans should include providing for the availability of support personnel and an appropriate signal system for calling for assistance.

In some cases, the abuser may routinely bring a weapon to the session. This usually takes the form of a pocket knife, possibly doubling as a key fob. It is therefore important to set the rule that no weapons of any kind be brought to therapy. Since it is not advisable to frisk patients, enforcement of this rule is somewhat voluntary. Therapists should also exercise caution in clearing potential weapons from the desk top. Such items as letter openers, scissors, paperweights, and note spindles are best placed out of sight in a desk drawer.

Couples characterized by violence may be particularly resistive to therapy. Often the abusive husband is, at best, a reluctant participant, coerced into participation either by the courts or by his wife's ultimatum. Consequently, the occurrence of violence during therapy may provide the husband with an excuse to discontinue therapy. It may be useful, therefore, to establish the ground rule that each spouse has a responsibility to come to each session. Meeting with one spouse in the absence of the other often can be divisive, facilitating the destructive impression of a therapeutic alliance.

Once the ground rules and a set of contingencies for rule violations have been established, the dual goals of attitude change and behavior change can be pursued. Attitude change is primarily a psychoeducational process. The following case example demonstrates how the therapist uses material presented by the abusive husband to reframe loss of control as instrumental behavior.

THERAPIST: Tell me how the violence occurs?

PATIENT: Well, usually we'd be having an argument and she wouldn't listen to anything I'd say, and she'd keep at me, and I'd just lose control. Before I knew it, I'd be hitting her.

THERAPIST: So what you're telling me is that you lose control and become violent. You feel you can't stop yourself from hitting her.

PATIENT: Yeah, that's right doc.

THERAPIST: Let's talk about the argument for a minute. If I understand what you're saying, when you and your wife get into an argument, you have a hard time getting her to listen to you.

PATIENT: Exactly, sometimes I can't get a word in edgewise.

THERAPIST: She just keeps after you, yelling and criticizing, and you can't get her to stop.

PATIENT: No way.

THERAPIST: Except by hitting her.

PATIENT: It's the only way to shut her up.

THERAPIST: So, actually, hitting her is your way of taking control of the argument.

PATIENT (*after an embarrassed silence*): Well, when you put it that way, I guess it is.

THERAPIST: It may be a little hard to take responsibility for the violence at first, but when you think about it, it's a lot less scary than being out of control.

Similarly, the therapist deals with issues of empowerment ("Your wife cannot make you either start or stop hitting her"), provocation ("Violence is never justified, regardless of your wife's behavior"), and legitimacy ("Violence is neither a marital right nor a role requirement"). Violence is construed as choice behavior. The husband chooses violence because effective nonviolent alternatives are not in his behavioral repetoire.

Behavior change is the other goal of intervention strategies for violent couples. Such change also involves two components: strategies aimed at directly controlling the violence and strategies aimed at resolving the marital conflict that sets the stage for the production of violence.

Violence-control techniques most commonly include (*a*) identifying the cues that violence is imminent; (*b*) learning to take a time-out; (*c*) engaging in nonviolent alternative behaviors; (*d*) self-talk; and (*e*) relaxation. These can be taught in the session and, if necessary, supplemented by a self-help manual (see *Aggress-Less* by Goldstein and Rosenbaum, 1982, and *Learning to Live Without Violence* by Sonkin and Durphy, 1982, for examples of self-help violence control books written for the lay public).

Maritally violent men generally report being able to identify cues that violence may be forthcoming. The first phase of Walker's 1979 cycle theory of violence is the tension-building phase. During this period there is an escalation of intrafamilial tension, which both spouses can identify. Tempers become short, the husband may throw or break objects, arguments become more frequent, minor violence may occur. Many husbands report physical symptoms, such as tension headaches, knotting in the stomach, and occasionally an aura (such as would precede a seizure). Behavioral symptoms include restlessness, anxiety, and hyperactivity. In some cases, the husband or wife may be able to identify cues days or even weeks in advance, whereas in others the warning may be only hours or minutes before the violent incident. It is not unusual for the violence to follow a pattern. One couple reported that the wife was always, and only, beaten on Christmas. Another couple observed a 6-week cycle, and since no corresponding pattern of environmental events could be identified, a self-fulfilling prophecy explanation could not be ruled out.

Once the couple has learned to identify the cues, the time-out is introduced. In contrast to therapy with nonviolent couples, where talking out the problems is preferred, the violent couple must disengage from the argument and physically separate when violence is imminent. Spouses are taught to call a time-out, and further, to respect a time-out called by the other, even if they are not feeling the need for one. Sonkin and Durphy (1982) suggest that the husband leave the home and return in exactly 1 hour. Regardless of the length of the time-out, there is general agreement that the important factors are that the time-out be sufficiently long to preclude the possibility of violence and that the couple have developed and agreed on a plan to continue the discussion as soon as they can do so without the threat of violence (Margolin, 1979). "Suspending the argument in this manner is very different from a unilateral cessation of an argument, for example, one person simply walking away from the other, which predictably enhances the other's rage" (Margolin, 1979, p. 17).

An additional problem with the time-out concerns the fact that many abusive husbands construe leaving an argument as "loss of face." It is important, therefore, to reframe the time-out in positive self-esteem terms. Suggesting that taking a time-out is the more difficult behavior, requiring more strength of character, is sometimes helpful.

The time-out period is important for several reasons. First, it reduces the likelihood of violence by physically separating the spouses from each other and terminating the escalation of the argument. It also serves to eliminate the excuse of impulsivity or loss of control. If the husband has time to think about his behavior, the volitional aspect becomes more apparent. For this reason, therapists often advise the wife to lock herself in the bathroom or run to a neighbor's house if the husband is not a participant in therapy. Lastly, it provides an opportunity for the husband to relieve some of the tension or "blow off some steam." Husbands are frequently advised to engage in some nonviolent exercise, such as jogging, during the time-out, in order to facilitate this latter function. Husbands must be cautioned not to drink or drive during the time-out. Many abusive husbands report driving either too fast or recklessly if they drive during this period. They must also be cautioned not to engage in any aggressive activities, such as punching a wall or punching bag, as it has been demonstrated that rather than produce a cathartic effect, such activities actually increase the probability of aggressive behavior (Bandura, 1973).

Violent couples often lack adequate communication skills. Although this issue is dealt with as a relationship enhancer, one aspect of this defect, failure of the husband to "check out" some of his "irrational beliefs," directly relates to the production of violence. Self-talk is commonly utilized as a violence-control technique with abusers. The following case example demonstrates both the problem and the technique:

> Mr. P. worked several jobs. He typically left for work at 6:00 a.m. and often didn't get home until 8:00 in the evening. The weekends provided him with his only opportunity to catch up on some sleep. Mrs. P., on the other hand, didn't drive and depended on Mr. P. to take her shopping on the weekends. Mr. P. was lying in bed at about 10:00 a.m. on Saturday when Mrs. P. began intentionally making noise by slamming doors, yelling at the kids, and so on. Mr. P. began to get angry, telling himself that she didn't appreciate how hard he worked, that she felt he wasn't entitled to sleep late, that she was an ingrate, that she was always putting him down. As his anger built, he felt that he was about to become violent. Instead, he stopped himself and began to challenge some of his negative self-talk. Perhaps the noise was not intentional, maybe the kids were just misbehaving. She was entitled to get angry and slam things sometimes. Not everything that happened related to him. Perhaps he should check out his anger with her. Mr. P. went downstairs and confronted his wife with his concerns. He stated that he was really getting angry because he thought she felt he was not entitled to sleep late. She calmly denied his concerns and told him that she knew he didn't get enough sleep and was usually glad that he could get some sleep on weekends; however, she had a doctor's appointment at noon and was afraid she was going to be late. His anger defused, Mr. P. assured her that he would get ready in plenty of time to get her to the doctor's office, went back to sleep for a little while, and then woke up, dressed, and took her out. He reported that instead of the violence that would have occurred in the past, positive self-talk (plus communicating with his wife) resulted in a nonviolent, satisfactory outcome.

Techniques for identifying and changing negative self-talk are adequately described elsewhere (see, for example, A New Guide For Rational Living by Ellis and Harper, 1975). Alternatively, it has been suggested that self-talk be utilized for cueing violence-control techniques (Sonkin & Durphy, 1982). When the husband identifies a cue that he is becoming angry, he utilizes statements such as "I'm getting angry. Maybe it's time for a time-out. I should get out of this situation before things get much worse. Maybe I should go out for a walk." Although these do not directly challenge the negative self-statements that may be escalating the anger, they do distract the husband from such negative self-statements, and increase the likelihood of employing a violence-control strategy.

It has been suggested that violence evolves out of a buildup of tension (Walker, 1979). Relaxation training provides a method of reducing the tension that eventuates in a violent episode. Effective therapist-guided (e.g., Goldfried & Davison, 1976) or self-help (e.g., Rosen, 1977) programs abound in the literature. Purdy and Nickle (1981) suggest that abusers use anger as a cue for the need to relax. Both spouses (abuser and victim) can benefit from relaxation training. The abused wife is usually under a great deal of stress. In their study of 60 battered women, Hilberman and Munson (1977–1978) describe the stress: "The women were a study in paralyzing terror which is reminiscent of the rape trauma syndrome (Burgess and Holstrom, 1974) except that the stress was unending and the threat of the next assault everpresent. . . . Agitation and anxiety bordering on panic were almost always present" (p. 464). It has even been suggested that some abused wives provoke the beating as a way of taking control of the situation and getting the inevitable over with (i.e., getting to phase 3 of Walker's (1979) cycle, which is characterized by loving and contrite behavior) and reducing the stress of uncertainty. Relaxation training can provide the abused wife with an alternative mechanism for reducing stress.

A final method of violence control that has proven useful involves application of stimulus-control procedures. Spouses can often identify the specific behaviors or situations that are productive of violence. Many abusers, for example, report that standing up is almost always a prelude to violence. It is helpful, therefore, to advise batterers to remain seated during arguments and to use standing up as a cue to take a time-out. Certain rooms of the house may be "violence prone," and couples should be cautioned against arguing in those places. Similarly, violent arguments may be more likely at certain times (e.g., evenings and weekends). Many abusive husbands report that violence is more likely if the agrument is protracted. Keeping arguments short by utilizing the time-out may help avert violence. The situations for each couple may differ, suggesting that the typology of violent arguments be discussed with each couple in order to identify any idiosyncratic stimuli that might profitably be manipulated. Both spouses should utilize these techniques. For example, it is more likely that the husband will stand up if the wife stands up; the wife can help to reduce the length of arguments and can avoid arguing in problem rooms or at problem times.

RELATIONSHIP ENHANCEMENT

A fundamental premise of marital therapy for abusive couples is that interspousal violence is unacceptable. Anger, however, is not only acceptable in a marital relationship, it is natural and expected (Margolin, 1979). An important goal of therapy, therefore, is to help spouses deal with anger and disagreement nonviolently. To this end, behavioral techniques such as communication training and problem solving have been utilized successfully. These techniques are complicated and have been articulated in detail elsewhere. Since the application of these techniques with maritally violent couples does not differ from that with nonviolent couples, the reader is referred to Jacobson and Margolin (1979) and Gottman, Notarius, and Markman (1976) for excellent descriptions of these strategies.

It has been noted that marriages characterized by violence are particularly unsatisfactory to the couple. Research incorporating standardized measures of marital satisfaction typically demonstrate abusive couples to have significantly lower satisfaction scores than nonviolent discordant couples (Rosenbaum & O'Leary, 1981). Displeasing events clearly outnumber pleasing interactions for these couples. It has been suggested that techniques aimed at increasing the frequency of positive interactions (e.g., love days, caring and sharing days) be employed to improve the tone of violent marital relationships (Margolin, 1979).

Although behavioral approaches to conjoint therapy for abusive couples have gotten a great deal of the attention, they are certainly not the only ways of dealing with this population. Geller and Wasserstrom (1984) describe an approach based on a family–systems orientation, which they claim to have employed successfully with over 250 couples. An important contribution of the systems approach is the incorporation of other family members (most commonly the children) into the therapy process.

Similarly, others have approached marital therapy with violent populations from nonbehavioral orientations with apparent success. Brown and Brown (1983) describe the strategies they employ at the Couples Conflict Project of the Community Counseling Center in Salt Lake City, Utah, as paradoxical, strategic, or therapeutic double-binds. Such techniques may be particularly useful given the resistive nature of abusive couples. Again, these techniques have been described in detail elsewhere (see, e.g., Weeks & L'Abate, 1982).

In addition to the difficulties normally encountered in the course of marital therapy with nonviolent couples, violent couples present some unique problems. Therapy with abusive couples usually follows a somewhat disturbing pattern. It is not unusual to find an almost immediate cessation of violence on commencing marital therapy. This period of nonviolent, positive (in contrast to previous relations) interaction has variously been characterized as a "flight into health" (Geller & Wasserstrom, 1984) or "honeymoon period" (Brown & Brown, 1983) and may last several months. Unfortunately, the period is often followed by a recurrence of violence. It is important for therapists to anticipate the possible recurrence of violence and prepare couples for it. Geller and Wasserstrom (1984) conceptualize this regression as resistance to change and suggest that therapists emphasize the importance of change to each of the spouses and implement a plan to facilitate change, thus defusing the instrumental use of violence as a strategy to avoid change and maintain homeostasis in the relationship. Sometimes, when the husband-toward-wife violence stops, the wife who has been abused becomes the abuser, directing her anger and violence at the husband. This provocative behavior is often perplexing to the therapist. One wife characterized it as follows: "At first it felt so good that he wasn't beating me. Everything was good between us. Then it started to bother me. It was as though he was saying O.K., now that period is over, let's start fresh.' But it wasn't O.K. We couldn't start fresh because we weren't even. I owed him fifteen years of fear, humiliation, and pain. I had to hurt him; then we could be even and start over."

The implications of this phenomenon for long-term success are unclear. Since many abusive husbands attribute their violent behavior to provocation by the wife, there is a high probability that the husband will respond to this violence in kind. It also raises questions concerning the long-term prognosis for abusive couples. There is a possibility that, like pathological jealousy, marital violence may be fatal to the relationship. There is insufficient outcome research, with acceptably long follow-up to answer this question at present.

THERAPIST ISSUES

The recency of research and clinical interest in marital violence, it has been noted, places our knowledge regarding many aspects of treatment at a rudimentary stage. One area that has been somewhat neglected concerns the key skills and attributes that therapists need to work effectively with this population. Although based largely on clinical experience, some suggestions do emerge.

Abusive husbands often report feeling out of control; consequently, it is important for them to feel that the therapist can deal with their violence. Firm limit setting is one way to demonstrate this. Abusers may test the therapist by threatening or by the suggestion of violence. Rather than show fear (a natural enough response to threat), the therapist should counter with the consequences of such behavior on the part of the husband. During a men's workshop session, for example, one of the participants took out a penknife and began paring his nails as he informed the workshop leader that he would "kill anyone who messed with his head." The leader inquired as to what "messing with his head involved," and the response was, "I don't know, but I'll know if anyone does it." A bit later he responded to a question asked by the leader with the remark: "I think you're messing with my head." The leader then informed him and the group that such threats impaired group functioning. He reiterated the rule that weapons were not permitted and asked the participant to put the penknife away. He further emphasized that if threatened, he would call the police and have the man arrested. Needless to say, there is more rationality and calmness in the retelling; nevertheless, firm limit setting and the threat of recourse to the authorities were effective in averting either violence or hysteria. If this example implies that therapists working with abusers are in a dangerous position, such was not the intent. Our experience reinforces the belief that working with wife abusers poses no extraordinary hazards. Therapists working with the abused wives, on the other hand, may be perceived as antagonists by the abusive husband, who might then pose a threat to the therapist.

It is important for therapists to be able to accept the batterer without accepting his behavior. Abusers often come to therapy with defective self-concepts, expecting to be rejected or condemned by the therapist. Resistance to treatment will be activated by therapeutic nonacceptance. On the other hand, it must be remembered that the behavior is unacceptable, and therapists must avoid being seduced into complicity with the batterer. The first author recently supervised a co-leader team, the female member of which was a probation officer. One of the group members was awaiting sentencing, having been found guilty of assaulting his wife, and faced up to 3 years in prison. Although the leaders (and their supervisor) did not know it at the time, group attendance was an instrumental manipulation intended to influence the judge to a reduced sentence. After several sessions, the female co-leader was informed that the probation department was recommending a jail sentence (to the dismay of both co-leaders), which the judge would likely enforce. Based on only a few group sessions, she tried to intervene with his probation officer to change the decision (a move that the male co-leader supported). It was necessary to remind both leaders that failure by the judiciary to treat domestic violence as a serious crime is one of the factors contributing to the proliferation of this problem. Moreover, it was important for the abuser to learn that his behavior had real and negative consequences. Just as it is important not to look at the batterer as reprehensible, so it is important not to look at him as "not responsible."

Therapeutic alliances present a serious problem in conjoint couples counseling. Therapists must be on their guard not only to avoid such alliances but to avoid the appearance of an alliance, which might alienate one of the spouses and threaten the therapeutic relationship. This problem is even more probable in working with violent couples because the ground rules (notably that the primary concern is the protection and safety of the victim) practically prescribe an alliance with the wife–victim. Clear specification of the rules and the reasoning behind them at the outset of treatment, and openness concerning the therapist's behavior with regard to enforcing the rules, may provide some help. It may also help to emphasize the distinction drawn between responsibility for the violence (which belongs to the abuser) and responsibility for the discord (which is shared by the spouses). This allows the therapist to align with the victim with regard to violence while stepping back into a more impartial role in dealing with the discord.

Family violence poses serious ethical and legal problems for the therapist. All states, for example, have mandatory reporting laws for child abuse, which obligate mental health professionals (among others) to report all incidents of known or suspected child abuse to designated government agencies. Although such reporting may jeopardize the therapeutic relationship, failure to report carries specific legal sanctions (differing from state to state), which may jeopardize the therapist (e.g., revocation of license, fines, civil penalties). Although there are no mandatory reporting laws for spousal abuse, a number of legal issues pertain.

It has been noted that spouse abuse and child abuse often occur in the same families; therefore, there is a higher than normal probability that child abuse may be an issue for spouse-abusive couples. If so, all the reporting requirements for child abuse pertain, along with the consequent jeopardy to the therapeutic relationship.

Even in the absence of child abuse, circumstances in which the therapist had knowledge that the spouse was in imminent danger would require notification of the police and, if necessary, the intended victim, according to the provisions of the *Tarasoff* decision (*Tarasoff* v. *Regents of University of California*, 551 P.2d 334, 1976), that is, that the therapist "bears a duty to exercise reasonable care to protect the foreseeable victim of that danger" (p. 345). Such concerns would apply in situations where a spouse called the therapist during a beating, as well as in situations where the abuser indicated his intentions to abuse either during a session or in the context of a telephone contact. It is important to note that these suggestions are based on interpretation of the *Tarasoff* decision (itself an interpretation of California statutes). There has not, to our knowledge, been a legal test of these issues specifically involving marital violence.

If, during the course of therapy, it becomes apparent that the violence cannot be brought under control and that the most therapeutic course would be for the couple to terminate the marriage, "it is the therapist's ethical and moral responsibility to abdicate the role of relationship advocate and help the threatened person find protection (Margolin, 1979, p. 14). The reader is referred to Margolin (1982) and Rosenbaum (in press) for more complete discussions of these and other relevant legal issues.

CONCLUSION

It should be clear that marital therapy for spouse-abusive couples presents some unique problems and involves more than merely applying traditional techniques developed for nonviolent couples. Unfortunately, at present there has been insufficient specialization and attention to this population by marital therapists for the development of unique treatment approaches. Currently, the majority of intervention strategies for abusive couples represent hybrids of traditional approaches combined with violence-control strategies, typically employed in men's groups or in individual therapy with aggressive individuals. There remains the question of the effectiveness of these therapeutic procedures in reducing or eliminating marital violence. Since, on average, marital violence typically does not occur more than "several times a year" (Rosenbaum, doctoral dissertation), and it is not uncommon to find couples going 3 or 6 months without a violent incident, even without treatment, it seems prudent to require therapy outcome studies to provide sufficiently long follow-up data to accommodate the potential infrequency of violent episodes. At the least, the nonoccurrence of violence for 6 months posttreatment would seem a reasonable demonstration of therapeutic effectiveness.

Unfortunately, collection of such data is particularly difficult with abusive couples, and there are few published outcome studies with acceptable follow-up periods. There are, however, some indications that group approaches with abusers can effectively eliminate violence. Purdy and Nickle (1981), for example, reported a 59% success rate for the elimination of violence after 6 months. We can report comparable results based on some preliminary findings regarding the effectiveness of the Men's Educational Workshop Program at Syracuse. We have routinely collected follow-up data from each workshop completer every 3 months, if possible. To date, we have data on 11 of the 12 men who completed the program between December 1982 and September 1983. The results appear promising. Only one of the men has reported a recurrence of violence, a single incident of slapping that occurred 4 months postgroup. Two of the men have remained nonviolent through 18 months, four through 9 months, two through 6 months, and two through 3 months. We are still in contact with eight men, but have lost contact with two after 3 months and one after 6 months, and it is not known if they remained nonviolent after those contacts. In sum, more than two-thirds of the men completing the group have remained nonviolent for at least 6 months postgroup, while the recidivism rate was less than 10%. Such results, though based on a relatively small sample, suggest that group programs can have a positive impact on spouse-abusive men.

Although such groups may help to reduce violence, it is not clear that reducing violence alone, or even in the context of marital therapy, will increase marital satisfaction. Our prognosis for violent couples must remain guarded. We hope that, as therapists become more aware of these issues, effective strategies for dealing with the specialized problems of abusive populations will continue to evolve.

REFERENCES

Bandura, A. (1973). *Aggression: A social learning analysis*. Englewood Cliffs, NJ: Prentice-Hall.

Brown, J., & Brown, J. (1983). Therapeutic tactics in the treatment of marital violence. Unpublished paper; available at Parents United of Salt Lake City, Inc., West Valley City, UT.

Burgess, A., & Holstrom, L. (1974). *Rape: Victims of crisis*. Bowie, MD: Brady.

Coleman, K., Weinman, M. C., & Hsi, B. P. (1980). Factors affecting conjugal violence. *American Journal of Psychology*, 105, 197–202.

Curley, A. P., & O'Leary, K. D. (1980). *Psychological correlates of spouse abuse*. Paper presented at the annual meeting of The Association for the Advancement of Behavior Therapy, New York.

Ellis, A., & Harper, R. (1975). *A new guide for rational living*. North Hollywood, CA: Wilshire.

Finkelhor, D. (1983). Common features of family abuse. In D. Finklehor, R. J. Gelles, G. T. Hotaling, & M. A. Straus (Eds.), *The dark side of families*. Beverly Hills, CA: Sage.

Frank, P. B., & Houghton, B. D. (1982). *Confronting the batterer: A guide to creating the spouse abuse workshop*. New City: Volunteer Counseling Service of Rockland County.

Ganley, A. L. (1981). Counseling programs for men who batter: Elements of effective programs. *Response*, 4, 3–4.

Gayford, J. J. (1975). Wife battering: A preliminary survey of 100 cases. *British Medical Journal, 1,* 194–197.

Geller, J., & Walsh, J. (1977–1978). A treatment model for the abused spouse. *Victimology, 2* (3–4), 627–632.

Geller, J., & Wasserstrom, J. (1984). Conjoint therapy for the treatment of domestic violence. In A. R. Robards (Ed.), *Battered women and their families: Intervention Strategies and treatment programs.* New York: Springer.

Goldfried, M. R., & Davison, G. C. (1976). *Clinical behavior therapy.* New York: Holt, Rinehart and Winston.

Goldstein, A. P., & Rosenbaum, A. (1982). *Aggress-less: How to turn anger and aggression into positive action.* Englewood Cliffs, NJ: Prentice-Hall.

Gottman, J., Notarius, C. I., & Markman, H. (1976). *A couples' guide to communication.* Champaign, IL: Research Press.

Hilberman, E., & Munson, L. (1977–1978). Sixty battered women. *Victimology, 2*(3–4), 460–470.

Hornung, P. A., McCullough, B. C., & Sugimoto, P. (1981). Status relationships in marriage: Risk factors in spouse abuse. *Journal of Marriage and the Family, 43,* 675–692.

Jacobson, N. S., & Margolin, G. (1979). *Marital therapy: Strategies based on social learning & behavior exchange principles.* New York: Brunner/Mazel.

Kalmuss, D. (1984). The intergenerational transmission of marital aggression. *Journal of Marriage and the Family, 46,* 11–19.

Margolin, G. (1979). Conjoint marital therapy to enhance anger management and reduce spouse abuse. *American Journal of Family Therapy, 7*(2), 13–23.

Margolin, G. (1982). Ethical and legal considerations in marital and family therapy. *American Psychologist, 37,* 788.

Maurer, A. (1976). Physical punishment of children. Paper presented at the California State Psychological Association Convention, Anaheim, CA.

Nye, R. I. (1978). Is choice and exchange theory the key? *Journal of Marriage and the Family, 40,* 219–233.

Pagelow, M. D. (1981). Factors affecting women's decisions to leave violent relationships. *Journal of Family Issues, 2,* 391–414.

Patterson, G. R., & Reid, J. B. (1970). Reciprocity and coercion: Two facets of social systems. In C. Neuringer & J. Michael (Eds.), *Behavior modification in clinical psychology.* New York: Appleton-Century-Crofts.

Purdy, F., & Nickle, N. (1981). Practice principles for working with groups of men who batter. *Social Work with Groups, 4*(3–4), 111–122.

Rosen, G. (1977). *The relaxation book: An illustrated self help program.* Englewood Cliffs, NJ: Prentice-Hall.

Rosenbaum, A. (1979). Wife abuse: Characteristics of the participants and etiological considerations. Unpublished dissertation, available at Department of Psychology, SUNY at Stony Brook, Stony Brook, NY.

Rosenbaum, A. (in press). Family violence. In W. J. Curran, A. L. McGarry, & S. A. Shah (Eds.), *Modern legal psychology and psychiatry,* Philadelphia: Davis.

Rosenbaum, A., Goldstein, D., & O'Leary, K. D. (1980). An evaluation of the self-esteem of spouse abusive men. Paper presented at the American Psychological Association annual convention, Montreal, Canada.

Rosenbaum, A., & O'Leary, K. D. (1981a). Marital violence: Characteristics of abusive couples. *Journal of Consulting and Clinical Psychology, 49*(1), 63–71.

Rosenbaum, A., & O'Leary, K. D. (1981b). Children: The unintended victims of marital violence. *American Journal of Orthopsychiatry, 51*(4), 692–699.

Russell, D. E. H. (1982). *Rape in marriage.* New York: Macmillan.

Sanson, B. E. (1979–1980). Spouse abuse: A novel remedy for a historic problem. *Dickinson Law Review, 84,* 147–170.

Sonkin, D., & Durphy, M. (1983). *Learning to live without violence: A book for men.* San Francisco, CA: Volcano Press.

Spinetta, J. J., & Rigler, D. (1972). The child-abusing parent: A psychological review. *Psychological Bulletin, 77*(4), 296–304.

Straus, M. A., Gelles, R. J., & Steinmetz, S. K. (1980). *Behind closed doors: Violence in the American family.* New York: Doubleday.

Tarasoff v. *Regents of the University of California,* 551, P.2d. 334 (1976).

Walker, L. (1979). *The battered woman.* New York: Harper & Row.

Wasileski, M., Callahan-Chaffee, M. D., & Chaffee, R. B. (1982). Spousal violence in military homes: An initial survey. *Military Medicine, 147,* 761.

Weeks, G., & L'Abate, L. (1982). *Paradoxical psychotherapy: Theory and practice with individuals, couples, and families.* New York: Brunner/Mazel.

Jealousy and Extramarital Sexual Relations

LARRY L. CONSTANTINE

Jealousy and extramarital sexual relations often go together, but there is no *necessary* connection between the two. Jealousy might never enter in when an affair has been kept secret or is approved of by the spouse. Yet jealousy may be triggered by a mere conversation, or even by a work involvement with an inanimate machine. There is, nevertheless, a conceptual relationship between sexual jealousy and extramarital sex. As concepts, both are related to the perceived sexual boundaries of relationships. On this basis we are justified in considering them together as issues confronting the marital therapist, though some of the analysis must nonetheless be separate and distinct.

A PARADIGMATIC APPROACH

The discussion of treatment issues outlined in this chapter is grounded in a theoretical framework that is both systemic and paradigmatic. Both marital and extramarital relationships are seen as imbedded in a systemic context. All relationships exhibit redundant patterns of collective behavior requiring collaboration to be maintained. Thus, both jealousy and extramarital relations are best understood within the context of the larger system, and the interventions at this level or that take the system into account are more efficient and more likely to succeed.

Larry L. Constantine. Private practice, Acton, Massachusetts.

Relationship Paradigms

The paradigmatic framework (Constantine, 1984; in press) is based on the work of Kantor and Lehr (1975) and Reiss (1981). Couples and families operate as if guided by relationship paradigms, overarching images of their relationship and of marriage and families in general. These images function as the point of reference against which experience can be checked, defining the priorities to be assigned to competing ends, the ground rules by which action is guided, and the values by which behavior is judged. A paradigm is, then, not only a model but also a world view through which experiences in relationships will be interpreted. Although it is possible to catalogue the basic themes on which relationship paradigms are built, this goes beyond the scope of this chapter (see Constantine, in press).

The meaning of behavior, including the initiation of an extramarital affair or a fit of jealous rage, depends on the relationship context in which it is imbedded; both the significance and the functions of behavior are best understood within this systemic context, including the paradigmatic basis of the system. In one marriage, a single incident of extramarital intercourse might be symptomatic of a profound breakdown of the marital relationship; in another, ongoing affairs may function as a form of enrichment experience essentially unrelated to a couple's problems, presenting or underlying.

By understanding a couple's basic assumptions and ground rules, their relationship paradigm, the therapist gains a concise formulation for understanding their patterns in jealousy and extramarital behavior. Couples whose relationships are built on different ground rules, whose marriages are guided by distinct paradigms, may need to be approached differently in treatment (Constantine, 1984).

Therapeutic strategy and technique follow from a thorough assessment of the relationship system. Technique is not, here, the central concern, as "customized" techniques can always be created *ad hoc* to fit uniquely a given situation. Once the therapist understands the relationship system and its paradigmatic basis, particular interventions suggest themselves.

Therapy and Change

Relationship paradigms are reflected in observable behavior through relationship *structures* that regulate behavior, maintaining redundant patterns (Sluzki, 1983). Therapy may intervene directly at the level of behavior or may seek to alter the controlling structures of the relationship. Change is unlikely to persist unless both levels are influenced in turn. Change that runs counter to a couple's guiding relationship paradigms may be possible but will be more difficult and will take more energy to sustain. Paradigms in themselves are very resistant to change. Thus an understanding of the relationship at all three levels—paradigm, structures, and process—serves the therapist.

A relationship system is disabled when it is ineffective in resolving problems, in meeting goals defined paradigmatically, or when significant individual needs and goals within the relationship are consistently unmet. The goal of therapy is to enable the system to overcome these problems. Success is defined within the system by its members and will, therefore, also depend on relationship paradigms.

Exclusive and Nonexclusive Paradigms

The treatment of problems involving jealousy and extramarital relations must take into account a couple's assumptions about the sexual exclusivity or nonexclusivity of their relationship. Jealousy is not only likely to mean very different things under these two assumptions, but can be of significantly different importance. Obviously, the appropriate treatment goals and approaches may be quite distinct.

There are many variants and elaborations. For example, conventional marriages and partnerships, which are likely to constitute the bulk of the caseload of most marital therapists, usually assume sexual exclusivity. In effect, there is a proviso that extramarital sexual relations, should they occur, are not to be disclosed to the partner. Once extramarital relations are revealed, they will "count as" complete failure of the marriage, and the spouse will feel betrayed. There is often an in-built sex difference. Under conventional assumptions, males are less monogamously oriented than females; therefore, transgressions by males may be more expected and forgivable.

Relationships not rooted in assumptions of sexual exclusivity may also take many forms, from tacit mutual permission to conduct separate affairs to an *inclusive* paradigm that seeks to incorporate other relationships into the primary relationship.

A MODEL OF JEALOUSY

Sexual jealousy can be considered from many points of view: as behavior or as emotion, as a situational and context-dependent response or as a trait or disposition within the individual, as a feature of a specific marital system or as an aspect of culture. At various times and for various purposes, each view has some utility for the therapist and should be integrated in a clinical model of jealousy.

Increasingly, therapists and researchers have come to regard jealousy as an emotional response to a perceived threat of loss in a significant relationship (Constantine, 1976). The felt response of jealousy may be expressed behaviorally in various ways that can be either functional or dysfunctional in a particular situation within a particular relationship. In itself, then, jealousy is neither good nor bad; and jealous behavior, like most behaviors, may serve almost any purpose in a relationship.

Jealousy, by this definition, involves at least three distinct components: recognition of loss or threat of loss, emotional response, and behavioral expression. All three aspects represent potential points of intervention or focuses for treatment.

Culture and Context

There is some debate about whether sexual jealousy is truly cross-culturally universal (Hupka, 1981; Reiss, 1983), but there is little argument that it appears in some form in nearly all cultures. The contexts in which it is more likely to appear and the behaviors by which it may acceptably be expressed vary substantially between cultures. Thus ethnicity must be taken into account (McGoldrick et al., 1982). Shouted attacks and threatened violence may be expected within a working-class Italian community on the East Coast. Such behavior would be rare and highly symptomatic among the more quietly stoic, middle-class Lutherans of the Midwest.

Individual Disposition

There is little doubt that some portion of jealousy may be attributed to individual traits or predispositions. The general propensity for jealousy, the specific situations perceived as threatening, and the particular behaviors by which jealousy may be expressed are all probably related to individual styles of participating in relationships.

A number of studies have consistently reported moderate but significant correlations between jealousy and various individual-trait measures. Jealous persons tend to be self-deprecating, dissatisfied and unhappy, anxious, dogmatic, and externally controlled (Bringle, 1981). Consistently over many studies, few differences between males and females have been found. A moderate but significant relationship exists between jealousy and androgyny: Individuals reporting more sex-stereotyped attitudes also reported more jealousy (Bringle, 1981; Hansen, 1983).

A therapist may be more or less disposed to see jealous behavior as characteristic of the individual. Regardless of the therapist's commitment to a "systemic formulation," individual dispositional factors need to be considered. Within couples, partners are more likely to see their own jealousy as situational while attributing their partners' jealousy to "personality." ("Oh, I get jealous under some circumstances, but Floyd is a jealous person.")

The Structure of Jealousy

Viewed systemically, jealousy involves three players: the jealous person, the partner with whom there is a valued relationship, and the rival or agent who precipitates the jealous response. The interaction of the partner and the agent are perceived as threatening or imbalancing the relationship so that something valued in the relationship is or might be lost by the jealous person. In systemic terms, this represents a threat to or violation of the boundary of the relationship between the jealous person and the partner (Constantine, 1976).

RELATIONSHIP BOUNDARIES AND THE THREAT OF LOSS

In assessing the seriousness or "reality" of the threat triggering jealousy, the therapist should keep in mind that *anything* valued in the relationship may be at stake: loss of face, status, or ego enhancement; loss of gratification, including, sexual, intellectual, and emotional; loss of control or power; loss of stability and predictability; loss of privacy or exclusive access; loss of time or contact. The entire couple relationship may not be at stake. The extramarital relationship as a whole may not be the threat. Exploring what is at stake is of obvious diagnostic value to the therapist and may help the clients find alternative arrangements that are less threatening.

JEALOUS BEHAVIOR

Jealous behavior may take many forms and be directed toward either the partner or the rival. Whitehurst (1971) classified a variety of jealous behaviors on the basis of their impact on relationships and relationship boundaries. Jealousy may be expressed through isolational behaviors—for example, withdrawal, withholding, or fight evasion—which do not enhance the relationship and which interfere with resolution of problems. Antagonistic behaviors—quarreling, intrusive interrogation, or taking revenge, for example—maintain contact between partners, though in a negative way that might neither enhance the relationship nor favor resolution. Redefinitional actions attempt to redefine threat through externalization, intellectualization, and ratio-nalization. The relationship boundary is strengthened as a couple unite in perceiving a common enemy in "the failure of marriage" or "temptations," but effective resolution may become deferred. Behaviors directed at resolution, including negotiation and joint problem solving, may be rare, but they support the relationship boundary while potentially moving the couple toward more effective functioning.

Recognizing jealousy as behavior and the variety of ways in which it may be expressed opens the option of working at the behavioral or process level to influence the couple system toward better functioning. Jealousy as an emotion need not be addressed.

EXTRAMARITAL SEXUAL RELATIONS

Although many behaviors have been classified under extramarital sexual relations and may be important in specific cases, sexual intercourse with someone other than a spouse remains the focal issue in most cases. To understand the clinical significance of extramarital sex (EMS), the therapist must be aware that EMS is a cultural anomaly, a behavior widely practiced yet still disapproved of by the vast majority of Americans (Christensen, 1973). It is a common fact of marital life. Estimates vary with samples and methodology, but reported EMS frequencies range from 30% to as many as 60% of men and from 25% to 40% of women (Libby, 1977). EMS could thus be a factor in more than three-quarters of all marriages. In client populations the frequency is likely to be comparable or even greater: Of the caseload of one sample of marriage counselors, 46% (Humphrey & Strong, 1976) involved EMS, and 60% of clients of another group of researchers eventually disclosed EMS (Green et al., 1974). EMS appears to be slowly on the rise, and, as with other sexual behaviors, the gap between women and men is narrowing.

Despite its ubiquity, between 70% and 75% of Americans consider EMS wrong under all circumstances. Marriage counselors and therapists apparently are no exceptions to double standards in this area. In one survey (Knapp, 1975), 31% of marriage counselors (clinical members of a major professional organization) reported having engaged in EMS, although, depending on the form it took, only 13% to 28% personally approved of EMS. In another sample from the same group (Humphrey & Strong, 1976), 38% of therapists admitted to having had an extramarital affair, though 58% opposed their spouses having an affair.

The therapist's manifest or implicit attitudes in therapy influences the likelihood of client disclosure. Despite its prevalence, some therapists may have little EMS reported to them. This may be especially true if only conjoint interviews are held; Humphrey (1982) has argued that some individual sessions are necessary if most cases are to be disclosed to the therapist. The clinical issues relating to EMS have not been considered extensively. A modest clinical literature has accumulated in recent years, much of it with a marital or couples therapy perspective (Constantine et al., 1972; Elbaum, 1981; Humphrey, 1982; Peck, 1975; Sprenkle & Weiss, 1978; Strean, 1976; Thompson, 1982).

Functions of EMS

Extramarital sexual relations, like any interpersonal behavior, may serve many different purposes and be interpreted differently by different couples. In some relationships, EMS may be regarded as symptomatic. It may serve neurotic needs or be an integral part of the relationship dysfunction. For other couples, EMS may be essentially irrelevant to treatment or even a positive and beneficial part of their relationship. It may be useful to keep in mind that behavior as common as EMS is, in some sense, "normal" and is extremely unlikely to be evidence of individual or relationship "pathology" in all cases (Thompson, 1982).

TREATMENT OF JEALOUSY
AND EXTRAMARITAL RELATIONS

To a considerable extent the treatment issues in jealousy and EMS overlap. Both have varied meanings and serve various purposes in different relationships. Moreover, EMS as a manifest problem is frequently accompanied by expressed jealousy.

The Choice of System

A systemic view highlights the therapist's choice of system on which to focus. The system in which jealousy is imbedded is always larger than the couple system and includes the precipitating agent. It is not necessary that this "outsider" be included in therapy sessions to be a part of the therapy. To understand the whole context, however, the therapist does need the larger purview. Inclusion of the precipitating agent in actual therapy should be considered as a possibility; it is consistent with a marital and family systems focus and can itself constitute a significant intervention.

> One husband's jealousy diminished markedly after a session in which he finally encountered his "rival" and got to see his wife with the man. The husband's fantasies about the man's superior attractiveness and personal magnetism vanished when it became clear how ordinary he was. The husband saw his rival's behavior with his wife as somewhat "wimpish" and ambivalent, while his wife readily expressed disapproval toward her lover. The husband concluded the affair presented little threat to him or his marriage.

The question of including extramarital partners in the therapy is a complicated but important one. Where EMS occurs, it is likely to be an important aspect of the relationship context. Ongoing affairs, especially, are a part of the couple system that can offset or undermine therapeutic gains unless understood and taken into account by the therapist. Varying advice has been offered on dealing with extramarital partners, ranging to the extreme of insisting in every case that all EMS contacts discontinue at the start of therapy (Elbaum, 1981). Teismann (1979) argues that the rival's "influence" must be "neutralized" to gain control over therapy, suggesting that this be accomplished by inviting the extramarital partner into therapy, an invitation usually declined. The therapist then insists that EMS should continue so that the problem can be thoroughly assessed. Such tactics used as formulas for general treatment can hardly be responsive to relationship paradigms or other differences among couples, although the tactic may be indicated in specific cases.

The question whether to draw extramarital partners into the therapy should not be confused with the issue of the therapist's approval or disapproval of the extramarital relationships. This distinction must also be made clear to the client couple. The therapist can stress that the purpose is strictly for the betterment of the couple's relationship, that they should look to this as an opportunity to understand each other better and strengthen their relationship. The therapist can clarify boundaries through the language used. ("I think we have a lot to gain at this point by inviting Daryl to come help in your therapy for a few sessions. The more he keeps coming up as an issue, the more you two seem to be confused. Having him 'come visit' a few times should help you two to straighten some of this out for yourselves.")

Perhaps because of the lack of precedents in normal social intercourse, therapists often feel at a loss as to what to do in a session where clients meet with an extramarital partner. However, the situation can be seen as not altogether unlike other family contexts more familiar to systems-oriented therapists—for example, a session that includes a child or other relative with whom one of the marital partners is intensely or overly involved and by whom the other partner is threatened. The extramarital partner and the threatened spouse may be encouraged to talk openly, as their engaging inexorably shifts the balance in the three-way relationship. The therapist's primary obligation remains to the client couple, but this must not preclude compassion and sensitivity toward the extramarital partner, who may be in an even more awkward and vulnerable position than either spouse. It is not ultimately functional for a couple's relationship to rest on the scapegoating of an outsider. A joint session used as a cathartic venting of hostility toward the "other woman or man" may be particularly destructive, regardless of how much it may seem to relieve some tension between the client couple. The therapist has the obligation to prepare the clients adequately to assure that joint sessions can be used constructively. Family sculpture can be useful to clarify multiple perspectives on the relationships, especially when discussions tend to degenerate into confrontation.

In sessions, the therapist might demonstrate alignment with the couple by sitting with them, facing the extramarital partner. Limiting the number of sessions involving the "visitor" is also good boundary setting; rarely would more than two or three be held unless there were a change in the "unit of treatment." (Occasionally a couple with an open marriage may request this.)

The inclusion of EMS partners in therapy sessions is usually indicated for couples with a nonexclusive relationship, especially the "inclusive" variety of an open marriage where a form of expanded-family network is formed. Although most therapists are reluctant to include EMS partners in therapy (Humphrey, 1982), doing so can give therapy a powerful boost. On the other hand, a careful assessment could indicate that a couple's overinvolvement with extrafamilial members helps sustain their disablement by deflecting attention from critical problems or by drawing outsiders into their conflicts.

The Moores complained of a lack of energy in their marriage and a perfunctory quality in their sexual relationship. Both complained of feeling overwhelmed by work and demands from children. Each had two regular EMS partners whom they saw once or twice a week, and they suggested that these partners, who were "part of the family," be brought in for joint sessions. The therapist, seeing the shortage of time for the couple to be alone together, declined, saying that he did not disapprove in principle, but could not himself deal with so much complexity and competing demands. His statement was a symbolic mirror of the couple's difficulties. Excluding the EMS partners from therapy was a structural intervention clarifying the couple's boundaries and creating time that was "just theirs."

Diagnostic Issues

Chronic jealousy, that is, expressed jealousy as a frequent and repeated pattern in a couple's interactions, can be approached with the same structural, strategic, and problem-solving tools used with any such pattern (Teismann, 1979; Im et al., 1983).

Extreme or "pathological" jealousy is a manifestation of chronic, seriously disturbed relationship patterns. The partner expressing the jealousy is easily seen as having deep-seated problems requiring intensive individual therapy. Although concurrent individual work may well be indicated, the marital therapist should not lose sight of the fact that the partners chose each other and are in a self-maintaining system. If the "victim" and the couple system are not also helped to change, progress in individual therapy may be impeded or may lead to the fracturing of the relationship.

The choice of approach to treating sexual jealousy is likely to be influenced by the clients' and the therapist's perceptions of the jealousy. If jealousy is seen as a symptom of "deeper" relationship difficulty or personal problems, the therapist is not likely to employ techniques or strategies aimed at "symptom relief," that is, intended directly and simply to reduce the frequency and intensity of jealousy in itself. Such approaches may appeal more generally to behaviorists, but may also be indicated for couples troubled by jealousy but with otherwise fairly functional nonexclusive marriages.

In general, the therapist should be interested in how jealousy or EMS fits in a given relationship: how it is generated and sustained and/or what function it serves in the system. The system that employs, generates, and sustains it includes, of course, not only the couple but also the extramarital partner(s) and/or the precipitating agent.

With respect to jealousy, specific key questions may affect the choice of tactic and strategy. Is the jealous behavior ego-syntonic or ego-dystonic for the jealous person? This can indicate a possible approach for individually focused intervention and may be predictive of the difficulty of change. If jealousy is experienced by the jealous client as uncontrollable yet undesired behavior or as behavior that is "basically not me," then behavioral and rational-emotive approaches may have a better chance of succeeding. Delivered with appropriate timing, the paradoxical technique of prescribing the symptom is often effective in bringing ego-dystonic responses under the individual's control, but is less likely to succeed in ego-syntonic cases.

A similar question is whether the jealousy is "syntonic" or "dystonic" with the paradigmatic basis of the relationship and with how the couple view themselves. Whether the relationship is intended to be exclusive, nonexclusive, or inclusive is, of course, an essential paradigmatic issue.

Except for those radically committed to an exclusively symptom-focused behavioral or problem-solving approach, most therapists will be interested in whether the jealousy or EMS is (a) essentially symptomatic of some other basic systemic disablement; (b) dysfunctional in and of itself; or (c) functional, that is, largely appropriate under the circumstances and for the most part useful for the couple. In the latter case, the old engineering maxim may be apropos: "If it works, don't fix it!"

Technique and Tactic

There is no shortage of techniques for treating or dealing with jealousy; a considerable array of them have been described by Ard (1977), Blood and Blood (1977), Constantine (1976), Francis (1977), Teismann (1979), Im et al. (1983), and others. Somewhat fewer tactics have been described specifically for dealing with EMS (e.g., Elbaum, 1981; Sprenkle & Weiss, 1978). The trick, as in all therapy, is to fit the technique to the situation. In fact, many of the techniques reported in the literature are variants of standard problem-solving and strategic techniques apparently modified to fit unique situations.

RELABELING AND REFRAMING

Jealous behavior may be relabeled as an expression of concern and caring. The therapist may use language suggesting positive aspects (Teismann, 1979), for example, referring to jealousy as passionate, involved, or sensitive, although the therapist needs to consider whether reinforcing conventional "sexual scripts" (Sprenkle & Weiss, 1978) is desirable in the long run in relation to the couple's relationship paradigm. Pejorative labeling of jealousy (e.g., as immature or a manifestation of insecurity or low self-esteem), whether by clients or therapists, is generally counterproductive.

Expressed jealousy may be regarded as a behavioral cue pointing to aspects of a relationship needing attention (Constantine, 1976). This nearly neutral reframing of jealousy is particularly useful for couples with relatively good communication skills whose paradigm supports explorative discussion of problems.

Where a couple or one partner is caught up in a sense of failure or betrayal engendered by an affair, positive relabeling of the EMS can be liberating. EMS may be reframed as a desperate attempt to draw attention and regain contact with the partner (Elbaum, 1981). An affair can be identified as a call for help that was successful in bringing the couple into therapy. The EMS itself or the failure to disclose it can be taken as a sign of commitment to the marriage: The "offending" partner "obviously" preferred the "burden of secrecy" or the "shame of an affair" or "to live with anxiety" or "to struggle with being pulled apart" rather than end the marriage.

An important strategy that may sometimes be the most effective way for dealing with highly charged marital and family issues is essentially to ignore them, at least temporarily, or to relegate them to a subordinate role in therapy. This can be especially useful where the issue is so "hot" that it becomes a trap, a constant distracter for the therapist as well as the family. Where the dysfunction that supports the disturbed behavior is pervasive and entrenched, focusing on the hot issue can detract from facilitating basic change.

The therapist reframes "the problem" as "not the problem" or "something else," in some cases telling the clients that the "real problems" are elsewhere. In difficult cases, the therapist may persuade clients that, bad as the EMS may seem, it is only the surface, hiding other problems. As the relationship improves, the hot issue becomes easier to deal with or may even disappear. Because of the strong taboos associated with it and the intense emotional reactions it may trigger, extramarital sexual relations may serve to detract both the clients and the therapist from addressing other issues. This is especially the case where affairs are actually in the past but the couple persists in fighting over them.

ROLE PLAYING AND ROLE REVERSAL

Role playing has several uses in treatment of jealousy and EMS. By having the couple act out actual or representative situations involving jealous behavior, the sequence of events involved in jealousy situations is more precisely and vividly revealed. In one case, role playing revealed that instances of jealousy by the husband occurred at meals he had cooked and at which he perceived his wife to be "far away." He was found to be in competition with her lover over who could "feed" her best. On the night after she had been to a fancy restaurant with her lover, the husband would try to cook a culinary masterpiece. If she was not sufficiently dazzled, he would get jealous.

Role playing can also be useful as a form of "desensitization," as well as a tool for training in better coping methods. The couple can be encouraged to role-play anticipated or imagined situations and to try various strategies for dealing with them (Ard, 1977).

Role reversals, whether as role plays in sessions or as between-session assignments, can disrupt interaction patterns and increase mutual empathy. Role reversal may be indicated where one partner's behavior (e.g., jealous interrogation) is more representative of the response desired from the other partner (Im et al., 1983). The jealous person, for example, may want attention and interest from the partner, attention that the rival seems to be getting. This desire is manifest in invasive interrogation of the partner. When the partner is told to take on that role, the jealousy diminishes. "Symptom transfer" is a specialized form in which the therapist attributes symptoms reported by one partner to the other and assigns the "helping" role to the originally symptomatic partner (Teismann, 1979). For example, a seething, vengefully jealous husband is told that his wife is like a volcano, waiting to erupt. His symptoms are thus attributed to her. The therapist engages the jealous client in the "arduous task" of helping her to deal with her anger more directly and productively. In order to coach her, the husband is learning new behaviors, for example, stress-management techniques that he will demonstrate to her.

Role reversal need not be bilateral. If one partner is more accessible, compliant, or committed to therapy and the relationship, he or she may be assigned a symptom reversal and directed to "pretend" to be the opposite. Carefully coached nonjealous behavior from a "jealous person" can interrupt an antagonistic spiral and lead to more positive responses.

Taking into account the entire "jealous system" clarifies the essentially complementary and collaborative nature of a couple's problems with jealousy. There are many variants. The jealous person may disown the jealousy or attempt to suppress it, but it becomes manifest in intrusive questioning, which the partner resents. The partner reciprocates with defensiveness and withholding of information. Once the jealous person owns the jealousy and expresses it directly, the need for defensiveness and evasion is reduced. This approach is especially appropriate where the real threat to the couple's relationship is minimal or nonexistent.

The partner may withhold information, often in the hope that this will avoid triggering jealousy. But the jealous person often feels left out and may be starved for information. In this informational vacuum, insecurity is increased and the jealous person becomes hypersensitive, which, in turn, justifies the partner's withholding. In such cases, "flooding" the client with information, as in the technique of "Scrupulous Honesty" (Im et al., 1983), disrupts the cycle and can help the couple develop more functional means of dealing with EMS and jealousy.

EXAGGERATION AND PRESCRIBING THE SYMPTOMS

Marital conflict may be escalated or jealous behavior exaggerated to absurd proportions at the urging of the therapist (Im et al., 1983). When a couple's problematic behavior is supported by a rigid internal logic that seems perfectly rational to them, they may be expected to reject the therapist's irrationality or fail in the absurd burlesque, settling into a new, more adaptive logic. More broadly, "prescribing the symptoms" is most effective when problematic behaviors are experienced as ego-dystonic or when the client reports an inability to control the behavior. For example, a husband reports that he doesn't know why he flirts so provocatively but can't seem to stop himself from doing it. He is told that this is an important part of himself, that he has something he is trying to learn, and that he should not stop, but should flirt deliberately. The wife is praised for understanding his need to find out about himself and is told to encourage his flirting by pointing out women she thinks he will find attractive. In this case, the threatened wife succeeds in her symptom reversal, but the husband is unable to carry out the assignment. The prescription is, of course, a therapeutic bind, because to continue flirtations would also put him in control of the symptoms.

Past but discontinued affairs can present numerous problems. Trust may be seriously eroded. Partners may be unable to overcome their sense of betrayal, which is generally stronger when a secret affair is finally disclosed than when an affair was conducted more or less openly from the start. The "injured party" may be unable to let go of feelings of hurt, rejection, or anger, while the "offender" may feel constrained and resentful that "reform" has not resulted in being "pardoned." A negative spiral is sustained, which may well push either party to another, possibly more detrimental, affair.

A ritual or rite of passage may be needed to help the couple start a new relationship. Picking up on the legalistic language couples often use, Im and colleagues (1983) have used the metaphor of "crime and punishment" to punctuate the end of the affair. The "offender" is "punished" by the "injured party" in a ritual that is actually a "benevolent ordeal" chosen to fit the "crime" and the relationship. (A husband was told that he must endure and disclose every detail of his affair in an interrogation by his wife. For her, this amounted to prescribing symptoms, as she was intrusively suspicious and distrusting of him.)

> One couple who appeared to be escalating their brief experiment with "open marriage" into divorce were told that the next session was going to be an enactment of their divorce to prepare them for what might happen. They were directed to prepare their "cases" during the week. The therapists conducted mock divorce proceedings, playing the roles of judge, witnesses, and attorneys. The "judge" asked the couple to explain what went wrong and why they should be granted a divorce. The question of custody of their young daughter was raised. The session resulted in a moving recommitment to the relationship.

IMAGE AND METAPHOR

The structure of jealousy highlights the significance of system boundaries in extramarital relations. Exploring and clarifying perceptions of individual and couple boundaries can be useful diagnostically as well as therapeutically. The most direct approach is through "imagistic" techniques which rely on spatial metaphors for relationship boundaries. Drawings and art constructions may be useful, but there is more experience with family sculpture (Duhl et al., 1973; Constantine, 1978) for dealing with jealousy and EMS.

In sculpture techniques, clients position themselves or representative objects to create a spatial metaphor for their relationship, thus clarifying the relationship and role of extramarital partners. Relationship sculpture can even be carried out on a game board (see, e.g., Cromwell et al., 1980).

> A husband chose the black queen to represent his wife ("the Queen of Sheba") and placed it in the center of a chess board. The pawn he used to represent himself was "in the corner." His paramour, represented by a white rook (a "castle"), was near the pawn but between it and the queen. ("She protects me, makes me feel safe.") This raised the important issue of what made him feel unsafe with his wife, what he felt he needed protection from, and

what it felt like to her to be the "big, powerful queen" with a "poor serf of a husband."

Personal-boundary sculptures have been effective in helping couples deal with issues of invasion and intrusion (Constantine, 1976). In this form of spatialization, the client is helped to map out the shape and extent of his or her personal space or "zone of comfort" by responding to repeated and varied approaches by the therapist or others. This is a metaphor that often closely reflects how a person responds to actual approaches by others (Duhl *et al.*, 1973).

After a woman indicated that she experienced her "personal space" to extend about 3 feet in front of her when she was simply approached by her husband with his hand outstretched, the therapist asked her husband to advance toward her with his lips pursed. She told him to back up; not until his back was against the wall did she say she was comfortable again. The therapist had noted the husband's expression before: whenever he was denying jealousy of one of her co-workers.

INDIVIDUAL FOCUS

Many techniques reported for treatment of jealousy are essentially focused on individuals. Among these are approaches based in the cognitive theories of emotion and in rational–emotive therapy as exemplified in the work of Ellis (1977). The object of this approach is to uncover and influence the basic beliefs and assumptions underlying the reaction, thus changing the interpretation given to events or to the individual's own emotional responses.

One of the rational–emotive concepts that has proven most useful in dealing with jealousy concerns the function of "rehearsal" in sustaining emotional experience. The basic assumption is that feelings are spontaneous reactions to situations and are self-limiting in the absence of continual "rehearsal" in which the individual thinks about the feeling or about things that regenerate the feeling. This approach seems to work best when the client reports jealousy as a prolonged, largely affective experience. The client is helped to become aware of the rehearsal process and the specific pattern of thoughts contributing to the ongoing affect.

In an approach resembling the common behavioral technique of systematic desensitization, another form of "rehearsal" used by Ard (1977) may be effective. In a carefully graded, step-by-step process a couple is encouraged to talk about and role-play anticipated and potential jealous situations.

NONEXCLUSIVE RELATIONSHIPS: SPECIAL ISSUES

In a recent national study (Blumstein & Schwartz, 1983), 15% of married couples reported having an agreement allowing for EMS. Most clinicians, however, report that nonexclusive relationships constitute only a few percent of their caseload; only a few attest to increases in open marriages in recent years, some reporting as many as 30–40% of clients with open marriages (*Marriage & Divorce Today*, 1973). Having dealt only with the therapeutic fallout from extramarital affairs and such alternative relationships as "open marriage," most clinicians have been understandably reluctant to grant the possible validity of relationships that are not sexually exclusive. Some attempts have been made to develop clinical perspectives that are more neutral toward variant sexual life styles and that do not either automatically defend these variants or universally view them as "pathological."

Developmental perspectives have been commonly used in the search for a broader framework. Coleman (1977) has drawn parallels between relationship development in nonmarital and marital dyads. Thompson (1982) has argued that both exclusivity and nonexclusivity may at different times be regarded as stage-appropriate behavior in the context of long-term marital relationship development. Clients' extramarital relations are not to be taken casually by the clinician, but neither are they to be automatically assumed to be detrimental, for they may play an important role in contributing to a couple's ability to understand the interrelationship of love, sex, and commitment.

Ryals and Foster (1976) employed the theory of ego development (Loevinger, 1966) in analyzing the demands posed by an open marriage as posited by O'Neill and O'Neill (1972). They argue that only individuals who have reached the rather advanced *autonomous* stage of ego development are likely to be successful in open marriages. The autonomous person recognizes the autonomy needs of others, has overcome excessive striving and overresponsibility, replacing moral dichotomies with an awareness of the complexity of real people and real situations. Peabody (1982) considers it essential for the clinician to assess ego development in order to understand the extent to which a particular sexual life-style choice is functional for a given couple.

Contractual Arrangements

Contracts or explicit, detailed agreements on the nature and limits of extramarital behavior are espoused by many therapists for dealing with EMS. These are assumed to be rational and concrete ways to regulate the impact of EMS on the couple, especially in the case of nonexclusive relationships.

The therapist needs to be aware of the tradeoffs involved when couples negotiate EMS contracts, since there are always both advantages and disadvantages to such agreements. The process of negotiation can be useful in itself, regardless of whether agreement is reached. The negotiation can help to clarify the partners' individual boundaries, how each perceives the boundaries of their relationship as a couple, what each may experience as threatening and what is perceived as "safe," what each has to gain from various kinds of extramarital relationships, and what the nature of their investment in the couple relationship may be.

An advantage of an explicit "contract" is that each partner knows specifically what is acceptable and unacceptable in outside relationships. A major disadvantage is that the negative impact of any "violation" of personal or couple boundaries is amplified. The "wronged" partner often feels hurt and betrayed because of the violation of the agreement itself, over and above whatever might otherwise be felt in a given situation. Anger and righteous indignation are often expressed, and the level of later distrust is increased. However explicit and detailed the agreement, there will always remain some ambiguity and room for interpretation. Violation of the agreement may be unintentional.

A very small departure from a highly explicit agreement may constitute a breach of contract. In the absence of a completely spelled-out contract, an isolated, situational departure from the understood norms for EMS might well be overlooked or forgiven. With a contract, it is almost invariably seen as breaking the agreement and an occasion for anger, depression, outrage, or revenge.

Relationships are also generally more fluid and evolving than are contracts. Even where it is understood that the contract is renegotiable, unless there is frequent reassessment of the viability of the contract, it is likely to lag considerably behind changing circumstances and personal development.

Clinical experience suggests that contracts, especially written ones, may in themselves often be symptomatic, at the least potentially indicating some lack of trust between the partners. Couples with a solid foundation of basic trust, who believe in each other's essential goodwill and intentions, probably have little need for elaborately constructed agreements. A general awareness of each other's vulnerabilities will suffice. On the other hand, a couple whose mutual trust is limited may be ill served by casting their insecurity in concrete, especially if they have already demonstrated their untrustworthiness in the relationship.

When personal boundaries are consistently respected, they diminish in salience. Respect for one's partner's vulnerabilities and insecurities builds trust. Isolated trespasses are more easily overlooked, and, with time, security in the relationship may replace insecurity, obviating the need for some self-protective restrictions on EMS.

Research does not support the general superiority of any particular set of ground rules (Buunk, 1980, 1981). However, clinical experience suggests that couples are likely to have trouble with ground rules that depart significantly from their relationship paradigm. Thus a couple with an essentially closed, traditional marriage may have trouble with a policy of complete openness and honesty, just as ground rules to regulate EMS strictly and keep everything about it private and unshared may be difficult in a marriage founded on openness and flexibility.

Tools and Skills

In general, communication skill building is best reserved for moderately troubled clients or for a late phase of therapy. In helping couples with nonexclusive relationships develop more effective interactions, tools and skills for problem solving and communication become especially important. This has been emphasized in much of the literature on dealing with jealousy and open relationships (e.g., Ard, 1977; Blood & Blood, 1977; Mazur, 1973; Constantine, 1976). Communication skills training (e.g., Miller *et al.*, 1975) is useful in an otherwise relatively sound relationship for increasing active or empathic listening and congruent, assertive communication.

If the assumption is that extramarital involvement will be a more or less permanent component of a couple's relationship, reducing jealousy and dealing efficiently and effectively with it when it does occur become paramount. Enhanced self-esteem and increased awareness of one's personal alternatives are associated with reduced jealousy (Hansen, 1983). It is appropriate for the couple to learn to acknowledge and appreciate gains from the partner's other relationships, and this may be facilitated in therapy through role plays and communication exercises that highlight and ritualize aspects of extramarital relationships which challenge conventional constructs (Constantine, 1976).

For example, the client couple are seated facing each other. The partner who is *not* involved in the outside relationship is told to talk about all the ways in which he or she personally gains or could benefit from the partner's outside relationship. ("The evenings you're with Gar have helped me learn something about how to be with just myself, instead of always relying on you to entertain me." Or, "You almost always are in good spirits when you return from seeing Gayle.") A fixed amount of time is allotted, all of it to be used. The therapist intervenes to make sure that things cited are genuine and not backhanded swipes at the partner. The partner may be asked to add to the list afterward.

In another variant, the one with the outside relationship is asked to "bring in gifts" to the partner: ways in which their perception of the partner or their relationship has been enhanced or improved by the "other relationship." ("By being with Tom, I've really come to appreciate what a good conversationalist you are. Tom may be very steady, but he doesn't sparkle at the dinner table anything like you do.")

Competing Paradigms

It is not uncommon for a couple to have failed to work out a consistent joint paradigm for their relationship. Of particular importance are cases where one partner sees or desires the relationship to be exclusive, and the other does not. It is very likely that the conflict in paradigms encompasses other areas as well, and unresolved struggles over paradigms can become central features of the relationship (Kantor, 1983). Therapists who have not made a clear separation of their own paradigmatic preferences from those of clients may have difficulty in these cases, as they are readily drawn into supporting, openly or covertly, the images of one partner at the expense of the other.

The therapist's job is to facilitate the couple's coming to a workable resolution out of their competing paradigms, an end served by assisting them in articulating these images and their origins in family experiences. Relationships with strong paradigmatic incompatibilities are not unworkable, but they may demand creativity and perseverance to find joint solutions. Concerning extramarital relations, the resulting structures may be somewhat complicated, nonstandard, or "messy," but may still be workable for that one particular couple.

THE THERAPIST

In the sensitive and controversial areas of jealousy and extramarital relations it is crucially important that therapists be clear about their own values and attitudes. This clarity is necessary if there is to be much hope of assessing the actual part jealousy or extramarital involvement play in a given couple's relationship.

The effects of clients' values and therapists' values as they impinge on each other can be very important and therefore must be taken into account. In the Knapp (1975) survey, only a minority of counselors indicated they would be professionally supportive of clients desiring to have a sexually open marriage, to engage in an affair, or to try "swinging."

This issue of professional support for clients working out relationship solutions within their own paradigms is probably more important than whether clients and therapist have similar or compatible values. Out of respect for the differing values of clients, therapists who cannot be supportive of client choices regarding EMS probably should make known their own values and offer to make an appropriate referral. Sprenkle and Weiss (1978) argue that a referral should be made in *all* cases where therapist and client values differ markedly. A willingness to support working solutions for clients independent of one's own personal values and life choices is especially important in cases where differing values within the relationship are themselves an issue (e.g., where one partner wants an exclusive relationship and the other does not).

Given the high incidence of EMS among counselors and therapists, coupled with stated disapproval of EMS, particularly for their spouses and clients, countertransference issues are likely to be substantial in many cases. Professionals for whom EMS is an unresolved issue or whose own life style and espoused values are incongruent may be less effective working with clients concerning issues of jealousy and EMS. In one case supervised by the author, the therapist was repeatedly drawn into focusing on his clients' extramarital activities to the exclusion of important presenting problems and the cycles that sustained these. Not until the therapist acknowledged his intensely conflicted secret affair with a co-therapist on another case could he deal with the envy he felt toward his clients, who appeared to have been more honest with each other about their outside relationships.

The most common treatment errors in dealing with jealousy are probably rooted in therapists' own relationship paradigms. It is almost always an error to try to change, through therapy, a couple's or family's relationship paradigm. Given the persistence of values and attitudes, to say nothing of modes of perception, attempting to influence the paradigmatic basis of a relationship is, at best, a waste of resources bordering on hopeless, and, at worst, a wedge driving a couple out of therapy.

Limited by their own strongly held world views, many marital therapists are prone to miss EMS altogether or, when it surfaces, to see it only in predefined terms that make it more difficult to assess its special role in a given relationship. They may then be easily trapped into exaggerating its importance. Both jealousy and EMS must be kept in perspective in the context of a real relationship whose basic premises may or may not resemble those of the therapist.

REFERENCES

Ard, B. N., Jr. (1977). Avoiding destructive jealousy. In G. Clanton & L. G. Smith (Eds.), *Jealousy*. Englewood Cliffs, NJ: Prentice-Hall.

Blood, R., & Blood, M. (1977). Jealousy workshops. In G. Clanton & L. G. Smith (Eds.), *Jealousy*. Englewood Cliffs, NJ: Prentice-Hall.

Blumstein, P., & Schwartz, P. (1983). *American couples*. New York: Morrow.

Bringle, R. G. (1981). Conceptualizing jealousy as a disposition. *Alternative Lifestyles, 4*, 274–290.

Buunk, B. (1980). Sexually open marriages: Groundrules for countering potential threats to marriage. *Alternative Lifestyles, 3*, 312–328.

Buunk, B. (1981). Jealousy in open marriage. *Alternative Lifestyles, 4*, 357–372.

Christensen, H. T. (1973). Attitudes toward marital infidelity. *Journal of Comparative Family Studies, 4*, 197–214.

Coleman, S. B. (1977). A developmental stage hypothesis for non-marital dyadic relationships. *Journal of Marriage and Family Counseling, 3*, 71–76.

Constantine, L. L. (1976). Jealousy: From theory to intervention. In D. H. L. Olson (Ed.), *Treating relationships*. Lake Mills, IA: Graphic Press.

Constantine, L. L. (1978). Family sculpture and relationship mapping techniques. *Journal of Marriage and Family Counseling, 4*(2), 13–23.

Constantine, L. L. (1984). Dysfunction and failure in open family systems, II: Clinical implications. *Journal of Marital and Family Therapy, 10*, 1–17.

Constantine, L. L. (in press). *Family paradigms: The practice of theory in family therapy*. New York: Guilford Press.

Constantine, L. L., Constantine, J. M., & Edelman, S. K. (1972). Counseling implications of comarital and multilateral relations. *Family Coordinator, 21*, 267–273.

Cromwell, R., Fournier, D., & Kvebaek, D. (1980). *The Kvebaek family sculpture technique*. Jonesboro, TN: Pilgrimage.

Duhl, F., Kantor, D., & Duhl, B. (1973). Learning, space, and action in family therapy. In D. Bloch (Ed.), *Techniques of family psychotherapy: A primer*. New York: Grune & Stratton.

Elbaum, P. L. (1981). The dynamics, implications, and treatment of extramarital sexual relations for the family therapist. *Journal of Marriage and Family Therapy, 7,* 489–494.

Ellis, A. (1977). Rational and irrational jealousy. In G. Clanton & L. G. Smith (Eds.), Jealousy. Englewood Cliffs, NJ: Prentice-Hall.

Francis, J. L. (1977). Toward the management of heterosexual jealousy. *Journal of Marriage and Family Counseling, 3*(4), 61–70.

Green, B. L., Lee, R. R., & Lustig, N. (1974, September). Conscious and unconscious factors in marital infidelity. *Medical Aspects of Human Sexuality,* 87–105.

Hansen, G. L. (1983, October). Perceived threats and marital jealousy. Paper presented at the National Council on Family Relations annual meeting.

Humphrey, F. G. (1982). Extramarital affairs: Clinical approaches in marital therapy. *Psychiatric Clinics of North America, 5,* 581–593.

Humphrey, F. G., & Strong, L. (1976, May). Treatment of extramarital sexual relations by clinical members of the AAMFC. Paper presented at the Northeast Regional Conference, AAMFC.

Hupka, R. B. (1981). Cultural determinants of jealousy. *Alternative Lifestyles, 4,* 310–356.

Im, W., Wilner, R. S., & Breit, M. (1983). Jealousy: Interventions in couples therapy. *Family Process, 22,* 211–219.

Kantor, D. (1983). The structural-analytic approach to the treatment of family developmental crisis. In H. A. Liddle (Ed.), *Clinical implications of the family life cycle.* Rockville, MD: Aspen Systems.

Kantor, D., & Lehr, W. (1975). *Inside the family.* San Francisco: Jossey-Bass.

Knapp, J. J. (1975). Some non-monogamous marriage styles and related attitudes and practices of marriage counselors. *Family Coordinator, 24,* 505–514.

Libby, R. W. (1977). Extramarital and comarital sex: A critique of the literature. In R. W. Libby & R. N. Whitehurst (Eds.), *Marriage and alternatives: Exploring intimate relatiosnhips.* Glenview, IL: Scott, Foresman.

Loevinger, J. (1966). The meaning and measurement of ego development. *American Psychologist, 21,* 195–206.

Marriage and Divorce Today. (1983, June). MDT reports "open marriage" no longer in favor with public. *Marriage and Divorce Today, 2.*

McGoldrick, M., Pearce, J. K., & Giordano, J. (1982). *Ethnicity and family therapy.* New York: Guilford Press.

Mazur, R. (1973). *The new intimacy: Open-ended marriage and alternative lifestyles.* Boston: Beacon Press.

Miller, S., Nunnally, E. W., & Wackman, D. B. (1975). *Alive and aware.* Minneapolis: Interpersonal Communications Programs.

O'Neill, N., & O'Neill, G. (1972). *Open marriage: A new lifestyle for couples.* New York: Evans.

Peabody, S. A. (1982). Alternative life styles to monogamous marriage: Variants of normal behavior in psychotherapy clients. *Family Relations, 31,* 425–434.

Peck, B. B. (1975). Therapeutic handling of marital infidelity. *Journal of Family Counseling, 3*(2), 52–58.

Reiss, D. (1981). *The family's construction of reality.* Cambridge, MA: Harvard University Press.

Reiss, I. (1983, October). A cross-cultural theory of human sexuality: Sexual jealousy. Paper presented in the Theory Construction and Research Methodology Workshop, National Council on Family Relations.

Ryals, K., & Foster, D. R. (1976). Open marriage: A question of ego development and marriage counseling. *Family Coordinator, 25,* 297–302.

Sluzki, C. E. (1983). Process, structure, and world views: Toward an integration of systemic models in family therapy. *Family Process, 22,* 469–476.

Sprenkle, D. H., & Weiss, D. L. (1978). Extramarital sexuality: Implications for marital therapists. *Journal of Sex and Marital Therapy, 4,* 279–292.

Strean, H. S. (1976). The extramarital affair: a psychoanalytic view. *Psychoanalytic Review, 63,* 723–725.

Teismann, M. W. (1979). Jealousy: Systematic problem-solving therapy with couples. *Family Process*, *18*, 151–160.

Thompson, A. P. (1982). Extramarital relations: counseling implications and a developmental perspective. *Australian Journal of Family Therapy*, *3*(3), 141–148.

Whitehurst, R. N. (1971). Violence potential in extramarital sexual responses. *Journal of Marriage and the Family*, *33*, 683–691.

19 Cross-Cultural Marriages

CELIA JAES FALICOV

If you are not going to marry the boy next door—
and if you do you may die of boredom
—then you are going to have to work much harder.
—MARGARET MEAD

Strictly speaking, we all intermarry, even if we marry the boy next door. Husband and wife belong to social units of one sort or another that differ in terms of family traditions, occupations, or political ideologies. Even the fact that the people marrying are of different sexes introduces discrepancies in world views and experiences. Since it is rare to find entirely parallel background experiences, all marriages necessitate some degree of mutual accommodation.

It is also probable that the inevitable accommodation may be longer and more complicated as the difference in background widens. With increasing frequency, marriages occur between partners of diverse ethnicity, religion, social class, race, or nationality (Gordon, 1964). The terms *intermarriage*, *intercultural* or *cross-cultural marriages* are used here to encompass those couples. Demographically, interethnic marriages are very common, interfaith marriages follow in frequency, with interracial marriages being the least frequent. Interclass marriages are comparatively rare (Barron, 1972; Cretser & Leon, 1982; Leslie, 1982; Schulz, 1976).

As interethnic, interfaith, and interracial marriages become more common, social tolerance increases; but within these marriages the diverse world views of the spouses produce strains and even serious conflict. Strains also can

Celia Jaes Falicov. San Diego Family Institute and Department of Psychiatry, University of California, San Diego, La Jolla, California.

429

come from the disapproval of family, friends and institutions. Families of origin may be quite different in values and rituals. One or the other family may object to the "cultural outsider." The new spouse may experience "culture shock" or feel ill at ease with the family of the other.

In spite of potential difficulties, a cross-cultural marriage offers unique possibilities for creative and functional matches. The factors that make for success or failure, happiness or unhappiness, are extremely complex and cannot be reduced merely to degrees of cultural commonalities and differences. Because of the enormous complexity and variety of cross-cultural marriages, it is extremely difficult to make generalizations that are useful to the clinician without delving further into the attendant family processes.

In this chapter we explore the conditions under which cultural differences interact with family processes to result in dysfunctional outcomes, such as are observed in clinical populations. First, a brief review of sociological theories about marital love and cultural consonance is presented. Second, the idea is introduced that couples who intermarry enter a form of *cultural transition* and have stylistic variations in the way that they adapt to their cultural differences; these variations have implications for the assessment of marital dysfunction. Third, three commonly found marital pictures in which cultural differences play a part are illustrated along with suggestions for therapeutic interventions that require different positions of the therapist vis-à-vis the cultural issues. The clinical examples emphasize the therapeutic use of culture as a valuable resource for change and highlight the dangers of dealing with cultural issues in a purely descriptive or explanatory manner.

MARITAL LOVE AND CULTURAL CONSONANCE

The ideology of American society dictates that marriages be based on a romantic foundation, that is, on the experience of mutual love. Some theories maintain that such love has a better chance of flourishing when the partners share similar backgrounds, while others are predicated on the opposite reasoning. According to Reiss (1976), the experience of rapport, so essential to the development of love, is greatly facilitated by commonality of social and cultural experiences: "One's social and cultural background is a key basis from which to predict the range of types of people for whom one could feel rapport. Broad factors such as religious upbringing and educational backgrounds would make one able to understand a person with similar religious and educational background, and thus make rapport more likely" (Reiss, p. 93).

Theories that focus on the importance of similarities for marital compatibility regard cross-cultural marriages pessimistically and cite the high incidence of divorce as proof of the difficulties involved in these marriages (Berman, 1968). In fact, most interfaith premarital counseling emphasizes finding areas of commonality between the prospective spouses.

Other theories about love are predicated on the importance of differences for individual need fulfillment in a relationship. A widespread belief is that "opposites attract" and complement each other (Winch, 1955). Most of the early computerized dating systems were based on this notion of complementary psychological needs (Schulz, 1976). Some authors view the cultural differences as mere masks behind which lie the partner's complementary needs.

> The bottom line is whether the union provides the necessary warmth, love, affection, excitement, caring, intimacy, and solidarity all human beings require. This is the prerequisite behind the masks of two racially different people. "It takes two to tango" and consciously or unconsciously a person selects a marriage partner who complements a particular dance step and road in life. (Jester, 1982)

Although the complementary differences referred to are personality differences, a similar argument might be used to find value in exposure to cultural differences (Falicov, 1982). Such a view would stress the oportunities open to cross-cultural marriages. For example, a workaholic, task-oriented WASP could benefit from marrying a person-oriented woman from a Latin culture. The integration of the two complementary backgrounds may produce a richer or more satisfying whole than if each had married a person within their own culture. A contemporary, positive view of intermarriage could propose that, like other types of "blended" families (Goldner, 1982), cross-cultural couples represent a newer, more complex form of marriage than the traditional endogamous relationships of preindustrial societies. These intercultural systems may come closer to what, Keeney (1983), borrowing from biology, calls an "ecological climax," an "vital balance" of diverse forms of experience and behavior in an ecosystem.

Both theories are valid at a sociological level and offer a broad perspective for the clinician, but they are of limited application when trying to distinguish the successful cross-cultural matches from the problematic ones. In the following section, a hypothesis is presented that links dysfunction to the couple's inability to develop a balanced view of their cultural differences in the context of their multiple differences and similarities.

CULTURAL TRANSITION AND VARIATIONS IN DEALING WITH CULTURAL DIFFERENCES

Metaphorically speaking, couples who intermarry enter a form of *cultural transition*. The main developmental task of this process of cultural transition is to arrive at an adaptive and flexible view of cultural differences that make it possible to maintain some individuated values, to negotiate conflictual areas, and even to develop a new cultural code that integrates parts of both cultural streams.

Cultural similarities and differences cannot be viewed in isolation from the total complex of a couple's other similarities and differences. One approach is to argue that the way in which a couple deals with their cultural differences is isomorphic to how the same couple deals with other sources of similarity or difference, such as their characterological attributes, age or occupational differences. But this view ignores the complexity of the marital system, namely, that it may function differently depending on the area or the problem. Moreover, any difference or similarity can be minimized or maximized at different times and in different areas for various purposes. Regardless of whether the cultural differences are large or small, what one usually observes is an outcome where difference and similarity stand in a fairly complex and comfortable balance or appear to be unbalanced. Couples vary in the degree of complexity and balance with which they view their cultural differences in the context of their other differences.

A Balanced View

Many intermarried couples offer a complex and balanced view of their relationship. This view encompasses experiences derived from their embeddedness in the spheres of family, social class, religion, occupation, historical moment, rural or urban setting, ethnic roots, or political ideology. Thus a husband and wife may attribute their similarities to the fact that they both were raised in a small nuclear middle-class family in an urban setting. They could point to differences in religious beliefs and practices, differences in the ethnic backgrounds of their grandparents or the political allegiances of their parents. Again, they can find similarities in their own contemporary historical and ideological moments or in the warmth of each of their mothers toward their children. Often, the aspect of culture a person selects to compare reveals that individual's own personal ideals. As one British-American Protestant man said about his and his Mexican-Catholic wife's backgrounds: "Our families' cultures were very similar in their traditions. On both sides, our parents slept in the same bed for fifty years." He underscored one definition of culture that mattered to him. Within a marriage possessing a balanced framework, cultural differences are more easily integrated, negotiated, or allowed to remain parallel or autonomous from other areas.

An Unbalanced View

Intermarried couples in distress are more likely to have only a limited number of frames through which to screen their similarities and differences. Their view about the complexity of similarities and differences appears to be impoverished, unbalanced, or distorted. These couples may be unaware of the impact of cultural differences on their interactions. Or they may selectively submerge or highlight their cultural differences and similarities in dysfunctional ways. Within an unbalanced framework, the couple may either overfocus on (maximize) the cultural differences or underfocus on (minimize) them.

Thus, cultural differences can be rather elastic and subjectively evaluated as foreground or background, depending on the other personal and social processes that are also present. In so doing, couples unwittingly use their differences and similarities in the service of function or dysfunction. The therapist then must be sensitive to the ways in which marital partners introduce or omit culturally related experiences in presenting themselves. It is very important to assess whether intercultural couples make a contextually balanced or unbalanced evaluation of their differences. This is not to imply that the unbalanced use of cultural differences is the cause of dysfunction, but it is a reliable indicator of problematic adaptation to the cultural transition. Attention to the styles of adaptation that maximize or minimize cultural differences also offer guidelines for appropriate therapeutic interventions, as is illustrated below.

CULTURAL DIFFERENCES IN THE CLINICAL SITUATION

Difficulties in adapting and resolving the state of cultural transition are manifested in a number of situations. Based on the author's clinical experience, three patterns are selected wherein the cultural differences appear to be unbalanced in the context of other marital processes. These patterns are (a) conflicts in cultural code; (b) cultural differences and permission to marry; and (c) cultural stereotyping and severe stress. In the first pattern, the marital conflicts are largely related to the lack of a shared cultural code. In the second pattern, the marital problems are tied to difficulties in the realignment of boundaries with the extended family, ostensibly because of the exogamous choice of marital partner. In the third pattern, the marital partners use their cultural differences stereotypically against each other to create a makeshift boundary that prevents painful emotional involvement in situations of severe stress.

These patterns can coexist simultaneously in the same couple; they can appear at different times in a couple's life span, or one pattern may be more salient than the others throughout their life. It also seems possible, but remains to be studied, that some patterns may be more typical of one developmental stage than another. Other clinical observations also indicate that individual and family life-cycle issues interact in the cross-cultural marital processes in complex ways (McGoldrick & Preto, 1984). For example, in the initial stages of a marriage there may be a focus on developing a common cultural code or on defending against the families of origin, while the third pattern could appear later, at the time of a threatened dissolution of the marriage through divorce, death, or other crises that exacerbate an already problematic adaptation to the original task of cultural transition. Another possibility is that any difficult developmental transition can unbalance the marital situation to the point that any or all of the three patterns can emerge.

The description of these patterns and the corresponding therapeutic strategies is illustrated in this chapter with clinical cases, followed by suggestions for making therapeutic use of the cultural issues in each case. Dangers inherent in dealing with cultural issues are underscored along with suggestions for avoiding a number of specific pitfalls that can result in an increased sense of hopelessness and rigidity.

In general, therapeutic interventions are guided by an assessment of structural aspects of the marital relationship. In the process of therapy a tactical use of culture is made. This use has been dubbed "cultural strategies" (Falicov & Karrer, 1984). Because of the variety and significance of cultural issues for cross-cultural couples, there are many possibilities for "cultural strategies." Special attention is paid both to the style of adaptation and the subjective evaluation the couple make of the cultural differences. The therapist, like the couple, also uses cultural differences as reality, as metaphor or as "camouflage," maximizing or minimizing them to serve therapeutic goals.

Conflicts in Cultural Code

Since it is extremely difficult to distinguish between conflicts linked to cultural differences and other marital conflicts, it is very helpful to avail oneself of a map or a conceptual framework to guide therapeutic assessment related to cultural matters. A framework of knowledge about the sociocultural characteristics of different ethnic, racial, or religious groups helps to raise relevant questions about cultural dissonances that otherwise may not be explored (McGoldrick, Pearce, & Giordano, 1982). The diversity of world views, interpersonal expectations, or child-rearing values could be so broad that skills in interviewing and conducting culturally sensitive inquiries are also essential. All inquiries about culture should be personal and nonstereotypic because enculturation and acculturation vary with the individual and may vary even more for those who intermarry. Guidelines for these clinical tools are offered by Lappin (1983), Faulkner and Kich (1983), and Schwartzman (1983).

When working with interethnic and interclass marriages, a conceptual framework focusing on differences in cultural values about marital and family organization is particularly helpful. Some cultural expectations about marriage emphasize values that maintain contact and continuity with the extended family, while others favor more discontinuity and emotional autonomy from the parental families. Many principles of family and marital organization stem from these two different value systems. The differences in rules governing inclusion and exclusion of others in the marriage (proximity–distance) and the rules about power and authority (hierarchies) are particularly important. These rules could be said to constitute a *cultural code* that organizes expectations about marriage both internally and in relation to other subsystems. For a detailed discussion of this topic, see Falicov and Brudner-White (1983).

Intermarried partners often come from family backgrounds that have different cultural codes. Many aspects of relationships are influenced by the spouses' individual cultural codes, from styles of communication to child-rearing values. These different expectations and world views could enter into a serious marital conflict. For example, some ethnic and religious groups have very high expectations regarding family interdependence, while others have normative expectations that emphasize greater autonomy and self-development. Using their circumplex model, Olson, Russell, and Sprenkle (1980) found that a frequent problem with many couples requesting treatment "is that each spouse is at the opposite extreme of the same dimension. On the cohesion dimension, one partner may want more cohesion in the relationship, while the other might want more autonomy and freedom" (p. 169). What often goes unrecognized by couples is that these expectations may stem from different cultural codes about relationships.

Couples who experience conflicts in cultural code may be separated by many objective differences, such as different ethnicity, race, religion, social class, nationality, and even language. They also share similarities, such as the same profession, or political or social ideologies. They may also complement each other in cultural or personality aspects.

In an effort to achieve mutual adaptation, the spouses either minimize or maximize the cultural differences and end up with only a superficial knowledge about the other's culture. This style prevents negotiation in important areas and impedes the development of a new cultural code. There are many covert misunderstandings, problems in communication, and covert and reciprocal anticipations of the other's behaviors. Errors based on either ethnocentric or stereotypic views of the other are common. Cultural traits may be mistaken for negative personality traits. An example (Case A) of a couple with these characteristics is given below.

A young American wife was shocked by her husband's family when they announced their move to the United States from Iran. Her husband, acting in a culturally syntonic manner, felt willing and obliged to install his family in his and his wife's apartment, even though they were both graduate students and had limited means and time available. The wife had many reasons not to want them to live in their apartment. Some were in her own self-interest. But others were considerate of the immigrant family's need to develop self-competence. The husband was extremely upset about what he thought was going to be perceived by his family as an unforgivable rejection. The wife finally compromised by agreeing to move to a building where the extended family could have a contiguous, separate apartment. But she remained covertly critical of her husband's "excessive attachment" to his family, and by implication superior to him.

Shortly after this incident, the wife attended a lecture focused on families in cultural context given by this author. After the presentation, the wife requested a couples interview. During this session, it was clear that there were other tensions between husband and wife. Each complained of not feeling understood and supported by the other. Up to the time of attending the lecture, the wife minimized the differences between herself and her husband, although there appeared to be many. She believed that "a world culture" prevailed nowadays, particularly among graduate students, whereby the similarities overpowered the differences in ethnic background. They were both liberal and agnostic, and from middle-class backgrounds, which further reinforced the ideological commonalities. She could not see how her cultural background could affect their relationship. Her grandfather had told her about her family: "We are all Yankees and that means we are the same as 90% of everybody else." The husband agreed with the wife in minimizing the cultural differences. Rather defensively, he described how, in spite of the present government's policies, Iran had continued to become Westernized. Many women now studied, worked, and were generally "liberated." For the husband, minimizing the differences was a way of not devaluing his country in comparison to his wife's.

The therapist continued to pursue a cultural theme by redefining the "world culture" as perhaps a goal for the future (a metaphor for their relationship). But at present, the therapist suggested, many couples are actually in "cultural transition." Continuing with the educational approach that had influenced the wife before, the therapist referred to cultural family organizations that modify definitions about marital boundaries with the extended family. Thus, what the wife considered to be her husband's "excessive attachment" to his family was normalized in a cultural framework.

Following this intervention, the husband said, "You are a product of your upbringing whether you like it or not, even if you don't agree with all the credos. The most important one that has stuck with me is that the man makes the decisions and the woman follows. I think deep down I don't really believe you can have two heads of household for everything." A lively discussion on different cultural codes about the levels of power of men and women ensued. The therapist facilitated a personal rather than an academic interaction between the spouses. It became clear that the husband had been fantasizing about having a baby, particularly after an Iranian friend's wife had just given birth. He felt quite inhibited about mentioning this to his wife because she had been so adamant about pursuing her career. He also said that her contraceptive routines had become upsetting to him, and he had begun wondering if she was rather cold or calculating. The wife felt hurt by this and claimed to be more affectionate than he was, a fact he could not deny.

The therapist reframed the wife's "cold and calculating behavior" in cultural terms, wondering if it could be "American practicality in pursuing goals." Furthermore, the therapist suggested that the wife's "calculating" could also be seen as an example of the determination women need to change their subordinate position, since sex roles are in transition everywhere. The husband's wish to have a baby was labeled by the therapist as bringing in "the missing part of a vital balance," the "heart" that complements the "intellect." The spouses' differences now stood in a complementary balance, and this intervention opened up a more positive climate for negotiation. After this session, the couple reported to be less disengaged and to have a greater sense of union and common purpose.

The Therapeutic Use of Cultural Issues

The couple in the case example began by minimizing their cultural differences, which in turn prevented disclosure in many important areas. The therapist maximized such differences in order to highlight, understand, and justify individual behaviors that the spouses had been covertly interpreting as personality traits. The locus of the problem was thus changed from the couple to the culture. The goal of this approach was to open up more productive communication and to help resolve conflictual issues.

The therapist assumed a role of cultural mediator, interpreter, or "clarifier" of values. Although this role is often helpful, there are several *pitfalls* to be avoided when using this approach.

First, "cultural clarification" is insufficient and even problematic if the discussion remains at a content level only. In developing restructuring goals for the couple, the therapist needs to attend to the process and select the cultural content accordingly. At a content level, the couple above professed to have an egalitarian relationship, but, process-wise, the wife initiated many interactions and the husband deferred to her. While this could have been partly due to the wife's superior knowledge of the culture and language, other marital processes (incongruent with their egalitarian goals) seemed to be at work. The clarification of cultural differences was orchestrated in a therapeutic context that addressed necessary structural changes in the marital relationship. For example, by facilitating the husband's expression of a desire for a baby and legitimizing it as temporarily supplying "the heart to his wife's intellect," the therapist made his contribution equal to his wife's. This complementary balance could be supported as part of the process of cultural and sex-role transition. A strict clarification of cultural content, without consideration for the complex hierarchical balance of this particular couple, could have led to interpreting the husband's desire to see his wife pregnant as a vestige of his culture's traditionalism in sex roles, and thus inadvertently diminish him further in his wife's eyes. Now both partners could be praised for their flexibility and their nonstereotypic sex roles.

Another pitfall of cultural clarification may occur when the therapist, in "raising consciousness" about cultural differences, unwittingly implies a sense of hopelessness about the possibility of change. A cultural reframing could unfortunately suggest that a particular behavior is unchangeable because it is rooted in the culture. ("He thinks a wife is only for making babies because of his Iranian upbringing." "She can't help being a Jewish American Princess." "He can't stop flirting—it's in his Latin blood.") This exonerates individuals from personal motivation or responsibility. It is better to view a cultural trait as a resource that can be used or not, depending on the circumstances, rather than an inflexible feature. In the foregoing example, reframing the wife's efficiency in avoiding pregnancy as "American practicality" did not imply rigidity or an inability to be romantic and less practical in other situations. In discussing hypotheses that marital partners formulate about each other's behaviors, Hurvitz (1975) coined the terms "terminal," that is, an explanation that suggests a behavior is unchangeable, and "instrumental," that is, an explanation that suggests something can be done about the behavior. Similarly, in cross-cultural situations the marital partners and the therapist run the danger of using culture as a "terminal hypothesis."

The third pitfall is to facilitate further marital disengagement by emphasizing the gap in cultural differences too strongly. These differences may then become the "kiss of death" that supports justifications for incompatibility. To avoid it, interventions that underline cultural differences can be balanced by finding other connections, common ideologies, or cultural complementarities or bridges. Perhaps the most effective way to prevent a static and disengaging use of culture is to label the couple as in cultural transition. In the example above, a notion of cultural transition, particularly transition in sex roles, served to unify the two cultures and to balance any implications that one culture may be superior to the other.

It is often helpful to define couples who experience conflictual codes as being in cultural transition. This definition encourages them to seek negotiations of their differences, and to encourage continuity with some of each spouse's traditions while developing a "new culture," one that is more personal, unique, and encompassing.

Cultural Differences and Permission to Marry

Although in Western cultures parents no longer play an overt role in arranging marriages, parental approval of the choice of marital partner one makes is of great psychological import for most individuals. Often, it is difficult to secure unconflicted extended-family support for intermarriage. The parental disapproval complicates the expected realignment of generational boundaries to include the new spouse and either halts or precipitates too rapidly the state of cultural transition. Each phase of the couple's life cycle is affected by the response of the extended family to the marriage (Faulkner & Kich, 1983). Interracial couples may be forced by their families to skip parts of the life-cycle rituals, such as the wedding ceremony. Or they may decide themselves to skip the rituals to avoid further family tensions. An assessment of intermarried couples should always include the extended network and even friends' reactions to the marriage and the subsequent relationships with the extended and the friendship networks.

Racial, religious, or ethnic differences could certainly increase the probability of parental disapproval, particularly in families where continuity over the generations is expected and endogamy is the rule. In many cases, however, the cultural prohibitions seem to be only part of the reason for the family tensions around the marriage. The disapproval may also stem from family processes that make it difficult for parents and their adult children to separate (Stanton, 1981; Friedman, 1982).

Stanton (1981) describes some of the family processes behind the parental disapproval of a marriage:

> Such disapproval can loom like a malevolent specter over a marriage. It may occur because one of the partners is instrumental in keeping his or her parents' marriage together, because a parent is undergoing bereavement and is giving the message that "I need you more than your spouse" to the partner, or for other reasons frequently tied into critical points in the family and parental life cycle. This disapproval is a way of not letting go of the son or daughter—they exert a pull on him/her—often because they feel their own needs are greater.(p. 22)

Cultural differences may not be the only or even the main cause of parental disapproval, but they certainly can provide a reinforcing concretization for the family's resistance to the marriage. Based on his extensive experience with intermarried couples, Friedman (1982) attributes the difficulties of religious or ethnic families in accepting cross-cultural marriages, not so much to a high degree of cultural commitment or religious devotion, but to other emotional processes. "Marrying out" represents an attempt to create emotional distance, usually initiated by the child who has been most important to the balance of the parents' marriage. For the parents, the cultural differences act as a justification to reject the outsider and, in Friedman's words, become "cultural camouflage" to avoid dealing with the emotional reactions to their son's or daughter's marriage.

Whether the content of the disapproval is ethnic or not, and the granting of the blessing religious or not, the more crucial problem is that a substantial number of intermarried couples suffer from a covert or overt lack of permission to marry, and this in turn may have repercussions on marital success. Stanton (1981) maintains that "80% of marriages that fail do so because one or both spouses have not had permission to succeed in the marriage." A similar point stressing the importance of parental approval for marital success is made by Boszormenyi-Nagy and Spark (1973).

In the case of intermarriage, it is as though the couple does not have permission to enter the state of cultural transition and begin to develop a new cultural code for their family unit. Instead, either a form of cohabitation takes place or a new code is developed at the expense of cutting off relationships with the families of origin.

Marital difficulties may be compounded by divided loyalties or unresolved family ties, but an *unhappy* cross-cultural marriage could also be a "solution" to problems in the family or origin of one or both spouses. On the one hand, the ties with the family of origin are slackened, since the cross-cultural configuration of the new couple draws a tighter boundary that excludes them from certain interactions with the extended family. Both parties, the parents and the married son or daughter, can blame the necessary distance on the cultural outsider. On the other hand, the marital difficulties themselves could ensure continuity of the family-of-origin patterns (cultural and idiosyncratic) if the son or daughter, by continuing to be the focus of parental attention, still detours parental problems, this time through his or her marital difficulties. A similar reasoning that interconnects the marital difficulties of the alcoholic or drug addict and his relationship with his parents (who refuse to accept his marriage) has been proposed by Stanton *et al.* (1978) and Stanton (1981).

Two contrasting styles of adaptation have been observed by this author in couples who do not obtain emotional permission to marry, ostensibly because of their cross-cultural union. The patterns may be distinguished by the boundary negotiations with the family of origin of one or both spouses, and the interpersonal boundaries within the marital subsystem. In the first pattern (Case B), the couple maximizes their cultural differences; in the second pattern (Case C), they minimize them.

MAXIMIZING DIFFERENCES

In the first pattern of adaptation, the couple seems to emulate the reactions of their families of origin. The spouses maximize their differences and do not blend, integrate, or negotiate their values and life styles. They lead parallel lives, each holding on to their culture and/or family of origin. Often, the counterpoint of the marital distance is an excessive involvement of one or both parties with the family of origin. There may also be unresolved longings for the past ethnic or religious affiliations, even if these were of little importance previously. The example below illustrates a couple (Case B) with these features.

> John and his wife, Pat, married for 18 years, came to therapy complaining of chronic marital dissatisfaction and severe alienation from each other. They had minimal daily contact, leading parallel lives, each with a separate group of friends and diverse interests. Their only common interest was the welfare of their 11-year-old daughter. Recently the husband made an extramarital affair public. This altered the marital balance and called for a definition about their future together.
>
> The couple had no explanation for their long-standing distance and lack of communication. They maximized their differences in personality, interests, life styles, cultural values—each vaguely blaming the other for not adjusting. The therapist focused the initial assessment on the beginning stages of the marriage with the purpose of restructuring by increasing their sense of connection through shared history. The following information was obtained.
>
> The husband was born in New York City of Italian background; the wife in upstate New York of French-Syrian parents. Both were Catholic families, but varied greatly in their adherence to religion. The husband's family was very devout. The wife's was not. The husband had been raised in an Italian neighborhood surrounded by "hundreds of intrusive relatives"; his nuclear and extended family lived together in a three-story apartment building. The wife had a lonely childhood, with almost yearly moves due to her father's position in the army. When Pat's father was stationed in

Europe, John was also in the army. The couple met then and married after a brief courtship just prior to John's completing his duty and returning to the United States.

Upon their return they went to live temporarily with John's family. There was tension between Pat and her in-laws. In addition to her not being Italian, she had shattered the parents' expectations of a big Italian wedding for their oldest son ("the prince of the family"). In fact, the husband purposefully avoided an Italian wedding (further rejecting his ethnic identification), but there are implications that he allowed his parents to blame his wife for depriving them of the wedding (and possibly for the subsequent marital problems).

With difficulty John acknowledged that at the time of the wedding he had wanted to create some distance with his family. In his words, "When you are faced with decisions, you have twenty-five relatives trying to help; they have your own good at heart, but they can drive you crazy." John's ambivalence about his family of origin and his wish to create some distance from them stemmed from two sources: an overly responsible, parentified role in his family plus a perception of ethnic confinement. Because his mother was often ill and his father frequently absent, almost all of the household responsibilities, child care, and the mother's emotional support fell on John. Pat also played a crucial role as her mother's confidant and detourer of marital conflicts. Her mother was chronically depressed and self-preoccupied. She sometimes blamed Pat for her problems, including marital ones.

Unlike Pat, who did not have a clear ethnic identity, and her parents, who minimized their own cultural differences, John lived in an intensely ethnic climate. Every person he came in contact with was Italian. All the stores, friends, people in the neighborhood were Italian. His father played and composed only Italian music. As a second-generation immigrant, John felt embarrassed by so much ethnic emphasis. He looked up to the Anglo world, particularly to bohemians and hippies. With her dark good looks and unconventional clothes, Pat looked like the Greenwich Village young women that he admired at a distance.

To avoid using culture to split or disengage, the therapist focused on the similarity of the positions of each spouse in their own families as being far greater than the cultural differences. The latter were reframed positively as the attraction of opposites: the diversity of Little Italy and Greenwich Village were used as a cultural metaphor for the interdependence and the freedom they were both seeking.

The therapist justified John's parents' behavior toward Pat as typical of Italian families' reaction to outsiders (Rotundo & McGoldrick, 1982), rather than a rejection of Pat as a person. John was able to verbalize his conflict of loyalties between his wife and his parents. Pat suddenly realized that her own French mother had never been accepted by her Syrian father's extended family: "She was never good enough for them."

The cross-cultural marriage could be seen as a partial solution to the husband's difficulties with his family of origin. Marriage to an Italian woman would have restricted him to interact only with his ethnic group and would have made it more difficult to disengage from his triangulated position with his parents. Marrying outside the ethnic group distanced him *from his family while he still maintained ties and was able to regulate the emotional distance. The unhappiness in the marriage perpetuated the closeness to his parents and provided a focus for John's parents' disagreements.*

Now, almost 20 years later, John still phones his parents from California weekly, visits them alone, and tells them about his marital problems. His parents put him in a no-win situation by disagreeing about how he should resolve his marital situation. About their position, John says: "My mother is in favor of us splitting up. I don't say me and Pat are miserable, but my mother looks at me and she says, 'I know you are not happy' and I know what she means, and she'll say one or two things about it and that's all. She does not insist, but I know where she stands. My dad can beat you to death with 'Don't break up the family.' " Although there had not been any cultural objections to her marriage, Pat also continued after her marriage to be overinvolved with her mother and her troubles.

To intervene in this situation, the therapist made the loyalty aspects of the distant and unhappy marriage explicit. With a paradoxical intention, she called the unhappy marriage a necessary and valuable sacrifice to the families of origin (Stanton 1981; Boszormenyi-Nagy & Spark, 1973). This positive reframing encompassed both past and present, and began to shift the couple's perception of their marriage and their motivation to work on modifying the boundary with their families.

The Therapeutic Use of Cultural Issues

Although there were many cultural differences in this case, this discussion was not considered to be therapeutic at the time because the couple was very disengaged and maximized their cultural differences dysfunctionally. In labeling and elaborating on the differences, the therapist could have unwittingly provided yet another ready-made perch on which to hang their unhappiness. The husband was ambivalent and defensive about his ethnic background, and felt put down by the wife on this issue. Since his ethnic roots were most intense, an emphasis on culture could have implied a criticism of what he brought into the marriage. The couple had made a negative use of cultural metaphors, comparing the marriage with two different countries, France and Germany. Here the therapist would expand the metaphor only if she could find a point of connection, such as the fact that France and Germany have a border, however small. Circumscribing the cultural issues to the extended family was more appropriate.

The cultural similarities and differences in values between generations (parents and adult children) and within generations (spouses) were minimized or maximized to create more appropriate boundaries (i.e., more consonance between partners) and greater differentiation between parents and adult children.

MINIMIZING DIFFERENCES

A second pattern of adaptation observed in couples who do not obtain emotional permission to marry consists of minimizing and even denying the cultural differences. They may join a third alternative "culture" and sever their cultural and family ties. These couples appear to have an attitude of "you and me against the world" or "we only have each other." The interface boundary with the families of origin then becomes too rigid. The individual boundaries of the spouses themselves are too permeable and diffuse.

The couple in the following example (Case C) illustrate this style of adaptation. The example also shows that the disapproval of the marriage is not always parental. In this case the lack of permission to marry was eventually found to arise from the children of a first marriage; it had a nearly devastating impact on a second marriage, and the symptoms abated only when this issue was confronted and resolved.

The wife was American and her parents were intermarried; her mother was German Catholic and her father English Protestant. The husband was American; his parents were Chinese and Indonesian. The spouses had met through their association with an Eastern-type religion. They shared many similar values and a holistic life style. They also had related occupations. Their original differences were certainly balanced by these ideological similarities, but the couple denied any cultural differences.

The couple had been married for 3 years and had a 1-year-old baby. They sought therapy because the wife was obsessed with the thought of the husband being unfaithful to her. Since they recently had a baby, the first probes the therapist made were based on a developmental hypothesis. After the birth of the baby, the wife was feeling unattractive, and the husband was so preoccupied with new responsibilities that he was less attentive to her. In this context, the therapist reframed the jealousy positively as a form of more intense romantic involvement with each other, and asked the husband to be more expressive of his love and attraction for his wife. The husband objected, arguing that because of his Oriental background he could not be very open with his feelings. By maximizing the differences, the husband seemed to be making a selective and possibly homeostatic use of culture. Not only was he highly acculturated, he was also quite expressive verbally. It soon became clear, however, that the spouses did not need to be more cohesive.

The second hypothesis the therapist tested was one that tied the symptom to a hierarchical imbalance (Madanes, 1981). The wife was older; she had been married before and had raised children, and she was the sole economic support of this new family. The husband, who had a history of drug involvement, procrastination in his studies, and job discrimination due to racial prejudice, stayed home to take care of the baby. He was attractive and articulate, however, and women were often interested in him. In this context, the jealousy could serve several balancing functions: The wife was the one with a problem now. Although they joked about the label, they both called her behavior "paranoid." The jealousy was a constant reminder of the husband's superiority in the area of sexual attractiveness. It was, in fact, a form of flattery toward him. The jealousy also allowed the wife more intensive supervision over the husband than would have been possible otherwise. Since the supervision was ostensibly due to the wife's symptom, the husband could be spared from any criticism about his problems, and thus save face.

The therapist felt that the most desirable correction of hierarchies was for the husband to get on with his studies and find a job. She used a reframing that normalized the wife's jealousy and made the husband's job a precondition for its disappearance. When he started working regularly, however, the symptom of jealousy flared up again. But this time there was an additional problem. The wife was very reluctant to leave the baby with a sitter and was convinced that the baby was now rejecting and turning away from her.

A third hypothesis was needed to account for the persistence of symptoms. Exploration of the beginning of this marriage provided some leads. The wife had left an unhappy marriage to get married to her present husband. After this decision, she became a total outcast not only from her first husband but also from her adolescent children and the two extended families. They scorned her for marrying into a different race and excluded her from family contacts. The couple encapsulated themselves behind an attitude of "you and me against the world." However, the wife felt terribly guilty toward her children and upset about their rejection. She said that although she had stopped being a Roman Catholic at age 12, she expected "punishment for her sins" and for "bringing unhappiness to so many people." What catastrophes would befall her? Since she was totally emotionally dependent on her new husband, in her view the most terrible thing that could happen would be if he left her for another woman. When her husband went to work and the baby was left with a sitter, she became fearful that this child, too, would end up disliking her, as her first children did.

The "lack of permission" from her children was thought by the therapist to be interfering with the trust and consolidation of the new couple. The jealousy was considered as a vulnerability that was maintained by marital processes, but it was also linked with the rejection by the wife's children. The wife seemed to be expressing her loyalty to her children by not trusting her husband completely, since her jealousy and mistrust of her new husband were similar to her children's.

Continuation of contact with her children was thought to be therapeutically necessary. Since she did not have direct access to them, the therapist suggested that perhaps a symbolic continuity could be attempted. Both husband and wife were encouraged to use their imagination to devise cultural rituals of continuity (Van der Hart, 1983). The custom of ancestor worship in the Chinese culture provided one type of model; the husband could help the wife with the rituals. Photographs and documents belonging to the maternal grandparents could be arranged chronologically in albums to be sent to the children at their high school graduation. Mementoes of when they were young could be saved to be given when they had babies themselves. Working on these projects would keep the connection with the children alive and decrease the wife's sense of powerlessness and impending doom.

In the following session, they both reported finding the task extremely difficult. The husband said he could not, in all honesty, help the wife atone for "sins she had not committed." He was extremely supportive of her and said that she had to leave her family for her own survival and sanity, but he would do what she requested from him. Christmas was near, and the wife felt that the best way to maintain continuity was to make gifts for her children and go to her own parents' home to deliver these on Christmas Eve. They would thus begin to "face the world." Husband and wife now became engrossed in the resolution of issues with her previous family and in planning the husband's continuation of his studies.

The Therapeutic Use of Cultural Issues

Cultural issues had been mentioned by each spouse (Catholic guilt feelings by the wife, Oriental lack of expressiveness by the husband) to understand or justify interpersonal behaviors, and as a homeostatic maneuver, to resist change. The therapist accepted, maximized, or minimized the cultural issues depending on the therapeutic goals. For instance, the therapist did not support the husband's claim that his lack of expressiveness resulted from his Oriental background primarily because supporting his cultural explanation would have justified his aloofness at an inappropriate time and place: early parenthood in a socially isolated couple. On the other hand, a ritual belonging to the culture of the husband was suggested to give legitimacy to the creation of a therapeutic ritual through association with time-honored traditions, and to include the husband in a task that concerned the wife's family.

Cultural and racial prejudices were also used by the ex-husband, the children, and the extended family to ostracize the mother, with whom they were all very angry for other reasons. Other cultural issues mentioned by the couple were based on realistic perceptions about societal prejudices. For example, hierarchical differences between husband and wife may have been partially connected with their differences in status in the society at large, but it would not have been therapeutically constructive to make these explicit.

The need to explore the relationships with the extended family became evident in this case. A dysfunction that superficially appeared to be exclusively marital could not be treated within the marital dyad. Only when the focus of treatment shifted from the couple to the relationship with other family members did the symptom take on a new meaning and became amenable to resolution.

Cultural Stereotyping and Severe Stress

Family members are quite capable of using cultural clichés against each other. This can be done in a friendly, humorous manner or in a distancing and disengaging fashion. In certain clinical situations, the presenting problem is accompanied by cultural explanations, usually of a negative tone, given by one spouse for the behavior of the other. There is a strong negative emotional component to the cultural hypotheses, an overfocus on and maximization of differences, or a polarization of views and values. Throughout their marriage, the spouses have handled, more or less successfully, a number of objective cultural differences (race, language, religion). At present however, the couple appear empoverished, offering simplistic explanations that maximize their differences. It seems possible that in dealing with the stage of cultural transition the couple adapted through a problematic attempted solution that breaks down under stress. When the person being blamed is a member of a foreign or minority subgroup, a first impression could suggest that the marital interactions replicate larger sociocultural tensions such as ethnic or racial prejudice. A closer (and necessary) examination reveals that other dysfunctional family processes are at work.

The distorted splitting content of the cultural explanation and the degree of emotional intensity gives the impression of a "cultural defense" or a massive denial that covers up other crucial processes. The question, 'Why is culture an issue now?' is essential for understanding these cases. The answer reveals severe underlying stress, such as impending loss of a spouse through divorce or death. In this light, a communication about culture can be heard as a metaphor for other relationship issues.

The notion that differences are maximized and "prejudice" increases in the face of stress has been the subject of many social psychology experiments (Kretch & Crutchfield, 1948; Simpson & Yinger, 1958). In the face of a situation that is hard to understand or accept, prejudices can be adopted to "explain" the crisis. These "situational prejudices" may be an attempt to bring meaning into a confusing and ambiguous crisis. They are a search for a reason, even an alibi, a way out for oneself of the other person. Consider Case D, which follows:

> A couple who had recently separated and were contemplating divorce consulted with the therapist as a last resort and with little hope, since previous marital therapy had not resulted in any changes. The wife, who was American with ancestors that went back 300 years in this country, spoke in a very derisive manner about her Cuban husband of 18 years, a successful engineer. She blamed many of his objectionable features on his ethnic origin and his minority status. The traits she focused on were: He had an "inferiority complex" and was "very insecure"; he was "insensitive and undemonstrative," "incapable of love," "selfish," "uncaring," "passive," and "crazy." She also said he was a poor Roman Catholic, although she herself was of Protestant background, and religion had never been an issue in their marriage.
>
> There were several surprising aspects to these statements. First, in spite of the cultural frame used, the traits did not really have any identifiable ethnic roots. Second, the couple had been married for almost 20 years with definite tensions due to cultural and language differences, but these had not been previously addressed by either one of them as insurmountable. If anything, the style of adaptation to their differences had been one in which the wife had joined the husband's culture—she had learned a little Spanish and had considerable knowledge of Cuban history. There had been many attempts at integrating the cultures, such as the children having two names each, one Spanish, the other English. Third, although the husband was visibly disturbed by the references to his ethnic background, he behaved like a gentleman and never returned in kind the cultural insults. In fact, he tacitly helped his wife to remain at this level of explanation for their problems.

The therapist did not question the content validity of the ethnic stereotypes or mention the previous adaptations made to the cultural differences because she sensed that something else was happening. To explore matters further, she interviewed the spouses separately. When alone, the husband said his marital dissatisfaction had been of long standing, but he had never expressed it. Recently, he had abruptly taken the initiative to move out of the house. He was living in an apartment with a younger Mexican woman, with whom he had fallen in love. His wife knew this but refused to take it seriously and had used every opportunity to invite him to move back with her.

In the context of this marital crisis, the use of ethnic stereotyping served several useful functions. First, by selecting to blame his background for his behavior, the wife protected herself from recognizing the possibility that she was no longer loved by her husband. This of course also excused him from responsibility for his behavior: "All Latin men have affairs." Second, in attacking the Latin culture, she was indirectly critizing her husband's choice of a new partner, who was Mexican. Third, the adjectives the wife used to describe her husband's character could be heard as metaphors for the feelings his behavior evoked in her: He was "insensitive" (toward her), "uncaring" (toward her), "incapable of love" (toward her), and "inconsiderate" (of her feelings toward him). Finally, the husband had been emotionally estranged from the wife for some time. The ethnic stereotypes she voiced were powerful and could provoke an emotional reaction on the husband's part.

To confront the wife with the distortions about her husband's culture by having an objective discussion about which of his traits were truly Hispanic, or how these traits clashed or fit with her own cultural preferences would have been therapeutically incorrect. It would have deprived this woman of a temporary means of protecting herself against the impending loss of her husband. Later, consideration for the children (two adolescent boys) and the type of balanced picture about the father that would benefit them in the future became a therapeutic avenue to help this woman search for her strengths and for a measure of equanimity.

A similar use of cultural stereotyping under conditions of severe stress due to impending loss is illustrated by Case E, which involves an interracial family.

The presenting problem was arguments between the mother and the 15-year-old daughter with the father acting as peacemaker. The father and the children blamed the mother's culture for the problem. They felt she was "too clean," "too particular" about the house, and that she "nagged people." The unspoken truth was that the mother had recently had a mastectomy and received frequent chemotherapy treatments that left her very tired. When she increased her demands for help with the house, the family group colluded to deny the reasons for the requests and instead attributed them to the mother's cultural traits, which had been acceptable for over 20 years. Temporarily, it was more protective for everybody to blame the mother's changes on the culture rather than recognize the nature of her illness.

The Therapeutic Use of Cultural Issues

In Cases D and E, culture, in the form of an alliance with negative public stereotypes, was being used in the family's domain to attempt to correct excessive deviations and thus gain a measure of psychological self-protection. The protective quality of using cultural stereotypes to explain the unexplainable or the very painful act should be given clinical consideration. In structural terms, the cultural stereotyping appears as a desperate boundary-making maneuver to prevent the passage of information and affect between people and thus create distance where there is too much proximity. From a therapeutic viewpoint, it seems better to respect this protective shield and work around it until it becomes possible to deal directly or indirectly with the thwarted information or the painful affect.

These cultural presentations need to be dealt with as an adaptation to family crises rather than take them at face value and focus on the cultural stereotyping or the cultural differences. The strengths inherent in the family system, both cultural and personal, need to be searched out and maximized to cope with the impending loss or other difficult transitions, and whenever possible, to halt the dysfunctional responses to stress.

SUMMARY

This chapter presents a framework for exploring the conditions under which cultural differences between spouses interact with other processes in dysfunctional ways. The hypothesis is advanced that cross-cultural couples undergo a form of cultural transition on entering marriage. The main developmental task of this aspect of the relationship is to arrive at an adaptive and flexible view of their cultural similarities and differences. This would make it possible to maintain some individuated values, to negotiate conflictual areas, and even to develop a new cultural code that integrates parts of both cultural heritages.

Couples in distress usually have an impoverished, unbalanced, or distorted view of their cultural similarities and differences, in the context of their many similarities and differences. Cultural differences are inappropriately focused on, either through maximizing and selectively highlighting them, or through minimizing and selectively submerging them. These signs are reliable indicators of problematic adaptation to the cultural transition.

Conversely, couples who achieve a balanced, complex, and appropriately focused style of dealing with their cultural differences are more likely to allow their cultural differences to remain relatively autonomous of other processes or to integrate them in a functional manner.

Three clinical patterns are described wherein the cultural differences are unbalanced. These are labeled as conflicts in cultural code, cultural differences and permission to marry, and cultural stereotyping and severe stress. Each pattern involves a different presentation of the role of the cultural differences in the marital problems. Special attention is paid to how the couple deal with their cultural differences, by maximizing or minimizing them, using them as reality, mask, or metaphor for their relationship issues. Each pattern requires a different therapeutic approach with varying focus on the cultural issues. Common pitfalls are described to help therapists avoid a focus on culture that becomes more a therapeutic liability than an asset.

Case examples illustrate a tactical use of cultural issues to progress toward a restructuring of the marital relationship, particularly in terms of interpersonal and intergenerational boundaries. Culture becomes foreground or background, depending on these goals, but it is always used positively, as a valuable resource for change.

ACKNOWLEDGMENTS

I would like to thank Lylian Brudner-White, PhD, Douglas C. Breunlin, MSSA, and Deborah Lapidus, PhD, for their helpful comments.

REFERENCES

Barron, M. (Ed.). (1972). *The blending American: Patterns of intermarriage.* Chicago: Quadrangle Books.

Berman, L. (1968). *Jews and intermarriage.* New York: Thomas Yoseloff.

Boszormenyi-Nagy, I., & Spark, G. (1973). *Invisible loyalties.* New York: Harper & Row.

Cretser, G., & Leon, J. (1982). Intermarriage in the United States. *Marriage and Family Review, 5.*

Falicov, C. J. (1982). Mexican-Americans. In M. McGoldrick, J. K. Pearce, & J. Giordano (Eds.), *Ethnicity and family therapy.* New York: Guilford Press.

Falicov, C. J., & Brudner-White, L. (1983). The shifting family triangle: The issue of cultural and contextual relativity. In C. J. Falicov (Ed.), *Cultural perspectives in family therapy.* Rockville, MD: Aspen Systems.

Falicov, C. J., & Karrer, B. (1984). Therapeutic strategies for Mexican-American families. *International Journal of Family Therapy, 6,* 1–18.

Faulkner, F., & Kich, G. K. (1983). Assessment and engagement stages is therapy with the interracial family. In C. J. Falicov (Ed.), *Cultural perspectives in family therapy.* Rockville, MD: Aspen Systems.

Friedman, E. (1982). The myth of the shiksa. In M. McGoldrick, J. K. Pearce & J. Giordano (Eds.), *Ethnicity and family therapy.* New York: Guilford Press.

Goldner, V. (1982). Remarriage family: Structure, system, future. In L. Messinger (Ed.), *Therapy with remarriage families.* Rockville, MD: Aspen Systems.

Gordon, A. (1964). *Intermarriage: Interfaith, interracial, interethnic.* Boston: Beacon Press.

Hurvitz, N. (1975). Interaction hypothesis in marriage counseling. In A. Gurman & D. Rice, *Couples in confict.* New York: Jason Aronson.

Jester, K. (1982). Analytic essay: Intercultural and interracial marriage. In G. Cretser & J. Leon, Intermarriage in the United States. New York: Haworth Press.

Keeney, B. (1983). *Aesthetics of change.* New York: Guilford Press.

Kretch, D., & Crutchfield, R. (1948). *Theory and problems of social psychology.* New York: McGraw-Hill.

Lappin, J. (1983). On becoming a culturally conscious family therapist. In C. J. Falicov (Ed.), *Cultural perspectives in family therapy*. Rockville, MD: Aspen Systems.

Leslie, G. (1982). *The family in social context*. New York: Oxford University Press.

McGoldrick, M., Pearce, J. K. & Giordano, J. (Eds.). (1982). *Ethnicity and family therapy*. New York: Guilford Press.

McGoldrick, M., & Preto, N. G. (1984). Ethnic intermarriage: Implications for therapy. *Family Process, 23*, 347–364.

Madanes, C. (1981). *Strategic family therapy*. San Francisco: Jossey-Bass.

Mead, M. (1968). We must learn to see what's really new! *Life*.

Olson, D. H., Russell, C. S., & Sprenkle, D. H. (1980). Circumplex model of marital and family systems, II: Empirical studies and clinical intervention. *Advances in Family Intervention, Assessment, and Theory, 1*, 129–179.

Reiss, I. (1976). *Family systems in America*. Hinsdale, IL: Dryden Press.

Rotunno, M., & McGoldrick, M. (1982). Italian families. In M. McGoldrick, J. K. Pearce, & J. Giordano (Eds.), *Ethnicity and family therapy*. New York: Guilford Press.

Schulz, D. (1976). *The changing family: Its function and future*. Englewood Cliffs, NJ: Prentice-Hall.

Schwartzman, J. (1983). Family ethnography: A tool for clinicians. In C. J. Falicov (Ed.), *Cultural perspectives in family therapy*. Rockville, MD: Aspen Systems.

Simpson, G., & Yinger, J. M. (1958). *Racial and cultural minorities*. New York: Harper & Brothers.

Stanton, M. D. (1981). Marital therapy from a structural/strategic viewpoint. In G. P. Sholevar (Ed.), *The handbook of marriage and marital therapy*. Jamaica, NY: S. P. Medical and Scientific Books (division of Spectrum Publications).

Stanton, M. D., Todd, T. C., Heard, D. B., Kirschner, S., Kleiman, J. I., Mowatt, D. T., Riley, P., Scott, S. M., & Van Deusen, J. M. (1978). Heroin addiction as a family phenomenon: A new conceptual model. *American Journal of Drug and Alcohol Abuse, 5*, 125–150.

van der Hart, O. (1983). *Rituals in psychotherapy: Transition and continuity*. New York: Irvington Publishers.

Winch, R. (1955). The theory of complementary needs in mate selection: Final results on the test of the general hypothesis. *American Sociological Review, 20*, 553–555.

An Introduction to Therapy Issues of Lesbian and Gay Male Couples

LAURA S. BROWN
DON ZIMMER

A couple is not a couple is not a couple. Although most experienced couples therapists would easily agree with this assertion, it is of particular significance when the couple in question is composed of two women or two men. The concrete issues confronted by most lesbian and gay male couples are, at first glance, similar to those dealt with by heterosexual couples: sharing of power, raising children, balancing relationship and career commitments, coping with in-laws. Yet beneath the surface, same-sex couples have very different sets of dynamics and issues when they come into therapy because their relationship is functioning badly. Those differences, and their sources, are necessary for understanding and working effectively with lesbian and gay male couples.

Two factors are of primary importance in understanding the differences. The first is the impact of gender-role socialization. In a same-sex couple, both partners possess the benefits and drawbacks of an essentially similar pattern of gender-role socialization. Whatever complementarity of roles that such socialization may create in a heterosexual couple is absent in most same-sex relationships. Rather, both partners are well-socialized members of their own, same gender. To work well with same-sex couples, a therapist must possess a clear comprehension of the strengths and deficits of each gender role.

The second factor that sets same-sex couples apart from their heterosexual counterparts is a phenomenon called *homophobia*. Homophobia can be defined operationally as the fear and hatred of same-sex intimacy, love, sexuality, and relationships, and of those individuals and institutions that

Laura S. Brown and Don Zimmer. Private practice, Seattle, Washington.

participate in, affirm, and support same-sex relating. Homophobia exists in a variety of ways. Externally and culturally, it has its visible manifestations in everything from laws that condemn same-sex sexuality to the phenomenon known as "queer-bashing," where vulnerable gays and lesbians are seen as legitimate targets of violence because of their sexual and affectional preferences. Internalized homophobia, the more subtle and thus more therapeutically problematic form of this phenomenon, represents the existence of homophobic values, some nonconscious, in an individual socialized in a homophobic culture. All lesbian and gay male relationships function in the context of homophobia, both cultural and internalized. The existence of a stable, happy, well-functioning same-sex relationship flies in the face of homophobia. In consequence, many problems faced by same-sex couples have their etiology in the homophobic settings in which the development of the couple has occurred. Because homophobia is never a factor in the healthy functioning of heterosexual relationships, and because the manifestations of internalized homophobia tend to be fairly subtle, the effects of homophobia are one of the more powerful sets of variables creating the differences between same-sex and heterosexual couples. They are, at the same time, most likely the factors ignored by therapists, whose own knowledge of homophobia and its manifestations is limited.

This chapter is designed to be a consciousness raiser and an introduction to common concerns and problems facing same-sex couples that differ from those faced by heterosexual couples. We wish to underline the introductory nature of this piece. Reading this chapter will not qualify the reader for competency in working with same-sex couples. Rather, we hope that the reader will become more aware of the large gaps in the training of most therapists where same-sex relationships are concerned, and thus will know how and where to seek further information. We hope that you will take the approach we offer of this being an introduction to a culture and life style that you may not have known thoroughly in the past. As with other cross-cultural endeavors, it is not possible to know the culture entirely from one brief literary excursion. We do encourage you to take this excursion and others like it. The lives and norms of the majority of lesbians and gay men have remained hidden from the view of most members of the helping professions. Information currently available in training is either biased or incomplete. Few reading this will know that you have lesbian or gay male friends, relatives, and colleagues. Yet most of you probably do; they are just not known to you. The invisibility of sexual-minority individuals has predisposed many otherwise well-meaning individuals to possess a vision of lesbians and gay men that is highly informed by myth and the media. It is imperative that helping professionals rid themselves of this mythology in order to serve sexual-minority clients adequately and ethically.

This chapter also does not prescribe any specific style or technique of couple counseling. We believe that the awareness of same-sex couple issues integrates well with any approach to couples therapy. We assume that readers seeking information or techniques will be able to find that information elsewhere in this handbook.

It has become axiomatic in scholarly work on lesbians and gay men to state that any such work cannot and does not represent the population because of serious limitations in our ability to sample. That caveat will most certainly apply here. The extent and demographic parameters of the population of lesbians and gay men are simply not known. This is an artifact of homophobia. As long as lesbians and gay men risk jobs, freedom, custody of children, and homes by being known, research and writing on this population will reflect the behaviors and values of those members of the population who are in a position to be visible, if only to other lesbians and gay men. Little systematic research is thus available on same-sex couple relationships (although by the time this volume is published, that may have changed; this is a field in constant flux). In addition, same-sex couples who are working class or people of color are, in tune with their heterosexual counterparts, less likely to seek therapy as a solution to problems in a couple relationship. This chapter thus describes work with a mostly white client group that is sufficiently comfortable with its sexual orientation to self-identify as lesbian or gay and to be open with a therapist. Both authors find that our experience in our own therapy practices is similar enough to that described by other therapists who work with this population that we feel confident that our recommendations reflect the reality and scope of same-sex couples in therapy.

As authors, we wish to make our own biases explicit. We bring to the writing of this chapter two important sets of experiences. Each of us is a therapist who has worked extensively with lesbian (LB) and gay male (DZ) couples. Each of us is also a partner in a long-term, committed, successful same-sex relationship, and we identify ourselves very clearly as a lesbian and a gay man. Therefore, both of us have perceptions, based on experience, that same-sex couples can and do work well over the long term, and each of us knows the challenges that a homophobic reality can throw in the paths of couples, even when the members of the relationship are both skillful communicators with a strong desire to make a relationship work well.

Another bias we hold jointly is that, because of the differences between male and female gender-role socialization, many of the issues faced by lesbian couples differ from those faced by gay male couples. We deal with those issues separately and lump problems in common only when we see them clearly shared by all same-sex couples. We also use the terms *lesbian* and *gay man* as our preferred nomenclature. Not all lesbians and gay men prefer these terms, and we encourage you to inquire of clients regarding their own preferred usage, as nomenclature has serious political and cultural meanings in the gay and lesbian community.

A final, and important, bias is that homosexuality is a minority rather than a deviant sexual and affectional preference. This setting is too brief a one in which to review and explore arguments regarding the etiology of such a sexual and affectional preference. We encourage the reader who does not share this bias to refrain from working as a therapist with same-sex couples. Essential to therapy with lesbian and gay male couples is the therapist's conviction that these couples are worth working on, capable of succeeding in therapy, and deserving of happiness. The therapist who sees such a couple as a substitute for, or second-best to, the "real" thing is likely to do harm to her or his clients in ways that would be ethically unacceptable to any helping professional, no matter what her or his attitudes toward homosexuality.

THE IMPACT OF HOMOPHOBIA ON LESBIAN
AND GAY MALE COUPLE FUNCTIONING

A problem that confronts all same-sex couples, no matter how well they are functioning, is homophobia. We address the impact on couples of both cultural–external homophobia and internalized homophobia, and identify some of the more common problems faced by same-sex couples as a result of this persistent phenomenon.

External–cultural homophobia has two levels of manifestation. The first is a punitive level. As of this writing (early 1984), 27 states carry statutes that make a felony of the sexual activities (i.e., oral–genital contact, anal–genital contact) most common in same-sex relationships. Lesbians and gay men are regularly fired from their jobs when their sexual preference becomes known. Lesbians and gay men in the armed services are discharged, irrespective of the quality and length of their service and commitment. Lesbians and gay men still routinely lose custody of or even visitation rights with children from previous marriages. In most jurisdictions, a lesbian or gay man can lose her or his rental home if sexual preference becomes known. Lesbians and gay men are unwelcome as worshippers.

The second level of cultural–external homophobia is that of invisibility. Lesbians and gay men cannot legally marry their same-sex partners. With the exception of insurance carried by the American Psychological Association and the *Village Voice* newspaper, insurance companies will not permit lesbians and gay men to add their partners as beneficiaries in the way that heterosexual men and women can add their spouses. Lesbians and gay men in relationships are not usually considered each other's family and thus can be excluded from visiting when their long-term partner is in intensive care or can have the wishes of a parent (often long-estranged) supersede those of the partner. Because of the risk entailed in having one's sexual preference known to an employer, lesbians and gay men are considered "single" and thus easily transferred from place to place or open to the endless matchmaking efforts of well-meaning friends and co-workers. Even at the level of the banal, lesbians and gay men suffer; there are rarely "wedding showers" for lesbian and gay male couples, even those who choose to solemnize their relationships in ways available to same-sex couples (e.g., the Holy Union service of the Metropolitan Community Church, a gay-oriented denomination).

The net effect of this on lesbian and gay male relationships is twofold. Because of the risks, few visible, happy, "Ozzie and Harriet"-style same-sex couples are available as models for lesbians and gay men of how to build a relationship between two women or two men. Unlike members of other minorities, who grow up among their own reference group, where culture and traditions can be transmitted in an affirmative manner, gay men and lesbians grow up trained to be heterosexual, with the expectations of a heterosexual relationship as their sole paradigm.

The meta-message of all this risk and invisibility is that the well-functioning same-sex couple does not and/or should not exist. Blumstein and Schwartz (1983) comment that the institution of marriage has as its symbolic function the official sanctioning and source of permission for a relationship between two people. The absence of that official blessing can often be interpreted by the lesbian or gay man as the prohibition to relate well. Cultural myths about lesbians and gay men complicate the matter; what images of lesbian and gay male couples are available are distorted, usually in the negative direction. Many lesbians and gay men have internalized the concept that same-sex relationships are brief, devoid of real feeling, and based primarily on sexual attraction. (As one lesbian activist put it, "We're told that we spend 22 hours a day doing drugs and alcohol and having sex, and the other 2 resting up to do it again"—Kathleen Boyle, personal communication, 1978.) This meta-message becomes internalized by almost all lesbians and gay men growing up in Western culture, no matter what their race or socioeconomic status. These factors can vary the intensity and negativity of the homophobia internalized, but will not take away from its presence.

Therapists should not make the mistake of believing that a lesbian or gay man with a conscious lack of homophobia will also lack nonconscious, internalized homophobia. Rather, in working with same-sex couples, it is important to probe for deeply held attitudes regarding the value of such relationships, and to be aware of ways in which internalized homophobia can be acted out. Some examples common to our experiences follow:

1. Members of a same-sex couple come into therapy with the focus of conflict being the merging, or not merging, of financial resources and/or household goods. In the therapy session, one partner talks about distrusting the other with her or his money; when questioned, she or he says, "But we'll break up some day, and then we'll have to disentangle it all." Planning to break up (as distinguished from holding a healthy awareness that any relationship can end) becomes the self-fulfilling prophecy in many same-sex relationships. Lack of trust can be, and often is, a symptom of internalized homophobia, particularly when there are no external, verifiable factors that would reduce trust between two partners. Saying that "this relationship will break up" becomes a code for saying, "Gay/lesbian relationships never last." Berzon and Leighton (1979) and Blumstein and Schwartz (1983) comment

on the relationship between longevity of same-sex relationships, satisfaction with same, and willingness to merge resources to some degree.

2. A same-sex couple enters therapy with one partner's extreme jealousy and/or possessiveness as the presenting complaint. One partner describes how the other will forbid her or him to have close friends who are also lesbians or gay men. In session, the couple talk about how, in their belief, all other lesbians and gay men are a threat to the relationship because "all your friends are potential lovers for your lover." This fear of infidelity can be a code for saying, "I don't believe that my partner could have a real commitment to me, since this is a gay–lesbian relationship, which by definition is based on the most fleeting of sexual attractions."

3. A couple seeks therapy because one member has a close friendship and/or infatuation with a heterosexual person of the same sex. It becomes apparent during the course of therapy that the fact of this individual's heterosexuality is the source of the threat; one member verbalizes it as, "If she could have someone who's straight, why would she want me?" Here, there is no code to break. Rather, it is explicit that a lesbian or gay man would be less valuable than a person who is not (or not identified as such).

4. A couple seeks therapy because although all is going well in other aspects of the relationship, there has been a serious diminishing of sexual frequency. Both partners express concern; both describe themselves as still attracted to and in love with their partner. Standard techniques used to increase and enhance couple sexual functioning seem to have little impact, even though motivation for change seems high, and both members of the couple begin to worry about whether the relationship can last if there is little or no sexual activity. This "worm in the bud" phenomenon, where a seemingly idyllic same-sex relationship contains one apparently fatal and insurmountable flaw, is one of the most subtle and challenging manifestations of internalized homophobia, yet one of the more common. The function of the problem is to communicate to the partners that a truly happy, functional, same-sex relationship, in which all components of relational functioning are satisfactory to both members of the couple, is an impossibility. This example illustrates that importance, for the therapist, of inquiring regarding the homophobic function of a lesbian or gay male couple's presenting problem. If the problem serves to communicate to the couple that their relationship is illegitimate, inconsequential, ephemeral, or otherwise less than equal to heterosexual relationships, then the chances are excellent that internalized homophobia will be a major, if not the only, source of the problem in functioning. One experienced therapist who works with lesbian couples puts it succinctly: "It's a wonder we have sex at all" (Gardner-Loulan, 1983).

It is important to stress that the best same-sex relationship will encounter glimmerings of internalized homophobia; both authors have had a number of occasions in their own well-functioning same-sex relationships where we have been able to make sense of an otherwise senseless issue by asking ourselves whether homophobia (our own or our partner's) had anything to do with what was happening. How much more likely, therefore, that a couple with problems will have to confront their mutual and usually non-conscious homophobic beliefs and values. This can be complicated severely if the therapist is unaware of and/or inattentive to her or his own internalized homophobia. Common manifestations of therapist internalized homophobia are these:

1. A lack of value for the couple's commitment; encouraging a couple to see their problems as insurmountable and to end the relationship more quickly than would be the case with a heterosexual couple with similar problems.

2. An overattachment to longevity of relationship as opposed to quality of relationship. This is a sort of reverse internalized homophobia. Because of the homophobic myth of the short, meaningless same-sex relationship, therapists as well as client couples can become overattached to the value of the longevity in a relationship. If you, as therapist, would aid in the healthy conclusion of a heterosexual relationship of similar longevity and avoid such a possibility with same-sex couples, you may be requiring your lesbian and gay male client couples to be your living proof that the myth is wrong.

3. A lack of serious attention to the issue and impact of substance abuse in a same-sex relationship. Several sources (Fifield, 1975; Swallow, 1983) document the high rates of substance abuse in sexual-minority communities. Both also attest to the neglect of that problem by the helping professions. Anecdotes arising from the gay–lesbian AA and Al-Anon communities point out that therapists have often neglected to take adequate substance use–abuse histories from same-sex couples, even in the face of the higher base rate of the problem in the gay–lesbian population.

4. Overglamorizing the same-sex relationship. Many well-meaning in-dividuals, both lay public and therapists, think that in order to combat homophobia we must assume that all same-sex relationships are wonderful and romantic. Telling your clients how "brave" they are to be having their relationship, or how wonderful it must be to have someone who can really understand you (the myth of intragender empathy, unfortunately given the countenance of scientific "fact" by Masters and Johnson's study of same-sex sexual functioning, is still really a myth) gives clients the meta-message that they must either underplay their problems in order to keep your image of gay men and lesbians intact or that there must be something dreadfully wrong with them because they are not romantic figures, but two ordinary people trying to learn how to communicate their anger more clearly.

A useful question for the therapist to ask herself or himself as a check against unexamined internalized homophobia is, "What message am I giving my clients regarding the meaning and value of same-sex relationships?" Denigration and pedestalization have equal potential for harm. It is important that a therapist working with lesbian or gay male couples strive to communicate the ordinary specialness of the relationship, its equal (not less or greater) value, its uniqueness as a same-sex relationship, and its banality as an intimate connection between two adults. The goal is for both therapist and client couple to take for granted the possibility of a happy, healthy, same-sex relationship in the way that happy, healthy, heterosexual relationships have long been taken for granted. It is particularly useful when working with same-sex couples to seek consultation early on from a therapist aware of, and experienced in working with, internalized homophobia. Our experience as therapists has been that our own internalized homophobia is not ever entirely apparent to us, and that despite our commitment to attend to it, we have been greatly aided by the eyes and ears of our equally aware colleagues. We find this caveat to be particularly true with therapists who are new to, or inexperienced in working with, same-sex couples, regardless of sexual orientation.

SPECIAL ISSUES AND CONCERNS OF LESBIAN COUPLES

One of the most salient facts regarding a lesbian couple is that it is made up of two women. This self-evident phenomenon is the richest source of both strengths and problems that lesbian couples bring into therapy. The therapist working with a lesbian couple is confronted with female gender-role socialization multiplied by two. Although each woman will vary in the degree to which she reflects this socialization, it is usually the case that even the most "masculine"-appearing lesbian will be quite well socialized when it comes to such issues as expressing and sharing power, expressing anger and hostility, initiation of sexual activity, and tolerance of conflict and difference. In order to work well with lesbian couples, a therapist should first have a thorough understanding of the development of female personality. A conceptual framework for understanding women, women's roles, and the expectations that women bring into relationships is a must for intervening in a problematic lesbian couple relationship. Readers are referred to Miller (1976) and Chodorow (1978) for a complete analysis of these topics. Without clearly comprehending the effect of women's socialization in a sexist culture in which women are devalued, it may be difficult for a therapist, no matter how skillful, to comprehend some of the more common problems faced by lesbian couples.

As with internalized homophobia, this phenomenon of the devaluation of women merits careful analysis in helping lesbian couples confront their problems. Lesbians, like other women, learn to have a low regard for the value of "feminine" ways of behaving: being nurturant, empathic, and concerned with comfort and the creation of a home. Blumstein and Schwartz (1983) comment that because the lesbians they studied are in the process of rejecting both traditional female and male roles, they are likely to experience more conflicts when it comes to the expression of behaviors in a relationship that are typically gender-role determined for heterosexual adults. Valuing the other woman in one's lesbian relationship because she is a woman challenges the deeply held sense, shared by most people socialized in this culture, that a woman is somehow second-best.

In problematic lesbian couple relationships, this issue is often expressed by means of perfectionistic expectations held by one member of the couple regarding the other (and often mutually held). In order to make up for her deficiency in not being a man, the female partner is required to be a perfect mirror, a perfect nurturer, and simultaneously totally independent and capable of meeting her own needs at all times. This double bind of expectation, in which ego-boundaryless empathy is to be merged with perfect interpersonal distance, becomes the rock on which many lesbian couples have foundered. A complicating factor in this phenomenon is that while women have been socialized to cope with such expectations when they come from men, they consider them unrealistic and often insulting when delivered by a (mere) woman. A case example may illustrate this phenomenon in operation.

> A lesbian couple seek therapy with a presenting complaint of lack of sexual activity. On initial interview, they share with the therapist that they have been sexual only four times in the course of a 5-year relationship. One of the women, who has often attempted to initiate sexual contact with no success, has become increasingly angry over the years but has restrained herself from expressing her feelings because she wants to "prove to my lover that I could handle anything that she did and still love her." This woman is in the process of acting out her anger by beginning a relationship with a new woman. This has served as a catalyst for the second woman, who has until now refused all sexual contact, to begin frequent initiation of sexual activity. The second woman is enraged at her partner, but primarily she is incredulous that her newly recovered interest in sex has not healed the wounds of the past 5 years. Her expectation, clearly stated, is that her lover will be able to understand and forgive. And if she can't, adds the second woman, then perhaps she isn't the truly understanding and caring person she has thought her to be.

This couple have agreed to and colluded with each other in creating and strengthening the expectation that one of them would and could be a perfect nurturer to the other, with all behaviors instantly forgiven, and no anger ever expressed. The couple saw conflict as an indication that one or the other woman had failed in her commitment to this perfection. The first woman, who prior to this lesbian relationship had been in a long-standing heterosexual marriage, revealed on questioning that, "I never would have put up with this kind of behavior from my husband." Somehow, each woman was giving the other the meta-message that it was expectable that she would be flawed, since female, but also equally expected that she would make up for these flaws by the perfection of her caring for her partner. Exploration during therapy revealed fantasies on the parts of both partners regarding "making it up to" the other woman by the demonstration of perfection at all times. The focus of therapy was on reshaping expectations and rewriting the relationship contract in such a way that each partner would accept her lover's "imperfections" rather than constantly hope for change to a perfect state. In this case, the client couple found it helpful to have the analysis of the effects of sexism and devaluation of women shared during therapy, as it allowed each woman to make better sense of behaviors that she had found hard to comprehend in herself and her partner.

Each woman's female sex-role socialization was a contributing factor in the development of their problem. Each had learned that women were not supposed to be interested in sex. Thus, the first woman's sexual interest and anger at lack of sexual activity were seen as deviations from role. Neither woman had learned that it was acceptable to express anger, even in fair and appropriate ways. Instead, each strove to be "nice," a "good girl," and defined anger as hatred rather than an expression of disagreement. Each expected a woman to be perfect in her empathic skills, and was critical of both herself and her partner when mutual mindreading did not transpire. In short, each expected herself and her partner to be a good "wife," and neither was given the chance to have the imperfections of the "husband" stereotype.

Another problem etiology common to lesbian couples (and to gay men as well) is the "age in gay life" or "who's a real lesbian" phenomenon. Because women come out and assume a lesbian identity at varying points during adolescence and adulthood, a couple with the same chronological ages may have very different ages in gay life. One woman may have identified herself as a lesbian since early adolescence, and have had little or no heterosexual experience but many relationships with other women. Her partner, on the other hand, may have been heterosexually married, borne children, and not become lesbian-identified until later adulthood (e.g., late 30s or early 40s). In couples where there is significant divergence in age in gay life, conflicts can become centered on this phenomenon. An example can be found in the following case:

> A lesbian couple who have been in a committed, monogamous relationship for 2 years seek counseling because one of the women is expressing an interest in taking a second lover and being nonmonogamous. The two women, both in their early 30s, have much in common: They come from similar ethnic and class backgrounds, they share many activities and interests, and they work in the same profession. One significant difference is that the woman who wishes to remain monogamous has been "out" as a lesbian since her late teens and viewed this relationship as her mature, adult attempt at settling down. Her lover is in her first lesbian relationship ever. The latter is feeling that she "missed her chance to try out other relationships with other women" and expresses some concern that she be able to respond to other women than her current lover. The second woman's request for a trial of nonmonogamy has been the source of great conflict and has polarized

the two women into their respective positions, with each quoting her favorite political tracts to support her position in the conflict.

In the course of therapy, the woman who was new to gay life expressed her desire simultaneously to remain committed to and in a relationship with her lover and to have her "lesbian adolescence," a phrase used by many lesbians to describe the adolescent-like period of sexual and relational experimentation experienced by many lesbians just following their coming out. Lesbian adolescence rarely corresponds in time with chronological adolescence (although as the stigma attached to lesbianism recedes, we can expect more lesbians to have their adolescent sexual experiences at a more age-appropriate time). The first woman, who had experienced a period of experimentation earlier in her own development, was more willing to understand her lover's request for a nonmonogamous contract when it was framed in terms of an adolescent acting-out period. The couple's conflict resolved when the second woman responded to this permission by dropping her request. Apparently, as with other adolescent rebellions, this had been a testing and request for limit setting as a way of being shown love and taken seriously. This woman commented that she felt more like a "real lesbian" if her partner truly thought her capable of relationships with other women, and she thus felt more equal in power to her partner, whom she had envied for her extensive experience with other women. Counseling continued with this couple with a goal of establishing more open, clear communication regarding symbolic issues, and the couple were referred to a support group for lesbian couples where they could have the opportunity to share experiences, problems, strategies, and solutions with other women.

The last sentence refers to another problem that exists for lesbian couples. A lack of role models, and the dearth of a mythology of how a happy, healthy lesbian couple would operate, has required the creation of support structures in which many couples may have access to the experience of others. In addition, in recent years some lesbian-couple-affirmative fiction has become available that serves to make models available to readers. The best of the genre, *Choices*, by lesbian psychologist Nancy Toder, does a superb job of describing the problems and solutions of garden-variety lesbians in a way that client couples can easily identify with. Creating support or couples therapy groups for lesbian couples represents a therapeutic strategy that expands the system of the lesbian couple and enlarges their view of how such a relationship might operate.

A final issue that complicates the life of even well-functioning lesbian couples is the boundary problem, often manifested as an intolerance for distance and difference within the lesbian couple. Chodorow (1978), Orbach and Eichenbaum (1983), and others have commented on how, in the development of female personality, women are left with permeable and poorly defined ego boundaries. The mother–infant daughter relationship becomes a paradigm for close and loving relationships between women, with the model including such features as perfect empathy, mutuality of needs, and poorly defined boundaries between the persons in the relationship. In the context of a heterosexual relationship, this poorly defined female ego boundary and heightened female capacity for empathy are functional when paired with a man, who has a well-developed boundary and less well developed interpersonal and intuitive skills (Orbach & Eichenbaum, 1983). But in a lesbian relationship, the presence of this personality configuration in both members of the couple can lead to problems and complications if not recognized.

It is extremely common for lesbian couples to describe their initial attraction in terms of a falling away of boundaries. For example, "We were so alike," "She understood me without my having to say anything," or "I felt merged with her." It is also common for couples in conflict to describe the etiology of their problems in terms of the development of differences between the two women. Intolerance of open conflict, differences of opinion and politics, styles of communicating—all of these appear with high frequency in troubled lesbian couples. They are often accompanied by a sense of terror on the part of both women that such differences have appeared. Problems also commonly develop when one woman wishes to spend leisure time apart from the other, or to have friends as an individual rather than in the context of the couple relationship. In problematic lesbian couples, such a bid for autonomy is usually defined as a desire to end the relationship by the member of the couple who is resisting the development of any distance. Enmeshment is thus perceived as a desirable goal, while appropriate interdependency is a threat. Problems often develop when a bid for greater autonomy on the part of one woman is met with increased demands for the meeting of dependency needs by the other, thus creating a cycle in which the autonomy-seeking partner finds herself feeling "trapped" (the word that most such clients use to describe their feelings at this juncture) by her partner's heightened demands for emotional and behavioral fusion.

This very common and delicate problem of lesbian couples is best approached by accurately diagnosing and naming to clients. Giving the client couple a clear theoretical explanation of what is occurring is often the most essential component of intervention. This seems to be true, in part, because the lesbian couple can see their problem as a normative one and as resulting from their socialization as women to participate in heterosexual relationships with men. Having this normative approach seems to reduce the fear associated with distance–difference issues so that they can be worked on in therapy in a constructive manner. When each woman can be clear that this struggle to establish boundaries is a sign of couple strength and health, rather than a portent of disaster, she is more likely to ally herself with the task of creating the healthy boundaries. Therapists working with lesbian couples need to differentiate clearly between behaviors associated with healthy bonding and those that indicate unhealthy fusion. Particularly important in this context are tools for teaching couples to bring anger and conflict to the surface for resolution, as well as tools for clarifying hidden and symbolic communications that would otherwise be consigned to the mindreading efforts of one or both women.

An invaluable tool for a therapist working with lesbian couples is knowledge of the dynamics of healthy and functioning lesbian couples. This can be accomplished in a variety of ways. For the lesbian therapist, having a network of social support that includes well-functioning couples besides one's own (if one is in a relationship) can aid in broadening the scope of conceptual possibilities for work with clients. For heterosexual or gay male therapists, affirmative contact with lesbian couples who are not your therapy clients may be necessary to begin framing a model of healthy lesbian couple functioning. Having a clinical feel as well as a behavioral model for a healthy lesbian couple will reduce the possibility that the therapist will be as confused about how a lesbian couple can work as her or his clients are.

THERAPY ISSUES WITH GAY MALE COUPLES

As with a lesbian couple, the juxtaposition of two socializations into the male gender role in a gay male couple acts as a source of both strength and problems. In many ways, men in Western culture are less well prepared by their gender-role socialization to be in an intimate relationship or to do the work of relationship maintenance (David & Brannon, 1976; Orbach & Eichenbaum, 1983; Pleck & Sawyer, 1974) than are women. Just as lesbians are socialized to expect the dynamics and norms of a heterosexual relationship, so are gay men. However, gay men learn to be "husbands": to control, express anger, be territorial, move for power, be sexual—but not to be empathic, nurturing, emotionally expressive, or to cook the meals. Many of the problems discussed in the section on lesbian couples are reflected in reverse here. Because gay men are men, the problems of gay male couples reflect the deficits built into the male gender role.

One of the most common problems faced by gay male couples is that of learning to do the work of relationship maintenance. Men are socialized in Western culture to respond sexually, and often a gay male couple will begin its life in a purely sexual context. Once the novelty of sex is reduced and the realities of relationship building are introduced, however, many gay male couples find themselves at a loss. The expression of tender feelings has been seen as wrong for men and, for many gay men, to be avoided as a way of avoiding the stereotype of the gay man as a "sissy" (Morin & Garfinkle, 1978). In addition, many gay men report that they experience some difficulty in maintaining sexual arousal in the context of a relationship and thus may avoid or sabotage long-term commitments in order to keep their sexual functioning at a comfortable level. An illustrative case example can be found in the following:

> *A gay male couple enter therapy with a presenting complaint of "poor communication." The two men have been lovers for 2 years and have lived together for the past 6 months, a point from which both men date the beginning of their problem. Neither has lived with a partner before, although both have extensive histories of relationships with other men. During therapy, it becomes apparent that neither man has skills for expressing dependency needs and tender feelings. Each becomes aware of some previously nonconscious expectations that a partner would know what he needed; neither feels comfortable with expressing vulnerability, seeing such behavior as "unmasculine." One man comments, "I want to be a real man for my lover, not some hysterical queen." Although each man has adequate skills for maintaining a dating relationship where contact is structured, infrequent, and centered on exciting and interesting activities, neither has a repertoire for coping with the requirements of increased physical proximity and emotional intimacy.*

Therapy in this case required confrontation of stereotypes about "masculinity" and male-appropriate behaviors. As internalized homophobia was a factor in this situation, both men were given the opportunity to see how their rigid thinking about masculinity was part of an attempt to avoid fitting homophobic stereotypes of gay men. In this case, as was the case with lesbian couples described previously, the therapist's presenting the problem as a normative issue in the development of gay male couples was a useful intervention, and allowed room for trial and error as each man learned to be more expressive of needs and feelings. It is often helpful, in working with gay male couples on issues of relationship maintenance, to connect the client couple with other well-functioning couples who are comfortable with emotional expressivity and can provide the clients with models of gay maleness that transcend stereotypes. This may be even more important than with lesbian couples, for male sex-role socialization seems to be more detrimental to couple maintenance than female sex-role socialization. Consequently, a gay male couple may be less likely than a lesbian couple to have models of well-functioning couples within their friendship networks, particularly if neither man has significant prior experience in long-term gay male relationships. Since many aspects of gay male culture have a "singles" flavor to them, it can be difficult for a gay male couple to value the benefits they obtain from a committed relationship when these are not culturally well supported. It may also be particularly important at this juncture for a therapist to examine her or his own beliefs about the value and likelihood of gay men being in committed relationships. Occasionally, the therapist may find herself or himself nonconsciously reinforcing a sense of hopelessness regarding the possibility of maintaining a long-term commitment because of the therapist's own internalized homophobia or acceptance of the myths that gay male relationships cannot last.

Another common issue that confronts gay male couples is that of defining relationship boundaries and levels of monogamy. It is very common for gay men to have a commitment that is one of simultaneous emotional monogamy and sexual nonmonogamy, with a clear contract between the partners regarding how nonmonogamous sexual behavior (often referred to as "tricking out") will take place. For example, "Don't bring them home," "Not with any of our friends," or "Only with our friends." The therapist who lacks experience with gay male couples may find it difficult to assimilate this apparent inconsistency within the relationship into her or his beliefs about monogamy and commitment, and thus may erroneously assume that the existence of such an arrangement is either the cause or symptom of problems within the relationship. It is important for such a therapist to accept that, for some gay male couples, this may be the very arrangement that allows their emotional commitment to function safely at all. This phenomenon helps to highlight the value of the therapist's being familiar with norms of gay male culture. At the same time, it is also worth exploring such a contract with a client couple with a mind open to the possibility that a tricking-out agreement may equally as likely be a source of comfort as it may be of relationship problems. Such a norm can become problematic for a couple when, for instance, one man is willing to be sexually monogamous and the other is not. When such an imbalance occurs, it is important to analyze and work with it from the perspective of a power imbalance within the relationship. A therapist must not assume that a commitment to sexual monogamy will be the only, or even the most likely, solution to an imbalance of this sort.

A case illustrating some therapy options for dealing with this issue is that of a gay male couple who entered therapy in the seventh year of a relationship that had been both emotionally and sexually monogamous. The couple entered therapy because one of the men had attempted to renegotiate the sexual monogamy contract. The couple was able to identify in therapy that a problematic issue had been the second man's fears about the open-ended, unpredictable nature of the new situation. Would he know when and with whom his lover was being sexual? Was it possible to do this? Were there any men who had made this agreement who did not end up leaving the relationship? In this case, therapy was used to help the couple negotiate a sexual nonmonogamy contract that gave equivalent weights to each man's needs and that created a trial period for experimentation with the new order of things. The therapist was able both to validate the fears and concerns of the second man and to make available to these clients models of gay male couples who had successfully integrated sexual openness into an emotionally committed relationship. In addition, the couple learned how to enhance their emotional expression, thus strengthening the outward manifestations of what each perceived to be a tight and secure bond of affection between them. What was important in this case was that the therapist was able to see this arrangement as both normative and feasible, and had a clear framework for working toward success for both members of the couple and the relationship itself.

A final issue common to gay male couples is that of competitiveness in the areas of power and status. Men in Western culture are often socialized to view their value as measured by the power, prestige, and income of their work, and to see other men as at best competitors and at worst the enemy in this game for status and power. In a gay male relationship, it is likely that one man will be in an occupation that has greater power, income, or status attached to it. The potential for feelings of competitiveness to emerge and to become a destructive thread in the fabric of the relationship thus exists. This competitiveness can operate in a variety of ways. For instance, the couple may present a problem of unequal sharing of chores or planning of social activities. On examination, what may often emerge is that the man with the greater culturally defined occupational value expects his partner to make up for his lesser status by doing more of the work of the relationship. The lesser-status partner may, in fact, be comfortable with the amount of energy he expends on the relationship and may be responding with discomfort to the unspoken messages regarding his lesser value as a human being secondary to his occupational status, rather than to the tasks he is performing.

In this situation, as with many other common problems presented in therapy by gay male couples, the therapist's thorough grasp of gender-role issues is essential to resolve the problem. It can be highly effective for the therapist to probe regarding the impact of differences in occupational status on the couple's functioning. Usually, the higher-status man is unaware of how his behavior is communicating devaluation to his partner. In fact, both men may have a spoken agreement that the lower-status man should have less power and more task responsibility in the relationship ("because it's only fair," to quote a commonly heard phrase spoken by both members of a couple in these situations). Because gay men are socialized to see a traditional heterosexual couple, with its imbedded (and equally unhealthy) power inequalities, as a relationship norm, neither may have questioned his taken-for-granted notions about how power is shared in a relationship. However, because each has been socialized to seek power in a relationship context, both members of the gay male couple need to be confronted with how this model works even less well for them than for heterosexual relationships, where one member of the couple (usually the woman) has been trained into submissive behaviors. It is important, when working with a gay male couple, for a therapist to ask how gender-role issues might be expressing themselves in the couple's presenting complaint. The two men may have very good skills at negotiating who takes out the garbage, but less comprehension of why taking it out feels so demeaning and problematic to the one who does the job.

Again, as for therapists working with lesbian couples, it is vital for a therapist working with gay male couples to have available to her or him models of healthy, well-functioning gay male couples. The authors cannot overstress the power of the effect of only seeing gay couples as one's therapy clients. The distorted image of gay male couple functioning that can result from such a skewed set of data may make it difficult for the therapist to help a gay male couple resolve their presenting problems successfully. Thus, we encourage therapists who are not familiar with the possibilities for gay male relationships to seek information. *The Male Couple*, by McWhirter and Mattison, is an excellent first step for therapists who are not in contact with the gay community. Written by a gay male couple, both therapists, it provides a range of examples of how well-functioning gay male couples, including that of the two authors, work.

CONCLUSION

Any two people who come into therapy to learn how to heal breaches in their relationship run a risk. The risk is that their couple system is not amenable to change in such a way that the system still operates. This holds true for lesbian and gay male couples just as much as it does for heterosexual couples. Neither author assumes that the only measure of effective therapy with lesbian and gay male couples is contained in the outcome of a good, ongoing relationship. Rather, we hope to have pointed out some common factors that may be obscured when a therapist's vision of lesbian and gay relationships has been formed by homophobic mythology. Our concern is that lesbian and gay male couples have an equal chance of success at remaining together, or success at ending a relationship in a fashion that opens doors to new possibilities for each person, to that of heterosexual couples.

In that regard, we wish to add a few words about the specific problems confronting lesbian and gay male couples who are ending relationships. Because legal marriage is not yet a possibility for same-sex couples, the legal ramifications of the end of a same-sex partnership are different from those of a married pair. Therapists are encouraged to obtain a copy of *A Legal Guide for Lesbian and Gay Couples* (Curry & Clifford, 1980) and to have a working consulting relationship with an attorney who is familiar with the legal issues in each jurisdiction regarding division of property and visitation and custody rights for children (this last becomes more essential as more lesbians, in particular, are giving birth to children by artificial insemination in the context of their couple relationships). We also encourage therapists working with a couple who are moving toward good functioning to examine the legal ramifications of their partnership. The shock of losing a shared home on the death of a partner merely because the relationship had never been formalized in a will, the pain of not having access to one's partner when she or he is ill because one has no legal right without previously arranged documents—these and other stressors on same-sex couples can be reduced when a therapist is aware of the possibilities and encourages clients to be legally prepared for the worst.

Same-sex relationships can be and are functional and viable systems, enriching the lives of lesbians and gay men in the same way that heterosexual relationships and marriage can be for heterosexual women and men. A troubled same-sex relationship can and should be equally supported by the helping professions, and the skillful couple therapist who is aware of the pitfalls put in her or his way by homophobia is likely to be able to lend that support.

REFERENCES

Berzon, B., & Leighton, R. (1979). *Positively gay*. Millbrae, CA: Celestial Arts.

Blumstein, P., & Schwartz, P. (1983). *American couples*. New York: Morrow.

Boyle, K. (1978). Personal communication.

Chodorow, N. (1978). *The reproduction of mothering*. Berkeley: University of California Press.

Curry, H., & Clifford, D. (1980). *A legal guide for lesbian and gay couples*. Reading, MA: Addison-Wesley.

David, D., & Brannon, R. (1976). *The forty-nine percent majority: The male sex role*. Reading, MA: Addison-Wesley.

Fifield, L. (1975). *On my way to nowhere: An analysis of gay alcohol abuse*. Los Angeles: County of Los Angeles.

Gardner-Loulan, J. (1983). It's a wonder we have sex at all. In J. Swallow (Ed.), *Out from under: Sober dykes and our friends* (pp. 93–101). San Francisco: Spinsters, Ink.

McWhirter, D., & Mattison, A. (1983). *The male couple: How relationships develop*. Englewood Cliffs, NJ: Prentice-Hall.

Miller, J. B. (1976). *Toward a new psychology of women*. Boston: Beacon Press.

Morin, S., & Garfinkle, E. M. (1978). Male homophobia. *Journal of Social Issues, 34*(1).

Orbach, S., & Eichenbaum, L. (1983). *What do women want?* New York: Basic Books.

Pleck, J., & Sawyer, J. (1974). *Men and masculinity*. Englewood Cliffs, NJ: Prentice-Hall.

Swallow, J. *Out from under: Sober dykes and our friends*. San Francisco: Spinsters Ink.

Toder, N. (1980). *Choices*. Watertown, MA: Persephone Press.

Suggested Additional Reading

Gonsiorek, J. (Ed.). (1982). *Homosexuality and psychotherapy: A practitioner's handbook of affirmative models*. New York: Haworth Press.

Mendola, M. (1980). *The Mendola report: A new look at gay couples*. New York: Crown.

Moses, A. E., & Hawkins, R. O. (1983) *Counseling lesbian women and gay men*. St. Louis: Mosby.

FURTHER REFERENCES

A selected bibliography of gay concerns for psychology: An affirmative perspective. Available from Committee on Gay Concerns, American Psychological Association, 1200 17th Street NW, Washington, DC 20036.

Further resource information can be obtained by writing to National Gay Task Force, 80 Fifth Avenue, New York, NY 10011. This group monitors national resource listings of all gay and lesbian organizations.

IV

MARITAL THERAPY AND SELECTED PSYCHIATRIC DISORDERS

Marital Therapy for Agoraphobia

R. JULIAN HAFNER

Although controversy exists about the nature of agoraphobia (Hallam, 1978), it is a disorder that can be defined adequately in operational terms such as those of the DSM-III: "The essential feature is a marked fear of being alone, or being in public places from which escape might be difficult or help not available in case of sudden incapacitation."

The central fear of incapacitation takes several forms. A majority of women with agoraphobia fear primarily the sudden onset of panic attacks, during which they are frightened of losing control in some way. A fear of loss of control through fainting or passing out is most commonly reported; others report a fear of "going berserk" and injuring or making a public spectacle of themselves. Agoraphobic men report panic attacks much less often than do agoraphobic women; instead, they are more likely to be preoccupied with fears of acute illness, sudden death, or alterations of consciousness when out alone, or with fears of loss of control of aggressive and self-destructive impulses (Hafner, 1981a, 1983a).

At least 60% of agoraphobics who seek treatment are married women. Half of the remainder are unmarried women; only about 20% are men (Vose, 1981; Doctor, 1982). Not only do the symptoms of agoraphobic men differ from those of women, but men respond less well to behaviorally oriented treatment programs and more commonly appear to be enmeshed in marriage relationships that perpetuate their agoraphobia (Liotti & Guidano, 1976; Hafner, 1981a). However, there is very little systematic data about marital systems or the value of marital therapy in agoraphobic

R. Julian Hafner. Department of Psychiatry, Flinders Medical Centre, Bedford Park, Australia.

men, and my own understanding of the area is embryonic. Therefore, this chapter focuses on agoraphobia in women.

MARITAL CONTRIBUTIONS TO AGORAPHOBIA

Anyone seeking to comprehend agoraphobia is confronted with a bewildering and seemingly unrelated variety of psychodynamic, behavioral, neurobiological, and interpersonal theories, of which the latter are the primary concern of this chapter. Ideally, theories are developed, tested, refuted or confirmed, and progressively modified, in the light of scientific research.

Research Findings

Systematic research into agoraphobia presents a number of extraordinary difficulties, of which the foremost involves patient selection. In routine clinical practice, it is unusual for agoraphobia to exist in isolation. Most patients present with a range of additional problems; the commonest are depression, hypochondriasis, generalized anxiety and obsessive–compulsive symptoms, social and general phobias, personality abnormalities, and marital difficulties. A recent factor analysis of a large clinical agoraphobic population (Hafner & Ross, 1984) showed that agoraphobic symptoms contributed only 16% to the variance in overall symptomatology. General symptoms contributed 28%, social fears 11%, and general fears over 30%.

Unfortunately, most systematic studies of agoraphobia, particularly those comparing two or more drug or behavioral treatments, deliberately exclude patients with significant additional problems. While this is necessary for methodological rigor, it means that most research on agoraphobia is conducted on unrepresentative populations. Such populations, because they are suffering from a single, relatively homogeneous disorder without major marital problems, generally respond to drug or behavioral therapies. If patients with significant additional problems are invited to participate in drug or behavioral treatment studies, they are often reluctant to do so, respond poorly, or drop out early, particularly if treatment includes exposure *in vivo* (confronting fears in real life). The unrepresentative nature of the patients who enter and remain in such studies is rarely emphasized by the authors. This has led to an over-valuation of behavioral and drug therapies in the treatment of agoraphobia and a neglect of dyadic and multimodal approaches. This widely held but distorted perspective is summarized in a recent overview (Rapp & Thomas, 1982): "In summary, we derive few clues about the nature of agoraphobia by studying the personalities, childhoods or marriages of patients."

Fortunately, there are now sufficient clinical dyadic studies of agoraphobia to act as a substantial counterweight to the mass of misleading research data obtained from unrepresentative populations.

Clinical Findings

I have reviewed elsewhere clinical dyadic studies of agoraphobia up to 1980 (Hafner, 1982) and therefore only summarize this area, including relevant clinical reports published since 1980.

There is a clear consensus among experienced, dyadically orientated agoraphobia therapists that severe, complex cases of agoraphobia in maritally dissatisfied women are best treated in a marital setting. Fundamental to such an approach is the idea of *assortative mating*, for which I have provided some empirical evidence (Hafner, 1977a, 1977b). From this perspective, the origins of agoraphobia lie in choice of marriage partner. For example, an unusually dependent woman who believes that she will be unable to manage life without a strong husband to protect and financially support her is likely to marry a man with the reciprocal belief that marriage is essentially a framework within which a "strong" man protects and financially supports a "weak," dependent woman. Agoraphobic symptoms emerge when one partner adheres more rigidly than the other to this initial, often tacit or unconscious, basis for the marriage. Classically, the husband becomes uncomfortable when his wife seeks to extend her interests beyond the purely domestic, and he undermines her attempts to do this. Since the husband's fears about his wife's greater autonomy are ultimately irrational, his attempts to confine her to a domestic environment are inevitably illogical, inconsistent, and confusing to her. Since she has already defined herself as an unusually dependent woman, abnormally reliant on her husband, she cannot reject her husband's viewpoint, however illogically or inconsistently it is expressed. In relation to this conflict she experiences anxiety symptoms, and, if she does defy her husband, suffers panic attacks when out alone.

Agoraphobia develops when situations outside the home are avoided, ostensibly because of the fear of panic attacks, although the precise mechanisms involved remain to be elucidated. Goldstein and Chambless (1978) have suggested that avoidance occurs through a process of classical conditioning: Panic attacks are extremely frightening, and this intense fear becomes strongly conditioned to the situation in which it occurs. Subsequently, the same or a similar situation, or even the thought of it, evokes fear and avoidance. This often appears irrational to the agoraphobic, since the situation itself is innocuous; thus the problem is not easily discussed or defined.

Classical conditioning weakens over time, however, whereas fear and avoidance in agoraphobia are often maintained for many years. To explain this remarkable persistence it is necessary to invoke *two-factor theory* (Tarpy, 1975), which proposes that avoidance is self-perpetuating because the consequent anxiety reduction reinforces the avoidance response. For example, if an agoraphobic woman panics and escapes from a crowded store, the sharp fall in her anxiety reinforces avoidance, and increases her fear of the store and similar places. If this is repeated, high levels of *anticipatory anxiety* develop. This is present in most agoraphobics and is characterized by a progressive buildup of fearfulness hours or even days before confronting feared situations. This central phenomenon has been called "fear of fear."

Since intrapsychic or interpersonal conflict is an additional, potent cause of anxiety, reduction of such conflict also may reinforce avoidant behavior. Where agoraphobia prevents a married woman from leaving home, her intrapsychic conflict about autonomy and independence within marriage is sharply reduced: She has no choice but to remain housebound. Marital conflict about her autonomy is also reduced. Reduction of these conflicts decreases anxiety and reinforces the avoidance response, perpetuating the agoraphobia. *Since the husband's behavior and attitudes are often central in maintaining both the patient's intrapsychic conflict and the marital conflict, he is frequently the key to therapeutic change.*

Goldstein and Chambless (1978), Holmes (1982), and Quadrio (1983) have demonstrated such marital interactions using rich and detailed clinical material. Holmes suggests that the husband "by denial of his own anxieties, may augment his wife's fears and so push her on towards illness. . . . If she can accept her husband's weakness, his denied anxieties—and if he is brave enough to reveal them—she may come to realise that she too has a hidden aspect, a strong side, and with it can start to overcome her fears."

Many married women with agoraphobia do not appear to be abnormally submissive and dependent, however, and may in fact be unusually assertive and *independent* before marriage (Hafner, 1983b). In such cases, agoraphobic symptoms emerge from predominantly intrapsychic rather than intramarital conflict. Nonetheless, once agoraphobic symptoms have become established, they are often perpetuated indirectly by husbands' attitudes and behavior. Precisely how this occurs is illustrated later.

Nonmarital Contributions to Onset

It is, of course, absurd to suggest that agoraphobia in married women always emerges primarily from marital interaction. In about 10% of cases, the patient is agoraphobic *before* marriage. Thus, although marital interaction may perpetuate the agoraphobia, it cannot be implicated in its onset. In a further 10–15% of cases, agoraphobic symptoms emerge for reasons that are largely or entirely unrelated to marital interaction. A common example of this is the occurrence of panic attacks and subsequent avoidance as part of an unresolved bereavement reaction.

Furthermore, many married women experience marital conflicts similar to those observed in agoraphobics, but do not develop agoraphobia. Hence, predisposing factors other than abnormal dependency are required for the emergence of agoraphobia from marital conflict. Genetic factors may be relevant here, and recent work on perceived parental rearing practices (Arrindell *et al.*, 1983) has shown some interesting differences between agoraphobics and social and height phobics.

Thus, like most psychological disorders, agoraphobia is a multidetermined condition, with biological, psychological, neurophysiological, and interpersonal factors contributing in varying degrees to each case. Once the symptoms are established, however, they may be reinforced by marital interaction. In my experience, husbands nearly always make some contribution to the maintenance of wives' agoraphobia. Such contributions range from very minor and largely irrelevant in perhaps one-third of cases to substantial and crucial in a further one-third. The persistence of the wives' agoraphobia reinforces in turn the husbands' unhelpful attitudes and behavior. These circular marital interactions are a major reason for the notoriously persisting nature of agoraphobia.

THE THEORETICAL BASIS OF COUPLES THERAPY

Effective therapy for complex cases of agoraphobia requires attention concurrently to (a) the patient's problems and symptoms; (b) any marital contributions to symptom maintenance; and (c) any relevant symptoms or problems in the husband.

The Patient's Symptoms and Related Personal Problems

It is unusual for agoraphobic symptoms to exist in isolation. In about one-third of cases, additional symptoms are fairly mild and constitute general anxiety and depressive symptoms, fears of illness or injury and of harmless or domestic animals, and fears of criticism.

In a further one-third of cases, additional symptoms are very severe and almost as troublesome and restricting as the agoraphobia. Patients in this group generally complain of a wide range of fears, especially social fears, fears of heights, fears of being left alone, and claustrophobia. They are often preoccupied with thoughts and fears of mental and physical illness, and complain of a range of associated bodily symptoms. Depressive and anxiety symptoms are often very severe, and many have significant obsessional symptoms and personality traits. Salzman (1982) has emphasized the close relationship between agoraphobic and obsessional symptoms, suggesting that many cases of severe agoraphobia are in fact primarily obsessional states and should be treated as such. There is some empirical support for Salzman's views in Hafner's (1977b) report of very high levels of hostility in agoraphobic women with high levels of overall symptomatology. Unexpressed hostility is a central feature of obsessional states (Barnett, 1969). If severe agoraphobia is sometimes an expression of an underlying obsessional state, then this explains the reluctance of such patients to enter and persevere with treatments based on exposure *in vivo* or drugs: Such therapies would directly challenge the patients' central fear of loss of control, evoking overwhelming anxiety.

Whether agoraphobia is the primary problem or merely one aspect of an obsessional state, it is often extremely difficult for patients' husbands to understand their wives' symptoms. This difficulty is generally compounded by the patients' reluctance to discuss their symptoms, either because they are concerned that this will result in the confirmation of their fears of "madness," or as one aspect of their obsessional personality structures. Involving husbands in conjoint therapy creates an opportunity for them to understand their wives' symptoms and learn to react more appropriately to their wives' requests for help in overcoming their fears and problems. This increased understanding is essential for the satisfactory cooperation of the husband in exposure *in vivo* programs.

As husbands learn more about their wives' symptoms, their attitudes often become more constructive. Overprotective husbands often become more willing to encourage their wives to enter and remain in feared situations; overcritical, detached, or unsupportive husbands become more willing to discuss their wives' symptoms constructively and engage with them in shared problem solving. Success in shared problem-solving activities improves the marital climate, which in turn contributes to further symptomatic improvement. Empirical support for these clinical observations comes from Cobb *et al.* (1980), who found that conjoint behavior therapy for maritally dissatisfied patients with severe agoraphobia and obsessional disorders significantly improved both the patients' symptoms and the marriage; in contrast, conjoint marital therapy improved only the marriage.

Marital Interaction

Fodor (1974) has argued convincingly that sex-role stereotyping and conflict are central to the development of agoraphobia. However, sex-role issues in agoraphobia have been largely overlooked by researchers and clinicians alike, and there is very little empirical data on this crucial area.

Although I have had a major interest in therapy and clinical research with agoraphobics since 1970, it was 8 or 9 years before the central roles of sex-role stereotyping and conflict became apparent to me. I now wonder at my obtuseness, which in retrospect I attribute to my own sex-role conditioning and an almost complete ignorance of women's issues. In fact, it was not until confronted by my own recent research data (Hafner, 1984) that I began systematically looking for sex-role issues in my patients. Thus, the following hypotheses and observations are preliminary.

A majority of agoraphobic women are involved in one of two distinct patterns of marital interaction, which for heuristic purposes I shall term *competitive* and *complementary*.

COMPETITIVE INTERACTION

Before marriage, and when free of agoraphobia and related symptoms, these women are unusually energetic, conscientious, well-organized, and independent; they score below normal on Eysenck's Neuroticism Scale and above normal on a measure of outward-directed hostility (Hafner, 1983b). Prior to marriage, they generally have responsible jobs that they enjoy greatly and that often involve supervising others. They highly value their employment as a major source of personal self-esteem and for the economic independence that it offers them. Because of their personal qualities, they are in turn highly valued by their employers.

Such women tend to marry men with *similar* personality traits—men who are highly extrapunitive and unusually free of neuroticism and psychological symptoms (Hafner, 1983b) and who are highly ambitious, competitive, and hardworking.

The wives' agoraphobic symptoms generally begin after 2–5 years of marriage, when their children are still dependent. These women crave the economic independence and personal freedom that they had before marriage. They miss greatly their rewarding and enjoyable jobs, which they relinquished in favor of childbirth. As a consequence, their self-esteem and self-confidence, which depended heavily on their work role, is considerably lessened. However, they are conscientious mothers and housewives, who set for themselves the same high standards in these areas that they did in their previous employment. They believe that in order to be good mothers they must be full-time mothers. This viewpoint is almost invariably reinforced by their husbands and their mothers, who nearly always have a "traditional," somewhat stereotyped, view of motherhood.

As good organizers, these wives manage their households in a small fraction of the weekly time available. They do not use their free time socializing with other mothers and young children, for they regard this as boring and trivial. Instead, they long to return to the work force, or to resume some other challenging and worthwhile activity beyond the domestic. However, they rarely have the opportunity even to go out in the evenings, since their husbands generally work long hours (as one aspect of their stereotyped view of the male role), and the couple generally cannot afford babysitters. These wives envy their husbands' freedom and fulfillment at work.

Thus these women experience a profound conflict between either remaining at home and living altruistically for and through their children and husbands or returning to the work force, with its personal, direct challenges and opportunity for fulfillment. Out of this conflict emerge anxiety and panic attacks, particularly when they are away from home. These women are not "avoiders," and they tend repeatedly to enter situations that precipitate panic attacks. They often leave prematurely, however, reducing their anxiety but reinforcing their fear and anticipatory anxiety (in accordance with two-factor theory). Once agoraphobia becomes established, their profound inner conflict and related anxieties diminish: They *cannot* resume work outside the home. Thus, once again in accordance with two-factor theory, *the agoraphobic symptoms are powerfully reinforced by the conflict reduction that they engender.*

When the agoraphobic symptoms are established, they become a displaced focus of dissatisfaction in the lives of these women, who blame themselves for their inability to overcome their disabilities. Their abnormally outward-directed hostility becomes redirected into excessive intropunitiveness, which is reinforced by their husbands' abnormal extrapunitiveness (Hafner, 1983b). For example, husbands tend to criticise their wives for their inability to overcome their symptoms, justifying this criticism on the basis that it will enhance their wives' motivation. Unfortunately, it serves merely to increase their wives' self-blame and decrease their self-confidence. Thus, instead of identifying the real origins of their symptoms, and engaging in appropriate problem-solving activities, wives continue angrily to blame themselves for their symptoms, adding self-dislike to their burden, and indirectly perpetuating their agoraphobia. These circular intrapsychic and intramarital processes are in my view best altered by couples therapy, details of which are provided later.

COMPLEMENTARY INTERACTION

Wives engaged in complementary marital interactions approximate the usual clinical description of agoraphobic women as dependent, anxious, timid, vulnerable, and unassertive. Strikingly often, their families of origin are characterized by an absent or emotionally or behaviorally withdrawn father and by a mother who brings up her children virtually singlehanded. These agoraphobic wives-to-be enter adulthood with the following central paradox to resolve: They crave a replacement for their absent, "weak," or emotionally withdrawn fathers. However, they have had no opportunity to learn from their fathers or parental dyads about nonpathological gender identity, sex roles, and male–female relationships. Thus their view of desirable men is based not on the reality of adequate male–female relationships but on a male sex-role stereotype: a composite image created by romantic and media-determined fantasies that have filled the vacuum left by the absence of a functional father.

These women see themselves ideally as complementary to the male sex-role stereotype. Their ideal is to be dependent, vulnerable, weak, and emotionally labile in order to attract a strong, assertive, capable, invulnerable, and emotionally controlled man who will meet their yearnings for the care and concern that they failed to receive from their fathers. Herein lies the paradox: These women identify primarily and strongly with their mothers, who, because they stood alone and managed without a man to support them, are the antithesis of the female sex-role stereotype. Thus, these ago-raphobic wives-to-be have a basic sense of identity as competent, strong, independent women that is totally incompatible with their ideal, sex-role stereotyped, images of themselves. As part of their attempts to resolve this paradox, agoraphobia emerges from their marital interaction in the following ways.

These women tend to marry early, usually between the ages of 17 and 19, often to escape their unsatisfactory families of origin. Maternal overprotection, poor self-esteem, and lack of self-confidence have denied them normal dating experiences, and they often marry the first "suitable" man who asks them. Unfortunately, it becomes clear soon after marriage that what they perceived in their husbands as silent strength was in fact shy and angry withdrawal. The husbands generally have families of origin similar to those of their wives. They seek to disguise their personal problems through marriage to a dependent, helpless woman, in relation to whom they feel strong and capable. Their reliance is heavy on the psychological defense mechanisms of *repression* of affects and *denial* of personal problems; they score below normal on measures of psychological symptoms (Hafner, 1984).

These husbands are much less ambivalent toward their male sex-role stereotyped images of themselves than are their wives to their female stereotypes of themselves. Having had absent, uninvolved, or withdrawn fathers, these men rely very heavily on a male sex-role stereotype for their sense of both personal and gender identity. They are driven to seek sex-role stereotyped women to complement and reinforce their own stereotyped self-images. Having had strong and dominant mothers, however, they are as ambivalent to the female sex-role stereotype as are their wives.

Within these complementary marriages, genuine intimacy is almost impossible because of the stereotyped nature of the couple's relationship and because both partners bring into their marriage major unresolved psychological and communication problems from their families of origin. Marital disputes are common initially. However, wives rapidly learn to defer to, or identify with, their husbands' views, and to suppress their anger toward them, especially after the children are born, since they then feel unable to leave the marriage. Eventually, the wives' supressed rage and frustration become uncontainable and emerge as panic attacks. Those occurring outside the home generalize to avoidance and agoraphobia. Agoraphobia resolves the central paradox in the lives of these women: Their symptoms render them dependent, helpless, weak, vulnerable, and emotionally labile, powerfully reinforcing and consolidating their sex-role stereotyped images of themselves, within which they become trapped. Their central identification with a competent, autonomous, and dominating mother becomes obscured by their symptom-related dependency on their husbands, with whom they identify instead. No longer do they struggle to resolve their inner conflict between competent autonomy and helpless dependency; they are forced to accept the latter. In handing over to their husbands the responsibility for their lives, however, these women relinquish their own problem-solving activities.

The emergence of agoraphobia reduces marital conflict, or displaces it onto the symptoms. Husbands' stereotyped images of themselves are reinforced by their wives' agoraphobic symptoms, and they become confident that their wives will not leave the marriage because of their agoraphobia. Similarly, wives believe that they could not manage without their husbands, and so they become extremely reluctant to risk alienating them by confronting them about any undesirable behavior and attitudes. In contrast, husbands, believing their wives to be unable to leave the marriage, feel free to treat them as they wish. In practice, however, husbands pay a considerable price for this "compulsory marriage" (Fry, 1962), since they are required to carry out many duties on behalf of their disabled wives.

By the time women engaged in complementary marital interactions see mental health professionals, they and their husbands have often come to regard the agoraphobia as an illness. Although coping with the effects of this "illness" creates a "pseudo-intimacy" within the marriage, it inhibits the couple's problem solving, since the couple have handed over responsibility for the agoraphobia to a mental health professional. Moreover, severe additional problems are commonly present: Patients in complementary marriages have greater dependency conflicts than those in competitive marriages and are much more likely to have significant anxiety, obsessional, hypochondriacal, and depressive symptoms, and social and general phobias. This makes couples therapy a highly challenging undertaking, but I believe the likelihood of success with this approach is much greater than with individual therapy.

OTHER TYPES OF MARITAL INTERACTION

About 75–80% of women who seek treatment are involved in predominantly competitive or complementary marriages, with roughly equal numbers in each. In practice, there is often considerable overlap between the two, with individual cases showing elements of both interactional types. Because women in competitive marriages generally have fewer additional problems and symptoms than those in complementary marriages, they are less likely to be excluded from systematic behavioral and drug studies, in which they are therefore overrepresented. Women in complementary marriages are probably overrepresented in the caseloads of experienced, multimodal agoraphobia therapists, since they gravitate to these after the failure or exclusion of unimodal approaches.

There remains about 20–25% of women who do not fit into either of the two main interactional patterns. In about half this population, sex-role stereotyping and conflict are obscured by the husbands' overt personal problems or symptoms. Thus, both partners are preoccupied with personal difficulties, and as a result the likelihood of effective shared problem solving is minimized. In the remaining half, although husbands are generally sympathetic, understanding, and concerned about their wives' symptoms, they lack the knowledge to help them. Such husbands often feel guilty and inadequate about their failure to help their wives, and may even blame themselves for contributing to their wives' symptoms and problems.

Husbands' Personal Problems

The average duration of agoraphobia prior to entering specialized treatment programs is about 8 years (Hafner & Marks, 1976; Doctor, 1982). Over these years, husbands have adapted to living with a partially disabled wife. Within *competitive* marriages, the wife's inability to return to the work force consolidates her husband's position as the sole family income-earner, with its built-in and somewhat stereotyped assumptions of meaning and purpose in life.

For many husbands, their work becomes dull and routine, sometimes because their wives' agoraphobia has prevented them from attending to aspects of their work role, such as interstate trips, which may lead to promotion. Similarly, wives' agoraphobia often hinders husbands' development of shared or individual leisure and recreational activities beyond the home. Thus these husbands are often unusually dependent for their self-esteem on the idea of being sole providers for their families; this consolidates within them an ambivalence to their wives' return to the work force, an ambivalence that is often a major problem to be resolved in therapy.

Within *complementary* marriages, husbands have often become firmly entrenched in a position of repressing feelings of frustration and vulnerability and denying personal problems. Their identification with the male sex-role stereotype of strength, invulnerability, calmness, competence, and fearlessness has become almost complete. Having for so long attempted to shoulder their wives' problems and deny their own, they have ignored their own personal development. Approaching their middle years, any questioning of their stereotyped attitudes and behavior is profoundly challenging, since it threatens to expose the sensitive, vulnerable, and emotional aspects of these men, which have been buried deep within them since early childhood.

For the reasons outlined above, it is generally difficult to engage husbands in couples treatment. Although they are usually willing to attend on one or two occasions, they tend to avoid serious personal commitment to the process of therapy. For example, Forrest (1969) was able to involve only 1 of 18 husbands in couples therapy. Exceptions to this are husbands who acknowledge personal problems or some personal contribution to their wives' agoraphobia. Because of husbands' general resistance to couples therapy, which they usually equate with marriage therapy, I have evolved an explicitly nonmarital couples approach termed "spouse-aided therapy" (Hafner, 1981b, 1982; Hafner et al., 1983).

SPOUSE-AIDED THERAPY

Spouse-aided therapy for agoraphobic women involves interviewing the patient and her husband individually and then conjointly, followed by a series of clearly defined strategies and interventions. These are explained now and described later with use of case material to illustrate their context and effect.

Engaging Husbands in Therapy

After assessing the patient individually, confirming the diagnosis, and obtaining her informed consent to spouse-aided therapy, it is necessary to engage the husband in the treatment process. This requires a mixture of reassurance and incentive. First, it is vital to reassure the husband that spouse-aided therapy is *not* a marriage therapy. Husbands in *complementary* marriages generally regard their marital commitment as unusually strong, since they have struggled over several years to protect and support a wife chronically disabled by agoraphobia. Any suggestion that their marriage may be challenged or scrutinized during therapy arouses deep resentment, which is nearly always expressed indirectly as refusal or reluctance to become involved. Such husbands are equally threatened by the idea that their *personal* idiosyncracies, vulnerabilities, and shortcomings may be exposed during therapy.

Although husbands in *competitive* marriages are generally willing to acknowledge and discuss marital conflict, they almost invariably attribute this to their wives' agoraphobia. Thus they are usually irritated or annoyed by the suggestion of marriage therapy, which they regard as irrelevant or misplaced. Instead, they almost always seek a direct therapeutic attack on their wives' symptoms.

For the above reasons, I emphasize to husbands from the start that the *agoraphobia* will be the main focus of therapy. At the same time I usually point out that their marriage must be unusually strong, since it has withstood the challenge of agoraphobia. Since most married agoraphobic women have received unhelpful individual therapy from a variety of agencies by the time I see them, I am able to emphasize to their husbands the manifest failure of an individual approach. I then state, clearly and unequivocally, that therapy is unlikely to be successful without the active help and support of the husband. Few husbands fail to respond to the idea of contributing to their wives' treatment in equal partnership with the therapist. Thus, the husband is initially engaged in spouse-aided therapy as a co-therapist or co-agent of change.

Forming a Therapeutic Alliance with the Husband

The first individual interview with the husband is critical, because it creates the opportunity of initiating a mutually honest and open relationship between husband and therapist.

There are several obstacles to such a relationship. First, the husband may have become alienated from the idea of therapy by previous treatment failures, which are very common in complex cases of agoraphobia. Second, personality factors may be a problem: Highly extrapunitive husbands tend to adopt an overcritical and suspicious attitude to others, including therapists; husbands relying on denial as a psychological defense mechanism find it difficult to accept the idea of working with the therapist, preferring the notion that the therapist will unilaterally deliver a cure. These personality problems often persist throughout therapy, but their power to disrupt progress is limited during the setting of treatment goals, outlined in the next section.

The third and most important obstacle is the "hidden agenda" of the husband's contribution to his wife's agoraphobia. Unless this is discussed, the therapist risks being duplicitous, since the focus of therapy has already been defined as the agoraphobia, which the husband considers to be his wife's problem.

I negotiate the first and third issues by congratulating the husband on his previous attempts at helping his wife cope with her agoraphobia and asking him for his thoughts on why the condition has nonetheless persisted. Most husbands admit at this stage to feelings of frustration, inadequacy, or helplessness regarding their wife's agoraphobia. I respond to this by stating that, in the absence of expert guidance, the most well-intentioned efforts of both husbands and professional therapists are often ineffectual and may even worsen the agoraphobia. In the ensuing discussion, I invite the husband's views on the origins and nature of the agoraphobia, and any other comments or questions. From this generally emerges an agreement that the husband needs to learn new, optimal strategies for helping his wife and that he is not to blame himself for his previous failures.

The remainder of the interview is used (a) to assess the husband's personal adjustment and give him the opportunity of discussing any personal problems and what help he may require in relation to these; and (b) to elucidate any obstacles to spouse-aided therapy, such as a lack of commitment to the marriage or clandestine extramarital liaisons.

Establishing Treatment Goals

After the individual interviews of patient and husband are completed, I invite both partners to a session aimed at establishing initial treatment goals, which are directly related to the agoraphobia. The first step is to reach agreement on the precise nature and severity of the patient's symptoms and problems. This is not usually a problem, since most husbands are well acquainted with their wives' symptoms. If they are not, then learning about their wives' problems often elicits a more helpful attitude. A second conjoint session may be required before initial treatment goals are agreed upon and fully operationalised.

It is vital for *both* partners to be actively involved in establishing treatment goals; if this does not occur, therapy is unlikely to be successful because the therapist cannot subsequently counter the husband's projection or denial, or the patient's avoidance. These and other resistances to therapy almost invariably emerge early in the couple's attempts at implementing treatment goals.

Implementing Treatment Goals

Initial treatment goals are aimed at facilitating systematic exposure *in vivo*, which is fundamental to recovery in most cases of agoraphobia. The following basic principles of exposure *in vivo* are outlined to the couple (for a very detailed description of basic principles, I recommend a manual by Mathews *et al.*, 1981):

1. Escape from a phobic situation while anxiety levels are high or rising reinforces avoidance and fear of that situation (two-factor theory) and must be avoided if possible. To minimize the likelihood of premature escape from phobic situations, construct a hierarchy of 10–20 items, with the most feared situations at the top progressing systematically downward to the least feared situations. Start exposure with the *least* feared situations, obeying the "75% rule," which states that *no phobic situation should be entered during systematic exposure unless there appears at least a 75% chance of the patient remaining in it long enough for anxiety levels to peak and then subside*. Once anxiety levels have fallen to moderate levels or below, it is possible to leave the feared situation without reinforcing fear and avoidance. Instead, fear is likely to be reduced; and a sense of mastery, rather than failure, emerges.

2. Progressing systematically up the fear hierarchy requires a great deal of time. Practice at exposure *in vivo* for a minimum of 4 hours a week is recommended. Patients should not be pushed into entering feared situations before they are ready. Since many agoraphobics lack assertiveness, they find it difficult to resist social pressure to break the 75% rule; it is therefore vital for husbands to help their wives adhere to it. This requires them to be systematically involved in their wives' exposure *in vivo* program, particularly in its early stages, since many wives are initially unable to enter phobic situations unless accompanied by their husbands or others.

Managing Resistance to Therapy

Problems in achieving treatment goals are almost inevitable and are usually blamed on the therapist. For example, the wife may accuse the therapist of expecting too much of her, causing her to break the 75% rule and experience an unsettling panic attack. The husband may blame the therapist for setting inappropriate treatment goals, or may deny some thoughtless or unhelpful act that reversed his wife's progress.

Dealing with these resistances is crucial to spouse-aided therapy, since it creates the opportunity of clarifying and confronting any marital and personality contributions to the persistence of the agoraphobia. Since both husband and wife shared equal responsibility with the therapist for setting treatment goals, the therapist can point this out, handing back responsibility to the couple for managing their problems through shared problem solving. Concurrently, since the therapist has by now established a working relationship with both partners, it is possible to confront either about unhelpful attitudes and behavior without alienating them from therapy.

Spouse-Aided Therapy in a Competitive Marriage

The patient, Mrs. Susan A., was a 29-year-old white woman who presented with moderately severe agoraphobia since the birth 4 years previously of her only child, a daughter. Her symptoms restricted her, when alone, to within 400 yards of her home, although she could travel several miles in a car or on public transport when accompanied by her husband or a close friend. Susan was unable to enter supermarkets or busy crowded places even when accompanied, but she managed to shop in a small store near her home. In addition to her agoraphobia, Susan had moderate general anxiety and depressive symptoms, and marked social fear and avoidance based on feelings of inferiority and fears of criticism and humiliation.

Susan's family of origin was characterized by a dominating, overcritical, and rejecting mother and a passive, unpredictable father who allowed himself to be dominated by his wife. Susan had survived an unhappy childhood by striving to behave impeccably and by supressing her anger toward her mother. She had worked hard at school in order to please her father, who was more sympathetic and tolerant toward her than her mother, and toward whom she felt strong affection.

On leaving school she had gained a good clerical job, and when she resigned prior to childbirth, she had been managing a department of five people for 18 months. She greatly valued and enjoyed her job.

Her husband, Mr. John A., was an extremely ambitious, hardworking man employed in the research section of a chemical engineering firm. He came from a large, working-class family of which he was the only member to have gone to a university, an achievement he greatly valued. John attempted to understand his wife's symptoms and help her, but often became impatient and shouted at her when she requested help or support. At other times, he would abuse her for her failure to overcome her fears. Although he later expressed remorse about these verbal assaults, they undermined his wife's trust in him and contributed to the couple's moderate marital dissatisfaction.

THERAPY SESSIONS 1 AND 2

Treatment goals were operationalized in Session 1, and in Session 2 Susan reported surprise at the success of exposure *in vivo* and her lack of anxiety throughout. Discussing his contribution to her success, John said, "I try and get Susan to accept that she's not a normal person, and that she must accept rewards for doing these things." I confronted John about his reinforcing Susan's view that she was "abnormal," stressing that this was unhelpful and likely to increase her social anxiety and avoidance.

THERAPY SESSION 3

Further success with exposure *in vivo* was reported and discussed. The discussion then shifted to Susan's brief previous experience with a psychiatrist, whom she regarded as sadistic and callous. Susan admitted to a strong fear that I might treat her in the same way; I reassured her, but pointed out that

I sometimes made mistakes during therapy and that I expected her or John to confront me about these as part of our agreement to work together. Susan was visibly taken aback by my comments, since they conflicted with her view that doctors were essentially authoritarian and expected unquestioning obedience from their patients. As a result, she became more willing to accept therapy as a process requiring her active participation. Toward the end of the session, Susan reported that her improvement had allowed her to plan to return to the work force.

THERAPY SESSION 4

Susan had started an evening course as a preparation for return to work, but she looked angry and weepy rather than pleased when she spoke about this. Marital conflict, which the couple attributed to John's anger and irritability, had increased sharply over the past week. John said, "Sometimes my feelings and my mind conflict. My mother did everything for me. I don't want this from Susan, but sometimes I want to take a step back in time to a mother who takes care of everything."

I suggested that John's conflicts about Susan's taking care of him were central to her agoraphobia, since they reinforced her ambivalence about relinquishing her exclusively domestic role. While discussing this, Susan for the first time told John about her real feelings toward him.

THERAPY SESSION 5

Their attempts over the previous week to discuss sex-role issues had led to fierce arguments, and for the first time they had seriously discussed separation. John had been both distressed and enraged by Susan's disclosure of her feelings of rage and envy toward him. Paradoxically, Susan looked more cheerful and relaxed than on any previous occasion, which she attributed to the greater honesty in the marriage. Issues of separation and divorce, and their alternatives, were discussed, with John and Susan finally deciding to continue working at their problems rather than separating.

THERAPY SESSIONS 6 AND 7

In Session 6, Susan ventilated a great deal of anger toward her parents, and after extensive discussion, the couple decided to visit them less often. In Session 7, Susan said that she had relinquished her hopes of a return to the work force because she realized that she could not cope with the sex-role conflict this would create. Also, she had become able to reconcile herself to a domestic environment for a few more years because John was now much more supportive and appreciative of her in this setting. John said, "I'm really trying to get more in touch with my feelings and to cling less to logic. I play it from the heart instead of thinking all the time what's the best angle."

THERAPY SESSIONS 8–12

These five sessions are summarized. First, Susan revealed a strong belief that her daughter would not survive to adulthood because of illness, assault, or an automobile accident. This belief clouded her general well-being and motivation to plan ahead. Second, she revealed a constant and consuming rage toward her previous psychiatrist. Third, she revealed her desire to "break" John emotionally, by which she meant getting him to weep and show his feelings. As an ultimate attempt to achieve this, she had fantasies of killing herself and her daughter.

All these areas were discussed, and John and Susan gradually learned to be more accepting of their own and each other's irrational feelings, beliefs, and behaviors. Role playing was used successfully to allow Susan to ventilate and resolve her angry feelings to her previous psychiatrist.

By the end of the twelfth session, Susan was virtually free of agoraphobia, although her social fears remained a problem. She planned to develop her social life, hobbies, and other interests, however. The couple believed their marriage to be greatly improved.

Comment. Initial success at exposure *in vivo* revealed sex-role conflict and other major marital and personal problems in both partners, which inhibited further improvement in the agoraphobia. As these problems were aired, discussed, and partly resolved, the agoraphobia improved again; systematic exposure *in vivo* remained a central aspect of this improvement. The improved marital climate allowed the couple to reveal to each other buried, irrational aspects of themselves that, once shared, became manageable problems rather than hidden conflicts. Had the patient not been able to resolve her own and her husband's sex-role conflict by choosing to remain at home, the course of therapy would have been much more difficult and prolonged.

Spouse-Aided Therapy in a Complementary Marriage

The patient, Mrs. Ann B., was a 36-year-old white woman with an 18-year-old son and a 16-year-old daughter. Her agoraphobia had started 12 years previously after she had narrowly escaped involvement in a serious automobile accident while driving her son to school. Subsequently, Ann had been unable to drive except when accompanied by her husband. Since she was also phobic of traveling alone on buses and trains, she was virtually housebound. In addition, Ann had major generalized anxiety and obsessional symptoms, and had on two previous occasions within the previous 4 years been admitted to a private psychiatric hospital in a state of exhaustion. Her referral to me was precipitated by her fears of an imminent readmission.

Of her mother, age 61, Ann said, "She was a very nervous woman, but she didn't suffer from depression. I loved her dearly. I couldn't have wished for a better mother, she was caring and loving. Just to see her there after school was like seeing an angel, I loved her so much. She didn't have much in life, but she dressed me beautifully; that was her only happiness."

Ann's mother had lost two babies, one at childbirth and one at 7 months of pregnancy, within 2 years of Ann's birth. This helps explain her overprotection and idealization of Ann.

Of her father, Ann said, "He loved me, but he couldn't show it, like a lot of men. He was always on shift work, and we never saw him during the week. At weekends he always went out and lived his own life. He liked to gamble and drink at the hotel. Often he came home drunk and fought with my mother . . . it was a regular thing. I suppose I was afraid. I listened, but I don't remember crying. Looking back, we really didn't have any family life at all . . . only with Mother. But I never felt any hatred for my father. I just swore I'd never marry any man that drank . . . my husband doesn't, he spends his spare time at home."

Ann had done poorly at school and had left at age 15 to become a sales assistant in a small store. She never enjoyed her work, mainly because of an obsessional fear of making mistakes with money. She was greatly relieved to be able to stop work when she married at 17.

Her husband, Mr. David B., was 39. His family background was characterized by a dominating mother, who ran the household, and a quiet, retiring, submissive father, who, like Ann's father, was away a great deal and uninvolved in family life, although he was not a heavy drinker. David was employed as a senior salesman by a large telecommunication company, and was successful at his job, so that the family was financially comfortable.

THERAPY SESSIONS 1–3

After a detailed fear hierarchy was established, it emerged that Ann had made an attempt to overcome her agoraphobia some 2½ years previously, when David had bought her an automobile. However, the vehicle had been gradually taken over by her son, Guy, so that now there were disagreements each time Ann sought to use it for practice. Since Guy nearly always won these disagreements, and no other car was available during the week, it became clear that exposure *in vivo* could not proceed until the ownership dispute was resolved. This required a detailed analysis of the family structure and relationships during Sessions 2 and 3, summarized as follows:

Mr. B. and the two children clearly regarded Mrs. B. as their personal servant. She was expected to wait on them hand and foot, and to disregard her own needs and feelings entirely. This she did. In spite of her attempts to please them, her children constantly criticized and ridiculed her, comparing her unfavorably with other mothers. If she complained to David about the children's tyranny over her, he was unsympathetic and tended to side with the children during family disagreements. This left her feeling isolated within the family. She devoted many hours to housework, dusting and cleaning extensively each day, and struggling to preserve her home in a state of meticulous order and cleanliness. Although free of major social fears, she had no close friends and no social life beyond her immediate family.

Thus, it became clear that David had a rigid, sex-role-stereotyped view of Ann, and a complementary stereotype of himself. He thought that it was entirely appropriate for Ann to act as a personal servant to her family, and to sacrifice entirely her own needs and wishes in favor of theirs. Ann shared this view but was plagued by guilt because of her constant inability to meet her family's needs adequately.

THERAPY SESSIONS 4–6

These sessions were basically educational, focusing on the couple's need to reappraise their sex-role-stereotyped views in order to create a framework within which Ann could regain some self-confidence and self-esteem. As a result, David and Ann began to work together; the ownership of the car was settled (Guy bought a motorcycle); the children were confronted about their tyranny; and systematic exposure *in vivo* was started.

THERAPY SESSIONS 7–11

These sessions were conducted over 11 weeks. Ann made good initial progress in overcoming her driving fears and fears of public transport. However, a new problem surfaced: She discovered that she had nowhere to travel to. This realization underlined her sense of social isolation and loneliness, and she temporarily ceased exposure *in vivo*, becoming depressed and withdrawn, feeling that life had passed her by and that it was too late for her to do anything useful or worthwhile or learn to enjoy life. Eventually Ann decided that a return to working outside the home was her only chance of sustained improvement, but she had grave doubts about her ability to find and retain a job, given her previous employment difficulties.

THERAPY SESSIONS 12 AND 13, FOLLOW-UP

Sessions 12 and 13 (4 weeks apart) focused on discussing work opportunities and developing Ann's self-confidence and interview skills. After applying unsuccessfully for several jobs, she obtained part-time employment as a sales assistant in a local store. During a 1-year follow-up she remained free of agoraphobia, and her depressive and anxiety symptoms largely resolved. Although she continued to be very obsessional, she had no problems handling money at work. She managed to establish a small circle of friends and acquaintances.

Comment. Although genuinely concerned about Ann, David had been so strongly imbued with a sex-role-stereotyped view of marriage that he was entirely unable to see the contribution that stereotyping had made to his wife's symptoms and problems. When confronted with a nonstereotyped perspective, he changed his views and subsequently became able to support his wife constructively in the goals she set for herself during and between therapy sessions. The quality of their relationship improved as a result, and this facilitated continuing improvements in their personal well-being.

OBSTACLES AND CONTRAINDICATIONS
TO SPOUSE-AIDED THERAPY

The contributions of sex-role stereotyping and conflict to the development and maintenance of agoraphobia have been emphasized in this chapter because of the need to redress their underrepresentation in clinical and research reports. There are, of course, other major contributing factors, of which personality is probably the most significant. Personality factors are also the most common obstacles or contraindications to spouse-aided therapy.

Personality Factors

Since the essence of spouse-aided therapy is the initiation or facilitation of couple's shared problem-solving activities, any personality factors that inhibit or prevent this are potential obstacles.

EXCESSIVE HOSTILITY

If, within competitive marriages, both marriage partners are overcritical, suspicious, mistrusting, and hostile toward each other, fierce marital disputes are very likely. Once the wife develops agoraphobia, and her excessive extrapunitiveness is transformed into abnormal intropunitiveness and self-blame, the intensity and frequency of marital disputes generally decrease. This is because some of the wife's anger is redirected from her husband on to herself, and her symptoms, rather than the marriage relationship, become the main focus of marital dissatisfaction.

As the wife's agoraphobia improves during spouse-aided therapy, and as her anger is redirected outward and on to her husband, the intensity and frequency of marital disputes often increases, and shared problem-solving becomes impossible. Couples may as a result decide that they are incompatible, and may initiate separation or divorce. Spouse-aided therapy contributes to this sometimes inappropriate outcome because (paradoxically) it is so effective in generating rapid changes in the patient's attitudes and behavior: The marital system cannot accommodate the rapid redirection of the patient's hostility. I am not suggesting that separation is always undesirable—merely that it may sometimes occur prematurely as a consequence of spouse-aided therapy. Thus, in highly extrapunitive couples, spouse-aided therapy is probably contraindicated. Instead, the patient and her husband should be offered concurrent individual therapy.

EXCESSIVE REPRESSION AND DENIAL

Within complementary marriages, although agoraphobic wives usually report high levels of hostile, critical, and suspicious thoughts, feelings, and impulses, these are generally not directed at husbands; even if they are, they are rarely expressed directly. Often, these feelings lack a focus and are dealt with using predominantly obsessional defensive operations, although concurrently they may be focused on those whom the patient regards as hostile, unsympathetic, or unhelpful to them.

Many husbands within complementary marriages rely heavily on repression and denial to cope with hostile and other unwanted feelings, thoughts, and impulses. Thus their capacity for empathy and emotional responsiveness toward their wives is very limited. However, shared concern about the patients' symptoms (or "illness," as they are commonly regarded within such marriages) creates a "pseudo-intimacy" that partially obscures the lack of emotional warmth and intimacy within the marriage. As patients' symptoms improve, they may become increasingly aware of their husbands' inability to meet their needs for genuine warmth, affection, and empathy. This inability is often increased during spouse-aided therapy because the husbands are being invited to reappraise their stereotyped views of marriage relationships; they commonly react to this challenge by increasing their defensive reliance on repression and denial. Consequently, once wives have achieved sufficient symptomatic improvement, they may decide to leave the marriage out of a premature conviction that their husbands will never be able to meet their emotional and companionship needs.

Thus, spouse-aided therapy is probably contraindicated when husbands rely very heavily on repression and denial as psychological defense mechanisms. In such circumstances, good results are more likely to be achieved if both partners enter individual therapy.

REJECTION OF COUPLES THERAPY

Where the patient or husband reject a couples approach, it is important to establish their reasons for this, and to decide whether they appear valid. For example, severely disabled women in complementary marriages are often extremely fearful of alienating their husbands; they sometimes reject couples therapy because it implies that the marriage is at fault, and hence some criticism of their husbands, any imputation of which these women are desperate to avoid. In about half of such cases, the patient readily responds to reassurance that the therapist will approach her husband with the utmost tact and discretion, and a personal invitation to the husband usually allows spouse-aided therapy to proceed.

In the remaining half, the patient does not readily respond to reassurance, and in these circumstances spouse-aided therapy should *not* be pursued: These women have good reasons for their wish to avoid couples therapy. If it becomes clear, as it often does in such cases, that individual therapy is likely to be a useless exercise, then the only honest approach is to tell the patient this and perhaps suggest that she consider accepting the *status quo* rather than continue a fruitless search for therapy (Hafner, 1979).

SUPPLEMENTS TO SPOUSE-AIDED THERAPY

Occasionally, once marital and personal contributions to the maintenance of agoraphobia have been exposed during spouse-aided therapy, one or the other partner reveals psychological difficulties that are best treated with individual or group therapy. The therapist should be sensitive to this possibility and willing to recommend appropriate supplementary treatment.

The presence of major psychological disorders in addition to agoraphobia is no obstacle to spouse-aided therapy, which may in fact be particularly suitable for treating the obsessional aspects of the condition. By facilitating communication and a more honest expression of feelings within marriage, central features of the obsessional state may be ameliorated.

Occasionally, agoraphobic women are so depressed that they are unable to set appropriate treatment goals, and in such cases the depression must be treated before spouse-aided therapy can proceed. In very severe, complex cases, it is best to regard spouse-aided therapy as a framework to which a range of therapeutic supplements may be added, including antidepressant and tranquilizing medication when appropriate. The severe social phobias that are frequent accompaniments of agoraphobia often require specific additional treatment. Although the spouse may contribute usefully to this, referral to specialized social-phobia treatment agencies is sometimes desirable.

In conclusion, I hope that this chapter encourages therapists to consider more often a couples approach to treating agoraphobia. Since the superiority of couples therapy for agoraphobia has yet to be demonstrated scientifically (Barlow *et al.*, 1981), more research in this area is clearly to be welcomed. Whether or not research ultimately demonstrates the superiority of couples therapy, one thing is certain: Spouse-aided therapy is a challenging, stimulating approach for therapists, patients, and spouses. It requires a flexible, innovative attitude to treatment, and therapists willing to attempt it are likely to be rewarded by increased enjoyment of their work in agoraphobia.

REFERENCES

Arrindell, W. A., Emmelkamp, P. M., Monsma, A., & Brilman, E. (1983). The role of perceived parental rearing practices in the aetiology of phobic disorders: A controlled study. *British Journal of Psychiatry, 143,* 183–187.

Barlow, D. H., Mavissakalian, M., & Hay, L. R. (1981). Couples therapy of agoraphobia: Changes in marital satisfaction. *Behaviour Research and Therapy, 19,* 245–257.

Barnett, J. (1969). On aggression in the obsessional neuroses. *Contemporary Psychoanalysis, 6,* 48–57.

Cobb, J. P., McDonald, R., Marks, I., & Stern, R. (1980). Marital vs. exposure therapy: Psychological treatments of co-existing marital and phobic-obsessive problems. *Behaviour Analysis and Modification, 4,* 3–16.

Doctor, R. M. (1982). Major results of a large-scale pretreatment survey of agoraphobia. In R. L. DuPont (Ed.), *Phobia: A comprehensive summary of modern treatments.* New York: Brunner/Mazel.

Fodor, I. G. (1974). The phobic syndrome in women: Implications for treatment. In V. Franks & V. Burtle (Eds.), *Women in Therapy*. New York: Brunner/Mazel.

Forrest, A. D. (1969). Manifestations of "hysteria": Phobic patients and hospital recidivists. *British Journal of Medical Psychology, 42*, 263–270.

Fry, W. F. (1962). The marital context of an anxiety syndrome. *Family Process, 1*, 245–252.

Goldstein, A. J., & Chambless, D. L. (1978). A reanalysis of agoraphobia. *Behavior Therapy, 9*, 47–59.

Hafner, R. J. (1977a). The husbands of agoraphobic women: Assortative mating or pathogenic interaction? *British Journal of Psychiatry, 130*, 233–239.

Hafner, R. J. (1977b). The husbands of agoraphobic women and their influence on treatment outcome. *British Journal of Psychiatry, 131*, 289–294.

Hafner, R. J. (1979). Agoraphobic women married to abnormally jealous men. *British Journal of Medical Psychology, 52*, 99–104.

Hafner, R. J. (1981a). Agoraphobia in men. *Australian and New Zealand Journal of Psychiatry, 15*, 243–249.

Hafner, R. J. (1981b). Spouse-aided therapy in psychiatry: An introduction. *Australian and New Zealand Journal of Psychiatry, 15*, 329–337.

Hafner, R. J. (1982). The marital context of the agoraphobic syndrome. In D. L. Chambless & A. L. Goldstein (Eds.), *Agoraphobia: Multiple perspectives on theory and treatment*. New York: Wiley.

Hafner, R. J. (1983a). Behaviour therapy for agoraphobic men. *Behaviour Research and Therapy, 21*, 51–56.

Hafner, R. J. (1983b). The marital systems of agoraphobic women: Contributions of husbands' denial and projection. *Journal of Family Therapy, 5*.

Hafner, R. J. (1984). The marital repercussions of behaviour therapy for agoraphobia. *Psychotherapy. 21*, 530–542.

Hafner, R. J., Badenoch, A., Fisher, J., & Swift, H. (1983). Spouse-aided vs. individual therapy for persisting psychiatric disorders: A systematic comparison. *Family Process, 22*, 385–399.

Hafner, R. J., & Marks, I. M. (1976). Exposure-in-vivo of agoraphobics: Contributions of diazepam, group exposure and anxiety evocation. *Psychological Medicine, 6*, 71–88.

Hafner, R. J., & Ross, M. W. (1984). Agoraphobia in women: Factor analysis of symptoms and personality correlates of factor scores in a clinical population. *Behaviour Research and Therapy, 22*, 441–444.

Hallam, R. S. (1978). Agoraphobia: A critical review of the concept. *British Journal of Psychiatry, 133*, 314–319.

Holmes, J. (1982). Phobia and counterphobia: Family aspects of agoraphobia. *Journal of Family Therapy, 4*, 133–152.

Liotti, G., & Guidano, V. (1976). Behavioural analysis of marital interaction in male agoraphobic patients. *Behaviour Research and Therapy, 14*, 161–162.

Mathews, A. M., Gelder, M. G., & Johnston, D. W. (1981). *Programmed practice for agoraphobia: Clients' manual*. London: Tavistock.

Quadrio, C. (1983). Rapunzel and the pumpkin-eater: Marital systems of agoraphobic women. *Australian Journal of Family Therapy, 4*, 81–85.

Rapp, M. S., & Thomas, M. R. (1982). Agoraphobia. *Canadian Journal of Psychiatry, 27*, 419–425.

Salzman, L. (1982). Obsessions and agoraphobia. In D. L. Chambless & A. L. Goldstein (Eds.), *Agoraphobia: Multiple perspectives on theory and treatment*. New York: Wiley.

Tarpy, R. M. (1975). *Basic principles of learning*. Glenview, IL: Scott, Foresman.

Vose, R. H. (1981). *Agoraphobia*. London: Faber and Faber.

22

Strategic Marital Therapy for Depression

JAMES C. COYNE

Discussions about how to treat depression tend to define the term broadly and assume a uniformity of the persons being identified. Even when care is taken to specify explicit, limiting criteria, persons labeled as depressed are likely to prove diverse in their complaints, circumstances, and responses to treatment. It is appropriate to begin this presentation of a strategic model of marital therapy for depression with a caveat: It is likely that every couple involving a depressed person will be somewhat unique in its problems, goals, attempted solutions, and susceptibility to particular interventions. Yet if we are justified in organizing an approach around the term *depression*, common themes and issues should arise.

It is generally accepted that the label of depression should represent more than just transient sadness or feeling blue, down in the dumps, or low. As defined in conventional diagnostic systems (American Psychiatric Association, 1980; Spitzer, Endicott, & Robins, 1978), depression involves mood disturbance that persists for more than a few days and additional complaints such as loss of appetite, sleep disturbance, social withdrawal, or evidence of impaired social functioning. Various schemes have been proposed to describe the differences among depressed persons, but considerable controversy persists. The current *Diagnostic and Statistical Manual of Mental Disorders* (DSM-III; American Psychiatric Association, 1980) provides a number of diagnoses for depressed persons, including major depression, single episode; major depression, recurrent; bipolar disorder, depressed; bipolar disorder, mixed; cyclothymic disorder; dysthymic disorder; and adjustment reaction with depressed mood. Yet these distinctions are inadequate for

James C. Coyne. Institute of Social Research, University of Michigan, Ann Arbor, Michigan.

many purposes, and interpersonally oriented therapists find that they fail to map many of their concerns.

There is a consensus that any form of psychotherapy is probably useful only as an adjunctive treatment for manic-depressive or bipolar depression (Rush, 1982). Beyond this, it is generally assumed that depressed persons differ in their responsiveness to therapy, but proven selection criteria are for the most part lacking. Many, but certainly not all, depressed persons show biological abnormalities, such as with the sleep electroencephalogram or the thyrotropin-releasing hormone or dexamethasone-suppression tests, but it has not been established that these are contraindications for therapy. The term *endogenous* has traditionally been invoked to differentiate depressions that are purportedly biological in etiology, without environmental precipitants, and that are less amenable to psychotherapy. This is to distinguish them from *reactive* depressions that are precipitated by environmental stress and suitable for therapeutic intervention. It now appears that the distinction is too simplistic. Careful interviewing generally reveals recent stressful events in the lives of endogenously depressed patients (Leff, Roatch, & Bunney, 1970). One study found that 42% of a sample of endogenous patients had maladjusted marriages and that their marital problems generally preceded the onset of their depressions (Birchnell & Kennard, 1983). Furthermore, recent clinical trials in which psychotherapy has proven superior to anti-depressant medication have included a considerable proportion of "endog-enously" depressed persons (Rush, Beck, Kovacs, & Hollon, 1977).

Dualistic thinking about the relationship between biology and social life have tended to leave marital therapists phobic about possible advances in our understanding of the biology of depression, while biologically oriented psychiatrists remain ignorant about the necessity of considering the interpersonal circumstances of depressed persons. As Klerman and Weissman (1982) note:

> Depression—regardless of symptom patterns, severity, the presumed biological vulnerability, or personality traits—occurs in a psychosocial and interpersonal context, and understanding and renegotiating the interpersonal context associated with the onset of symptoms is important to the depressed person's recovery and possibly to the prevention of further episode. (p. 88)

DEPRESSION AND MARRIAGE

Depression tends to be a disorder of the married and formerly married. Depression and marital disturbance have been found to be associated in a number of studies (for a review, see Coyne, Kahn, & Gotlib, 1985). Not being able to confide in one's spouse is a significant vulnerability factor for depression (Brown & Harris, 1978), and an increase in arguments with the spouse is the most frequent recent life event reported by depressed women (Paykel *et al.*, 1969). The marriages of depressed women are characterized by friction, poor communication, dependency, and a lack of affection

(Weissman & Paykel, 1974). Hostility is frequently overt, and even when it is not, the unspoken misery of wives is viewed by their husbands as an accusation (Bullock, Siegal, Weissman, & Paykel, 1972). These difficulties may persist well beyond the acute episode. While there has been an increasing number of studies examining the marital relationships of depressed women, there has been less attention to depressed men, and almost no attention to the spouses of depressed persons (Coyne et al., 1985). Nevertheless, it has been noted that "the spouse of the depressed person cannot be considered neutral. He or she becomes solicitous, or angry, or withdrawn emotionally" (Rush, Shaw, & Khatami, 1980, p. 105).

Based on their laboratory observations of couples with a depressed partner and the couples' reports of how they handle disagreements in general, Kahn, Coyne, and Margolin (in press) have suggested that the marriages of many depressed persons are characterized by periods of inhibited communication and tension punctuated by arguments involving intense negative affect and then withdrawal, with little constructive problem solving. The aversiveness and futility of efforts to resolve differences encourages avoidance of confrontation until an accumulation of unresolved issues precipitates another negative encounter. This circular pattern is given considerable attention in the treatment approach presented in this chapter.

Many, but not all, depressed persons present with marital problems. Some report that they are not dissatisfied with their marriages, and home observations of these depressed persons interacting with their families reveal few differences from the family interactions of nondepressed persons (Hops et al., 1983). In our work at the MRI Mood Disorders Center, we have frequently noticed that distinctive interactive patterns are apparent when these persons are *not* depressed. Before becoming depressed, and frequently after recovery, these persons face overwhelming responsibilities and little support or appreciation. To paraphrase Bateson's (1971) classic comments on the sober life of some alcoholics, the reasons for some people being depressed lie in what their lives are like when they are not depressed. Whether or not depressed persons report dissatisfaction with their marriages, they tend to be facing difficulties renegotiating their relationships so that they meet their wants and needs as they define them, and this recurs as a common theme in therapy with them.

Any theoretical model of depression should acknowledge that the disorder frequently occurs in the context of marital dissatisfaction, disruption, or dissolution, but that it is not limited to these situations. In the therapy approach described here, it is assumed that depression or depressive interactions arise from the mismanagement of life transitions or the accumulated mishandling of everyday hassles (DeLongis et al., 1982). Regardless of its origin, a depressive episode tends to be self-limiting (Stern & Mendels, 1980), and the further assumption is made that it persists only as a result of the inappropriate coping of depressed persons and key members of the immediate social environment. The complaints of depressed persons are likely to reflect their involvement in situations that are intractable or are even exacerbated by their ways of coping (Coyne, Aldwin, & Lazarus, 1981). However, the intractability of their situations and the apparent ineptness of their coping may well depend on the response they receive from significant others, and in the case of married depressed persons, their spouses.

Coyne (1976a, 1976b) has described how depressive behavior can be interwoven or concatenated with the response of significant others. The distress and dysfunction of depressed persons can prove aversive but, at the same time, guilt inducing and inhibiting. Depressed persons elicit displays of support, reduce demands, and inhibit hostility from others by conveying their distress. Significant others, for their part, temporarily reduce the aversiveness of depressed persons by seemingly providing what is being asked, even while their growing impatience, hostility, and withdrawal leak to the depressed person. The subtle and overt hostility and rejection that depressed persons thus receive elicits further expression of distress, strengthening the pattern.

The approach described here does not assume that the marital unit must have been the initial source of the patient's difficulties in order to become the focus of treatment. Regardless of the precipitants for someone's feeling or acting depressed, others tend to become involved as helpers, opponents, critical commentators, and, too often, sources of frustration and disappointment. As we frequently state to spouses of depressed persons, one does not have to be a "cause" of a problem to be a vital part of its solution (Coyne, 1984a). Even when we implicate family members in the perpetuation of depressive interactions, however, it is not assumed that they have any compelling investment in the status quo or that depressive behavior serves a function in the larger system. Indeed, glib functional accounts of depressive interaction pose the risk that therapists will ignore or minimize the profound distress and deprivation that depressed persons and those around them inflict on each other.

A THEORY OF THERAPEUTIC CHANGE

As used here, the term *strategic* applies to a brief, interactional therapy that conceptualizes clinical problems as aspects of ongoing interpersonal systems (Coyne & Segal, 1982; Watzlawick, Weakland, & Fisch, 1974). Based on the assumption that depression persists as a result of ineffective coping, therapy is directed toward the modification of what depressed persons and their spouses are doing about their problems—or how they are coping with the difficulties each's problem-solving efforts pose for the other. In an important sense, it is neither depression nor depressing circumstances but the couple's problem-maintaining solutions that are the focus of treatment.

Why do people persist in behavior that preserves an unsatisfactory situation or even makes it worse? The assumption is made that they have come to see the problem in a way that what they are doing seems to be the best that can be done. Change comes about when they are provided with an experience that shifts their point of view or framing of the situation. These experiences are most compelling when the couple believe that they are the result of their own behavior when they occur in their daily living, rather than in the artificiality of the therapy session.

Preparing the couple to act differently is therefore given priority over the development of insight or the exploration of feelings. The therapy session is used to gather information, redefine problematic situations, set goals, and plan antidepressive events, rather than to enact problems and solutions. Therapeutic goals are typically small but strategic changes in behavior intended to instigate change of a more generalized nature. Extensive use is made of homework assignments accompanied by direct and indirect suggestions, often of a paradoxical nature. A key ingredient of most interventions is reframing (Coyne, 1984b; Watzlawick et al., 1974). The therapist works to grasp the language with which the target person describes a problem, actively acknowledges this perspective to him or her, and then extends or turns this view in a direction that allows new behavior to be initiated. Thus, for example, if a spouse can come to view the depressed person's resistance to influence as the last refuge of pride and self-respect, rather than as stubbornness and a personal affront, it is more likely that the spouse will behave in a supportive manner.

THE STRUCTURE OF THERAPY

In work at the MRI Mood Disorders Center, we have developed a strong preference for initially interviewing the depressed person and spouse separately. Either only one partner will be asked to the first interview or, more likely, it will be split with each partner getting half of the session. One important reason for interviewing members of the couple separately is that it allows the therapist to explore each partner's commitment to the marriage.

An additional reason for meeting with each spouse separately in the beginning is that it is frequently easier to get clear information about each one's perspective on critical incidents in the absence of the other. Together, they tend to lapse into a pattern of inhibition and withdrawal or, alternatively, emotional outbursts, characterological criticisms, and accusations. This pattern is clinically relevant, but a brief report of its occurrence is as informative as a drawn-out enactment in the therapy room. Furthermore, there is no guarantee that disagreements in a therapy session are reliable representations of what occurs at home; the partners may be taking into account the availability of the therapist as a commentator, referee, or potential ally.

No matter who is seen first, there is a basic plan for the information to be gathered in the first sessions (Fisch, Weakland, & Segal, 1982). An explicit statement is requested as to how the person sees the problem for which help is being sought, how it arises in everyday life, and what has been done to deal with it. An attempt is then made to formulate some concrete, minimal goal for treatment with answers to the question, "What would it take to indicate to you that you were on the right path, even if you were not yet out of the woods?"

Usually there are some discrepancies among the goals of the two partners. Frequently the depressed person focuses on the distressing marital relationship, whereas the spouse will argue that the depressed person's distress and dysfunction are ruining what otherwise would be a good relationship. This does not necessarily pose a problem, particularly when the likelihood is that these differences will dissolve as the couple's situation is reframed and there is improvement in both the depressed person's level of distress and the quality of the marital relationship. Goal discrepancies need to be made explicit and negotiated only when they are fundamental, such as when the couple has contradictory notions about how specific role responsibilities are to be reallocated. What is important is that each partner feel that he or she is working toward a personally meaningful goal and that progress can be marked with identifiable behavioral accomplishments.

If spouses are frequently seen separately and there are sometimes discrepancies in the goals that they are pursuing, how is this different from the spouses' merely receiving individual therapy from the same therapist? Many writers would identify conjoint interviews as the *sine qua non* of couples therapy. Our perspective is that an interactional system approach does not require that all persons composing the system attend therapy together; indeed, an interactional system approach encourages consideration of how appropriate changes in a subsystem (one member of the couple) can bring about major changes in the entire system.

In many cases, it is more practical to attempt to work separately with the spouses to obtain to such changes than to work with them together in a way that requires that they reach an agreement as to how to define the problem and who is at fault. Yet, unlike a situation in which both spouses are in individual therapy, our approach gives particular attention to how each one's behavior is part of a recursive pattern involving the other—the locus of the problem lies with neither partner but in what they do together. Furthermore, unlike individual therapy, it is stressed that goals and interventions must be ecological, in that they should take into account how each spouse is likely to react and what new problems and possibilities this will pose.

Finally, it is important that the couple be aware that therapy is time limited and that a lack of progress will not justify more treatment. It is assumed that both the therapist and the couple will make the best use of their time together if they are aware that it cannot continue indefinitely. An arbitrary 10- or 12-session limit can be set. Alternately, it can be established that therapy will not continue beyond some trial period—for instance, 6 sessions—only if some small goals have been met and some new ones can be set. More therapy is thus justified only with visible improvement. Otherwise, termination or a referral will be offered.

SPECIFIC INTERVENTIONS

For the purposes of discussion, we can distinguish among three foci for interventions: the depressed person's distress, the response of the spouse, and the marriage. The three are interdependent, however, and changes in one area tend to have a direct impact on the others. Which area becomes critical depends largely on the opportunities provided by the couple.

The Distress of the Depressed Person

Perhaps the most basic rule in working with depressed persons is never dispute their right and privilege to remain depressed. People around them, their spouses in particular, have probably provided them with considerable practice in arguing this issue, usually to no one's benefit. One of the first therapeutic interventions to be made is typically an active acknowledgment to them that they have good reason to be depressed. Even the simple question, "Why are you depressed?" can sound accusatory if it is badly timed, and "Who or what is depressing you?" is usually a better alternative. To focus on the depressed person's resources, it is also useful to inquire, "What accounts for your not being more depressed?"

Depressed persons generally can find in their inept handling of situations evidence that they are irresponsible and incompetent. In attempting to compensate for this, however, they frequently take on too much, fail, and confirm their negative view of themselves. In indicating that a depressed person should proceed slowly and in small steps, the therapist can suggest that being depressed has obvious drawbacks but that it can serve to restrain someone from trying too hard when resources are depleted. The therapist can then suggest that the depressed person's immediate task is to find methods of self-restraint that can be substituted for a depression and might just lift when it is most needed. Comments such as "Some people have excuses, others take breaks or vacations, and others get depressed" or "Depression is like a leaky vacation cottage, and you never know when you are going to get evicted" may bolster this point of view.

Such discussions often lead to a focus on the role of the spouse as an observer, source of demands, or critical commentator. It can be suggested to the depressed person that there are obvious disadvantages to flaunting her improvement. First, it may catch the spouse off guard and prove unsettling. The spouse may be unprepared for a partner who acts competently and independently, and who can assert needs and wants. The spouse may be left feeling unneeded, and may be forced to face his inadequacies. Second, the demonstration of obvious improvement can produce demands for more

improvement: "If you can do A, now you can do B, C, D, and E."
Furthermore, the spouse may develop the logic that "If that is so easy, why
didn't you do it weeks ago when I asked you?" Finally, it can be pointed
out that depression serves to inhibit negative responses from others (Coyne,
1976a, 1976b), and it is sometimes true that others unleash pent-up resentment
just when depressed persons are feeling a bit better.

Suggestions such as these point out some realistic contingencies in the
marriages of depressed persons. From a strategic point of view, however,
they provide the depressed person with a rationale for not struggling so hard
to change. Moreover, they help the depressed person disengage from the
spouse's demands and criticisms and begin to appreciate that the spouse too
has vulnerabilities and limitations. As the depressed person accepts this point
of view, it can be further proposed that "When one is making a transition
from patienthood, one is often called upon to be exceptionally patient and
charitable toward others. Other people do not always cope well. It is a lot
to ask of you, and you certainly cannot be expected to be perfect, but please
be easy on your spouse."

Such framings of the drawbacks of improvement should be accompanied
by specific homework assignments. The depressed person might be asked
to hide certain accomplishments, leave specific tasks undone, or make
ritualized statements of distress or need to the spouse at predetermined times.
The alternative may also be posed that the depressed person could initiate
some activity that would both be reassuring to the spouse and enjoyable.

A fundamental strategy underlying many of these suggestions is that it
is advantageous to frame depression as an active, dignified practice, but one
that is costly and even self-sacrificing. It is easier to get a woman to shift
activity than to rouse her from passivity to activity. Therefore, an effort is
made to reframe the depressed person's distress and dysfunction as having
instrumental value, at least for the spouse and the marriage, if not for the
depressed person. For instance, "You're like a canary in a coal mine,
registering problems in the relationship that your spouse does not yet notice,
and that he may even be too defensive to admit, and at the same time,
you're showing him how miserable you can get and still stick it out."

If the depressed person complains about how uncommunicative and
defensive the spouse is, the therapist can agree and suggest that this reflects
the spouse's vulnerability and that being depressed is a way of protecting
the spouse. When the depressed person produces an account of an incident
in which the spouse reacted negatively to assertiveness, decisiveness, or
independence, the therapist can accept this and volunteer, "Depression may
be a way of shooting yourself in the leg so that you don't wander off or
otherwise threaten your spouse." Having identified specific negative actions
or thoughts that the depressed person sees as maintaining her plight, the
therapist can indicate that they might continue to do more of the same over
a period of a few more weeks in order to protect the spouse and the marriage.
If the depressed person agrees to this, some self-indulgence should be planned.
"If you are not paid, you are unlikely to stay on the job."

A variation on the theme of depression as a protective practice is that it can be a deliberately chosen alternative to asserting wants and needs or expressing hostility. Before prescribing specific assertive tasks, the therapist may propose *in vivo* thought assignments that make the choice explicit. As an example, a woman who felt unappreciated by her husband and oppressed by her housework was asked to prepare a meal of leftovers and place it on the stove as usual. She was then asked to turn on the burner as high as it would go and to imagine the food becoming a stinking, charred mass. She would say to her husband, "Dear, somehow our dinner was ruined, and I'm sorry, but you must take us out to eat." With this brief fantasy completed, she should then turn the burner down, complete the preparation of the meal, and serve it with a smile. The key features of such assignments are that they require little effort or risk and involve imagining making demands that the depressed person can see as patently unreasonable and out of character. Yet, despite their absurdity, these assignments make explicit the depressed person's existing choice not to be assertive or confrontative. Very frequently, depressed persons who have received them report spontaneously taking more assertive actions in dealing with their spouses. Furthermore, more reasonable assertive tasks become more palatable.

The Response of the Spouse

Initial work with the spouse requires that the therapist grasp and acknowledge the frustration, misunderstandings, and miscarried helping efforts that may have already occurred. Also, in an effort to avoid conflict and further displays of distress by the depressed person, the spouse may have made unnoticed and unappreciated concessions, such as a reduction in independent activity, a deferring of plans, and a stifling of complaints. Interventions are unlikely to be successful without taking them into account. In defining and pursuing specific concrete goals, the therapist's general goals are to (*a*) assist the spouse in achieving a moderate level of involvement, neither hostilely withdrawing nor becoming overinvolved in well-meant but inappropriate efforts to help; and (*b*) legitimize the needs and wants of the spouse, particularly as expressed in activities that do not involve the depressed person.

Frequently, the spouse's initial encouragement and reassurance have given way to advice, and when this does not make a difference, to coercion and characterological attack. It is as if the spouse becomes more committed to getting the depressed person to engage in a particular activity than to have her achieve the original end (i.e., feeling better). Reports of such interactions should be elicited in detail. The therapist should acknowledge the spouse's good intentions, and how, as if by negative magic, they resulted in the persistence of the depressed person's dysfunction. The therapist may further concede that the depressed person seems stubborn, but suggest that this could be a positive sign because stubbornness and resistance to influence are the refuge of pride and self-respect. The spouse may then be asked to utilize the partner's stubbornness in an experiment. In specific situations, the spouse should attempt to encourage the depressed partner with discouragement. A mildly obstructionist attitude, "Go slow, you are attempting too much," should be adopted, and the results carefully noted.

When the spouse reports becoming frustrated, the therapist might acknowledge this and ask, "Have you ever had another roommate or a coworker who became depressed? Did he or she recover without your taking charge?" An experiment can be suggested in which the spouse reacts as a spouse on some days but as a roommate or co-worker on others. If the spouse is particularly frustrated, the therapist can frame the "roommate" days as letting the depressed person stew in her own juices.

Spouses often become inhibited in the expression of their negative feelings toward depressed partners, only to overreact in a rather noncontingent manner later. When the spouse has reacted with withdrawal and alienation, the therapist can comment that this has a useful element of autonomy in it and then suggest that if getting upset is what is needed to allow such distance, then the spouse should get upset at least once a week whether it is spontaneous or not—unless, alternatively, he is able to get some distance or do something independently without getting upset.

The Marital Situation

Whether or not depressed persons and their spouses report marital turmoil, they generally have a difficult time negotiating arrangements by which the needs and wants of both can be met. Frequently, both partners have a sense of having given as much as they can give, and the therapist should be cautious about requesting unilateral change. At first, the therapist may see numerous opportunities to negotiate a settlement of some concrete issues, and it may be puzzling that the couple have not done so themselves. Sometimes such negotiations are successful, but, more often, new problems are then identified by the couple as more pressing, any change that results is seen as trivial, and characterological attacks and displays of distress result as one or both members of the couple assert a new set of demands.

It has been our experience that an active problem-solving orientation on the part of the therapist often produces a passive, help-rejecting, complaining stance on the part of the couple (Coyne, 1984a). Our general preference has been for the therapist to take a "one-down," temporizing position. Rather than attempt to settle specific issues, the therapist concentrates on positively connoting whatever disagreements are occurring between the couple and, if they occur with any great frequency, prescribing more of the same in a way that allows a playful or even absurd element to be introduced.

How disagreements are to be positively connoted depends on the specific framing that the couple have placed on their disagreements. Generally, the therapist comments on the passion, commitment, romanticism, or rejection of a more banal existence that is implicit in their efforts. When it is acknowledged that the couple have been fighting and withdrawing for a considerable period of time, it can be suggested that they are not as intimate as they once were, and that arguments are a defense against "precipitous intimacy." Provocation of an argument by one member of the couple is labeled as a miscarried effort to get close too quickly. "You two porcupines are going to get stuck on each other's quills if you try to snuggle up."

Prescription of continued arguments is indicated when they are already highly frequent events, as well as when the couple have focused on their occurrence as a sign that their marriage is in jeopardy. The general strategy is to reframe such occurrences so that they are transformed from intense, deadly serious confrontations with no constructive problem solving to more playful exchanges that benefit the relationship. A more detailed statement about this class of interventions is available elsewhere (Coyne, 1984b).

Basically, interventions involve introducing elements of make-believe, exaggeration, repetition, or a preplanned positive outcome. The therapist should first elicit detailed accounts of recent arguments. In doing so, particular attention should be paid to what the couple view as the most negative element of these encounters: their intense negativity, lack of resolution, repetitiveness, or the sense of distance with which they leave the couple. The therapist should then acknowledge the couple's efforts to avoid such confrontations or achieve more positive outcomes. It should be emphasized to them that change can be difficult but that some of the sting of these encounters might be reduced. The couple are then asked to stage such arguments on their own time, but with a specific small change that contradicts or challenges the aspects of the arguments that they find most distressing. A couple distressed about the suddenness and unpredictability of their arguments might be asked about how many such arguments they have had in the past few weeks. They would then be asked to meet their weekly average in the first 3 days of the next week and, because this is a sacrifice for therapy, to reward themselves if they meet their quota on time.

As an example, a man was extremely critical of his depressed wife's social *faux pas*. Her feeble apologies for herself seemed only to invite more devastating attacks and, in turn, an embroilment in which each screamed at the other. Furthermore, the more the woman attempted to avoid making mistakes, the more negatively self-focused she became, and the clumsier she acted. The couple agreed that all spontaneity had been lost from their relationship. He blamed her social ineptness, and she blamed his hyper-criticalness for their plight. They were asked to reduce the spontaneity of their negative encounters in order to clear the way for spontaneous positive events. The woman was specifically asked to make a visible social blunder with a flourish, and the man was asked to overreact. It was noted that to make a blunder would be a sacrifice, and because of this, she should at least have the compensation of doing it at a very good restaurant. To comply, she started a dinner by ordering a gin and tonic with a raw egg. She broke the egg over the drink, toasted her husband, and sucked the egg off the top of the drink. He was too taken aback to do his part of the assignment, and they proceeded to enjoy the meal together with a lightness and sense of closeness that they had not experienced in a long time.

In marital relationships characterized, not by turmoil, but by each partner's being overconcerned with avoiding the distress of the other, a different plan is adopted. The therapist should repeatedly and actively acknowledge that the couple do not engage in the destructive conflict that many others do, but that as a result of being this way, they are making numerous unnoticed sacrifices to the quality of their marriage. The general thrust of interventions is to connote positively the couple's existing arrangements, even while preparing for change in the direction of their being less overconcerned about each other.

The following set of assignments is often given in the guise of an exercise for the purpose of assessment. Each partner is asked to perform one act of self-indulgence and to make one contribution to the couple or family as a sacrifice to therapy. This is to allow for a subsequent assessment in which each person is to be quizzed in a separate interview about what the other has done in the name of therapy. The couple are further cautioned that only ambiguous feedback is to be given in return. After a few weeks of this, the couple are told to decide whether the assignment is in need of doing, but not to inform the spouse. Subsequent assignments are likely to involve each member of the couple's being given a coupon good for one overreaction to their partner. However, they are not to tell the spouse when the coupon is about to be used.

In many of these couples, signs of independence and autonomy may be misconstrued as alienation. An overreaction from at least one partner is a probable event, and when it does occur, the second assignment may provide a benign explanation. Often the couple become quite enthusiastic about these assignments and utilize them to do things that they have wanted to do but were too guilt-ridden and intimidated to attempt. Very often, preexisting but unspoken disagreements become explicit. If this is the case, the therapist might point to this as a clear accomplishment, positively connoting it (e.g., "You are now feeling comfortable enough with the relationship to risk disagreement"), and urge the couple to go slow. It might be suggested that the depressed person can relapse to preserve the harmony of the relationship if she so chooses. To the spouse, it might be suggested that the choice between a depressed partner and some disagreement can be a troubling one, but that the couple have a history of looking after each other on which to fall back.

THE ROLE OF THE THERAPIST

The traditional individual therapy literature contains numerous references to the difficulties and discomfort presumed to be inherent in working with depressed persons (Jacobson, 1954; Cohen et al., 1954). Elsewhere (Coyne,

1976a), I have presented a representative case example in which a reacted with hostility and rejection when her unrealistic reassurance tan... to improve the mood of her depressed patient. In general, a therapist working with a depressed patient faces the same task as that which confronts the patient's spouse: to avoid overinvolvement without resorting to withdrawal and rejection, and to remain concerned about the welfare of the depressed person without becoming demanding, coercive, and condemning. It is easy to become more agitated about the patient's remaining depressed than the patient is, but once this has occurred, the therapist is much more likely to personalize the continued distress of the depressed person: "How dare she remain depressed when I am doing such fine therapy?" Unintentionally, two psychoanalysts have provided a classic example of therapists falling into such a trap in their depiction of the depressed person as "truly aggressive toward others through the very medium of the manifestations of his depression. His suffering is an accusation. His sense of incurableness is a reproach. His demands are perhaps humble, but devastating. His dependency [is] tyrannical" (Nacht & Recamier, 1960, p. 486).

Less attention has been given to the difficulties of working with the spouse of a depressed person. Frequently, however, therapists may choose to ignore a spouse's clear statement that nothing is wrong with the marriage except that the partner is depressed. The therapist then proceeds as if there is a mutual contract to improve communication or some general feature of the marriage, while the spouse has not identified such a problem. Alternatively, the therapist may join with the depressed person in attempting to reach an emotional response from the spouse, perhaps a revelation of a purported masked sadness or depression. Such tactics generally serve only to increase reticence and encourage defection from therapy.

In working with the couple, one potential problem is that the therapist will take sides and become unable to join and disengage from each partner as the tasks of therapy require. The therapist may see the spouse as the hapless victim of the depressed person or, alternatively, the depressed person's plight as the result of the spouse's machinations. A therapist who is able to identify a pure victim and a pure victimizer in a couple is unlikely to be of much help.

A problem that is specific to strategic marital therapy with depressed persons is the possibility that the obvious distress of one or both partners will prove either so absorbing or threatening that the therapist cannot adopt an appropriately balanced attitude of dead-serious play (Haley, 1963) in dealing with them. Therapists who experience discomfort using paradoxical injunctions, symptom prescriptions, and other standard techniques of strategic therapy are more likely to have difficulty when one member of a couple is depressed. Certainly, if a therapist is uncomfortable with a particular intervention, then he or she should not employ it. Furthermore, if a therapist communicates a sense that a particular intervention or reframing is not personally acceptable, then the couple will find added reason to reject it.

One does not have to believe that there are genuine drawbacks or disadvantages to improvement in order to make interventions that take this as a premise, but it helps.

One is probably in the best position to be an effective strategic therapist with depressed persons and their spouses if one is thoroughly convinced of the ironies and paradoxes of depression and recovery from it: Depressed persons are powerful in their powerlessness; one sure way to make oneself miserable is to try too hard to be happy; there is a considerable amount of comfort to be found in the familiar certainty of the depressed person's discomfort; and whatever advantages there are to recovery, it is likely to present new problems (this is presented to depressed persons as "Every silver lining has at least some wisps of black cloud attached to it"). It is likely that much of the effectiveness of strategic therapy is derived from its recognition and exploitation of these departures from conventional wisdom.

SPECIAL ISSUES IN TREATING DEPRESSION

Three issues, each likely to arise with some regularity in work with depressed persons and each worthy of extended discussion, can be noted only briefly within the limits of the present chapter: the threat of suicide or divorce, and the use of antidepressant medication concurrently with therapy.

The possibility of suicide is best explored in a frank discussion with the depressed person and, if doubts remain, with the spouse in an individual interview. When there is a definite threat of suicide, the following interventions with the depressed person may become important: (a) Indicate that probably neither the therapist nor anyone else can prevent someone determined to commit suicide from doing so; (b) obtain, as a condition of therapy, an antisuicide contract in which the depressed person agrees not to make an attempt, and, in the event that she feels that this agreement can no longer be kept, what actions (such as voluntary hospitalization) will be taken; (c) reframe the suicidal person's situation in a way that is respectful and suggestive of alternative ways of coping.

Unrealistic reassurances about the therapist's availability, overreactions, and threats may all increase the possibility that a depressed person will become locked into suicidal gestures as a way of structuring the therapeutic relationship. The therapist needs to avoid seeming to offer more than he or she is able to provide and also to avoid denying depressed persons' power to enact a suicidal gesture. It is likely that many suicide attempts and completions arise out of depressed persons' rebellion against threats and constraints that prove to be more feeble than they first appear (Kobler & Stotland, 1964). "The paradox is that to assume total responsibility for the safety of this type of patient and to react to every evidence of suicidal behavior with an unwillingness to take risks may . . . ultimately increase the risk of suicide" (Flinn, Slawson, & Schwartz, 1978, p. 126).

Reframings of suicidal situations may center on the person's dilemma as a reflection of something positive. For instance, a woman felt that she had disgraced her family with an extramarital affair and the neglect of her children and that she had disappointed her boss and co-workers with her absenteeism. She had already made one serious suicide attempt when she had tried to make up for lost time at work only to become overwhelmed and despondent. She monotonously reiterated her complaint that she was irresponsible. The therapist suggested that she was overly responsible and stubbornly conscientious to the point of its being a deadly vice. Most people would have taken refuge in excuses of some kind in order to avoid the heroics of trying to right her situation in the way that she was attempting— most people would have accepted that a bit more "irresponsibility" in the face of overwhelming demands was defensible. After she agreed to call her boss and ask for a leave of absence, the therapist suggested that her most serious problem was that she seemed to be a bit relieved—feeling better, she might believe that she was now able to tackle all her problems at once again. Discussion then followed as to how she might protect herself from her conscientiousness in case her depression lifted when it was most needed.

Work with the spouse of a suicidal person should include efforts to prevent suicidal gestures from becoming a way for the suicidal partner to influence the spouse. It is best that any antisuicide contract be between the depressed person and the therapist, rather than with the spouse. This is particularly important if there is marital conflict in which the threat of abrogation of the contract can become a tactic. The therapist might indicate to the spouse that no one has the absolute power to prevent another from committing suicide and suggest that someone who accepts this difficult point is more likely to be of help. Some effort might then be made to connote positively the suicidal person's dilemma. Beyond this, however, the therapist should seek to reduce the tendency of the spouse to overreact to the suicidal person and of the couple to make the threat of suicide the central issue in the relationship.

Like suicide, separation and divorce are salient possibilities as outcomes of depression; and like suicide, their potential should be discussed early in the course of treatment. If marital dissolution is raised as something that is likely, the therapist may acknowledge that this is understandable, given the circumstances, but indicate that treatment is more likely to prove beneficial if separation is not an immediate issue. If one partner cannot agree to this, the therapist should indicate that it is unclear how marital therapy can be helpful. In this situation, a therapist who is open-minded but skeptical about the usefulness of either therapy or the continuation of the marriage is more likely to elicit a commitment from the couple than one who makes a strong case for either.

It is sometimes the case that the dissolution of the marriage has already been discussed, and uncertainty about the future has served to immobilize one or both partners so that they are ill prepared either to take steps to improve the viability of the relationship or to adapt to a separation. One of them, usually the nondepressed spouse, may have withdrawn to "wait and see" what changes the partner will make. Whether or not the therapist has only one partner with whom to work, therapy can be structured around answers to the question, "Could you identify some small goals that could allow you to look back on this period with a sense that it had been well spent—no matter what the outcome of the marriage?" If no workable answer is forthcoming, the therapist can shift to, "What are some small ways in which we could attempt to reduce the pain and cost of this difficult period for you?" Either way, it is useful to identify concrete goals that would also serve to reduce the intensity of the negative involvement of the couple.

Depressed persons often seek therapy while they are receiving antidepressant medication. Evidence is mounting which suggests that even when drug treatment results in an improvement in mood, there is little reduction in marital problems (Klerman & Weissman, 1982). It is important that all professionals involved in the treatment are aware of the others' participation, but beyond that, there may be little necessity for making concurrent drug treatment an issue in strategic marital therapy for depression. There are legal and ethical problems when therapists who are not physicians attempt to make decisions about termination of medication. Patients, spouses, and biologically oriented psychiatrists may all be most comfortable with an arrangement whereby marital therapy is framed as either a concurrent treatment for depressing circumstances or as a way of assisting the couple in being more supportive. Often the depressed person soon wishes to reduce or eliminate the medication, but this is left as an issue between patient and physician.

REFERENCES

American Psychiatric Association (1980). *Diagnostic and statistical manual of mental disorders* (3d ed.). Washington, DC: Author.

Bateson, G. (1971). The cybernetics of "self": A theory of alcoholism. *Psychiatry, 34*, 1–18.

Birchnell, J., & Kennard, J. (1983). Does marital maladjustment lead to mental illness? *Social Psychiatry, 18*, 79–88.

Brown, G. W., & Harris, T. (1978). *Social origins of depression.* New York: Free Press.

Bullock, R., Siegel, R., Weissman, M. M., & Paykel, E. S. (1972). The weeping wife: Marital relations of depressed women. *Journal of Marriage and the Family*, 488–492.

Cohen, M. B., *et al.* (1954). An intensive study of twelve cases of manic-depressive psychosis. *Psychiatry, 17*, 103–137.

Coyne, J. C. (1976a). Depression and the response of others. *Journal of Abnormal Psychology, 89*, 186–193.

Coyne, J. C. (1976b). Toward an interactional description of depression. *Psychiatry, 39*, 28–40.

Coyne, J. C. (1984a). Strategic therapy with married depressed persons: Initial agenda, themes and interventions. *Journal of Marital and Family Therapy, 10*, 53–62.

Coyne, J. C. (1984b). *Frames and reframing.* Unpublished manuscript, Mental Research Institute, Palo Alto, CA.

Coyne, J. C., Aldwin, C., & Lazarus, R. S. (1981). Depression and coping in stressful episodes. *Journal of Abnormal Psychology, 90*, 439–447.

Coyne, J. C., Kahn, J., & Gotlib, I. (1985). Depression. In T. Jacobs (Ed.), *Family interaction and psychopathology*. New York: Pergamon Press.

Coyne, J. C., & Segal, L. (1982). A brief, strategic interactional approach to psychotherapy. In J. Anchin & D. Kiesler (Eds.), *Handbook of interpersonal psychotherapy*. New York: Pergamon Press.

DeLongis, A. M., Coyne, J. C., Dakof, G., Folkman, S., & Lazarus, R. S. (1982). Daily hassles, uplifts, and the prediction of health states. *Health Psychology, 1*, 119–136.

Fisch, R., Weakland, J. H., & Segal, L. (1982). *The tactics of change: Doing therapy briefly*. San Francisco: Jossey-Bass.

Flinn, D. E., Slawson, P. F., & Schwartz, D. (1978). Staff response to suicide of hospitalized psychiatric patients. *Hospital and Community Psychiatry, 29*, 122–127.

Haley, J. (1963). *Strategies of psychotherapy*. New York: Grune & Stratton.

Hops, H., Biglan, A., Sherman, L., Arthur, J., & Friedman, L. S. (1983, August). *Direct observation study of family processes in maternal depression*. Paper presented at the annual convention of the American Psychological Association, Anaheim, CA.

Jacobson, E. (1954). Transference problems in the psychoanalytic treatment of severely depressed patients. *Journal of the American Psychoanalytic Association, 2*, 595–600.

Kahn, J., Coyne, J. C., & Margolin, G. (in press). *Depression and marital conflict*: The social construction of despair. *Journal of Social and Personal Relationships*.

Klerman, G. L., & Weissman, M. M. (1982). Interpersonal psychotherapy: Theory and research. In A. J. Rush (Ed.), *Short-term psychotherapy for depression: Behavioral, interpersonal, cognitive, and psychodynamic approaches*. New York: Guilford Press.

Kobler, A. L., & Stotland, E. (1964). *The end of hope: A social–clinical study of suicide*. New York: Free Press.

Leff, M., Roatch, J., & Bunney, L. E. (1970). Environmental factors preceding the onset of severe depression. *Psychiatry, 33*, 298–311.

Nacht, S., & Recamier, P. C. (1960). Symposium on depressive illness: II: Depressive states. *International Journal of Psycho-analysis, 41*, 481–496.

Paykel, E. S., Myers, J. K., Dienelt, M. N., Klerman, G. L., Lindenthal, J. J., & Pepper, M. P. (1969). Life events and depression: A controlled study. *Archives of General Psychiatry, 21*, 753–760.

Rush, A. J. (1982). Diagnosing depressions. In A. J. Rush (Ed.), *Short-term psychotherapies for depression: Behavioral, interpersonal, cognitive, and psychodynamic approaches*. New York: Guilford Press.

Rush, A. J., Beck, A. T., Kovacs, M., & Hollon, S. (1977). Comparative efficacy of cognitive therapy and Imipramine in the treatment of depressed outpatients. *Cognitive Therapy and Research, 1*, 17–37.

Rush, A. J., Shaw, B., & Khatami, M. (1980). Cognitive therapy of depression: Utilizing the couples system. *Cognitive Therapy and Research, 4*, 103–113.

Spitzer, R. L., Endicott, J., & Robins, E. (1978). Research diagnostic criteria: Rationale and reliability. *Archives of General Psychiatry, 35*, 773–782.

Stern, S. L., & Mendels, J. (1980). Affective disorders. In A. E. Kazdin, A. S. Bellack, & M. Hersen (Eds.), *New perspectives in abnormal psychology*. New York: Oxford University Press.

Watzlawick, P., Weakland, J., & Fisch, R. (1974). *Change: Principles of problem formation and problem resolution*. New York: Norton.

Weissman, M. M., & Paykel, E. S. (1974). *The depressed woman: A study of social relationships*. Chicago: University of Chicago Press.

Marital Therapy in the Treatment of Alcoholism

TIMOTHY J. O'FARRELL

ALCOHOLISM AND MARITAL RELATIONSHIPS

In DSM-III (American Psychiatric Association, 1980), an individual with an alcoholism problem can receive a diagnosis of alcohol abuse or alcohol dependence. Criteria for a diagnosis of alcohol abuse are (*a*) a pattern of pathological use of alcohol; or (*b*) impairment in social or occupational functioning as a result of alcohol use. To merit a diagnosis of alcohol dependence, the individual must show evidence of physical addiction to alcohol (i.e., either tolerance or withdrawal) in addition to meeting the criteria for alcohol abuse.

Marital Discord and Abusive Drinking: A Reciprocal Relationship

MARITAL ISSUES CONTRIBUTE TO ALCOHOLISM

Marital relationship issues contribute to the development and maintenance of alcohol problems. An unhappy marriage can lead to increased drinking and, in a susceptible individual, to the development of alcoholism. Marital conflict as a primary etiology of alcoholism, although more common among women than men, is rather infrequent. Once an alcohol problem has developed, however, marital interactions very frequently contribute to the maintenance of alcoholism. Often the alcohol problem becomes the focus

Timothy J. O'Farrell. Department of Psychiatry, Harvard Medical School, Boston, Massachusetts and Veterans Administration Medical Center, Brockton, Massachusetts.

of much of the couple's interactions. The couple becomes entangled in a self-defeating struggle over the alcoholic's abusive drinking. The nonalcoholic spouse, in attempts to change the alcoholic's drinking, often unwittingly attends primarily to alcoholic behaviors while virtually ignoring positive nondrinking behavior. Nonalcoholic spouses also often provide financial, emotional, and other forms of rewards when the alcoholic is drinking heavily, thus providing consequences likely to maintain drinking. The alcoholic often is unassertive when his or her spouse complains and argues about the excessive drinking, and this leads to bottled-up rage in the alcoholic, which often is dealt with by drinking. The alcoholic also can use the repeated nagging and complaints about drinking by the spouse as an excuse to avoid examining his or her drinking problem, choosing rather to blame the excessive drinking on the spouse's behavior. In addition to conflict about alcohol, conflicts about other issues in the marriage also may lead to abusive drinking. As McCrady (1983) has noted, the difference between alcoholic couples and other couples experiencing marital distress is that in the former drinking is a high-probability response to marital conflicts. Finally, even when recovery from alcoholism is well under way, marital conflicts can precipitate renewed drinking by abstinent alcoholics (Hore, 1971a, 1971b; Marlatt & Gordon, 1978).

ALCOHOLISM PRODUCES MARITAL DISCORD

Alcoholism contributes to marital discord, among the more serious consequences of which are separation or divorce (O'Farrell, Harrison, & Cutter, 1981) and spouse abuse (Hanks & Rosenbaum, 1977), in a number of ways. An actively drinking alcoholic often is unpredictable and undependable, making household and family management and decision making difficult and chaotic. Alcohol abuse can contribute to many marital stresses including embarrassing incidents, financial problems, job difficulties and losses, verbal and physical abuse, and inadequate parenting and sexual functioning by the alcoholic. The negative effects of the excessive drinking leads the couple into an intense, hostile struggle in which the nonalcoholic spouse tries desperately to control the alcoholic's drinking, and the alcoholic, although at times promising to reform, keeps on drinking. Such repeated unkept promises to change and short-lived periods of improvement followed by a return to abusive drinking lead to a high level of anger and mistrust on the part of the nonalcoholic spouse and a decrease in the time and activities shared with the alcoholic. Finally, the alcohol abuse exacerbates non-alcohol-related marital conflicts and differences because it (a) obscures the cause of the problems by virtue of the couple's tendencies to attribute all difficulties to the alcohol problem; and (b) prevents resolution of the problems by interfering with communication about them.

Nondyadic Factors in Alcoholism

Despite the importance of marital factors in alcoholism, other nondyadic factors frequently play an important role in both the etiology and maintenance of alcoholism problems. For example, individuals reared with an alcoholic parent are at risk for developing alcohol problems due to both genetic factors and faulty role modeling. Similarly, learning to drink to cope with stress and exposure to stressful situations outside the marriage (e.g., job pressures) can contribute to alcoholism. The importance of factors other than the marital relationship in alcoholism means that marital therapy often is adjunctive to individual treatment for the alcoholic. In all cases, even when marital therapy is the sole treatment modality, recent thinking about stages in the process of change for a person with a drinking problem (Goldstein & Marlatt, in press; Prochaska & DiClemente, 1983) is useful for organizing the different marital therapy interventions required to meet the varied needs of alcohol-troubled couples. Briefly stated, the process of change for someone with a drinking (or other addictive behavior) problem has three stages: (a) initial commitment to change—recognizing that a problem exists and deciding to do something about it; (b) the change itself—stopping abusive drinking and stabilizing this change for at least a few months; and (c) the long-term maintenance of change.

After briefly presenting goals and preparations for marital therapy with alcoholics, this chapter discusses marital therapy interventions for use in the second and third stages of change in the alcoholism problem. Techniques are grouped according to primary focus, either on the drinking problem itself or on marital relationship issues other than drinking. Also, common obstacles to successful marital therapy with alcoholics are considered. Types of cases not usually helped by marital therapy and some recently suggested solutions also are discussed. Like the author's work on behavioral marital therapy (BMT) for alcoholics (O'Farrell, 1979; O'Farrell & Cutter, 1977, 1979, 1984a, 1984b) much of the material in this chapter is based on a social learning perspective.

GOALS AND PREPARATIONS FOR MARITAL THERAPY WITH ALCOHOLICS

Goals

Once the alcoholic has decided to change his or her drinking, marital therapy has two basic objectives in order to stabilize short-term change in the alcohol problem and in the alcoholic's marriage. The first goal is to reduce or eliminate abusive drinking and support the alcoholic's efforts to change. To this end, a high priority is changing alcohol-related interactional patterns (e.g., nagging about past drinking but ignoring current sober behavior) presumed to maintain abusive drinking. Clinical experience suggests that one can get abstinent alcoholics and their spouses to engage in behaviors more pleasing to each other, but if the alcohol-related interactional patterns are not changed, they soon return to arguing about past or "possible" future drinking. Frequently such arguments lead to renewed drinking (Hore, 1971a, 1971b; Marlatt & Gordon, 1978). They then feel more discouraged about their relationship and the drinking than before and are less likely to try pleasing each other again. The second goal involves altering general marital patterns to provide an atmosphere that is more conducive to sobriety. This involves helping the couple repair the often extensive relationship damage incurred during many years of conflict over alcohol, as well as helping them find solutions to relationship difficulties that may have predated the alcoholism. Finally, the couple must learn to confront and resolve relationship conflicts without the alcoholic's resorting to drinking. After the change in the alcohol problem has been stable for 3 to 6 months, the goals of marital therapy in contributing to long-term maintenance of change are to help the couple prevent relapse to abusive drinking and deal with marital issues frequently encountered during long-term recovery from an alcohol problem.

Assessment Procedures

In the initial interview with the couple, the therapist needs (a) to determine at what stage the alcoholic is in the process of changing his or her alcohol abuse; (b) to assess whether there is a need for crisis intervention prior to a careful assessment; and (c) to orient the couple to the assessment procedures. If the alcoholic already has initiated changes in the drinking or at least clearly recognizes that a problem exists and may want to change it, then proceeding with the assessment makes sense. If the alcoholic has not yet made a firm decision whether or not to change the drinking, then facilitating this decision becomes one of the goals of the assessment. In terms of the need for crisis intervention, the therapist evaluates whether any serious negative consequences are likely to occur if two or three assessment sessions are conducted before taking action on the couple's presenting complaints. For example, crisis intervention is necessary for cases in which violence or divorce seem likely risks of delayed action or cases in which an alcoholic is ready to stop drinking but needs immediate hospitalization for detoxification and starting alcoholism treatment. Often the usual assessment can be conducted after the crisis has been resolved.

In the present author's practice, pretreatment assessment consists of (a) the husband and wife being interviewed separately about the alcoholic's drinking history and in detail about the drinking in the previous year (Timeline Drinking Interview; O'Farrell, Cutter, Bayog, Dentch, & Fortgang, 1984); (b) each spouse completing the Michigan Alcoholism Screening Test (MAST; Selzer, 1971) about themselves and about their spouse to determine the extent to which their drinking habits and consequences resemble those of alcoholics; (c) each spouse completing separately a series of questionnaires about their marriage including the Marital Adjustment Test (Locke & Wallace, 1959) to determine overall relationship satisfaction and areas of disagreement, the Marital Status Inventory (Weiss & Cerreto, 1980) to assess steps toward separation and divorce, the Areas of Change Questionnaire (Margolin, Talovic, & Weinstein, 1983) to establish relationship changes desired, the Conflict

Tactics Scale (Straus, 1979) to assess the extent of verbal and physical abuse, and a Sexual Adjustment Questionnaire (O'Farrell, Kleinke, & Cutter, 1984); and (d) a videotaped sample of communication while the couple discuss a current marital problem. Each spouse is interviewed separately to review their questionnaire responses and provide an opportunity to clarify anything that is ambiguous.

After the assessment information has been gathered, the couple and therapist meet for a feedback session in which the therapist shares impressions of the nature and severity of the drinking and marital problems and invites the couple to respond to these impressions. A second goal of the feedback session is to decide whether or not the couple will begin short-term marital therapy and prepare them for the marital therapy if that is the decision. Assuming the decision is to start marital therapy, the therapist usually emphasizes the value of marriage counseling in achieving sobriety and a more satisfying marriage and tries to promote favorable therapeutic expectations. Verbal commitments are obtained from the husband and the wife to live together for at least the initial course of therapy, not to threaten divorce or separation during this period, and to do their best to focus on the future and the present (but not the past) in the therapy sessions and at home. In addition, the couple is asked to agree to do weekly homework assignments as part of the therapy. Finally, the therapist gives an overview of the course of therapy and tells the couple in more detail about the content of the first few sessions.

Typical Structure and Sequence of Marital Therapy Sessions

Marital therapy to help stabilize short-term change in the alcoholism and associated marital discord usually consists of 10 to 15 therapy sessions each of which lasts 60 to 75 minutes. Like other BMT practitioners, the present author's sessions tend to be highly structured, with the therapist setting the agenda at the outset of each meeting. A typical session begins with reviewing the homework assignment from the previous session; moves on to new material, such as instruction in and rehearsal of skills to be practiced at home during the week; and ends with the assignment of homework and answering questions. Generally, the first few sessions focus on decreasing alcohol-related feelings and interactions and increasing positive exchanges to decrease tension about alcohol (and the risk of abusive drinking) and to build good will. Both are necessary for dealing with marital problems and desired relationship changes in later sessions using communication and problem-solving skills training and behavior change agreements. The following section describes typical interventions used.

Once the alcohol problem has been under control for 3 to 6 months, the structure and content of marital therapy sessions often change as the emphasis of the therapy becomes maintaining gains and preventing relapse. This phase of therapy is described later in the chapter.

PROCEDURES FOR STABILIZING CHANGE IN
THE ALCOHOLIC'S DRINKING BEHAVIOR
AND MARITAL RELATIONSHIPS

Alcohol-Focused Interventions

After the alcohol abuser has decided to change his or her drinking, the spouse can be included in alcohol-focused interventions designed to support the alcohol abuser in adhering to this difficult and stressful decision. The first purpose of such treatment is to establish a clear and specific agreement between the alcohol abuser and spouse about the goal for the alcoholic's drinking and their respective roles in achieving that goal. If abstinence is the goal, the minimum desired length of time during which the alcoholic plans to abstain should be specified. If reduced drinking is the goal, the acceptable quantities and conditions (e.g., where, when, with whom), along with the consequences of excessive drinking, must be established, preferably in writing. Of course, individual treatment for the drinking, including possible attendance at AA and Al-Anon meetings when applicable, also must be agreed upon.

The second general purpose of alcohol-focused treatment with couples is to specify other behavioral changes needed in the alcohol abuser or the spouse that would help achieve the drinking goal. Although needed changes vary widely from case to case, certain issues occur with sufficient frequency that they should probably be addressed with most cases. For instance, possible exposure to alcohol beverages and alcohol-related situtions should be discussed. The couple should decide if the nonalcoholic spouse will drink alcoholic beverages in the alcoholic's presence, whether alcoholic beverages will be kept and served at home, if the couple will attend social gatherings involving alcohol, and how to deal with these situations. Particular persons, gatherings, or circumstances that are likely to be stressful should be identified. Couple interactions related to alcohol also need to be addressed, for arguments, tension, and negative feelings can precipitate more abusive drinking. Therapists need to confront such patterns and provide specific procedures for the couple to use in difficult situations. For example, Lazarus (1968) and others (Cheek, Franks, Burtle, & Laucius, 1971) have used relaxation training and systematic desensitization to help spouses control their fear and anger about the alcoholic's drinking. Similarly, Eisler (Eisler, Miller, Hersen, & Alford, 1974) taught the alcoholic to request assertively that the spouse refrain from comments about drinking. The therapist frequently will need to deal with other situations identified by the couple as likely to cause difficulty. Finally, if the therapist identifies positive consequences of the drinking (e.g., facilitation of sexual interaction), then specific strategies for obtaining these satisfactions without drinking will need to be planned (Davis, Berenson, Steinglass, & Davis, 1974). The remainder of this section describes specific methods and examples of how to achieve the general goals described.

BEHAVIORAL CONTRACTING

1. Reducing abusive drinking. Peter Miller (1972) used contingency contracting with an excessive drinker and his wife to shape controlled drinking and reduce arguments about drinking. The 44-year-old husband had been consuming 4 to 6 pints of bourbon per week for 2 years prior to treatment and could not specify any anxiety-producing situations preceding his drinking episodes. He did, however, report that his wife's frequent critical comments and disapproving glances about his drinking increased his consumption. The couple signed a contract that required the husband to limit his drinking to between 1 and 3 drinks a day (in the presence of his wife before the evening meal) and the wife to refrain from negative verbal or nonverbal responses to her husband's drinking. Each partner agreed to pay the other $20 if he or she broke the agreement. Each spouse received a few fines during the first few weeks of the contract, but the infractions rapidly diminished when each partner learned that the contract would, in fact, be enforced.

The alcohol abuser treated by Miller was employed, showed no medical damage from his excessive drinking, and the negative impact of his drinking was confined to the marital relationship. These factors suggested an attempt to reduce rather than eliminate the drinking. Therapists need to choose carefully in each individual case whether the goal of treatment should be controlled drinking or total abstinence. Although empirical data on which to base this decision are still being gathered, rational guidelines are available (Heather & Robertson, 1981, pp. 215–240; Miller & Caddy, 1977) and should be used prior to implementing such a behavioral contracting procedure.

2. Antabuse contracts to promote abstinence. Antabuse (disulfiram), a drug that produces extreme nausea and sickness when the person taking the drug ingests alcohol, is widely used in alcoholism treatment for persons with a goal of abstinence. Antabuse therapy often is not always effective because the alcoholic discontinues the drug prematurely (Lundwall & Baekeland, 1971). The Antabuse Contract, a procedure adapted from the work of Peter Miller (Miller & Hersen, 1975) and Nathan Azrin (Azrin, 1976; Azrin, Sisson, Meyers, & Godley, 1982), is designed to maintain Antabuse ingestion and abstinence from alcohol and to decrease alcohol-related arguments and interactions between the alcoholic and his or her spouse. Before negotiating such a contract, the therapist should be sure that the alcoholic is willing and medically cleared to take Antabuse and that both alcoholic and spouse have been fully informed and educated about the effects of the drug.

In the Antabuse Contract, the alcoholic agrees to take Antabuse each day while the spouse observes. The spouse, in turn, agrees to record the observation on a calendar provided by the therapist and not to mention past drinking or any fears about future drinking. It is extremely important that each spouse view the agreement as a cooperative method for rebuilding trust that has been lost and not as a coercive checking-up operation. More details on how to implement the Antabuse Contract and how to deal with common resistances to this procedure are available elsewhere (O'Farrell & Bayog, 1984).

Maintenance of the Antabuse agreement is facilitated by monitoring compliance with the procedure at the beginning of each session. The couple brings the calendar on which the observations are recorded to each session, and the therapist probes for, and discusses, any lapses in compliance. The couple can be asked to role-play the sitations that interrupted the performance of the agreed-on behavior and provide alternative strategies for dealing with such sitations in the future. Midweek phone calls to monitor the agreement also can be very useful in getting the procedure firmly established. Monitoring compliance with the Antabuse Contract is especially important in the first month of the agreement, since most couples seem to have some difficulty with the procedure during this period. In later therapy sessions, a brief review of the calendar and a reminder to contact the therapist if the Antabuse ingestion is not observed for 2 consecutive days and to refill the prescription when needed usually suffice. Finally, the therapist should contact the couple a few weeks prior to the expiration of the agreement to set an appointment to discuss whether or not the couple wants to renew the contract.

3. *Structuring the spouse's and the alcoholic's role in the recovery process.* The following examples of written behavioral contracts, although different in many specific aspects of the agreements, have a number of common elements that make them useful. The drinking behavior goal is made explicit. Specific behaviors that each spouse can do to help achieve this goal are also detailed. The contact provides alternative behaviors to negative interactions about drinking. Finally, and quite important, the agreement decreases the nonalcoholic spouse's anxiety and need to control the alcoholic and his or her drinking.

Daniel Kivlahan and Elizabeth Shapiro (personal communication, May 18, 1984) have male alcoholics who are not taking Antabuse and their spouses engage in what they call a Trust Contract. Each day, at a specified time, the alcoholic initiates a brief discussion in which he reiterates his desire not to drink that day and then asks the wife if she has any questions or fears about possible drinking that day. He answers the questions and attempts to reassure the wife as best he can. The wife is not to mention past drinking or any future possible drinking beyond that day. The couple agrees to refrain from discussing drinking at any other time, to keep the daily trust discussion very brief, and to end it with a positive statement to each other.

> When he consulted the present author, a male alcoholic recognized he had an alcohol problem, has abstained for 3 months in the past year, but was trying to engage in "social drinking." Periodically he would drink heavily for a period of 3 to 5 days. The binge would end with the alcoholic being very contrite and pledging to stop drinking after an intense fight with his wife in which the husband became verbally abusive and the wife threatened to terminate their relationship. After two serious binges in a 6-week period, Antabuse was being considered. After a third binge, the husband insisted

he wanted to abstain for at least 6 months, and obtained but did not want to start taking Antabuse, preferring to "do it on my own if I can." At a conjoint session with the wife, various alternatives were considered and the following agreement was negotiated: (a) the husband's goal was at least 6 months' abstinence from alcohol; (b) if he drank before then, he would start daily Antabuse and continue it at least to the end of the 6-month period; (c) if the wife thought he had been drinking, she would remind the husband of their agreement and ask him to start the Antabuse; (d) if the husband refused, the wife would refrain from arguing or threats and leave their home until the husband had stopped drinking and started the Antabuse. The agreement was posted in the couple's home on the inside of the cabinet where the Antabuse was kept. Two weeks after the agreement was negotiated, the husband drank and then voluntarily started the Antabuse. Both husband and wife were pleased that their customary intense argument was not necessary to terminate the drinking. They went on to negotiate an Antabuse Contract as described above, and the husband refrained from drinking as he had planned.

A retired male with a long history of alcoholism and serious liver cirrhosis was being seen in weekly outpatient sessions after being hospitalized for alcoholism treatment. He reported good progress, indicating that he was looking for part-time work, attending AA regularly, and abstaining from alcohol. However, he complained that his wife was accusing him of drinking, and they were arguing about how to solve their financial problems and how to spend their time together. At about the same time, liver function tests had been performed in order to encourage the patient to remain abstinent by giving him medical evidence about the improvement of his liver status. The results of this liver test showed elevated liver enzymes, most likely indicating recent drinking. Conjoint sessions with the alcoholic and his wife were begun and the following agreement was established: (a) each evening the husband would take an alcohol breath test using a Mobile Breath Alcohol Tester (Mobatt; Sobell & Sobell, 1975) to verify he had not been drinking; (b) the wife would refrain from accusations about current drinking or complaints about past drinking; (c) liver function tests would be performed monthly, and the daily Mobatt review would continue until normal liver test results and no evidence of drinking were achieved for 2 consecutive months; (d) the couple would continue in conjoint sessions about their other relationship problems. After this agreement was negotiated, only two isolated instances occurred in which the Mobatt indicated the husband had been drinking that day. The couple, with the therapist's help, decided on a solution to their financial difficulties and began planning their time together more satisfactorily.

DECREASING SPOUSE BEHAVIORS THAT CUE OR REINFORCE ABUSIVE DRINKING

McCrady and Noel (1982) describe procedures to decrease spouse behaviors that cue or reinforce abusive drinking. McCrady (1982) described the implementation of these procedures in a case study of a male alcoholic and his wife seeking abstinence. The couple identified many of the wife's behaviors that cued further drinking, including threatening to leave her husband because of his drinking, saying the children would lose respect for him, pouring alcohol down the sink or getting rid of it in other ways, hiding alcohol, and questioning her husband about where he had been. The husband reacted to these behaviors by becoming angry or depressed and drinking more. The wife unwittingly reinforced drinking by protecting her husband from the consequences of his drinking (e.g., by attempting to make him comfortable when drunk, cleaning up after him when he drank, getting him to bed, bringing him up from the car if he passed out).

As part of a multifaceted behavioral treatment program, McCrady worked with the husband and the wife to find mutually comfortable and agreeable methods to reverse the wife's behavior that inadvertently promoted drinking. First, the couple discussed and role-played ways the wife could express her fears and negative feelings about the husband's drinking in an assertive and constructive manner that would not make him feel more like drinking. The wife also rehearsed new alternative behaviors to counter her tendency to protect the husband when he was drinking. Finally, the wife was taught to provide positive reinforcers (such as verbal acknowledgement, going to movies and flea markets together, making special dinners and snacks) contingent on the husband's not drinking rather than in her previous noncontingent manner.

DEALING WITH RELAPSE

Relapses to abusive drinking often occur during marital therapy with alcoholics. The probability of dealing therapeutically with a relapse is increased if the therapist intervenes before the relapse goes on for too long a period. Having the alcoholic keep a daily record of urges to drink (and any drinking that occurs) and reviewing this record each session can help alert the therapist to the possible risk of a relapse. Between-session phone calls to prompt completion of homework assignments can also alert the therapist to precursors of a relapse episode or to a relapse already in progress. Therapists' goals once a relapse has occurred should be to get the drinking stopped and the couple to the therapist's office as soon as possible for a conjoint conference to use the relapse as a learning experience. At the couple session the therapist must be extremely active in defusing negative hostile or depressive reactions to the relapse. It should be stressed that relapses do not constitute total failure, that inconsistent progress is the rule rather than the exception. The therapist also should try to help the couple identify what couple conflict (or other antecendent) had led up to the relapse and generate alternative solutions other than drinking for similar future situations. Finally, the therapist should help the couple decide what they need to do to feel sure that the relapse is over and will not continue in the coming week (e.g., restarting Antabuse, going to AA and Al-Anon together, reinstituting a Trust Contract).

Interventions to Improve the Marital Relationship

Once the alcohol abuser has begun successfully to control or abstain from drinking, the therapist and the couple can turn their attention to the couple's marital relationship. The nonalcoholic spouse's resentment about past abusive drinking and fear and distrust about the possible return of abusive drinking in the future, coupled with the alcoholic's guilt and desire for recognition of improved drinking behavior, frequently lead to an atmosphere of tension and unhappiness in the marital relationship. Few positive interactions or enjoyable activities occur, and both the alcoholic and wife may become aware of extensive relationship problems. There are problems caused by drinking (e.g., bills, legal charges, embarrassing incidents) that still need to be resolved. There is often a backlog of other unresolved marital problems that the drinking obscured. Relationship problems may be perceived as increasing with drinking improvement due to greater problem recognition and the removal of alcohol as an excuse. The alcoholic and spouse frequently lack the communication skills and mutual positive feelings needed for problem resolution. As a result, many marriages break up during the first 1 or 2 years of the alcoholic's recovery, and marital conflicts often trigger relapse and a return to abusive drinking by the alcoholic (Marlatt & Gordon, 1978; Hore, 1971a, 1971b). Many alcoholics need assistance to improve their marital relationships once changes in drinking have begun.

The two major goals of interventions focused on the alcoholic's marital relationship are (a) to increase positive feeling, goodwill, and commitment to the relationship; and (b) to resolve conflicts, problems, and desires for change. The marital therapy procedures used by the present author to achieve these goals are similar to behavioral marital therapy (BMT) procedures used with nonalcoholics. These methods are not presented in this chapter because BMT procedures (Holtzworth-Munroe & Jacobson in this volume; Jacobson & Margolin, 1979; Liberman, Wheeler, de Visser, Kuehnel, & Kuehnel, 1980; Stuart, 1980) and their application to alcoholics (O'Farrell, in press; O'Farrell & Cutter, 1984a, 1984b) have been described in detail elsewhere.

MARITAL THERAPY TO PROMOTE LONG-TERM MAINTENANCE OF CHANGE

Relapse Prevention

Marital therapy methods to help ensure long-term maintenance of changes in alcohol problems have received very little attention and need considerable development. The present author has a few general methods that he uses during the maintenance phase of treatment, defined somewhat arbitrarily as the phase that begins after at least 6 consecutive months of abstinence or consistent nonproblem drinking have been achieved. Maintenance must be planned before the termination of the active treatment phase. As a first step, a therapist can review the previous marital therapy sessions with the clients to determine which therapeutic interventions (e.g., Antabuse Contract, communication sessions) have been most helpful. Once these have been identified, the therapist and couple can plan how long the couple wants to continue the new behavior and how to ensure that they will be likely to engage in the desired behavior when needed. A second method is to discuss and rehearse possible coping strategies for dealing with (a) high-risk situations for relapse that may occur after treatment; and (b) a relapse if and when it occurs (including creating a time delay after the first drink, calling the therapist, and thinking rationally about the slip [Goldstein & Marlatt, 1984]). A specific couple "relapse episode plan," written down and rehearsed before ending active treatment, can be particularly useful. Early intervention at the beginning of a relapse episode is essential and must be stressed with the couple. So often, couples wait until the drinking has reached dangerous levels again before acting. By then, much additional damage has been done to the marital relationship and other aspects of the drinker's life.

Continued contact with the couple via planned follow-up sessions at regular and then gradually increasing intervals for 3 to 5 years after a stable pattern of recovery (e.g., 6-months' abstinence) has been achieved is also very useful. This frequent and ongoing contact helps the therapist monitor progress, assess compliance with planned maintenance procedures, and evaluate the need for an unplanned preventive session. The therapist must schedule and remind the couple in advance of follow-up sessions and place agreed-upon follow-up phone calls if these procedures are to be completed successfully. The rationale given to couples for the continued contact is that alcohol abuse is a chronic health problem that requires active, aggressive, ongoing monitoring to prevent or to treat relapses quickly. The follow-up contact also provides the opportunity to deal with marital issues that surface after a period of recovery.

Marital Issues in Long-Term Recovery

Many alcohol abusers continue to experience significant marital difficulties after a period of stable recovery has been established. Although a wide variety of issues can present difficulties during long-term recovery, a number of concerns and life patterns predominate. Difficulties in role readjustment occur when the spouse resists the alcohol abuser's efforts to regain important roles in the relationship (e.g., disciplinarian to children, equal partner, and parent) that were lost through drinking. Nearly all couples with a serious alcohol problem face this problem early in the recovery process and although many resolve it on their own, some will need help. Couples often present problems with sex and intimacy (O'Farrell, Weyand, & Logan, 1983) after many of the most severe hardships due to alcohol abuse have been repaired and roles have started to restabilize. Problems with children, especially communication and behavior management with adolescents, frequently become a focus for intervention during long-term recovery. Finally, couples during the recovery process seem particularly vulnerable to stresses created by critical transitions in the family life cycle (e.g., children leaving home), external life change events (e.g., job loss), and/or developmental changes in any of the family members (e.g., midlife crisis). A few case examples illustrate these points.

A male alcoholic with 5 years' sobriety, who had seen the author in marital therapy early in the recovery process, now had yearly couple sessions to review current status and renegotiate an Antabuse Contract. The wife called for help when the husband refused to participate in the Antabuse observation, despite their agreement, and threatened to drink and to end the marriage. Contact with the husband revealed that he was still taking Antabuse, although he would not give his wife the satisfaction of knowing this. A few crisis intervention sessions revealed the factors that had precipitated the marital crisis. Serious sexual problems had concerned the couple for a few years. The husband's fiftieth birthday was approaching, and he wanted to have more sexual fulfillment and closeness in the marriage or the freedom to seek it in a new relationship "before it is too late." In addition, the couple had a mentally ill son in his early 20's who had shown in the previous year that he was not going to be able to support himself or to live outside a sheltered setting.

In another case, a male alcoholic with 12 years' sobriety, achieved through AA for himself and Al-Anon for his wife, sought help after becoming involved in an extramarital affair with a co-worker. The husband had discontinued his participation in AA a number of years previously and currently did not have any inclination to drink, although his wife remained a regular Al-Anon participant. The wife attributed her husband's affair to his "alcoholic personality," meaning that although he wasn't drinking, he was still lying and sneaking around and that the affair was a substitute for the drinking. Further assessment indicated that in the previous year the wife had started to work outside the home, and increases in stress and required overtime on the husband's job had made him quite irritable. These changes disrupted activities previously enjoyed by the couple, and the wife withdrew affection and communication in response to the husband's irritability, choosing to use her Al-Anon friends for support instead. When the husband turned to the woman at work, the couple's problems escalated.

In both examples, marital therapy was successful in resolving the marital crises. The issues in these cases certainly are not unique to alcoholics' marriages. When such issues are presented by alcoholic couples during long-term recovery, however, the therapist must consider two factors not evaluated with other couples. First, the therapist must carefully determine if a relapse is imminent so that necessary preventive interventions can be instituted immediately. Second, the therapist must (a) determine each spouse's view of the relationship between the former alcohol problem and the current marital difficulties; and (b) carefully assess whether or not he or she shares the spouse's view. The latter is important because spouses often continue to attribute relationship difficulties to the previous alcohol problem rather than to current life events and relationship behavior. For example, in the second case presented above, the wife's attribution of the husband's marital affair to his alcoholic personality (after 12 years of sobriety) and her insistence that he return to regular AA attendance were not accepted by the present author during the marital therapy.

COMMON OBSTACLES TO SUCCESSFUL MARITAL THERAPY WITH ALCOHOLICS

Alcohol-Related Crises

Despite their seeming suitability for marital therapy, many alcoholics and their spouses will present the therapist with substantial obstacles. A common problem encountered during assessment or early in therapy are pressing alcohol-related crises (e.g., actual, impending, or threatened loss of job or home, or major legal or financial problems) that preclude a serious and sustained marital therapy focus. The therapist can help the couple devise plans to deal with the crisis or refer them elsewhere for such help, often after establishing a couple agreement about drinking and alcohol-related interactions (e.g., Antabuse Contract). Other marital therapy interventions can be started when the crisis has been resolved.

The Blaming Spouse

A very common obstacle early in therapy is the nonalcoholic spouse who insists on carrying on conversations about past or possible future alcohol-related events, while the alcoholic listens passively and frequently says as little as possible. Interpreting the spouse's behavior as an attempt to punish the alcoholic or sabotage the alcoholic's recovery, or in other ways overtly disapproving of the spouse's behavior, usually is not helpful. The therapist needs to empathize with the spouse. Often this can be done by reframing the spouse's behavior as trying to protect the couple from further problems due to alcohol. From this perspective, the spouse's conversations about the past are intended to be sure the alcoholic (a) knows fully the negative impact of the drinking (and this is plausible since often the drinker does not remember much of what happened); and (b) is aware of the full extent of the problem so his or her motivation toward sobriety will be fortified. Similarly, talk about "possible" future drinking is intended to make the alcoholic forearmed against relapse and lapses in motivation. If the therapist sympathetically interprets the nonalcoholic spouse's intent for the repeated alcohol-related conversations as just described, most often the spouse agrees that she or he has been correctly understood. Frequently the spouse then becomes more receptive to the therapist's suggestion that the spouse has been "doing the wrong thing for the right reason" and to suggestions about more constructive methods to achieve the same goal.

Negative Escalating Cycles and Potential Violence

Many alcoholic couples whose negative interactions escalate quickly have difficulty containing conflict between sessions and pose a potential for violence in some instances. Responses to the Conflict Tactics Scale (Straus, 1979) and the videotaped communication sample help identify many such couples during the pretherapy assessment. Once identified, these couples have conflict containment as an explicit goal of their therapy from the outset. For couples with a history of interspousal violence, it is important to determine whether the violence was limited to occasions when the alcoholic had been drinking. If so, then methods to deal with the alcohol abuse may relieve much of the couple's concern about violence. Nonetheless, an additional procedure described by Shapiro (1984) can be very useful in cases where violence still seems likely. This involves a written agreement that spouses are not to hit or threaten to hit each other, and that if they do, one of the spouses (designated in the agreement) will leave the home and go to a place designated in the agreement for 48 to 72 hours. Another procedure the present author often uses to contain conflict is a "time-out" agreement. In this procedure if either party gets uncomfortable that a discussion may be escalating, he or she says, "I'm getting uncomfortable. I want a 5-minute time-out." Spouses go to separate rooms, where each relaxes (deep breathes) and tries to stop thinking about the argument. Afterward, the couple may restart the discussion if both desire it. If a second time-out is requested, then the couple definitely must stop the discussion.

Repeated Drinking Episodes

Although relapse to abusive drinking is an expected occurrence in marital therapy with alcoholics, couples in which repeated drinking episodes occur can present a particularly difficult challenge. As indicated above, each drinking episode should be used as a learning experience, and depending on what is discovered, different strategies may be helpful. Sometimes a careful analysis will show that the drinking is being precipitated by factors outside the marital relationship, such as work pressures or job-related drinking situations. Individual sessions with the alcoholic to devise methods to deal with the nonmarital precipitants often can be useful in such cases. Another nonmarital factor that can lead to repeated drinking episodes is the alcoholic's ambivalence about whether to stop drinking or attempt to drink "socially." Often an individual session with the alcoholic helps the therapist establish the alcoholic's ambivalence as the basis for the repeated drinking and matter of factly lay out the choices facing the alcoholic about his or her drinking behavior.

At times, repeated drinking episodes are related, at least in part, to marital relationship issues. Analysis of the relapse episodes may reveal that the drinking has adaptive consequences for the relationship (e.g., facilitates sexual interaction or emotional communication for one or both spouses). The main strategy here is to identify this phenomenon for the couple, get them to accept this view, and strengthen controls against drinking while working intensively with the couple to attain the same adaptive relationship consequences without the aid of alcohol. For other couples, repeated drinking episodes are a response to recurring, intense marital conflicts. Relatively favorable long-term outcomes can often be achieved if the therapist can help the couple (a) devise specific methods tailored to their idiosyncratic needs that they can use to contain conflict and that the alcoholic can use to avoid drinking; (b) strengthen nonmarital alcohol coping mechanisms (e.g., AA, Antabuse); and (c) learn alternative communication and problem-solving skills. However, a certain type of couple has presented nearly insurmountable problems in this author's experience. These couples have been unhappily married for many years, and the husband's alcoholism has been a chronic problem that has only been under control for a few short periods after the wife made credible threats of separating or did separate. In addition, the husband frequently denies he has a drinking problem and attributes his excessive drinking to his unsatisfactory marriage. The wife blames the marriage problems on the drinking and insists the drinking must be stopped for an extended period before the marriage can improve. These relationship dynamics are not uncommon in marriages of alcoholics and their wives. The intensity, chronicity, and durability of the marital power struggle over drinking are what appear to characterize these most difficult cases.

Successful Sobriety and the Bankrupt Marriage

A final problem encountered all too frequently is that even though the alcohol problem is under control, the course of therapy reveals that the marriage is no longer viable. Spouses may have grown apart, or one may be unwilling to set aside the past hurts. Whatever the reason, facing the emptiness and inevitable dissolution of the marriage often precipitates a dangerous crisis for the alcoholic and spouse. If there has been a strong tendency to blame the alcoholic for relationship problems, there is a strong push to want the alcoholic to drink again to provide the reason for the marital breakup. The therapist can try to help the couple confront separation and divorce without requiring the alcoholic to fail again and be the scapegoat for the breakup. If the couple can separate without the alcoholic's drinking, the alcoholic's future relationship with his or her children may be preserved, and both spouses may be able to obtain a realistic assessment of the basis for their divorce. Unfortunately, many couples cannot do this.

LIMITATIONS TO THE USE OF A MARITAL THERAPY APPROACH WITH ALCOHOLICS

A marital therapy approach is not very useful when the alcoholic has not yet made an initial commitment to change and/or is uncooperative and refuses to enter therapy. Recently, two methods have been described for dealing with such cases: the Johnson Institute Intervention and Unilateral Family Therapy. Also, cases where the couple is separated or both spouses have an alcohol problem, although relatively common, may render much of the marital therapy procedures described about inappropriate.

The Johnson Institute Intervention for Denying Alcoholics

Vernon Johnson of the Johnson Institute in Minneapolis has developed an "intervention" procedure to assist family members of alcoholics who deny their alcohol problem (Johnson, 1973; Thorne, 1983). The intervention process consists of preparatory sessions with the family members followed by a confrontation session with the alcoholic and the family. The usual first session is an educational meeting about alcohol's effects on the drinker and the family. The second and third sessions are held to gather further information about alcohol-related problems in the family. The fourth session is the rehearsal for the confrontation session with the alcoholic during which family members rehearse as if the alcoholic were present and discuss strategies to counteract the drinker's excuses and alibis. Session 5, the intervention itself, is held with the alcoholic. He or she is confronted with the data about the negative effects of his or her drinking. The alcoholic is also asked to seek professional help. If refused, other efforts are made, and undesirable alternative consequences are presented (e.g., "If you don't get help, John, I can't go on living with you anymore"). The intervention session ends with the alcoholic's acceptance of the first treatment plan (usually hospitalization), agreeing with an alternative plan (outpatient counseling or attendance at Alcoholics Anonymous meetings), or rejecting all treatment. The counselor meets with the family after the session to discuss future means of family involvement or, when the alcoholic rejects help, to consider alternatives and to provide support.

Unilateral Family Therapy for the Uncooperative Alcoholic

Edwin Thomas and colleagues at the University of Michigan (Thomas & Santa, 1982; Thomas, Santa, & Bronson, 1984) have been developing a unilateral family therapy approach to reach and to change the uncooperative alcohol abuser by working exclusively with a cooperative family member, usually the spouse. This approach emphasizes helping the nonabusing spouse to strengthen his or her coping capabilities, to enhance family functioning, and to facilitate greater sobriety on the part of the alcohol abuser. After helping the spouse deal with such individual difficulties as anxiety, lack of assertiveness, depression, anger, and emotional overinvolvement, the unilateral therapist works to enhance marital and family functioning. The relationship enhancement component of the unilateral approach is designed to improve the working relationship between the marital partners and increase the capability of the spouse to influence the alcohol abuser. The therapist and spouse choose a series of particular behaviors designed to improve the attractiveness of the marital relationship. Such efforts have produced more pleasant and harmonious interactions and have facilitated the later efforts of the spouse to influence the alcohol abuser to change the drinking (Thomas et al., 1984).

Sobriety facilitation involves educating the spouse about alcohol abuse, removing spouse or family conditions that promote the drinking, and inducing the abuser to change the drinking. In the final part of the unilateral family therapy approach, getting the abuser to change his or her drinking behavior, previously unsuccessful methods are reviewed, and the spouse is told to stop such behaviors. Specific advice is given on influencing the drinker to change. Available information (Thomas et al., 1984) indicates that some alcohol abusers will initiate efforts to change their drinking in response to the changed spouse behavior by seeking treatment, joining AA, starting a formal self-control program using a self-help manual (e.g., Miller & Munoz, 1982), or devising their own idiosyncratic method. For cases in which previous steps have not produced a change in the drinking, the final step in the unilateral approach is a programmed confrontation, patterned after the Johnson approach and adapted for use with an individual spouse. A very important contribution of the unilateral family therapy approach is that it provides a series of graded steps to use prior to confrontation that may be successful in their own right or at least pave the way for a positive outcome to the programmed confrontation experience. Thomas et al. (1984) provide a more detailed account of each step of this innovative unilateral family treatment method and the specific criteria that need to be met for its successful use.

The Separated Alcoholic

Marital separations, most often instituted by the nonalcoholic spouse and maintained to provide a "trial period" during which the alcoholic is given the opportunity to demonstrate that he or she wants and can maintain sobriety, are more common in alcoholics' than in other marriages (McCrady, 1983; O'Farrell, Harrison, Schulmeister, & Cutter, 1981). Many of the marital therapy procedures described above are not applicable or require considerable modification for use when the couple is separated. In such cases a marital agreement cannot be used to strengthen the alcoholic's commitment to abstinence, and an individual program must be devised for the alcoholic (e.g., AA, alcoholism counseling). It is important that the spouse be made aware of what steps the alcoholic is taking to deal with the drinking problem. Also, it is helpful to clarify exactly what signs, in addition to not drinking, the spouse will use to determine it is safe to attempt a reconciliation. If the couple is willing, a structured separation therapy following guidelines suggested by Stuart (1980) can be attempted to help the couple decide if they wish to reconcile or maintain their separation. Such an approach involves a time period during which they definitely will not reconcile, while they spend preplanned time together at least twice weekly. In the present author's experience, such an approach can be very helpful, but it is particularly difficult to implement in two types of cases. One is the hostile dependent male alcoholic who, despite agreeing explicitly not to do this, continues to badger and plead with his wife to take him back each time they are together. Either the wife takes his behavior as evidence of continued immaturity and rejects the alcoholic or gives in and takes him back against her better judgement; neither decision bodes well for the alcoholic or the marriage. A second case is the female alcoholic whose husband has temporary custody of the children. Often she feels that reconciliation may be her only realistic chance to regain her children. However, the stress of returning to a difficult marriage, which has been part of the reason for her alcoholism and which she really does not want, may be more than she can handle without drinking.

Both Spouses Alcoholic

The situation in which both spouses residing together have an alcohol problem presents a difficult clinical challenge. Very often, the drinking of one spouse affects the other's drinking, and seldom are both spouses interested in changing their drinking habits at the same time. Clinicians often develop an individual treatment program for the spouse who is willing to change. Frequently this involves at least a temporary removal (through hospitalization or a stay in a halfway house or residential treatment center) from the home environment in which the other spouse continues to drink abusively. Some of the time one spouse's stopping drinking will precipitate improvement in the other partner's drinking. Nonetheless, marital interventions need to be developed for the situation in which both spouses have an alcohol problem. Such situations are not uncommon, but treatment solutions are rare in the published literature. An exception are two interesting examples presented by Hay (1982) and Murray and Hobbs (1977) for the rather rare case in which both spouses have an alcohol problem, drink together almost exclusively, and seek treatment together with a goal of reduced drinking.

THE ROLE OF THE THERAPIST

Certain therapist attributes and behaviors are essential to successful treatment of alcoholics' marriages, and certain related therapist errors occur rather frequently. From the outset, the therapist must recognize the alcohol problem and structure treatment so that control of the alcohol abuse is the first priority, before attempting to help the couple with other problems. It is not unusual for referrals to the author's Counseling for Alcoholic Marriages program to have had previous unsuccessful experiences with marital therapists who either did not diagnose an alcohol problem or saw the couple in marital therapy without dealing with the alcohol abuse. The hope that reduction in marital distress will lead to improvement in the drinking problem usually is not fulfilled. More typically, recurrent alcohol-related incidents and interactions undermine whatever gains had been made in the marital relationship.

A related therapist attribute is the ability to structure and take control of treatment sessions, especially in the early assessment and therapy sessions. Alcoholics and their spouses often act out their feelings, lead chaotic lives, and have seldom attempted a rational, orderly approach to dealing with their many life problems. The BMT method of therapy used by the present author requires highly structured therapy sessions with a directive, active therapist. However, recent empirical evidence on marital therapy for alcoholics suggests that the need for a high degree of structure is not just a component of a BMT approach. A somewhat less structured "interactional" couples therapy showed no advantage over individual therapy for alcoholics' marriages (McCrady, Paolino, Longabaugh, & Rossi, 1979); a more, as compared with a less, directive, structured, focused approach to couples therapy produced superior outcomes (Steinglass, 1979); and BMT was equal or superior to a type of therapy that pursued the same goals as BMT but in a much less structured fashion (O'Farrell, Cutter, & Floyd, 1985). Many of the errors of beginning therapists involve difficulty establishing and maintaining control of the sessions and responding to the myriad of resistances and noncompliances presented by couples. Therapists must steer a middle course between lack of structure and being overly controlling and punitive in response to noncompliance. Clearly establishing and enforcing the rules of treatment accompanied by a "shaping attitude," in which the therapist acknowledges approximation to desired behavior despite significant shortcomings, is what the author attempts to teach his students.

Therapists need to take a long-term view of the course of change of an alcoholism problem and associated marital distress. Serious alcoholism problems may be helped substantially only by repeated efforts that include some failed attempts. Such a long-term view may help the therapist encounter relapse without becoming overly discouraged or engaging in blaming and recriminations with the alcoholic and spouse. As mentioned, the therapist also should maintain contact with the couple long after the alcohol and marital problems apparently have stabilized. A frequent error is for therapists to leave such contacts to the couple, a practice that usually means no follow-up contacts occur until the couple is back in a major crisis again.

CONCLUDING COMMENTS

The present chapter has provided an overview of current marital therapy procedures derived mainly from a social learning perspective for use as part of treatment for alcoholism. In the next few years considerably more data should be available on which to base marital therapy with alcoholics. Current work in progress includes both outcome studies of marital therapy with alcoholics and studies of the marital interactions of alcoholics. The results of such research should tell whether or not the marital therapy methods for alcoholics described in the present chapter prove fruitful and provide a further basis for developing clinically useful marital therapy procedures for alcoholics and their spouses.

REFERENCES

American Psychiatric Association (1980). *Diagnostic and statistical manual of mental disorders* (3d ed.). Washington, DC: Author.

Azrin, N. H. (1976). Improvements in the community-reinforcement approach to alcoholism. *Behaviour Research and Therapy, 14,* 339–348.

Azrin, N. H., Sisson, R. W., Meyers, R., & Godley, M. (1982). Alcoholism treatment by Disulfiram and community reinforcement therapy. *Journal of Behavior Therapy and Experimental Psychiatry, 13,* 105–112.

Cheek, F. E., Franks, C. M., Burtle, V., & Laucius, J. (1971). Behavior modification training for wives of alcoholics. *Quarterly Journal of Studies on Alcohol, 32,* 456–461.

Davis, D. I., Berenson, D., Steinglass, P., & Davis, S. (1974). The adaptive consequences of drinking. *Psychiatry, 37,* 209–215.

Eisler, R. M., Miller, P. M., Hersen, M., & Alford, H. (1974). Effects of assertiveness training on marital interaction. *Archives of General Psychiatry, 30,* 643–649.

Goldstein, S. J., & Marlatt, G. A. (in press). Building self-confidence, self-efficacy, and self-control. In W. M. Cox (Ed.), *Treatment and prevention of alcohol problems: A resource manual.* New York: Academic Press.

Hanks, S. E., & Rosenbaum, P. C. (1977). Battered women: A study of women who live with violent alcohol-abusing men. *American Journal of Orthopsychiatry, 47,* 291–306.

Hay, W. M. (1982). The behavioral assessment and treatment of an alcoholic marriage. In W. M. Hay and P. E. Nathan (Eds.), *Clinical case studies in the behavioral treatment of alcoholism* (pp. 157–182). New York: Plenum Press.

Heather, N., & Robertson, I. (1981). *Controlled drinking.* London: Methuen.

Hore, B. D. (1971a). Life events and alcoholic relapse. *British Journal of Addiction, 66,* 83–88.

Hore, B. D. (1971b). Factors in alcoholic relapse. *British Journal of Addiction, 66,* 89–96.

Jacobson, N. S., & Margolin, G. (1979). Marital therapy: *Strategies based on social learning and behavior exchange principles.* New York: Brunner/Mazel.

Johnson, V. A. (1973). *I'll Quit Tomorrow.* New York: Harper & Row.

Lazarus, A. A. (1968). Behavior therapy and marriage counseling. *Journal of the American Society of Psychosomatic Dentistry and Medicine, 15,* 49–56.

Liberman, R. P., Wheeler, E. G., de Visser, L. A., Kuehnel, J., & Kuehnel, T. (1980). *Handbook of marital therapy: A positive approach to helping troubled relationships.* New York: Plenum Press.

Locke, H. J., & Wallace, K. M. (1959). Short marital-adjustment and prediction test: Their reliability and validity. *Journal of Marriage and Family Living, 21,* 251–255.

Lundwall, L., & Baekeland, F. (1971). Disulfiram treatment of alcoholism. *Journal of Nervous and Mental Disease, 153,* 381–394.

McCrady, B. S. (1982). Conjoint behavioral treatment of an alcoholic and his spouse. In W. M. Hay & P. E. Nathan (Eds.), *Clinical case studies in the behavioral treatment of alcoholism* (pp. 127–156). New York: Plenum Press.

McCrady, B. S. (1983). Marital dysfunction: Alcoholism and marriage. In E. M. Pattison & E. Kaufman (Eds.), *Encyclopedic handbook of alcoholism* (pp. 673–685). New York: Gardner Press.

McCrady, B. S., & Noel, N. E. (1982, November). Assessing the optimal mode of spouse involvement in outpatient behavioral treatment of alcoholism. In T. J. O'Farrell (Chair), *Spouse-involved treatment for alcohol abuse.* Symposium conducted at the annual meeting of the Association for the Advancement of Behavior Therapy, San Francisco.

McCrady, B. S., Paolino, T. J., Longabaugh, R., & Rossi, J. (1979). Effects of joint hospital admission and couples treatment for hospitalized alcoholics: A pilot study. *Addictive Behaviors, 4,* 155–165.

Margolin, G., Talovic, S., & Weinstein, C. D. (1983). Areas of Change Questionnaire: A practical approach to marital assessment. *Journal of Consulting and Clinical Psychology, 51,* 920–931.

Marlatt, G. A., & Gordon, J. F. (1978). *Determinants of relapse: Implications for the maintenance of behavior change.* Alcoholism and Drug Institute, Technical Report No. 78-07, University of Washington.

Marlatt, G. A., & Miller, W. R. (1983). *The drinking profile: A questionnaire for the behavioral assessment of alcoholism.* Albuquerque, NM: University of New Mexico Press.

Miller, P. M. (1972). The use of behavioral contracting in the treatment of alcoholism: A case report. *Behavior Therapy, 3,* 593–596.

Miller, P. M., & Hersen, M. (1975). *Modification of marital interaction patterns between an alcoholic and his wife.* Unpublished manuscript. Available from Peter Miller, Hilton Head Health Institute, P.O. Box 7138, Hilton Head Island, SC., 29938–7138.

Miller, W. R., & Caddy, G. R. (1977). Abstinence and controlled drinking in the treatment of problem drinkers. *Journal of Studies on Alcohol, 38,* 986–1003.

Miller, W. R., & Munoz, R. F. (1982). *How to control your drinking.* Albuquerque, NM: University of New Mexico Press.

Murray, R. G., & Hobbs, S. A. (1977). The use of a self-imposed timeout procedure in the modification of excessive alcohol consumption. *Journal of Behavior Therapy and Experimental Psychiatry, 8,* 377–380.

O'Farrell, T. J. (1979). Behavioral marital therapy for alcoholics and spouses: A comprehensive annotated bibliography. JSAS *Catalog of Selected Documents in Psychology, 9,* 8–9.

O'Farrell, T. J. (in press). Marital and family therapy for alcohol problems. In W. M. Cox (Ed.), *Treatment and prevention of alcohol problems: A resource manual.* New York: Academic Press.

O'Farrell, T. J., & Bayog, R. D. (1984). *Antabuse contracts for married alcoholics and their spouses: A method to insure Antabuse taking and decrease conflict about alcohol.* Unpublished manuscript, Veterans Administration Medical Center, Brockton, MA.

O'Farrell, T. J., & Cutter, H. S. G. (1977). Behavioral Marital Therapy (BMT) for alcoholics and wives: Review of literature and a proposed research program. Paper presented at the NATO International Conference on Experimental and Behavioral Approaches to Alcoholism, Bergen, Norway. *Resources in Education,* November. (ERIC Document Reproduction Service No. ED 155 531).

O'Farrell, T. J., & Cutter, H. S. G. (1979). A proposed behavioral couples group for male alcoholics and their wives. In D. Upper and S. M. Ross (Eds.), *Behavioral group therapy: An annual review* (pp. 277–298). Champaign, IL: Research Press.

O'Farrell, T. J., & Cutter, H. S. G. (1984a). Behavioral marital therapy couples groups for male alcoholics and their wives. *Journal of Substance Abuse Treatment, 1,* 191–204.

O'Farrell, T. J., & Cutter, H. S. G. (1984b). Behavioral marital therapy for alcoholics: Clinical procedures from a treatment outcome study in progress. *American Journal of Family Therapy*, 12, 33–46.

O'Farrell, T. J., Cutter, H. S. G., Bayog, R. D., Dentch, G., & Fortgang, J. (1984). Correspondence between one-year retrospective reports of pretreatment drinking by alcoholics and their wives. *Behavioral Assessment*, 6, 263–274.

O'Farrell, T. J., Cutter, H. S. G., & Floyd, F. J. (1985). Evaluating behavioral marital therapy for male alcoholics: Effects on marital adjustment and communication from before to after therapy. *Behavior Therapy*, 16, 147–167.

O'Farrell, T. J., Harrison, R. H., & Cutter, H. S. G. (1981). Marital stability among wives of alcoholics: An evaluation of three explanations. *British Journal of Addiction*, 76, 175–189.

O'Farrell, T. J., Harrison, R. H., Schulmeister, C. A., & Cutter, H. S. G. (1981). A Closeness to Divorce Scale for wives of alcoholics. *Drug and Alcoholic Dependence*, 7, 319–324.

O'Farrell, T. J., Kleinke, C. L., & Cutter, H. S. G. (1984). *Sexual adjustment of male alcoholics: Changes from before to after receiving alcoholism counseling with and without marital therapy.* Manuscript submitted for publication.

O'Farrell, T. J., Weyand, C. A., & Logan, D. (1983). *Alcohol and sexuality: An annotated bibliography on alcohol use, alcoholism and human sexual behavior.* Phoenix, AZ: Oryx Press.

Prochaska, J. O., & DiClemente, C. C. (1983). Stages and processes of self-change of smoking: Toward an integrative model of change. *Journal of Consulting and Clinical Psychology*, 51, 390–395.

Selzer, M. L. (1971). The Michigan Alcoholism Screening Test: The quest for a new diagnostic instrument. *American Journal of Psychiatry*, 127, 1653–1658.

Shapiro, R. J. (1984). Therapy with violent families. In S. Saunders, A. Anderson, C. Hart, & G. Rubenstein (Eds.), *Violent individuals and families: A handbook for practitioners* (pp. 112–136). Springfield, IL: Charles C Thomas.

Sobell, M. B., & Sobell, L. C. (1975). A brief technical report on the MOBAT: An inexpensive portable test for determining blood alcohol concentration. *Journal of Applied Behavioral Analysis*, 8, 117–120.

Steinglass, P. (1979). An experimental treatment program for alcoholic couples. *Journal of Studies on Alcohol*, 40, 159–182.

Straus, M. A. (1979). Measuring intrafamily conflict and violence: The Conflict Tactic (CT) Scales. *Journal of Marriage and the Family*, 41, 75–88.

Stuart, R. B. (1980). *Helping couples change: A social learning approach to marital therapy.* New York: Guilford Press.

Thomas, E. J., & Santa, C. A. (1982). Unilateral family therapy for alcohol abuse: A working conception. *American Journal of Family Therapy*, 10, 49–60.

Thomas, E. J., Santa, C. A., & Bronson, D. (1984, March). *A treatment program of unilateral family therapy for alcohol abuse.* Paper presented at Council on Social Work Education Annual Program Meeting, Detroit.

Thorne, D. R. (1983). Techniques for use in intervention. *Journal of Alcohol and Drug Education*, 28, 46–50.

Weiss, R. L., & Cerreto, M. C. (1980). The marital status inventory: Development of a measure of dissolution potential. *American Journal of Family Therapy*, 8, 80–85.

24

Marital Therapy with Schizophrenic Patients

CAROL M. ANDERSON
DOUGLAS J. REISS
JOHN F. CAHALANE

While the goals of marital treatment with schizophrenic patients are influenced by the general level of functioning of the patient and the spouse, and the phase and severity of the illness, the overall philosophy of intervention must be based on an integrated psychosocial–biological understanding of schizophrenia. Without a consistent integrated approach to the illness, treatment efforts of any sort are likely to be variable, inconsistent (May, 1975), or even detrimental (Van Putten & May, 1976; Goldberg, Schooler, Hogarty, & Roper, 1977).

Schizophrenia is a complex disorder, or group of disorders, with biopsychosocial underpinnings (Group for the Advancement of Psychiatry, 1984). The complexity of these syndromes makes it difficult to state a simple, distinctive diagnostic pattern. However, the American Psychiatric Association (1980) states that "the essential features of this group of disorders are: the presence of certain psychotic features during the active phase of the illness, characteristic symptoms involving multiple psychological processes, deterioration from a previous level of functioning, onset before age 45, and a duration of at least six months" (p. 181). The course of the illness is defined as having a prodromal phase, an active phase, and a residual phase characterized by affective blunting and an impairment in role functioning. Hirsch (1976) underlined the difficulties associated with the course and treatment of schizophrenia, in this way: "The primary handicap for schizophrenics can be seen as an extraordinary vulnerability, like walking a tightrope, with the dangers of an understimulating environment leading to negative symptoms of social

Carol M. Anderson, Douglas J. Reiss, and John F. Cahalane. Western Psychiatric Institute and Clinic, University of Pittsburgh, Pittsburgh, Pennsylvania.

withdrawal and inactivity on one side, and the dangers of overstimulation leading to florid symptoms and relapse on the other" (p. 461). The underlying philosophy that governs the series of marital interventions described here is based on research findings, collected over the past half century, which have identified a "core psychological deficit" in schizophrenic patients (e.g., see Rabin, Doneson, & Jentons, 1979; Silverman, 1972; Tecce & Cole, 1976; Venables, 1964, 1978), which makes them vulnerable to stimulation.

Many different sorts of stimulation seem to have an impact on the course of schizophrenia, including that of the patient's cultural, therapeutic, and family environment. For instance, complex, technologically advanced societies appear to have higher rates of schizophrenia (Torrey, 1973), while course and outcome seem worse in "developed" countries and better in "developing" countries (Sartorius et al., 1977). Within our own culture, stressful life events, such as induction into military service (Steinberg & Durrell, 1968) or membership in socially disadvantaged classes (Kohn, 1973), have been associated with higher rates of schizophrenia.

In the therapeutic environment, certain patients have been observed to relapse more quickly in intensive social therapy (Goldberg et al., 1977), as well as in more dynamic day-treatment centers (Linn et al., 1979). Within the home environment, data suggest that aspects of the patients' family and marital life may influence the course and outcome of the illness. Patients returning to highly conflictual home situations (Hogarty et al., 1979) or whose family members exhibit high rates of "expressed emotion" also have higher relapse levels (Brown, Birley, & Wing, 1972; Vaughn & Leff, 1976). In general, then, it can be hypothesized that stimulating environments, be they natural or therapeutic, have the ability to exploit the vulnerability of many schizophrenic patients, precipitating, in turn, a cycle of hyperarousal, distraction, disattention, and eventual relapse.

Little attention has been paid to the issue of how these factors might impact on the marriages of these patients, perhaps because a relatively small percentage of schizophrenic individuals marry (Watt & Szulecka, 1979), and those who do tend to be patients with better premorbid functioning (Gittleman-Klein & Klein, 1968; Held & Cromwell, 1968; Turner et al., 1970). For those patients who marry, the relationship issues are highly significant. Marriage is complex and stressful, even for healthy individuals, and patients who are vulnerable to stimulation may have particular difficulty negotiating the vicissitudes of marital life. Furthermore, spouses dealing with any chronic illness in their partner are often overwhelmed by sadness, fear, anxiety, and a sense of loss of control. With schizophrenia, these common reactions to illness are probably intensified by the unpredictable nature of the behaviors and symptoms associated with schizophrenia and the need for a relatively long-term rearrangement of role responsibilities within the home. The onset of a psychotic illness or episode usually brings with it not only bizarre, inconsistent, and unpredictable behaviors but also a decrease in general functioning, a decrease in financial earning power, and at least the temporary loss of a companion and sexual partner for the spouse. While the degree of impact of the illness on the marriage will depend on its chronicity and the quality of the patient's functioning between episodes, it is not surprising that many spouses have been found to become less tolerant and more resigned over time, and that many of these marriages end in separation or divorce (Johnston & Planansky, 1968).

Although there is no evidence to show a causal relationship between marital interaction and psychosis, clearly there is probably some connection between the patient's context and the course of the illness. Early on, many professionals tended to view the patient's marriage as a pathogenic force. For example, Alanen and his colleagues (1968) stated: "Factors related to marital dynamics in these cases formed an important link in the pathogenesis of schizophrenia. The immature and unsatisfactory relationships between the spouses had led to frustrations which were contributory factors in the psychotic development in a vulnerable person. After the illness had become overt, the marital interaction deteriorated further" (p. 299). Other researchers and clinicians have emphasized the concept of assortative mating, that is, the tendency for people with similar characteristics to be attracted to each other, marry, and then interact pathologically (Crago, 1972; Kreitman, 1962; Nielsen, 1964; Turner et al., 1970). The implication is that even if marital issues do not cause psychotic disintegration, these relationships would be, at best, pathological, as a result of the characterological makeup each partner brings to the selection process and the union. Thus, if patients are somehow able to emancipate from a pathologic family of origin, they are doomed to experience a pathologic marital relationship. In fact, some marital therapists operate as though the patient's symptoms not only play a function for the marital system; they go so far as to suggest that spouses actually wish to keep patients sick. Unfortunately, only rarely is there any attention given to the possibility that some of the marital problems experienced by schizophrenic patients may be a response to the illness and the inevitable stresses it places on patients and spouses (Johnston & Planansky, 1968), or even the possibility that love and understanding may *increase* as patients and spouses are helped to deal with the psychosis (Dupont et al., 1971).

It makes sense that any severe and chronic illness involving one spouse will have an impact on a marriage and that the marriage, in turn, will have an impact on the illness. The question is whether this reciprocal and recurring cycle is inevitable or if it might be possible to help patients and their spouses to cope in such a way as to avoid exacerbating stresses and eventual marital dissolution. The marital treatment proposed here is based on the assumption that it is easier and more direct to help patients and spouses develop coping mechanisms to deal with the immediate problems caused by the illness, or the problems that might perpetuate it, before assuming the existence of long-term pathogenic patterns of marital interaction and attempting to deal with them. Thus, this model of marital treatment is based on the assumption of "least pathology" until proven otherwise (Pinsof, 1983).

Nevertheless, it appears likely that almost all couples in which one member has schizophrenia would benefit from *some* treatment. This is *not* because their relationships are pathological, or at least any more pathological than most other marital relationships, but because the illness is a severe one. Information, support, and coping skills can be invaluable to couples attempting to deal with illness. Help in establishing a home with increased structure and in facilitating the patient's gradual resumption of roles and responsibility are also almost always appropriate. Following these basics, the amount of additional marital treatment and its specific goals must be related to the impact of the illness on each couple and their desire for continued change or growth.

TREATMENT GOALS

Treatment of marriages in which one member has schizophrenia differs from more traditional forms of marital therapy because it requires attention to the symptoms and course of the illness in addition to attention to the marriage itself. Depending on the amount of time a therapist has to work with such patients and spouses, it may be possible to alter the course of the illness and even to enhance the satisfaction each partner receives from the marital relationship. Thus the treatment approach must first help to decrease the patient's vulnerability to stimulation through the use of medication and to decrease the amount of stimulation in the environment. Simultaneously, the treatment approach must address the pain and suffering of the marital partner as he or she attempts to cope with the illness and its unique impact on marital roles and interactions; and finally, the treatment must address the marital relationship itself.

Treatment can be divided into three relatively distinct phases, each with its own primary goal. The interventions of the first phase of marital treatment are conducted during acute episodes of the illness with the goal of helping patients and spouses deal with the psychosis. This requires imparting information about the illness, supporting the spouse during the crisis, and increasing the amount of structure and control available in the home environment. The second phase of marital treatment occurs during the post-psychotic stage when most patients suffer from the negative symptoms of schizophrenia (amotivation, lethargy, depression, and disinterest). The goals of treatment at this time are to help patients and spouses come to grips with this deficit state, cope with frequent dysfunctions in role behaviors and the frustrations that result, and gradually help patients to resume basic responsibilities. The third phase of marital treatment occurs when patients have regained sufficient energy and strength to begin to perform more normally in the marital relationship and in general. The goals of marital treatment at this time are to deal with the chronic recurring nature of the illness while focusing on more typical marital issues of concern to the couple, such as sexuality, finances, parenting, and control. Whether a couple is offered all three phases of marital treatment depends on an assessment of the patient, the spouse, the marriage, and the contract they are willing to make with the therapist.

This assessment must be multifaceted. It must determine the extent of the patient's current dysfunction, as well as the couple's level of distress and ability to cope. By conducting a review of the course of the illness and past treatment experiences, it is possible to judge the long-term impact of the illness on the couple and the effectiveness of various past treatment interventions. Finally, the assessment must determine environmental and relationship stressors and strengths that may affect the course of the patients' illness and, in turn, the marriage.

As issues arise during the early assessment sessions, whether and when they are addressed depends on how they are evaluated in regard to three questions:

1. Is this crucial to the patient's or spouse's immediate survival?
2. Is this issue crucial to the patient's return to basic functioning?
3. Is this issue crucial to the couple's satisfaction and happiness?

These questions allow the therapist to rank issues in a hierarchial list that relates to the timing of interventions. Issues that relate to immediate survival must be dealt with in the first phase of treatment. Issues that interfere with the patient's return to basic functioning should primarily be addressed in the second phase of treatment, while issues related to general satisfaction can be reserved for the final phase.

PHASE 1: ADJUSTING TO THE ILLNESS

Helping couples to develop a better understanding of schizophrenia, including its symptoms, possible causes, and course and treatment, can decrease anxiety and offer both partners an increased sense of control. Many couples will have dealt with this illness and its inevitable impact for years with only minimal guidance and support from professionals. Most therapists do not share information about the illness, and better ways of coping are almost never a part of the treatment agenda. The sense of isolation and lack of knowledge often interfered with the ability of spouses to help patients, and may also have led to the development of coping behaviors that unwittingly interfered with recuperation and rehabilitation. Ultimately, this approach to treatment may have actually made both the patient and the marriage less functional over time. Thus, in and of itself, information that increases the spouse's understanding of the patient's symptoms and problems can decrease stress, fear, and anxiety. In fact, with greater insight into this illness and the potentially negative interaction between marital stress and symptomatology, couples often spontaneously use their own initiative to develop ways of coping better, as well as ways of toning down the home environment.

There are other reasons for helping the couple develop a better understanding of the patient's problems. First, information can help to maintain the patient in treatment. Since up to 50% of patients with schizophrenia fail to connect with aftercare services or discontinue treatment after just a few visits (Taube, 1974), treatment compliance is a major issue. Information that helps both patient and spouse to accept the fact that schizophrenia is an illness that requires a long-term commitment to both chemotherapy and psychotherapy can be an essential step in increasing treatment compliance. Second, the patient's spouse and even his or her children often fear that they have contributed to the patient's schizophrenia. Past treatments may have unwittingly reinforced this view. The simple process of collecting a thorough psychiatric history with its usual focus on precipitating or negative events often exacerbates feelings of guilt on the part of family members. Thus it is important to decrease these feelings by sharing appropriate information. Third, information also can lay the groundwork for teaching the couple to identify the patient's specific prodromal signs, which in turn can help them to cope with the current episode, manage possible future ones, and selectively attend to the patient's signals of distress. For instance, recent research has suggested that enhancing patient and family recognition of prodromal, or "early warning," signs of episodes can lead to increased ability to manage the illness and short circuit the development of psychotic symptoms (Goldstein et al., 1978).

Another primary task of the first phase of marital treatment involves helping the couple build increased structure into their home environment. Since stress can be a precipitant of psychotic symptoms in a vulnerable individual, it is important to help the couple create an environment that is less chaotic and more predictable than that of most households. Although this "toned down" environment may not be normal, it is useful in a time of crisis. Using the couple's newly acquired knowledge about the patient's vulnerability to stimulation, early sessions can focus on determining which common household events are experienced as most stressful. In so doing, it is important not only to focus on the patient's early signals of overload or stress but also to determine the spouse's early signals of decreasing tolerance and "burnout." Recognition of these factors can be used to establish rules or guidelines that operationalize the principles of maintaining a temporary low-key environment in the couple's day-to-day life.

It is particularly crucial during this time to provide adequate support to the patient's spouse. During the crisis of an acute episode, professional attention tends to be directed toward the stabilization of the patient. Frequently, the needs of the spouse are viewed as secondary or are overlooked altogether. Spouses themselves often ignore their needs; they come to expect little from the patient or even from other possible support systems. Yet, the spouse's ability to cope is essential. Without attention and support, spouses can become resigned, hopeless, less able to cope, and less able to help the patient over time.

PHASE 2: ADJUSTING TO THE DEFICIT STATE

It is natural for a spouse to become a caretaker when his or her partner becomes ill. In fact, this caretaking role can be very helpful during the acute illness and the phase immediately thereafter. During an acute psychotic episode, and often for months afterward, a patient may be unable to perform the roles expected of a spouse in a marital relationship. Over time, however, treatment must help the patient in the resumption of these roles and at the same time take into consideration any realistic temporary or permanent loss of functioning due to the illness.

Since the aftermath of an acute episode of schizophrenia is often characterized by so-called negative symptoms, patients with schizophrenia and their spouses are especially vulnerable to slipping into a chronic patient–caretaker pattern. During the course of any chronic illness, there is a risk of nonfunctional habits and secondary gains becoming sufficiently reinforcing to inhibit the patient's motivation to "get better," as well as to inhibit the spouse's ability to see the patient as other than dysfunctional or to give up the power inherent in the caretaker role. The resumption of more balanced role responsibilities between partners thus is often unexpectedly difficult. Therefore, treatment must begin by helping the couple temporarily structure their relationship to allow a relatively low level of functioning on the part of the patient while beginning a gradual push for him or her to accept greater responsibility as he or she becomes more capable. Unfortunately, the discrepancy between past and present functioning may be significant, especially if the initial psychotic break occurred sometime after the marriage. Thus the therapist must help the couple to mourn past competencies and assess, negotiate, and eventually assume redefined temporary functional and expressive roles. This task must be accomplished in a way that does not allow the patient role to come to dominate the patient's or spouse's view of the patient or the marriage, since role performance may be more important than the illness prognostically.

PHASE 3: DEALING WITH MARITAL ISSUES

Although it would be easy to relate all the marital and individual problems experienced by these patients to the presence of a mental illness, it is probable that many of these marriages have the same problems and strengths as most other marital relationships. Typical issues that arise once the crisis has passed include lack of joint and/or independent social networks for each partner, communication difficulties, child-rearing disagreements, dependence, sexual dysfunctions, and power struggles.

The chronic recurring nature of schizophrenia is, however, a complicating factor in resolving many of these issues. The occurrence of an acute psychotic episode by its nature influences the level of the patient's functioning and consequently requires continual readjustment by the patient and spouse. Since the couple must live with the ongoing threat of another episode, in some ways making these relationships work demands greater skill than that required of "normal" couples. Both partners must learn to play multiple roles dependent not only on the life stage of the marriage but also on the independent intrusion of a recurring illness.

For these reasons, these general marital issues are dealt with only after the patient has stabilized and has begun to reassume his or her basic responsibilities. Whether and how these issues are handled in this phase depends on their significance as ongoing stresses for either partner, whether or not they were present before the illness and a part of the marital "understanding," the likelihood that they will constitute problems in the future, and each partner's desire for their resolution. As in all marital therapy, only more so, it is particularly important not to establish the goals of treatment based on a conception of an "ideal" marriage. In many cases, the most realistic goals are limited ones, such as the restoration of a "previously marginal symbiotic stability" (Kern, 1967). Thus the therapist must also assess the couple's overall strengths and weaknesses, and discuss with them whether they desire changes in any areas sufficiently to contract for ongoing marital treatment.

THE STRUCTURE OF TREATMENT

It is necessary for a person with a chronic physical ailment to be in some form of medical treatment for the rest of his or her life. When the illness is a psychiatric one, however, there is often a sense that brief treatment is appropriate. It is naive to assume that an illness as severe, debilitating, and chronic as schizophrenia can be dealt with adequately in brief treatment. In reality, short-term treatment contracts have the potential of creating unrealistic expectations about the pace of change, exacerbating the patient's vulnerability to stimulation, and precipitating relapse or increased discouragement. Unless the need for a long-term contract is emphasized, both patient and spouse may discontinue treatment after the acute psychosis, wishing to put the episode behind them and hoping that the patient is "cured."

Thus, it is only the first phase of this marital treatment (information and support) that can or should be viewed as possible to accomplish in a short-term contract (i.e., during an inpatient stay), and even then it probably should not be viewed as an end in itself. To deal adequately with the issues described in either Phase 2 or Phase 3 of this treatment, a longer-term contract is both beneficial and necessary. An initial commitment to a treatment contract of at least a year is desirable. Most couples should be seen for at least 2 years.

On the other hand, while long-term treatment is necessary for most patients with schizophrenia, there is rarely a need for weekly sessions. In fact, frequent sessions may give the covert message that rapid progress is anticipated, and can thus stimulate frustration and anger. It is suggested, therefore, that during the acute crisis the sessions be frequent, once or twice a week. During the recuperative period, sessions can be much less frequent, perhaps biweekly or even monthly, with the time between sessions gradually extended as stability and structure are reestablished. On the other hand, during times of change, heightened stress, or increased ability to work on marital issues, sessions should be more frequent.

Each therapy session in all phases is best structured into four basic components. These are the social contact, a discussion of current concerns and tasks assigned at the previous session, the development of resolutions to problems, and task assignment. Conducting sessions with this regular format makes therapy more predictable and further helps to provide the structure that ensures a low-key therapeutic environment.

Sessions should predominantly involve both husband and wife, since the majority of issues directly or indirectly involve both partners and require joint input to negotiate successfully. There are three exceptions to this rule. First, while the patient still is acutely psychotic, the spouse should be seen individually to give him or her a chance to deal with the upset related to the psychotic episode. Not only does the spouse need support at this time, but sessions with an acutely psychotic member are usually not helpful (Anderson, 1977; Mueller & Orfanidis, 1976). Second, if the couple has children, or if there are other relevant family members, they should be seen alone at least once or twice early in treatment and on an "as needed" basis thereafter. Many times, these individuals have concerns they cannot share with the patient. Giving them a chance to begin without the patient present can open up issues to be dealt with later by the couple or in larger family sessions. Third, there may be occasions when either marital partner would benefit from some time alone with the therapist. These times usually occur when one spouse is extremely frustrated with the slowness of change in treatment. Sometimes frustration can be diffused and continued cooperation gained more easily in an *ad hoc* individual session.

SPECIFIC TECHNIQUES

Perhaps the only unique aspect of this marital treatment is the educational component, and the belief that information is a useful and essential tool for coping with illness. The rest of the treatment approach is a highly structured one that pulls from many theoretical schools: the structural use of joining and assignment of tasks that attempt to change alliances and boundaries, the behavioral specificity of goals, and the strategic use of positive connotation and reframing—all are employed in this model.

Nevertheless, the manner in which all these techniques are applied differs from more general marital therapy. For instance, most marital therapists would work to establish a relationship between therapist and couple in which there is a genuine working alliance. This task is especially important with this population, since many couples will have had previous treatment experiences that have not been useful. Thus, extra effort must be made to "join" with each partner before attempting change-producing interventions (Minuchin, 1974), to take the time to develop a therapeutic system and establish the therapist's own credibility. In addition to general techniques of joining, initial discussions must include attention to the problems and themes specifically related to both living with the symptoms of schizophrenia and attempting to find adequate mental health care. These discussions, along with the demonstration of genuine concern and empathy with the couple's struggle and the sharing of information about the illness and its treatment, help the therapist communicate to the couple that their opinions will be respected and that they will be regarded as equal partners in the process of treatment. In this way, the therapist diminishes the couple's natural tendencies to exclude him or her, to resist his or her interventions, or to discontinue treatment prematurely.

The following clinical example comes from the third therapy session with the wife of a hospitalized patient still acutely psychotic.

THERAPIST: How are you doing?

WIFE: I'm O.K. How's Jim doing?

THERAPIST: A little better. Before we get into that in detail, I've got to say that you look less than O.K. In fact, you look exhausted.

WIFE: Well, I guess I am. Even with Jim in the hospital, I can't seem to get enough rest. And now, Jessica [her 4-year-old daughter] has the flu and is keeping me up all night.

THERAPIST: Boy, I bet you're exhausted. I just went through that with my daughter and I'm still tired. And I had my wife to help me.

WIFE: What can you do? When you're a parent, you've got to get up and function no matter how tired you are.

THERAPIST: I know—wouldn't it be nice if someone did that for us when we got sick?

WIFE (smiling): The life of a parent.

THERAPIST (smiling): Yup.

Later, the session refocused on the patient, Jim.

THERAPIST: As I said, Jim's doing a little better, but he's still balking about taking his meds.

WIFE: Not again! That's what started him off again. He said he didn't need to take that stuff. He thought it was "poison." That was four months ago and now look at him.

THERAPIST: Does it go well when he takes his meds?

WIFE: A hell of a lot better. I mean there are some rough spots, but it's a lot better.
THERAPIST: It must be upsetting when he stops.
WIFE: I want to kill him—or myself. I don't know if I can handle it.
THERAPIST: After our first couple of meetings, I've been amazed with how well you have handled it. You've coped with an awful lot, and from the sounds of it, done a really good job.
WIFE: Thanks. I've really tried. But it gets tough sometimes.

During these interactions, the therapist connected with the patient's wife through a discussion about a mutual life experience (i.e. the responsibility of parenting), as well as by demonstrating a genuine concern for how *she* was feeling, before focusing on the patient's issues. In addition, he began to emphasize her abilities to cope, labeling her as a strong person who has been dealing with a difficult and painful situation over a long period.

The sharing of information about schizophrenia and its management is a cornerstone of this approach to marital treatment. Whatever the facts may be, facts are easier to deal with than coping with the unknown. As stated, information helps spouses to see symptoms as part of an illness rather than as attempts to manipulate, helps to develop a sense of cognitive mastery over a chaotic and seemingly uncontrollable situation, and helps in the development of more realistic expectations and plans for the future. Information can be provided in a number of ways. It can be given on an ongoing basis during regular sessions, partially in response to questions from the couple and partly at the initiative of the therapist. It also can be given in a series of multiple-family group sessions or in a day-long workshop format (Anderson *et al.*, 1980). The latter two formats are particularly beneficial in that they can also begin the process of de-isolation, destigmatization, and peer-group support for couples not connected with a relevant support system.

Although the specific content of the educational component may vary depending on the belief system of the therapist, certain topics should be discussed, since they are of universal concern to all who must live with a mental illness. Information about the phenomenology of the illness, as well as what is known about its etiology, course, and outcome, should be shared. Since a medication regime is usually important in managing this illness, compliance with a drug program usually is necessary. Thus it is important for the couple to understand how drugs work, why they are needed, and their potential temporary or permanent side effects. Discussing the purpose and effectiveness of treatments in general is also important and helps the couple decide about their participation in marital treatment.

Information also should be shared about what spouses and family members can specifically do to help. In our program, this includes detailed suggestions of coping strategies in the following areas: revising expectations, setting limits, creating barriers to overstimulation, recognizing signals for help, and normalizing the family routine. All this information helps in laying the groundwork for specific therapeutic interventions that will occur in marital therapy over the course of time. The impact of imparting this information is almost always a powerful one. Following her attendance at an all-day workshop, the wife of a patient shared her reactions:

> I would look at him when he was getting sick and say, "Oh, boy, we have to go through this again," and that was selfish. I learned not to be selfish. It was always from my point of view, you know. "I've got these kids to take care of; he's laying up there," and it was just *frustrating*. That's what I thought, but when I come home from the workshop, I took a long look at my husband, and for the first time in a long time felt sympathy and understanding because I was made a little aware of what went on inside his head when he got ill.
>   . . . We found out that day, he really cannot control it. It is something that you have no control over, and that was a rude awakening for me. That reality never hits until its explained to you. Then you can go on. You can build from there. If you have that fact right in front of your face. You know, this is a chronic illness, it's not going to go away. It's like having cancer or liver disease or heart disease. This is the way we will help you deal with it. . . . You don't know how I appreciate that.

During Phase 2 of the marital treatment, the focus moves to maintaining the patient outside a hospital setting, gradually moving him or her toward increased functioning, and supporting the spouse during this difficult period. Without a good deal of support, most spouses become discouraged by the low level of personal fulfillment they experience and the high level of responsibility they must assume (Barlow, 1979). Tasks are used to reinforce concretely the themes of sessions, to help prolong the impact of sessions, and to give the couple a focus and a sense of progress over time. In addition, information about whether or not the task was completed, and how well it was done, is used to provide the therapist with valuable feedback about the patient's current level of functioning and the couple's progress toward their goals. This, in turn, gives information about the appropriateness of the pace at which treatment is proceeding.

Tasks used in this phase of the marital treatment should be very specific, well defined, and involve only one theme or area of change during a particular session or over a specific period of time. In the following example, the task assigned evolved out of Nancy's anger at her husband's lack of personal hygiene.

THERAPIST: You seem really upset about Dave's lack of self-care.
NANCY: I'm embarrassed for him—more than that it turns me off. I mean he doesn't brush his teeth or wash and then he comes on to me. I hate to say it, but I don't want to be near him when he's that dirty.
THERAPIST: Dave?
DAVE (*sullenly*): She doesn't love me.
NANCY: You don't *hear* me. I do love you and want you, but not when you're filthy.
THERAPIST: Did you hear what she said?
DAVE: I guess.

THERAPIST: Any thought about what to do?

DAVE: I don't know.

THERAPIST: Well, it seems that this is a problem we can work on. I'd like our homework task this time to focus on it. It seems that you each would like something from the other, but there are some roadblocks to getting it. Any thoughts about how to resolve this?

NANCY: I hate to nag. Sometimes I think I'm his mother instead of his wife. And I do want him. If he would just take better care of himself.

DAVE: Like how?

NANCY: Like brushing your teeth before bed— and showering.

DAVE: And then . . .

NANCY: And then I'd be with you.

THERAPIST: What do you say, Dave? Would you do those things?

DAVE: If she really means it.

NANCY: Oh, Dave, I do.

In this case, hygiene was related to a larger issue of sex and intimacy. Although the task decided on seems a simple one, the therapist met the patient at his own level and reinforced a task designed concretely to develop in Dave a greater sense of self, as well as greater intimacy for the couple.

Sexual problems occur frequently, often resulting from a lack of desire on the part of the patient. It is sometimes difficult to determine whether these issues preceded the illness or are a part of it. Certainly many schizophrenic patients, especially males, report decreased sexual interest and functioning caused by either the illness itself or the psychotropic medications (Lyketsos et al., 1983). Furthermore, the need for the spouse to play a caretaking role over time tends to de-eroticize the marital relationship. During this phase, some attention to the issue of sexuality is usually essential, although not always with the goal of increasing interest or performance. Some couples are quite content to put sex temporarily, or even permanently, on a back burner. The crucial issue is whether the couple is in agreement both about the importance of the sexual issue and what to do about it. In general, if the issue is raised by either spouse before the patient is functional, it is labeled as a problem that will be addressed when the crisis has passed.

In most sessions, the couple is asked to participate in defining problems and deciding what should be done about the issues raised. When resolutions are reached or coping mechanisms learned, they are made explicit to allow for generalized learning to other situations. In the following example, Ron raised the issue of Susan's parenting abilities:

THERAPIST: I understand your concern. When Susan goes back to bed after you leave for work that leaves Jimmy [their 5-year-old son] to fend for himself. However, I think I overestimated your wife's readiness to get up by herself so early and take care of your breakfast and then be with Jimmy until it's time for school.

SUSAN: I want to do these things—but I can't seem to do it.

RON: That's a wife's job (angrily).

THERAPIST: It sounds like Susan agrees that's her job, but she needs a little help right now to get back on track. I think she'll eventually be able to do it. Right now, though, I wonder if the two of you would be willing to try to come up with a temporary solution.

SUSAN(*after some coaxing to come up with a suggestion*): If Ron could just help a little bit with Jimmy in the morning, I wouldn't feel so overwhelmed.

THERAPIST: How do you feel about that, Ron?

RON: I guess it's O.K., if you're sure it's not permanent.

THERAPIST: O.K., let's try it for two weeks as a trial, and see how it went when we get back together.

The discussion continued in exploring Ron's feelings about helping his wife with parenting tasks, focusing on potential concerns and problems. For Ron, the idea of doing "women's work," not the tasks themselves, made it difficult for him to help. Once it was stressed that his assistance was required on a temporary basis because of the illness, not his wife's purposeful shirking of her duties, he was able to agree to help. It is important that such agreements be genuine and reasonable ones, since failure in tasks tends to escalate stress, leading couples to feel badly about themselves or angry at the therapist.

During the course of ongoing treatment, the marital therapist can make frequent use of the technique of reframing. Since many couples dealing with chronic illness have feelings of hopelessness that increase their sensitivity to negative experiences, it is important that, within realistic limits, the therapist reframe events and behaviors positively. For instance, the strengths and coping skills of both partners can be emphasized, since they must be present for the couple to have dealt with this illness over time. In addition, when tasks do not go well, therapists can assume responsibility for the failure, labeling an unaccomplished task as having been too difficult or inappropriate for the couple at this time. Failure at one task then can be followed by the assignment of one that has a greater potential for success.

Good communication skills are helpful in developing and maintaining a healthy marital relationship. Thus, an important component of marital treatment involves monitoring the interactions of the couple, and assessing them particularly for clarity and simplicity. Both spouses are encouraged to take responsibility for their own statements and to be supportive to each other. Since an intensive effort in communication training may tend to increase anxiety, most of the therapist's work in this area can be done informally. Early in the course of marital treatment, the patient is encouraged to make sense, while the spouse is encouraged to limit bizarre communication and insist on clarity. In the following example, the therapist gently encourages more functional communication in this way.

NAOMI: I'd love to get out to a movie with him.

THERAPIST: What do you think about that, Art?

ART: The force will control the scene and laser radiate animals.

NAOMI: Huh. . . . Oh, he must mean when we saw *Star Wars*. We really liked that. I guess he wants to go.

THERAPIST: Wow! That's incredible. To be honest, Art, I didn't understand what you said. (*To Naomi.*) Did you really understand him?

NAOMI: Well, I guess not. It's just easier sometimes to try to make sense out of it than to ask.

THERAPIST: I'm sure it is. It must be tough to follow sometimes. But, I think it would help Art if we ask him to answer more clearly. Not everyone he talks to is going to have your patience.

NAOMI: I guess not.

THERAPIST: Would you ask him again.

NAOMI: Would you like to go to the movies with me?

ART: O.K.

The therapist helped Naomi to see the need to limit Art's psychotic communication and help him to be more clear, and at the same time offered understanding about her frustration in having to deal with Art's strange messages on a day-to-day basis. Finally, he gave the implicit message to Art that he was capable of communicating more appropriately.

Over the course of time, as the patient gets better, the focus of marital treatment shifts toward developing better tools for conflict resolution, dealing with sexual problems, dealing with the patient's resuming major role functioning and developing an intimacy based on increased equality between husband and wife roles. Although the specific therapeutic techniques do not change, these issues are likely to be more emotionally charged. Thus, when these topics are approached, there is a greater risk of escalating stress and stimulating conflict. For this reason, the structured, task-oriented approach is continued. The therapist helps the couple translate their complaints and concerns into measurable and achievable goals. This concrete focus helps prevent the issues from becoming overwhelming or out of control. In the following example, taken from a session 16 months after Angela's hospitalization, Paul raised an issue that had surfaced a number of times in the past.

PAUL: I've said it a hundred times. I feel like I'm all alone in the battle. Angela's more like my daughter than my wife.

THERAPIST: I know you've brought that feeling up before, and I've put you off because I didn't feel you both were ready to deal with it. But things are going well now, and I think it's important to discuss it and see if the problem can be resolved. Could you be more specific about what you would like to see different, Paul?

PAUL: I don't know. It's just a feeling I have.

THERAPIST: I understand. Could you give me an example of when you feel that way so that Angela and I can understand?

PAUL: Well. . . . Like, if I have a rough day. Like two days ago, I had a lousy day at work. I came home from work and started telling Angela—looking for sympathy, I guess—and she just didn't want to hear about it. But not nasty. More like she was a kid who you shouldn't tell your problems to.

THERAPIST: In other words, you turned to your wife for support, and she was unable to give it.

PAUL: Yeah. I mean it's lopsided. I need strokes too.

THERAPIST: I agree. Angela, do you remember the time Paul is talking about?

ANGELA: How can I forget? He wouldn't talk to me for the rest of the night. I don't know. . . . I want to help, but. . . . I don't know.

THERAPIST: What keeps you from helping?

ANGELA (*pause*): I guess I feel guilty. If I were better, then he wouldn't have his problems. I guess I feel like I'm the cause of his problems. When he's miserable, I feel like I caused it and then I get scared that he'll figure it out too and leave. Sounds crazy. . . . Well, they say I'm crazy.

THERAPIST: It doesn't sound crazy to me. Are you saying that if you felt less responsible, you'd be more comfortable in being supportive?

ANGELA: I guess.

PAUL: But it had nothing to do with you. It was just a lousy day. I just wanted you to listen.

ANGELA: I get scared and don't hear that.

THERAPIST: O.K., if I understand this, Paul, you're asking for support and caring from your wife, and, Angela, you think you could give it if you didn't feel responsible for causing his problems.

PAUL: Yes.

ANGELA: Yes.

This session went on to clarify further the respective needs of each spouse with the therapist continuously helping the couple to state their messages in simple and concrete terms. From there, the couple, with the therapist's help, developed a task that continued the focus on building better communication and understanding.

THE ROLE OF THE THERAPIST

This model of marital intervention requires therapists to be highly active and directive, both in limit setting and in creating and assigning tasks. Thus it is important that they both be comfortable with the use of power and aware of the dangers of becoming overly responsible for the work of therapy. Therapists also must be able to establish their credibility clearly and be comfortable in the role of expert. This requires an up-to-date awareness of major research findings about schizophrenia and its management, including a solid understanding of theories relating to the etiology and course of the illness, and relating to medication and other treatments. Finally, it is essential that therapists have an understanding of the pain and difficulty associated with having a serious mental illness or living with someone who does.

Although this model of treatment is designed to be relatively straight-forward, it is important that the therapist have certain specific qualities and skills. First, to do well, two types of therapeutic experience are necessary: experience working with severely disturbed patients and experience working with couples. Without firsthand knowledge of psychotic illnesses, there is a tendency for therapists to have unrealistic goals and expectations. When therapists expect progress to be rapid and consistent, they become frustrated with the limitations of these patients and the inevitable slowness of change. Successful treatment requires carefully planned interventions and long periods of waiting.

Similarly, experience in working with couples is essential. Viewing the couple as a system helps in understanding the reciprocal impact of the illness, other life stresses, and the couple's interactions. The therapist must accept the importance of the involvement of both spouses in treatment without having an attitude that blames the spouse for the patient's problems, or vice versa.

Even when therapists have these skills and attributes, problems occur in treatment. One set of problems relates less to what occurs within a session than to the difficulties in working cooperatively with other professionals in managing a serious illness. For instance, frequently the patient's medication is managed by one professional, the marital treatment by another, and vocational rehabilitation by a third. Lack of communication between members of such a treatment team, and/or the lack of a unified philosophy of treatment, can cause professionals to work at cross purposes or send contradictory messages to the couple. Inevitably, such situations cause confusion, frustration, and even anger at therapists that eventually can lead to resistance or non-compliance with treatment.

Another set of treatment problems occurs because the therapist has become emotionally involved in the couple's system. For instance, due to the highly dichotomous presentation of many couples (one spouse being obviously ill and the other appearing significantly more healthy), it is easy for a therapist who is unaware of his or her own issues to begin to align covertly with one partner. If this sort of alignment is a transient phenomenon, it does not tend to cause more trouble. If it continues over time, however, it can act to impede therapeutic progress. This model of marital therapy requires that the therapist not assume an adversarial role with either partner. Thus it is essential that his or her allegiance be neither to the patient nor to the spouse, but to the couple and to helping them cope. There are times, however, when spouses must be helped to make decisions about their commitment to the marriage, times when continuing in the marriage will probably mean a lifetime commitment to a caretaking role. Some spouses are willing to make this commitment, others are not. If the marriage is to dissolve, the therapist must help the partners to separate with a minimum of stress and chaos, optimally some time after an acute episode.

Finally, the slow pace of treatment often creates frustration for the therapist. At those times, the therapist is often tempted to focus on dynamic issues that the couple is not yet ready to face. Unfortunately, this is countertherapeutic in that it escalates the intensity of sessions and adds another stress at an already stressful time. Early in treatment, a dynamically oriented, emotive approach to working with these couples has the potential for precipitating crises, heightening marital distress, and/or increasing positive symptomatology. These issues should be reserved for the latter phases of treatment, being discussed only after the patient's stabilization has been clearly achieved, and even then, only if the couple demonstrate both the commitment and ability to work in this way.

CLINICAL ISSUES

This model of marital treatment does not attempt to cure schizophrenia or even offer a permanent solution to the marital problems associated with it. Rather, it offers a marital couple better ways of understanding and coping with a difficult problem and ways of enhancing their relationship given the need to cope with problems that are likely to be chronic ones. Schizophrenic patients who marry are in a minority. Most male schizophrenic patients never marry, and most female schizophrenic patients are unable to sustain the marriages they make (Johnston & Planansky, 1968; Watt & Szulecka, 1979). Thus, patients who are married are likely to be among the better skilled and adjusted of this population. Even so, patients with this illness require more than marital therapy. Most individuals with schizophrenia require ongoing or periodic psychotropic medication, and many must be involved in other treatment modalities, such as day treatment, social skills training, or vocational rehabilitation.

Resistance and noncompliance to treatment are already significant issues for the patient with schizophrenia and his or her spouse. These problems emanate from a number of sources. First, many patients and families have had bad experiences with past treatment providers, which leaves them skeptical as to how any treatment will help. Second, many patients have difficulty in accepting that they have an illness. Since their reality is altered by the illness, many patients have difficulty believing, for instance, that there is no systematic plot against them. Third, some spouses do not want to be involved in treatment because they see the illness as their partner's "problem," not their own.

Whatever the source of resistance, it is common during the initial phases of treatment, becoming somewhat less so after information has been shared. If the resistance is related to past bad treatment experiences, it is important that the therapist not attempt to defend other therapists or facilities but be empathic about the problems that have occurred and reassuring that every attempt will be made to make this experience a different one. If the spouse is resistant initially, the therapist may emphasize his or her concern for the spouse's welfare and make suggestions for easing current stresses that may or may not be related to the patient's illness. Finally, it sometimes helps decrease resistance to treatment by reframing marital treatment as a way of dealing with problems that the patient is invested in addressing, such as getting a job or improving the sexual adjustment. This offers the patient or the couple alternative and more palatable reasons for getting involved in therapy.

SUMMARY

We have described a model of marital intervention for couples in which one member has schizophrenia. This model, to be used in conjunction with a medication regime, includes the provision of information that helps couples to understand the illness and that provides couples with a rational guide for living with it. Ongoing treatment includes the facilitation of a structured environment and the development of coping skills that reduce possible environmental precipitants of relapse while gradually enhancing and restructuring the marital relationship. Marital dynamics are rarely a direct focus early in this model, and perhaps not even in the later phases. However, interpersonal boundaries and marital interaction seem to change for the better as the patient and the marriage become more functional over the course of treatment. While the marriages of psychotic patients are at high risk, it is our belief that many of these marriages can be preserved and even become satisfying to both partners over time.

REFERENCES

Alanen, Y. O., Hagglund, V., Harkonen, P., & Kunnunen, P. (1968). On psychodynamics and conjoint psychotherapy of schizophrenic men and their wives. *Psychotherapy and Psychosomatics, 7*, 299–300.

American Psychiatric Association. (1980). *Diagnostic and statistical manual of mental disorders* (3d ed.). Washington, DC: Author.

Anderson, C. M. (1977). Family intervention with severely disturbed inpatients. *Archives of General Psychiatry, 34*, 697–702.

Anderson, C. M., Hogarty, G. E., & Reiss, D. J. (1980). Family treatment of adult schizophrenic patients: A psycho-educational approach. *Schizophrenia Bulletin, 6*(3), 490–505.

Barlow, M. D. (1979). Communication, commitment, and decision-making in the marital relationships of schizophrenics. *Dissertation Abstracts International, 40*(4-A), 2268–2269.

Brown, G. W., Birley, J. L. T., & Wing, J. H. (1972). The influence of family life on the course of schizophrenic disorders. A replication. *British Journal of Psychology, 121*, 241–258.

Crago, M. A. (1972). Psychopathology in married couples. *Psychological Bulletin, 77*, 114–128.

Dupont, R. L., Ryder, R. G., & Grunebaum, H. U. (1971). An unexpected result of psychosis in marriage. *American Journal of Psychiatry, 128*, 91–95.

Gittelman-Klein, R., & Klein, D. F. (1968). Marital status as a prognostic indicator in schizophrenia. *Journal of Nervous and Mental Disease, 147*, 289–296.

Goldberg, S. C., Schooler, N. R., Hogarty, G. E., & Roper, M. (1977). Prediction of relapse in schizophrenic outpatients treated by drug and social therapy. *Archives of General Psychiatry, 34*, 171–184.

Goldstein, M. J., Rodnick, E. H., Evans, J. R., May, P. R., & Steinberg, M. (1978). Drug and family therapy in the aftercare treatment of acute schizophrenia. *Archives of General Psychiatry, 35*, 1169–1177.

Group for the Advancement of Psychiatry. (1984). *Research and the complex causality of the schizophrenias.* New York: Brunner/Mazel.

Held, J. M., & Cromwell, R. L. (1968). Premorbid adjustment in schizophrenia. *Journal of Nervous and Mental Disease, 146*, 264–272.

Hirsch, J. R. (1976). Interacting social and biological factors determining prognoses in the rehabilitation and management of persons with schizophrenia. In R. Cancto (Ed.), *Annual review of the schizophrenic syndrome* (Vol. 4). New York: Brunner/Mazel.

Hogarty, G. E., Schooler, N. R., Ulrich, R., Mussare, F., Ferro, P., & Herron, E. (1979). Fluphenazine and social therapy in the aftercare of schizophrenic patients. *Archives of General Psychiatry, 36,* 1283–1294.

Johnston, R., & Planansky, K. (1968). Schizophrenia in men: The impact on their wives. *Psychiatric Quarterly, 42,* 146–155.

Kern, J. W. (1967). Conjoint marital psychotherapy: An interim measure in the treatment of psychosis. *Psychiatry, 30,* 283–293.

Kohn, M. L. (1973). Social class and schizophrenia: A critical review and a reformulation. *Schizophrenia Bulletin, 1*(7), 60–79.

Kreitman, N. (1962). Mental disorders in married couples. *Journal of Mental Science, 108,* 438–446.

Linn, N. W., Caffey, E. M., Lett, C. J., Hogarty, G. E., & Lamb, H. R. (1979). Day treatment and psychotropic drugs in the aftercare of schizophrenic patients. *Archives of General Psychiatry, 36,* 1055–1066.

Lyketsos, G. C., Sakka, P., & Mailis, A. (1983). The sexual adjustment of chronic schizophrenics: A preliminary study. *British Journal of Psychiatry, 143,* 376–382.

May, P. R. A. (1975). Schizophrenia: Evaluation of treatment methods. In A. M. Freedman, H. I. Kaplan, & B. J. Sadock (Eds.), *Comprehensive textbook of psychiatry* (Vol. 1). Baltimore: Williams & Wilkins.

Minuchin, S. (1974). Structural family therapy. In S. Arieti (Ed.), *American handbook of psychiatry* (Vol. 2). New York: Basic Books.

Mueller, P. S., & Orfanidis, M. M. (1976). A method of cotherapy for schizophrenic families. *Family Process, 15,* 179–191.

Nielsen, J. (1964). Mental disorders in married couples (assortive mating). *British Journal of Psychiatry, 110,* 683–697.

Pinsof, W. M. (1983). Integrative problem-centered therapy: Toward the synthesis of family and individual psychotherapies. *Journal of Marital and Family Therapy, 9,* 19–35.

Rabin, A. L., Doneson, S. L., & Jentons, R. L. (1979). Studies of psychological functions in schizophrenia. In L. Bellak (Ed.), *Disorders of the schizophrenic syndrome.* New York: Basic Books.

Sartorius, N., Jablensky, A., & Shapiro, R. (1977). Two year follow up on the patients included in the WHO International Pilot Study of Schizophrenia. *Psychological Medicine, 7,* 529–541.

Silverman, J. (1972). Stimulus intensity modulation and psychological disease. *Psychopharmacologia, 24,* 42–80.

Steinberg, H. R., & Durell, J. (1968). A stressful social situation as a precipitant of schizophrenic symptoms. *British Journal of Psychiatry, 114,* 1097–1105.

Taube, C. (1974). Readmissions to inpatient services of state and county mental hospitals, 1972. Statis note 110. Biometry Branch, NIMH.

Tecce, J. J., & Cole, J. O. (1976). The distraction-arousal hypothesis, CNV, and schizophrenia. In D. I. Mostofsky (Ed.), *Behavior control and modification of physiological activity,* Englewood Cliffs, NJ: Prentice-Hall.

Torrey, E. F. (1973). Is schizophrenia universal? An open question. *Schizophrenia Bulletin, 7,* 53–59.

Turner, R. J., Dopkeen, L. S., & Labreche, G. P. (1970). Marital status and schizophrenia: A study of incidence and outcome. *Journal of Abnormal Psychology, 76,* 110–116.

Van Putten, T., & May, P. R. A. (1976). Milieu therapy of the schizophrenias. In L. J. West, & P. E. Flinn (Eds.), *Treatment of schizophrenia.* New York: Grune & Stratton.

Vaughn, C. E., & Leff, J. P. (1976). The influence of family and social factors on the course of psychiatric illness. *British Journal of Psychiatry, 129,* 125–137.

Venables, P. H. (1964). Input dysfunction in schizophrenia. In B. A. Maher (Ed.), *Progress in experimental personality research* (Vol. 1). New York: Academic Press.

Venables, P. H. (1978). Cognitive disorder. In J. K. Wing (Ed.), *Schizophrenia: Towards a new synthesis.* New York: Academic Press.

Watt, D. C., & Szulecka, T. K. (1979). The effects of sex, marriage and age at first admission on the hospitalization of schizophrenics during 2 years following discharge. *Psychological Medicine, 9,* 529–539.

25

Marital Therapy
for Narcissistic Disorders
MELVIN R. LANSKY

NARCISSISTIC DISORDERS AND RELATIONSHIP ISSUES

The concept of narcissism has undergone considerable evolution since it was first described as a perversion, an erotic attachment to the self. Referring to the psychoses, Freud (1914) described narcissistic, as opposed to transference neuroses, as those so characterized by self-attachment and self-absorption that a utilizable transference could not be formed. This early conceptualization is not the same as that in current usage. Narcissism no longer is felt to distinguish psychoses qualitatively from neuroses. The word narcissism now applies colloquially to persons who are self-centered, needy of admiration, and high strung, with tendencies toward exhibitionism and omnipotence and a sensitivity to humiliation. The psychoanalytic usage has evolved considerably. Abraham (1919) first described the humiliation-prone patient in analysis, and the difficulties of this character trait as an obstacle to psychoanalytic treatment. In recent years, attention has been centered on narcissistic personality organization. Kernberg (1975) considers it a type of borderline organization. Kohut (1971) has pointed to the special transferences, idealizing and mirroring, formed by narcissistic patients in the analytic situation, and the need for such patients to establish and perpetuate self-object relationships, ones in which others are used as extensions of the self, rather than experienced as independent sources of initiative.

The treatment of narcissistically injured and narcissistically vulnerable persons requires a high tolerance in the therapist, for countertransference

Melvin R. Lansky. Department of Psychiatry, UCLA Medical School, Los Angeles, California and Brentwood Veterans Administration Medical Center, Brentwood, California.

problems, such as boredom and irritation, a sensitivity to shame and its dynamics, and an ability to empathize with the patient's world, even in the pressures of the treatment situation, provoke the therapist to react with blame or sympathy rather than with empathy. For the marital therapist, narcissistic organization in the personalities of spouses poses special difficulties for treatment.

It is common to find that if one spouse has narcissistic pathology, both spouses, and often others in the family, do too. It is also the rule that the narcissistic vulnerability—that is, the proneness to personality disorganization and fragmentation, loss of control, and sense of shame because of these vulnerabilities—becomes masked. The main defensive operations of such persons are often collusive. Persons with similar defensive needs cooperate in transpersonal defenses. The aim of defenses is to keep persons involved in collusive activities from being exposed as out of control, empty, fragmentation prone, and needy (Lansky, 1980a). Narcissistically vulnerable persons also have a need to keep people from getting too close or too far away in a more rigidified way than do people without narcissistic features prominent in their personality organization (Lansky, 1982, 1983). These difficulties, masking, humiliation proneness, a tendency to form collusive relationships, and a need for pathological distance regulation, all provide special difficulties for treatment and increase the risk of treatment failure with such persons.

Relationship issues contribute in many ways to the individual pathology of the spouses. In the early history of such patients, there is often sustained neglect on the part of one or both parents, emotional absence, involvement of the patient in catering to the emotional needs of one or both parents or as a surrogate parent or mediator in the midst of parental conflict, or sustained physical or sexual abuse with the knowledge of one or both parents (Lansky, 1980b). Such experiences serve to leave the future narcissistic patient with an enduring sense of shame, a vulnerability to fragmentation, a feeling of being incomplete, and a developmental arrest that is usually countered or defended against in adult life by various collusive and pathological relationships that prevent the patient from disorganizing, getting out of control, or becoming exposed as defective. Such collusive relationships come at enormous cost to well-being and satisfaction, and serve mainly to ward off exposure that intensifies the spouses' shame. Relationship patterns, however painful, are often mutually reinforcing and self-perpetuating, rigid, enduring, and un-gratifying. Forms of such relationships include chronic conflictual marriages that endure despite continued misery. I have elsewhere referred to these as "blaming" couples (Lansky, 1980a). Alternatively, one may see dysfunction in one spouse, who is either depressed or symptomatic. Symptoms are often impulsive actions, such as wrist slashing, binge drinking, overdosing, or compulsive gambling (Lansky, in press). The couple may project their difficulties on to children, who become symptomatic in a similar way (Bowen, 1966).

Or, among constantly preoccupied spouses, one may see close, caring, and responsible but emotionally absent relationships that have a devastating effect on children.

The individual problems and the marital problems then dovetail; the individual pathology tends to mask and bury itself in the collusive relationship, and the relationship is held together by the fact that such people need each other to avoid decompensation or exposure because of their personality defects. Fragmentation-prone, humiliation-prone, narcissistic patients with incohesive senses of self collude over the same defensive needs. There are often differing styles of defense at the surface, say, with one member of the family blaming, another preoccupied, and yet a third with a life style characterized by habitual impulsive action. On close scrutiny, these prove to be modes of pathological distance regulation that keep members from becoming too close when intimacy and exposure is a danger, and too far away when separation runs the risk of precipitating personality disorganization and subsequent flooding with anxiety and shame. The rigidity of these defensive operations comes at a high cost.

Patterns of defense have a typical impact on the interpersonal surroundings that may be of diagnostic and even of prognostic significance. *Preoccupied* couples often are high achievers and successful in the area of work, social, and community relations. Obligations outside the family may rationalize an inability to tolerate intimacy. Marriages characterized by pathological preoccupation are very difficult to change. Often, the offspring of such marriages suffer considerably more than parents. *Blaming* couples show surprising cohesiveness, despite the outward show of disruption; often there is some mixture of *impulsive action* in the picture, with one spouse inviting blame by drinking, slashing, committing infidelities, or gambling compulsively. These marriages are more treatable than early impressions might lead one to think. Some habitually *demanding* and *devaluing patients* may alienate their families entirely. Moderate-length hospitalization is often decisive in treatment of such patients. Chronic daily substance abuse or manipulativeness (Bursten, 1972) requires more than psychotherapy (in any combination) for successful results (Lansky, Bley, Simenstad, *et al.*, 1984).

The model for treatment set forward here is intimately involved with dyadic relationships in childhood, marriage, and the therapeutic situation, but does not presume that treatment is exclusively dyadic. Dyadic relationships are important in the etiology of such disorders; usually the history of nurturance is such to predispose the patient to shame and personality disorganization, and the notion of oneself as cheated, incomplete, and in need of attention or recompense. The propensity of the personality to disorganize and the need for pathological distance regulation are personality features conducive to the endurance of an unhappy dyad. The collusive relationships in adult life prevent disaster but also prevent growth. It is then incumbent on the therapeutic relationship or dyad to prevent disaster while promoting growth.

A THEORY OF THERAPEUTIC CHANGE

The rationale for this treatment approach follows in most details from this theoretical psychopathological model. It is assumed that some degree of developmental arrest is behind the personality disorder; that the effects of this arrest are perpetuated in part by collusive defensive systems; and that growth may resume, under proper circumstances, at least partially. It is also assumed that some degree of improvement may occur if the rigid collusive protective system is loosened in a way that does not threaten the psychic survival of the spouses. This, of course, is easier said than done. Many such couples improve when the pressure is eased, others do not, and yet others cannot even endure the humiliation inherent in seeing themselves entering or staying in treatment. Nonetheless, treatment results for such couples are improved immensely when specific pitfalls are avoided and obstacles to treatment are foreseen.

Treatment strategies, which may take a variety of directions in persons without significant narcissistic vulnerability, must be aimed at specific treatment obstacles: personality disorganization, pathologic distance regulation, masks, shame and humiliation, lack of observing ego in collusive relationships, overreactivity, and lack of empathy. The therapist must create, as much as possible, a safe place where lengthy treatment can attempt to restore enough of a sense of well-being so that a developmental arrest can be at least partially acknowledged and compensated for, where the cost of defenses can be apprised, and where spouses can get beyond the panic underlying the need for encompassing protectiveness and actually get some satisfaction out of their marriages.

The therapist's overall strategy, then, is to create a safe environment; one that both sides experience as empathic and just, and one in which each feels understood. In this environment, vulnerabilities and shortcomings can be explored in an atmosphere as free of blame as possible, and each spouse can take sustenance from the therapist and, as treatment develops, from each other.

A major goal of such therapy, and one that is often neglected, is to free succeeding generations from the tendency of such disorders to replicate themselves over generations. Often what appears to be a hopeless marital situation may so involve children, even grown ones, that they find extreme difficulty in working, loving, and feeling whole, and they do not understand why. Often a few sessions with such children present may help emancipate them from malignant features of the process, and set them on a pathway to restoration (see Case F).

It is often possible to facilitate differentiation and allow for separate experiences of growth for spouses. These treatment conditions are not easily achieved. The therapist, in deciding to employ strategies that are specific for narcissistic vulnerability in the marital dyad, must first assess the clinical situation. The presence of difficulties in early nurturance outlined above, collusive relationships, the need for pathological distance regulation, the presence of blaming, impulsive action, or extreme preoccupation may alert the therapist to the fact that ordinary didactic, instructional, or communication-enhancing techniques will not suffice. Nor will brief therapy. For narcissistically vulnerable persons, communication and attendant exposure is often a very real and mortifying danger, and should not be approached offhandedly as a value of the therapist to be embraced unquestioningly by the couple. A goal that *can* be immediately stated is the importance for the marriage and the work for each spouse to feel understood, and to feel that his or her world has been entered by the therapist (and, one hopes, by the other spouse), as a thing valued in itself and with no attempt to coerce, change, or manipulate it. The conduct of therapy varies, depending on whether symptom, system, or personality is being addressed (Lansky, 1981a). For situations in which impulsive action such as suicidality, drinking, or violence is in the picture, some control of the symptom, whether through medication, hospitalization, or other means, must be attained before the system, and finally the personality system, are addressed. If, however, it is agreed that the marriage or family *is* being worked on, the therapy must be designed to avoid, as much as possible reactivity (spouses to each other), collusion, and humiliation, and to enhance the empathy that is so vital to growth and change in such patients. This technique is described in detail in the next section.

TREATMENT TECHNIQUES AND ISSUES

When it is agreed that the marital system is to be the focus of therapeutic attention, the therapist is usually better employed as a "conductor" than a "reactor". Following Bowen (1966), I have found that with patients who are overreactive and prone to get into collusive stalemates, facilitating communication is not useful as a major technical task. It is usually better for the therapist to pair off with each individual. They will "communicate" with each other soon enough when they feel understood. This technique is not easily done with a co-therapist because so much structure is necessary that coordination is very difficult, and one therapist usually assumes a clearly auxiliary role. Weekly sessions for a good number of months, even years, often yields major gains and the ability to compensate for developmental arrests in both spouses. The therapist must be aware of the constant sense of injustice and the enduring need for empathy in such patients, even if it is not at the surface. While these are universal therapeutic requirements, they are especially crucial in the treatment strategies of narcissistically vulnerable patients. It is also important for the therapist to convey clearly the sense that the marriage is important, as are both people in it. Indifference to the marriage (as opposed to therapeutic neutrality about the issues raised) is as out of place in the treatment of couples as indifference to outcome in the treatment of suicidal persons.

Establishing an Empathic Connection

A major design of the treatment is to enable each spouse to receive empathic understanding when he or she communicates with the therapist, and for the task of the spouse who is listening to be defined as an attempt to put aside his or her complaints and empathically enter the world of the other. As illustrated in Case A, I begin with one spouse, and instruct him or her to tell me his or her view of things, so that I can enter into that spouse's world.

> A couple came for therapy of long-standing marital difficulties, which had increased in severity over the past year. They had recently moved from New York at the same time that their son, their only child, went to college on the East Coast. Mr. A. was a screenwriter, age 45, and Mrs. A., a photographer, age 44.
>
> I began by saying that I wanted to hear from both of them, but one at a time, concerning the areas of tension, what the marriage had been like, where their private fulfillment was, what their families of origin were like, what unfinished business they had brought into the marriage, and anything else that might be on their minds. I asked one of them to begin, with no attempt to be fair to the other, and to share his world with me, while the other was to attempt to deal with a more difficult task: listening. I explained that the reason I was talking to the other spouse was to create an opportunity for the listening person to really listen, without preparing an argument, and to take note of the conditions under which such listening became impossible. I then proceeded to talk to Mrs. A., having prescribed empathic contact as the task of the listening spouse, noted that this would be a difficult task, and set about trying to provide it myself as a model. My assumption here is that by fostering the emotional nurturance in which each is so lacking, I also promote growth, goodwill, and modeling that generalizes.

MRS. A.: I'm tired of being intimidated by Burt. I still love him, but he is volatile and self-centered. He explodes in rages, and scares me to death, and that's been getting worse and worse.

THERAPIST: Since when?

MRS. A.: Since we were married, since we were dating, but much worse in the last year.

THERAPIST: What's gone on since then?

MRS. A.: Well, we came out to Los Angeles, and then Arthur has gone to college. I used to spend a lot of time with him, and we used to do a lot together. Burt wouldn't explode so much then. But now that it's just me and Burt, it's terrible, and there is a new city. I don't have any of my friends. I don't have my son. I live in terror all the time. I try to please him, I've always tried to please him. But I'm just terrified by his temper. . . .

MR. A.: You've got it all wrong, Alice! You've got it all wrong (shouting). You make me furious. (Alice freezes.) You don't realize what sets me off. You don't know what you do. You shut me out. You start it. You pull away—

THERAPIST (*interrupting*): Is this typical?

MR. AND MRS. A.: (*Both nod.*) Yes. (*Mr. A. attempts to continue, but therapist interrupts.*)

THERAPIST: I presume this has gotten you nowhere, hasn't it, or you wouldn't be here.

MR. AND MRS. A.: (*Agree in unison.*)

THERAPIST: It goes that way when there is tension in a marriage; that's why I want to talk to each of you in turn and not have you talk to each other. When things are better, when you both feel understood, then you can talk to each other; but in the meanwhile, talk to me first. When you talk to each other like this, you'll never resolve anything. I'll talk to you first (*nods to Mrs. A.*) and then to him (*turns to Mr. A.*). Yours is the harder task. I want you to listen. That won't be easy. I mean, to really get in her world, with all the hurt that I presume you've gone through, you'll be tempted to correct the record almost every time she starts talking, and to set her straight. But it won't do you any good, it won't resolve anything. It only gets you in the same stalemate. No one in a marriage that hurts really wants to understand, they only want to be understood— but I want you to try while I'm talking to her—because nothing's going to change until you each do that for each other, and you each have the real feeling of being understood, and that isn't easy. So try to look at yourself, and see what Alice does that sets you off and pushes your buttons, and makes you want to correct her. With a lot of tension in the marriage, buttons are very easy to push. (*Turns to Mrs. A.*) Now, tell me—

MRS. A.: It's been awful. He yells at me, you know, just like he did then. He expects me to deal with the businessmen, with the bills. It's always up and down with his career, when a contract comes through, when he sells a script. There are bill collectors. I take care of him. He works at home, I make him sandwiches and call the creditors, and he yells at me. There is nothing to protect me—I've given him my whole career. He does that—he frightens me, he frightens me—

MR. A. (*interrupting*): You don't know what you're doing (*escalating, hysterical*). You drive me crazy, Alice, you pull away, you freeze up, you leave me in the cold, I'm just twisting in the wind and I start screaming, and you don't know how to, how to— anything.

The task of empathic listening is not always successful at first. Often the listening spouse will intrude with a statement that the talking spouse has gotten the facts wrong, or ignores certain things, or is like a parent, or is simply impossible. I then repeat the direction and note that, however difficult it is to listen, the alternatives to listening have gotten nowhere or the couple would not be here, and encourage the listening person to try again. We then try to begin looking at a system so organized that people must correct the record or defend themselves rather than make each other feel understood. I am neither tentative nor shy about putting forward the need to understand and be understood as a goal and a necessary condition of any increase in marital satisfaction. I try to make it my goal to deal with one spouse's failure of empathic contact in an empathic way.

THERAPIST: I can feel the hurt and helplessness and anger when she keeps talking and you feel misunderstood and tuned out. I don't know if it's possible for you to get beyond that right now, because the feelings are so intense. But perhaps you will be able to sometime. (*Mr. A. calms.*)

MRS. A.: Just like that. I die on the inside. It's gotten worse, but it was always like this.

THERAPIST: So what did you see in him in the first place?

MRS. A.: I liked him. He had life. At Ann Arbor he had a reputation for being the most explosive guy in town, and also the most brilliant. I guess that turned me on.

THERAPIST: Let's hear about how it turned you on.

MRS. A.: My life before Burt was so dull.

THERAPIST: What was it like?

MRS. A.: I came from a family that was so boring.

THERAPIST: Tell me about it.

MRS. A.: I'm from Minnesota. My father was a doctor. My mother was so dedicated to him. They were both very religious. All he ever did was become absorbed in his practice. And she backed him up.

THERAPIST: No life to it. And Burt here was just the opposite, I take it.

MRS. A.: Yes.

THERAPIST: And that really turned you on.

MRS. A.: Yes.

THERAPIST: Turned you on, and now really scares you to death.

MRS. A.: Yes, it kind of excited me. I mean, that's a part of my life that's always been missing.

THERAPIST: Maybe a part of your life that you can't provide for yourself.

MRS. A.: Yes. I'm always too reasonable, that's the way it is in the marriage. I wish I were more explosive.

THERAPIST: But you just freeze up and pull away.

MRS. A.: Yes.

THERAPIST (*to Mr. A.*): And that has an effect on you?

MR. A.: Yes. It drives me crazy.

THERAPIST: Let's hear.

MR. A.: She pulls away, she's cold and aloof, and judgmental.

THERAPIST: So what did you see in her in the first place?

MR. A.: She had real class. I was used to dating these mousey little busybodies, who kept gibbering all the time. She had real class.

THERAPIST: Real class was important to you?

MR. A.: Yes.

THERAPIST: Any idea why?

MR. A.: Yeah. I grew up in an apartment house in Chicago. There was no class in our family. My mother had a big mouth; my father—well, my father was a mouse.

THERAPIST: Tell me, what was it like?

MR. A.: My father was a mouse. They used to argue all the time; in fact I used to sort of run the show—it was like they were in court, and I was the judge.

THERAPIST: That makes you kind of a big shot, kind of the authority in the family, doesn't it?

MR. A.: Yes. I was a special customer. I had writing ability—my father didn't. My mother really valued that. She had wanted to write. I mean, she married him, and he had the barber shop and did well, but it wasn't enough for her.

THERAPIST: So you were the glint in mother's eye, and the special customer—her man, so to speak?

MR. A.: Yes, that's right.

THERAPIST: But she wasn't your kind of lady?

MR. A.: Hell, no. Big mouth and intrusive and obnoxious—

THERAPIST: Not with a lot of cool and class, like Alice.

MR. A.: That's right.

THERAPIST: But the same kind of cool you sometimes experience as aloof and judgmental, not just classy.

MR. A. (*thinking*): Yes, I guess so.

It is not uncommon to find that the same thing that attracts couples about each other is the very source of the marital complaint. In the case of the A.'s, his volatility and assertiveness and her cool, detached demeanor were both intensely attractive to the other. In modified form, they are the very same things that are wrong with the marriage.

Creating an Intergenerational Perspective

A serious problem in many cases of severe narcissistic vulnerability is the proneness to humiliation that so typifies these patients. With such patients, I have found it particularly useful to use an intergenerational approach specifically for minimizing shame. Very often, a focus on the family of origin, especially with unconscious identification with the same-sex parent, provides the clue to why one or both spouses feel so humiliated and so desperate (Dicks, 1967). Identification with the same-sex parent, and the patient's struggle against it, is an important issue, even if a surface comparison between parent and child seems preposterous. Consider Case B, which follows:

> A couple in their early 40s were in conjoint therapy for severe marital tensions. Mr. B., an attorney in solo practice, worked long and indefinite hours and defiantly refused to give his wife any reliable schedule of his time that she could count on. He also made her aware of his extramarital affairs; she became angry, and to his way of thinking, controlling and domineering. This stalemated situation appeared in a different light when understood intergenerationally.
>
> He was the only son of successful immigrant parents who lavished praise on him and found fulfillment in his accomplishments. His mother, an overbearing woman, held his father in open contempt. The father, despite his financial successes, colluded with this devalued view of himself and doted on the son.
>
> Mrs. B. came from a family with a dominant, insensitive father and a helpless mother, whom she at first portrayed vaguely. Mrs. B. later mentioned offhandedly that when she was an adolescent, her mother had committed suicide.
>
> The B.'s current marital tensions could be better understood as reflecting deep-seated, but consciously disowned, identifications of each spouse with the parent of the same sex. Mr. B., fearing the contempt and control that had been his father's lot; Mrs. B., responding by overcontrol and domination to the helplessness, desperation, and fear of abandonment that had driven her mother to suicide. The marital struggle was a battleground for the unconscious struggle against identification with each same-sex parent. The cost of the struggle was enduring marital misery.

Often, very accomplished and competent people struggle with an unconscious identification with a parent of the same sex who, in the parental marriage, was felt to be helpless or was held in contempt (Greenson, 1954). Often issues in early nurturance shed light on features that make the patient very ashamed in adult life: vulnerability to separation, extreme neediness, loss of control, tendencies to either blame or emotionally withdraw when the pressure is on. When these experiences in the family of origin are understood, discussion of them in the family of procreation is less humiliating. Consider Case C, which follows:

> A 45-year-old man viciously berated his wife of 20 years for appearing 10 minutes late to a conjoint session. Her tangential, vacuous explanation seemed to amplify his anger, which continued for most of the session. Both spouses agreed that such tirades were typical in the marriage and not due to special circumstances.
>
> Mr. C. had been orphaned in wartime Europe and had been raised by several aunts and a grandmother. His caretakers resented him and passed him back and forth. Mrs. C., the youngest of three daughters, was the only child to remain with her alcoholic mother after the parental marriage broke up. Her mother could not manage with her, so she went with her father and resentful older sisters. Mr. C.'s vulnerability to personality disorganization when he was left for even a short time was a source of panic and shame. His vehement blaming attacks were a response to the panic, disorganization, and shame, and expressed his anger at all the female caretakers who had let him down and whom he held responsible for his vulnerabilities and difficulties in life. Mrs. C.'s apparent submissiveness served the same binding and palliating function with her resentful husband as it had with her resentful sisters. Her actions, however subtle, which provoked her husband to blame, and in the apparently pathetic style with which she egged him on, emerged as her method of control and vengeance over those who had so humiliated her over the years.

With an intergenerational perspective, each spouse may reach an understanding of self as an unfolding (and vulnerable) process, not just as a clingy, controlling, or angry person who is ashamed to have his or her protective activities exposed.

As noted earlier, it quite often happens that the very thing that spouses say attracted them to the partner in the first place is in only slightly modified form what the marital complaint is about (see Case A). Some notion of the patient's idea of justice in the family of origin is crucial. Patients may feel either that the same-sex parent was held in contempt or that one sex or another was undermining, bullying, or undercutting or that one child or another got more than they should have, at the patient's expense. These issues, as Boszormenyi-Nagy (1972) has eloquently emphasized, are crucial determinants in what people feel entitled to and what they feel accountable for.

It is useful to understand that there are traumatic absences as well as traumatic presences. An absent psychotic, depressed, or constantly preoccupied parent may provide a devastatingly traumatic model; often a patient who has dealt with such a parent of the opposite sex may feel a lack of worth, a lack of ability to assume leadership in the marriage, and depression in dealings with the spouse. Consider Case D, which follows:

> An unmarried couple, both physicians in their late 30s, came for treatment for the purpose of deciding whether to marry. The man, a misanthropic, cynical, tactless person, alienated friends and family with immature intellectual snobbery. The woman admitted that she found it almost impossible to get angry, and at times vicariously enjoyed her boyfriend's petulance. Over the years, the enjoyment wore thin, and she realized that she resented him almost constantly. Her response to his insensitive conduct was a silent, depressive withdrawal, which lasted for days on end. She herself felt futile over her inability to take the lead in shaping the relationship, or to leave it. Her failure in this area was in sharp contrast to her leadership abilities in her profession. This woman had strong identifications with a competent mother, who had supported the family while caring for her father, a man who had suffered a stroke in his 30s and remained aphasic and paralyzed. He had been chronically psychotic and withdrawn even before the cerebrovascular accident. His daughter's failure to acquire a repertoire of competent behaviors with her father had left her with deficits in asserting herself in her own intimate life. Some of the effects of this developmental arrest were worked through in the conjoint sessions with a male marital therapist.

Emotional absences such as withdrawal, depression, or inattentiveness in one spouse may provoke or precipitate emotional turbulence and impulsive action on the other (see Case B). In general, the intergenerational approach should be seen as a tool to minimize shame and view marital issues in an unfolding perspective.

Understanding the Dynamics of Shame

Shame dynamics are much more difficult to grasp than guilt dynamics. What a patient feels guilty about because he or she has done something hurtful—transgressions often involving attack or control—is more easily understood than the patient's vulnerability to being seen, or seeing himself or herself, as defective, out of control, inadequate, or empty. Shame is often so mortifying that the patient will take almost any action to avoid it. Violent outbursts, suicide attempts, drinking bouts, and sexual escapades (about which the patient may feel guilty) often cover over subtle bouts of personality disorganization (about which the patient feels ashamed). Consider Case E, which follows:

A 35-year-old man and his 50-year-old wife appeared for evaluation after he had beaten her. He asked for admission to the hospital to decompress the dangerous situation and to get control over his propensity to be violent. He talked with appropriate horror about his violent outburst, noting that his wife could really "push his buttons." As he told of his difficulties in life, his touchiness with authorities, his despair over consistent job losses, Mrs. E. interrupted constantly with disorganizing and humiliating reminders of his failures and inadequacies. This repeated exposure to deliberate debunking was reminiscent of his relationship to a cruel father, who publicly shamed him on many occasions. His wife's debunkings shamed him, both by reminding him of his failures and by having an immediately disorganizing effect on him that added to his humiliation. The violence was more understandable as a response to, and an attempt at control of, this mode of relating. The violent behavior, and his guilt about it, as well as his wife's fear and disorganization, all took attention away from his intense and enduring shame and his inability to pull his life together.

Persistent shaming of the patient by the therapist, often rationalized as feedback or responsibility enhancement, is responsible for many treatment interruptions.

Identifying Boundary Issues

Something must be said about boundary issues in framing the therapy. Properly handled marital therapy of persons with narcissistic disorders is almost always compatible with other forms of therapy. I rarely see spouses individually for more than one or two sessions while I am seeing them as a couple, but I encourage individual therapy with another therapist. I avoid any sustained individual contact for a variety of reasons. Such contact may increase both spouses' uneasiness about what has been said in private and increase the temptation to see the therapist as the one responsible for communication between the two. The individual treatment, which should always have the potential to evolve into definitive intensive psychotherapy, is usually kept from flowering by fantasies surrounding the conjoint sessions and remains limited to supportive contact. Quite apart from these limitations on both patients, it is not possible for me, as therapist, to function maximally in either role in the midst of shifts in loyalty (Boszormenyi-Nagy, 1972) and the ever-present potential for unexpected conflicts over secrecy and exposure. If I do have an individual session, I make it clear in advance that I do not keep secrets that constitute a betrayal from the other spouse and that I will not engage in continuing therapy. I insist on using my discretion about what is confidential. I will usually not mention something that is not current, for example, if I am told about a past homosexual encounter, an abortion in adolescence, or sexual behavior prior to the current relationship. I will not agree to keep secret an ongoing affair unknown to the spouse or definite plans to leave the marriage that have not been shared.

Intensive psychotherapy in combination with marital therapy usually has a synergistic effect if the therapists can avoid competing with each other. Often the marital therapist, by providing a situation that is more immediately gratifying than the responsibility-enhancing and self-scrutinizing individual work, may be competing, upstaging, or outright sabotaging the individual work.

In work with couples, I am mindful of the malignant effects of their interactions on the narcissistic equilibrium of their children. I tend to be much more directive in issues involving children, especially involvements of children as allies in marital disputes. Too often, children are perpetrators, exploiters, and ultimately victims of marital difficulties, as confidantes to one spouse or the other, as scapegoats, parentified objects, or as persons who sacrifice themselves so that parental focus may be on them rather than on a difficult marriage.

It often makes sense to bring children into the therapy for a few sessions in an attempt to have them understand, and to emancipate them from the process. This is true of children of any age, even grown-ups. I never presume at such times that it is safe for them to talk. I insist on parental agreement that children may speak or not, according to whether they are comfortable, but need not be required to talk. Consider Case F, which follows:

> A couple in their late 50s were seen conjointly while the husband's bizarre fetishistic sexual escapades and his depressed mood were addressed and treated in the hospital. When he talked to his wife, he talked slowly and tangentially, provoking her to hysterical, hyperexcitable blaming bouts. Neither could be induced to look at the process, or to modify what they did, even when transactions were directed through the therapist. A chance remark outside of a session from one of the couple's two daughters about her own difficulties prompted the therapist to include both daughters in a number of the marital sessions. The harangue continued between Mr. and Mrs. F., and the daughters felt angry, depressed, and helpless but at the same time responsible for the chaos. Over the din of the parents' quarreling, both daughters' sense of responsibility for the marriage was addressed. Both felt responsible, not only for the marriage, but for each parent separately. The F.'s marital difficulties did not resolve, but both daughters were successful in using subsequent individual therapy to emancipate themselves from the malignant marital process that had so engrossed them, at such a devastating cost to their capacity for satisfying relationships.

I take the attitude that children are hurt by the marital rift, that they become politically sensitive to marital tensions, that they exploit the rift, and that symptoms in children very often serve a defensive function for all in the family.

Transference and Countertransference Issues

I deal somewhat cautiously with transference of the couple toward me. I do not presume that transference interpretation is always a major vehicle of cure in marital therapy. Nonetheless, understanding the transference may be a clue to understanding the couple's deep anxieties about the therapist. When a couple engage in their habitual mode of defense (e.g., *preoccupation* with outside obligations, *blaming* or provoking blame, or exclusive focus on *impulsive action* of one person), this often points to anxiety about the therapist or therapeutic situation. Consider Case G, which follows:

> A chronically impulse-ridden man with violence, irresponsibility, and binge drinking among his difficulties was discharged following a hospitalization of many months. That hospitalization had been of considerable value, stabilizing him and settling him at work in an ongoing outpatient therapy. His wife, a woman with a similar degree of personality instability, responded to his new-found stability with suicidal bouts and threats to leave the marriage. Mr. G.'s therapist attempted to see the couple conjointly, and finally found time in her schedule when both could come in. They appeared at the therapist's office on the wrong day and at an extremely awkward time. The error evoked feelings of helplessness and anger in the therapist. She did not respond with disorganization or blame, but arranged another time with the G.'s. Her continued empathy, during the disruption, served as a test that allayed the couple's (well-founded) anxieties that only an especially strong, stable person could really tolerate them. Both later reported volatile, overwhelming parents who could not tolerate untimely demands with the composure that had been displayed by the therapist. The therapy continued conjointly, with some gains despite continued manifestations of instability.

Any boundary difficulties—over time, money, phone calls, or special arrangements—may represent transference anxieties or outright testings of the therapist that should be acknowledged or explored. Most of the time, however, therapy focuses on the transferences between the spouses and not toward the therapist.

The therapist may find countertransference problems in, for example, competing with the same-sex spouse, as either spouse or parent. There are also complementary countertransferences (Kernberg, 1975), in which the therapist may become swept up in blaming, in rationalized emotional withdrawal, or in impulsive attempts to control one of the spouses. The therapist may then unwittingly participate in collusive activity, such as preoccupation, blame, or impulsive action, or may shame the patient. In general, any consciously felt aversion to the patient should be an object for the therapist's scrutiny. Often when the patient is understood intergenerationally, rigid attacking behaviors become more understandable as protective and less immediately repugnant to the therapist. Consider Case H, which follows:

A couple, both in their mid-50s, appeared for conjoint treatment when their marriage seemed near collapse. As Mr. H. was recounting his feeling attacked, devalued, and belittled for 30 years, his wife belligerently and consistently interrupted with a blast of cutting remarks that ignored his feelings completely. The therapist felt, but did not act on, considerable revulsion for Mrs. H., and did address her inability to tolerate Mr. H.'s feelings. Her attacking and controlling became intelligible after she talked of her mother's early death, and her being sent from orphanage to orphanage early in life. Her husband's emotional withdrawal, lack of leadership, and threats to leave the marriage were stimuli to the obnoxious behavior that he so much complained about, and that affected the therapist. Her attacking and devaluing regularly subsided after she felt understood and valued, for even a few minutes. This atmosphere of acceptance and understanding, provided by the therapist, added a stabilizing ingredient to the marital dyad that could be fully understood only when Mr. H.'s need to disorganize her came into focus.

A constant danger as a countertransference problem is the likelihood that the therapist will become averse to devaluation, emotional absence, and subtle debunkings in the process, or to emotional turmoil that is low key and unrecognized. Many therapeutic errors are made by therapists who do not recognize such dangers as characteristic of the transactional behavior of narcissistically vulnerable persons and become reactive to patients and subtly or overtly reject them.

Defining the Marital System as Problematic

The failure of the couple to agree that the system itself is a problem constitutes a serious difficulty. One or both may view a dysfunctional spouse or child as the symptomatic one, and focus on the symptom itself. Such difficulties are familiar to every family therapist but are exaggerated in narcissistically vulnerable families. Persons in individual psychotherapy may avoid responsibility in a marriage in a similar fashion by perpetually *complaining* about a spouse, without taking responsibility for what they do in a relationship or including the spouse in the treatment. Within the marital therapy context and elsewhere, collusive defenses without a utilizable observing ego, too much humiliation-proneness, paranoia, or a tendency to become so lost in detail or impulsive action all work against a utilizable treatment alliance. Any attempt to change the patient may result in preoccupied withdrawal, paranoid blaming, or increased impulsive symptomatology. The sensitivity to shame in such patients may surprise the inexperienced therapist. Almost any comment tending toward responsibility enhancement or pointing to the patient's role in marital difficulties, however understanding or tactfully it may be worded, may produce a mortifying experience of shame in patients with extreme narcissistic vulnerability.

The method of marital therapy sketched here is limited basically by what the patients themselves can tolerate. If one spouse cannot bear to look at self, then marital therapy becomes extremely difficult. It is not uncommon for an extremely dysfunctional spouse, say, a drinker or suicidal or violent person, to be willing to look at self, whereas the apparently normal spouse emerges as the one who is unable to tolerate shame and will refuse to cooperate in an honest scrutiny of the marriage. Often, treatment combinations are necessary, either to control symptoms, for example with hospitalization or drugs, or to aid in personality growth. The latter include individual therapy, psychoanalysis, multiple-family groups or couples groups.

THE ROLE OF THE THERAPIST

The clinical skills required of the therapist draw from psychoanalysis, family therapy, and general psychiatry. The therapist must assess, treat, and deal with symptoms, system, and personality at varying times. The therapist should have empathy for both sexes, or at least an awareness of blind spots in empathy. These blind spots are often best found by intergenerational therapy of the therapist, and are often the result of specific injustices in the therapist's own family of origin. The therapist must be able to face and utilize inevitable countertransference reactions; either the inability to bear affect, emotional absence, depression, devaluation, or other difficult affects and defenses from patients or the need to use patients for narcissistic purposes, for example, to please the therapist—to improve, to validate theories, to give up symptoms quickly. The therapist must also watch for collusion in relationships that essentially constitute emotional absences and preoccupied states, blaming, impulsive action, or shaming transactions.

Therapists must do considerable personal work and undergo considerable disillusionment, disorganization and growth before they are able to control anger at patients; struggle over symptoms with a need to control them for the therapist's narcissistic reasons, as opposed to sincerely wishing to help patients control them; develop a tolerance for neediness, depression, stubbornness, emptiness, despair, or emotional turmoil; develop a sensitivity to shame, patience with the time it takes for emotional growth; and avoid collusion in the sorts of malignant defensive processes outlined above. Thus, therapists who, for defensive reasons of their own, cannot appreciate the complexity of such a clinical situation and behave like a stereotype of excessive analytic passivity or excessive behavioristic need for control, will be unable to help such families. Neither will therapists who cannot tolerate feeling anxious, empty, depressed, or helpless and who respond as though the spouses were no more than ignorant or inexperienced and can be helped by simply giving them didactic learning experiences or specific behavioral exercises. These countertransference errors should, of course, be distinguished from more sophisticated analytic and behavioral techniques that respond to the patient's needs and not the therapist's unacknowledged anxieties. In general, therapists who are unable to give up omnipotent or narcissistic roles will have the same unfortunate effect on people in such marriages as did their own upbringings, that is, at best a neutral, and at worst a disastrous, effect.

A FINAL CLINICAL ISSUE: TREATMENT COMBINATIONS

It is not possible to overcome every serious treatment obstacle in conjoint work with every narcissistically vulnerable couple. The major factor in the therapist's success or failure with such marriages is often the therapist's ability to recognize and deal with issues that shame the couple. To treat such spouses, the therapist must be able to point to narcissistic defenses, collusion, the need for pathologic distance regulation, and so forth without criticizing, without implying that defenses can be dispensed with immediately, and without the need to strip them away before it is safe to do so. The therapist should appreciate that, in narcissistically vulnerable persons, communication is not always a relief and an opportunity; it is often a mortification and a real danger. Therapists wedded to the idea that communication is in and of itself beneficial, necessary, and always of great value for a marriage can do considerable damage. People do not like to see themselves as empty, damaged, clinging, needy, or controlling, even if they are. Communication that exposes protective tendencies must be done in a tactful, supportive, and well-timed way that is commensurate with the patients' capacity to understand what they do, and to begin to appreciate anxieties behind these maneuvers in a safe, supportive environment.

Marital therapy is part of the treatment of narcissistically vulnerable persons and addresses only the (important) systems aspects. When interventions other than marital therapy are used with a couple in treatment, their narcissistic significance within the marital system must be understood. For control of extremely dangerous symptoms, hospitalization, medication, or other modalities may be required. For some humiliation-prone spouses, the suggestion that they should take medication, no matter how clear the indications, or that they should go into individual therapy, is experienced as fully the equivalent of blame and must be understood as having that possible significance. For others, medication or individual sessions may leave the other spouse feeling that he or she did not get something that the mate got (Lansky, 1981b). Medication may be experienced as a wish on the part of family members or the therapist to be rid of the patient's turbulence, or of his or her humanity altogether, or as a method of buying off, palliating, and disposing of chaos. Such a view may be colored by past behavior of a parent who could not tolerate emotional turbulence. A tendency to overregulate even a seriously disturbed suicidal patient may be experienced as a kind of vengeful overcontrol. All this is not to say that any of these maneuvers are contraindicated, only that their narcissistic significance in intimate relations must be understood properly to ensure that their effective use is maximized.

My own view is that individual therapy and marital therapy done in a noncompetitive way are almost always synergistic and provide the opportunity for self-scrutiny in the most intimate of relationships, and at the same time in the safety of the therapeutic dyad. In lengthy experience treating couples who may also be in individual therapy or psychoanalysis, I have never had an individual therapist tell me that the marital therapy was anything but helpful. Similarly, I have never felt that the individual therapy, when done competently, is anything other than helpful to the marital therapy. Sometimes the process of healing is finished in the context of long-term individual therapy or analysis. The marital therapist need not feel abashed or second rate when other modalities are employed. Commonly the marital therapy is the decisive and liberating ingredient in an overall picture that may include all of the therapeutic possibilities currently known, but center in the marital unit as the center of therapeutic strategy.

REFERENCES

Abraham, K. (1919). A particular form of neurotic resistance against the psychoanalytic method. *Selected papers on psychoanalysis*. London: Hogarth.

Boszormenyi-Nagy, I. (1972). Loyalty implications of the transference model in psychotherapy. *Archives of General Psychiatry, 27*, 374–390.

Bowen, M. (1966). The use of family theory in clinical practice. *Comprehensive Psychiatry, 7*, 345–374.

Bursten, B. (1972). *The manipulator*. New Haven: Yale University Press.

Dicks, H. (1967). *Marital tensions*. New York: Basic Books.

Freud, S. (1914). On narcissism. *Standard Edition XIV* (pp. 67–104). London: Hogarth.

Greenson, R. (1954). The struggle against identification. *Journal of the American Psychoanalytic Association, 2*, 200–217.

Kernberg, O. (1975). *Borderline conditions and pathological narcissism*. New York: Jason Aronson.

Kohut, H. (1971). *Analysis of the self*. New York: International Universities Press.

Lansky, M. R. (1980a). On blame. *International Journal of Psycho-Analytic Psychotherapy, 8*, 429–456.

Lansky, M. R. (1980b). On the idea of a termination phase for family therapy in the hospital. In L. Wolberg, & M. Aronson, *Group and family therapy 1980—An overview*. New York: Brunner/Mazel.

Lansky, M. R. (1981a). Treatment of the narcissistically vulnerable marriage. In M. R. Lansky (Ed.), *Family therapy and major psychopathology*. New York: Grune & Stratton.

Lansky M. R. (1981b). Medication and family process. In M. R. Lansky (Ed.), *Family therapy and major psychopathology*. New York: Grune & Stratton.

Lansky, M. R. (1982). The role of the family in the evaluation of suicidality. *International Journal of Family Psychiatry, 3*.

Lansky, M. R. (1983). Masks of the narcissistically vulnerable marriage. *International Journal of Family Psychiatry, 3*, 439–449.

Lansky, M. R. (in press). *The explanation of impulsive action. International Journal of Psychoanalytic Psychotherapy*.

Lansky, M. R. , Bley, C., Simenstad, E., et al. (1984). The "absent" family of the hospitalized "borderline" patient. *International Journal of Family Psychiatry, 4*, 155–171.

26

Marital Treatment of Eating Disorders

SHARON W. FOSTER

To date, virtually no attention in the clinical literature of family therapy has focused on applications of marital therapy to the treatment of patients with eating disorders. Numerous authors have described the use of marital therapy for parents of patients with eating disorders, usually adolescents, but the use of marital therapy with couples in which one of the spouses is symptomatic has rarely been addressed (excepting Madanes, 1981; Schwartz, Barrett, & Saba, 1983). At the same time, the reported increase in the incidence of eating disorders, particularly in college-age and slightly older women (see below), raises the possibility that couples therapy may increasingly be considered as an appropriate and useful therapeutic intervention. The aims of this chapter are to (*a*) suggest a conceptual framework for marital assessment and intervention for couples with an eating-disordered spouse; (*b*) provide guidelines on indications for and specific intervention strategies with such couples, particularly regarding the issues of combining individual and couples treatment and the relationship between interpersonal–systemic and symptom foci; and (*c*) offer clinical illustrations of the utility of couples therapy with eating-disordered patients who are married.

THE SCOPE OF THE PROBLEM

Epidemiological data to date have not been widely generalizable because of small or restricted samples and variation among diagnostic criteria. None-

Sharon W. Foster. Department of Pediatrics, University of Wisconsin Medical School, and University of Wisconsin Hospital and Clinics Madison, Wisconsin.

theless, existing data suggest that the prevalence of anorexia nervosa, bulimia, and related eating disorders has increased (Duddle, 1973; Jones, Fox, Babigan, & Hutton, 1980; Halmi, 1974; Halmi, Falk, & Schwartz, 1981; Kendell, Hall, Hailey, & Babigan, 1973; Pyle, Mitchell, & Eckert, 1981; Sours, 1969; Theander, 1970). There has also been growing evidence that eating disorders are occurring with increasing frequency in older women (Garfinkel & Garner, 1982; Jones *et al.*, 1980; Kendell *et al.*, 1973).

The symptomatology of eating disorders has been discussed in detail elsewhere (Bruch, 1973; Crisp, 1980; Dally, 1969; Garfinkel & Garner, 1982; Minuchin, Rosman, & Baker, 1978; Russell, 1970; Selvini-Palazzoli, 1978). Nomenclature for differentiating among eating disorders subtypes has varied among writers. The American Psychiatric Association DSM-III distinguishes between anorexia nervosa and bulimia. The DSM-III criteria explicitly require a differential diagnosis between anorexia nervosa and bulimia: Patients cannot be diagnosed as both anorexic and bulimic. Further, purging behavior (by self-induced vomiting or abuse of laxatives, diuretics, etc.) is not required for a diagnosis of bulimia. Clinically, bulimia is frequently used to refer to a symptom cluster involving both binging and purging. Other writers have used *bulimia nervosa* (Russell, 1979), *bulimarexia* (Boskind-White & White, 1983), and *bulimic anorexic* (Garfinkel & Garner, 1982) to refer to symptom clusters that include characteristics of both anorexia nervosa and bulimia. The variety of terms used by writers to describe various subgroups of eating-disordered patients in part reflects a recognition of the heterogeneity of behaviors and clusters of behaviors exhibited by such patients. Following conventions increasingly established in the research literature, the term *restricter* is used in this chapter to refer to patients who severely restrict dietary intake as a primary means of attempting to control their weight, the term *bulimic* to normal-weight-range patients who binge and purge, and *bulimic anorexics* to refer to patients who meet the criteria for both anorexia nervosa and bulimia.

Increasingly, investigators have provided both conceptual and empirical evidence suggesting that subtypes of eating disorders are distinguishable on the basis of both symptom cluster and individual and interpersonal functioning. Studies of restrictor and bulimic anorexic subgroups have characterized the latter as showing a higher probability of impulse disorders such as drug and alcohol abuse and stealing; use of diuretics, diet pills, laxatives and/or vomiting to control weight; more lability in mood, anxiety, depression, and suicidal gestures or attempts; and to be more socially outgoing, more sexually active, and less withdrawn than restricters (Casper, Eckert, Halmi, Goldberg, & Davis, 1980; Garfinkel & Garner, 1982; Garfinkel, Moldofsky, & Garner, 1980; Garrow, Crisp, Jordan, Meyer, Russell, Silverstone, Stunkard, & Van Itallie, 1975; Russell, 1979; Strober, Salkin, Burroughs, & Morrell, 1982). Although marital status *per se* has until recently not been a major focus of attention, one team has reported that in a sample of 97 bulimic anorexics and 96 restricters, 22.7% of the former group and 11.5% of the latter were married (Garfinkel & Garner, 1982, p. 44). Affective disorders and alcohol abuse have been found to be more prevalent in families of origin of bulimic anorexic than restricter patients (Cantwell, Sturzenberger, Burroughs, Salkin, & Green, 1977; Halmi & Loney, 1973; Kalucy, Crisp, & Harding, 1977; Winokur, March, & Mendels, 1980). Studies of the incidence of such disorders in spouses of identified patients have not been conducted, and could be informative. The personality structures of eating-disordered patients typically have been described as involving obsessional features for all subgroups; and histrionic, schizoidal, and borderline characteristics have been variously ascribed by different writers to one or a variety of eating-disordered subtypes. From a more clinical perspective, restricters have been viewed as isolated, withdrawn, and perfectionist, with little sense of self and a rigid denial of pain or conflict. Their denial and self-restraint is complemented by the family's avoidance and denial of conflict, emphasis on achievement, enmeshment, overprotectiveness, and disconfirmation of direct expressions of affect or autonomy in the service of maintaining the family status quo. In bulimic anorexic individuals and families, by contrast, there is a greater expression of affect and impulses, but without resolution or understanding, and a general sense of hostility and chaos.

While investigation has been directed primarily to commonalities among patients within eating-disordered groups, there are also crucial differences not only between but also within groups. Eating disorders occur on a continuum with respect to both symptomatology and individual and interpersonal functioning (Fries, 1977; Garfinkel & Garner, 1982; Swift & Stern, 1982). Eating-disordered patients display a remarkable heterogeneity with regard to the type, severity, and duration of symptoms and the nature and severity of psychological difficulties. This diversity has critical implications for prognosis (Crisp, Kalucy, Lacey, & Harding, 1977; Garfinkel, Moldofsky, & Garner, 1977; Goetz, Succop, Reinhart, & Miller, 1977; Hsu, 1980; Hsu, Crisp, & Harding, 1979; Morgan & Russell, 1975; Pertschuk, 1977). For example, later age of onset, the presence of bulimic as well as restricting behavior, duration of illness, and previous hospitalizations were found to be associated with continued symptomatic behavior on follow-up. Moreover, although there have been no controlled-treatment outcome studies of which treatment modalities (individual, marital, family, or group therapy) are most effective for which patients, such considerations are important in the clinical tasks of assessment and intervention. It is erroneous to apply one method or technique of treatment across what, in many ways, is a diverse population. As such, in conceptualizing the factors critical to the nature, assessment, and treatment of eating disorders, both commonalities and differences among patients must be taken into account.

A FRAMEWORK FOR ASSESSMENT AND INTERVENTION

The development of a conceptualization of the focal conflict in couples in which there is a spouse with an eating disorder requires recognition of both object relations and interpersonal–systemic contributions. The basic issues involve how both partners perceive themselves and their relationship, and how their actual interpersonal behavior functions to preserve those perceptions. Assessment and intervention efforts thus must be directed to discovering and modifying both the couple's definitions of self and other and the structure of their interpersonal behavior.

The relationship between the eating-disordered patient and his or her spouse can be conceptualized as analogous to the identified patient's relationship with his or her family of origin. (Given that eating disorders have been exhibited primarily by females, for the sake of simplicity the identified patient (IP) will hereafter be referred to as "she"). Unresolved conflicts with the IP's family of origin are displaced to, and enacted within, the context of the marital relationship. Such conflicts occur primarily around separation–individuation issues, with the IP ambivalently attempting to assert autonomy and submitting, often resentfully, to what are perceived as the demands or needs of the spouse. The IP's deficit in ability to identify and express her own feelings, thoughts, and wishes, that is, her "false self" (Winnicot, 1965), is often complemented by the spouse's tacit acceptance of the IP's presentation of false self. The IP's lack of autonomy and ego strength are often masked by a superficial competence expressed, for example, in attention to the needs of the spouse or other family members, performance in career or avocational pursuits, and so on. Often it is only when the symptomatic behavior of the IP becomes so severe as to interfere with these other activities that the spouse expresses concern about the IP's well-being. In such marital relationships there is little ability to engage constructively in well-directed metacommunication about relationship issues. While the partner may be controlling at the level of overt behavior, he may exhibit an inattention to his own needs and a rigidity and denial that is parallel to that of the IP. Such spouses are often ambitious and hardworking, and they derive a primary sense of satisfaction from such endeavors. The relentless, driven quality of their actions may reflect a fundamental sense of inadequacy and lack of self-efficacy. Each spouse may view the other as both a source of satisfaction vis-à-vis their own depleted sense of self and a withholding or controlling of such resources. The symptomatic behavior functions so as to focus the couple's attention on the need for initiative on the part of both spouses in developing an increased ability to pinpoint their own inner states and examine the dysfunctional interpersonal "contract" (Sager, 1976) with the other.

The IP's conflicts regarding autonomy in the marital relationship often are compounded by a continuing, frequent, and intensive "close" relationship with one or both parents in the family of origin or with the family as a whole. The continuing enmeshment with the family of origin not only compromises the boundary between the marital dyad and the family but also may impair whatever ability the couple may have to distinguish their own perceptions of their relationship issues from those of extended-family members. The boundary between the marital and extended-family systems may be particularly vulnerable at times of developmental change within the marital relationship or in the increased responsibility or individuation of the IP. Such events as the birth of a child, the couple's move to a point geographically distant from the family of origin, or a change or promotion in a job may precipitate an exacerbation of symptoms.

While the above describes some of the similarities that may be exhibited in eating-disordered couples, there are also areas of important differences. These differences may be in both the type and the degree of psychological dysfunction. In couples in which there is a restricting IP, the degree of conflict avoidance may range from moderate to markedly severe. The couple may rigidly deny any area of conflict, may admit to difficulties in relatively trivial content areas but without significant emotional tone, may describe areas of conflict but only with difficulty articulate their own positions, or may show periods of identifying affects and cognitions followed by relatively "blank" exchanges. In bulimic anorexic or bulimic couples, the couple's interaction is more likely to be overtly hostile and chaotic. As with restricter couples, such interactional characteristics may differ in degree across couples. There may be a sense of conflict and hostility that only occasionally is stated openly by either partner; repetitive cross-complaining; or open, direct expressions of anger and attack accompanied by threats of separation or divorce. In couples with a spouse presenting with a borderline level of personality organization, such threats may be followed by destructive acting out between sessions.

In sum, the core dysfunction in eating-disordered couples may be conceptualized as existing on a continuum with respect to separation–individuation. While the IP spouse displays inattention to her own needs most strikingly in the medically dangerous symptomatic behavior, both spouses exhibit a developmental deficit with regard to identifying, articulating, and engaging in constructive behavior regarding their own thoughts and feelings. The developmental dysfunction is reflected in the couple's type and degree of affective expression, characteristic defenses, cognitive behavior, and ability to engage in personally rewarding, goal-directed behavior. Intervention with such couples requires a careful assessment of the couple's deficits and strengths with respect to all these dimensions.

STRATEGIES FOR ASSESSMENT AND INTERVENTION

The utility of marital therapy with eating-disordered patients depends on the therapist's ability to elicit and aid the couple in developing a focus on the function of the symptomatic behavior within the context of the marital relationship. With a patient population presenting several potentially defensible decisions regarding treatment modality (e.g., individual, marital, family), assessment of which treatment is most appropriate for which patient is an important step in the treatment process. In addition, while in theory one modality may be used throughout the therapy, in practice several modalities may be used concurrently or in sequence. Such options should be considered at the outset of treatment and require at least intermittent reevaluation as therapy progresses. Decision making about such options centers on (a) indications and contraindications for marital treatment; (b) the methods and areas of assessment; and (c) aims and techniques of marital therapy with eating-disordered patients.

Indications and Contraindications for Marital Therapy

Positive indications for marital therapy are fourfold: (a) onset of symptoms immediately before or during the development of the relationship, or marked exacerbations in previously existing symptoms at change or crisis points in the relationship; (b) the failure of previous individual therapy, with patient having been and at present in an ongoing couples relationship; (c) the individual's report of marital conflict as a problem; and (d) evidence of the partner's ability to tolerate interpersonal change without personality decompensation. Of these criteria, the first is the most important. To the extent that onset or variation in symptoms can be documented as associated with relationship stressors, the more marital therapy is appropriate.

Contraindications to marital therapy are any of the following: (a) a history of brief and/or unstable previous relationships that is attributable to a moderate or serious character disorder; (b) strong resistance on the part of the IP or her partner to marital therapy that would interfere with the development of a therapeutic working relationship; (c) evidence that the patient would benefit more from some other psychotherapeutic modality, at least in the short term. Patients with major personality dysfunction may receive more benefit from individual therapy. Such patients may benefit more, at least initially, from individual treatment aimed at aiding the patient in developing a more stable and positive introject and alternatives to self-destructive behavior as a method of dealing with stress. Patients involved in relatively stable, even if unsatisfactory, relationships, however, should be strongly considered as candidates for marital therapy, recognizing that the interpersonal and individual dysfunctions are highly likely to be functionally related. The third criterion is the one least likely to be met, given that, empirically, there is strong evidence for the efficacy of conjoint as contrasted with individual treatment for problems that are interpersonal in nature (Gurman & Kniskern, 1981). As noted, eating disorders are prototypic of interpersonal–systemic dysfunction (Minuchin, Rosman, & Baker, 1978; Selvini-Palazzoli, 1978).

In addition to determining whether marital therapy is the initial treatment of choice, consideration should also be given to whether and in what sequence individual and/of family-of-origin sessions may be appropriate in addition to the marital therapy. Individual therapy alone may be necessary for patients who present with extreme psychological deficits and little sense of identifiable conflict, patients with severe affective disorders, or patients in whom obsessiveness is so extreme as to constitute an obsessive–compulsive disorder. Such patients show little or no insight into the nature of the eating disorder, and much preoccupation with symptoms. A primary goal of such therapy would be to increase the individual's ability to identify affective states and describe them verbally. Psychotherapeutic medication may also be appropriate for some patients. Marital therapy in the above cases is best deferred until the person is more able to describe experiences in interpersonal terms. Such situations, however, will be rare even among hospitalized populations. If there is a question whether to recommend individual or marital therapy, the latter is generally preferable. Individual therapy may be sought by either spouse as an adjunct to marital therapy, and the spouse's rationale for the request may be explored in the marital sessions. Individual therapy may also be useful following completion of marital therapy, particularly if the partners decide to divorce.

Inclusion of the family or families of origin may benefit individuals who report continuing, frequent interactions with the family of origin. Those who may have achieved some separation from the family, but who have recently become more intensively involved (e.g., due to the death of a parent), are good candidates for family-of-origin sessions in addition to the marital therapy. Third, if there is a significant slowing of progress in marital therapy using conventional interventions, inclusion of the family of origin may prove helpful in providing a wider context of understanding for the couple's difficulties. A reasonable rule of thumb is that whenever there is an exacerbation of an individual's eating-disordered symptoms, detailed inquiry about any psychological precipitants and reevaluation of the current therapeutic regimen is in order. At such times, the decision may be to increase the frequency of the current treatment, adjunctively to add another kind of treatment, or to move to another (usually more inclusive) therapy modality exclusively.

Areas and Methods of Assessment

Assessment is directed to three major areas: (a) the symptomatic behavior, including an analysis of onset and changes in symptoms as a function of psychological events; (b) individual assessment, including psychiatric status and tentative psychodynamic formulation; and (c) marital and family functioning. The evaluation should also include medical evaluation of the patient's physical status. Critical to the assessment task is differential diagnosis regarding both symptomatology and intrapsychic–interpersonal functioning. Throughout the initial evaluation, both the structure of the assessment and the specific questions asked can be developed to emphasize to the patient the psychosomatic nature of the disorder. Beginning the assessment by interviewing the IP individually, for example, serves two functions. It gives a message both to the IP and to the spouse that the IP is a separate individual and that her medical status and initial opportunity to talk about her emotional and physical concerns are a matter between her and the staff. Second, it permits a more thorough and systematic psychological assessment of the individual's strengths and weaknesses individually, which can later be compared with her functioning in the marital dyad. Within the psychological assessment, such questions as, "What stresses or changes occurred at the time that you began having difficulties with [type of symptomatic behavior]?" or straightforward reflections of relationships between previously elicited information, such as, "So it appears that your eating problems were one way you had of dealing with your parents' divorce," aid in establishing the psychosomatic nature of the disorder.

Individual assessment begins with an evaluation of the patient's eating-disordered behavior. This inquiry may be helpful in corroborating the medical staff's assessment and aiding in differential diagnosis. It also facilitates the development of a therapeutic alliance by allowing the patient to talk about what is often the central issue around which the patient will admit strong feelings. The type and severity of the eating disorder has dispositional and prognostic implications, as discussed earlier. Age of onset, sex, duraction and severity of disorder, a history of previous treatment failure, premorbid psychological status, and the existence of psychiatric disorder in other family members have all been cited as factors associated with outcome (Garfinkel & Garner, 1982). Prognosis is more favorable, for example, for females than for males, for younger than for older IPs, for patients with relatively recent onset and no previous treatment history, for patients who are restricters rather than bulimic anorexics, and for patients with good premorbid functioning and no history of psychiatric disorder in other family members. As such, symptom assessment should be directed in detail to obtaining a history of the patient's symptoms, including (a) methods of weight control used (e.g., restrictive dieting, binge eating and vomiting, use of laxatives, diuretics, diet pills, excessive exercise); (b) frequency and duration of symptomatic behavior; (c) body image, including assessment of changes in the patient's menstrual pattern and her feelings about such changes and their potential consequences; (d) the patient's perception of the degree to which there is a serious illness; (e) any previous self-initiated change efforts and their results; and (f) any previous treatment history and outcome. The goal is to develop a reading of the type, severity, duration, and patient perception of the symptomatic behavior.

The transition to the assessment of the patient's psychological functioning can be effectively made by exploring the correlations between onset and/or changes in the symptomatic behavior and issues in the marital and family systems. Useful questions are, for example, what the patient hoped to change about herself at the onset of her symptoms, what changes had occurred in her life and especially in the marriage since the onset of her symptoms, which person expressed the greatest concern about the symptoms and how that concern was expressed, how the spouse had tried to "help" the IP regarding the symptom, and how the patient imagines the marital relationship would be different if the symptomatic behavior ceased. It is also often informative to ask the patient directly whether she views the symptom as serving some emotional function, and if so, what she construes that function to be. The individual assessment should also include exploration of the patient's range of affect, degree and manner of cognitive disturbance (particularly with regard to Beck's 1976 description of cognitive distortions), characteristic defenses, perception of self, extent and depth of peer relationships, and education–vocational competencies and involvement. An evaluation of the patient's psychiatric status and history should be obtained, as well as the psychiatric history of family members. Patients for whom there is evidence of an affective disorder may be referred for evaluation for psychopharmacological treatment adjunctively, especially in the light of recent data suggesting that some antidepressant medications may contribute to symptomatic improvement in bulimics (Hudson, Pope, & Jonas, 1983; Johnson, Stuckey, & Mitchell, 1983; Pope, Hudson, & Jonas, 1983; Pope, Hudson, Jonas, & Yurgelun-Todd, 1983; Walsh, Stewart, Wright, Harrison, Roose, & Glassman, 1982). A marital and family history should be obtained with the purpose of eliciting the patient's sense of similarities between her role in her family and her role in the marital relationship. Finally, the patient's motivation and capacity for insight may be evaluated by a brief trial therapy in which the patient's response to low-level interpretations is assessed. For example, the interviewer may seek to assess whether, in degree of specificity, the patient recognizes the eating disorder as a reflection of emotional conflicts, the patient views current emotional issues as centering on her relationship with her husband, and/or the patient views the symptom as her way of rejecting her role as dependent and helpless and seeks a more egalitarian relationship with her spouse.

In the marital assessment, the spouse is not informed of any of the specifics regarding the IP's assessment. The emphasis is on assessing the spouses' ability to disengage from a focus on the symptom and explore the function of the symptom in the context of their interactions. The questions suggested earlier regarding perceptions of associations between onset and exacerbation or other changes in the symptomatic behavior, and changes in the couple's relationship, may be addressed to the husband and to the couple together. Eliciting such perceptions on the part of the couple also provides the interviewer with an opportunity to observe the couple's interaction. These observations may be offered to the couple, and their responses noted. For example, spouses may address their comments exclusively to the interviewer, without communicating about the issue between themselves. They may also compete with each other for the therapist's attention by interruptions and disqualification of the other's reactions. Such behavior is an important source of hypotheses about the nature of the issues, of which the eating disorder may be a function. Particularly important is what happens, in terms of both the interaction process and the content of the couple's interaction, that is immediately followed by their return to a focus on the eating disorder as "the only problem" in their relationship. As in the individual interview, provisional hypotheses or trial interpretations are suggested to the couple. Their ability to respond both cognitively and affectively to such formulations about the conflicts in their relationship provides data about their likely initial responses to marital therapy. The couple's resistance at this point is complemented by the degree of distress they have experienced regarding the symptom and the relationship issues that have been denied through the symptom. The couple may thus show some understanding and relief because of their wish for change and their anticipation of help. The couple may temporarily disavow any such understanding once the IP is receiving help with the symptom, but this behavior usually responds to firm, straightforward, and warm confrontation.

To be most effective, the recommendation regarding marital therapy is made concurrent with recommendations for medical treatment. Depending on her physical status, hospitalization of the IP may be necessary. Regardless of whether the IP is to be managed medically on an outpatient or inpatient basis, the presence of both medical and psychological staff simultaneously during presentation of the recommendations regarding both medical and psychological treatment can be a powerful communication to the couple about the psychosomatic nature of the eating disorder.

AIMS AND TECHNIQUES IN MARITAL THERAPY WITH EATING-DISORDERED COUPLES

The usual therapeutic aims are fourfold: (a) to disengage the couple from their focus on the symptom; (b) to provide them with an opportunity for exploring other issues in the marital relationship that have been obscured by their attention to the symptom; (c) to allow the couple to decide whether they wish to work on effecting change on such issues; and (d) to offer the IP aid in symptom management.

In the psychosomatic marital relationship, interpersonal–systemic issues have become confounded with a focus on the symptom. As such, separation of the medical and psychological aspects of treatment is preferable as a way of establishing appropriate boundaries between psychological and somatic treatment foci. A nurse or physician experienced in the application of behavior modification principles with eating-disordered patients may provide symptom management in consultation with the therapist. The consultation may be useful in developing ways of tailoring the specific expectations and interventions with the IP to the particular needs and capabilities of the IP. Ongoing consultation between medical and psychological personnel also provides a gauge for assessing the effectiveness of marital therapy interventions.

The flexible use of a variety of therapeutic techniques is helpful and likely to be necessary. Structural, strategic, systemic, and behavioral techniques have all been reported to have demonstrated clinical efficacy with this population in family, and at times in individual, treatment. What is essential is that specific techniques be employed in the context of a relatively well developed conceptualization of the interpersonal conflicts in the marital relationship, and that the utility of the techniques be evaluated in the light of their ability to effect change in the basic interpersonal behavior and experience of the spouses. Although the conceptualization may evolve over the course of the therapy, it is important to recognize that the fundamental issues being negotiated by the couple are how they define themselves and the relationship; it is the impact of the interventions on these negotiations that will effect systemic change.

The strategy for intervention will differ depending on the "psychosomatic diagnosis" of the couple. For IPs who present with serious character disturbance, such as a borderline personality disorder, explicit written contracts may be useful, especially in the initial stages of therapy. Such contracts clarify not only the specific expectations involved in the patient's treatment but also provide a structure in which it is clear that the patient has a major responsibility for effecting change. Such contracts should include the frequency and type (marital) of sessions, the frequency and duration of the IP's contacts with the professional conducting the symptom management, expectations regarding both spouses' participation, and a statement about desired short-range goals. It is important with all couples, but especially with couples who may behave impulsively and attempt to split the treatment team, to emphasize that the medical–symptomatic and psychotherapeutic treatments are mutually contingent. Symptom management will not be offered without marital psychotherapy, and vice versa. With an extremely emotionally constricted couple, to go to the other end of the continuum, it may be important to allow for some "play" in the treatment plan. For example, in one highly rigid, emotionally reserved couple, the female IP stated that her parents would be visiting the following week, and the couple would therefore have to skip the next session. The therapist solemnly agreed that family responsibilities could be difficult. As such, the therapist recommended to the couple that they invite the wife's parents to attend the following session with them.

Treatment goals may also vary as a function of the assessment of the couple's strengths and deficits. In more severely disturbed couples, the eating disorder may represent a defense against marked turmoil and even decompensation. With such couples, a treatment goal may be to effect some change in simulus control regarding the symptom so that only a decrement or plateau to a less medically dangerous level would be effected. Maintenance of the symptom at that plateau may need to be sustained for some time before sufficient relationship change has occurred and enough other supports have been found to allow cessation of the symptoms. In well-integrated patients, firm expectations regarding relatively rapid symptom change may be developed parallel to the couple's ability more readily to make interpersonal–systemic change.

For the majority of couples with relatively midrange dysfunction, a useful strategy is to tailor the technique to the degree of observing ego or integrative capability in the spouses. Stated another way, the therapist may begin with fairly direct and "straight" interventions and progressively employ techniques developed for use with more resistant patients as the resistance is encountered in the therapy. For example, the therapist may begin by intervening with regard to the couple's communication behavior and proceed by attempting to elicit direct statements about what each spouse would like more of from the other (e.g., time together, talking about relationship issues). If serious resistance is met at this point, the therapist may proceed to direct the couple to explore some of the ways in which they have "agreed not to agree" with each other via their fundamental relationship "contract" (Sager, 1976). This may also allow the couple to be more "in charge" of their treatment (e.g., if the spouses are each asked to write their own contracts outside of sessions). If further resistance is met, the couple may be tacitly suggesting that it is difficult for them to work together as a couple and that their primary allegiances continue to be to their families of origin. Exploration of each spouse's experiences in the family of origin, and possibly including extended-family members in the sessions, may be useful.

Throughout the treatment, it is important for the therapist to foster a climate in which each spouse's autonomy and integrity are respected. Given that not only the IP but her spouse are likely to have come from families in which the dominant rule was that they meet others' expectations or fit some norm, firm limit setting regarding indirect, disqualifying, or mindreading communication, negative attributions from one spouse to another about the other's intentions, or appeals to the perceived authority of the therapist is important. The couple must be allowed to set the pace of their exploration, with room for fantasy and "play." Affective expression is crucial, within tolerable bounds. Positive connotation of each spouse's attempts to define his or her perception of self and needs from the relationship are important, recognizing that such expressions may be modified over time to more realistic and constructive ones. For many couples, if the isolation of affect is not too extreme, appeal to their cognitive capabilities, in terms of "willingness to engage in experimentation," may be a useful way to frame behavior-change efforts.

The specific interventions used by the therapist will differ depending on the type and severity of the IP's symptomatic behavior. With restricter couples, the therapist initially, clearly and firmly, should establish a focus on the couple's expression of their thoughts and feelings, and positively connote such expressions. Resistance in the early stages of therapy is likely to take the form of the couple's focusing on symptomatic behavior and attempts to elicit the therapist's expectations or prescriptions about what the couple "should" do. Such resistance should be identified and redirected to what ideas the couple have about how the therapy might be helpful to them. It is important positively to connote emotional expressions on the part of either spouse and to reflect feelings accurately. Moreover, it is important not to direct or "lead," for such patients have been likely to have been exquisitely sensitive to others' implicit demands, and to expect and reject mindreading on the part of significant others. Increasingly, the therapist encourages more specificity and elaboration of the spouses' thoughts and feelings about themselves as individuals and as a couple. As suggested earlier, if an apparent hiatus is reached, inclusion of one or both families of origin may aid not only in supplying additional information but also in prompting more immediacy in the spouses' experience of their hopes and disappointments for the marital relationship in the context of their experiences in their families. As the spouses become progressively more able to pinpoint inner states and communicate this to the spouse, the couple may resist any "heating up" of their interaction. At this point, more systemic interventions may be appropriate. For example, the therapist may summarize an interaction in which one spouse has been expressing anger about the other spouse's apparent reluctance to express affection by saying, "It appears that each of you is aware of a need for a balance between risk taking and trust in your relationship, and that each of you contributes in different ways toward this balance. I concur with your wise decision to go slowly in deciding how best to achieve this, and believe it is important for you to proceed carefully in making changes in this balance." Systemic interventions may be complemented at the latter stages of therapy by the therapist's straightforward reflections of his or her belief in the spouses' autonomy and ability to work through their feelings, perceptions, and behavior toward each other on their own. Criteria for termination include weight gain and maintenance and improvement in other symptomatic behavior on the part of the IP; increased autonomous functioning in terms of affect, cognition, and actual behavior on the part of both spouses, as manifested in the couple's development of more direct and unambiguous patterns of communication; their ability to disagree and resolve conflicts openly; an increase in the spouses' capacity for a wider range and intensity of affective experience and expression; the formation of more appropriate boundaries between the spouses and their families of origin; and each spouses's development of a stronger sense of self, more resourcefulness, experimentation, and increased self-efficacy. Often, although not necessarily, termination will be at the couple's initiation.

With bulimic couples, a more structured approach is helpful in order to aid the couple in containing and modulating the lability of affect and behavior. In couples in which there are multiple types of impulse or addictive disorders (e.g., alcoholism, stealing, physical and/or sexual abuse) or affective disorders, encouraging the couple to seek appropriate outside resources may be considered. The rationale for this recommendation is that while management of a patient's multiply symptomatic behaviors is certainly possible, the therapist is more able to confront the function of these behaviors effectively when their management is undertaken by professionals especially skilled in working with such disorders. Techniques useful in working with bulimic couples include, first, containing repetitive and escalating hostile exchanges by straightforwardly interrupting such interactions and pointing out their ineffectual character. Such interactions, characterized by hostile affect, belittling, and attack, and little resolution of any of the multiple conflicts raised, are highly typical in bulimic and bulimic anorexic couples, and are not productive. Direct teaching of alternative methods of coping with tension (e.g., relaxation training, time management) and regarding communication and problem-solving skills may be directed to the spouses both as individuals and as a couple. Not only useful in their own right, such interventions may also provide the couple with an increased behavioral repertoire and sense of effectiveness in exploring the interpersonal function that their symptoms and dysfunctional interactional behavior have had. Bulimic couples may also benefit from interventions confronting discrepancies between affect and behavior, or what is said and what is done. While verbally spouses may request fewer attempts to manage each other's behavior, their dysfunctional behavior often constitutes an implicit request to be taken care of. Such discrepancies may be systemically construed as the spouses' attempts to learn how autonomously to request nuturance from each other.

While eating-disordered couples have in common dysfunction in the area of separation–individuation, they tend to differ in how such conflicts are expressed, with restricters more likely to behave interpersonally in a hostile, withdrawn, conflict-avoiding manner, and bulimic or bulimic anorexics with openly hostile, repetitive interactions with little conflict resolution. Such differences are illustrated in several cases below.

Case 1

> Denise presented as a 36-year-old married woman with a 7-year history of weight loss by restricting. At the time of her initial clinic evaluation, she exhibited severe malnutrition and weighed 69 pounds. The IP had previously been involved in individual therapy, without significant change. Assessment of the marital relationship revealed that the couple's interaction was virtually centered on issues related to the IP's symptoms. There was no evidence of affective disorder or severe personality disorder in either partner. The recommendation was for weekly marital therapy, and strict contingencies for the IP's weight gain were made to test her ability to make progress on an outpatient basis.

The spouses agreed to engage in marital therapy. The IP showed relatively rapid initial weight gain, which was monitored by a nurse; weight plateaued after approximately 8 months. Given that the systemic function of the symptom was difficult to identify initially, sessions were focused on each of the spouse's roles in their families of origin, and their models for their own marriage.

> The IP reported a lack of expression of affection in her family and described her mother as highly overtly controlling. The IP had lost weight and become

amenorrheic at age 22, following her sister's marriage. The husband had experienced a serious depression following the death of his father when the husband was 16 years old. The husband had felt obligated to adopt a caretaking role vis-à-vis his mother, and his adolescent experiences were curtailed during his final 2 years of high school as a result. He continued to live at home and take care of his mother during his first year of college, attending a nearby university. He decided to move away from home for the remainder of college, and became progressively less interpersonally isolated and less depressed. When the couple met, the husband admired Denise's independence, and she sought from him the nurturance and affection she felt she had been unable to receive from her own family. Denise married Paul against the wishes of her family, and particularly against her father's strong objections.

Initially seen biweekly due to the couples' protestations about other commitments, the sessions were increased to a weekly frequency to aid the couple in containing and directing the emerging experiences. After several months of therapy focusing on family-of-origin issues, the couple became increasingly willing to explore marital issues. The husband appeared to seek a highly symbiotic union in which both spouses' individuality was submerged with "the marriage." At the same time he had a controlling influence on the relationship, particularly regarding an issue that emerged only after several months of therapy. The couple revealed that the husband had a strong wish for children, about which the wife was highly ambivalent. Her weight loss and amenorrhea had effectively temporarily obviated the issue of children. The wife's fears about becoming pregnant covaried with a plateau in weight gain. When this issue was confronted, and an explicit contract regarding the couple's treatment goals made, the wife made some initial improvement, then had an accident in which she fractured her hip. She thus returned to a sick role, allowing her husband to engage in caretaking.

Subsequently, the couple became increasingly able to express feelings about relationship issues, including the issue of children. It became increasingly apparent to the IP that she had maintained her role as the "good daughter" that had interfered with her efforts in developing the marital relationship. Her concern was that she might move from being the "good daughter" to being the "good wife."

As of this writing, the couple continue to be actively engaged in marital therapy. The wife has increased her weight to 109 pounds, and has been able to maintain at that weight. Both Denise and Paul struggled with depressed feelings regarding the loss of an ideal relationship. While they question the viability of the marriage, their efforts are directed to developing a more realistic and more satisfying marital relationship.

Case 2

Joanna came to the initial assessment at the clinic unaccompanied. She presented as a 26-year-old married female with a 5-year history of binging with laxative abuse and occasional diuretic use. At age 11 she had lost 40 pounds in 3 months, followed by weight gain, but weight fluctuations occurred during alternating periods of restricting and overeating. She previously had attended a weight-loss clinic, which she had not found helpful. She had also been involved in psychotherapy following her father's death a few years prior.

The patient was initially seen for individual psychotherapy as well as symptom management contacts, given that family-of-origin issues seemed more prominent than marital ones. The patient had been quite attached to her father, and felt much guilt about individuating regarding what had been an overly close relationship. She also reported guilt about not having lived up to his unrealistically high expectations of her. The patient had also been intensely competitive with her sisters.

As the patient achieved more emotional separation from her family of origin, she increasingly voiced dissatisfaction with her marriage. Couples therapy was initiated, and both spouses agreed to this recommendation. The individual therapist (female) added a male co-therapist to the treatment team. The couple had met and decided to be married during the period of Joanna's father's illness. Joanna had become reliant on her husband, but felt a lack of emotionality in their relationship. Communication training and attempts to elicit from each spouse what was wanted from the other (modified Ps and Ds) were conducted, as well as exploration of the couple's roles and expectations within the larger family system. Joanna had become asymptomatic at this point, and concomitantly voiced strong feelings about the unsatisfactory nature of the relationship, particularly regarding sexuality issues. The couple agreed to separate. The families of origin were invited, and in spite of strong disapproval on the part of her family, Joanna proceeded with a divorce. Follow-up individual sessions were offered to each spouse. David terminated therapy after a few sessions; Joanna continued individual therapy for several months. She developed more extensive friendships with both men and women, and became involved in a heterosexual relationship that she regarded as satisfying. Joanna completed a professional degree with honors and found a job that she viewed as befitting her level of competence. She successfully terminated therapy after 15 months from the time of intake.

Case 3

Mary presented as a 27-year-old married female with a 5-year history of weight fluctuations, binging and vomiting, laxative, diet pill, and alcohol abuse. Frequency of binging and vomiting was 5 to 6 days per week, up to 4 times per day. Onset of the symptomatic behavior reportedly occurred during a period when Mary's supervisor in a training program was, in Mary's view, highly critical of her. The patient was referred to the clinic by her previous individual therapist, who after working with Mary for over a year felt that no significant change had been effected.

Mary came across like a young girl, speaking distractedly in a high-pitched voice. She was frequently self-deprecating and yet seemed eager to please. She was strikingly obsessive, perfectionist, and reported much compulsive behavior. A previous trial of antidepressant medication had been unsuccessful in modifying either her mood or her eating-disordered symptoms.

Mary had been married shortly after graduation from college and reported an acrimonious relationship with her husband. Their sexual relationship was infrequent and unsatisfying. Mary seemed to adopt a role of deference and submission to her husband but was covertly highly critical of him. He expressed a willingness to "do whatever was necessary to help Mary." Given the previous unsuccessful individual therapy and the reported marital concerns, weekly marital therapy and symptom management contacts were recommended.

The couple were seen for approximately a year by a male–female co-therapy team. A variety of techniques, including behavioral and strategic interventions, were used within a predominantly interpersonally oriented conceptual framework. The husband, a hardworking dentist, denied any personal conflicts and viewed the marital discord as primarily stemming from the IP's symptoms. His belief was that if the symptoms ceased, the relationship would improve considerably. Mary, who had discontinued working in a teaching position and become involved in managing her husband's office, overtly sought support and direction from her husband but covertly was intensively engaged in power struggles with him both at work and at home. Mary increasingly reported sexual associations to her symptomatic behavior, and "flirted" when at social functions with other men. The husband grew increasingly frustrated in the sessions, and Mary requested individual therapy. At the time of this writing, Mary has shown a marked reduction of symptoms, although she still exhibits eating-disordered behavior. Marital issues continue to be voiced by Mary, although she continues her individual treatment and shows some improvement.

As suggested in the above examples, change is not accomplished quickly. Significant interpersonal–systemic change may require a year or more of weekly couples sessions, although session frequency may be decreased as the couple become more able to take on the interpersonal issues on their own.

Therapist characteristics important in working with such couples are interpersonal flexibility and the ability to use a variety of specific techniques within the context of a solid conceptual foundation. Setbacks and plateaus in couples work must be tolerated. Experience in working with adolescents may provide a basis for understanding the interpersonal function of the symptomatic behaviors. The ability to work from a team approach may also be helpful with some patients, especially if hospitalization is required.

While marital therapy has been demonstrated clinically to be useful with eating-disordered couples, as yet there has been no empirical controlled-outcome research on the efficacy of marital as compared with other treatments for eating-disordered patients. Such research is needed, and would constitute an important contribution to the literature.

ACKNOWLEDGMENT

The author would like to thank Drs. Nadine Kaslow and Randy Flanery for providing some of the case examples.

REFERENCES

Beck, A. T. (1976). *Cognitive therapy and the emotional disorders*. New York: International Universities Press.

Boskind-White, M., & White, W. C. (1983). *Bulimarexia: The binge/purge cycle*. New York: Norton.

Bruch, H. (1973). *Eating disorders*. New York: Basic Books.

Cantwell, D. P., Sturzenberger, S., Burroughs, J., Salkin, B., & Green, J. K. (1977). Anorexia nervosa: An affective disorder? *Archives of General Psychiatry, 34*, 1087–1093.

Casper, R. C., Eckert, E. D., Halmi, K. A., Goldberg, S. C., & Davis, J. M. (1980). Bulimia: Its incidence and clinical importance in patients with anorexia nervosa. *Archives of General Psychiatry, 37*, 1030–1034.

Crisp, A. H. (1970). Diagnosis and outcome of anorexia nervosa: The St. George's view. *Proceedings of the Royal Society of Medicine, 70*, 464–470.

Crisp, A. H. (1980). *Anorexia nervosa: Let me be*. London: Academic Press.

Crisp, A. H., Kalucy, R. S., Lacey, J. H., & Harding, B. (1977). The long-term prognosis in anorexia nervosa: Some factors predictive of outcome. In R. Vigersky (Ed.), *Anorexia nervosa* (pp. 55–65) New York: Raven Press.

Dally, P. (1969). *Anorexia nervosa*. New York: Grune & Stratton.

Duddle, M. (1973). An increase of anorexia nervosa in a university population. *British Journal of Psychiatry, 123*, 711–712.

Fries, H. (1977). Studies on secondary amenorrhea, anorectic behaviour, and body image perception: Importance for the early recognition of anorexia nervosa. In R. Vigersky (Ed.), *Anorexia nervosa*. New York: Raven Press.

Garfinkel, P. E., & Garner, D. M. (1982). *Anorexia nervosa: A multidimensional perspective*. New York: Brunner/Mazel.

Garfinkel, P. E., Moldofsky, H., & Garner, D. M. (1977). The outcome of anorexia nervosa: Significance of clinical features, body image and behavior modifications (pp. 315–329). In R. Vigersky (Ed.), *Anorexia nervosa*. New York: Raven Press.

Garfinkel, P. E., Moldofsky, H., & Garner, D. M. (1980). The heterogeneity of anorexia nervosa. *Archives of General Psychiatry, 37*, 1036–1040.

Garrow, J. S., Crisp, A. H., Jordan, H. A., Meyer, J. E., Russell, G. F. M., Silverstone, T., Stunkard, A. J., & Van Itallie, T. B. (1975). Pathology of eating, group report. In T. Silverstone (Ed.), *Dahlem Konferenzen*, Life Sciences Research Report 2. Berlin.

Goetz, P. L., Succop, R. A., Reinhart, J. B., & Miller, A. (1977). Anorexia nervosa in children: A follow-up study. *American Journal of Orthopsychiatry, 47*, 597–603.

Gurman, A. S., & Kniskern, D. P., (1981). Family therapy outcome research: Knowns and unknowns. In A. S. Gurman & D. P. Kniskern (Eds.), *Handbook of family therapy*. New York: Brunner/Mazel.

Halmi, K. A. (1974). Anorexia nervosa: Demographic and clinical features in 94 cases. *Psychosomatic Medicine, 36*, 18–25.

Halmi. K. A., Falk, J. R., & Schwartz, E. (1981). Binge-eating and vomiting: A survey of a college population. *Psychological Medicine, 11,* 607–706.

Halmi, K. A., & Loney, J. (1973). Familial alcoholism in anorexia nervosa. *British Journal of Psychiatry, 123,* 53–54.

Hsu, L. K. G. (1980). Outcome of anorexia nervosa. *Archives of General Psychiatry, 37,* 1041–1048.

Hsu, L. K. G., Crisp, A., & Harding, B. (1979). Outcome of anorexia nervosa. *Lancet, 1,* 61–65.

Hudson, J. I., Pope, H. G., & Jonas, J. M. (1983). Treatment of bulimia with antidepressants: Theoretical considerations and clinical findings. *Psychiatric Annals, 13,* 965–969.

Johnson, C., Stuckey, M., & Mitchell, J. (1983). Psychopharmacological treatment of anorexia nervosa and bulimia: Review and synthesis. *Journal of Nervous and Mental Disease, 171,* 524–534.

Jones, D. J., Fox, M. M., Babigan, H. M., & Hutton, H. E. (1980). Epidemiology of anorexia nervosa in Monroe County, New York: 1960–1976. *Psychosomatic Medicine, 42,* 551–558.

Kalucy, R. S., Crisp, A. H., & Harding, B. (1977). A study of 56 families with anorexia nervosa. *British Journal of Medical Psychology, 50,* 381–395.

Kendell, R. E., Hall, D. J., Hailey, A., & Babigan, H. M. (1973). The epidemiology of anorexia nervosa. *Psychological Medicine, 3,* 200–203.

Madanes, C. (1981). *Strategic family therapy.* San Francisco: Jossey-Bass.

Minuchin, S., Rosman, B. L., & Baker, L. (1978). *Psychosomatic families: Anorexia nervosa in context.* Cambridge, MA: Harvard University Press.

Morgan, H. G., & Russell, G. F. M. (1975). Value of family backround and clinical features as predictors of long-term outcome in anorexia nervosa: Four-year follow-up study of 41 patients. *Psychological Medicine, 5,* 355–372.

Pertschuk, M. J. (1977). Behavior therapy: Extended follow-up (pp. 305–314). In R. Vigersky (Ed.), *Anorexia nervosa.* New York: Raven Press.

Pope, H. G., Hudson, J. I., & Jonas, J. M. (1983). Antidepressant treatment of bulimia: Preliminary experience and practical recommendations. *Journal of Clinical Psychopharmacology, 3,* 274–281.

Pope, H. G., Hudson, J. I., Jonas, J. M., & Yurgelun-Todd, D. (1983). Bulimia treated with imipramine: A placebo-controlled, double-blind study. *American Journal of Psychiatry, 140,* 554–558.

Pyle, R. L., Mitchell, J. E., & Eckert, E. D. (1981). Bulimia: A report of 34 cases. *Journal of Clinical Psychiatry, 42,* 60–64.

Russell, G. F. M. (1970). Anorexia nervosa: Its identity as an illness and its treatment. In J. H. Price (Ed.), *Modern trends in psychological medicine* (Vol. 2). London: Butterworths.

Russell, G. F. M. (1979). Bulimia nervosa: An ominous variant of anorexia nervosa. *Psychological Medicine, 9,* 429–448.

Sager, C. J. (1976). *Marriage contracts and couple therapy.* New York: Brunner/Mazel.

Schwartz, R. C., Barrett, M. J., & Saba, G. Family therapy for bulimia. Paper presented at the annual conference of the American Association for Marriage and Family Therapy, Washington, D.C., October, 1983.

Selvini-Palazzoli, M. (1978). *Self-starvation: From individual to family therapy in the treatment of anorexia nervosa.* New York: Jason Aronson.

Sours, J. A. (1969). Anorexia nervosa: Nosology, diagnosis, developmental patterns, and power control dynamics (pp. 185–212). In G. Kaplan and L. Levovivi (Eds.), *Adolescence: Psychosocial perspectives.* New York: Basic Books.

Strober, M., Salkin, B., Burroughs, J., & Morrell, W. (1982). Validity of the bulimia-restricter distinction in anorexia nervosa. *Journal of Nervous and Mental Disease, 170,* 345–351.

Swift, W. J., & Stern, S. (1982). The psychodynamic diversity of anorexia nervosa. *International Journal of Eating Disorders, 2,* 17–35.

Theander, S. (1970). Anorexia nervosa: A psychiatric investigation of 94 female patients. *Acta Psychiatry Scandanavia* (Suppl.), *214,* 1–194.

Walsh, B. T., Stewart, J. T., Wright, L., Harrison, W., Roose, S. P., & Glassman, A. H. (1982). Treatment of bulimia with monoamine oxidase inhibitors. *American Journal of Psychiatry, 139,* 1629–1630.

Winnicot, D. W. (1965). Ego distortion in terms of true and false self (pp. 140–152). In *The maturational process and the facilitating environment.* New York: International Universities Press.

Winokur, A., March, V., & Mendels, J. (1980). Primary affective disorder in relatives of patients with anorexia nervosa. *American Journal of Psychiatry, 137,* 695–698.

V

SPECIAL ISSUES

The Effectiveness of Marital Therapy: Current Status and Application to the Clinical Setting

27

DONALD H. BAUCOM
JEFFREY A. HOFFMAN

Attempting to understand marital discord and assisting distressed couples are challenging tasks. The therapist and investigator are presented with two people who are unique individuals. Together they form a marital unit that appears different from the sum of the two people, and as a married couple, they are a part of a larger family system. As evidenced by the preceding chapters in this volume, numerous conceptualizations of marital discord and treatment interventions have been developed. These conceptualizations have implications for empirical investigations, including how the unit of analysis is defined (e.g., each spouse separately, the couple as a unit); whether data from husbands and wives are combined and if so, how; and what dependent variables are believed to be worthy of investigation. These complexities, in addition to the difficulties inherent in conducting any treatment-outcome research, have resulted in reluctance among many marital therapists to evaluate the effectiveness of their procedures.

In spite of these difficulties, within the past few years there has been a major thrust in the empirical evaluation of the effectiveness of marital therapy. This attempt has been led primarily by the proponents of behavioral marital therapy (BMT), but advocates from other theoretical orientations are also beginning to evaluate systematically the effectiveness of their treatments. The purpose of this chapter is twofold: first, to summarize and evaluate the current empirical status regarding the effectiveness of different approaches to marital therapy; and second, to provide suggestions as to how clinicians

Donald H. Baucom and Jeffrey A. Hoffman. Department of Psychology, University of North Carolina, Chapel Hill, North Carolina.

might more effectively evaluate the effectiveness of marital therapy in applied contexts.

A number of articles have been published that evaluate the effectiveness of marital therapy. Some of these reviews have been impressively exhaustive, including results from numerous unpublished dissertations and "hard to locate" papers (e.g., Gurman & Kniskern, 1978). (In fact, there is now a well-written article that reviews the other review articles [Williams & Miller, 1981]!) The current chapter includes a number of recent studies unavailable at the time of previous reviews and focuses only on evaluating rather well controlled outcome investigations. By "well controlled," we mean that the investigations must at least contain the appropriate comparison groups to allow for a test of the investigators' hypotheses, as well as random assignment of couples to treatment conditions. Further, they must define the content of the treatment; for example, we question the utility of investigations that compare the relative effectiveness of conjoint marital versus conjoint-group marital therapy when the content of the treatment is unknown. Moreover, although marital enrichment programs are being recognized for their potential preventive effects and the increased quality of life they may provide to married persons (Markman, 1984), the current review focuses solely on the treatment of distressed couples. And since the focus of the chapter is to evaluate the effectiveness of treatment as it might actually be applied to distressed couples, analogue studies based on short treatment unrepresentative of clinical practice (four treatment sessions and under) are not considered. Finally, the review is limited to treatments designed to have applicability to a broad range of maritally distressed couples and does not include treatments designed for more focal concerns, such as particular sexual dysfunctions.

At present, the most popular frameworks for conceptualizing and treating marital distress include (a) behavioral; (b) systems; (c) psychodynamic; (d) communication; (e) cognitive; and (f) experiential approaches. The current review evaluates the empirical status of each of these orientations. Unfortunately, there is very little research on the systems, psychodynamic, cognitive, and experiential approaches, and the few studies evaluating these treatments were typically conducted by investigators from behavioral and communication orientations. Consequently, few conclusions regarding the relative effectiveness of these four approaches can be drawn.

BEHAVIORAL MARITAL THERAPY

By far the majority of controlled-outcome investigations in marital therapy have involved BMT. In the late 1960s and early 1970s, BMT treatment programs were developed by the Oregon group (Patterson & Hops, 1972; Patterson, Hops, & Weiss, 1975; Weiss, Hops, & Patterson, 1973), by Stuart (1969a, 1969b), and by Azrin, Naster, and Jones (1973). The initial findings were encouraging and thus set the stage for a number of subsequent controlled investigations that have focused on various issues: (a) the effectiveness of BMT versus a waiting-list control group; (b) the effectiveness of BMT versus a nonspecific treatment condition; (c) the relative effectiveness of different BMT treatments; (d) the impact of varying noncontent parameters of BMT such as single versus co-therapists; (e) the magnitude of relationship change produced by BMT; (f) the predictors of treatment effectiveness; and (g) the relative effectiveness of BMT versus other orientations to marital therapy.

Baucom (1983) has proposed a two-stage approach for assessing the effects of skills-oriented marital therapies. First, one may ask whether couples learn and implement the specific skills and behavior changes taught in treatment. Second, one can assess whether learning these skills led to changes in marital adjustment or satisfaction. In order to address these issues directly, correlations between changes in specific skill areas and relationship adjustment would need to be provided. This information would allow us to know whether learning skills and changing specific behaviors are related to changes in relationship adjustment. Unfortunately, such correlations are not provided in the literature. Therefore these issues are addressed as follows:

1. Does a treatment group learn specific skills?
2. Does the group alter specific behaviors, including presenting problems?
3. Does the group report overall change in relationship adjustment?

The various issues explored in BMT are assessed according to these questions. Consequently, some dependent measures included by investigators but not focal to these issues are not included in this evaluation.

BMT versus Waiting-List Couples

The primary skills taught to couples in BMT are (a) communication and problem solving;[1] and (b) behavior change, usually based on contracts. In the eight investigations that taught communication skills and provided direct behavioral observation measures of communication, all but two (O'Farrell, Cutter, & Floyd, 1983; Turkewitz & O'Leary, 1981) demonstrated a significant decrease in frequency of negative communication, such as complaining and criticizing, relative to the waiting list (WL). However, teaching distressed couples to increase positive communications (e.g., accepting responsibility, offering problem solutions) appears to be much more difficult. Among these same studies, only Jacobson (1977, 1978a) has *consistently* demonstrated an increase in positive communication for BMT relative to WL couples.

1. The communication skills typically taught in BMT have been oriented toward assisting the spouses to become more efficient problem solvers. This focus is somewhat different from "communication" therapies in which expression of emotion and listening skills are the focus of attention.

Other investigators either have found no changes in positive communication relative to WL couples (Hahlweg, Schindler, Revenstorf, & Brengelmann, 1984; Turkewitz & O'Leary, 1981) or have obtained mixed results (Baucom, 1982; Baucom & Lester, 1982; Mehlman, Baucom, & Anderson, 1983; O'Farrell et al., 1983).

BMT has also focused on behavior change in areas other than communication that the couple view as problematic for the marriage (i.e., presenting complaints); these concerns have typically been assessed through self-report questionnaires. Of the 10 investigations that include such data (Baucom, 1982; Baucom & Lester, 1982; Boelens, Emmelkamp, MacGillavry, & Makvoort, 1980; Ewart, 1978a; Girodo, Stein, & Dotzenroth, 1980; Hahlweg et al., 1984; Jacobson, 1984; Johnson & Greenberg, 1984; Mehlman et al., 1983, O'Farrell et al., 1983), all but two (Girodo et al., 1980; O'Farrell et al., 1983) indicate that BMT resulted in a significant decrease in reported problem areas or requests for behavior change relative to WL.

Finally, on self-report measures of marital adjustment (in the United States, the Marital Adjustment Scale [MAS, Locke & Wallace, 1959] and the Dyadic Adjustment Scale [DAS, Spanier, 1976] have typically been employed), 10 of the 13 BMT investigations indicated significantly increased marital adjustment relative to WL; in addition, Ewart (1978b) found that distressed wives, but not husbands, showed increased marital adjustment relative to WL.

In summary relative to WL couples, couples receiving BMT show decreases in negative communication assessed in the therapy setting, decreases in reported problem areas and requests for behavior change, and increases in overall marital adjustment. The predominant lack of change in positive communication is a source of concern, since behavioral marital therapists certainly want couples to communicate with each other in more positive ways. This inconsistent change in positive communication could result from the observational coding systems employed (see Baucom & Adams, in press, for a discussion of current coding systems and assessment of communication), but the lack of change has been found using different coding systems. From our own treatment studies and our knowledge of others' studies, we believe that the treatment is at least in part responsible for this finding. The communication skills taught are generally aimed at problem solving. Thus, a number of destructive communications that interfere with the process often tend to be emphasized (e.g., couples must not interrupt, become sidetracked, blame). It is easier to teach couples to eliminate these behaviors than to force couples to say positive things to each other while problem solving (e.g., compliment, agree, accept responsibility). In order to have meaning, many positive communications must be spontaneous, emerging from the person's internal thoughts and feelings about the partner or the topic; however, the therapist can almost always find a legitimate basis for altering specific negative communications.

BMT versus Attention and Nonspecific Control Groups

Three investigations have compared the effectiveness of BMT to marital therapy not emanating from a specific theoretical orientation (Azrin, Besalel, Bechtel, Michalicek, Mancera, Carroll, Shuford, & Cox, 1980; Crowe, 1978; Jacobson, 1978a). The purpose of these latter treatment conditions has been to serve as a control for receiving treatment and focusing on problem areas. In these nonspecific treatments (Jacobson & Baucom, 1977), couples have typically been encouraged to discuss their problems, express their feelings and attitudes, and explore solutions; however, couples are not taught specific behavioral skills or guidelines. Jacobson (1978a) provided the only data on behavioral observations of communication and found that BMT was superior to the nonspecific treatment on observational measures of communication. In terms of problem checklists and presenting complaints, Azrin *et al.* and Crowe found BMT to be superior to the nonspecific treatments at posttest, and Crowe noted these differences continued at follow-up. However, the findings with regard to group differences in marital adjustment and happiness are mixed. Azrin found significant group differences favoring behavioral treatment at posttest. Jacobson obtained similar findings that continued at follow-up on one self-report of marital satisfaction; however, on another self-report of marital happiness, there was no difference between treatments. Crowe found no between-group differences at posttest, but the behavioral treatment was superior during some follow-up periods.

Overall, the superiority of BMT over nonspecific and attention control groups is equivocal. Based on limited findings, BMT has been found to be more effective than nonspecific treatments in altering communication and other specific behaviors of concern to the couple. However, these specific changes did not consistently result in greater increase in marital adjustment and happiness than a nonspecific treatment.

Relative Effectiveness of Different BMT Treatments and Components

BMT usually consists of more than one treatment procedure. Several investigations have been conducted to determine (*a*) the most effective multiple component treatment; (*b*) the relative effectiveness of specific treatment components; and (*c*) the order in which the treatment components should be presented. In the first sizable outcome study of BMT, Jacobson (1978a) compared two BMT treatment approaches that differed only in type of contingency contracting: (*a*) communication–problem solving followed by good-faith contracting; (*b*) communication–problem solving followed by *quid pro quo* contracting. Contracting involves the use of contingencies for behavior change. In *quid pro quo* contracting, the contingent reward for a change in one spouse's behavior is a change in the other person's behavior. In good-faith contracting, the reward for a behavior change is some outside reinforcer, not a behavior change by the partner. Both treatments were effective but did not differ from each other on communication changes or reported marital satisfaction, the latter also evaluated at follow-up. Jacobson questioned whether the contracting component was of use. Later, questions were raised regarding the usefulness of contracting unless it is preceded by communication training (Liberman, Levine, Wheeler, Sanders, & Wallace, 1976) or whether contracting might actually be destructive (Jacobson, 1978b). Subsequent investigations indicated that contingency contracting is an effective treatment strategy in producing behavior change. Ewart (1978a) found that when preceded by communication training, goal setting (without contingencies), good-faith, and *quid pro quo* contracts produced meaningful targeted behavior change beyond that produced by the communication training, and all three strategies were equally effective in producing behavior change. Furthermore, the couples stated that they enjoyed the contracting and valued it. However, husbands did not report increased marital satisfaction, and only some of the wives showed significant increases in marital adjustment (i.e., those for whom contingencies were involved in the contracting). Further support for contingency contracting was found by Emmelkamp, van der Helm, MacGillavry, and van Zanten (1984) in a cross over design comparing contracting followed by communication–problem-solving training with communication–problem-solving training followed by contracting. Each treatment component was equally effective in altering targeted problems and marital satisfaction; order did not matter.

An additional strategy has been to conduct treatment component investigations in which some couples receive only one treatment component. (The largest BMT outcome investigation conducted to date is a component study [Hahlweg *et al.*, 1984]; however, since the results are dependent on treatment format, they are discussed in a later section.) Baucom (1982) compared the effectiveness of (*a*) communication–problem-solving alone; (*b*) *quid pro quo* contracting alone; and (*c*) communication–problem-solving plus contracting. Jacobson (1984) has conducted a similar comparison that used a behavior exchange component with no contingencies, rather than *quid pro quo* contracts. Both investigations found the treatments to be effective but essentially no between-group differences at posttest on self-reported requests for behavior change and marital adjustment. Baucom also found the three active treatments did not differ from each other on communication changes. Whereas Baucom reported no significant differences between the groups at follow-up, Jacobson found trends indicating that couples receiving behavior exchange only were deteriorating at follow-up.

In summary, the findings overall do not support major differences in the effectiveness of different BMT treatment procedures when used as a combined package, when used in isolation, or when the order of presentation is varied. The appropriate use of contracting in BMT is unclear. Several investigations have found that couples treated with contracting alone or in combination with other treatment procedures improve; on the other hand, Jacobson's

1984 findings question the permanence of such changes. Our clinical observations are that some couples find contracting appealing and helpful, and other couples do not like or benefit from contracting. Thus far, however, no studies have been conducted to validate this observation or identify which couples might profit from contracting.

Effects of Altering Noncontent Parameters of BMT

In addition to changing the content of treatment, investigators have evaluated the effects of other treatment characteristics. Two broad noncontent parameters of BMT treatment have been investigated: (a) who will be present at a treatment session; and (b) the timing of the treatment. Regarding who will be present, much has been written extolling the potential merits of co-therapists in treating a distressed couple (e.g., Bellville, Raths, & Bellville, 1969). However, in treating distressed couples with BMT, Mehlman et al. (1983) found no significant differences between a single therapist and two co-therapists in helping couples alter requested behavior change, observed communication, and marital adjustment at posttest or follow-up.

The effects of altering the number of distressed spouses present has also been investigated. Hahlweg et al. compared the effectiveness of BMT in conjoint therapy (one couple present) with conjoint-group therapy (several couples present). They used (a) a communication component (CT) of a BMT treatment package; and (b) a broader BMT treatment, which in addition included positive reciprocity training, problem solving, contracting without contingencies, and crisis management. BMT in both formats was successful in altering presenting problems, observed communication, and marital satisfaction. Conjoint BMT was superior to conjoint-group BMT in producing improvement in the couples' self-report of relationship problems and general happiness with the relationship.

Bennun (Bennun, Margolin, & Christensen, 1983) has also compared conjoint BMT with conjoint-group BMT. In addition, he developed a behavioral marital treatment in which only one spouse received treatment. All three treatments reduced targeted problems and increased marital adjustment, but there were no significant differences between treatments on these measures.

The second major parameter investigated thus far deals with the timing for providing BMT. Because of limitations on professional time in applied settings, couples are often placed on a waiting list; similarly in research settings, a waiting-list condition usually serves as a control group. It is important to know whether having couples wait for several months alters the effectiveness of treatment once it is provided. Mehlman et al. (1983) found that, in terms of behavior change requested, observed communication, and marital adjustment, there were no significant differences between couples receiving BMT immediately after requesting treatment compared to couples who received BMT after being placed on a 10-week waiting list.

Overall, manipulating these treatment parameters did not meaningfully alter the impact of BMT. However, at this time, we do not know if other noncontent parameters might boost treatment effectiveness.

Magnitude of Change Produced by BMT

The investigations discussed thus far indicate that BMT is effective in statistically significantly reducing requests for behavior change, altering at least some aspects of communication and increasing marital adjustment. However, these results are limited in describing the magnitude of change that has occurred and the percentage of couples responding to treatment. Recently, additional analyses have been conducted to provide supplementary information regarding degree of change in the couples. Hahlweg and Markman (1983) submitted the findings of 17 BMT outcome investigations to meta-analysis using the "effect-size" method introduced by Smith and Glass (1977). For a given dependent measure, the effect size is equal to the mean difference between the treated and control couples after therapy divided by the standard deviation of the control couples. Thus an effect size of one would indicate that the mean of the treated couples was one standard deviation above the mean of the control couples. The 81 dependent measures within the 17 studies showed an average effect size of 0.92. Assuming a normal distribution of scores, these findings suggest that the average couple receiving BMT was more improved than 82% of the couples receiving either no treatment or nonspecific treatment. The findings also indicate that the changes were essentially identical for both self-report and observational measures and that the effect size remained stable during follow-up.

While providing useful information, the effect-size data presented thus far do not clarify whether the changes produced by therapy are "clinically significant" or meaningful in magnitude. One way to seek such data is to determine the extent to which couples move from the distressed to the nondistressed category in their self-reported marital adjustment. Using a rounded-off cutoff score of 100 on the MAS and 92 on the DAS, there are nine investigations which use the standard versions of these scales, present mean group scores, and have pretest means in the distressed range. Of these, only four studies showed BMT posttest means in the nondistressed range, and three of these are from the same investigator (Jacobson 1977, 1978a, 1984; O'Farrell *et al.*, 1983). The remaining five studies have mean posttest scores in the distressed range; two additional studies, which did not report group means, did state that BMT did not increase MAS and DAS scores more than a waiting-list condition. Consequently, based on mean marital adjustment scores, results suggest that a substantial proportion of couples are still distressed at the end of BMT and that this finding is common across a number of settings where BMT has been employed. Additional effect-size analyses corroborate this conclusion (Hahlweg & Markman, 1983).

In order to examine this issue further, Jacobson, Follette, Revenstorf, Baucom, Hahlweg, and Margolin (in press) reanalyzed the data from four previous BMT outcome investigations to evaluate more precisely the percentage of couples moving from the distressed to nondistressed range based on self-reported marital adjustment scores. Taking the reliability of the marital adjustment measures into account, this rather stringent criterion indicated that 60–65% of the couples either remained somewhat distressed or failed to change during treatment. During follow-up, approximately 10% of the couples showed further improvement compared to posttherapy marital adjustment, while the others either remained relatively stationery (two-thirds of the couples) or experienced relapse (18.1%).

It should be noted that the criteria used in this reanalysis are quite stringent, and the results should not be compared to improvement rates using other criteria. Still, *the mean posttherapy marital adjustment scores and the estimates of the percentage of couples satisfied with their marriages after treatment are consistent in indicating that many couples still experience some notable distress following short-term BMT (averaging 14 sessions).*

Predictors of Response to BMT

Given the wide variability in couples' responses to BMT that have been noted (e.g., Turkewitz & O'Leary, 1981), several investigators have begun attempts to isolate variables that will predict treatment effectiveness. First, demographic characteristics of the couples have been investigated. Several studies indicate that younger couples benefit more from BMT than do older couples (Baucom, 1984; Hahlweg et al., 1984; Turkewitz & O'Leary, 1981). Although Crowe's (1978) findings do not support a relationship with age, he did find that education was negatively correlated with response to BMT.

The couple's attitudes toward the marriage have also been found to be predictive of response to BMT. Those couples thinking of and acting toward divorce prior to treatment were (a) more likely to drop out of treatment (Ewart, 1978b); (b) less likely to evidence increased marital satisfaction at the end of treatment (Beach & Broderick, 1983; Ewart, 1978b; Hahlweg et al., 1984); and (c) more likely to separate after treatment (Crowe, 1978).

The role of communication in predicting response to treatment has been investigated, with mixed results. Hahlweg et al. (1984) found that, as expected, couples' self-report of satisfactory communication before treatment predicted increased pleasure with the marriage after therapy. However, contrary to expectations, they also found that couples who showed *more* negative communication before treatment (based on coders' ratings of the couples' interactions) showed greater marital happiness at the end of treatment. Also perplexing, Baucom and Mehlman (1984) found that couples who showed more positive communication (based on direct observations) at the end of treatment were *more* likely to separate during follow-up.

Several relationship behaviors other than communication have been found to be somewhat more consistently related to treatment response. That is, "quality of emotional affection" has been found to be "more important than the amount and handling of conflict in predicting therapy outcome" (Hahlweg et al., 1984, p. 27). More specifically, they found that when, before therapy, sexual intercourse was infrequent, both partners reported lack of tenderness, and the wife sensed a lack of "togetherness" and communication, then the couple was unlikely to report marital happiness after treatment.

Similar findings have also resulted from investigations based on a trait perspective (Baucom & Aiken, 1984). They found that the higher the wife's self-reported femininity before treatment, the more she and her husband both reported an increase in marital satisfaction in response to BMT. The measure of femininity used (Baucom, 1976) includes a heavy focus on valuing interpersonal relationships and experiencing and expressing emotions.

One difficulty in interpreting these findings is that many of the non-demographic predictor variables mentioned may be confounded with marital satisfaction and adjustment. That is, spouses who report a lack of tenderness in their relationship and have taken steps toward divorce before treatment may simply be very dissatisfied couples. A greater understanding of the factors predictive of response to treatment could be attained if investigators would conduct their analyses to determine whether specific variables offer additional predictability of marital adjustment at posttest, once the initial global distress level of the couple was taken into account (e.g., partial correlations or stepwise regression procedures).

BMT versus Other Treatment Approaches

BMT has been compared to (a) a systems approach (Boelens et al., 1980; Emmelkamp et al., 1984); (b) a group-analytic strategy focusing on the here-and-now (Crowe, 1978); (c) a group interaction approach (Liberman et al., 1976; O'Farrell et al., 1983); (d) communication training emphasizing emotional expressiveness and listening skills (Girodo et al., 1980; Hahlweg, Revenstorf, & Schindler, 1982; Turkewitz & O'Leary, 1981); (e) cognitive restructuring plus BMT (Baucom & Lester, 1982); and (f) an experiential intervention (Johnson & Greenberg, 1984). With certain exceptions, few significant differences have been found between BMT and these other approaches. Based on meta-analysis, Hahlweg and Markman (1983) also concluded that BMT and other approaches produce essentially equivalent effects but that BMT shows a trend toward more stable effects at follow-up.

Although replications are greatly needed, three notable exceptions to this general conclusion have been found. First, Hahlweg et al. (1982) found that conjoint BMT and conjoint-group BMT were superior to conjoint-group communication therapy in altering presenting problems, some observed communication, and marital adjustment. Second, O'Farrell *et al.* (1983) found that BMT was more effective than an interaction group in increasing some observed positive communication and self-reports of marital adjustment, when they treated outpatient male alcoholics and their wives in a Veterans Administration setting with either conjoint-group BMT or an interactional approach often used with alcoholics. The latter approach emphasized sharing of feelings, general discussion of problems, and verbal insight into the couple's relationship. (However, in a similar comparison of treatment approaches with nonalcoholic distressed couples, Liberman *et al.* [1976] found few differences between the two treatments.) Third, when Johnson and Greenberg (1984) compared BMT that taught problem-solving and communication skills with an experiential approach that used Gestalt and client-centered techniques to identify the couple's negative interaction style and unacknowledged feelings underlying the interaction, they found the experiential approach to be superior to BMT in reducing presenting complaints and increasing marital adjustment at posttest; the difference in marital adjustment continued at 8-week follow-up.

Interestingly, all of the outcome investigations that have found one treatment approach to be superior to other approaches have been conducted by investigators aligned with the more successful approach. It is unclear whether this finding is coincidental, whether the results are influenced by the investigators' enthusiasm for one approach or the expertise with which the treatments are delivered, or whether some other factor has contributed to this pattern of results. However, these findings point out the necessity for future comparative outcome investigations to demonstrate that all treatments are conducted with a high level of expertise. See Johnson and Greenberg (1984) for a discussion of several strategies aimed at reaching that goal.

COMMUNICATION THERAPY VERSUS WAITING-LIST AND OTHER TREATMENT APPROACHES

There are now five studies involving distressed couples that compare CT to a waiting-list condition (Ely, Guerney, & Stover, 1973; Epstein & Jackson, 1978; Girodo *et al.*, 1980; Hahlweg *et al.*, 1984; Turkewitz & O'Leary, 1981). *Summarizing the results of these studies, it appears that compared to no treatment, CT results in improved communication but has little overall effect on marital adjustment.* However, most of the couples received CT in a conjoint-group modality, and there is some evidence to suggest that CT given in a conjoint modality increases marital adjustment (Hahlweg *et al.*, 1984). Thus our conclusions are consistent with Beach and O'Leary's (in press) that CT appears less effective with distressed couples when used in a group format. *When CT has been compared to treatment approaches other than BMT, there have been no significant differences between treatments in increasing marital adjustment, although treatments teaching a specific skill often evidence greater change in that aspect of the couple's relationship.* For example, Epstein and Jackson (1978) found that CT that emphasized assertiveness skills was more effective than an interaction insight format in increasing assertive requests. Similarly, Epstein, Pretzer, and Fleming (1982) reported that cognitive marital therapy focusing on faulty attributions and unrealistic expectations was superior to CT in altering problematic expectations and attributions. Finally, Jessee and Guerney (1981) found that CT was more effective than a Gestalt approach in improving self-reports of communication.

SYSTEMS, INSIGHT, AND COGNITIVE BEHAVIORAL APPROACHES

To date, there are five studies comparing systems, insight-oriented, and cognitive behavioral approaches to various control conditions (Baucom & Lester, 1982; Boelens *et al.*, 1980; Crowe, 1978; Epstein & Jackson, 1978; O'Farrell *et al.*, 1983). Each of these studies has been discussed above in the comparisons between BMT and other approaches, so we will only briefly summarize additional findings. Unfortunately the systems approach was combined with the other treatment condition (BMT) in comparing it to the WL condition (Boelens *et al.*, 1980). The two treatments together were superior to the WL in reducing presenting problems and increasing marital adjustment but not on direct observations of communication. Crowe found that the group-analytic approach was not significantly different from a supportive control group in altering presenting problems, and no persistent differences between the two groups on marital adjustment were found. Relative to a waiting-list condition, Epstein and Jackson's five-session interaction insight training group was significantly improved on only 1 out of 11 observed communication variables, and no difference was found on their self-report measure of marital satisfaction. Similarly, O'Farrell *et al.* (1983) found that their insight interaction approach was not superior to a WL condition in improving observed communication or marital adjustment. In their progress report, Baucom and Lester (1982) noted that, compared to a WL condition, cognitive restructuring followed by BMT was significantly more effective in increasing self-reported marital adjustment, decreasing the amount of behavior change requested by the spouse, and altering observed communication in two of three areas; these findings were identical for husbands and wives.

Consequently, because of the extremely limited amount of data currently available, drawing conclusions about the effectiveness of systems, insight-oriented, and cognitive approaches relative to WL and supportive control groups is premature.

CAUTIONS IN EVALUATING THE RESULTS
OF MARITAL THERAPY OUTCOME RESEARCH

We have included in this review only controlled-outcome investigations in which distressed couples were randomly assigned to treatments regardless of types of presenting complaints. This research design imposes a major limitation regarding the implications of the results for clinicians treating individual couples. We are limited in our ability to determine what type of treatment would be most effective for any particular individual couple. Clinicians in applied, nonresearch settings typically formulate a treatment for each couple, taking into account the unique characteristics of that couple. It is critical to realize that *the current research findings do not indicate that when a particular couple requests marital therapy, the treatment approach employed does not matter.* The results simply indicate that if the unique characteristics and needs of the couple are not considered, then no theoretical approach has demonstrated superiority. To assist clinicians in tailoring treatments for specific couples, outcome investigations are needed that systematically evaluate whether specific couples respond differently to various treatments.

A second factor that may be contributing to the general lack of significant differences between treatments is the small sample sizes often employed in the above studies. It is not atypical to have only 5–10 couples receiving a given treatment. Even if there are true overall differences in effectiveness between the treatments, such differences are unlikely to be observed with small sample sizes. If one couple does not respond to treatment because it is not the optimal treatment and another couple deteriorates due to a severe environment stressor such as a job loss, the general effectiveness of the treatment may be disguised if only five couples received the treatment. Since different couples seem to vary in their response to a specific treatment (c.f. Turkewitz & O'Leary, 1981), the very small sample sizes often employed create research designs that lack the statistical power to detect actual treatment differences which may exist.

EVALUATING TREATMENT EFFECTIVENESS
IN APPLIED SETTINGS

In addition to gleaning useful information from the results of controlled-outcome investigations, clinicians can learn about changes occurring during treatment by assessing their own clients. In most applied settings, clinicians have neither the desire nor the means to conduct controlled-group outcome investigations as discussed above. However, we agree with others that much useful information can be obtained from a careful look at the treatment of individual couples in applied contexts (Barlow, Hayes, & Nelson, 1984; Hayes, 1981; Hersen & Barlow, 1976; Kazdin, 1981). The case study method may be both feasible for the clinician and capable of supplying information about the effectiveness of treatment with specific couples. In fact, a series of carefully conducted case studies might yield as much if not more information about treatment effectiveness than the studies discussed above. A primary reason for this is that the group design studies discussed thus far are not totally representative of how treatment is typically applied in clinical contexts; for example, the above studies typically employed a predetermined number of sessions and a certain sequencing of treatment strategies.

The Case Study

The case study has typically involved intensive study of one couple. The clinician describes the couple, the treatment involved, and the observed effects of treatment. Heretofore, case studies have been generally rejected in academic circles, partly because of the vague, unclear way in which they have been conducted and presented in the literature.[2] Just as experimental investigations vary greatly in quality and applicability, Kazdin (1981) has shown that case studies vary similarly. The ultimate goal in designing a single case study is the same as the goal of controlled-outcome investigations: to provide data suggesting that therapy is responsible for treatment change and to rule out as many alternative explanations as possible (Kazdin, 1981). In order to provide optimal information from a case study, several measurement issues must be addressed.

THE CONTENT OF ASSESSMENT DATA

First, the content to be assessed must be determined. For example, is the clinician interested in global marital adjustment and satisfaction, specific communication patterns within the session, noncommunication behavior outside of the session, or certain cognitions that may contribute to marital distress? This question must be answered according to the clinician's specific goals; still, there is likely to be some overlap in what various marital therapists wish to know about the effects of treatment.

Regardless of theoretical orientation, most clinicians will be interested in the changes in marital adjustment and satisfaction that each spouse believes have occurred during therapy. This can be accomplished by asking each spouse to complete a standardized marital adjustment scale, such as the MAS or DAS, before and at the end of treatment. These scores for the particular couple can then be compared to various reference groups. Cutoff points for these scales have been established that differentiate between distressed

---

2. However, the reliance on clinical experience and case studies even by treatment outcome investigators should be obvious when we realize that there are almost no controlled outcome investigations to justify the recommendations in marital therapy books and workshops on how to work with specific types of couples, how to handle resistance, and so forth.

and nondistressed couples; thus, the clinician can evaluate whether the couple seems to have joined the ranks of the nondistressed. Further, since the DAS and MAS have been used in a number of marital therapy outcome investigations, the clinician can also compare the amount of change evidenced by a specific couple with the average amount of change shown by distressed couples participating in outcome investigations. Another recently devised inventory, the Marital Satisfaction Inventory (MSI, Snyder, 1981), might also be useful. The MSI contains a Global Distress scale, as well as a Validity scale and nine content-based problem area scales, and it yields an MMPI-type profile for each spouse, comparing the spouse to a general community sample of married persons. Thus, standardized self-report measures of marital distress and adjustment and several comparison groups are readily available for assessing change during therapy.

Considering controlled-outcome investigations, Baucom (1984) has suggested that we can help to clarify whether we have isolated the factors critical to marital adjustment if we assess each specific aspect of the relationship focused upon in treatment. The same logic applies to the case study method. For example, assume a cognitive marital therapist focuses treatment on a couple's attributions for relationship problems. If the couple shows an appreciable gain in marital adjustment from pre- to posttherapy but little pre–post change in attributions, the clinician must question whether the content of the treatment was the critical factor in the couple's improvement in adjustment. (The difficulty comes in establishing cause–effect relationships, should the couple improve on both measures.) Numerous chapters (cf. Weiss & Margolin, 1977) and books (cf. Filsinger & Lewis, 1981; O'Leary, in press) detail specific standardized assessment instruments developed to evaluate different aspects of marital relationships.

THE SOURCE OF ASSESSMENT DATA

Not only must the clinician define the content to be assessed, but the method or source of data must also be determined. In marital outcome research, it is becoming the norm to include several sources of information (e.g., self-report, spouse evaluation, outsiders' ratings of behavioral interaction, and therapist's evaluations). Obtaining data from more than one source is a sound approach, and the clinician should select those sources based on the particular information desired. For example, findings indicate that trained raters' evaluations of a couple's communication during a specific interaction do not appear to correspond with (a) the couple's evaluation of their communication in that same interaction; or (b) the couple's evaluation of their communication in general (see Baucom & Adams [in press] for a review). The clinician must decide which kind of information is important—the couple's perception of their own interaction, some more "objective" outsider's assessment, or both. Since a couple's communication is a major focus in many marital therapy approaches, a further discussion of this content area is in order.

Behavioral coding systems for couples' communication, such as the Marital Interaction Coding System (MICS, Hops, Wills, Patterson, & Weiss, 1972) and the Couples Interaction Scoring System (CISS, Notarius & Markman, 1981), have generated much useful research data; however, they are clearly too time-consuming and expensive for clinicians to use on an ongoing basis in applied settings. However, the Verbal Problem Checklist (VPC) is feasible and potentially beneficial for clinicians to use (Thomas, 1977; Thomas, Walter, & O'Flaherty, 1974). It consists of 49 verbal communication problems, each of which the clinician can rate for frequency and severity for a particular couple. If the clinician is interested in assessing the congruence between the intent of a speaker's communication and the impact of the communication on the partner (each rated positive to negative), a procedure based on Markman's (1982) communication box can be used. After a person speaks, the speaker holds up a card marked from 1 to 5 to indicate how positive to negative the message was intended to be; independently, the listener holds up a similar card, rating the impact of the message. Thus, information is provided about each spouse's evaluation of a given interaction. Similarly, each person's perception of the couple's communication *in general* can be assessed using standardized self-report measures such as the Primary Communication Inventory (Navran, 1967) and the Marital Communication Inventory (Bienvenu, 1970). Consequently, low-cost strategies are available for evaluating the clinician's perception of the couple's communication, the couple's perception of a given segment of their communication, and the couple's global evaluation of their communication patterns.

In treatment-outcome research, particularly from a behavioral orientation, the value judgment is often expressed that observed behavior is objective, scientific, and therefore preferred over self-reports or ratings by the couple, which are subjective, prone to bias, and merely accepted as a compromise when actual behavioral observation is not possible. Our view is that both methods can provide useful information, and whatever method best supplies the information desired should be selected. In marital assessment, when the couple's actual behavior is of interest, behavioral observation is the method of choice. However, at other times the subjective evaluations of the two partners may often be of major importance, such as when a husband perceives as negative his wife's statement, which she intended as positive. In such a case, the husband's negative perception may have more bearing on the relationship than an outside rater's positive evaluation of the wife's statement. Indeed, Markman (1981) has shown that subjective-impact ratings by spouses are highly predictive of marital adjustment 5 years later. Also as Kazdin (1977) has suggested, discrepancies between outsiders' ratings based on behavioral observations and spouses' subjective evaluations can provide information regarding whether behavior changes occurring during therapy have reached a socially meaningful level.

THE INTERPRETATION OF ASSESSMENT DATA

Most psychological measures gain meaning by comparing a couple's obtained scores with other couples' scores; that is, usually a given couple's scores on a variable are compared to some norm group to obtain a sense of the couple's relative standing on that variable. There is no absolute norm group for assessing couples' data on marital adjustment and distress. However, comparisons can be made, for example, with nondistressed couples, with initially distressed couples who have received therapy, or with a representative sample of couples from the general population. Various comparisons provide different information, and the norm group should be selected carefully to provide the desired information.

Other strategies can also be used to help the clinician interpret the effects of treatment. The couple can explicitly define their own norms in terms of their own relationship and the degree of change they view as necessary and optimal. Goal-attainment scaling or some variant can be used for this purpose (Kiresuk & Sherman, 1968). After an initial assessment but before treatment, the couple and therapist can decide on several specific, clearly defined problem areas that would serve as foci of treatment. As a variant of the standard goal-attainment scaling approach, the couple can define what they consider to be moderate improvement, extreme improvement, no change, moderate deterioration, and extreme deterioration in each problem area. The clinician would assist to ensure that the goals of treatment are reasonable. At the end of treatment or at various periods during therapy, the therapist and couple could assess the extent to which various treatment goals have been reached. This strategy would allow for comparing improvement across different content areas and different couples, while acknowledging that treatment criteria have been used for each problem area and each couple. Thus the approach is not oriented toward a comparison of *absolute* change across problem areas and couples; rather, it is oriented toward a comparison of the extent to which individualized standards have been met. As such, conclusions based on traditional statistical tests must be made cautiously (Ihilevich & Gleser, 1979).

THE FREQUENCY AND TIMING OF ASSESSMENT DATA

Thus far, the suggestion has been made that assessment data be gathered before and at the end of treatment. We believe this is the minimum to allow the clinician to make any educated guess about the effects of treatment; in addition, follow-up data are clearly needed to assess maintenance of change. Also, periodic evaluation during the course of therapy can be useful to clarify when changes are occurring. Periodic evaluation can be particularly useful when the clinician shifts from one treatment technique to another. For example, assume treatment began with communication training and after several sessions, a shift is made to the couple's maladaptive cognitions. Assessing both communication and cognitions at this point in therapy can help clarify what changes occurred at which times during treatment.

OVERALL QUALITY OF THE CASE STUDY

In order to clarify how the above strategies and options can provide useful information about the impact of treatment, the above recommendations for case studies of marital therapy are viewed within the context of Kazdin's more general recommendations for case studies in order to eliminate competing explanations for change. First, Kazdin noted the importance of the type of data obtained. More specifically, anecdotal information about the couple creates less confidence about treatment change than more standardized, quantifiable assessment strategies. A number of specific standardized measures have been mentioned above with some guidelines regarding the selection of particular measures.

Second, past and future projections of the course of a disorder can help to clarify whether treatment was influential in creating change. Thus, if on entering marital therapy a couple reported having had problems rather consistently for several years and having undergone marital therapy twice in the past with no success, the change occurring during the current therapy can more confidently be related to treatment. On the other hand, if the couple reported that their relationship seems to cycle with several bad months followed by several good months, the clinician must be cautious in attributing change during the therapy to treatment itself.

Future projections can also prove useful by knowing the likely course of a disorder; that is, what is the likelihood that the couple will improve without treatment? Marital therapy-outcome investigations indicate that only a small percentage of waiting-list couples show clinically meaningful improvement (Jacobson et al., in press); similarly, but somewhat less pertinent, waiting-list couples as a group rarely show statistically significant improvement on any of the dependent variables employed in previous outcome investigations. An examination of waiting-list data would allow for some rough estimate of how much change could be expected during a given time period without formal treatment, and the clinician could then compare changes from a given treatment couple to change in the absence of treatment.

Third, Kazdin noted that the more immediate the change and the greater the magnitude of change, the more likely the treatment helps to account for change. Since controlled-outcome investigations provide means and standard deviations of changes that result from treatment, a clinician's case can be compared with those norms to have some basis for evaluating typical magnitude of change.

Fourth, Kazdin recommended gathering assessment data at various points relative to therapy. Specifically, he recommended frequent assessment before, during, and at the conclusion of treatment.

Even if the above strategies and guidelines are used, a specific couple may have improved during marital therapy for reasons unrelated to the therapy itself. Greater confidence can be placed in the effectiveness of treatment if the results are replicated with other couples. The characteristics of the types of couples included in the clinical replication will determine what information is obtained. If the clinician focuses on couples with the greatest similarity in background characteristics and presenting problems, then the findings will help to clarify whether a given form of marital therapy is effective with a specific, homogeneous subgroup of distressed couples. If the couples are rather heterogeneous, then the clinician will be focusing on the generalizability of the effectiveness of treatment across divergent couples.

Thus far, we have focused primarily on the dependent measures to be gathered, and the foregoing discussion points out that for the clinician to optimize learning from treating couples in an applied setting, a careful description of the couples treated is necessary. This is important not only for descriptive purposes but because different couples are likely to respond differently to various treatments. Providing guidelines for what that description of couples should include is somewhat premature, since there is no agreed-upon nosology of marital distress. However, we would offer the following tentative guidelines: First, we recommend that demographic and background characteristics of the couple be obtained, including such variables as age, length of marriage, number and ages of children, religious affiliations, education, previous marriages, and income level. Second, specific, atypical aspects of the relationship should be noted; for example, due to the husband's travel, the couple see each other only two days per week. Third, we suggest that information be obtained on variables known to be significant predictors of treatment outcome, such as steps taken toward divorce. Finally, any factors that seem to be affecting the course of treatment should be recorded; for example, the husband's anger regarding the wife's recent affair has apparently resulted in his unwillingness to behave positively toward his wife. Despite possible bias in deciding which factors to record, the process is critical in helping to clarify which couples respond to specific marital therapy approaches.

Barlow et al. (1984) have noted that if clinical replications are to be optimally effective, clearly defined intervention procedures also are necessary. Clinicians will typically tailor treatment to particular couples, and such tailoring is both expected and appropriate. What becomes important is that the clinician be able to describe the intervention clearly; without that, the clinician will remain only vaguely aware of "what seemed to work," and sharing this information with others will become impossible.

Finally, attending to treatment failures and cases with only limited improvement is important (Barlow et al., 1984). Understandably, treatment failure is a topic that couples, clinicians, and researchers prefer to avoid. However, a careful analysis of such cases can clarify when treatment is likely to be unsuccessful. Although there will be unique circumstances for each case, the clinician's task is to look for trends across couples. For example, in one of the well-known examples of clinical replication with couples, Masters and Johnson (1970) noted the importance of religious orthodoxy in the success rate of treatment for secondary impotence. By delineating the factors related to treatment failures, we can possibly reach greater understanding of marital distress, institute appropriate interventions for different couples, and develop new treatment strategies when needed.

Single-Subject Experimental Designs

Using the above guidelines and recommendations, the case study can be a strategy for learning a great deal about the effects of marital therapy conducted in a clinical setting. However, the clinician may wish to have more confidence in attributing a particular couple's changes to a specific intervention. As Hayes (1981) has pointed out, a single-subject experimental design can be used to replicate *within* the one couple, the changes that have been assumed to result from treatment. Thus, the single-subject experimental design can be seen as an extension of the case study method described above (Barlow *et al.*, 1984). Several excellent sources are available that provide detailed descriptions of the use of numerous single-subject designs in applied contexts (Barlow *et al.*, 1984; Hayes, 1981; Hersen & Barlow, 1976), and we here only briefly touch on one design—the multiple-baseline technique—which holds promise for evaluating specific changes in marital therapy.

"In the multiple-baseline technique, a number of responses are identified and measured over time to provide baselines against which changes can be evaluated. With these baselines provided, the experimenter then applies an experimental variable to one of these behaviors, produces a change in it, and perhaps notes little or no change in the other baselines" (Baer, Wolf, & Risely, 1968, p. 94). "Subsequently, the experimenter applies the same experimental variable to a second behavior and notes rate changes in that behavior. This procedure is continued in sequence until the experimental variable has been applied to all the target behaviors under study" (Hersen & Barlow, 1976, p. 226). Jacobson (1977, 1979) has used multiple-baseline procedures to demonstrate the effectiveness of both problem solving and contracting in BMT. For example, one wife complained (*a*) that her husband seldom talked to her; and (*b*) that when he did speak, he made a number of demanding statements (Jacobson, 1977). The frequency of each behavior was assessed daily for a 2-week baseline period during which no intervention occurred pertaining to these areas. Then the couple formed a contract in which the husband agreed to talk with his wife an hour a day, and for doing so he earned points toward watching sports events on television. The amount of conversation dramatically increased immediately and continued throughout treatment. However, the frequency of demanding statements did not decrease until 2 weeks later when a new contract was formed focusing on demanding statements.

Single-subject experimental designs seem particularly useful when specific behavioral changes are the focus of intervention; they may be less pertinent at other times. In addition, the frequent data gathering can be time-consuming for both the couple and the clinician, and this approach is likely to be unrealistic in many applied settings. As mentioned earlier, the single-subject experimental design is an extension of the case study method and is an additional strategy the clinician can use to gain confidence that a specific intervention resulted in a specific change in a given couple.

CONCLUSIONS

This is an exciting period in the evaluation of marital therapy. Controlled-outcome investigations have reached increasingly higher standards in the past few years. Conducting such investigations has benefited the field in several ways. One, outcome research has necessitated clarification of treatment strategies employed within different theoretical frameworks. Second, these outcome investigations have also answered some basic questions about the effectiveness of treatment with distressed couples which should be of interest to all marital therapists. Finally, the existing outcome data provide some norms to which clinicians can compare a specific treated couple. Optimally, as current and future outcome investigations address more complex issues, such as combining and integrating different treatment strategies or applying existing treatments to more specific populations, the usefulness of marital therapy research to clinicians will be augmented further.

Moreover, it is clear that the transmission of knowledge occurs in both directions. Findings from carefully designed case studies and single-subject experimental studies conducted in applied settings not only hold great promise of providing useful data on treatment effectiveness but also are likely to form the basis for some of the most meaningful hypotheses to be addressed in future controlled-outcome investigations.

Thus, clinicians in applied settings and researchers really do have the potential for a happy marriage. As we have so often told distressed couples, "You two have much to offer each other. If you will each behave positively and constructively toward the other, I think you will find your efforts reciprocated."

ACKNOWLEDGMENT

This chapter was supported by National Institute of Mental Health Grant #MH37118 to Donald H. Baucom.

REFERENCES

Azrin, N. H., Besalel, V. A., Bechtel, R., Michalicek, A., Mancera, M., Carroll, D., Shuford, D., & Cox, J. (1980). Comparison of reciprocity and discussion-type counseling for marital problems. *American Journal of Family Therapy, 8,* 21–28.

Azrin, N. H., Naster, B. J., & Jones, R. (1973). A rapid learning-based procedure for marital counseling. *Behavior Research and Therapy, 11,* 365–382.

Baer, D. M., Wolf, M., & Risley, T. R. (1968). Some current dimensions of applied behavior analysis. *Journal of Applied Behavior Analysis, 1,* 91–97.

Barlow, D. H., Hayes, S. C., & Nelson, R. O. (1984). *The scientist practitioner: Research and accountability in clerical and educational settings.* New York: Pergamon Press.

Baucom, D. H. (1976). Independent masculinity and femininity scales on the California Psychological

Inventory. *Journal of Consulting and Clinical Psychology, 44,* 876.

Baucom, D. H. (1982). A comparison of behavioral contracting and problem-solving/communications training in behavioral marital therapy. *Behavior Therapy, 13,* 162–174.

Baucom, D. H. (1983). Conceptual and psychometric issues in evaluating the effectiveness of behavioral marital therapy. *Advances in Family Intervention, Assessment and Theory, 3,* 91–117.

Baucom, D. H. (1984). The active ingredients of behavioral marital therapy: The effectiveness of problem-solving/communication training, contingency contracting, and their combination. In K. Hahlweg & N. S. Jacobson (Eds.), *Marital interaction: Analysis and modification.* New York: Guilford Press.

Baucom, D. H., & Adams, A. (in press). Assessing communication in marital interaction. In K. D. O'Leary (Ed.), *Assessment of marital discord.* New York: Lawrence Erlbaum Associates.

Baucom, D. H., & Aiken, P. A. (1984). Sex role identity, marital satisfaction, and response to behavioral marital therapy. *Journal of Consulting and Clinical Psychology, 52,* 438–444.

Baucom, D. H., & Lester, G. W. (1982, November). *The utility of cognitive restructuring as a supplement to behavioral marital therapy.* Paper presented at the annual meeting of the Association for the Advancement of Behavior Therapy, Los Angeles.

Baucom, D. H., & Mehlman, S. K. (1984). Predicting marital status following behavioral marital therapy: A comparison of models of marital relationships. In K. Hahlweg & N. S. Jacobson (Eds.), *Marital interaction: Analysis and modification.* New York: Guilford Press.

Beach, S. R., & Broderick, J. E. (1983). Commitment: A variable in women's response to marital therapy. *American Journal of Family Therapy, 11,* 16–24.

Beach, S. R., & O'Leary, K. D. (in press). The current status of outcome research in marital therapy. In L. L'Abate (Ed.), *Handbook of family psychology and psychotherapy.* Homewood, IL: Dow Jones-Irwin.

Bellville, T. P., Raths, O. N., & Bellville, C. J. (1969). Conjoint marriage therapy with a husband-and-wife team. *American Journal of Orthopsychiatry, 39,* 473–483.

Bennun, I., Margolin, G., & Christensen, A. (1983, December). *The treatment targets of behavioural marital therapy: Application to specific populations.* Paper presented at the annual meeting of the Association for the Advancement of Behavior Therapy, Washington, DC.

Bienvenu, M. J. (1970). Measurement of marital communication. *Family Coordinator, 19,* 26–31.

Boelens, W., Emmelkamp, P., MacGillavry, D., & Markvoort, M. (1980). A clinical evaluation of marital treatment: Reciprocity counseling vs. system-theoretic counseling. *Behavioral Analysis and Modification, 4,* 85–96.

Crowe, M. J. (1978). Conjoint marital therapy: A controlled outcome study. *Psychological Medicine, 8,* 623-636.

Ely, A. L., Guerney, B. G., & Stover, L. (1973). Efficacy of the training phase of conjugal therapy. *Psychotherapy: Theory, Research and Practice, 10,* 201-207.

Emmelkamp, P., van der Helm, M., MacGillavry, D., & van Zanten, B. (1984). Marital therapy with clinically distressed couples: A comparative evaluation of system-theoretic, contingency contracting and communication skills approaches. In K. Hahlweg & N. S. Jacobson (Eds.), *Marital Therapy and Interaction.* New York: Guilford Press.

Epstein, N., & Jackson, E. (1978). An outcome study of short-term communication training with married couples. *Journal of Consulting and Clinical Psychology, 46,* 207–212.

Epstein, N., Pretzer, J., & Fleming, B. (1982, November). *Cognitive therapy and communication training: Comparison of effects with distressed couples.* Paper presented at the annual meeting of the Association for the Advancement of Behavior Therapy, Los Angeles.

Ewart, C. K. (1978a, August). *Behavior contracts in couple therapy: An experimental evaluation of Quid Pro Quo and good faith models.* Paper presented at the meeting of the American Psychological Association, Toronto, Canada.

Ewart, C. K. (1978b, November). *Behavioral marriage therapy with older couples: Effects of training measured by the Marital Adjustment Scale.* Paper presented at the annual meeting of the Association for the Advancement of Behavior Therapy, Chicago.

Filsinger, E. E., & Lewis, R. A. (Eds.). (1981). *Assessing marriage: New behavioral approaches.* Beverly Hills, CA: Sage.

Girodo, M., Stein, S. J., & Dotzenroth, S. E. (1980). The effects of communication skills training and contracting on marital relations. *Behavioral Engineering, 6,* 61–76.

Gurman, A. S., & Kniskern, D. P. (1978). Research on marital and family therapy: Progress, perspective, and prospect. In S. L. Garfield & A. E. Bergin (Eds.), *Handbook of psychotherapy and behavior change* (2d ed.). New York: Wiley.

Hahlweg, K., & Markman, H. J. (1983, December). *The effectiveness of behavioral marital therapy: Empirical status of behavior techniques in preventing and alleviating marital distress.* Paper presented at the annual meeting of the Association for the Advancement of Behavior Therapy, Washington, DC.

Hahlweg, K., Revenstorf, D., & Schindler, L. (1982). Treatment of marital distress: Comparing formats and modalities. *Advances in Behaviour Research and Therapy, 4,* 57–74.

Hahlweg, K., Schindler, L., Revenstorf, D., & Brengelmann, J. C. (1984). The Munich marital therapy study. In K. Hahlweg & N. S. Jacobson (Eds.), *Marital interaction: Analysis and modification.* New York: Guilford Press.

Hayes, S. C. (1981). Single case experimental design and empirical clinical practice. *Journal of Consulting and Clinical Psychology, 49,* 193–211.

Hersen, M., & Barlow, D. H. (1976). *Single case experimental designs: Strategies for studying behavior change.* New York: Pergamon Press.

Hops, H., Wills, T. A., Patterson, G. R., & Weiss, R. L. (1972). *Marital interaction coding system.* Unpublished manuscript, University of Oregon and Oregon Research Institute.

Ihilevich, D., & Gleser, G. C. (1979). *The progress evaluation scales.* Unpublished manuscript.

Jacobson, N. S. (1977). Problem-solving and contingency contracting in the treatment of marital discord. *Journal of Consulting and Clinical Psychology, 45,* 92–100.

Jacobson, N. S. (1978a). Specific and nonspecific factors in the effectiveness of a behavioral approach to the treatment of marital discord. *Journal of Consulting and Clinical Psychology, 46,* 442–452.

Jacobson, N. S. (1978b). A stimulus control model of change in behavioral couples therapy: Implications for contingency contracting. *Journal of Marriage and Family Counseling, 4,* 29–35.

Jacobson, N. S. (1979). Increasing positive behavior in severely distressed marital relationships: The effects of problem-solving training. *Behavior Therapy, 10,* 311–326.

Jacobson, N. S. (1984). A component analysis of behavioral marital therapy: The relative effectiveness of behavior exchange and communication/problem-solving training. *Journal of Consulting and Clinical Psychology, 52,* 295–305.

Jacobson, N. S., & Baucom, D. H. (1977). Design and assessment of nonspecific control groups in behavior modification research. *Behavior Therapy, 8,* 709–719.

Jacobson, N. S., Folette, W. C., Revenstorf, D., Baucom, D. H., Hahlweg, K., & Margolin, G. (in press). Variability in outcome and clinical significance of behavior marital therapy: A reanalysis of outcome data. *Journal of Consulting and Clinical Psychology.*

Jessee, R. E., & Guerney, B. G. (1981). A comparison of Gestalt and relationship enhancement treatment with married couples. *American Journal of Family Therapy, 9,* 31–41.

Johnson, S. M., & Greenberg, L. S. (1984). *The differential effects of experimental and problem solving interventions in resolving marital conflict.* Manuscript submitted for publication.

Kazdin, A. E. (1977). Assessing the clinical or applied importance of behavior change through social validation. *Behavior Modification, 1,* 427–452.

Kazdin, A. E. (1981). Drawing valid inferences from case studies. *Journal of Consulting and Clinical Psychology, 49,* 183–192.

Kiresuk, T. J., & Sherman, R. E. (1968). Goal attainment scaling: A general method for evaluating comprehensive community mental health programs. *Community Mental Health Journal, 4,* 443–453.

Liberman, R., Levine, J., Wheeler, E., Sanders, N., & Wallace, C. J. (1976). Marital therapy in groups: A comparative evaluation of behavioral and interaction formats. *Acta Psychiatrica Scandinavica, 266,* 1–34.

Locke, H. J., & Wallace, K. M. (1959). Short marital-adjustment and prediction tests: Their reliability and validity. *Marriage and Family Living, 21,* 251–255.

Markman, H. J. (1981). The prediction of marital distress: A five-year follow-up. *Journal of Consulting and Clinical Psychology, 49,* 760–762.

Markman, H. J. (1982, November). *Couples' observation of their own communication: Implications for the assessment, prevention and treatment of marital distress.* Paper presented at the annual meeting of the Association for the Advancement of Behavior Therapy, Los Angeles.

Markman, H. J. (1984). The longitudinal study of couples' interactions: Implications for understanding and predicting the development of marital distress. In K. Hahlweg & N. S. Jacobson (Eds.), *Marital interaction: Analysis and modification.* New York: Guilford Press.

Masters, W. H., & Johnson, V. E. (1970). *Human sexual inadequacy.* Boston: Little, Brown.

Mehlman, S. K., Baucom, D. H., & Anderson, D. (1983). Effectiveness of cotherapist versus single therapists and immediate versus delayed treatment in behavioral marital therapy. *Journal of Consulting and Clinical Psychology, 51,* 258–266.

Navran, L. (1967). Communication and adjustment in marriage. *Family Process, 6,* 173–184.

Notarius, C. I., & Markman, H. J. (1981). The couples interaction scoring system. In E. E. Filsinger & R. A. Lewis (Eds.), *Assessing marriage: New behavioral approaches* (pp. 112-127). Beverly Hills, CA: Sage.

O'Farrell, T. J., Cutter, H. S., & Floyd, F. J. (1983). *The class on alcoholism and marriage (CALM) project: Results on marital adjustment and communication from before to after therapy* (Tech. Rep. No. 4-1). Brockton, MA: Brockton/West Roxbury Veterans Administration Medical Center.

O'Leary, D. K. (Ed.). (in press). *Assessment of marital discord.* New York: Lawrence Erlbaum Associates.

Patterson, G. R., & Hops, H. (1972). Coercion, a game for two: Intervention techniques for marital conflict. In R. E. Ulrich & P. Mountjoy (Eds.), *The experimental analysis of social behavior* (pp. 424–440). New York: Appleton-Century-Crofts.

Patterson, G. R., Hops, H., & Weiss, R. L. (1975). Interpersonal skills training for couples in early stages of conflict. *Journal of Marriage and the Family, 37,* 295–303.

Smith, M. L., & Glass, G. V. (1977). Meta-analysis of psychotherapy outcome studies. *American Psychologist, 32,* 752–760.

Snyder, D. K. (1981). *Marital Satisfaction Inventory (MSI): Manual.* Los Angeles: Western Psychological Services.

Spanier, G. B. (1976). Measuring dyadic adjustment: New scales for assessing the quality of marriage and similar dyads. *Journal of Marriage and the Family, 38,* 15–28.

Stuart, R. B. (1969a). Operant-interpersonal treatment for marital discord. *Journal of Consulting and Clinical Psychology, 33,* 675–682.

Stuart, R. B. (1969b). Token reinforcement in marital treatment. In R. D. Rubin & C. M. Franks (Eds.), *Advances in behavior therapy* (pp. 221–230). New York: Academic Press.

Thomas, E. J. (1977). *Marital communication and decision-making.* New York: Free Press.

Thomas, E. J., Walter, C. L., & O'Flaherty, K. (1974). A verbal problem checklist for use in assessing family verbal behavior. *Behavior Therapy, 5,* 235–246.

Turkewitz, H., & O'Leary, K. D. (1981). A comparative outcome study of behavioral marital therapy and communication therapy. *Journal of Marital and Family Therapy, 7,* 159–169.

Weiss, R. L., Hops, H., & Patterson, G. R. (1973). A framework for conceptualizing marital conflict. In L. A. Hamerlynck, L. C. Hardy, & E. J. Marsh (Eds.), *Behavior change: Methodology, concepts, and practice.* Champaign, IL: Research Press.

Weiss, R. L., & Margolin, G. (1977). Assessment of marital conflict and accord. In A. R. Ciminero, K. S. Calhoun, & H. E. Adams (Eds.), *Handbook of behavior assessment.* New York: Wiley.

Williams, A. M., & Miller, W. R. (1981). Evaluation and research on marital therapy. In G. P. Sholevar (Ed.), *The handbook of marriage and marital therapy.* Jamaica, NY: Spectrum.

28

Ethical Issues in Marital Therapy

GAYLA MARGOLIN

As this book attests, marital therapy has come of age. The battle we have waged to be recognized as a viable clinical practice has been won, and our time no longer needs to be spent attempting to gain a foothold in the world of traditional psychotherapy. However, with the recognition that marital therapy can be a powerful psychotherapeutic tool comes the responsibility for how that tool is used. One of the major challenges currently facing us is that of self-evaluation and self-scrutiny so that marital therapy is used ethically, responsibly, and with an eye toward accountability.

This chapter highlights ethical issues pertinent to the practice of marital therapy. Ethical matters, according to Webster's dictionary, involve "conforming to professionally endorsed principles and practices." Ironically, however, there are no universally accepted principles or practices of marital therapy. Furthermore, although marital therapy is a subcategory of the more general profession of psychotherapy, the ethical guidelines of this umbrella category do not always apply. As argued by O'Shea and Jessee (1982), there are basic philosophical and ideological clashes between individually oriented theories of psychological disturbance and dyadically oriented and systematically oriented models that emphasize the interpersonal context. All told, there are serious lacunae in formalized guidelines for the professional practice of marital therapy.

According to Webster's, ethical issues also involve "questions of right and wrong." While the inherent ambiguity of psychotherapy makes it difficult, if not impossible, to identify clear-cut standards of right and wrong, there has been a tendency to avoid some rather fundamental questions: Under

Gayla Margolin. Department of Psychology, University of Southern California, Los Angeles, California.

what conditions is it "right" to recommend marital therapy? Are there specific marital therapy practices that are "wrong" to use under certain conditions or with certain clients? These fundamental questions have no easy answers but are essential to our being able to respond to questions of consumers, public policymakers, and our own trainees (Gurman, 1983).

This chapter focuses on ethical and value-oriented issues that are likely to arise in marital therapy. The sheer practicalities of seeing two as opposed to one client, as well as the theoretical implications of an interpersonal as opposed to individual model, complicate and create new kinds of ethical and value dilemmas (Margolin, 1982; O'Shea & Jessee, 1982). Specific issued addressed here include therapist competence, confidentiality, informed consent, therapist responsibility, and cultural and sex-role values. Although the focus of this chapter is on marital, as opposed to family, therapy, there is considerable overlap between issues addressed here and issues pertinent to multigenerational therapy. A more extensive look at the additional ethical considerations for family work is found in Margolin (1982).

THERAPIST COMPETENCE

The ethical practice of marital therapy, or any psychotherapy for that matter, ultimately boils down to a question of the therapist's competence. The difficulty lies in defining areas of competence, the way competence is demonstrated, and methods for measuring competence.

Initially, one acquired the title of marital therapist simply as a consequence of choosing to work with couples. Over time, as the number of identified marital therapists grew, the trial-by-fire approach gave way to tutelage with experienced clinicians, either through workshops, apprenticeships, or post-degree training institutes. More recently, there have been attempts to regularize both training in and the practice of marital and family therapy. The Commission on Accreditation for Marriage and Family Therapy Education of the American Association for Marriage and Family Therapy (undated) has set forth guidelines for graduate-level and postgraduate-level courses of study. Individuals in the field also have recommended model curricula (Everett, 1979; Nichols, 1979; Winkle, Piercy, & Hovestadt, 1981). The gist of the training recommendations is that the marital and family therapist should receive specialty training. Becoming competent requires a particular conceptual background (e.g., systems theory, social learning theory, family sociology, developmental theory), as well as good deal of supervised "hands on" experience. Training recommendations generally portray marital therapy as a subset of family therapy without making distinctions in requisite areas of studies. For the most part, the theoretical and substantive issues relevant to marital and family therapy are identical. Moreover, from a practical perspective, expertise in both forms of therapy is needed to handle instances in which marital and family problems are interwoven.

The risk of not receiving specialized training is balanced by the risk of becoming so specialized that the therapist lacks a general background in psychotherapy. Training is needed to know the benefits as well as the limitations of individual psychotherapy and to be knowledgeable about individual psychopathology. First-generation marital and family therapists evolved their interactional perspective from a knowledge of, albeit also their frustration with, individual dynamics. For later-generation marital therapists, it is important that specialty training not supersede basic training in abnormal psychology; in personality theory; in human sexuality; in child, adolescent, and adult development; and in models of individual assessment and therapy. With the broad perspective that comes from being a psychotherapist first and a marital therapist second, the clinician can make informed decisions on each case about the merits of a dyadic focus versus an individual focus. Without that broad perspective, the clinician is likely to offer a therapeutic intervention with which she or he is most familiar and most comfortable, regardless of its appropriateness.

The need for a broad-based approach also applies within a marital therapy approach. There is an unfortunate tendency at both the graduate and postgraduate levels for training programs to promote one particular approach to marital therapy. In students' early stages of learning, this may be helpful as a way to develop a model from which to conceptualize cases and make clinical decisions. The drawback, however, is well communicated in Maslow's 1966 observation: "If the only tool you have is a hammer, (you tend) to treat everything as if it were a nail" (pp. 15–16). The more parochial the therapist is in theoretical orientation, the greater likelihood that his or her cases will be construed to fit into that system.

Within a given theoretical framework, discussion and debate tend to take on a rather provincial quality. Systems theorists may debate the best way to construct a family genogram. Social learning theorists might argue about the most effective type of behavioral contract. While these discussions are important, they pale in contrast to questions about when such procedures should or should not even be used. Gurman and Kniskern (1978) argue that too strong a focus on technology risks losing sight of basic therapeutic principles.

As Becvar, Becvar, and Bender (1982) point out, while we need theory to give meaning to what we observe, we must refrain from believing our theory is good for all people: "Any theory is circular in that its assumptions and concepts guide feelings and actions which logically follow from its basic premises. Such actions tend to confirm the fundamental assumptions and concepts of the theory" (p. 388). These authors go on to suggest that the clinician be conversant enough with a variety of theories to ask himself or herself the following: "Though I largely advocate theory X, *if* I were to view the client system using theory Y and theory Z, what might I *do* differently with them? Given these *action* alternatives, which are likely to be most helpful/least harmful in this case?" (p. 390).

The best guarantee against becoming too wedded to any one explanation of marital distress or any one type of intervention is found in broad-based assessment procedures that actually guide the therapist toward one or another type of intervention. This presumes that the assessment procedures represent more than one model of marital distress and are used to choose among various options rather than simply to confirm the therapist's preconceptions about what treatments are applicable for most marital cases.

WHOSE AGENT ARE WE?

Just as we must guard against strict adherence to a particular theoretical bias, we also must refrain from automatic assumptions about who is our client. When dealing with the marital dyad, it generally is understood that the therapist has a commitment to both spouses. One of the most obvious, yet also one of the most difficult, tasks for the marital therapist is not taking sides with one individual. Napier and Whitaker (1973) indicate that this is particularly important in the beginning stages of therapy.

It is impossible constantly to balance one's attention and support for the two clients. By virtue of the fact that the couple are in therapy, it is likely that they have conflicting goals and needs, which often cannot be met simultaneously. Faced with this situation, the marital therapist must ensure that, at a minimum, improvement in one spouse does not occur at the long-range expense of the other. "Long-range" is the key word here, since, in unbalancing a stuck marital system, the asymptomatic spouse may become symptomatic; while we can hope this is not a permanent condition, we cannot always predict the ramifications of our systemic interventions.

Definitions of success reveal a precarious balance between improvement of a system versus improvement of one or both individuals within that system. The process of improving the marital system may precipitate a crisis, leading to increased discomfort in one or more individuals. As stated elsewhere (e.g., Bloch & LaPerriere, 1973; Jacobson, 1983), a systems-oriented therapy is a political act. The family therapist "interferes directly in the family political system, making covert operations explicit, and, on occasion, shifting his weight in the direction of redistributions of power of various sorts" (Bloch & LaPerriere, 1973). The problem, in many distressed couples, is that both persons feel powerless and as though they have no impact. The therapeutic strategy in such cases is to help each spouse recognize his or her power and use the power more effectively. In other couples, however, the power differential is very real and may be recognized as being destructive to the marriage. Here, the therapeutic focus may indeed lead to a redistribution of power with one person actually relinquishing part of his or her power base.

There is, in addition, the very real possibility that improvement for one or the other spouse can come about only through the demise of the relationship system. The self-esteem and sense of personal efficacy experienced by one spouse may improve dramatically only if he or she is to leave the relationship *system* (Jacobson, 1983).

There are very real dilemmas involved in defining oneself as an advocate of the relationship versus an advocate of the individual. As a relationship advocate, the therapist reframes the goals of individual partners into problem definitions and intervention strategies that serve the couple as a unit. However, as Framo (1981) warned, the objectives of the therapist as relationship advocate may actually be at variance with those of the client. While the therapist and individual spouses are likely to agree on the ultimate goal of improved relationship adjustment, they may have different ideas about what actually constitutes that goal and what steps are necessary to reach that goal. Moreover, maintaining the stance of relationship advocate may result in an insensitivity to one spouse's desires that contradict the overriding goal of relationship improvement. A therapeutic alliance based on the ostensible goal of "relationship improvement" is countertherapeutic, for example, if one spouse seeks therapy as a way to exit from the relationship or to ease the burden of announcing a decision to separate. An emphasis on relationship improvement in this instance would lead to increased hope and emotional investment on the part of one individual, with an ultimate result of greater disappointment and sense of failure (Weiss & Birchler, 1978).

On the other hand, marital therapy is almost doomed to failure if the therapist does not get beyond viewing the couple as two separate individuals. To avoid "perpetrator" and "victim" labels, the couple can be viewed as a system in which spouses both affect and are affected by one another. Lacking that perspective, the therapist is likely to develop an unequal empathy for one spouse over the other or a countertransference reaction that immobilizes the therapy process. Moreover, by taking the role as advocate of one or the other individual, the marital therapist is likely to experience the same futility as the spouses in terms of the seemingly irreconcilable nature of their positions. To be effective, the marital therapist must be able to conceptualize problems in a way that gets beyond the spouses' initial complaints and to consider the impact of any intervention on the relationship as a whole. In doing this, the therapist must be aware of and take into account each spouse's long-range goals for the relationship and not become overwhelmed by the couple's immediate frustrations.

The question about therapeutic responsibility also extends to persons who may not even be present in the therapy session. It is a well-accepted assumption that children of a maritally distressed couple are at risk for their own problems. Since children are unlikely to initiate a therapeutic contact on their own, the marital therapist is in a unique and important position of assessing the children's welfare (Margolin, 1981). In some instances, this simply translates into inquiries of the parents as to the impact of the marital problems on the child. However, in working with parents who are highly distraught about their own situation and who may not be able to objectively evaluate the impact on the children, the therapist might wish to intervene more directly and meet with the children in a family session or in an individual session. Similar considerations may arise regarding other members of the extended family who, in some way, are involved in the couple's problems. If one source of conflict is an elderly parent who resides with the couple, the therapist may help the couple arrive at a solution that reduces their own stress but that has major impact on the parent. Rather than maintain a myopic focus on the couple's welfare, the therapist also must address the repercussions on this other family member either by direct contact or by ascertaining through other means that she or he has a sufficient support system.

CONFIDENTIALITY AND PRIVILEGE

The translation of ethical principles from an individual client to a marital dyad proves to be most difficult surrounding issues of confidentiality. Exceptions regarding confidentiality are relatively straightforward in a one-on-one client–therapist relationship: It is the therapist's responsibility to safeguard information obtained in the therapy session except in the specific circumstance in which a breach of confidence is needed to avoid imminent and serious danger to the client or to others (e.g., the Tarasoff decision). The same basic tenet also holds regarding the way the therapist treats information from the conjoint session.

An issue that is less clear concerns the way that the spouses themselves handle therapy-related information vis à vis outsiders. The *sequelae* are entirely personal for the individual deciding whether to discuss with others the content of therapy or even whether to mention that she or he is in therapy. The couple, however, are subject to mutual consequences if one spouse discusses therapy material with an outsider. Whether or not this constitutes a breach of confidentiality depends on how the spouses themselves define the boundaries of their confidentiality. This issue, of course, is not limited strictly to the therapy situation. Information from therapy is only one of the many possible examples in which material considered private by one spouse might be revealed to a third party. However, the difference with therapy material is that the therapist has the option of recommending specific guidelines regarding confidentiality rather than leave this matter to the spouses' individual predilections or to their own unsuccessful negotiations.

The other, typically more pressing, issue for marital therapists is how to handle the separate confidences of individual spouses. As discussed elsewhere (Margolin, 1982), there are two divergent positions on this question. One preference is for the therapist to treat each spouse's confidences as though that person were an individual client. Following this strategy means that information obtained during a private session, an individual telephone call, or written correspondence is not divulged to the partner. The other strategy is explicitly to discourage the sharing of any information that is not available for use in the conjoint session. This stance is adopted to block the formation of a special alliance with one person to the exclusion of the mate.

Taking either one of these firm positions—provided, of course, that the position is made clear to both spouses—prevents some of the quandaries that occur when working in a conjoint context. In many instances, however, it is easy to find oneself without a clear-cut position on confidentiality or to find oneself having to face confidentiality issues before stating a position to the couple. Clients, if they have thought at all about this question, generally enter therapy with their own presuppositions about how confidentiality is likely to be handled. A client may simply act on the basis of his or her own preconceptions, for example, revealing private information to the therapist without checking on how this information will be received.

Since there is no one "right" ethical position, decisions about sharing individual spouse confidences typically reflect the therapist's overall clinical strategy. The decision to maintain confidences may elicit rich clinical material that helps the therapist better understand that particular spouse. Without being able to use that material openly, however, there may be no advantage to having obtained the information. The therapist can always encourage, but will not necessarily succeed at getting, the secret holder to reveal the information to the spouse. Failing at that strategy, the therapist may find his or her therapeutic options reduced rather than expanded. The secret holder actually has acquired more power by virtue of his or her special relationship with the therapist. The therapist, in turn, has lost power, since she or he no longer is controlling the flow of information or even maintaining the type of relationship she or he desires with the uninformed spouse.

As illustrated in Margolin (1982), one of the most difficult confidentiality situations occurs when one spouse reveals an affair and the other has made "no affairs" the condition for continuing the marriage:

> If confidentiality has been promised, the therapist may find himself/herself in a position of concealing information that is crucial to the wife's decision about remaining both in therapy and in the marriage. When the wife learns about the affair, she may believe that the therapist has neglected her welfare in favor of the husband, and may even accuse the therapist of keeping her in therapy for personal gain. Even if the therapist were to terminate the case, an explanation is owed to the wife, which is likely to compromise the husband's confidentiality. (p. 792)

Since Karpel (1980) describes a very similar dilemma surrounding affairs, we may conclude that this is not a rare therapeutic situation. He points out that emotionally the therapist "may feel guilty for deceiving the unaware, resentful of the secret holder for having revealed the secret, anxious about the complications developing in the case, and powerless to do anything about them" (p. 301).

Part of the clinical decision making regarding secrets surrounds the question of what will be gained versus what will be lost if this information were to be shared. There are certainly situations in which it is not necessarily advisable that all information, particularly details from the distant past, be shared. On the other hand, one must also question who is being protected when information is not shared. Karpel (1980) persuasively argues that the uninformed spouse no longer can be protected from the betrayal itself, since that already has occurred: "What bears comment is that when the secret-holder claims to be trying to protect the unaware, s/he does so *without consulting the person himself/herself*. What may be extremely important decisions about a person's life are being made for the person, not with the person" (Karpel, 1980, p. 299). Such decisions simply constitute another level of betrayal. Careful attention must be paid to whether such decisions are based on overly protective or "convenient" presumptions regarding the uninformed spouse's ability to cope with difficult information. While it is true that the sharing of relationship secrets may precipate a relationship crisis, it also may precipitate relationship growth. Unfortunately, we tend to be quite limited in our ability to predict the outcome of such important interventions.

Who makes the decision about whether or not secrets are to be shared? It is the therapist's responsibility to inform spouses about how confidentiality will be handled. As such, it is best to anticipate this issue before a dilemma arises and to include this as a standard part of the therapist's description to both spouses of the conditions of therapy. If this has not been done, it is likely that questions will arise indicating that a confidentiality issue may be in the offing. Inquiries about whether or not there will be individual sessions with each spouse provide a good opportunity to discuss how information from such sessions, if they do occur, will be handled. When one spouse telephones the therapist or lingers a few minutes after a session, the therapist should preempt that client's message by informing him or her how private information will be handled.

There is an important distinction between refusing to guarantee confidentiality and refusing to meet separately with the spouses. In many instances, even when the policy is not to guarantee confidentiality from the other partner, one or both spouses still will request individual sessions with the therapist. Such requests may signal that the spouse is looking for guidance in how to broach a difficult topic. Similarly, there is a big difference in seeking spouses' opinions about whether to meet individually versus seeking spouses' opinions on how information from such meetings will be handled. If one spouse favors sharing information while the other opposes it, the therapist is caught in the middle of an important relationship issue without even knowing what that issue is. Yet once a confidentiality policy has been established by the therapist, there generally is little to be lost and often much to be gained by having spouses participate in the decision about whether or not they want individual sessions.

Finally, related to the clinical and ethical issue of confidentiality is the legal issue of privileged communication. Clients, as holders of privilege, determine whether or not information from therapy will be introduced as evidence in a legal proceeding. Laws regarding privilege vary considerably from state to state (Sporakowski & Staniszewski, 1980) and many states still lack clear policies regarding the holder of privilege in marital therapy.

The question that arises in marital therapy is who holds privilege: either wife or husband, both wife and husband, or neither. With the first option, privilege can be waived at the request of one spouse and against the wishes of the other. In a divorce proceeding, for example, one spouse could subpoena the therapist even if the other spouse does not want the therapist to testify. The second option, in contrast, would require the separate permission of each spouse before privilege would be waived. The third option really reflects two alternatives: Either privilege is not subject to waiver or else there is no privilege. In certain states, privilege is said not to apply at all, since, with a third party present in conjoint therapy, the necessary one-on-one condition for privilege is lacking. In other states, privilege applies only for certain professionals (e.g., for psychologists and psychiatrists but not for marriage and family therapists).

Privilege is most frequently an issue when a marriage therapy case goes to divorce proceedings. Although husband–wife communication was one of the very first examples of privileged communication, there have been recent court decisions that the husband–wife privilege does not hold in divorce proceedings (*Ellis* v. *Ellis* as reported in Gumper & Sprenkle, 1981). In the light of this decision, one spouse can reveal the therapy communication of another spouse in the special circumstances of adjudication around divorce. In addition, patient–therapist confidentiality in conjoint sessions also might be in jeopardy if marital therapy ends up in divorce proceedings. Based on a case recently heard in California, divorce proceedings may become a new exception to patient–therapist privilege (G. Heymann, personal communication, December 5, 1983). If this should come to pass, therapists could be required to testify in such proceedings regardless of whether or not a spouse waives privilege.

In sum, when it comes to questions of confidentiality and privilege in marital therapy, therapists cannot assume that they can fall back on predetermined guidelines. The therapist needs to set his or her own guidelines regarding confidentiality between spouses and then communicate these guidelines to the couple. Similarly, marital therapists cannot assume that they are protected from disclosure in judicial proceedings in the same fashion that they are protected with individual clients. It is important to be familiar with the laws in one's own state and to keep abreast of any changes in these laws.

INFORMED CONSENT

Informed consent is a systematized way of informing the client how therapy will proceed. Even therapists who do not use informed consent procedures discuss, with varying degrees of comprehensiveness, what is likely to occur in therapy. By using more formal consent procedures, the therapist guarantees that specific points will be discussed with each client, regardless of whether clients request that information. Informed consent also implies that the therapist actively seeks clients' acknowledgment and acceptance before proceeding to implement an intervention.

Informed consent in marital therapy is at least as important (if not more important) as in individual therapy. When the two partners have discrepant ideas about what therapy will entail, informed consent procedures serve to highlight any points of dissension or misinformation. Divergent ideas about confidentiality, for example, could be explored and dealt with in informed consent procedures. Informed consent procedures also help to equalize the situation when one spouse is more familiar with therapy than is the other spouse, a common occurrence when a partner is brought into what previously was individual therapy.

The primary consideration regarding informed consent is that a therapeutic contract between client and therapist is endorsed by each spouse (Margolin, 1982). Even if one spouse has been the principal initiator of therapy, this procedure sets up a structure whereby each spouse must make his or her own decision about whether to enter therapy. These procedures do not necessarily imply that the two spouses enter into identical agreements with the therapist. One spouse, for instance, may enter into an agreement that includes working on some individual issues that do not involve the partner. What it does ensure is that each has come to some agreement and entered into some formalized relationship with the therapist.

Recent reviews of informed consent (Everstine, Everstine, Heymann, True, Frey, Johnson, & Seiden, 1980; Hare-Mustin, Marecek, Kaplan, & Liss-Levinson, 1979) recommend that the following issues be discussed as part of informed consent procedures: (a) an explanation of the procedures and their purpose; (b) the role of the person who is providing therapy and his or her professional qualifications; (c) discomforts or risks reasonably to be expected; (d) benefits reasonably to be expected; (e) alternatives to treatment that might be of similar benefit; (f) a statement that any questions about procedures will be answered at any time; and (g) a statement that the person can withdraw consent and discontinue participation in therapy.

Some of these points apply without question across all models of marital therapy, while others tend to vary somewhat depending on the therapist's theoretical position. Item b, which calls for providing clients with information about the therapist, should be available to all clients. Also, regardless of how strongly a therapist endorses one particular mode of therapy, the therapist should be able to offer information about other forms of therapy or alternatives to therapy altogether (Item e).

Since couples often enter therapy with ideas about what type of therapy they want, the therapist should be able to compare and contrast his or her therapeutic strategy with what the couple requests. As therapists, we may discern that the couple's expectations for therapy are not necessarily in their best interests and that it is worth their while to try our approach. Certainly we can make a compelling case for our preferred mode of therapy as long as the couple are given an opportunity to decide whether to try something they did not anticipate.

What complicates informed consent procedures is the difficulty inherent in actually describing certain procedures (Item *a*). It generally is easy enough to give an overview of the objectives (e.g., better marital adjustment), as well as to describe the format of therapy (e.g., how often sessions will be held). It may be difficult for some therapists to provide more details, however, particularly if the success of their interventions relies on mobilizing the oppositional tendencies of clients (Margolin, 1982).

Similarly, detailed information about benefits and risks (Items *c* and *d*) is difficult to provide because therapists rarely (if ever) have accurate data on the outcome of their therapy. Even behavior therapists, who have collected considerable treatment-outcome data, do not attempt to predict the outcome for a given couple with a given therapist. Moreover, as mentioned previously, an outcome may be welcomed by one spouse and feared by the other. In view of these considerations, the best we may be able to do is to discuss with couples *the range of possible outcomes* and have the spouses tell us which of those outcomes is desired or undesired.

The remaining item to consider concerns the issue of voluntariness of participation (Item *g*). Each spouse has a right to withdraw from therapy as well as a right to receive therapy. One spouse's participation cannot be used to coerce the other spouse to become involved but can be used as the basis of an encouraging invitation to enter therapy. While one spouse's decision to end therapy should not mean that the other is denied therapy, it may mean that therapy will take a very different course and, in some cases, that therapy should not continue with the same therapist.

In sum, informed consent is best viewed as a general approach rather than a specific procedure. Descriptions of therapy generally evolve over time as the therapist becomes clearer about the direction that therapy should take. Thus the information available in the first few sessions often is less accurate and less specific than what the therapist can provide after a thorough assessment has occurred. The therapist who follows the general spirit of informed consent procedures continues to update clients as to what therapy is about and continues to seek their consent to further interventions. When complete openness would undermine a particular intervention, then a complete description and full consent are not possible. That fact does not negate an overall attitude on the part of the therapist that clients have the right to be consulted on important decisions regarding their treatment.

THERAPIST VALUES

It is belaboring the obvious to point out that all couples have values and that all therapists also have values. Values affect almost every dimension of how a couple choose to live their lives together and very often are the source of conflict for the couple. As Framo (1968) poignantly illustrates, the values that surface in marital and family therapy are the same values that cause therapists most anguish and concern in their own lives. Thus, therapists' value systems, as well as the individual and collective value systems of the couple, are part and parcel of the decisions made and the actions taken in the marital therapy session.

Cultural Values

Rather than universal truths about what is normal versus what is deviant in couples, we find distinct and important differences based on culture. Tavris (1982) illustrates this with the following example:

> The young wife leaves her house one afternoon to draw water from the local well. She saunters down the main street, chatting amiably with her neighbors, as her husband watches from their porch. On her return from the well, a stranger stops her and asks for a cup of water. She obliges, and in fact invites the man home for dinner. He accepts. The husband, wife, and guest spend a pleasant evening together, and eventually the husband puts the lamp out and returns to bed. The wife also retires to bed—with the guest. In the morning, the husband leaves early to bring back some breakfast for the household. Upon his return, he finds his wife again making love with the visitor. (p. 46)

Tavris, citing the work of Ralph Hupka, goes on to explain how husbands of different cultures would react to this situation. A century ago, a Pawnee Indian husband would bewitch any man who dared even to make the original request of a cup of water from his wife. For an Ammassalik Eskimo husband, a show of proper hospitality includes inviting his guest to have sex with his wife. The guest would have exceeded the bounds of this invitation, however, by having sex with the wife again in the morning. In the polyandrous Toda tribe, the events described would be acceptable as long as the stranger had obtained permission from both spouses and had negotiated a yearly fee for this liaison. In middle-class American households, most husbands would be incensed with both the guest and the wife. Tavris notes, however, that some couples explicitly seek out these arrangements and maintain that such sexual experimentation is essential to their overall marital adjustment.

What couples present as marital problems, what we as therapists choose to treat, and how we actually conduct the treatment all are affected by the cultural values that we bring to the therapy session. In considering relationship norms and their role in therapy, Walsh (1983) points out the difference between felt deviance and externally defined deviance. Felt deviance refers to a lack of correspondence between the spouses' behavior and their own social norms; for example, the couple who are uncomfortable with overt displays of conflict find themselves reverting to such conflict tactics. Externally defined deviance refers to a lack of correspondence between a couple's behavior and standards held by others, most notably, the therapist. One such example is found in the differences between couples' values and therapists' ideas about the necessity and intensity of boundaries between the couple and their extended family. Rogers and Leichter (1964) found that although 63% of the Jewish couples in their study valued close contact with families of origin, only 3% of the therapists approved of these close ties. Recommendations by these therapists to become more distant from the extended family would have been a direct affront to the couples' beliefs and traditions.

In view of the cultural diversity of most metropolitan centers, as well as the emphasis on recruiting clinical trainees of various ethnic backgrounds, there is an ever increasing likelihood that clinicians and couples in therapy will be from different cultural backgrounds. Falicov (1983) identifies two types of errors that can be made in this situation. The Type I, or false positive, error occurs when the marital therapist underestimates the impact of culture and incorrectly attributes dysfunction to a pattern that is normative in that couple's culture. A Type I error would occur, for example, when a therapist labels as dysfunctional the Asian woman's reluctance to be forthright about her dissatisfactions in the marriage and her tendency to defer to her husband. The Type II, or false negative, error occurs when, on the basis of cultural stereotyping, the therapist fails to recognize dysfunctional family processes. The therapist might mistakenly assume, for example, that the acculturated couple who fit the majority culture are well adjusted, while failing to address the couple's unresolved issues regarding acculturation or the conflicts that acculturation raises with their extended families. In like manner, when faced with a couple from two different cultures, the therapist may attribute their problems to the cultural differences without doing a more complete assessment to rule out other, nonculturally related issues.

The cultural balancing act is not solely limited to instances in which the therapist and couple are from different cultures. According to Lappin (1983), there are a different set of risks when the therapist and the family are culturally syntonic. The expectations for being able to understand the situation readily and know what to do are higher for the therapist from the same cultural background. That therapist also bears the risk of making false assumptions of similarity of values on the basis of a similar cultural background.

Making cultural values a positive, as opposed to a negative, force in the therapy session depends on the same steps for working with other values as well. It is essential that the therapist become aware of his or her culturally based values. What is the culture's prejudices about members of other cultures? What is the culture's view about marital adjustment? How have these views been altered by being a member of the academic or professional culture? Lappin (1983) underscores the difficult nature of this task, since cultural influence is so ingrained and subtle that it is difficult to recognize and evaluate. Therapists also should become familiar with the values of other cultures. Part of this comes from learning about and interacting with members of these cultures. The rest depends on being comfortable with asking for help from clients in understanding their culture and its impact on marital functioning.

Traditional Versus Nontraditional Relationships

Blumstein and Schwartz (1983) suggest that couples have changed more in the past 30 years than in the previous 250 years. Probably the most significant change revolves around a lessening in role differentiation for men and women. What we are witnessing is not an evolution from one type of sex-role patterning to another but an overall broadening of sex-role patterns. Societal change from rigid to more flexible gender roles has resulted in considerably more options for all couples, which translates into increasing complexity in the therapy situation.

To what extent does the marital therapist tamper with a couple's sex-role values versus show acceptance of whatever values the couple brings to therapy? This dilemma is a prime example of the therapist's having to decide how extensively to overhaul the relationship based on his or her own values and model of marital adjustment. At one extreme are therapists who explicitly endorse a particular model of sex roles, be it traditional or nontraditional. Overt endorsement of nontraditional relationships, for example, may take the form of working toward a balance of power, as well as equal control and access to relationship resources. Endorsement of traditional relationships would be exhibited if treatment recommendations resulted in the wife better fulfilling typically feminine relationship functions and the husband better fulfilling typically masculine functions. Such a highly directive stance, regardless of whether it is in a traditional or nontraditional direction, can be criticized for going well beyond the couple's problem definition or their ideas about how to resolve the problem. A positive aspect of such a stance is that the therapist's values are quite apparent. Thus the couple can decide whether to accept these suggestions and continue working with that therapist.

In most instances, however, the reinforcement of sex-role patterns is much more subtle. By redefining all problems as interactional (e.g., overtly helpless behavior actually serves the function of being protective of the spouse), one denies that actual injustices exist in the marital system (Hare-Mustin, in press). Similarly, emphasizing relationship enhancement as a general goal may be destructive to the spouse who is struggling with issues of disengagement (Jacobson, 1983). On the other side, the therapist can err by promoting assumptions about egalitarianism in a relationship that do not exist. At the least, such a therapist will be viewed as insensitive (Margolin, Talovic, Fernandez, & Onorato, 1983). The potential also exists for more harmful outcomes if the couple adopt certain problem resolutions that simply do not fit their life style; for example, a therapeutic injunction for the wife to exercise more control, if she is not prepared to do so, may backfire and leave her feeling misunderstood and incompetent.

Another rather common strategy is for the therapist to attempt to leave his or her values outside the therapy room and accept whatever sex-role values the couple present. Not only is this strategy unlikely to work; it may be most harmful in that sex-role issues get ignored altogether. Jacobson (1983) concludes: "The net effect of the therapist conducting value-free marital therapy would be to reinforce whatever values the clients bring into the therapy arena. By accepting whatever values the spouses exhibit as legitimate, the therapist is in effect tacitly endorsing them. Even if tacit endorsement is not the intent, such passive acceptance is likely to be perceived as endorsement by the couple" (p. 14). Furthermore, in situations in which the two spouses do not share a common perspective, the therapist's own values are likely to agree more closely with one or another of the family members. Since attempts at neutrality in this situation are unlikely to succeed, the therapist needs to be clear about his or her own values and how these values may affect therapy.

In addition, it must be recognized that little goes on in marital therapy that does not touch on the topic of sex roles. Disagreements in instrumental problem areas such as finances and household management typically reflect sex-role conflict over decision-making control or the distribution of responsibilities. Disagreements surrounding affectional and emotional issues may be an outcome of sex-role socialization. Because spouses often are unaware of the unifying themes in their complaints and are confused about directions for change, they may not label issues as related to sex-role considerations.

Therapists can compound this oversight by failing to recognize sex-role conflict as the underlying issue in spouse's discontent. By accepting complaints at face value, there is the danger that therapy simply will change behavior within a role rather than change the role itself (Gurman & Klein, 1983). By having the husband wash dishes three nights a week, for example, he simply "helps out" the wife in her household responsibilities; there has been no meaningful redistribution of responsibilities.

As reviewed elsewhere (Gurman & Klein, 1980; Hare-Mustin, in press), all major forms of marital therapy, as currently practiced, run the risk of inadvertently perpetuating stereotyped sex roles. Hare-Mustin (in press) observes that, at times, marital therapy may be practiced in a nonsexist fashion, but that is a long-way from practicing feminist therapy in which societal oppressiveness is viewed as a determiner of behavior. Simply understanding marital problems as a result of sex-role socialization does not necessarily resolve the problem, but does at least offer the couple alternative attributions regarding the source of their frustration. On the other hand, overlooking sex-role implications has the unfortunate consequence of constricting the potential usefulness of marital therapy for both males and females. Attempts to improve marital adjustment may falter if spouses are suffering from the burden of restrictive, prescribed sex roles or are experiencing confusion as a result of societal and personal changes in sex-role patterns.

Recommendations on how to make sex-role issues a constructive force in therapy take several forms (e.g., Berger, 1979; Gurman & Klein, 1980, 1983; Hare-Mustin, 1978; in press; Jacobson, 1983; Margolin et al., 1983). It is recommended that marital therapists examine their own values related to sex roles and examine their therapeutic models in the light of traditional versus nontraditional roles. Therapists then are likely to be more alert to the possibility of role confusion and role conflict as part of couples' presenting concerns. Since it is impossible to provide equal benefit to both spouses, therapists must ask themselves if they are differentially sensitive to the needs and goals of one sex over the other. The major point is actively to address and assess sex-role issues. An adequate assessment does not mean that a commitment has been made to intervene in this area. It simply provides the therapist and couple with the necessary information on which to decide whether such an intervention is warranted.

CONCLUSION

Initial developments in marital therapy were highly focused on practical and theoretical issues, but the passage of time has allowed for reflection on ethical, political, and value-oriented issues as well. Conducting conjoint therapy or seeing each spouse in separate sessions constitutes much more than simply a change in therapeutic format from individual therapy. This change elicits specialized ethical considerations regarding confidentiality and therapeutic responsibility. With the change to a focus on the marital unit, it also is inevitable that important value considerations will be brought forth, with cultural and sex-role issues being two very compelling examples. It has been heartening to see increasing attention paid to these topics in the professional literature and at professional conferences. Nonetheless, marital therapy continues to face a significant challenge. At the same time that it is necessary to continue defining marital therapy as a specialty area with the need for specialty training, marital therapy must guard against becoming too remote from the mainstream of psychotherapy. We must strike a balance that recognizes the uniqueness of marital therapy but that still attends to, and reaps the benefits from, the discoveries and mistakes of psychotherapy more generally.

REFERENCES

Becvar, R. J., Becvar, D. S., & Bender, A. E. (1982). Let us first do no harm. Journal of Marital and Family Therapy, 8, 385–392.
Berger, M. (1979). Men's new family roles—some implications for therapists. Family Coordinator, 28, 638–646.
Bloch, D. A., & LaPerriere, K. (1973). Techniques of family therapy: A conceptual frame. In D. A. Bloch (Ed.), Techniques of family psychotherapy: A primer. New York: Grune & Stratton.

Blumstein, P., & Schwartz, P. (1983). *American couples*. New York: Morrow.

Commission on Accreditation for Marriage and Family Therapy Education. (undated). *Manual on accreditation*. Upland, CA: AAMFT.

Everett, C. A. (1979). The master's degree in marriage and family therapy. *Journal of Marital and Family Therapy, 5*, 7–13.

Everstine, L., Everstine, D. S., Heymann, G. M., True, R. H., Frey, D. H., Johnson, H. G., & Seiden, R. H. (1980). Privacy and confidentiality in psychotherapy. *American Psychologist, 35*, 828–840.

Falicov, C. J. (1983). Introduction. In J. C. Hansen & C. J. Falicov (Eds.), *Cultural perspectives in family therapy* (pp. xiii–xix). Rockville, MD: Aspen.

Framo, J. L. (1968). My families, my family. *Voices, 4*, 18–27.

Framo, J. L. (1981). The integration of marital therapy with sessions with family of origin. In A. S. Gurman & D. P. Kniskern (Eds.), *Handbook of family therapy*. New York: Brunner/Mazel.

Gumper, L. L., & Sprenkle, D. H. (1981). Privileged communication in therapy: Special problems for the family and couples therapist. *Family Process, 20*, 11–23.

Gurman, A. S. (1983). Family therapy research and the "new epistemology." *Journal of Marital and Family Therapy, 9*, 227–234.

Gurman, A. S., & Klein, M. H. (1980). The treatment of women in marital and family conflict: Recommendations for outcome evaluation. In A. Brodsky & R. T. Mustin (Eds.), *Women and psychotherapy*. New York: Guilford Press.

Gurman, A. S., & Klein, M. H. (1983). Women and behavioral marriage and family therapy; An unconscious male bias? In E. A. Blechman (Ed.), *Contemporary issues in behavior modification with women*. New York: Guilford Press.

Gurman, A. S., & Kniskern, D. P. (1978). Technology, methodolatry, and the results of family therapy. *Family Process, 17*, 275–281.

Hare-Mustin, R. T. (1978). A feminist approach to family therapy. *Family Process, 17*, 181–194.

Hare-Mustin, R. T. (in press). Family therapy: A feminist perspective. In B. Haber (Ed.), *The women's annual: 1982—The year in review*. Boston: G. K. Hall.

Hare-Mustin, R. T., Marecek, J., Kaplan, A. G., & Liss-Levinson, N. (1979). Rights of clients, responsibilities of therapists. *American Psychologist, 34*, 3–16.

Jacobson, N. S. (1983). Beyond empiricism: The politics of marital therapy. *American Journal of Family Therapy, 11*, 11–24.

Karpel, M. A. (1980). Family secrets: I. Conceptual and ethical issues in the relational context: II. Ethical and practical considerations in therapeutic management. *Family Process, 19*, 295–306.

Lappin, J. (1983). On becoming a culturally conscious family therapist. In J. C. Hansen & C. J. Falicov (Eds.), *Cultural perspectives in family therapy* (pp. 122–136). Rockville, MD: Aspen.

Margolin, G. (1981). The reciprocal relationship between marital and child problems. In J. P. Vincent (Ed.), *Advances in family intervention assessment and theory: An annual compilation of research* (Vol. 2). Greenwich, CT: JAI Press.

Margolin, G. (1982). Ethical and legal considerations in marital and family therapy. *American Psychologist, 37*, 788–801.

Margolin, G., Talovic, S., Fernandez, V., & Onorato, R. (1983). Sex role considerations and behavioral marital therapy: Equal does not mean identical. *Journal of Marital and Family Therapy, 9*, 131–146.

Maslow, A. H. (1966). *The psychology of science: A reconnaissance*. New York: Harper & Row.

Napier, A. Y., & Whitaker, C. (1973). Problems of the beginning family therapist. In D. A. Bloch (Ed.), *Techniques of family psychotherapy: A primer*. New York: Grune & Stratton.

Nichols, W. C. (1979). Education of marriage and family therapists: Some trends and implications. *Journal of Marital and Family Therapy, 5*, 19–28.

O'Shea, M., & Jessee, E. (1982). Ethical, value, and professional conflicts in systems therapy. In J. C. Hansen & L. L'Abate (Eds.), *Values, ethics, legalities and the family therapist* (pp. 1–22). Rockville, MD: Aspen.

Rogers, C., & Leichter, H. (1964). Laterality and conflict in kinship ties. In W. Goode (Ed.), *Readings on the family and society*. Englewood Cliffs, NJ: Prentice-Hall.

Sporakowski, M. J., & Staniszewski, W. P. (1980). The regulation of marriage and family therapy: An update. *Journal of Marital and Family Therapy, 6,* 335–348.

Tavris, C. (1982). *Anger—the misunderstood emotion.* New York: Simon & Schuster.

Walsh, F. (1983). Normal family ideologies: Myths and realities. In J. C. Hansen & C. J. Falicov (Eds.), *Cultural perspectives in family therapy* (pp. 1–13). Rockville, MD: Aspen.

Weiss, R. L., & Birchler, G. R. (1978). Adults with marital dysfunction. In M. Hersen & A. S. Bellack (Eds.), *Behavior therapy in the psychiatric setting.* Baltimore: Williams & Wilkins.

Winkle, C. W., Piercy, F. P., & Hovestadt, A. J. (1981). A curriculum for graduate level marriage and family therapy education. *Journal of Marital and Family Therapy, 7,* 201–210.

Author Index

Numbers in italic indicate pages on which the complete references can be found.

V

van der Hart, O., 444, *450*
van der Helm, M., 602, 606, *618*
van Deusen, J. M., 75, 101, 102, *103, 104*
Van Itallie, T. B., 576, 592
Van Putten, T., 537, 556
van Zanten, B., 602, 606, *618*
Vanzetti, N., 179, *194*
Vaughn, C. E., 538, *556*
Venables, P. H., 538, *556*
Verhulst, J., 364, 376, *384*
Vincent, J. P., 30, 67, 69, 70, 180, *193*
Vogelsong, E., 153, 158, 167, *171, 172*
Vollmer, M., 29, 61, 69
von Bertalanffy, L., 14, 27, 74, *103*
Vose, R. H., 471, *493*

W

Wackman, D. B., 423, *426*
Waldo, M., 158, *172*
Waldron, H., 40, 69, 219, 236
Walker, L., 313, *319*, 322, 323, 325, 338, 340, 343, 344, 395, 397, 398, *405*
Wallace, C. J., 602, 606, 607, *619*
Wallace, K. M., 181, *194*, 516, *534*, 600, *619*
Walsh, B. T., 583, *593*
Walsh, F., 632, *638*
Walsh, J., 389, *403*
Walter, C. L., 612, *620*
Wampold, B. E., 30, 60, 69
Wasileski, M., 387, *405*
Wasserstrom, J., 399, *404*
Watson, C., 210, *215*
Watt, D. C., 538, 554, *556*
Watzlawick, P., 253, 262, 276, 498, 499, *511*
Weakland, J. H., 78, 88, *103*, 498, 499, *511*
Weeks, G., 399, *405*
Weiler, S. J., 367, *384*
Weinglass, J., 200, *215, 216*
Weinman, M. C., 387, *403*
Weinstein, C. D., 516, *534*
Weinstein, J. P., 297, *299*
Weiss, D. L., 412, 416, 424, *426*
Weiss, R. L., 29, 30, 32, 33, 34, 40, 44, 67, 69, 70, 180, *193, 194*, 198, *216*, 516, *535*, 598, 611, 612, *619, 620*, 625, *638*

Weiss, R. S., 293, 299
Weissman, M. M., 496, 497, 510, *510, 511*
Welch, G. J., 298, 299
Weyand, C. A., 524, *535*
Wheeler, E. G., 29, 40, 69, 523, 533, 534, 602, 606, 607, *619*
Whitaker, C. A., 100, *104*, 238, *251*, 284, 299, 364, *384*, 624, *637*
White, M., 86, *105*
White, R. A., 368, *384*
White, S. W., 282, 293, 298
White, W. C., 576, 592
Whitehurst, R. N., 411, *427*
Wieman, R. J., 153, 154, *172*
Wile, D. B., 61, 62, 70
Wile, D. E., 258, 262, 276
Williams, A. M., 243, *251*, 598, *620*
Williams, J. E., 345, *359*
Williamson, D. S., 143, 145, 146, *146, 147, 148*
Wills, T. A., 33, 70, 612, *619*
Wilner, R. S., 415, 416, 417, 418, 419, *426*
Winch, R., 431, *450*
Winer, L. R., 144, *148*
Wing, J. H., 538, *555*
Winkle, C. W., 622, *638*
Winnicot, D. W., 578, *593*
Winokur, A., 577, *593*
Wisemann, R., 198, *216*
Wisneski, M. J., 239, 240, *250*
Wolf, M., 616, *617*
Wolinsky, F. D., 219, *236*
Wolman, B. B., 3, *11*
Wood, L. F., 29, 70
Wright, J., 364, *384*
Wright, L., 583, *593*
Wyden, P., 336, *344*

Y

Yalom, I. D., 238, 240, 243, *251*
Yinger, J. M., 446, *450*
Yoppi, B., 180, *193*
Yurgelun-Todd, D., 583, *593*

Z

Zilbergeld, B., 364, 371, *384*
Ziskin, J., *427*
Ziskin, M., *427*

Subject Index